Publications of the
Modern Humanities Research Association

Volume 9

Traditions of Heroic and Epic Poetry

Founded upon the Transactions of the London Seminar on Epic
1964–1972

In Two Volumes

General Editor: A. T. Hatto

Previous Publications in this series

Sortie from the Trojan Horse

TRADITIONS OF

HEROIC AND EPIC POETRY

VOLUME ONE
The Traditions

Presented by: the late Robert Auty, H. W. Bailey, C. R. Bawden,
G. F. Cushing, C. J. Dunn, J. B. Hainsworth, L. P. Harvey,
A. T. Hatto, H. F. Morris, D. J. A. Ross, and J. D. Smith

Under the general editorship of
A. T. HATTO

LONDON
The Modern Humanities Research Association
1980

Published by

THE MODERN HUMANITIES RESEARCH ASSOCIATION

Honorary Treasurer, MHRA
KING'S COLLEGE, STRAND
LONDON WC2R 2LS
ENGLAND

ISBN 0 900547 72 3

Printed in England by
W. S. MANEY & SON LIMITED
HUDSON ROAD LEEDS

CONTENTS

ACKNOWLEDGEMENTS

We, the Contributors, wish to thank fellow Members of the Seminar who were not able to contribute to this volume (see the list which follows) for seven years of animated discussion, talk, and good companionship. We also thank the distinguished Guest Speakers (see the list of Papers read to the Seminar) for reading us their brilliant and stimulating essays and for their company afterwards at dinner.

We thank John Smith for joining us after the last session of the Seminar with his contribution on Old Indian epic.

Our grateful thanks are due to Dr Phyllis Auty and Professor Anne Pennington for reading the proofs of the late Robert Auty's contribution 'Serbo-Croat'.

We further wish to thank Mr Brian Hickman, B.A., Assistant Librarian in charge of the Japanese and Korean Collection of the School of Oriental and African Studies, University of London, for valuable bibliographical assistance with the Ainu contribution.

We record our thanks to the Authorities of King's College, Queen Mary College, The School of Oriental and African Studies, and University College, all of London, for meeting the expenses of Guest Speakers within the United Kingdom during 1965–72.

We thank Messrs George Allen and Unwin (Publishers) Ltd, for permission to quote from Arthur Waley, *The Secret History of the Mongols and other pieces* (1963), in the Ainu contribution.

The contributors thank the Director and Staff of the German Archaeological Institute in Athens for furnishing a reproduction for the Frontispiece and the Department of Antiquities and Restoration, Athens, for permission to publish it. We also thank the Trustees of the British Museum for permission to publish the illustration which appears on the dust-jacket and facing p. 165.

We thank the Modern Humanities Research Association for so generously enabling us to publish our studies, for the patience of the Officers while we got our second wind, and in particular the Honorary Treasurer Professor Roy Wisbey (himself no mean critic of heroic and epic poetry) for his vigilant sponsorship and reassuring understanding of the fact that the pace of a co-operative work of scholarship must be that of the slowest contributor.

Professor Wisbey read, amended and normalized the typescript of the entire volume with uncommon discrimination and accuracy; he later read the galleys with unremitting attention to detail; finally, he reviewed the page-proofs. The General Editor relied heavily on the Honorary Treasurer's unwearying expert support in this area, without which the Association's standards would not have been met. To state these facts is to acknowledge a profound debt.

We account ourselves fortunate that our book has had the benefit of Mr A. S. Maney's close personal attention at every stage and thank him warmly for the care he has lavished on it.

MEMBERS OF
THE LONDON SEMINAR ON EPIC

Auty, R.‡	*Serbo-Croat*
Bailey, Sir Harold (26.2.68)	*Ossetic*
Bawden, C. R. (2.11.64)	*Mongol*
Browning, R. (26.2.68)	*Modern Greek*
Collas, J.-P.‡	*Old French*
Combridge, Rosemary (Hon. Secretary) (2.11.64)	*Medieval German*
Cushing, G. F.‡	*Mansi (Vogul) and Hanti (Ostyak)*
Dunn, C. J. (19.5.69)	*Ainu*
Gandjei, T. O. (14.3.66–11.11.68)	*Persian and Turkish*
Hainsworth, J. B. (29.11.65)	*Ancient Greek*
Harvey, L. P.‡	*Medieval Spanish*
Hatto, A. T.*‡ (Chairman)	*Germanic (Medieval German); Kirghiz*
Henderson, Eugénie (2.11.64)	*Linguistics*
Lang, D. M. (25.10.65–9.3.70)	*Georgian*
Lewis, B.*‡ (until 11.10.67; guest 1.6.70)	*Arabic and Turkish*
Mead, W. R. (2.11.64)	*Finnish*
Morris, H. F.‡	*Runyankore of Uganda*
Ross, D. J. A. (14.3.66)	*Old French*
Saggs, H. W. F. (14.12.64–27.6.66)	*Sumerian and Akkadian*
Simmonds, E. H. S.*‡	*Thai*
Stanley, E. G. (2.11.64–21.3.72)	*Germanic (Old English)*
Wiseman, D. J. (2.5.66)	*Akkadian and Hebrew*
Wright, J. C. (17.10.66)	*Sanskrit*

* Proposer Member (16.6.64)
‡ Founder Member (22.6.64)

A single date in brackets indicates the time of a Permanent Member's enrolment, not necessarily his first attendance.

PAPERS READ TO THE
LONDON SEMINAR ON EPIC

(An asterisk indicates that the paper was read by a Guest)

2 November 1964	A. T. Hatto and E. G. Stanley: The Germanic heroic lay.
15 February 1965	R. Auty: The heroic poems of the Serbs and Croats.
15 March 1965	K. H. Jackson: The poems of Aneirin.*
13 May 1965	Sir Maurice Bowra: The shorter heroic poem in Greek.*
25 October 1965	C. Stief: The Russian *byliny* as evidence for heroic poetry.*
29 November 1965	L. P. Harvey: The shorter heroic poems in Spanish.
7 February 1966	E. H. S. Simmonds: Characteristics of Thai narrative poetry.
14 March 1966	H. W. F. Saggs: Sumerian precursors of Akkadian epic.
2 May 1966	V. M. Zhirmunskiy: *Alpamysh* and *Odyssey*: the Return of the Husband in the epic tradition of Central Asia.*
9 May 1966	W. R. Mead: The Lemminkäinen theme in *Kalevala*.
6 June 1966	G. F. Cushing: Vogul and Ostyak heroic epic.
28 November 1966	H. F. Morris: Bahima vaunts with particular reference to the attributes of the hero.
13 January 1967	J.-P. Collas: Heroic poetry and the realities of feudalism. The problem explored with reference to the Old French *chansons de geste*.
20 February 1967	S. Piggott: Conditions for epic in pre-history.*
8 May 1967	J. B. Hainsworth: Homeric ideals, gods, and societies.
5 June 1967	C. R. Bawden: The decline of the Mongol epic.
6 November 1967	A. L. Lloyd: Techniques of epic performance in South-East Europe. (Illustrated by tape-recordings)*
26 February 1968	D. M. Lang: The Knight in the Panther-skin.
18 March 1968	D. J. A. Ross: The Old French Epic.

6 May 1968	A. L. Lloyd: The sung hero-tale in Rumania. (Illustrated by tape-recordings)*
11 November 1968	A. T. Hatto: Kirghiz heroic poetry of the Mid-Nineteenth Century.
25 November 1968	J. Knappert: The epic in Swahili.*
18 March 1969	J. C. Wright: The Ancient Indian epic. (Illustrated with tape-recordings)
19 May 1969	R. Browning: The Medieval Greek Epic of Digenis Akritas.
10 June 1969	Eugénie Henderson: In search of the physical and acoustic correlates of various types of vocal delivery.
20 June 1969	Sir Harold Bailey: Ossetic Nartä tales.
4 December 1969	S. M. Pandey: The tale of Lorīk and Candā.*
9 March 1970	C. J. Dunn: The Ainu epic.
16 March 1970	C. S. Bird: Heroic and epic poetry in the Mande.*
1 June 1970	F. Gabrieli: Epic elements in ancient Arabic poetry.*
21 March 1972	Le Rév. Père Thomas Bois: La forteresse Dim-Dim (Kurdish).*

A NOTE ON THE TWO ILLUSTRATIONS

Apart from their vitality and interest, the two illustrations were chosen as reflecting in the field of visual art the comparativist approach of the Seminar to problems of heroic and epic poetry.

The frontispiece is from a neck-panel of a Relief Pithos now in the Museum at Mykonos and dated *c.* 675 B.C. (Late Geometric/Early Archaic). The general subject of the panel is the emergence of Greek warriors from the interior of the Wooden Horse at the Siege of Troy. The subject of the part selected for our frontispiece has been aptly described thus: 'A peculiarly splendid warrior . . . mounts a wheel to receive a large scabbard sword, handed down by the warrior in the foremost body of the horse' (Miriam Ervin, 'A relief pithos from Mykonos', Ἀρχαιολογικόν Δελτίον, 18 (1963), p. 41 and Pinax 20a).

The subject of the second illustration (between pp. 164 and 165), which also appears on the dust-jacket is taken from a panel (four times repeated from the same die) of the Sutton Hoo Helmet, restored. It is dated at the second or even first half of the sixth century A.D. Dr Rupert Bruce-Mitford, F.B.A., who was responsible for the final restoration of the design from six fragments in all, refers to the subject as follows: (a) 'dancing warriors'; (b) 'the two men, although carrying sword and spears, seem to be dressed in civilian or cere-monial dress and not in war-gear' (R. Bruce-Mitford *et al.*, *The Sutton Hoo Ship-burial*, II (London, British Museum, 1978), 186 f.). Elsewhere, Dr Bruce-Mitford has referred to the two figures as 'twin male figures engaged in a ritual dance' (*Aspects of Anglo-Saxon archaeology. Sutton Hoo and other discoveries* (London, 1974), p. 200, referring to Plate 14b).

The common element of the two illustrations is that the Greek and Germanic warriors are each carrying a pair of spears, beyond all doubt throwing not thrusting spears. The Greek warrior can be directly related to extant epic poetry in Greek, since the Lay sung by Demodokos in the Eighth Book of the *Odyssey* looks back to the stratagem of the Wooden Horse, of which the *Iliad* falls short. Moreover, 'a pair of spears' is canonized as a concept in the use of the dual number δοῦρε in Homeric arming scenes, as in the great Arming of Agamemnon at the beginning of *Iliad*, XI: the poet describes greaves, breast-plate, shield (for this must go on next, being slung from a baldric), and helmet, and concludes εἵλετο δ'ἄλκιμα δοῦρε δύω, κεκορυθμένα χαλκῷ 'he took up a pair of stout spears tipped with bronze'. On the other hand, the ritual dance of the two Germanic figures is without parallel in extant Germanic heroic poetry; the dual number in nouns had died out in Germanic in any event, and 'pairs of spears' are not otherwise indicated verbally. Nevertheless, there is a passage of

Germanic heroic poetry which throws much light on the question as to why Greek and Germanic warriors should be depicted holding pairs of throwing spears. It occurs in the Old High German *Hildebrandslied* (see pp. 167–69, below). As the tragic battle between Hildebrand and his son Hadubrand is joined

63 do lęttun se ærist askim scritan,
    scarpen scurim: dat in dem sciltim stont.

(First they let glide their ashen spears in sharp showers: these stood fast in the [others'] shields.)

The warriors then close the range to fight with swords, which have soon whittled away the shields down to the boss. The language is marvellously elliptical. While closing the range each warrior must have hacked away the heavy spears transfixed in his shield. 'Sharp showers' is both hyperbolic and impressionistic. It is certainly not literal. How many spears could a warrior safely grip in one hand? *Iliad*, xvi. 139, εἵλετο δ'ἄλκιμα δοῦρε, τά οἱ παλάμηφιν ἀρήρει offers some guidance: 'He then laid hold of a pair of stout spears that suited his grip'. The grips of warriors are unlikely to have varied by as much as the thickness of a spear-shaft. And how many spears would warriors fighting on foot have time to hurl between coming into effective range and engaging the adversary with shield and sword? The answer would again seem to be 'two'. There are, then, logistical reasons for carrying 'a pair of spears' (as many as possible) to battle, in order to seek a tactical advantage before close-combat, reasons that applied equally (though *mutatis mutandis*) to ancient Greek and Germanic warriors. Though the context of the Sutton Hoo panel, like that of other Swedish panels, is ritual dance, war and its logistics are remembered, if not directly invoked, in the warriors' gesture. In numerous depictions of warriors holding a pair of spears in Geometric and sub-Geometric art, it was the convention to hold them parallel to one another as in our frontispiece. The fewer examples in Germanic art do not permit of a generalization, for crossed spears, as in our helmet-panel, and parallel spears occur. Whether the crossing of spears has ritual significance or is solely in order to provide a pleasing visual motif would be hard to tell for lack of evidence, though some have argued the analogy of crossed swords laid on the ground in sword dances. A final point that emerges from this confrontation of two famous traditions is that they developed the same synecdoche for 'spear' under the logistical compulsion of the best wood available for spear-shafts — the ash. *ask* in the *Hildebrandslied* verses quoted above (= Old English *æsc*) is matched by the Homeric μελίη 'ash', then 'spear', used of the great weapon of Achilles, by the formulae δόρυ μείλινον and μείλινα δοῦρα and by the epithet (mostly of King Priam himself) ἐϋμμελίης 'he of the good ash spear'.

J.B.H.
A.T.H.

GENERAL INTRODUCTION

THE TWO VOLUMES of which this is the First, offer the fruits of a co-operative enterprise of scholarship in the field of comparative literature in the broader sense.[1]

The leading idea behind Volume One was to present a variety of heroic and/or epic traditions in general terms in their own right, some for the first time in English.[2] The intention in Volume Two, in the main, is to afford technical support to Volume One. In it, for example, it is planned to include detailed investigation, quoting original texts, of problems of diction, prosody and versification, observations on voice-production of bards, and other specialist papers not suitable for inclusion in Volume One, documentation of the Seminar's brief history, and an index to both volumes.

After a symposium on 'History and epic: their mutual relationship' on 29 October 1963 at Queen Mary College with a party from the School of Oriental and African Studies as guests, the suggestion was made that the joint discussion of epic poetry should continue indefinitely by means of a seminar. The suggestion was well received, and the London Seminar on Epic was founded. A more detailed account of its foundation, of the devising of its rules and the manner of conducting its business will be found in Volume Two, together with some early documents, so that it suffices to say here that the first ordinary meeting, with a paper followed by discussion, took place on 22 June 1964 and the last on 21 March 1972. A list of the titles of papers read to the Seminar, and of their authors, whether Members or distinguished Guests, forms part of our Acknowledgements, as does a list of permanent and sometime Members. The latter shows that as the result of widening interest and the translation of some of its Members, their academic homes came to be the apices of the triangle Oxford–Cambridge–London. They were thus still able to meet the requirement that members of such a seminar should live and work within easy reach of one another.

It would take a separate study to establish this Seminar's ancestry, a study not to be embarked on here. Whilst allowing for such forerunners as V. V. Radlov (W. Radloff), on a scale not yet fully realized by other than Turcologists, Domenico Comparetti, Viktor Zhirmunskiy, who cited A. N. Veselovskiy as his forerunner, and Zhirmunskiy's pupil, our contemporary, E. M. Meletinskiy, we can note a strong 'Anglo-Saxon' strain in the comparative study of heroic and epic poetry, with W. P. Ker, the Chadwicks, Milman Parry, Sir Maurice Bowra, and A. B. Lord. Some great German specialists — Th. Nöldeke (for Persian), R. Thurneysen (for Old Irish), R. Trautmann (for the Russian *byliny*) and Andreas Heusler (for Germanic) — wrote as though well attuned both to each other and to the comparative problem; but it was left to G. Gesemann, who had the good fortune to be captured — and captivated — by the Serbs during the First World War, to venture far into the region of generalization. It was an expression of the Seminar's awareness of its particular line of descent and of the point it judged the subject had reached, that Sir Maurice Bowra was invited to address it at its Fourth Ordinary Meeting on 13 May 1965.

The geographical range of the traditions studied by the Seminar is marked by the trapeze Iceland–Uganda–Thailand–Mongolia, that is in the main Eurasia, the classic area of heroic and epic poetry. There seems to be no prospect as yet of a gathering together of the fragments of the indigenous heroic poetry of America to set beside fine collections from Siberia (compiled by Finnish, Scandinavian, Hungarian, as well as Russian and native scholars of the nineteeenth and twentieth centuries), whereas the quest in Africa, though belated, is at least well begun.[3]

Historically, our enquiries reached back to ancient Sumer and Babylon, and it is a matter for keen regret that although papers from this field were read and discussed, no contribution is included in Volume One.

'When I think of epics', said Arthur Waley on being told of the founding of the Seminar, 'I think how different they all are'.[4] It was a challenge which Members have never lost sight of in the course of their many discussions. For we were agreed that our approach should be empirical and that while emptying our minds of prejudice and broadening our ideas through contrasts we should compare only what is comparable. This procedure necessarily implied that we must postpone the quest for a definition of the epic genre, though criteria were noted on the way.[5] In order to heighten the incidence of comparable features it was also agreed to exclude 'secondary epic'.[6] Another limitation, and in the present writer's eyes one of cardinal importance, was to focus attention on what might be called the heroic pole of epic poetry — a notion which requires explanation.

The concept of 'heroic societies', that is of societies whose ruling class, at least, were imbued with an 'heroic ethos', is firmly established; and it is equally well established that poetry expressive of such ethos should be named and studied as 'heroic poetry'. The wide field of heroic poetry, however, is made up of various genres both major and minor, such as 'heroic boast' (see H. F. Morris's contribution for Runyankore of Uganda, pp. 350–57, below), 'heroic lament', 'heroic elegy', 'heroic behest',[7] 'heroic lay' — and 'heroic epic'. As to epic, not all epic need be 'heroic' in the technical sense.[8] There are, then, two axes which intersect, 'the heroic' and the 'epic'. The nearer the poems approach to the notional point of intersection the more comparable they must be.

The impression of simplicity induced by this analogy must be dispelled at once. Heroic and epic traditions are the products of culture in the highest degree. Their bearers, whom we term 'bards', cultivate their repertoires unceasingly in terms both of the experience of their societies and of the latent potential of their languages, with the result that to the best ability of its bards each tradition presents an extreme case. As long as little else was known, the Homeric poems were regarded as norms for epic, a view buttressed by the authority of Aristotle. Yet had Aristotle collected 'barbaric' epic poems as open-mindedly as he collected 'barbaric' constitutions and had he studied them as profoundly, he must have placed Homer differently. Comparisons such as those undertaken by the London Seminar on Epic show the Homeric poems to be as extreme and idiosyncratic as those of any other tradition, irrespective of aesthetic quality.

It may be conceded that comparison of two epic poems from diverse traditions could be fruitful and sometimes very fruitful, thanks to fortuitous parallelism of plot, types of hero or heroine, style, and manner of performance: such opportunities occur and can be exploited with zest and profit. But if one retreats from individual heroic epic *poems* to consider *traditions* of heroic epic poetry one finds oneself on firmer ground for comparability owing to the higher degree of generality and integration with the social background. It is from some angles possible to discuss an individual epic *poem* without reference to performer and audience, and indeed where no data on such matters are available one is compelled to do so. On the other hand, it would be difficult to discuss a *tradition* of epic poetry without such reference. To make this point quite plain: it would surely not be possible to speak of a Sumerian tradition of epic poetry in the same sense in which we speak of a Serbo-Croat or Ostyak tradition, or even of a medieval French or German tradition.

It is only when traditions of epic poetry as distinct from specimens of such traditions are compared that certain fundamental paradoxes are perceived with their salutary warnings against facile generalization from the armchair. Approached through its tradition, the Ahīr epic of *Lorikī* in Hindī is challenging. The scholar who has examined it assures us that the contents have no connexion whatever with the Ahīr past, so that one surmises that its at times bellicose narrative in some way expresses the cockiness of high-caloried Ahīr dairymen towards their half-starved neighbours.[9] Comparison with the extraordinarily 'realistic' Mohave epic, sole surviving specimen of its tradition and likewise said to be ahistoric,[10] shows *Lorikī* to be the richer in fantasy and romance. In comparing epic traditions for 'historicity' and 'realism', clearly, any scale of estimation, however crude, must range from nil to a high count, with the proviso in the case of 'historicity' that the frontiers of 'heroic epic' with 'historical poetry' or 'historical legend' be not overstepped.

Comparisons of traditions of heroic epic poetry in an empirical sense will lead on naturally to classifications of traditions based upon a number of criteria: on for example the status of bards; their manner of composition and performance; the nature, style and function of epithets for heroes, heroines, accoutrements, the living environment; the ethos informing the actions of the characters; the attitude towards time and the past.

This method of classification and grouping is inspired by a desire not to go beyond the facts. It had already proved useful in dealing with the far more manageable minor genre of the *alba*.[11] Whether or not type-situations will emerge in which heroic epic traditions took shape (the nearest we could ever come to 'origins') will be discussed in Volume Two. Cyclization, and the relationship (if any) of 'lay' to 'epic' will also be discussed there; but this much may be anticipated here, that in one tradition at least, the Spanish, a shorter form follows a longer.

Many strands of comparison in epic will not run the whole way: yet overlap of strands running part of the way will make a serviceable rope.

Comparability may also be found in the more rarefied aesthetic aspects of the subject. Epic poetry is apt to condense long-drawn tensions into brief scenes of dramatic power enhanced by visual magnificence, that is, 'epic moments'. And it is of high significance that beyond the confines of uttered epic poetry, such moments occur, for example, in Indian and Indonesian dance-drama, with the living, not inward eye as witness. This offers a clue to the phenomenon, since South and South-East Asian dance-drama cannot be severed from the epic mode; and I fancy that most of the great moments of spoken epic could be danced impressively in costume. Are there not seeds (and for all we know flowers) of dance-drama in the Sixteenth Book of the *Iliad*, when Patroklos, masked in the armour of a greater warrior than he, thrice scales the walls of Ilion, and Apollo, terrible in his splendour, thrice hurls him down, thrusting away the bright shield with immortal hands, then at the fourth attempt quells him with a vatic shout? And, later, at Patroklos's fourth demonic onrush, when Apollo stands behind him and strikes his shoulders with the flat of his hand so that the mortal's eyes start from his head and his borrowed helmet flies into the dust? Or in the moment in which Roland at last and too late blows his horn with a blast so strong that his temples burst and Charles hears it beyond the mountains in sweet France?[12] Or in the two linked moments in the *Nibelungenlied*, the seemingly quiescent moment when young Kriemhild weeps tears of blood over Siegfried's corpse, and the other, frenzied moment, when she has Hagen bound and at her mercy and sees at his side the sword her sweetheart wore when she last saw him — which she now draws in vengeance at long last for the abrupt end to her happiness?[13] That such moments do not need to be the result of fine writing is amply shown by the occurrence of similar passages, comparably situated, in oral epic. Indeed, so far as the post-oral but publicly performed *Nibelungenlied* is concerned, it has been demonstrated by comparison of more and less archaic versions of the narrative that its outstandingly visual passages can be apportioned to two contrasting styles of different date, the later (the property of the literate 'Last Poet'), in which *scenes* with implied visual and aural space with décor provide a setting for the enactment of whole episodes; and the earlier (shared more or less by the whole oral epic tradition), in which tense dialogue culminates in *gestures* of great symbolic power.[14] Both techniques are associated with epic moments; but it is significant that at least one *scene*, that in which Hagen refuses to rise to greet the Queen, incorporates an old *gesture*, that of the Avenger of the Kindred with his sword across his knees, which is at least as old as the Finn episode in *Beowulf* (lines 1143 f.).[15] I have dealt elsewhere on an epic moment in the Ostyak 'Song of Golden Hero-prince'. 'Tall-cap's elder brother is killed in his town. The younger, sole survivor among the defenders, is wounded. In the night there is a knock at Tall-cap's door. His younger brother enters. He stems his bow against his chest, his head with its flowing locks is bowed to the dark earth. "Elder brother Tall-cap-with-swan-brim, listen now! Look, my fingers are broken! Take me into your house as your servant!" Tall-cap's wife offers him food and drink. He declines and resumes the fight. The scene is repeated. And again. The fourth time the young hero shuts his brother's door "forever" and dies fighting with his back to it. Only then does the aged hero bestir his limbs a little, span his bow, don his magic snow-shoes and lazily clean up the enemy. He then restores his younger brother's life and finally sits in his shrine as a god.'[16] In the mid-nineteenth-century Kirghiz epic of *Semetey*, the hero has been treacherously slain, and his wife Ay-čürök, six months gone with child, has fallen to the slayer Er Kïyaz. After twelve months of heroic gestation Ay-čürök bears a son. Er Kïyaz now comes with drawn sword to take off the babe's 'apple-head': but the mother tells Er Kïyaz that although six months were Semetey's, six were his, so that he might well spare the boy. Then, revealing herself as a battle-maiden, Ay-čürök threatens to don her swan-mask and fly off to fetch her father Akïn-khan with his armies. This is the structural peak of *Semetey*, since Kïyaz is cowed, and the boy lives to avenge his true father. Ay-čürök's gesture is inspired by the pen's gesture of fierce threat when defending her brood.[17] In their astonishing epic, the Mohave, too, have their 'moments', despite its sober garb of everyday, shrouding what its editor, the ethnographer A. L. Kroeber, designates as pure fantasy.[18] After raids, abortive invasions and strange dormancies, possession of the Mohave Valley is disputed by the great chiefs Nyītše-vilye-vave-kwilyêhe and Umase'āka and their peoples:

Umase'āka's people stood without shooting. Nyītše-vilye-vave-kwilyêhe's people stood without shooting. Nyītše-vilye-vave-kwilyêhe stood there: Umase'āka went to him: they met. They did not hit each other with stick clubs; they did not thrust with head clubs. Both of them wore long kovešo shells hanging from their noses. As they stood facing each other, breast against breast, Umase'āka swallowed Nyītše-vilye-vave-kwilyêhe's nose ornament, fell down and died; Nyītše-vilye-vave-kwilyêhe swallowed Umase'āka's nose ornament, fell down and died. Umase'āka fell with his head to the south: Nyītše-vilye-vave-kwilyêhe fell with his head to the north. . . .

In his note on this striking passage — an unmistakable epic moment — Kroeber infers that to the Mohave themselves this was the climax of the whole Umase'āka cum Nyītše-vilye-vave-kwilyêhe episode, since it is also featured in an isolated fragment of this duel obtained from another informant. 'Why swallowing the opponent's nose ornament should kill (Kroeber asked himself rather rationalistically) . . . and whether as poison or mutilation is not clear; but some species of magic is evidently involved. Later on . . . having the pendant drop into one's own mouth is an omen of death.'[19] The swallowing of nose pendants is mutual and simultaneous, so that it is impossible to disentangle cause and effect: yet there can be little doubt that in some way the nose pendant stood for the vital self, to swallow which was to end it, and probably oneself as well.

Epic moments are highly charged narrative ganglia, and it is suggested here as one of the fruits of comparative study that possession of them in memory confers power on the mature bard to build up an episode or even a string of episodes. In other words, it is suggested that epic moments, in addition to being great poetry are mnemonic elements of epic of an order altogether superior to that of 'themes' or 'formulae', now so well-discussed: and that they will therefore mark or help to mark the structures of epics.[20]

To return from general theory to the project in hand. In the present volume, specialists have as it were laid their contributions side by side with the grain, and with little more cross-reference than was required by historical adequacy. In another volume planned, we were to have abandoned our specialisms and dealt across the grain with aspects common to all traditions such as have already been referred to. In the course of six or seven years of regular meeting we had heard some thirty-five different traditions introduced by specialists, had discussed them together and had doubtless read and thought about yet others; and it was judged that in treating aspects common to all or some traditions known to us we could hope to transcend our specialisms in print as we had so often done in discussion. Such a volume was, alas, not to be achieved by us, for at a plenary meeting on 29 June 1976 it was resolved not to put the plan into execution. Nevertheless the concept of a non-specialist investigation 'across the grain' was not entirely abandoned, since at the same meeting I was authorized to salvage the Seminar's best general ideas in a contribution to be included in Volume Two. In any case, the contributors have shaped their essays to respond to the same questions, and it is obvious that whilst preserving their individual freedom and safeguarding the uniqueness of their material they have become

attuned to each other over the years and to the requirements of the joint enterprise in a way not possible in the best planned and conducted symposia-for-the-
nonce.[21] Thus although a comparativist approach did not emerge explicitly
in a separate volume at the theoretical level, it must needs be implicit in this
First.

It was mentioned above how comparative studies have flourished in this
country. This may be due, as I believe, to the urbanity of its scholars, no misers
of their knowledge, and to the learned pursuits of its administrators and missionaries returning from a once far-flung empire. Yet despite their flourishing,
comparative studies are little esteemed in Britain, a situation which will only
improve when suspicious specialists are made, by the quality of comparative
studies, to perceive that these have a discipline every bit as stringent as their
own. It is highly improbable that a specialist who also engages in comparative
studies would or could apply a double standard of truth and accuracy as he
moves between his specialism and the wider field. In any case, it is only through
such inter-communication as the 'universal' type of comparative studies has
to offer that there can be any return from specialization (which began as a
sub-division of labour for a common goal) to a detached philosophical outlook
worthy of the *Universitas*.

No rigid normalization of exotic names has been attempted as between
contributions, since to have done so might have broken the unity with a contributor's other writings. Thus 'Genghis Khan' in one section is the same as
'Chinggis-khan' in another, and so it is with 'Kalmuck' and 'Kalmak'. Scholars
also very understandably cling to that particular transliteration of cyrillic
which has served them best in the past.

The scholars and institutions to whom the Seminar is indebted are named in
our Acknowledgements, yet one debt must be recorded here. We express our
gratitude to our incomparable Secretary, Dr Rosemary Combridge, a distinguished scholar in her own field, who selflessly took down in long hand more
of the essence of our discussions than others could possibly have got down in
short, and in so well-digested and elegant a form that reading her Minutes
afterwards we sometimes marvelled at the sayings she attributed to us and asked
whether, like the bards, we had found eloquence in our cups. Dr Combridge's
Minutes typed in foolscap have been bound and will repose one day in the
Archives of the School of Oriental and African Studies, next the centre of the
University of London.

A. T. Hatto

NOTES

1. See *EOS. An enquiry into the theme of lovers' meetings and partings at dawn in poetry*, edited by Arthur
    T. Hatto (London–The Hague–Paris, 1965), p. 5 (Preface).
2. Those on heroic narrative in Ainu, Kirghiz, Mongol, Ossetic, and Ostyak.

3. The standard was set by H. F. Morris in *The heroic recitations of the Bahima of Ankole*, The Oxford Library of African Literature (Oxford, 1964), in which the author gives texts with translations and commentary, together with detailed investigation of praise-names and formulae in their linguistic-prosodic setting.

4. Arthur Waley had himself translated one-sixth of an Ainu epic, see pp. 332–34, below.

5. These criteria will be listed in Volume II.

6. Cf. C. S. Lewis, *A preface to Paradise Lost* (London, 1942). The *Aeneid*, *The Lusiads*, and *Paradise Lost* are clear instances of 'secondary epic'. On the other hand, if it should ever be shown that the Homeric poems had far closer parallels in Asia Minor or further afield than have been adduced until now, and if it were ever agreed that they were composed with the help of writing, oral bardic style and tradition are so powerfully present in them that it would be absurd to classify them as 'secondary epic'. The same is only some degrees less true of the *Nibelungenlied*, see p. 170, below.

7. By the genre of the 'heroic behest' is meant a long and detailed command, in the case of a dying leader a testament to a comitatus or a people, couched in more or less 'heroic' terms. This genre underlies, for example, parts of the Old Turkic runic inscription to the memory of Toñukuk (*c.* A.D. 720) in a strongly exhortatory and moralizing style. More clearly it underlies passages in Kirghiz epic, notably in the testament (*kereez söz*) uttered to his Nogay people by the dying Khan Kökötöy (see *The memorial feast for Kökötöy-khan, Kökötöydün ašı*. Edited and translated by A. T. Hatto, London Oriental Series 33 (Oxford, 1977), verses 53–162. *kereez söz* are worked into epic at apposite moments in much the same way as are heroic laments, which also form their own genre.

8. The contests in the version of the Tibetan *Gesar* communicated by Alexandra David-Neel are settled entirely by supernatural means in a way that wholly transcends, say, the interventions of Athene in the *Odyssey*. Even when Gesar has met his match in Petul, and they go through the regular sequence of arrowfire, sword-play, dismounting, hand-to-hand on foot, the issue is decided by Gesar's superior concentration of thought, summoning Manene and Padma Sambhava to his aid (*The superhuman life of Gesar of Ling* (London, 1959[2]), p. 225). Similarly, there are 'heroic' touches in the Mandinka epic of *Sunjata* occasionally, but the general tone accords with the turning-point ushering in the victory and reign of Sunjata, when his sister wheedles the secret from the evil Susu Sumanguru that he could only be overcome if his father, a seven-headed *jinn*, were shot with an arrow tipped with a white cock's spur (e.g. G. Innes, 'Sunjata', *Three Mandinka versions* (London, 1974), pp. 73 ff.). The effect of constant and measureless hyperbole in the Mongol poems presented by C. R. Bawden below is similarly to reduce their 'heroic' — and 'epic' — impact to a minimum.

9. On 4 December 1969, Dr S. M. Pandey read a paper to the Seminar entitled 'The tale of Lorīk and Candā: a "national epic" of the Ahīr peasantry'. See further: S. M. Pandey, 'The Hindī oral epic *Canainī* or *Lorikī*', *Orientalia Lovaniensia Periodica*, 2 (1971), 191–210.

10. A. L. Kroeber, 'A Mohave historical epic', *Anthropological Records*, 11 (1951), i–v; 71–176. See further pp. 5 f., above.

11. *EOS*, pp. 47–68 (Chapter 3, 'The "origins" of dawn poetry').

12. Laisses 133–35, out of a total of 298: thus a centrally placed culmination.

13. Strophes 1069 and 2372 f.: thus placed very near the ends of the First and Second Parts respectively.

14. Hugo Kuhn, 'Über nordische und deutsche Szenenregie in der Nibelungendichtung', in *Edda, Skalden, Saga. Festschrift für Felix Genzmer* (Heidelberg, 1952), pp. 279–306. Reprinted in: Hugo Kuhn, *Dichtung und Welt im Mittelalter* (Stuttgart, 1959), pp. 196–219.

15. See Marianne Wynn, 'Hagen's defiance of Kriemhilt', in *Mediaeval German studies presented to Frederick Norman* (London, 1965), pp. 104–14.

16. *Shamanism and epic poetry in Northern Asia*. Foundation Day Lecture 1970. School of Oriental and African Studies, University of London, 1970, pp. 7–8.

17. A. T. Hatto, '*Semetey*. Part II', *Asia Major*, 19 (1974), 32; *The swans*. By [Sir] Peter Scott and the Wildfowl Trust (London, 1972), Plate 6 (opposite p. 39).

18. See note 8, above.

19. Op. cit., p. 87 (para. 79); p. 105 (para. 184); p. 158, note 33. It also accords that a faithless wife who wishes to return to her lover tears out her husband's nose ornament: p. 92 (para. 107).

20. See notes 12 and 13, above.

21. As, for example, recorded in the following interesting publications: *Volksepen der uralischen und altaischen Völker*, Vorträge des Hamburger Symposiums vom 16.–17. Dezember 1965, herausgeben von W. Veenker, Ural-Altaische Bibliothek 16 (Wiesbaden, 1968), pp. i–ix; 1–86; *La poesia epica e la sua formazione* (Roma, 28 marzo–3 aprile 1969), Accademia Nazionale dei Lincei, Anno CCCLXVII–1970, Quaderno N. 139 (Rome, 1970), under the Presidency of Enrico Cerulli, pp. 1–876. To these may be added the following, which appeared after the present work was concluded: *Heroic Epic and Saga. An Introduction to the World's Great Folk Epics*, edited by Felix J. Oinas [Introduction by Richard M. Dorson.] (Indiana University Press, Bloomington & London, 1978). It is reviewed by the present writer in the *Slavonic and East European Review*, 58 (1980), 274–76. See also J. Opland, *Anglo-Saxon Oral Poetry. A Study of the Traditions* (New Haven and London, 1980), and the same author's Ph.D. dissertation, 'A Comparative Study of the Anglo-Saxon and Xhosa Traditions of Oral Poetry, with Special Reference to the Singer Theory' (University of Cape Town 1973).

INTRODUCTION TO VOLUME ONE*
The Traditions

THE AIM of this First Volume is to acquaint the reader with some traditions of heroic/epic poetry from a point of vantage gained by the joint efforts of the various contributors and of others. As stated in the General Introduction, the prime object of study was to be not individual works (though some outstanding examples are cited) but the traditions which sustained them. For those who wish to make comparisons there is more to compare between traditions than between their constituent works, since traditions of poetry are expressive of their mother-cultures, and in similar circumstances cultures may run somewhat parallel to one another: whereas works of poetic art, whose very fabric is a linguistic *idiom*, tend more towards uniqueness the greater the art bestowed on them.

Nevertheless, the traditions presented here are a very mixed bag, so much so that it was not at all clear in which order the essays should come. Should genetically simpler specimens come first and the more complex follow after? It might have carried conviction had one set the Bahima tradition of vaunts on the cattle-raid before the Ancient Greek on the grounds that one such boast of Nestor recalling his youth[1] is but a petty trait of an epic *Iliad* encompassing many other minor genres on its march. But what is genetic simplicity? What is genetic progression? Must for example the shorter 'lay' form always precede the longer epic on the evolutionary plane? The history of the Spanish tradition provides an exception.[2] By analogy with other traditions one turns to the Mongol hero-songs of the present and recent past in the expectation of finding at least echoes of the mightiest empire ever founded on warlike deeds — deeds reflected in many an epic sequence in the otherwise prosaic *Secret History of the Mongols* of *c.*1240. Yet as far as the modern songs are concerned, Chinggis and his house lived and fought in vain, for the farthest our contributor goes back is to an ill-defined but post-Yüan time of warring khans.[3] The tendency of his analysis is to deny the songs all but the name of heroic epic and leave them the status of 'hero-tales or songs'. Has there been a reverse movement here? Or with the reduction of the feudal nobility and the inception of ethnographic field-work has a type of hero-tale emerged to view which was more or less there all the time for the entertainment of simpler folk?[4]

---

* It was of course not planned by the Seminar that the General Editor should furnish an introduction to Volume I in addition to his introduction to the whole work: it became his inescapable duty to do so. The Contributors edited each other's contributions under the eye of the General Editor.

A plausible arrangement of our contributions would have been to set them in a progression from purely oral to fully literary traditions, e.g. (i) oral: Ainu, Bahima, Kirghiz, Mongol (largely), Ob Ugrian, Ossetic, Rājpūt[5] (largely), Serbo-Croat (largely); (ii) sub-oral: Homeric?; (iii) post-oral: Old French, Medieval Spanish?, and German. The categories may overlap, and the terms need some expansion. 'Oral tradition' covers both oral composition-cum-performance and oral transmission of memorized poems composed orally,[6] with the admission already implied that as in Mongolia and Yugoslavia, where there was a concomitant literate culture, written texts might intrude fitfully. 'Sub-oral' tradition is coined here to imply that the Homeric poems were near enough in date of composition to the introduction of alphabetical writing into Greece to have profited from its powers of fixation, even though the Homeric manner as such is wholly explicable in terms of oral tradition.[7] 'Post-oral', for example, is appropriate to epic poetry in medieval Europe, where such poems as the *Nibelungenlied*, indubitably composed and transmitted on parchment, nevertheless preserved many features of an earlier oral style — as well they might, since they were publicly performed. The term 'literary' or 'literate' epic would imply the possibility of reading by eye less than the breaking of stylistic links with prior oral tradition. However, since the Seminar's interest was focused on the nature and influence of oral tradition, we had to exclude from consideration in these pages such self-consciously literary master-pieces as the Georgian *Knight in the Panther-skin*, the *Aeneid* and *Paradise Lost*, some of which class have also been styled 'secondary epics'.[8] The final literate form of the *Mahābhārata* is held to encapsulate oral and post-oral elements.[9] As to the *Rāmāyaṇa*, which was composed 'in the manner of an epic — presumably the *Mahābhārata*', since our contributor stops just short of including it among 'secondary epics'[10] yet another term might have to be found for it.

Faced with such problems and rejecting the facile solution of throwing these essays into the reader's face in alphabetical order of languages or contributors' names, I decided on a rough order in time free from all genetic implications and accepting that this arrangement too would be bedevilled by such anomalies as the recurrence in India of certain evolutionary sequences from ancient to modern times.[11]

It was the declared purpose of the contributors to introduce their various traditions of heroic/epic poetry in a form that can be easily assimilated and also to present them in their most attractive light with suitable passages in translation. It may serve, however, if some points are emphasized here in rapid review as they come, with no attempt at systematization.

The assessment of Homeric style has undergone a revolution in our own times. Our contributor, who has himself made a notable contribution to this branch of Homeric studies,[12] gives us his appreciation of what can be safely accepted in this very complex field fifty years after Milman Parry, as well as many other cool judgements of controversies once as heated as they are famous. The shape of the hexameter makes the economy of formulaic style in Homer surely the most complex and demanding on record and thus the most revealing example. The relations of gods and heroes in Homer may also be the most challenging. The fact that 'Homer' became the tutor of the Greeks for behaviour banishes forever the suspicion that students of heroic epic poetry may be still living out boyhood fantasies.

In the contribution on Indian epic the author (who, alas, was too young to be a member of the Seminar during its talkative days) approaches the *Mahābhārata* and *Rāmāyaṇa* with insights gained from his own studies, in the field, of living Rājpūt traditions of epic — of the dacoit Ompurī and the brigand Pābūjī[13] — the only oral traditions touched on in this volume that are not moribund, galvanized or stone dead. Without wishing to press the analogy further than it will go, he sees comparable sequences from the heroic through the mythic to the deific and from the oral–traditional to the scribal–canonical both in the processes that formed the *Mahābhārata* and *Rāmāyaṇa* and in those which formed and are forming the texts of the Rājpūt cults. He also gives a brief critical appreciation of the work of Dr Mary C. Smith, who with the help of the computer seeks to isolate the cores of the two great Old Indian epics on the basis of metrical-cum-thematic analysis.

If the outstanding product of the medieval German tradition, the *Nibelungenlied*, looks back from the feudal age and sometimes recaptures the spirit of the Germanic past, the Old French epics as a group, whilst feigning to look back to the Carolingian age, express the feudal concerns of their own, and this in three great cycles, each with its own ramifications. These concerns in various ways have to do with baronial autonomy versus central authority, the late outcome of which issue in German lands postponed unification for seven centuries. In other words, the *chansons de geste* treat of raw rebellion, or conversely in a minor key not devoid of pathos, the abandonment of a loyal vassal by a feckless sovereign. Thus the extant *Roland*, composed half a century before the extant *Nibelungenlied*, seems the more 'modern', even when the crusading elements of the former are set aside. In his account, our contributor barely touches on the Germanic past of the Franks, nor does he need to, beyond what has been absorbed into the feudalism of the *langue d'oïl*. His iconographical expertise, coupled with his knowledge of armour and tactics, dwelt on at some length in his contribution, have enabled him elsewhere to add firmness to the dating of *Roland* and to recognize passages of probably earlier date.[14] In the Old French epic tradition it is the internal enemies who provide serious opposition, whereas thanks to religious fervour the Saracens go down at a cheap rate, an epic weakness not to be overlooked. In the Guillaume-cycle the divide is bridged by the love and marriage of the Christian marcher-lord Guillaume and the Saracen Orable, who left a husband and family for Guillaume and the Christian faith — a situation and a relationship which the German knight Wolfram von Eschenbach seized on in its rude strength to make a world masterpiece.[15] Of the medieval epic traditions, the Old French alone had its works adapted into foreign tongues, thanks partly to their own quality but in the main to the prestige of medieval French culture. The tense figure of Roland provides a touchstone for the crusading spirit as an absolute. On the other hand Guillaume is the pattern of relaxed 'human' warriors. There is some evidence in France of a cult of alleged heroic ancestors perhaps rather as the lords of Peilstein in Austria adopted Rüedeger from the *Nibelungenlied* into their necrology.

The less usual evolutionary sequence of epic to shorter heroic poem, in this case the Spanish *romance*, has already been remarked upon.[16] It seems that in Spain the interval between historical events and the epics which reflected them was shorter than elsewhere. This would go well with the later disintegration of epic through its inability to outlast the rise of vernacular chronicles. Nor does this intimate link between history and epic poetry in Spain end here, since chroniclers were given to cannibalizing epic for their accounts, so that now students of epic are decannibalizing the chronicles. Heroic epics, however, were also distilled into *romances*, with a heightening of certain poetic qualities. Some influence of French epic is admitted. Influence of Arabic writing in the heroic vein is found to be not proven — we are indeed fortunate that our Hispanist is conversant with Arabic and Hebrew and so able to assess the arguments at first hand. His essay on the metrical irregularities of the *Cantar de Mio Cid*, published in the year before our Seminar was mooted,[17] aired the view that the *Cid* was an oral poem which, exceptionally, had been taken down from dictation, thus cramping the singer's feel for metre. This is a point that all must bear in mind who deal with oral texts recorded before the introduction of the more discreet tape-recorders. The confinement of epic to Old Castile is even tighter than that of the *chanson de geste* to the *langue d'oïl*: both examples serve to remind us that there are epic regions inhabited by epic peoples.

The Medieval German contribution has no claims to originality or even to novelty. Surviving scholars of older schools may find it something of a massacre. Yet it is only marginally more radical than accounts now published in Germany[18] in its assessment of what in the great mass of 'Heldendichtung' is truly heroic poetry. Those who taught the subject in France or Britain in the 1930s came to such assessments then, prompted by some of the distortions prevailing at that time. Now that the true heirs have caught up it has been hinted that interest in the Germanic past on the part of German and Austrian scholars can be a stumbling-block. It is the prayer of this contributor that the present comparative study, in confirming again the great and timeless worth of some medieval German heroic poetry will play its small part in bringing that pendulum to rest. The only other point to be made here is that ancient

Germanic formulations of the heroic ethos, and not least those preserved in Old English poems, provide a classic norm by which to measure others.

The Serbo-Croat tradition is one of the most strongly stylized both in ethos and form, with standing epithets which, however, remain simple in structure when compared, say, with the Homeric, Ob Ugrian or Kirghiz. Among oral traditions the Serbo-Croat was probably the earliest to attract the attention of romantic scholars, patriots and poets, and therefore to be recorded in the field. The tension which it was sought to achieve in the short heroic poems of this tradition restrained it from expanding into epic either by inflation and broadening or by amalgamation of plots, even in Muslim areas where Ramadan boredom had to be catered for. We thus have an independent tradition of 'heroic lays' of a single-stranded, episodic nature to set beside the Germanic, with a similar personalizing treatment of the historical events which underlay them.

Here one may pause to consider how bardic treatment of episodes selected for their narrative-dramatic qualities argues for greater maturity than narration of a long sequence of events, say, from the hero's birth onwards (as in the Inner Asian schema), which would tend to smother any memorable action involving a clash of wills. Even at 'epic' length, viable episodes, as distinct from 'biographical' sequences, preserve their dramatic force, as in the loss of Roland, or the death of Siegfried and the fall of the Nibelungs embedded in the quasi-'biographical' extant *Nibelungenlied*, not to mention the mood of Achilles called his 'Wrath'. Despite the subjectivity which some may find in the concept of 'maturity' as applied to the cultivation of the episode, it is suggested here that it provides another marker for fruitful comparisons. Another, related marker could be 'the possibility of tragedy' such as must always lurk in heroic poems which, like the Serbo-Croat, aim at tension.

The fine contribution for Serbo-Croat is one of the last writings of the late Robert Auty, F.B.A. Our pride in publishing it is mingled with sorrow that he did not live to see it in print among the other contributions of a seminar of which he was a loyal and well-loved member.

The Ob Ugrian epics, appropriately introduced by a professor of Hungarian, are quite remarkable, both for their own unique style and for the questions they pose to students of other traditions. With performance by a bard-shaman possessed by a hero narrating in the first person, and with that hero's assumption of godhead and thus the heightening of his epic into myth — a myth justifying the sacrifices he prescribes — we have a perfect paradigm of which other traditions seem to have parts. Perhaps the nearest analogy in this respect is found in the Tibetan epic of *Geser*, where bard-shamans sought possession by the hero and other divinities, and where the hero after his beneficent exploits on earth returned to his heavenly sphere. The formulae of the Ostyak and Vogul epics are elaborate and based on acute observation of objects in the real world.

Their vision of the past embraces a hippic phase, for which they have an accurate nomenclature.

Despite the efforts of distinguished scholars who have given their attention to Ossetic heroic narrative in the past, the present contribution cuts so deep that it must be called a pioneering essay. If field-workers now and again astonish and delight us by bringing back from distant regions unsuspected traditions, Sir Harold Bailey has achieved a similar effect from distant times by the application of his unrivalled knowledge of North Iranian to the names and functions of the Nartä heroes and heroines, showing how, through Ossetes to Alans and beyond, they reflect aspects of the Old Iranian Great Household.[19] The framework of the Caucasian Nartä tales is thus definitively underpinned in terms of Saka Ossetic. In the long run such exact scholarship will do more to allay the anxieties of the Qabards, Adyge, Ubykh and the others, who also have their Narts and are rightly proud of them, than accommodations from on high to keep the peace. Sir Maurice Bowra included Nartä material in his *Heroic poetry* as verse without question. Prosodically at times this seems to be such a near thing that he might well have enhanced his rich haul by also including Old Irish cattle-raids and destructions (in which one may in any case find encapsulated verse) by virtue of their unprosaic prose. This Seminar had no such doubts. It was only the sad neglect of Old Celtic literature at the universities of south-east Britain which caused us to forego its beauties.[20]

The ahistoricity of modern Mongol epic was mentioned above. The Mongol tradition is also baffling in some other respects. The boundaries of the genre are fluid, on the one hand towards book-narrative, on the other towards *märchen* and other kinds of tales. It employs a well-developed alliterative and formulaic technique, comparable in detail with that of the Kirghiz and some other Turkic traditions, to convey simple goody-baddy plots. Because of the fundamentally invincible nature of heroes faced with appalling monstrosities our contributor is inclined to deny to these heroes' ethos the term 'heroic' as used in the present work. One might even go further and withdraw the English term 'epic'[21] in favour of 'hero-song', despite the presence of a vehicle obviously capable of carrying weightier matter. Whether the problems suggested by these observations and other salient problems of 'Mongol epic' can ever be solved is now the preoccupation of a continuing 'Rundgespräch' of the Central Asian Seminar in Bonn under the direction of Professor Walther Heissig, of which our contributor, together with the distinguished senior Mongolist Nicholas Poppe, is a member.[22] It remains to be noted that styles of performance of the Mongol hero songs vary widely and that these are dealt with in our Mongol contribution in unusual detail based on knowledge from the field.

Except to those conversant with Japanese, the epics of the Ainu have remained enigmatic for too long. The glimpse offered by the missionary John Batchelor in the fascinating tale of 'Pon-ya-un-be' was tantalizingly prolonged by Arthur Waley in his beautiful — some also said beautified — version of about one-sixth of *Kutune Shirka*, leaving us to wonder what the other five-sixths contained. Our contributor for Ainu not only put the Seminar out of its misery by reading us his translation of the missing portions from Kindaichi's parallel Japanese rendering, and depositing it in our archive, but he has now also very generously furnished the present account knowing that a major publication of Ainu oral poetry in English translation by another is imminent. He has further provided a valuable multiple bibliography based on the catalogue by B. Hickman, of the Library of the School of Oriental and African Studies, to which he wrote the foreword.

The study of Kirghiz epic poetry of the mid-nineteenth century has exercised a considerable influence on comparative studies, if the truth be known an influence as great as that of the more famous Serbo-Croat or Finnish traditions. This is because the pioneer of Turkic studies V. V. Radlov (W. Radloff), who recorded the bulk of known Old Kirghiz epic in 1862 and 1869, perceived its bearing on the Homeric problem most acutely and recorded his perceptions in impressive detail in the introduction to his edition of Kirghiz texts in 1885. Milman Parry's working hypothesis on the nature of the Homeric diction is already here in nuce — as distinct from Parry's phenomenal demonstration — and he scrupulously acknowledged his debt to Radlov by quoting him in full in his epoch-making paper. The strength of the Old Kirghiz epic tradition, however, lies not only in its rich store of well-structured formulae (set to a far less demanding metre than the Homeric) but also in its tense dramatic plots. Virtually alone among the Turkic epic traditions and against the general background they provide, at least now, the Kirghiz has achieved the maturity of episodic treatment spoken of above.[23] Among such themes dealt with in Old Kirghiz epic (and still apparent in the more bookish effusions of twentieth-century bards) are: (i) a propitious hero from abroad is accused by his feckless patron of an affair with the latter's faithful wife (compare the first part of the *Nibelungenlied*, which, however, is more complex);[24] (ii) a memorial feast for a great khan followed by a horse-race, games and heroic brawling (compare the Twenty-Third Book of the *Iliad*); (iii) the revenge of the scandalized ancestor-spirits on an impious younger generation of khans, leaving the women to bring the family through. With a relaxed ethos there is the epic–cum–mock–epic of the gargantuan Joloy. The present writer believes that he is the only scholar engaged in study of this unspoilt *Old* Kirghiz tradition. So far as the West is concerned this is odd, though it is not so for the East, where a new-found delicacy of conscience rejects the rapacious gusto of these poems.

African traditions have not often been invoked in comparative studies of heroic/epic poetry. Sir Maurice Bowra, naturally, was open to them and has some suggestive things to say in his *Heroic poetry* of 1951; yet some of his appreciations are over-generalized and unwarranted, due to the absence of published texts. Had our contributor's *Heroic recitations of the Bahima of Ankole* (1964) and even the paperback *Sundiata: an epic of Old Mali* (1965) been available to him, Bowra would have been the first to divine their significance for the problems with which he was concerned. He noted the resemblances between panegyric or lament and heroic poetry and thought there must be a relation, with 'historical priority' probably belonging to panegyric. The Bahima material introduces the sub-genre of 'auto-panegyric' — let us call it 'the boast' or 'vaunt'. This opens up another theoretical sequence that links up with Bowra's: for self-praise to become praise little more than pronouns and their verbal correlatives need changing and accommodating to the metre, and for praise to become primitive epic only tenses require alteration. We may agree with Bowra that Africans seem not often to have made the transition to a historic past in heroic poetry, but if his view that 'the intellectual effort required for such an advance seems to have been beyond their powers' has any truth in it, a more positive formulation would be that the lack of detachment spoken of stemmed from sheer abundance of lyrico-musical gifts. In any case, at least one age of vanished imperial glory is enshrined in an African narrative in the third person and that is the Mandinka *Sunjata*, sung in various areas of what was Old Mali, now distributed among various modern states. Here the heroic tone is somewhat diluted by low-grade magic.[25] Under Islamic influence in the East there are now the Swahili epics, intensively studied by J. Knappert. The theme of the Bahima metrical boasts is deeds done about the cattle-herds, whether lifting or defending them, a theme widespread in heroic literature since ancient days.[26] Another aspect of the recitations of the Bahima that will strike the comparativist concerns the highly stylized diction: some of the formulae come close in structure to the Germanic kennings.

The essays presented here differ much despite the common underlying scheme not only because of the different personalities who composed them and the widely differing traditions they deal with, but also because these traditions have been studied for very different periods of time and at very different levels of intensity. At one extreme there is the Ancient Greek tradition which in its Homeric manifestation has been studied as a superlative achievement of human genius for some two and a half millennia and for both ethical and aesthetic reasons. At the other extreme there is, for example, the Bahima tradition, brought from the field in the years of its decline by a discerning Officer for Native Affairs and introduced to scholarship in a pioneering thesis, and then book, which set a standard of philological accuracy.[27] Over towards the former extreme are the medieval European traditions, objects of close investigation for scarcely more than two centuries, yet very intensively studied for reasons of patriotic pride and because the age which turned its attention to them was experiencing a great broadening and deepening of scholarly disciplines. Fortunately, too, native scholarship in the various lands was enriched by the interest of others in what was, after all, a shared and for the most part Christian European tradition. In the period in which such studies began there was a feeling abroad that every European nation[28] should have its epic, a feeling so strong that where there was none an epic was, if not invented, nevertheless somehow got together and produced. Various recent peoples of the Soviet Union are now going through a similar phase with regard to their poems of heroes, and it will be interesting to see how soon they catch up in the acceptability of their editions with the European scholars of the eighteenth to twentieth centuries, many of them Russians,[29] and all, naturally, heirs to a long tradition of Classical and Biblical scholarship.

A. T. HATTO

NOTES

1. *Iliad*, xi, 670–761.
2. The *romance* comes after epic, see p. 161, below.
3. See pp. 272 ff., below.
4. See p. 276, below.
5. The modern field adduced by the contributor for Old Indian, see p. 54, below, and his 'The singer or the song? A reassessment of Lord's "Oral Theory"', *Man*, 12 (1977), 141–53.
6. As in the Rājpūt texts of Pābūjī, see previous footnote, and as has been inferred for the Germanic lay.
7. See pp. 31 ff., below.
8. By C. S. Lewis, who launched the concept in his *Preface to Paradise Lost* (London, 1942).
9. See p. 51, below.
10. p. 73, below.
11. p. 55, below.
12. J. B. Hainsworth, *The flexibility of the Homeric formula* (Oxford, 1968).
13. See pp. 54 ff., below and note 5, above. Publication of a work on the Pābūjī texts by Dr John D. Smith et al., is imminent.
14. See the studies cited in notes 81, 84 and 85 to the contribution for Old French, p. 129, below.
15. See p. 185, below.
16. p. 10, above.
17. *Bulletin of Hispanic Studies*, 60 (1963), 137–43.
18. See note 1 to the contribution for Medieval German, p. 194. below.
19. See also H. W. Bailey, 'A half-century of Irano-Indian Studies', *Journal of the Royal Asiatic Society*, 1972, pp. 108–10.
20. In the Third Paper read to the Seminar, Professor Kenneth Jackson preferred to address us on the subject of the 'The poems of Aneirin' (15 March 1965). In the Preface to his book '*The Gododdin*'. *The Oldest Scottish poem* (Edinburgh, 1969), Professor Jackson states that it is an expansion of the paper he read to us.
21. English 'epic' stands closer in meaning to the Aristotelian ἐπο-ποιία than do German 'Epos' or Russian 'эпос', which after Herodotus and Pindar, strictly speaking, ought to be the plural 'ἔπεα'. The fact that German scholars have classed Arthurian romances as 'Ritterepen' would be no justification at all for regarding them as 'epics'. Similarly it is very convenient that various traditions of hero-tale in verse in the Soviet Union should be called 'эпос', but that does not necessarily make them into 'epics' in the English and Aristotelian sense.
22. The present writer has been privileged to attend.
23. p. 14.
24. See A. T. Hatto, 'Almambet, Er Kökčö and Ak Erkeč'. An episode from the Kirgiz heroic cycle of Manas, a. d. 1862', *Central Asiatic Journal*, 13 (1969), 169–71.

25. The hero's evil opponent can be killed only by a doctored spur of a white cock. See G. Innes's fine 'Sunjata'. *Three Mandinka versions*. [Mandinka texts, English translations and notes] (London, School of Oriental and African Studies, 1974). It is arguable, reciprocally, whether unique vulnerability in the heel or shoulder-blade is on a higher magical level. See also note 8, to the General Introduction, above. On 'epic' in Africa, cf. Dr Morris's note 9, p. 374, below.
26. See the Foreword by A. T. Hatto, to H. F. Morris, *The heroic recitations of the Bahima of Ankole* (Oxford, 1964), pp. v–xii.
27. Dr Morris was the pupil of Professor A. N. Tucker.
28. The contributor for Medieval Spanish notes that the speakers of each distinct language of Iberia aspired to an epic, see p. 134, below.
29. Z. N. Kuprianova's bilingual edition of Samoyed heroic songs *Épicheskie pesni nentsev* (Moscow, 1965) has set a standard in the Siberian and Central Asian heroic/epic field that has never been surpassed.

ANCIENT GREEK

By J. B. HAINSWORTH

THE ANCIENT GREEK EPIC TRADITION is represented for us by two long poems, *Iliad* and *Odyssey*, attributed to Homer, and by a long list of poets, fragments, and titles of works no longer extant. There is good reason for supposing that the *Iliad* and *Odyssey*, the integrity of whose text we must assume, are exceptionally fine products of their tradition. A distinction should accordingly be drawn between 'Homer', i.e. the two extant epics, and the rest of a long and often dreary epic tradition. This distinction is implicit in the following discussion.

I.   The setting of the Greek tradition

It is likely, though other views have been canvassed, that an Indo-European people began to penetrate the Greek peninsula soon after the beginning of the second millennium B.C. This movement introduced, or at least popularized, a characteristic pottery, now called 'Minyan', and an important animal, the domesticated horse.[1] In archaeological terms this movement is marked as the passage from the Early Helladic (EH) to the Middle Helladic (MH) periods of the Greek Bronze Age.

The MH period (*c.*1900–1580 B.C.), dull and undistinguished, was ended by the contacts its people established with the artistically brilliant culture, called Minoan, which had been developing on the island of Crete. The Minoans were in no sense Greek, but the mainlanders may now be safely so called, having fused with the earlier inhabitants and having developed their language into a form that will soon prove to be unmistakably Greek. At various points on the mainland, at Thebes, Athens, and especially at Mycenae, centres of power had been established which now in the Late Helladic (LH) period (*c.*1580–1100 B.C.) found the taste and means to acquire the arts of civilization. The acquisition was sometimes a little direct. Already in LH I Crete with the great centres of Cnossos and Phaistos, their native power shattered by the effects of the volcanic cataclysm that exploded the nearby island of Thera *c.*1500 B.C., had been seized. In LH II Mycenaean colonists landed in Rhodes and Cyprus, merchants visited Syria and Egypt. In LH III adventurers penetrated to Sicily and Italy, buccaneers raided the lands of the Hittite emperor, and an ancient and wealthy fortress in the north-east Aegean, known to legend as Ilion or Troy, was sacked. That it was the Mycenaean Greeks who sacked it cannot be certainly affirmed by archaeology, but legend is nowhere clearer: the blame lies squarely on the shoulders of one Agamemnon, King of Mycenae, and his confederate chiefs. For the LH period, especially the LH III B (*c.*1300–1200 B.C.), is the archaeological term for the Greek Heroic Age.

For the archaeologist the Mycenaean culture visible to us (which is to say the culture of the ruling classes) appears self-confident, receptive, and open-minded, especially in contrast with what went before and what was to come after. Men were aggressive and military: they enjoyed luxury and beauty. Gods were reverenced, of course, but the supernatural was inconspicuous. Palaces, not temples, dominated the settlements. Many tastes in art, many practices in government and religion have demonstrable analogues in the Near East. Indeed the Aegean may be regarded as a peripheral part of the Levantine world of the late second millennium B.C. There was literacy, or at least numeracy, in the local Linear B syllabic script. Bureaucratic organizations occupied themselves with the details of economic life, especially with the production of wool and cloth. Just occasionally the archives permit a glimpse of the men for whom this wealth was produced: the *wanax* (king), the *lawagetas* (army-leader), the *e-qe-ta* (companion or 'count'): and how they spent it, on gold and chariots.[2] Many years later, at the end of the eighth century B.C., the didactic poet Hesiod recognized the special quality of the Mycenaean age. In his dismal account of the decline of the human race he marks a reversal of the trend:

But when earth had covered this generation also, Zeus the son of Cronos made yet another, the fourth, upon the fruitful earth, which was nobler and more righteous, a god-like race of hero-men who are called demi-gods, the race before our own, throughout the boundless earth. Grim war and dread battle destroyed a part of them, some in the land of Cadmus at seven-gated Thebes when they fought for the flocks of Oedipus, and some when it had brought them in ships over the great sea gulf to Troy for fair-haired Helen's sake. (*Works and Days*, 156–65)

Geographically the Mycenaean was a mainland culture centred on the triangle Thebes–Athens–Mycenae but strong throughout the Peloponnese and with important outposts in Thessaly to the north and in Crete and the Dodecanese to the south and east. It did not penetrate Asia Minor. Ethnically the people were known as Achaeans. Their dialect of Greek has obvious affinities with the classical Arcado-Cypriot dialect. Their literature would be in a form of this Mycenaean dialect, a fact with important implications for the history of the Greek epic tradition.

According to the most recent excavator, Professor Blegen, Troy VII A fell at an archaeological horizon to be translated into our reckoning as *c.*1250 B.C. It may have been a little later. If the Achaeans were the destroyers, the sack marks the peak of Mycenaean power. Soon, in LH III C, the quality of art declines, its unity gives way to regionalism, wealth diminishes. There are signs of unease, soon to be justified. About 1200 B.C. the unprotected suburbs of

Mycenae were destroyed, Pylos and many lesser sites were obliterated. Finally Mycenae too fell. Of all the centres of Mycenaean culture, only Athens remained untouched.

Who wrought this destruction? Legend tells a story of a dynastic quarrel at Mycenae. The Pelopids expelled the Heraclids. The Heraclids put themselves at the head of the Dorians, a Greek tribe dwelling beyond the northern limits of the Mycenaean world, and 'returned'. The Dorians are archaeologically invisible, but they are a plain fact. In classical times they held the great cities of Megara, Corinth, Argos and Sparta. But the end of the Mycenaean age was one of general disturbance throughout the Levant. Some have tried to discern profound climatic changes which ruined the economic base of Mycenaean strength and depopulated the country. (The depopulation seems to be a fact.) Into the vacuum would have moved the Dorians, as the Slavs moved into a similar vacuum in the sixth century A.D.

Whatever its cause the collapse was complete and permanent. The centuries that followed the fall of Mycenae have long been known as the Dark Age (c.1100–700 B.C.). Archaeologically it comprises the Proto-Geometric and Geometric periods.[3] Despite the introduction of iron it was a mean period. Hesiod describes it:

Thereafter would I were not among the men of the fifth generation, but either had died before or been born afterwards. For now truly is a race of iron, and men never rest from labour and sorrow by day and from perishing by night; and the gods shall lay sore trouble upon them. (*Works and Days*, 174–78)

Thucydides, the late fifth-century historian, infers the period's miserable economic condition, its incessant disorder and piracy (*History*, I. 5). Thucydides was arguing from the analogy of backward districts in his own day, but his argument and inferences are exactly the same as we should make ourselves.

Amid these disorders the Greek world was reconstructed, and its balance significantly altered. About 1000 B.C. the Asiatic shore of the Aegean began to be intensively colonized, and the cities planted there — Smyrna, Colophon, Ephesus, Miletus, Halicarnassus — soon achieved a size and importance not far short of that of the cities of the mainland. In the Asiatic colonies the linguistic and ethnic divisions of the Greeks were sharply defined: Aeolic Greeks held the north, Ionians the centre, Dorians the south. The same divisions were recognized on the mainland also. The Achaean name survived, but the Achaeans themselves were scarcely any more counted a separate branch of the Greek people. The prestigious race was the Dorian. Culturally the meanness of the Dark Age is emphasized for us by the loss of literacy. We expect little of it. But this could be a mistake.[4] What we cannot discover from the meagre remains is the spiritual condition of the people. Hesiod's gloom is that of a peasant and a pessimist. Against him we can set all the signs of incipient resurgence visible in the eighth century. The decentralized, tribal political organization which the fall of the Mycenaean dynasties had left behind was replaced by the city state. The alphabet was introduced from Phoenicia. And about the middle of the century among the Ionians of Asia Minor the two remarkable poems were produced, the *Iliad* and the *Odyssey*.

The Dark Age gave way to the Archaic period (*c.*700–500 B.C.). The wealth of the Greek world steadily increased. A new wave of colonists descended on Cyrenaica, Sicily, Italy, the north Aegean, the Marmora and the Black Sea. From the very beginning of the period the political unit was typically the city and the political problem was the social stability of the city. Some cities had kings, now called *basilees*, but the kingship was often titular, temporary, and elective. Aristocracies of birth, often boasting descent from the heroes who fought at Troy, struggled with diminishing success against oligarchies of wealth. The first experiments in popular government were made. In this environment the epic tradition continued. It did not fade out until the fifth century B.C.

II. Literary situation

In the Mycenaean age literacy was cumbrous and specialized; in the Dark Age there is no evidence that it even existed. 'Literature' was thus of necessity oral. Doubtless many forms existed. Homer himself refers to choral part songs (*Il.*, 1. 603–4), and to dirges (*Il.*, 19. 282 ff.), as well as to epic lays (*Od.*, 8. 74, 499). But the impression that Homer gives is that the epic has no serious competitor. And this is probably right. The names of other epic poets of the late eighth century are known, Arctinus, Lesches, Stasinus. The earliest non-epic poet known to Greek literary history is Archilochus (*c.*650 B.C.).

After Homer, and while the epic tradition continued, the range of visible literature widens rapidly. The 'Hymn', in the Greek sense of a short narrative (up to *c.*600 lines) celebrating a divinity, appears almost immediately, followed soon (*c.* end eighth century) by the didactic, theological, and cataloguing verse of the mainland Hesiodic school. This poetry has no diction of its own, and its content does little more than add a few footnotes to the great epic tradition.

Literary independence is first asserted by the hortatory and reflective poetry of the elegists, but here too the dependence upon the epic is heavy. The elegy in any case was not a pretentious genre. It could not threaten the dominant epic. The challenge came in the late seventh century in the shape of the choral lyric of Stesichorus and Alcman. This lyric developed a new diction. Its content was typically mythological narrative. Its manner was formal, its tone elevated and moral. It had the advantage also of strong links with cults and festivals. For a hundred and fifty years the choral lyric was the leading literary form of Greek art. The last poet of the old epic seems to have been Panyassis in the early fifth century; after him the next epicist of note, Antimachus of Colophon (*c*.390 B.C.), shows all the signs of secondary, literary epic.

The Archaic period knew no prose literature and no drama.

Writing is common enough from the beginning of the sixth century to sign a name or perpetuate an epitaph, but Greek society in general did not practise literacy. Poetry was recited or sung, not read. However, the Archaic period did make an important step in the direction of literature in the strict sense. The old epic poets had been equipped with a technique for extempore composition. One may guess that their performances of the 'same' poem varied considerably. But this is not the case with the lyric. There the words are fitted into a strict and complicated metre. The poem may be composed entirely in the head and published and transmitted by mouth, but its text is fixed from the start. We know that in the Archaic period the idea of the fixed text came to be applied to Homer. It must also have affected the continuing epic tradition, but how it did so there is no direct evidence to show.

III.   Place of epic in the general literary situation

We have noted already that in the Dark Age epic poetry was the sole significant literary form, acceptable to all levels of society. Genius would naturally express itself through an epic poem. That was the genesis of the *Iliad* and *Odyssey*. But apart from the two Homeric poems the reputation of epic poetry among the Greeks of classical times and later did not stand very high. Homer was all. His poems were carried all over the Greek world by professional reciters, and their performance became a regular feature of certain festivals, such as the Panathenaea at Athens. Other epicists were despised for the shapeless plots and jejune style — men who began each sentence with the words *autar epeita* ('and thereafter . . .'). But the influence of epic continued wide and deep. This is true in detail. The hymnal and didactic genres share the epic metre and diction. The elegists have a similar metre and use epic diction regularly. The metres of lyric are various, but the use of epic and epic-inspired diction is a normal form of embellishment. Yet the influence works also at a deeper level. Throughout the Archaic period art expresses itself through narratives. Lyrists and vase painters alike stole the epic poet's clothes, pushed him slowly into the background, and left the genre with no exponents of real genius.

IV.   The general nature of Greek epic

(a)   *Content*

What Greek epic is about is defined by Homer as *klea andrōn*, glorious deeds of heroes. Hesiod neatly summarized the typical circumstances (*Works and Days*,

156 ff., quoted above, p. 21). The staple was martial exploits about a besieged town in pursuit of booty or vengeance. A straightforward cattle-raid is the subject of one of Nestor's tales in the *Iliad* (11. 670 ff.). Journeys to distant lands were recounted in the story of the Argonauts and the Returns of the Heroes from Troy. For an army the highest exploit was to carry the enemy's fortifications by assault (cf. the Trojan assault on the Greek camp, *Il.*, 12. 88 ff.); for the individual hero it was to slay a worthy opponent in single combat. Against this background the content of the *Iliad* appears typical and homogeneous. The special character of the poem is that it selects a particular episode out of the siege story and tells it at length. The *Odyssey*, however, is clearly somewhat exceptional. In essence the poem is an elaborately told *nostos*, or Return Home from Troy. The Return was a regular epic theme, cf. the song of Phemius, *Od.*, 1. 326, and the Cyclic Epic *Nostoi*,[5] and the climax is a spear fight in the Iliadic manner, but for the rest the net is cast rather wide and relies quite heavily on elements of folktale. This is especially true of the Wanderings of Odysseus (*Od.*, Books 5–13) the greater part of which takes place in fairyland. The hero then becomes a disguised beggar in his own palace and reveals himself by passing an ordeal. Until its last moments therefore the *Odyssey* seems to be a poem about cunning rather than prowess.

Culture heroes, e.g. Palamedes, are known to Greek mythology, but did not much interest the epic tradition until its last days when poems about Heracles and Theseus (who rid the earth of plagues) and the founders of cities became popular.

(b)   *Ethos*

The Homeric ethos is summed up in the famous line with which fathers sent forth their sons: 'Be always best and pre-eminent beyond all others' (*Il.*, 6. 208; 11. 784). The qualities of mind are not despised, but the pre-eminence is primarily physical and to be displayed in battle, cf. Nestor's compliment to Diomedes: 'Son of Tydeus, in war indeed you are very mighty and in counsel too you surpass all your generation' (*Il.*, 9. 53–54). Coming from Nestor that is a compliment indeed. For Homeric counsel is the wisdom that is the fruit of experience; it is not intelligence, and certainly not cleverness. The *Iliad* is especially clear on this point. Nowhere is the intellectual level of the heroes represented as any higher than plain common sense. No one attempts any tactical tricks or strategic ploys. Most striking of all, Achilles is made to repudiate lying: 'As hateful to me as the gates of Hell is that man who hides one thing in his heart, and speaks another' (*Il.*, 9. 312–13). Generally the Greeks were admirers of the Big Lie.

On the other hand valour is everywhere. It is the indispensable virtue of the hero and the greatest single obligation upon him. 'Why are we honoured with

precedence and maintenance in Lycia?' asks Sarpedon (*Il.*, 12. 310 ff.), and
the answer is, 'because we stand amid the front ranks of the Lycians and
encounter the heat of battle, so that one of the Lycian warriors may say, "Not
inglorious are the kings who lord it over Lycia and consume the rich flocks and
sweet wine" '. In the intervals of battle the hero's prowess displays itself in
athletic contests (*Il.*, 23, 257 ff.; *Od.*, 8. 104 ff.).

It is important that the hero should be successful. Sometimes, it is true,
warriors of unimpeachable valour retreat in the face of odds to fight again on a
more auspicious day, but the true Iliadic note is that sounded by Poseidon (*Il.*,
13. 232 ff.). Even if all seems black, that is no excuse for cowardice: the brave
man takes up his spear and turns to face the enemy. The greatest warrior,
Achilles, does not retreat at all, or meet with any reverse at the hands of human
opponents. His career on the battlefield (*Il.*, Books 20–22) is one successful
slaying after another, culminating in single combat with the greatest of the
Trojans, Hector.

The idea, therefore, of the glorious failure, the gallant fight against insuper-
able odds, is not Homeric. The fact that a worthy opponent must fall before the
great warrior means that the idea is often latent, and may present itself to our
minds, e.g. in the deaths of Patroclus (*Il.*, Book 16) and Hector (*Il.*, 22). But
Homer does not see it that way: Patroclus was trapped by his folly, and Hector's
kin see nothing in his death but unmitigated disaster.

Success wins for the hero glory (*kydos* or *kleos*); and to have *kydos* is to receive
honour (*timē*). *Timē* does not mean respect in the sense of an emotion, for the
Homeric world tends to externalize the mind: *timē* is receiving precedence,
holding possessions, accepting gifts. That is why the seizure of the girl Briseis by
Agamemnon or the behaviour of the Suitors in the palace were to Achilles and
Odysseus insufferable insults which their code required them to avenge.

To these standards a partial exception is formed by the middle books of the
Odyssey, the Wanderings. Once Odysseus has passed Cape Malea on his home-
ward journey he ceases to do any fighting. His heroism is expressed in endurance
and in guile. He lies freely to everyone he encounters. He suspects everything,
often with good reason. His opponents are monsters and ogres. He overcomes
these by cunning, magic, or special favour, but finally through the sacrilege of
his companions he is reduced to a naked castaway. Then from this utter
nothingness he returns to seize back his throne.

Other exploits and virtues play a very subordinate role. Heroes are generous
and hospitable, but they care little for justice and mercy. Acts which to us seem
vindictive and cruel, such as the killing of a man who asks for quarter, are told
as if ferocity were a natural adjunct of valour. Women's virtues are chastity
and faithfulness, but Homer attributes to women little will and drive, so that
it is difficult to imagine an active female role. Penelope survives by avoiding a
confrontation with her suitors. (In the epic tradition there were such formidable

ladies as Clytemnestra, who, for vengeance, slew her husband and usurped his throne.) Since women have no will no credit can attach to overpowering it; Homer has no seducers. This is not prudery; it is just that women's bodies are men's property.[6] Like other facts of life, blood, sweat, filth, Homer accepts sex straightforwardly and makes nothing of it.

Lastly, because Greek heroes are but strong men without magical or absurdly superhuman powers, it is possible for them to be heroic not merely in their deeds but also in their deep attitudes of mind. Odysseus esteems his home of higher value than immortality and the embrace of a goddess. Achilles chooses vengeance for a friend in the face of the early death he knows that this will bring upon him. In the great duels that climax the passages of battle, it is not the details of the combat that matter (these are quite ordinary), but the spirit of the warriors, the proud words on their dying lips.

(c) *Powers of the hero*

Homeric heroes are normal human beings cast on a very large scale. There is no absurd exaggeration of their strength; occasionally we are told that some hero hurled a rock with ease that two men of our own generation could not lift, or that Odysseus was nine days swimming in the sea, but for long stretches of narrative there is no exaggeration at all. However, the story has a continuous supernatural accompaniment. Gods are everywhere. In the *Odyssey* especially the hero is constantly attended and assisted by the goddess Athene. Apart from gods supernatural phenomena are extremely rare. True, both leading heroes have weapons which only they can wield, Achilles a great spear and Odysseus a bow. But these are simply special weapons appropriate to their owners' heroic strength. They are not magical, and do not have their own names. Achilles is addressed at a solemn moment by his horse and is visited, in a dream, by a ghost. The *Odyssey* has a fine description of second sight (20. 350 ff.). (Again we must make an exception of the Wanderings with their witches, spells, and magic ships.)

Greek gods were beings anthropomorphic in mind and appearance whose constitution lacked all the ills that human flesh is heir to. They were immune from fatigue, illness, or death.[7] Though not omnipotent or omniscient, they embodied in high degree all the physical virtues of strength, skill, and beauty. Their seed was never without issue. They might transform themselves, render themselves unseen, alter the course of that part of the world that fell within their province. On the moral side they seemed to later ages to be deficient. But later ages saw morality in terms of justice and temperance, whereas the epic gods are heroic beings on the largest scale. Like heroes, the gods are unconcerned in general with notions of justice, but at helping their friends and harming their enemies they are very good indeed.

c

Since it is so conspicuous, it is important to understand the divine element in epic correctly. In one sense the gods are obviously fiction. Mermaids do not rise out of the sea. If they are represented as doing so we are in the presence of 'literature' not 'life'. To a pious audience this would not be mere ornament. The introduction of gods would invest an episode with complex religious emotions that are now beyond our grasp. In another sense, however, the gods are fact. No Greek in the eighth century, or for centuries afterwards, doubted so manifest a truth as the existence and activity of gods: winds rose or fell, spears hit or missed, warriors went berserk or got a second wind. To tell a story without mentioning gods would be like telling it without mentioning the heroes, or their weapons, or some other essential element. So we may ask a factual question: on what occasions do Homeric heroes have recourse to religious language? These defined, we should then be able to translate the Homeric expressions into a contemporary mode.

First, the gods provide an explanation for the general course of events, especially if these are contrary to expectation. As a rule, the gods are not thought to control the world or set limits to human achievement. That was the business of *Moira* (Fate). But the gods are powerful and unpredictable beings, and they may decide for their own reasons, as Zeus does in the first book of the *Iliad*, that this week the Trojans are to have the upper hand. One becomes aware of this by failure (cf. *Il.*, 13. 222 ff.). Failure, of course, might be due to cowardice, but if one has taken special precautions to expose and eliminate cowardice, and still does not succeed (and in human affairs this does happen), then what other explanation can there be than the decree of heaven (cf. *Il.*, 2. 362 ff.)? If necessary, this conclusion can be confirmed by consulting professional diviners, such as Calchas (*Il.*, 1. 68) or Theoclymenus (*Od.*, 15. 256).

Second, the result of any particular action whose outcome is unpredictable may be attributed to divine intervention. If I sail safely into an uncharted harbour, some god must have guided me (*Od.*, 9. 142). If I throw my spear and it misses, Athene must have deflected it (*Il.*, 5. 843). But this language is not obligatory, and even if it is used, it is not taken to diminish the credit of success or to excuse failure.

These usages may be compared with modern notions of chance, luck, and 'form'. They are pseudo-explanations which restate the event in more colourful language.

Third, just as 'being on form' is a way of expressing a fine performance, so speaking of a god in Homer may express excellence. Thus Pandarus *made* himself a *fine* bow (*Il.*, 4. 104 ff.), so it was *given* him by Apollo (*Il.*, 2. 827). No literal gift is implied.

In poetry 'literature' sometimes invades 'life' and the gods are made to act on the same stage as the heroes. This may be quite trivial, as when Athene stiffens Telemachus's resolve in *Od.*, Book 1 (which might mean that his resolve was, unexpectedly, stiffened) and the suitors see her (cf. the invisible Athene of *Il.*, 1. 198) and ask questions about her. It might be colourful, as when Diomedes engages Ares and Aphrodite in *Il.*, Book 5. It might also constitute an excuse (as the gods cannot be in 'life'), as when the death of Patroclus is attributed to the act of Apollo in *Il.*, Book 16. The last is exceptional.

(d)   *Believed historicity*

Homer himself and the poets that he mentions claim to be the mouthpieces of the goddesses of poetry, the Muses. In bald language this means that they have the special skill that being an epic poet requires. Now Homer invokes the Muse not only at the very beginning of his poems, when it is reasonable that he should summon up his poetical skill, but also at certain points within them. These points are not moments of climax, as if the poet were calling for inspiration, but arid catalogues whose recital might constitute a feat of memory, but little else. In other words the Muse assists the poet to get his 'facts' right. Her qualification is that she has knowledge, whereas men have but hearsay. Fortified by her aid, Homer proceeds with sublime self-assurance, and normally without apology.[8]

The fictional nature of much epic was apparently perceived by Hesiod who makes his Muses say: 'We know how to speak many false things as though they were true; but we know, when we will, to utter true things' (*Theogony*, 27–28). He makes truth the hallmark of his own, didactic genre. But this was an eccentric view. Otherwise in archaic or classical Greece the literal truth of Homer was taken for granted. The Archaic period was indeed the heyday of the hero-cult.[9] Not all of these heroes were epic ones, but many were, and the cults, tombs, and the politically-inspired traffic in bones, could not have existed without a belief in the literal existence of the heroes and the historical reality of their deeds. Even the political geography of *Iliad*, Book 2 was quoted in support of territorial claims. The sceptical historian Thucydides accepted Homer as a historical source with little qualm. Aristotle recommended epic tales to tragedians because tragic plots should be 'probable', and what has *actually happened* is inherently probable.

Of course, it is one thing to believe in the historicity of the siege of Troy, and another to believe that on a certain day in the tenth year Meriones killed Phereclus with a thrust in the guts, and yet another to believe in Cyclopes and Circes. We do not know where the line was drawn, if at all. The concept of 'fiction' is a sophisticated one, and did not begin to be elucidated in Greece before Aristotle. For the Archaic period the opposite of truth was falsehood: and no one wished to say that Homer was a liar.

In the Hellenistic age (after 300 B.C.) the usual scholarly assumption, reasonably enough, was that the main events, taking place as they did at familiar places were true, but that the Wanderings of Odysseus were fictional and set in a fictional landscape.[10]

(e) *Times presented*

The Greek epic was concerned with the exploits of men believed to have belonged to two or three generations living *c.* 1275–1175 B.C., the men, that is, in the words of Hesiod, who fought at Thebes and Troy. The salient exploits and personages were made so familiar by the epic tradition as to become canonical. By Homer's time there was no doubt at all where a given personage belonged and what his relationship was to others. The salient features of the material background to the Heroic age were also well known and canonical, especially where they differed from the contemporary scene of the late Dark Age. The poet lived in Asia, in a Greek world without a dominant political centre and ethnically divided into Dorian, Ionian, and Aeolian Greeks, whose people used iron tools, did their fighting mostly on foot, and lived at a relatively low economic level. He described a world in which Asia was non-Greek, Greece dominated by the King of Mycenae, ethnically unified under the Achaean name, using bronze and fighting with chariots, whose rulers enjoyed great wealth and luxury. At this level the description is remarkably consistent, and, except in one particular, historically accurate. The exception is that the Mycenaean age buried its dead in fine built tombs, whereas Homer's heroes are cremated and a mound of soil heaped over their ashes. There is no obvious explanation why this anachronism should have successfully penetrated the epic's picture of its world. Nonetheless, the exclusion of the Dorian Greeks and the insistence on the use of bronze show that the epic tradition had a definite notion of the otherness of the Heroic age.

As may be expected, the peculiarities of the Heroic age are confined to general matters. In detail, e.g. in the shapes of shields or the decoration of swords, Homer is full of anachronism and is careless of consistency. So at *Il.*, 6. 117 Hector's shield is the great body-shield of early Mycenaean times stretching from neck to ankle. A little later, at *Il.*, 7. 238, the same hero boasts to Ajax of his skill at the parrying movements used with the small, hand-gripped target of the late Dark Age. But there is no reason to suppose that in this and dozens of similar details Homer realized that he was admitting a modernism. It is likely that if he had appreciated what he was doing he would have avoided the anachronism: for there are a few details which are mentioned in similes, such as riding horseback and the use of the trumpet, and are excluded from the narrative where in fact they would be anachronistic.

As a result of the great number of small innovations in its tradition, the Greek epic has no real idea what the Mycenaean age was like. Indeed Homer was far more ignorant than we are ourselves after more than a century of archaeological exploration and the recent decipherment of the Linear B archives. Oddly enough Homer tends to underestimate the material civilization of Mycenae. For him a great palace needed the enormous number of fifty maids to run it (one can almost hear the audience gasp at such luxury):[11] the king of Mycenaean Pylos commanded the services of many hundreds.

For the Greek epic the times represented were clearly in the past and had to be represented in a certain way. Homer himself occasionally contrasts the Heroic age with the present, but he gives no clue as to its distance in the past. His audiences could easily have worked it out if they had wished to: the aristocrats of Ionia and Aeolis had only to count up their ancestors. But within the poems themselves the action is not located in a chronological framework that includes the present. Like all aspects of his personality the poet's attitude to the past is obscure, for the convention of Homeric narration is rigidly objective. There is no overt nostalgia for the passing of the Mycenaean civilization, no malice towards its destroyers, no expressed pride in national achievement.

(f) *Manner of composition*

Nothing, of course, can be directly known about the methods of composition used by Homer and his successors, and the inferential arguments, as commonly presented, include a comparative element. Homer himself has no comment, or rather a number of non-comments. 'The Muse moved the bard to sing' (*Od.*, 8. 73). 'The god has set many lays in my heart' (*Od.*, 22. 347). These are quite uninformative. More helpful is the fact that Demodocus, the bard of *Od.*, Book 8, is blind. He, personally, got along without writing, but it is left uncertain whether he improvised or memorized.

The inferential arguments are drawn essentially from three facts:

(i)   the high totals of demonstrable formulae in Homer,

(ii)   the schematization of the formulae into extensive but economical systems,

(iii)   the quality of the result.

'Formula' has been defined in various ways, usually with a view to increasing the number of expressions in the texts that can be counted formulaic. A repeated phrase is certainly a formula, and Homerists often add, as 'formulaic expressions', 'formulae by analogy', or 'structural formulae', expressions that have something other than verbal identity in common with each other, such as metrical shape and syntax. Formulae are of all sorts, sets of lines, whole lines, half lines, subjects + verbs, verbs + objects, epithets + nouns. By far the most conspicuous type to the ordinary reader is the last, the epithet being often of a highly colourful sort, e.g. 'Apollo of the silver bow', 'cloud-gathering Zeus', 'dark-prowed ships', 'fair-maned horses'.

The density of formulae in the text varies with the subject matter: battle scenes are more formulaic than speeches or similes. How densely formulaic depends on how the formula is defined. But even if the term is defined very narrowly there are few lines in the average passage that do not contain at least one formula. If the term is stretched to include 'structural formulae', whole sections may be dubbed totally formulaic.

If the expressions for a much used concept, e.g. 'wine', are gathered together we obtain a set ('system') of half a dozen phrases or thereabouts, e.g. in order or increasing length:

> sweet mead
> r e d   w i n e
> gleaming wine
> honey-sweet wine
> wine sweet to the mind
> wine made of fine grapes

The arrangement indicates the natural positions of these formulae in the verse. Between them they fill all the metrical shapes that the poet commonly needs for a nominal phrase. This fact constitutes the 'extension' of the formulaic system. It will be noted that the extension is bought at some cost. The shortest formula can only be constructed by using as a synonym a rather rare word, *methy*, which for clarity more than accuracy I have rendered 'mead'. Synonyms are very frequently pressed into service in this way, but Greek epic seldom uses paraphrase and true kennings are virtually unknown.

For each metrical shape there is only one formula. This is the 'economy' of the system. In the Greek the formulae 'red wine' and 'gleaming wine' (*woinon erythron* and *aithopa woinon*) have indeed the same length but begin with different types of sound, a vowel or a consonant. In a quantitative metre such as Homer's this is an important metrical difference, for which the formula-systems make frequent provision.

This schematization of the formulae, repeated as it is for scores of proper names and common nouns, is a decisive argument for the traditional character of the Homeric diction. It is also easily turned into a powerful argument that the diction which Homer inherited was an instrument perfected for the tricky task of orally improvising verses. Why else should we have this curiously refined situation in which the greatest number of metrical needs are met with the least number of formulae?

Much else falls into line with this argument. When it is treating certain subjects, as for example battles, Greek epic is very repetitive. Scenes are built up out of typical details and arranged in typical sequences. So we may imagine that 'in composing [Homer] would do no more than put together for his needs phrases which he has often heard or used himself, and which, grouping themselves in accordance with a fixed pattern of thought, come naturally to make the sentence and the verse; and he would recall his poem easily, when he wished to say it over, because he would be guided anew by the same play of words and phrases as before'.[12] Some hesitation has been caused, however, by point (iii) above: the quality of the result. Homer always contrives to give the impression of gushing spontaneity, fired by an alert and vigorous imagination. Both poems are also excellent dramatic narratives, of a standard *perhaps* inconsistent with improvised composition of any sort. So it has been *guessed* that Homer was a traditional poet who learned to write and to exploit the advantages of the new tool (M. Bowra, *Heroic Poetry* (London, 1952), pp. 240–41), or that he dictated his poems at a slow and reflective pace to an amanuensis (Lord, 1953; see note 12, above).

The fragments of post-Homeric epic are too small to permit the sort of analysis to which the Homeric diction has been subjected. There is some suggestion that the rigidity and economy of the old formula-systems was broken down. If this was in fact the case it would imply a diminished reliance on extempore composition. However, the truth is that we are in almost complete ignorance of the character of Greek epic in the later stages of its long tradition.

There is no extant account of how a poet acquired his skill. None of the poets mentioned in Homer is accompanied by an apprentice. Usually the art of song is simply described as a gift of the gods. The most elaborate statement is that of Hesiod:

And one day [the Muses] taught Hesiod the glorious art of song as he was shepherding his lambs beneath holy Helicon . . . and they plucked and gave me a rod, a branch of sturdy laurel, marvellous to see, and breathed into me a divine voice that I might celebrate things that shall be and things that were before; and they bade me sing of the race of the blessed gods that are eternally. (*Theogony*, 22–33)

(g) *Manner of performance*

All our knowledge for the performance of traditional epic in the Dark Age derives from the *Odyssey*, chiefly from Book 8. There a minor king, Alcinoos, gives an entertainment in his court consisting of feasting, sports, and poetical recitations. A bard is sent for. (The palace of Odysseus on Ithaca appears to have a resident bard.) After the meal the bard, prompted by the Muse, begins to sing. He accompanies himself on the *phorminx* (syn. *kitharis*), a multistringed lyre, apparently remaining seated. His song makes the guest weep, so the king brusquely suspends the performance. 'That's enough of music. Now let's go out and watch some wrestling.' A special dance is then put on, accompanied 'in the midst' by the bard. Then (or perhaps during the dance) the bard sings the hilarious tale, *The Love of Ares and Aphrodite*. He is rewarded with a dish of viands sent down from the High Table. He then sings another heroic tale, this time at the suggestion of the guest, but once more, as in the case of the first performance, the song has a disastrous effect, and is suspended.

It is hard to date the picture drawn in this vignette. It might even be Mycenaean. A famous fresco from the great hall of the palace at Pylos shows a lyre-player holding a five-stringed *phorminx*. But I should guess that it is contemporary with Homer, and reflects the conditions of some epic performances in the eighth century B.C. Statuettes and vase-paintings of the Geometric period represent seated lyre-players solo and standing lyre-players amid dancers.

It is clear that the epic in its heyday was sung in the strict sense of the word. With the close of the eighth century a change set in. Describing his 'call' in the *Theogony*, Hesiod says that the Muses gave him a staff, not a lyre. In Homer the staff is the implement of the orator, later it was familiar as an accoutrement of the professional reciters (not composers) of epic poetry, the 'rhapsodes'. A diverting picture of a late fifth-century rhapsode is given in Plato's dialogue *Ion*.

(h) *Style*

The salient features of Greek epic style are objectivity and formality. The poet is pure narrator, using the third person and the past tense throughout.[13] Having transported us into the Heroic world he is careful to keep us there, allowing no reference to the present and none to the audience. History and prophecy are not excluded, but their chronological limits are those of the Heroic world. Homer has nothing comparable to the great speech of Anchises in the sixth book of Virgil's *Aeneid*. The poet refers to himself only in a very formal way, as in an appeal to the Muse for aid, and hides his personality behind the elaborate and artificial diction in which custom (and the needs of improvised composition) required Greek epic to be expressed.

The metre is a repeated line, the dactylic hexameter, the same metre as was later used by the poets of the literary epic in both Greek and Latin. There is no stanza or any other external articulation. There is no structural rhyme or assonance. The rhythm is based on syllabic quantity. The fundamental element is the metrical foot, called a dactyl, consisting of one 'long' syllable followed by two 'shorts'. The line is made up of six of these feet except that the last is shortened by one syllable (a common feature of clausulae). What, however, gives the metre its versatility is the fact that a single long is accepted as the syllabic equivalent of the two shorts of the dactyl. This equivalence is freely used in the first four feet of the line, but is rare in the fifth, for at the end of the verse it is desirable to permit the metrical form clear expression. There are thus sixteen metrical variants in common use. Moreover the length of the line (thirteen to seventeen syllables) means that short sentences fall within its length. Bearing in mind that enjambement is a regular feature, it follows that the relation of sentence to metre is almost infinitely flexible. The general effect is one of great variety, ease, and speed.

The epic metre and the epic diction went hand in hand. Selected parts of the diction might be borrowed by other genres, but in archaic and classical times the use of the hexameter is restricted to the epic and its close relatives, the hymnal and didactic genres.

The language of Homer is very artificial. The predominant element is Ionic Greek, but a liberal infusion of formations from the Aeolic dialect, archaisms, and arbitrary combinations is allowed. The ancient view was that the motive for this admixture was aesthetic: it produced grandeur and solemnity. No doubt the effect was aesthetically gratifying, but in fact the admixture of dialectal, archaic, and artificial formations is governed by the same technical factors as govern the formulaic diction. For any given grammatical form, non-Ionic formations are admitted if, and only if, they are metrically different from the Ionic. The poet thus obtains extension: several formations of the same sense but different shape, and, at the same time, economy: for a given shape only one formation. Even the colourful and characteristic composita have a very close relation to the needs of metre and formulae. They very often, for example, exactly fill the last two feet of the verse.

An improvising composer does not have the same scope for varying his style of composition as a writer, because he works with traditional elements. Homer looks stylistically very even. This is deceptive. His pace especially he can vary. The first sixty lines of the *Iliad* pour out with breathless speed. Odysseus's boat is built in twenty lines (*Od.*, 5. 241 ff.), with hardly a single ornamental epithet. On the other hand it requires nearly 1800 lines, from the beginning of *Iliad*, Book 2, to bring the Greeks and Trojans into battle. Aptly chosen vocabulary can give a majestic or horrendous effect to passages of description, for example:

Foam formed about his mouth, his eyes blazed beneath the glowering brows, and about his temples his helmet shook dreadfully as Hector fought; for Zeus himself from heaven was his helper. (*Il.*, 15. 607–10)[14]

There are also passages that are flat and jejune, where end-stopped lines succeed each other and traditional phrases are used with imprecision and redundancy.

The unit of construction in narrative is the brief 'episode', told in from half a dozen to twenty lines or more, of the type How A slew B, How X exhorted Y. Here too the poet can be very laconic, or he can elaborate the episode to great length by adding more and more elements: compare the very brisk manner of *Il.*, 16. 306 ff., a series of slayings, with the similar but leisurely passage *Il.*, 5. 37 ff., and that with the elongated duel scene *Il.*, 16. 419 ff. Episodes arrange themselves in fairly predictable sequences. Thus if an army has to be got into action we are likely to find (i) a council of war, (ii) a sacrificial meal, (iii) a parade, (iv) a harangue, (v) the charge, (vi) a series of slayings by various warriors, (vii) a series of slayings by one hero, (viii) a rally, and the sequence repeated from (iv) for the benefit of the other side. The narrative is always sequential, and events which must be supposed to take place simultaneously are narrated as if they followed each other.

The poet focuses his attention so sharply on the episode he is narrating, that at times the logical connexion between adjacent episodes (or their balance) may be weak. This is nowhere clearer than in the characteristic similes. The battle-passages especially are interspersed with these elaborate comparisons, which are often remarkably fine, and as often developed in a way irrelevant or inapposite to their context: e.g. at *Il.*, 8, 553–59 the watchfires of the Trojans (a most ominous sign to the Greeks) are compared to the stars on a clear night, when all the crags and trees stand out clearly *and the shepherd's heart rejoices*. In a series of parallel scenes, such as the adventures of Odysseus on his wanderings, one (e.g. the Cyclops episode, or the chariot race in the Games of Patroclus) may receive very much more elaborate treatment than the others.

In such large works as *Iliad* and *Odyssey* the tone naturally varies. Homer permits himself humour (e.g. *Il.*, 23. 306 ff., Nestor's advice to his son on how to cheat) even smutty humour (*Od.*, 8. 334 ff.). But generally the tone is dignified without becoming pretentiously solemn. The tone is also moral. Homer clearly intended to portray what he believed to be virtue. However, ideas of virtue and dignity change. Hellenistic critics found fault, for example, with Agamemnon's passion for a concubine, and frank allusion to what she was to be kept for. They also took offence at Achilles's abusive language towards Agamemnon. That is merely their squeamishness. It is easy also for us to think that Homer is a little too free with his gore, that he dwells too gloatingly on the deaths of men. That would be our squeamishness; we are, generally, unfamiliar with the Homeric emotion *kharme*, battle-lust. Yet Homer seems to recognize that there is a pornography of blood, and avoids it.[15] He will specify the site of wound, he will describe in detail the course of a spear-point through the vital organs, but slayings are brief and told at a fast pace. Extended similes frequently relieve the mind. Deaths are instantaneous. Corpses are seldom mutilated. Achilles's treatment of Hector's body is the only example of abuse of the dead, and this is recognized to be excessive, expressive of his frantic lust for vengeance. Judicial execution and mutilation is practised only on disloyal slaves. The passage (*Od.*, 22. 431 ff.), for an inegalitarian age, is hardly an exception to the general tone.

(i) *Social function*

The social function of Greek epic down to and including Homer can only be surmised. The usual verb associated with minstrelsy is *terpein* 'please', and audiences are represented as 'entranced', not as stirred up to valour and admiration. The epic is serious and moral in tone, but it does not preach. Heroes are brave and imperious, wives faithful and submissive, young men courteous and deferential — but not more so than the story requires. However, the epic was for several centuries the sole important art of its community. As such it inevitably incorporated and served to transmit the ideals and experience of the people. The epic poet was the custodian of the past. Even so it is something of a quirk of chance that throughout the archaic and well into the classical period Homer's poetry enjoyed an almost biblical reputation. It became the staple of education and shaper of opinion, for which reason it was bitterly attacked by the moral philosophers from Xenophanes to Plato. It is natural therefore that during this period the later epic poets should attempt to exploit this reputation. Eumelus promoted the glory of Corinth, Asios Boeotia, the author of the *Theseis* Athens, and so on.

(j) *Audience*

At one point (*Il.*, 9. 189) Achilles himself is represented as singing the mighty deeds of heroes to the lyre. He is relieving the boredom of his self-imposed idleness, and his audience consists only of himself and his companion Patroclus. Otherwise poetry appears to be in the hands of professional bards. The best descriptions are in *Od.*, Books 1 and 8. At one time these accounts were doubtless apposite. They represent the audience as the guests of a princeling at dinner. The audience was therefore male and aristocratic. The bard's employers were his social superiors, and treated him with scant respect. But already epic was not confined to the palaces. Demodocus had to be summoned from the market place. Bards, like other professionals, might be itinerant (*Od.*, 17. 384). In later times, when biographies of Homer were invented, it was thought plausible to represent him as wandering from city to city and reciting his poems in the market places. Another occasion for poetry was the funeral games of the aristocracy, where a competitive element entered. Hesiod remarks how he won the prize against all comers at the obsequies of Amphidamas at Chalcis in Euboea (*Works and Days*, 654 ff.). A heroic lay would have been appropriate, but Hesiod does not specify the nature of his entry. His extant work is of a moralizing or theological kind. Recitations also took place at religious festivals, such as that on the island of Delos (*Hymn to Apollo*, 169 ff.), attended by all, irrespective of sex or status. The festival has been peculiarly tempting to Homeric scholars, since it seems to offer an occasion of sufficient duration and an audience sufficiently captive to explain the great length of the Homeric epics, which each require at least twenty hours for their performance.[16] Unfortunately, apart from this convenience, there is no evidence to connect the epics with the festivals in the age of their composition. Who actually formed Homer's audience is thus not known, but on the wider view it is not very material to know who they were, for it is clear from the way in which epic matter permeates the whole of the archaic culture of Greece that the audience was effectively the sum of the population.

(k) *Length*

Apart from the probabilities of the case, there is some evidence in the songs of Demodocus in *Od.*, Book 8, in the episodic cataloguing poetry of Hesiod, and in the scale of the major Homeric Hymns (*c.*300–600 lines) that the short lay was known to the Greek tradition. But it is scarcely now visible to us. The normal assumption in Greece was that an epic poem would be a substantial work. In the summaries of the Trojan Cycle recorded in Proclus's *Chrestomathy*, lengths of two to eleven 'books' are noted (Iliadic books average *c.*600 lines). The two Homeric poems, of twenty-four books each, are clearly of outstanding length. This great length has no obvious explanation within the Greek tradition. It is there in full perfection in the earliest extant works, and was never subsequently rivalled. Nor is the scale achieved by mere linear addition, at the expense of form. Expansion is contrived within the plot.

V. Development of the tradition

That Homer is the flowering of a tradition is obvious. This fact is really the sum of our knowledge regarding the development of Greek epic. The diction certainly began to develop in the Mycenaean period itself, because certain formulae, such as the 'silver-studded sword', describe objects only to be found in limited archaeological contexts. The singer is depicted in the palace frescoes. Interestingly, siege-scenes occur in Mycenaean vase-painting. But since vase-painting becomes less and less pictorial in the sub-Mycenaean phase we soon lose this possible clue to the content of literature.

This Mycenaean epic tradition died out on the mainland, but before it did so it had been carried over the Aegean to the colonies of Ionia and Aeolis, and there it stayed until the end of the eighth century B.C. We reckon therefore with a development of at least 400 years before Homer. During this time the Greek language underwent many changes in the course of normal linguistic evolution, but the formulaic diction lagged behind, for the new forms might make the old formulae unmetrical. But new formulae were created continuously, and many took advantage of linguistic changes. The dialect situation in Mycenaean Greece is obscure and it would be hazardous to guess in what dialectal form the epic tradition had its birth. The main part of its development, however, was certainly in the Ionic form of Greek.

What use Homer made of his tradition is the domain of the abstruser kind of Homeric scholarship. It is a field where there are obviously few certainties. One of them (to stress it again) is that the Greek tradition blossomed into a flower of exceptional size and colour. Homer dominated Greek epic. As they are recorded for us, the poems of the Cycle group themselves around the *Iliad* and *Odyssey* and complete the tale of Troy. Outside the Cycle very little is known. Fragments are few and brief. But they reveal one thing: the epic diction had become ossified in its Homeric form, and had lost the capacity to renew itself. The decline was slow and prolonged, but during it, with one exception, the epic maintained a serious aspect, it did not shade off into romance or melodrama. The exception is the *Margites*. Margites was an anti-hero, a buffoon who fails in everything. The interest of this parody of the epic ethos is that the poem was very likely early. Epic could already seem funny at the beginning of the seventh century B.C.

VI.   Appreciation

There is little evidence in Homer of the criteria by which his audiences would have judged his poems, and what there is is trivial. The popularity of the 'new song' is noted at *Od.*, 1. 351. Odysseus comments that Demodocus recounted the woes of the Achaeans 'in due order' (*Od.*, 8. 489).

The great critics of antiquity lived long after the demise of the epic tradition, and in a very different social and literary world. Their criticism is of great interest, but of no special authority. Aristotle's discussion (*Poetics*, ch. 23–24) is a postscript to his analysis of the tragic drama and applies the critical principles worked out with that genre in mind. Accordingly he stresses the dignity and nobility of epic, and the dramatic force of the Homeric poems. The episodic plots of the Cyclic epics are condemned. 'More than eight tragedies could be made out of the *Little Iliad*', he remarks scornfully. But *Iliad* and *Odyssey* are dramatic unities, though diversified by digression and embellishment.

Longinus, in the typical cataloguing manner of an ancient grammarian, lists five sources of the 'sublime' in literature: command of full-blooded ideas, inspiration of emotion, proper use of 'figures', nobility of phrase, general effect (*De Sublimitate*, ch. 8). The *Iliad* is found supreme on all five counts. His views on the *Odyssey* are interesting. It does not live up to the grandeur and intensity of the *Iliad*. But, implies Longinus, it should have done. Therefore the *Odyssey* shows a great genius in decline. Homer was old, garrulous, more taken up with character than action, and produced an epic that was a Comedy of Manners. 'Yet if I speak of old age, it is nevertheless the old age of Homer.'[17]

My own appreciation is in three sections, considering (i) a fragment of the *Little Iliad*, (ii) *Iliad*, Book 16, and (iii) the *Odyssey*.

Fragment 19 of the *Little Iliad* reads as follows:

But the glorious son of great-hearted Achilles took the wife of Hector down to the hollow ships. Her son he took from the bosom of his fair-tressed nurse, and seizing him by the foot flung him off the tower, and dark death and stern fate took hold of him having fallen. And he took out Andromache, the well-girdled wife of Hector, whom the chiefs of the Achæans had given him as a pleasing gift.

This passage will serve to illustrate the great difference between Homer and the rest. Lesches, the alleged author of the *Little Iliad*, is jejune and matter-of-fact in his relation of this frightful incident to a degree that convicts him of a woeful failure in poetical imagination. Homer would have mentioned the mother's premonition (cf. *Il.*, 22. 447), her pleas, the hero's stern rejection (cf. *Il.*, 21. 98 ff.), the mother's laments. These are all typical themes, but the point is that Homer knows how to use them, and has an enormous number crowding his mind.

The effect of this Homeric fecundity is well seen in *Iliad*, Book 16. The essential content of the book is briefly told. Achilles, alarmed for the Greeks, sends Patroclus to drive back the Trojans. Patroclus suceeds brilliantly, but in the moment of victory is killed. To tell this Homer takes 867 verses. Of course, the scale of the *Iliad* demands that the Patrocleia, a crucial turning point in the plot, should be related at adequate length. An elaborated battle narrative might have been sufficient for that purpose, but in fact *Iliad*, 16, more than any other part of the *Iliad*, is the *Iliad* in miniature.

The book opens with Achilles and Patroclus in conversation. About 250 lines of the book are direct speech, a normal Homeric proportion. But this conversation is rather special. A few yards away the Trojans are storming the last Greek defences. What will Achilles do? The conversation brings out the tensions in his mind: loyalty to friends versus obstinate affronted pride. For Achilles is a man for whom everything should be attainable, yet by pursuing it he attains nothing. Now, by seeking to vindicate his honour by refusing to fight for Agamemnon he has almost destroyed the Greeks. He relents to the extent of permitting Patroclus to lead his men, the Myrmidons, back to the battle, but warns him not to attack Troy itself. The conversation was a sort of council scene and we now follow the usual joining battle and battle sequence through the death of Sarpedon, Trojan rally, and Greek counter rally to line 683. The narrative has many stylistically brilliant passages. A fine simile compares the Myrmidons to wolves:

They came like flesh-devouring wolves with unspeakable fury in their hearts which have killed a great horned stag in the mountains and rend it in pieces, and all their jowls run with blood, and in a pack they go to lap with their lean tongues the dark surface of a spring of black water, belching gore. Their bellies are stretched full, but their heart is untamed in their breast. (156–63)

(This simile has enriched the English language with the modern connotation of 'Myrmidon'.) A catalogue of the Myrmidon leaders follows, to lend impressiveness to the scene. The clash of the Greek and Trojan armies (306–50) is a brilliant tour de force. It is, as usual, a list of slayings, naming the warriors on each side, but the compression and vigour are exceptional. The effect is not really translatable, for it depends on the handling of formulae and on enjambement to achieve its breathless effect of cut and thrust, blood, and confusion. These short individualized scenes are the favourite form of Homeric battle narrative; general descriptions of battle are used sparingly, e.g. 364–93, and the most successful ones are built up around some striking image. Here it is the wreck of the Trojan chariots in the Greek trench, while the immortal horses of Patroclus leap over.

Battle narrative is enlarged and relieved by a change of scene to Olympus, by similes, by short biographies of the slain, by the boasts and imprecations of the warriors, by unusual modes of fighting (such as hurling huge boulders), and by set duels between the major heroes.

By line 683 Patroclus has slain Sarpedon and routed Hector. Nothing stands between him and the wall of Troy. Now would be the time to heed Achilles's warning. Patroclus could have done so without discredit: Diomedes and Hector among others heeded warnings to hang back. But the ways of the gods are inscrutable: in his folly Patroclus rushes on (684–97). We know that he cannot succeed, for we are expressly told that the gods are summoning him to his death, and in typical fashion Homer has foreshadowed the end of this episode at the beginning (250). Patroclus might have been presented as dying from a surfeit of heroism, defying fate, in much the same way as Achilles goes out to avenge him knowing his own doom is near. But he is not so great a man as Achilles. Three times he mounts on the glacis of the wall (a fine touch), only to be thrust back by Apollo. He pauses, and the Trojans recover. Finally, in a passage (788 ff.) unique in Homer the god Apollo in person strikes him helpless, and Hector delivers the mortal wound. Patroclus dies defiantly, prophesying Hector's doom.

Patroclus is a man who fights hard and comes within an ace of success, but in the end he is overcome by the mysterious will of the gods.[18] Homer recognizes the brilliance and glory of heroism, but he does not shrink from the pain and misery that heroism brings in its train:

'You remind me, friend, of the misery we Achaeans suffered and how we fought about the town of Priam, where all the best were slain. There lies Ajax, there Achilles and Patroclus, and there my own dear son, Antilochus. Who of mortals could tell all the woes we suffered?' (*Od.*, 3. 103 ff.)

The invocation of the Muse at the beginning of the *Odyssey* begs the goddess to take up the story 'at some point'. The poet then plunges *in medias res*. The

Iliad begins similarly. The first books of both epics are indeed very skilful settings of the scene, but there is no formal introduction of the characters or explanation of what they are doing.[19] It is not necessary. The audience knew the tale of Troy as well as the poet. The two epics have also another feature in common, a very compressed time-scale. The *Iliad* relates the events of fifty-five days, the *Odyssey* of forty, but both include long stretches of time, periods of nine, twelve, or eighteen days, in which there is no action. This compression contributes to the effect of dramatic concentration, and it is not certain that it was shared by other Greek epics. Some certainly covered a time-span of several years. But the *Odyssey* contrives to have it both ways: by the device of putting a first person narrative into the mouth of the principal character it not merely alludes to, but actually narrates the events of the preceding ten years.

Including the first person narrative, and stated in their chronological order, the events of the *Odyssey* are as follows. Odysseus, laden with booty, leaves Troy for home. He meets many adventures on the way, but by his guile he surpasses every obstacle. Bit by bit, however, his glory and booty slip away, until he is cast away alone on a distant island. After many years he is permitted by the grace of heaven to escape, only to be cast away again, this time on an island paradise whose hospitable inhabitants despatch him home. Arrived home, he finds chaos reigning, his wife besieged by suitors, his son absent in search of him. By guile he outwits the suitors, avenges himself on them, and is reunited with his wife. As a plot this story has obvious romantic and melodramatic possibilities. The hero passes from triumph to despair and back to triumph. Again and again he is on the point of disaster. There is ample opportunity for suspense and surprise. But by beginning where it does, and in the way that it does, the *Odyssey* foregoes these possibilities, except in a minor way.

The poem begins with the announcement that Odysseus is on his distant island and that the gods have at last decided that he shall return home. So much for suspense, a romantic device in which the Greek epic takes almost no interest. In place of it we are introduced to brooding gods. Zeus mentions the fate of Aegisthus who in his folly violated the due order of things, wedded Clytemnestra, and with her murdered Agamemnon: in due time retribution followed. Standing as it does at the very beginning of the poem this passage is clearly programmatic, and it stamps the *Odyssey* as a serious and moral work. It begins with chaos, it ends, under the guidance of heaven, with the restoration of the proper order of society.

The structure of the plot is ternary, consisting of the Telemachy, the Wanderings, and the Vengeance. The Telemachy, or Journey of Telemachus, is in the nature of a vast digression: its incident contributes all but nothing to the advancement of the poem's action. Driven to despair by the arrogance of his mother's suitors, Odysseus's son Telemachus goes in search of his father, visiting Nestor at Pylos and Menelaus at Sparta. He discovers nothing of value, and his father's return takes place while he is away. The description of the situation within Odysseus's palace is very well done, with some good characterization: Telemachus as the touchy adolescent (1. 345 ff.), Antinoos and Eurymachus as insolent and hypocritical. But the point of the digression is moral. It establishes Telemachus, a character with no role in the wider epic tradition, as a worthy helper of his father, and it contrasts the breakdown of society on Ithaca with the peace and order of Pylos and Sparta. After the riotous and churlish scenes on Ithaca this is how Telemachus and the goddess Athene (disguised as Mentor) arrive at Pylos:

They came to the meeting place of the Pylians. There sat Nestor with his sons, and about them their companions prepared the feast, roasting and skewering the meat. And as soon as they saw the strangers they came all together and welcomed them with their arms and bade them be seated. (3. 31 ff.)

The *Odyssey* in fact is particularly good at the evocative description of scenes of peace and beauty, giving the lie to the slander that the Greeks had no eye for landscape. Compare the account of the island off the land of the Cyclopes:

On it there were meadows by the shore of the grey sea, moist and soft, where the vine would never wither. There was level plough-land too, where men would reap a deep crop every harvest, for fat was the soil beneath. By it was a safe harbour, where there was no need of moorings, no need to drop anchors or make fast cables, but only to beach the boat and stay till the wind blew and their spirit moved the sailors. (9. 132 ff., cf. the gardens of Alcinoos, 7. 112 ff.)

Such descriptions pose a problem about the nature of the poet's imagination. It is easy to show that the accounts are cast in generic terms — the diction is highly formulaic — yet they have such an air of strange precision that more than one observer travelling in Mediterranean lands has convinced himself that he was standing on the very spot visited by Odysseus.

The Wanderings follow the Telemachy abruptly and a little awkwardly. It would be natural, to the modern mind, to have Odysseus begin the last stage of his journey home simultaneously with Telemachus's departure on his journey. But Homer prefers to narrate sequentially. So Telemachus is left in Sparta to do nothing for several days while Odysseus tells his story to Alcinoos in the paradise land of Phaeacia. For those who know the poem only by report, these deep sea yarns often *are* the *Odyssey*. There is no denying that each touches on something of permanent fascination to the human mind; drugs, ogres, cannibals, witches, the world of the dead, divine mistresses. 'In fact this Odysseus of the sea-adventures makes too strong an impression for the good of the whole poem' (Kirk), and that although only four books (9–12) are assigned to them. The compression is very tight, especially in comparison with the slow pace and discursive character of the parts that come before and after, thus

D

showing the poet's concern for the overall balance of his poem, and his wish to subordinate the Wanderings to it.

Phaeacia is one of the earliest examples in the world's literature of a Utopia. Its fruits ripen at all seasons. Its people know no war or toil; their skill in the arts and crafts is unrivalled. Their city stands on a peninsula with two harbours (the ideal site sought by Greek colonists). It has a temple of quarried stone. The king is courteous and keeps open house — he also has a fascinating nubile daughter. His palace has bronze walls and golden doors guarded by magic watch-dogs of gold and silver. The general idea is one of luxury combined with ease.

The dovetailing of the Telemachy and the Wanderings is rather intricately done, with several changes of scene between Ithaca where Odysseus has just landed and Sparta where we left Telemachus at the end of Book 4. The problem is to bring together two narratives which it is the convention to narrate as if sequential. Chiefly by mentioning features common to both narratives, Homer does this to the normal reader's (and certainly hearer's) satisfaction. Only a careful check reveals that we have lost a day out of Odysseus's life.

	Odysseus	Telemachus
Night 1	Asleep in Ithaca	Asleep at Sparta
Day 1	?	Journey to Pherae
Night 2	?	Asleep at Pherae
Day 2	In Eumaeus's hut	Journey to Pylos
Night 3	Talk with Eumaeus	Voyage to Ithaca
Day 3	Odysseus and Telemachus meet	

The preliminaries to Odysseus's vengeance on the suitors are long. The main point is to bring out the desperate circumstances of Odysseus and his complete lack of resources. His ultimate success has, of course, been foreshadowed and he is attended throughout by the symbol of success, the goddess Athene. But first he must enter his palace disguised as a beggar and meet with various humiliations. Besides this various minor scenes contribute a general air of pathos. Eumaeus, the faithful swineherd, tells the story how he, a prince's son, was stolen away to become a slave (15. 390 ff.). As Odysseus approaches his palace his aged hound Argus, lying neglected before the doors, recognizes him through his disguise (17. 290 ff.). A slave-woman, weaker than the others and kept working until dawn to grind corn for the young lords, prays aloud for the destruction of the suitors (20. 105 ff.).

The vengeance is introduced by the ordeal of the bow. Prompted by Athene, Penelope, who does not yet know the identity of the beggar, challenges the suitors to shoot through a line of axe-heads and undertakes to marry the winner. One by one the suitors fail to string the bow. Telemachus has the bow passed to the beggar Odysseus. He strings it, sends an arrow through the axes and the next through the throat of Antinoos. The slaughter, by bow and spear, is told with Iliadic zest and speed.

When the debris has been cleared away Odysseus and Penelope meet. Recognition is not instantaneous. The crafty hero has a worthy wife, and is put through another test. Penelope calls for the marriage bed to be brought out of its chamber. But Odysseus knows the secret; the bed cannot be moved:

'There was the long-leaved trunk of an olive-tree within the court, flourishing exceedingly: and it was thick like a pillar. About it I built my chamber, till it was finished, with close-set stones, and roofed it well above, and I put in the doors, close-fitting. Then I cut the leaves off the olive tree, and trimmed the trunk truly from the root up with the axe, and set it true by the line to fashion my bed-post, and drilled all the holes with my drill'. (23. 190 ff.)

Only then does Penelope fling herself into his arms.

In Hellenistic times certain learned men supposed that the *Odyssey* ended soon afterwards at 23. 296, with husband and wife safely in bed again after their twenty years of separation. The Hellenistic age was not without romantic feeling, and if the *Odyssey* were a romance this would be a good point to stop. But we must not forget that Odysseus is returning to his home and kingdom as well as to his wife, and there are still some loose ends to tie up before peace and order are restored on Ithaca. Odysseus must bring back his father from his enforced retirement, and the blood feud begun by the slaying of the suitors, 'the noblest men in Ithaca', must be settled. The existing ending is marked by a falling off in quality, and the last lines, where Athene stops the feud, are an especially crude use of the *deus ex machina*. 'Great natures in their decline are sometimes diverted into absurdity' (Longinus). 'The last book of the *Odyssey* exhibits a manifest decline in force, as if the mind and hand of the master were conscious that their work was done, and coveted their rest' (Gladstone). I should prefer to wonder, in a work devoted to comparative literature, if the art of the good ending does not imply a poet's assurance that his audience would allow his poem to run its full course. If so, the well finished ending would be one of the late achievements of literature, and not likely to evolve until literary composition was undertaken in calmer circumstances than the noise of the princeling's court or the distractions of the market place.

NOTES

1. The horse is actually attested in Greece only from the latter half of the Middle Helladic period. See Emily Vermeule, *Greece in the Bronze Age* (Chicago, 1964), p. 261.
2. Mycenaean society abounded in obligations, but it is not clear that any of these are feudal in a strict sense. Any trace of feudalism in Homer, and it is not certain there are any, would be a memory of Mycenæ. Translators' use of terms like 'count' and 'squire' must not be taken strictly. See M. I. Finley, 'Homer and Mycenæ: property and tenure', *Historia*, 6 (1957), 133–59, reprinted in *Language and Background of Homer*, ed. G. S. Kirk (Cambridge, 1964), pp. 191–217.

3. So called from the characteristic style of pottery decoration.
4. For a use of comparativist argument in favour of the poetical possibilities of the Dark Age see G. S. Kirk, *The Songs of Homer* (Cambridge, 1962), pp. 126–38.
5. The term 'Epic Cycle' is used to denote the group of poems (*Cypria, Aethiopis, Little Iliad, Sack of Troy, Nostoi,* and *Telegony*) in which the tale of Troy and its aftermath was told.
6. The usual double standard permits the male what is denied to the female. Morally, male sex is neutral.
7. Yet the gods may be wounded and feel pain, at any rate for the purposes of literature.
8. Some have thought that the destruction of the Achæans' wall by Poseidon and Apollo (*Il.,* 12. 13 ff.) was an attempt to forestall the objection that there was no physical trace of this fortification in the Troad.
9. In the Archaic period the term 'hero', which in Homer means simply a valorous warrior, came to be used for the illustrious dead who (contrary to Homeric belief and practice) received worship at their tombs and gave aid in need to their devotees.
10. This is substantially the modern opinion too, with appropriate reservations. On the historicity of the Trojan War see M. I. Finley, J. L. Caskey, G. S. Kirk, and D. L. Page, 'The Trojan War', *Journal of Hellenic Studies,* 84 (1964), 1–20.
11. Like many Homeric expressions of number the fifty maids are formulaic. (The same number serves both Alcinoos and Odysseus.) Fifty signifies a large number, but it also defines what the Homeric notion of a large number was in this context.
12. M. Parry, 'Studies in the Epic Technique of Oral Verse-making: I. Homer and the Heroic Style', *Harvard Studies in Classical Philology,* 41 (1930), 73–147, now reprinted in *The Making of Homeric Verse,* The Collected Papers of Milman Parry, ed. Adam Parry (Oxford, 1971), pp. 266–324. A. B. Lord, 'Homer's originality: oral dictated texts', *Transactions of the American Philological Association,* 84 (1953), 124–34.
13. Rhetorical questions are occasionally used, but no direct address is made to the audience. Certain heroes are apostrophized, but only in special formulae where the device renders metrical the otherwise intractable names of Eumaeus and Patroclus. Again in special circumstances, in the appeal to the Muse, the poet alludes to himself in the first person.
14. This quality is especially Iliadic, and infuses many similes. In the construction of such similes the *Odyssey* is strikingly less felicitous.
15. The death of Adamas (*Il.* 13. 567 ff.) is perhaps the most gruesome slaying: 'Meriones pursued and as he withdrew struck him with his spear between the privates and the navel, where warfare brings greatest pain to wretched mortals. There did Meriones fix his spear. And writhing about the shaft Adamas gasped, like an ox that herdsmen bind with ropes in the mountains and drag along against his will: so, being wounded, did he gasp for a little while.' We are not usually so invited to visualize the agony.
16. If recited at the rate of *c.*12 lines per minute. This is the rate a modern European will normally adopt. The singing speed would presumably be much slower.
17. The facts underlying Longinus's judgement are undeniable. Behind the similarity in style there are considerable differences in interests and attitudes between the *Iliad* and the *Odyssey.* It is an open question (in my view) whether the difference is enough to postulate separate authorship.
18. The idea that Patroclus should be conceived as a weak or effeminate character is quite unhomeric.
19. The Iliadic *Catalogue of Ships* is delayed until the second book. There are other cataloguing passages at 3. 161–242 and 4. 250–421. The *Catalogue* seems to be a traditional list; it does not introduce all the *Iliad*'s characters, and introduces some that do not appear. The *Odyssey* has no catalogues of this kind.

ADDITIONAL LITERATURE

The scholarship devoted to Homer is very voluminous. The best guide through its intricacies is A. Lesky, *Homeros* (Sonderausgaben der Paulyschen Realencyclopädie der classischen Altertumswissenschaft) (Stuttgart, 1967). J. B. Hainsworth, *Homer,* Greece and Rome, New Surveys in the Classics, No. 3 (Oxford, 1969), is composed with a more popular audience in mind.

An excellent comprehensive book is the work quoted in note 4, G. S. Kirk, *Songs of Homer* (Cambridge, 1962) (abridged as *Homer and the Epic*, 1964), especially if it is balanced by T. B. L. Webster, *From Mycenæ to Homer* (London, 1958) (reprinted with corrections 1964). The *Companion to Homer*, edited by A. J. B. Wace and F. H. Stubbings (London, 1962), was many years in preparation; leading authorities contributed but some articles are dated. Useful things are also to be found in C. H. Whitman *Homer and the Heroic Tradition* (Cambridge, Massachusetts and Oxford, 1958), and in the more popular work of C. R. Beye, *The 'Iliad', the 'Odyssey', and the Epic Tradition* (London, 1968). Among older books C. M. Bowra, *Tradition and Design in the 'Iliad'* (Oxford, 1930), remains invaluable.

The post-Homeric epic is examined by G. L. Huxley, *Greek Epic poetry from Eumelus to Panyassis* (London, 1969).

The writings of Milman Parry, who single-handed changed the course of Homeric studies, have been reprinted and translated under the title of *The Making of Homeric Verse* (see above). Comparativists will also be interested in the work of his pupil A. B. Lord, *The Singer of Tales* (Cambridge, Massachusetts and Oxford, 1960).

OLD INDIAN
The Two Sanskrit Epics
By JOHN D. SMITH

BY THE TWO SANSKRIT EPICS I mean the *Mahābhārata* and the *Rāmāyaṇa*. It is, by now, universally accepted that these two compositions represent the only two surviving instances of early Indian epic, and that, no matter what textual form one is inclined to assign them, they not only predate but also predispose later writing in a genre that could lay claim to the title 'epic'. The later *mahā-kāvyas* or 'great poems' — Kālidāsa's *Raghuvaṃśa* and *Kumārasambhava*, or the even later and more 'literary' examples such as the *Rāghavapāṇḍavīya* — bear much the same literary relationship to the two early epics as does Virgil to Homer, or Milton to Virgil. The *Mahābhārata* and the *Rāmāyaṇa* are only Sanskrit claimants to the name of 'primary epic': the great poems which followed on them and drew from them are, without question, 'secondary' creations, courtly epics. Above all and in particular, they are poems deliberately *written* by poets consciously operating within known, and more-or-less well-documented, aesthetic canons. Whatever the exact nature and genesis of the two 'primary' Sanskrit epics, they are assuredly not the work of trained, self-conscious literary technicians.

Both the *Mahābhārata* and the *Rāmāyaṇa* are in Sanskrit, the later form of attested Old Indo-Aryan; but both — especially the *Mahābhārata* — display many grammatical divergences from 'classical' Sanskrit, which is, approximately, the form of speech used by courtly writers of a later period, who were well aware of the teachings of the grammatical texts that developed during the last centuries B.C. Sanskrit continued in ritual and courtly use long after its demise as anybody's natural mother-tongue, and no doubt remained for a long time comprehensible even to those who could not speak it 'correctly'; so that there is nothing strange in the (attested) popularity of epic recitation even into the second half of the first millennium A.D., and nothing unnatural about the insertion into the epics of later, non-'original' material *in Sanskrit*. This is not the place to enter into controversial speculation on the date of composition of the two epics: there is every reason to assent to the consensus view that both took several centuries to reach their final forms, and no particular reason to dissent from the consensus view that the formative period of the *Mahābhārata* was *c*.400 B.C. to *c*. A.D. 400, that of the *Rāmāyaṇa* *c*.200 B.C. to *c*. A.D. 200 (give or take a century or so in each direction — there are limitations on what we *can* know).

Prior to the epics, the extant Old Indo-Aryan literature is uniformly Brāhmaṇical, that is to say, it is the 'property' of the Brāhmaṇ caste, the priests and law-givers of early Indo-Aryan society. The Vedic hymns themselves and the later ritual, speculative and exegetical texts are all firmly priestly in tone and intention. It is certain that the earlier of these works were composed at a time before the introduction of writing in India, and were initially transmitted (more-or-less) intact by memory: they were *śruti*, the divine revelation *heard* by the first Brāhmaṇical *ṛṣis*, and it was found desirable from an early period to guarantee them against accidental textual corruption by means of various mnemonic devices. But there can be no doubt at all that by the time of the grammarians a fully-developed script was known (the earliest *surviving* written Indo-Aryan is represented by the Aśokan inscriptions of the third century B.C.), for the first grammarian, Pāṇini, whilst continuing to use the mnemonic *sūtra* style, employed as notational symbols letters such as *ñ* and *ḷ*, whose phonemic status is very doubtful, but which the script called into being. Priestly literature had thus reached a stage of advanced development by the time at which it is supposed that the *Mahābhārata* began to take shape: it contained hymns, incantations, learned theses, and narrative both didactic and heroic; it used both prose and verse for its media; and it was acquainted with writing.

Viewed against this background the *Mahābhārata* represents, as it were, a return to the beginning. It was an oral composition; it was purely heroic in character; and it dealt with people and events of which the earlier Brāhmaṇical literature had taken practically no notice. References to the Kurus as a race are, it is true, not wanting in the earlier texts, and certain names appear, including that of Dhṛtarāṣṭra;[1] but for the names of the Pāṇḍava heroes we have to wait until Pāṇini, who also (*Aṣṭādhyāyī*, 6.2.38) knows the name *Mahābhārata*. The reason for the very marked dichotomy between the *Mahābhārata* and what had preceded it is not difficult to ascertain. As the Vedas and their supporting literature were the 'property' of the Brāhmans, so the epic was the 'property' of the Kṣatriyas, the caste of warriors and princes. The epic dealt with 'their' legendary heroes, and put forward 'their' code of conduct: it was the statement of 'their' mythology. The two leading castes were not merely concerned with different events, personages, and conventions of behaviour; they were often, it would appear, specifically antagonistic towards one another. Thus we read in the *Mahābhārata* (1.180.1–3) that when Arjuna, disguised as a Brāhmaṇ, claimed the hand of the princess Draupadī, the assembled Kṣatriyas fell upon her father Drupada, who had consented to the match; and we may recall also the myth of Rāma Jāmadagnya (Paraśurāma), the Brāhmaṇ incarnation of Viṣṇu who annihilated the Kṣatriyas no fewer than twenty-one times.

The *Mahābhārata* may have 'belonged to' the Kṣatriyas, but it was not composed by them. There are numerous Sanskrit terms for 'bard', 'singer [of narrative]', 'panegyrist', etc., but the creators and transmitters of the great epic were, it seems certain, the Sūtas, a particular caste which enjoyed a symbiotic relationship with the Kṣatriyas apparently very similar to that between medieval Rājpūts and their Cāraṇ court-poets. The Sūtas would have performed not only 'ancient tales' but also songs of their own composition, and have accompanied themselves on the instrument called *vīṇā*.[2] It is worth noting that at this early stage of its development the *vīṇā* was not the sophisticated instrument or class of instruments to which the name is given today, but was rather a simple stick-zither: it is nowadays very widely the case that singers of oral epic accompany themselves either on a one-stringed or two-stringed fiddle (a later form of instrument) or on a plucked stick-zither or long-necked lute.[3]

The poem which is known at the present day — indeed, the poem known fifteen centuries ago — by the name *Mahābhārata* does not, however, bear much resemblance to the original bardic epic. Between its oral composition and the literary redaction that underlies the entire known manuscript tradition, the text of the *Mahābhārata* underwent a massive expansion which not merely at least quadrupled its size but also radically altered its character. Great quantities of didactic material, long tales, numerous priestly myths were inserted, at some points wholly submerging the epic story, and sometimes resulting in bizarre inconsistencies and self-contradictions. By the end of the process, the text had, so to speak, changed hands: it was now the 'property' of the Brāhmaṇs, and came even to be dignified as 'the fifth Veda'.[4]

Something not dissimilar happened to the *Rāmāyaṇa*, albeit on a much smaller scale. The earlier Vedic literature contains the names of a few characters who appear in the epic, but seems not to know any narrative connexion between them.[5] The only extant text containing an older version of the story is, significantly, Buddhist not Brāhmaṇical: the *Daśaratha-jātaka*.[6] This, however, deals only with the banishment and return of Rāma; the war with Rāvaṇa is not mentioned at all, and the Sanskrit *Rāmāyaṇa* is the earliest extant version of the 'full' story. But modern scholarship has achieved near-unanimity in declaring the first and last books (and also some other parts) of the existing text to be later additions; and it is in these added passages that the Kṣatriya hero Rāma is identified with the Brāhmaṇical god Viṣṇu. Like the *Mahābhārata*, the *Rāmāyaṇa* thus ended up as a holy text, and it is indeed precisely as a holy story that Indian tradition has interpreted it: the very numerous *Rāmāyaṇas* of later times and divers languages are above all religious works, retaining little of the epic character of their great forebear.

The available texts of the two Sanskrit epics are thus — and this is especially true of the *Mahābhārata* — gargantuan hodge-podges, literary pile-ups on a grand scale; and it is hardly surprising that scholarly reactions to them have differed greatly and in many ways. For some native scholars it is still a point of crucial significance whether or not the events related in the *Mahābhārata* and the

Rāmāyaṇa took place in historical fact. The majority of western orientalists, together with many Indians, have devoted much of their work to attempts at determining what is 'original' and what 'spurious' in the surviving manuscripts. Other western scholars, principally the comparative mythologists, have preferred to sift through the existing texts for patterns of mythological 'thinking' that may be paralleled elsewhere. There is, of course, nothing fundamentally wrong in any or all of these approaches; indeed, it is surely a sign of health in a subject that it can be treated in so many different ways. Unfortunately, however, it is in practice the case that the different types of scholarship in question start from differing assumptions of various kinds which are mutually irreconcilable: thus it becomes necessary to belong to one or another 'school' — surely a sign of ill-health in a subject. This is the disadvantage of regarding the two epics as history, as literature, or as myth; they may be all these at once and yet remain, above all, something apart.

As far as the question of historicity is concerned, there is little that *can* be said — and this is itself the chief thing that *must* be said. As in many other contexts, it is here desirable to put the two epics on two different sides of a dividing-line. I do not see very much merit in attempts at interpreting the *Rāmāyaṇa* as a history in which one 'tribe' has become the monkeys and another the demons; the story of Rāma is chiefly mythic, only secondarily heroic, and only tertiarily historic.[7] The *Mahābhārata*, on the other hand, contains a great deal that was probably regarded as historical fact by the early bards and their literate successors; which is not to say that it bears any discoverable relationship to what *we* might regard as historical fact. 'Euhemerism', writes Henige in a work which has profound implications for epic studies (1974, p. 49), 'died hard in the western world'. In at least some parts of the East it never died at all. At an indeterminate point in the remote past, in the North-West of India, there may have been a dynastic struggle between people calling themselves Kauravas and Pāṇḍavas; or there may not. We have no way of knowing.

Textually speaking, both epics present a problem. Conventional text-criticism may be applied to the extant manuscripts (which are all very much later than the presumed dates for completion of composition), but the resulting texts are, quite clearly, the end-products of processes of interpolation that have already been described. Conventional techniques are not capable of reaching back beyond the final, inflated texts. There can be no doubt whatever that these texts were themselves the immediate product of the pen, not the tongue: as usual, the *Mahābhārata* provides the extreme case, with the interpolation en bloc of evidently old but originally separate passages of considerable bulk (the *Bhagavadgītā* is the most obvious instance). This can only have been the work of a literate 'editor'. How, exactly, the old oral epic came to form the nucleus of the inflated written text is something we shall never know: it is imaginable, but by no means certain, that at some stage there was interaction between oral and written versions. But this could only have taken place after 'Brāhmaṇization' had already occurred; and it cannot be observed in, or even deduced from, the critical editions prepared with such care and devotion in Poona and Baroda.

Even before these editions, which represent the sum of available manuscript evidence, had been published, or indeed dreamed of, scholars had begun the perilous task of trying to isolate the 'original' texts. Their efforts involved the use of unconventional critical techniques, and they were in constant danger of falling into the mire they wished to dredge. (The comparison made by Mary Carroll Smith (1972, p. 63) between epic text-criticism and archaeological 'digs' is uncomfortably apt.) As early as 1846, Adolf Holzmann Senior sought to give (in German translation) an 'original' version of the *Mahābhārata*. But his effort was based purely on an attempt to achieve narrative consistency, a wholly subjective criterion. Winternitz kindly spoke of Holzmann's 'enviable self-confidence' (1963, p. 287); yet he too was compelled, on the very next page, to launch into his own summary of 'the principal narrative'.

Clearly, objective criteria are essential if we are to go beyond what the manuscript-tradition can tell us, and such criteria are provided by internal evidence and by the proportionate frequency of particular metrical forms. Jacobi (1893, pp. 31–59, 24–31) applied both criteria to the *Rāmāyaṇa* with great skill and success, and his findings have formed the basis of all later work in this field. For the *Mahābhārata*, Hopkins (1898; 1901, pp. 191–362) made use of the same criteria in a tour de force of scholarship which remains as daunting now as it must have seemed at the turn of the century. The summary given above of the manner in which the two poems evolved into their attested forms is based principally on the work of Jacobi and Hopkins. But — at any rate in the case of the *Mahābhārata* — the subject is by no means exhausted. The latest attempt to reach back to an 'original' text was made in 1972 in an unpublished Ph.D. dissertation by Mary Carroll Smith.[8] She remarks (p. 2) 'Hopkins associated diversity of metre with diversity of authorship and date. He said further: "It appears to be a heterogeneous collection of strings wound about a nucleus almost lost sight of. The nucleus, however, is a story" [Hopkins, 1901, p. 363]. Hopkins seemed not to have associated the story nucleus with a metrical nucleus which could be detected by scansion.' Dr Smith's own work seeks, precisely, to sift the evidence for a correlation between narrative and metrical patterns, and it is interesting that she finds that correlation not in the *śloka* verses, by far the commonest metre to occur in the *Mahābhārata*, but in the *triṣṭubhs*, and even more particularly in the 'irregular', pre-classical *triṣṭubhs*: 'I have found that the metrical irregularities are clues to complete kernels of story elements. The computer aids in tracing the irregularities but further analysis is necessary to identify the development of the narrative elements. The connexion of groups of triṣṭubh verses from one Book of the epic to the other appears much more striking when the triṣṭubhs are excised [i.e. excerpted]'

(p. 7). 'The Indian tradition has preserved a nucleus of old Vedic-type ['irregular'] verses. The nucleus contains the basic story of the Gambling Match, the embassies for peace, and the final battle. Encrusted over the nucleus are successive layers of stories which can be identified by increasing occurrences of the upajāti ['classical'] pattern of triṣṭubh metre. The "Great Epic" has evolved from a nucleus which is still extant' (p. 65). This 'nucleus' consists of some 3,000 verses, as contrasted with nearly 75,000 in the Poona critical edition.

One hopes that this work will be published and expanded upon: if Dr Smith is not completely right (which she may well be), she is certainly following a good scent. But her work, like that of Hopkins and others before her, places later scholars in a quandary. When we talk of 'the *Mahābhārata*', are we talking of an excerpted 'original'? or of the existing text? or of some stage in between, perhaps after the expansion of the epic narrative (Dr Smith convincingly demonstrates that the four battle-books of the epic contain, in turn, increasingly high proportions of non-'original' material, the fourth, the *Śalya-parvan*, being wholly secondary) but before the insertion of the lengthy didactic passages? An indication of the problems involved may be given by comparing the attitudes of two modern scholars. Dumézil bases much of his 'trifunctional' argument on the ascription to the five Pāṇḍava brothers — and also to other characters — of divine fathers and consequent semi-divine status: Yudhiṣṭhira is the son (and thus 'a part') of Dharma, Bhīma of Vāyu, Arjuna of Indra, and the twins Nakula and Sahadeva of the Aśvins; Bhīṣma is the son of the river Gaṅgā, Karṇa the son of the Sun-god. Van Buitenen, on the other hand, regards this divinization of the heroes as not merely secondary in time but also somehow inferior in quality: he seems almost irritated by it, speaking of 'inept mythification' (1973, p. xx) and 'this decaying mythology' (p. xxi); and he writes, 'There is no reason at all why Bhīṣma should be the son of the river goddess, why Karṇa should be the offspring of the Sun, why the Pāṇḍavas should have been begotten by various deities. Certainly, these heroes are superhuman in the baronial tradition of epics everywhere . . . It could have been left at that . . . As usual in such pious transformations, the results are less than gratifying . . .' (p. xix).

This attitude is, I believe, unhelpful: it simplistically confuses the ancient with the 'authentic', when what is in question is a process, not a state. 'It could', indeed, 'have been left at that'; but it was not. Both the Sanskrit epics *developed* over a period of time from one thing into another. It is the text-critic's job to try to chart the process of development; the comparative mythologist, for his part, must recognize that the ideology with which he is confronted was a dynamic, not a static phenomenon. The reason for the development, the force activating the dynamism, is clearly of primary concern to both disciplines. The Sanskrit texts themselves, as has already been noted, offer no help here: it may therefore be useful to look briefly at observable processes of text-expansion and 'mythification' at work in present-day Indian oral epic and heroic narrative.

In December 1976, during a visit to western India, I recorded a well-known local song about the death of a dacoit called Ompurī. It described his betrayal at the hands of a peasant to whom he had given quarter, the arrival of the military, the escape of his nephew and confederate Lālpurī, his battle single-handed with the forces surrounding him, and his final suicide to prevent the ignominy of capture. I was surprised to learn from a retired senior civil servant that these events had taken place only some twenty years before (he had in fact himself known Ompurī personally); but, as he rather acidly remarked, 'They don't sing that Lālpurī disguised himself as a woman to make his escape'. It was true, they did not; and in addition, the song contained self-evident elements of the stuff of legend, rather than history: the two dacoits had gone out to rob against the pleas of Ompurī's wife; they had encountered bad omens as they rode; they had violated the *dharma*[9] of good dacoits by robbing some women; Ompurī had fought alone down to the last cartridge, which he had used on himself; the doctor who performed the post mortem examination was terrified at the appearance of the body; Ompurī's heart was found to weigh $2\frac{1}{2}$ lb.; and so on. Within a mere two decades, then, the story had shed all disagreeable features of historical fact, and had embellished itself with suitably heroic motifs. It had also, even more significantly, provided a cosmic meaning and coherence for human actions: Ompurī died *because* he had committed a breach of *dharma*, and his death was inevitable and preordained — his wife had foreseen it, and the omens foretold it. The historic has given way to the heroic, and the heroic has been supplemented by the mythic. Ompurī has not as yet achieved divine status, but there is now nothing to prevent his doing so.[10]

The same performers from whom I recorded the song of Ompurī are also, by profession, epic-singers: their bread-and-butter occupation is to sing the epic of Pābūjī.[11] Pābūjī was, in historical probability, a fourteenth-century Rājpūt brigand-chieftain, and thus not far removed in nature from Ompurī. But the present-day oral epic recounting his deeds is, specifically, a religious ritual, for Pābūjī has achieved full deification, being widely worshipped by pastoral (non-'Brāhmaṇized') communities in western India. His story, as the singers present it, plays down the brigandish elements, but is full of the same apparatus of Indian myth-making as is beginning to appear in the song of the dacoit: warnings and omens, with their suggestion of preordination, and also vows, curses, and systematic revenge-taking. The cosmic underwriting of his actions has become complete, but it is, significantly, not textually explicit: the epic-singers are, to a greater or lesser degree, able to *explain* the 'higher purpose' behind the events of the narrative, but they do not *sing* of this purpose, and the less competent among them are indeed unaware of it. But the epic text (which

is fixed and memorized), and its deeper meaning, are not static: singers learn
story-episodes and story-interpretations from one another — I have myself
directly observed this process at work. Each performer's version is capable of
expansion as he learns more, and each performer's knowledge of the divine
nature of the hero increases from his contacts with other singers. With the epic
of Pābūjī, the mythic has been supplemented by the divine, and an intricate
incarnation-system links the characters of the story to figures from the orthodox
Hindu religious pantheon. The provision of this connecting network — surely
unconscious but certainly purposeful — opens the door to a future incorporation
of Pābūjī himself into the Brāhmaṇical pantheon; but this is yet to come.

The songs of Rāmdevjī — sung by, among others, the performers of Pābūjī's
epic — bring us to the beginning of the final stage. Rāmdevjī has acquired
wide acceptance as a god among folk of greatly-differing social rank, and at least
a limited acceptance among the Brāhmaṇs;[12] and his songs, once solely the
'property' of lower-caste illiterate singers, are now beginning to appear in
print:[13] the literary redactor has been at work, and the tradition is shifting from
the oral to the literary, from the heterodox to the orthodox. The heroic and the
mythic are now firmly linked with the divine; the pen, or printing-press, is now
copying, imitating, and 'improving on' the earlier work of the tongue; and
the priesthood has begun to accept the *fait accompli*. Rāmdevjī has achieved
respectability as a god, as once did Kṛṣṇa, as did Rāma, as may Pābūjī . . . as
may Ompurī?

I must stress that the relevance of the modern western Indian material to the
two Sanskrit epics is not direct: there is no question of a single continuing
tradition 'beginning' with the *Mahābhārata* and 'ending' with the song of
Ompurī; nor, of course, do the unlettered present-day singers know or understand any Sanskrit texts (indeed, their accounts of the earlier myths often
diverge sharply and interestingly from the available Sanskrit versions). I am
putting forward the modern tradition merely as a possible *paradigm* to aid our
understanding of the processes at work in shaping and reshaping the ancient
poems. If that paradigm is accepted, then what is involved is a progression from
songs about noteworthy human beings to canonical written texts concerning
Hindu deities. En route, the narratives acquire successive accretions of heroic,
mythic, and deific elements; they pass from the oral to the written or printed;
their chief characters become assimilated to the figures of the prevailing
Brāhmaṇical pantheon through divine parentage or divine incarnation; and the
cults of the old deified heroes finally achieve orthodox acceptability ('Brāhmaṇization'), while the texts deriving from the old songs become part of a
canon. The observations on the *Mahābhārata* and *Rāmāyaṇa* which follow are
suggested in part by the proposed paradigm and its implications; but it is no
part of my task to put forward any new 'sectarian' viewpoint, and I hope that
nothing I say may appear to be tendentious. The pattern of development which

can be seen in the modern songs is, I believe, suggestive; but it is certainly no more than that.

One further word of caution is required. It is by no means easy to draw clear dividing-lines between the heroic and the mythic, or between the mythic and the deific: to do so would require hard-and-fast definitions which would inevitably themselves be largely ad hoc creations. Nor is there the slightest reason to suppose that all heroic elements existed in the texts before any deific elements were introduced (and so forth); on the contrary, it seems certain that the processes of textual expansion and mutation continued simultaneously at every level for a considerable period of time. The exceedingly numerous — and often significant — 'interpolations' noted, but textually rejected, in the critical editions indicate that the texts continued to be expanded with material of many different kinds until the very end of their periods of composition. Often, whatever the evidence of the manuscripts, one cannot help regretting an omission.

*   *   *   *   *

There is no one single type of epic hero in Sanskrit. Rather we find, in both the *Mahābhārata* and the *Rāmāyaṇa*, a group of heroes characterized more or less sharply by differing sets of qualities. In some cases the characterization is slight: one can see little 'shape' to the twins Nakula and Sahadeva in the *Mahābhārata*, for instance, or to Śatrughna in the *Rāmāyaṇa*. Bharata, on the other hand, is clearly depicted: he is Rāma's loyal and faithful half-brother, refusing the throne that is Rāma's by right even when he is offered it, ruling in Rāma's stead because it is necessary, but placing a pair of the latter's sandals in ultimate authority, and even putting to them matters of state (*Rāmāyaṇa*, 2.107.22). Many of the other figures in the two texts are equally clearly charac-terized. It would, of course, be a mistake to suppose that the authors of the epics consciously created particular characters and set about depicting them as fully and convincingly as possible, as a western playwright or novelist might; what is involved is the representation by the various different figures of various different aspects of the heroic. The heroes are thus largely 'stock' characters: they do not develop, and they are not presented 'in depth'; we learn about them from the consistency with which their words and deeds (and often their names) conform to particular models. Of the great mass of occurring types I have here selected three on which to concentrate, not only because of their prominence and importance, but also because they recur more than once in similar guise in the two epics (and, indeed, elsewhere): they seem, between them, to represent the complete span of possible epic heroic character. Finding brief names for the three is by no means easy, but some idea may be given by the following: the immense and impetuous; the quiescent king; the warrior prince.

The immense and impetuous type is seen at its full development in the character of Bhīma ('the Terrible') in the *Mahābhārata*. He is possessed of a giant's strength, fears nothing and no one, and fights with dreadful violence; whatever he does, be it vowing (and exacting) vengeance, or eating, or helping his family on an arduous journey, is done with a superhuman and unrestrained vigour. He has no exact parallel among the 'stock' characters of western literature: one may, according to one's literary upbringing, think of Rabelais's Frère Jean des Entommeures or of Desperate Dan; but there is nothing comic about Bhīma. His weapon is a part of his character: it is a club.

When Draupadī, gambled into bondage by Yudhiṣṭhira, is insulted by Duḥśāsana ('the Ungovernable'), who attempts to strip her naked in public, Bhīma makes a terrible vow. In the following passage he fulfils it (8.61.1–10):[14]

The prince Duḥśāsana, fighting in that tumultuous battle, did a hard deed;
with his arrow-blade he cut off Bhīma's bow, and further pierced his
    charioteer with six arrows.

Then that great man most swiftly pierced Bhīma with many excellent arrows;
whereupon he [Bhīma], weaving along like a wounded snake, hurled his club
    at him in the battle.

With that club Bhīma overcame Duḥśāsana, casting it ten bow-lengths;
struck by that speeding club, Duḥśāsana fell, quivering.

O prince,[15] his horses and charioteers were killed by that club as it fell, and his
    chariot was reduced to dust;
he writhed, tormented by intense pain, his armour, his ornaments, his clothing
    and his garlands destroyed.

Then the violent Bhīma, remembering the [acts of] family-hostility performed
    by your sons,
leaped down from his chariot on to the ground, fixing his eye eagerly upon him.

Drawing his sharp sword with its excellent blade, and treading upon the throat of
    the writhing man,
he cut open his breast as he lay on the ground, and drank his warm blood.
Then, having quaffed and quaffed again, he looked [up] and spoke these words
    in his excessive fury:

'Better than mother's milk, or honey with ghee, better than well-prepared mead,
better than a draught of heavenly water, or milk or curd, or the finest buttermilk,
today I consider this draught of the blood of my enemy better than all of these.'

With these words he rushed forward once more, bounding on in exhilaration
    after his drink;
and those who saw him then, they too fell down, confounded with fear.

And even those men who did not themselves fall, their weapons dropped from
    their hands;
and they howled loudly in their fear, and closed their eyes when they saw
    the [scene].[16]

Those on all sides who saw Bhīma there, drinking that blood of Duḥśāsana,
all fled, overpowered by fear; and they said, 'This is no mortal man'.

Bhīma is a violent, hot-tempered and impetuous figure; the other Pāṇḍavas
frequently find it necessary to prevent him from wreaking carnage upon his
foes at an unsuitable time or place. He is also capable of feats of enormous
strength and endurance, as here, where he assists the escape of his family from
the inflammable house of lac in which their enemies had sought to burn them
alive (1.136.15–19):

> And the Pāṇḍavas too, O king, much distressed, escaping
> with their mother through that tunnel, went on in secret, unnoticed.
>
> Then, impeded by drowsiness and frightened, the Pāṇḍavas,
> destroyers of their enemies, could not go on with haste.
>
> But, O prince of kings, Bhīma of terrible speed and valour
> took [up] all his brothers and his mother too, and went on.
>
> That hero, carrying his mother on his shoulder, the twins [Nakula and
>   Sahadeva] on his hip,
> and the two mighty brothers [Yudhiṣṭhira and Arjuna], sons of Pṛthā,
>   in his hands,
>
> went rapidly on, breaking trees with the speed of his advance and
>   splitting open the earth with his feet
> — the valiant Wolf-belly, swift as the wind.

Bhīma is, literally, as swift as the wind, for he is the son (and thus 'a part') of
Vāyu, the wind-god. The name Wolf-belly (*Vṛkodara*) derives from another
aspect of his gargantuan character, his ravenous appetite. This appetite,
together with his fondness for boasting about his own strength, is the reason
Yudhiṣṭhira offers him for his final (apparent) downfall on the road to Heaven
in the closing stages of the epic (17.2.23–25). Bhīma is a combination of heroic
excesses, and passages such as the one above might even suggest an excessive
size — that he might be, physically, a giant. This does not, however, seem to
be so: in the middle of a long and worried reflection about him, Dhṛtarāṣṭra,
father of the Kauravas, compares his stature to that of a palm-tree in a conventional hyperbole, but adds that he is 'a few inches taller than Arjuna' (5.50.19).
    If we look at the *Rāmāyaṇa*, it does not take long to discover there a hero
whose nature is very similar to that of Bhīma. (It is not the *same* nature — we

are not talking about an exact replication of Bhīma — but it is of the same *kind*, 'a combination of heroic excesses'.) The monkey Hanumat is immense and impetuous, and is an important ally of Rāma. Any doubts about the proposed 'connexion' are allayed by the very important fact that the great monkey, like Bhīma, is a son of the wind-god; and, in addition, we may consult the text of the *Mahābhārata* itself, in which Bhīma actually meets Hanumat and recognizes his strength (3.146–50), and (in a rejected stanza: *Udyoga-parvan*, p. 266, stanza 341*) arranges for him to place his own image on Arjuna's banner. Hanumat does not seem to be a glutton or a boaster, and he is distinguished from Bhīma in being able (in both epics) to become a giant at will. But, like his half-brother, he fights with a club, to excellent effect; although in the following passage he has abandoned it in favour of his bare fists (*Rāmāyaṇa*, 6.64.12–16, 22–23):

> The mighty Nikumbha, with arms like iron clubs, brought down
> his iron club, bright as the sun, on the breast of the mighty Hanumat.
>
> On his firm, broad chest that club broke into a hundred pieces,
> shattering violently apart like a hundred meteors in the sky.
>
> The great monkey staggered under that blow;
> the club made him shake as a mountain might shake in an earthquake.[17]
>
> Struck in this way by that [club], Hanumat, best of monkeys,
> tremendous in might, firmly clenched his first.
>
> The valiant hero, swift and powerful as the wind, raising his fist,
> struck vehemently at the breast of Nikumbha . . .
>
> Throwing Nikumbha down with great exertion, he crushed him;
> then, leaping quickly up, the heroic Hanumat fell upon his chest.
>
> He seized hold of his neck with both arms and, running round in a circle,
> he ripped off Nikumbha's dreadful great head in the midst of his cries.

Hanumat also has the superhuman strength of Bhīma, his innocent fidelity and transparency of emotion. Things always present themselves to these two characters in the simplest black-and-white terms, and problems are solved by the simplest expedient — exertion of their enormous physical strength. Here Hanumat has gone to the mountain of herbs in order to fetch back medicines to revive Rāma and Lakṣmaṇa, who lie unconscious on the battlefield; but the herbs he needs have concealed themselves (*Rāmāyaṇa*, 6.61.59–62):

> Then the great Hanumat, unable to see them, was enraged and roared
>   loudly in his fury;
> unforbearing, his eyes bright as fire, he addressed these words to that
>   prince of mountains:

E

'How is this, that you make up your mind not to feel pity for Rāghava
    Rāma?
Prince of peaks, see now, overcome by the strength of my arm, your
    own self torn apart.'

Seizing its summit, covered with trees and with elephants, full of
    gold and thousands of mineral ores,
he uprooted it swiftly and violently, breaking off its pinnacles and
    making its highest ridges shake.

Ripping it off, he leaped into the air, terrifying the [three] worlds[18]
    with the gods and the princes of gods;
acclaimed by the many sky-travellers, he went swiftly forth, full of
    Garuḍa's[19] terrible might.

— and after taking the mountain to his master and seeing him and Lakṣmaṇa
recover, Hanumat thoughtfully returns it to its original place.

The *Rāmāyaṇa* contains in addition a figure who strikes one as almost a parody
of the immense and impetuous hero. Kumbhakarṇa does nothing by halves: he
is mountainous in size, and eats and drinks accordingly; he sleeps, thanks to a
curse, for six months at a time, and no amount of noise, beating with mallets,
etc., will wake him; he boasts at length of his own prowess, and is reprimanded
for his lack of 'political' understanding. His apparently parodistic quality may
well be no accident, for he is a Rākṣasa, brother of Rāvaṇa the demon king of
Laṅkā, and it is possible that he is actually intended as the inversion of a well-
known heroic pattern. In the end he is killed by Rāma.

In case it should be imagined that the existence in both Sanskrit epics of
immense and impetuous heroes might be a matter of coincidence, it is worth
underlining the pervasiveness of the type by pointing to its occurrence in the
present-day epic of Pābūjī. Like Bhīma and Hanumat, Ḍhĕbo ('the Fat') is a
major assistant to the chief hero. He drinks a well-ful of opium-water, and eats
the food prepared for an entire wedding-party; when his horse grows weary he
picks it up and carries it under his arm; he annihilates whole armies single-
handed, and has to be restrained from killing an enemy who must not be slain
under any circumstances. His link with the Sanskrit 'son of the wind' is indeed
recognized by the epic-singers, for they specifically say that he is an incarnation
of Hanumat.

If Bhīma and Hanumat seem to us like heroes endowed with great strength
but deprived of a sense of proportion or propriety, Yudhiṣṭhira in the *Mahābhārata* seems the exact opposite: he is the rightful king, his is the cause for which
the great war takes place, and yet he himself does more or less nothing. In the
course of what must be one of the bloodiest epics ever composed, Yudhiṣṭhira
('the Firm in Battle') kills only Śalya and his younger brother (9.16.47–62),
and this occurs in a passage — indeed in a book of the *Mahābhārata*, the

Śalya-parvan — which is almost certainly a later addition (see p. 53 above). His quiescence is almost total; van Nooten writes (1971, p. 56): 'In Yudhiṣṭhira the contrast between the Hindu hero and the Western hero shows clearly, in that the admirable part of his character lies not in what he does, but in his abstention from acts of violence. Even when injustice is committed and his interference might save the honor or the life of another human being, as in the case of Draupadī's disrobement, as a true hero he refuses to act.' I do not, myself, accept this explanation of royal quiescence (the appeal is to *ahiṃsā*, the Hindu principle of non-violence) — as we have just seen, not *all* Hindu heroes abstain from acts of violence — but the point is well-made. The reason for it is more likely to lie in the deep-rooted belief that the king is above the hurly-burly of human action, whether violent or otherwise: to plunge like Bhīma into the fray would detract from his dignity. During the course of the war, Yudhiṣṭhira orders the disposition of his forces — and is, of course, obeyed, for he is the king — but takes hardly any part in the actual fighting: it is, quite simply, not his job to do so.

Things happen *to* Yudhiṣṭhira: he loses his kingdom and his liberty, together with that of his brothers and their joint wife; he loses in two successive gambling matches where his opponent cheats him consistently without incurring any rebuke; his wife is publicly insulted and ill-treated; he is compelled to spend years in exile in the forest, and to assume a false identity for a further year; finally he discovers that war with his cousins is inevitable. He does not complain (unlike Bhīma, who is ready to lash out at the slightest provocation); rather he accepts everything with a resignation which may seem like feebleness to us, but which is intended to be the highest virtue. 'Resignation' is not quite the right word, for it suggests that he is mere putty in the hands of Fate, whereas in fact he is seeking to make sure that the workings of Fate play themselves out to the end. To secure this aim he is willing to cross the battlefield before the start of the war and ask four of his greatest enemies to assist him in gaining the victory; and his enemies, being as noble as himself and as intent on bringing about the 'right' outcome, are willing to do so, though they remain forced by circumstances to fight against him. In the following passage Droṇa explains how he himself may be overcome and killed (later Bhīṣma will do Yudhiṣṭhira the same service) (6.41.46–52, 56–61):

> Yudhiṣṭhira greeted Droṇa, and [respectfully] circumambulated him;
> and he spoke aloud to that unconquerable one words uniquely suited to
> his own interest:
>
> 'Lord, I salute you. I shall fight without sin
> and conquer all my enemies, if you permit me, O Brāhmaṇ.'

Droṇa said:[20]

'If you had not come to me after making up your mind to fight,
I should have cursed you, O king, to utter defeat.

But, sinless Yudhiṣṭhira! I am pleased with you and honoured by you.
I give you permission: fight and obtain the victory!

And let me perform what you desire: tell me what it is you want.
With things as they stand, O king, what — other than [my withdrawal
    from] the fight — do you wish?

Man is the slave of money, but money is no man's slave.
I speak the truth, O king: I am tied by money to [your enemies] the
    Kauravas.

And so it is that I say to you impotently, "What — other than [my
    withdrawal from] the fight — do you wish?"
I shall fight on the Kaurava side, but I shall pray for your victory.'

. . . Yudhiṣṭhira said:

'Best of Brāhmaṇs, I ask you — listen to what I wish to say —
how I may in the battle defeat you, who are invincible.'

Droṇa said:

'There is no victory for you as long as I continue to fight in the battle.
Strive with your brothers for my speedy death!'

Yudhiṣṭhira said:

'Alas! Then tell me, strong-armed hero, the way in which you may be killed:
my teacher, I fall before you and ask it of you. Honour be to you!'

Droṇa said:

'I know of no enemy, sir, who might kill me while I stand in the battle,
fighting in fury, pouring forth torrents of arrows like rain.

Only when I am prepared for death, my weapon laid down, my mind
    removed elsewhere,
may [anyone] kill me in this warriors' battle: I tell you this truthfully.

And I shall lay down my weapon in the battle when I hear ill news
from a man whose word I can trust: I tell you this truthfully.'

I noted above (p. 50) that the narrative of the *Rāmāyaṇa* consists of an older
part (the story of the banishment) found also in the *Daśaratha-jātaka*, and a later
part (the story of the war with Rāvaṇa). In the transition from older to later
the character of Rāma seems to change: when he fights Rāvaṇa he is highly
active, but his conduct in the earlier story is dominated by quiescence. Like
Yudhiṣṭhira he is an embodiment of virtue, seemingly more acted upon than

acting; he too is the rightful ruler but accepts the loss of his throne with equanimity; and he too is banished to the forest. He hears of his exile on the eve of his installation as crown-prince, from the very woman who has brought it about, his stepmother the queen Kaikeyī, and his reaction is almost bland in its acceptance of Fate (2.16.18-28):

> [Rāma said,] 'If it were the king's command I should even jump into fire;
> I should eat deadly poison, or plunge into the very sea,
> if [so] instructed by my *guru*, my father, my king or my friend.
>
> So tell me, O queen, what is the king's desire;
> I shall do it, I swear: Rāma does not speak twice [does not change his mind].'
>
> Then to the righteous and truthful Rāma
> the ignoble Kaikeyī spoke these terrible, harsh words:
>
> 'Once, in the war of the Devas and Asuras, O Rāghava, your father
> was pierced by a spear in the great battle. I looked after him and he granted
>   me two wishes.
>
> And so I have asked the king for the installation of [my son] Bharata [as
>   crown-prince in your stead],
> and for your exile to the Daṇḍaka forest this very day, O Rāghava.
>
> If you wish your father to be true to his promise,
> and you [likewise], best of men, then listen to my words.
>
> Act on the king's command, as he swore:
> you must go into the forest for nine years and five.
>
> Dwell for seven years and seven in the Daṇḍaka forest,
> forgoing this installation-ceremony, and wearing matted hair and ragged
>   clothes [like an ascetic].
>
> In the city of Ayodhyā, let Bharata rule over this Earth,
> filled as it is with numerous jewels and with horses, chariots and elephants.'
>
> Hearing those deadly, inimical words, Rāma, the slayer of enemies,
> was not perturbed, and spoke thus to Kaikeyī:
>
> 'So be it: I shall go hence to dwell in the forest,
> wearing matted hair and ragged clothes; thus I shall keep the king's oath.'

Once again we may seek a parallel in modern western Indian epic, and in this case we find it in the figure of Pābūjī himself. His elder brother has taken the title and the trappings accompanying it, and never gives him any assistance in his exploits; so that he too is somewhat 'disadvantaged', although not so severely as Yudhiṣṭhira or Rāma. Throughout the story he is almost passive, allowing Fate to act upon him against his own apparent interests; and, like Yudhiṣṭhira, he takes very little part in the fighting: indeed, the only killing attributed to him is admitted by the epic-singers to be non-historical, a piece of narrative exaggeration.

The third type of heroic character to occur in readily-isolable form in the Sanskrit epics, that of the warrior prince, requires rather less comment than either the immense and impetuous or the quiescent king; the reason being that the figure is likely to be far more familiar to the reader of western literature than either of the two so far described. Arjuna in the *Mahābhārata* and Lakṣmaṇa in the *Rāmāyaṇa* actually seem to us to behave like heroes, without the apparently negative qualities of Bhīma and Hanumat, or Yudhiṣṭhira and Rāma. Neither is himself the king: both are junior princes, half-brothers to the king. Both are brave and fearless, but without the unrestrained violence and brute strength of the 'son of the wind'.[21] Both have severe qualms about the propriety of some of their masters' actions (Arjuna about fighting his cousins, Lakṣmaṇa about allowing Rāma to pursue the 'deer' which is the evil Mārīca in disguise), but both ultimately accept the decisions that have been taken. Of the two, Arjuna is unquestionably the greater, partly perhaps because in the later part of the *Rāmāyaṇa* story Rāma himself begins to act as warrior prince, thus diminishing Lakṣmaṇa's stature. It is Arjuna who (3.38–49) visits the celestial regions to obtain the divine weapons which figure so prominently in the fighting, and upon which, indeed, victory depends. The dying Bhīṣma remarks to a disconsolate Duryodhana ('the Unfightable', chief of the Kauravas) (6.116. 38–39):

'The divine weapons of Agni, Varuṇa, Soma, Vāyu, Viṣṇu,
Indra, Paśupati, Brahmā, Parameṣṭhin the Lord of Creatures,
Dhātṛ, Tvaṣṭṛ and Savitṛ — all these

are known to Arjuna alone in the whole world of mortals;
Kṛṣṇa son of Devakī too knows them, but no-one else.
Sir, these Pāṇḍavas cannot be defeated in battle in any way.'

Arjuna's nobility — like Yudhiṣṭhira's kingliness — can perhaps best be seen in his dealings with his enemies, and the events immediately preceding the passage just quoted form a very good illustration. Bhīṣma, the enemy general but also the revered 'grandsire' of the Pāṇḍavas themselves, has fallen to Arjuna's arrows; Arjuna immediately comes to pay his respects to the dying man and to minister to his needs. Bhīṣma asks for a pillow for his head, and various luxurious pillows are produced, but he spurns them and asks Arjuna to provide him with what he requires; and Arjuna, understanding the request, constructs a more appropriate headrest out of arrows shot into the ground. Later, much the same thing happens when Bhīṣma feels thirst (6.116.10–14, 19–24):

'My body is afire with the arrows, and I am fainting with their burning;
I desire water,' he said to those kings.

Then, O king, all those Kṣatriyas brought him
various foodstuffs and pitchers of cool water.

When he saw those things brought, Bhīṣma son of Śaṃtanu said,
'Sir, today I cannot eat any mortal foodstuffs

from [the hands of] mortal man. I lie on a bed of arrows,
and remain, awaiting the cessation of sun and moon.'

After saying this, O son of Bharata, Śaṃtanu's son, his voice filled with distress,
spoke to those princes about the strong-armed Arjuna.

. . . [Arjuna comes, and Bhīṣma again requests a drink of water] . . .

The heroic Arjuna assented, and, mounting his chariot,
forcefully strung his bow Gāṇḍīva and drew it.

Hearing the sound of the bowstring against his palm, which sounded like the
    roar of a thunderbolt,
all creatures were afraid, and so were all the princes.

Then that best of chariot-fighters circumambulated with his chariot
the prostrate [Bhīṣma], finest of Bharata's line and best of all weapon-bearers.

The glorious Arjuna then fixed a blazing arrow [to his bow] and consecrated it;
while the whole world watched, he aimed his Parjanya weapon
and split open the ground to the right side of Bhīṣma.

From that place arose a pure, clear torrent of water,
cool, ambrosial, and of divine scent and taste.

Thus Pṛthā's son Arjuna of divine deeds and valour assuaged the thirst
of Bhīṣma, bull of the Kauravas, with a torrent of cool water.

In Sanskrit epic, then, we find kings who are too kingly to muddy their
hands by any kind of action, but who, at another level, are intent on permitting
Fate to run its course without intervention. Among their immediate retinue we
find two types of hero: one loyal, noble and temperate; the other violent, unruly
and fantastically strong. We find that a very similar situation occurs also in a
modern oral epic sung in western India.[22] The characteristics of the heroes as I
have tried to delineate them are, without doubt, subject to some permutation
and variation, but the three types nevertheless form together a distinct and
recurrent pattern.

Of the characterization of the villains there is little to say: they do not seem
to answer to set types in the same way as the heroes, although we have already
noted (p. 60) a possible instance of the deliberate 'parodying' of a 'stock' heroic
model. In the *Mahābhārata* the issue is complicated by the fact that many of those
who take the side of the Kauravas are not themselves villains at all, indeed are
specifically objects of veneration: they are 'tied by money to the Kauravas' (see

p. 62). Those who are, on the other hand, truly villainous seem to be distinguished only by being more or less evil (Duḥśāsana is worse than Duryodhana);
although it is probably fair to add that what may appear to be bad 'political'
judgement on the part of the leading villains is in fact as much a part of their
necessary role as is the quiescence of Yudhiṣṭhira: they are blind to the workings
of Fate, and are destroyed in consequence.

Much the most remarkable feature of the hero/villain antithesis in the two
epics is, however, the frequent apparent reversal — in 'ethical' terms — of the
goodies and the baddies. In the *Mahābhārata* this is so extreme as to have led to
the so-called 'inversion theory', according to which the Kauravas were actually
the original heroes and the Pāṇḍavas the original villains. There can be few
now who would adhere to this theory — Duryodhana and Duḥśāsana are ill-
equipped to serve as epic heroes — but the facts for which it sought to account
remain to trouble us. Taking only the most notorious examples, three of the
four Kaurava generals are killed by utterly 'unfair' means: Arjuna shoots
Bhīṣma whilst using as a shield Śikhaṇḍin, who in a previous birth had been a
woman (Ambā) and against whom Bhīṣma had therefore vowed that he would
not fight; Droṇa is killed after laying down his weapon and abstracting his
mind on hearing from a man whose word he can trust (Yudhiṣṭhira) of the
death of his son Aśvatthāman (see pp. 61–62) — yet the news is false, for the
dead Aśvatthāman was merely an elephant; and Karṇa dies whilst the wheel of
his chariot is stuck fast and after his energy has been largely sapped by the
taunts of his charioteer Śalya, who is acting at the instigation of Yudhiṣṭhira.
The hero of the *Rāmāyaṇa* is no freer from seeming moral taint: his own justification for the murder of the monkey Vālin is far from convincing, and the
mutilation of Rāvaṇa's sister Śūrpaṇakhā is an act of apparently senseless
violence which, though carried out by Lakṣmaṇa, takes place in Rāma's
presence, draws no rebuke from him, and was indeed largely 'set up' by him.

For some of these seemingly villainous deeds it is possible to discover acceptable motives. Bhīṣma and Droṇa are, as already noted, not baddies but
goodies who are compelled to fight on the 'wrong' side; and it is probably the
case that, being both good and powerful, they *cannot* be killed by normal means:
certainly both acquiesce in their own deaths by explaining in advance how they
may be dispatched. Similar, though not identical, considerations apply to
Karṇa. So whilst it may be that Yudhiṣṭhira's chariot-wheels, which had always
previously travelled off the ground by reason of his truthfulness, come down to
earth after he has lied to Droṇa about Aśvatthāman, we must also remember
that Droṇa had, quite literally, asked for it; and Yudhiṣṭhira thus retains his
role of instrument rather than agent.

For many of the bad deeds of the epic goodies there is, on the other hand, no
discernible justification (a fact which evidently caused as much anxiety to the
ancient text-compilers as it does to modern scholars). 'The solution of the

problem', however, 'is seen in the vanishing of the problem'. Surprising it may or may not be, but it is the case that in Indian mythology from the Vedas to the present day, there has been no inbuilt necessity for the goodies to be morally good and for the baddies to be morally bad. In the modern epic of Pābūjī, the hero rides out in pursuit of the 'wicked' Khīcī, who is making off with a herd of stolen cattle; yet not long before, he had himself been busy rustling camels. The facts of the story would thus seem to allow us impartiality or a preference for either of the two parties; yet it happens that we are supposed to be 'on Pābūjī's side'. Much the same applies to the conflict between Rāma and Rāvaṇa: Rāvaṇa's actions are precipitated by the savage mutilation of his sister Śūrpaṇakhā (see p. 66), and we might be tempted to feel tha the was justified in his battle against Rāma. But it is not 'permissible' to take his side. As early as Vedic myth the misdeeds of the gods, principally Indra, are well known; and one once again feels that it is, as it were, arbitrary which side one takes, although once again, of course, there is no question of actually choosing the 'wrong' side.[23] It is worth quoting Wendy Doniger O'Flaherty at some length on this point (1975, p. 270):[24]

'The battle between gods and demons, the central theme of Hindu mythology, sets the stage upon which all of the gods . . . play their roles . . . The battle lines are blurred by the lack of distinction between gods and demons, who share not only their superhuman powers . . . but also their anthropomorphic moral ambivalences. In terms of cosmic symbolism, the battle may represent the conflict between light and darkness, but in actual myths there is little to distinguish between the two opposed forces. By definition, by status and official function, the gods are "right" and right must triumph, but the nature of this "right" and the method of the triumph underwent major transformations in the three broad periods of Hindu mythology. The heroic measures which the Vedic gods employ came gradually to be superseded by treacherous stratagems in the Epic period and finally, in the Purāṇas, by outright and elaborate deceptions which had been originally categorized as "demonic".'

What applies to the gods in heaven applies no less to their partial or total incarnations on earth. There is no implicit compulsion upon the Pāṇḍavas or upon Rāma to act virtuously: their job is the battle.

*   *   *   *   *

Their job is the battle: the *dharma* of the epic heroes is to play out the roles which Fate has allotted them to the — often bitter — end. This is, of course, one of the primary teachings of the *Bhagavadgītā*; but it raises further problems. In all the material I have mentioned, from the modern song of Ompurī the dacoit to the Sanskrit *Mahābhārata* itself, there is a powerful element of pre-ordination; and yet the heroes (and villains) must be assumed to be independent actors, for the stories would otherwise be meaningless tautologies. The question thus reveals itself to be a new form of the all too well-known problem of determinism versus free will.[25]

The answer, roughly speaking, seems to be as follows: it is Fate (*daiva*, the will of the gods) which assigns a role to a character in the cosmic 'drama'; it is the character's own chosen actions and their repercussions (*karman*) which determine the course that that 'drama' will take; but the characters act in the full knowledge of their role and with the awareness that their task (*dharma*) is to act in accordance with the will of Fate. Rather as it is possible to *imagine* taking the 'wrong' side in the stories, so it is possible to *imagine* a different version of those stories in which the characters are in breach of the prescribed *dharma* and act in the 'wrong' way, resulting in the overthrow of the cosmic plan. But this does not, of course, happen: perhaps it would be right to say that it *could* not happen, though no such suggestion is explicitly made. The consequence is that human actions and their results become a part of the mechanism of Fate: viewed from this standpoint — which is, without question, the intended standpoint — narrative interest is sustained less by who kills whom and why than by the permanently-present *possibility* that an aberrant human action will violate the workings of Fate. Hence, no doubt, the inclusion of the immense and impetuous heroes who often so *nearly* err — but are never actually allowed to do so.

Though direct access to the Sanskrit texts is nowadays restricted to a small learned minority, their narrative and mythic content is still well known, and indeed forms a fruitful source for further myth-making. In this process the actual content and purpose of the original material is subjected to reshaping. The reputed author of the *Rāmāyaṇa*, Vālmīki, would no doubt have been shocked by the following exceedingly heterodox account of the cosmic 'logic' underlying the story of Rāma (and so too would many excellent present-day *paṇḍits*); but it is interesting in that it offers a new explanation for old 'facts', one which is perfectly in accord with the spirit of the epic: earthbound individuals (including demons) act in accordance with their *dharma* to produce the result required by Fate. In this version[26] the gatekeepers of Viṣṇu's heaven, Jaya and Vijaya, refuse entry to the four Kumāras, sons of Brahmā, who imperiously assume the right to an audience with Viṣṇu. Infuriated by being denied access, the Kumāras curse Jaya and Vijaya to become Rākṣasas (demons). Viṣṇu himself is unable to revoke or even to mitigate a curse uttered by another, but he promises his aid to his servants in a different way: they will be reborn as Rāvaṇa and Kumbhakarṇa, and it will be their task — their *dharma* — to behave in so abominable a fashion as to necessitate a divine incarnation to destroy them — and thus to terminate the curse. Jaya, now Rāvaṇa, acts accordingly, and Viṣṇu incarnates himself as Rāma; at the same time the Goddess (specifically Śiva's consort, not Lakṣmī consort of Viṣṇu)[27] incarnates herself as Sītā, knowing that without her aid Viṣṇu-Rāma will not be capable of defeating Rāvaṇa. She carries out her plan by causing herself to be abducted by Rāvaṇa, who has himself also recognized that to steal Rāma's wife is the only action that will goad Rāma into a war of destruction. Rāvaṇa's *dharma* in this interpretation is thus to seek his own death, Rāma's is to administer that death, and Sītā's is to force Rāma into doing so.

In its details this account is highly deviant from what we know of the Sanskrit 'cosmic plan' behind the *Rāmāyaṇa*, but it is a complete and coherent statement using elements typical of Hindu 'mythification'. It is interesting that in two thousand years the patterns of mythological thought have changed so little: Vālmīki might, as I have suggested, have been shocked by the modern account, but he would not have found it alien. He would have recognized the initial fault[28] that causes seemingly endless repercussions before it can at last be neutralized; the working of Fate, inexorably connecting event to event from the beginning of the story to its conclusion; and the apparatus of curses and incarnations used by Fate to make the necessary connexions.

If we turn our attention towards the purely human side of the *Rāmāyaṇa*, we find much the same pattern — an initial breach of *dharma* followed by an inexorable and inevitable chain of events. The whole of the narrative is traced back to two occurrences, neither of which is given much prominence, but in each of which Rāma's father Daśaratha commits a fault. One is his foolish promise to Kaikeyī (referred to by her in the quotation on p. 63 above); the other is his accidental killing of the young ascetic (unnamed by Vālmīki but known to later tradition as Śravaṇa Kumāra), whose grief-stricken father curses Daśaratha to the loss of his own son and subsequent death (*Rāmāyaṇa*, 2.57–58). From these two seeds the whole story grows, proceeding by unavoidable steps until it is at last played out. If Daśaratha had not granted two wishes to Kaikeyī and had not been cursed by Śravaṇa's father, then Rāma would not have been banished to the forest; if Rāma had not gone to the forest, then Śūrpaṇakhā would never have laid eyes upon him; if Śūrpaṇakhā had never seen Rāma, then she would have remained unmutilated; if she had not been mutilated, then Rāvaṇa would not have decided to act against Rāma — and so on. (The story is not, as this description might suggest, unilinear: if Rāma had not gone to the forest, then he would never have encountered Hanumat; and if he had not had the assistance of Hanumat, then he would not have been able to defeat Rāvaṇa — and so on.)

I have referred now more than once to the 'apparatus' of myth-making as being constituted by incarnations, vows, curses, etc. The function of an incarnation (total or partial) is, I imagine, fairly unambiguous: it is the device whereby the cosmic 'drama' may be brought down to Earth. It is, however, worth commenting briefly on three other clear-cut 'devices', for they are all closely similar in format, and they all serve a single purpose in more or less a single way: each consists of an utterance, and each permits the establishment of a direct causal link between events widely-separated in time. Generally speaking, of course, cause and effect are immediate in the epic as in real life — Rāma is hurt so Hanumat goes (there and then) for medicine — but it not infrequently happens that the causal link has to operate over an extended period. In such cases, the 'energy' required to bring about the necessary effect is, so to speak, 'stored' in a *form of words*. Not everybody can speak such words: Kumbhakarṇa may talk at length of his forthcoming destruction of Rāma's forces, but he does not achieve it; and from time to time heroic 'boasts' are made, even by major characters, that remain unsubstantiated. The uttering of a *curse* or *vow* and the granting of a *wish* (in the conventional jargon of Sanskritists, a 'boon') require a certain personal stature and a certain deliberate commitment; but, granted these conditions, they preordain the future with absolute certainty. All three 'forms of words' cannot fail to come true, and therefore all three demand power from the person who utters them. (This power may exist amongst gods, saints, heroes or demons — for differing reasons.) Śravaṇa's father curses Daśaratha to lose his son, and therefore, later, Rāma is banished. Bhīma vows to drink Duḥśāsana's blood, and therefore, later, he comes to do so. The Yakṣa Sthūṇākarṇa grants a wish to Ambā (reborn as the girl Śikhaṇḍinī) (*Mahābhārata*, 5.192.23–30), and therefore she becomes a man (and therefore, later, Bhīṣma dies). It is worth noting that, whilst all three 'forms of words' demand power from the speaker — the uttering of curses and the granting of wishes often act to his acute disadvantage — the making and keeping of vows also *confers* power. Bhīṣma acquires his name ('the Awesome') and his con-comitant power as the result of his vow to remain celibate and allow the king-dom to pass on to his half-brothers; although admittedly his original name — Devavrata ('of Divine Vows') — had anticipated the event.

We are now reaching a point at which it becomes possible to attempt some generalized statements about the mythic elements in the narrative of the two Sanskrit epics. We have seen that the animating force of that narrative is the dichotomy between preordination on the one hand and independent human actions on the other; and we have also seen that both these disjunct elements are themselves only parts of a mechanism established by Fate for the acting-out of a cosmic 'drama' on Earth. It follows from this that the events of the epics are doubly accountable: they must make sense as deeds performed by human beings, and they must make sense as components of the cosmic plan. Any single event in the vast chain of events must, in theory, have two motives: a human motive looking to the past, and a cosmic motive looking to the future. So, Sītā is seized by Rāvaṇa, because Śūrpaṇakhā desires the dishonour and death of Rāma, because Rāma caused her to be mutilated, because . . . ; and at the same time Sītā is seized by Rāvaṇa, because it is necessary that Rāma and Rāvaṇa shall fight, because it is necessary that Rāvaṇa die, because . . .

This principle of double accountability forms the crux of the two epics, but we are, alas, cursed to only a very incomplete understanding of it. The information we are given about accountability at the cosmic level is extremely scanty, so that any picture of the overall plan that we may draw is bound to be either highly fragmentary or highly conjectural.[29] If we return to our paradigm, the epic song of present-day western India, we find a reflex of the same situation: as I remarked earlier, the epic-singers are, to a greater or lesser degree, able to *explain* the 'higher purpose' behind the events of the narrative, but they do not *sing* of this purpose, and the less competent among them are indeed unaware of it. After making several recordings of the epic of Pābūjī, I had still only the haziest notion of the cosmic plan that underlies it, and it took a number of interrogation sessions before I was able to reach a reasonable understanding. The modern text, then, is silent on what is, in effect, its own raison d'être — and so, for the most part, are the Sanskrit texts. Under these circumstances, and in particular with no modern paradigm to aid him, it is greatly to the credit of Georges Dumézil that he has so clearly understood the nature of the crux of the *Mahābhārata*; writing of *Causalités superposées*, he says (1968, p. 209):

'Il est *a priori* probable que, comme les types et les carrières individuels de chacun des principaux héros, cette succession de drames dans laquelle ils sont collectivement engagés est, elle aussi, de la mythologie transposée en épopée; probable que la succession des événements, si bien motivée qu'elle soit par le jeu des passions humaines, obéit d'abord aux convenances de la transposition, reproduit pour l'essentiel l'économie interne d'un mythe. De quel mythe?'

I cannot, however, accept the answer he gives to his own question, largely because no reason is offered for the 'transposition', and it is by no means easy to supply one (Dumézil, p. 218): 'le Mahābhārata transpose en une crise presque mortelle de la lignée et de la royauté des Kuru une crise de l'histoire du monde, ce que la mythologie hindouiste appelle la "fin d'un yuga" [i.e. one of the periodic and cyclic "ends of an age of the world"].' This is, I believe, at once very general and very speculative: an interesting and perhaps illuminating interpretation, but not definitive, not 'the final solution of the problems'. My own contention is much less positive: I do not believe that we *can* ever know with certainty the full cosmic meaning of either of the two Sanskrit epics, for those who could have told us are all long-dead. The hand of Fate is much in evidence in both stories, but its intentions remain largely obscure.[30]

One of the most important ways in which Fate manifests itself in the *Mahābhārata* is in the person of Kṛṣṇa. If the cosmic plan is likened to a drama, then Kṛṣṇa is the stage-manager: abstaining from an active part, particularly in the fighting, he nonetheless guides the Pāṇḍavas along the paths they have to take, inciting them to many of their morally devious actions, but also discoursing to Arjuna on the nature of *dharma* in the *Bhagavadgītā*. He is almost all-pervasive: without his presence the story would fail to take the 'right' course. He is thus, in a sense, Fate's own representative in the action which Fate has instigated, simultaneously involved in events and aloof from them. He has no equivalent in the *Rāmāyaṇa*, where Rāma seems to be able to do the right thing without guidance; but he has — in his role as stage-manager, not in his personality — a strong resemblance to Deval, a major character in the epic of Pābūjī. Deval is an incarnation of the Goddess, and her purpose in the story is to make sure that the 'right' outcome is secured. Deval is in fact more active (to a point approaching aggression) in her role than Kṛṣṇa, but her task and function are equivalent to his.

Kṛṣṇa is, however, much more than Fate's stage-manager: he is also, of course, the great god of the epic, Viṣṇu incarnate. As we have seen, all the major heroes of the *Mahābhārata* are sons, and thus partial incarnations, of various gods, and they were no doubt accorded due veneration (in Hinduism, the word 'worship' may mean anything from a deferential nod towards a red-painted stone at the foot of a tree to human sacrifice); and Arjuna in particular, together *with* Kṛṣṇa, seems to have been the object of some devotion. But it is Kṛṣṇa himself who is *the* god of the *Mahābhārata*: the epic is his theophany. Similarly in the *Rāmāyaṇa*, Rāma is *the* god, and he too is held to be an incarnation of Viṣṇu: of the other characters, Lakṣmaṇa (according to later tradition an incarnation of Śeṣa, the snake on which Viṣṇu sleeps) attracts some devotion — rather like Arjuna — for his closeness to *the* god, while Hanumat has remained an important folk-deity, though with few theological pretensions. It is worth mentioning, in order to refute, the commonly-held view that, since it is generally in passages of evidently later date that Rāma is identified with Viṣṇu, the identification was itself therefore late, and its establishment was the chief purpose of the secondary additions to the main poem. This is not a tenable conclusion. It is clear that the later material — chiefly the first and last books — was added to satisfy a need, not to propose an aggrandisement of the hero: it really makes no sense to suggest that the composition of a few thousand lines of verse can, of itself, confer deity on a man, however heroic he may have been.[31] In the *Rāmāyaṇa* the chief hero is also the chief god (and it is overwhelmingly likely that this was the case from the beginning, i.e. from Vālmīki onwards); whereas in the *Mahābhārata* this is not so, and we do not hear of a cult of Yudhiṣṭhira, much though the epic makes of him (especially towards the end). In the modern epics too, the person of the god may or may not coincide with that of the central hero: in the epic of Pābūjī it does so, but in that of Devnārāyaṇ, a similar epic sung in the same region, the chief god is the avenger who 'settles the score' after the death of the king and all his confederates — a figure with an exact, but undeified, counterpart in the Pābūjī epic. It is not easy to see why the 'choice' of the deified figure should vary thus: several types of explanation may be offered — perhaps even the unknown facts of a remote history?

*   *   *   *   *

The chief proposal made in this article — one which has few claims to originality — is that the Sanskrit epics, as we have them, represent the end-products of processes of textual inflation and change which have converted oral songs about famous men into the canonical theophanies of Hindu gods, and that these same processes work by subjecting the 'facts' to 'reinterpretation' along fairly standardized heroic and mythic lines, the great god achieving deification at some point along the way. I have also suggested that the similar processes observably at work today on the oral songs of western India may be viewed analogically; and in the attempt to describe the Sanskrit material, resemblances to the modern songs have been found at various specific points.

The two Sanskrit epics are not, however, exact equivalents in this respect. The 'core' of the *Mahābhārata*, whether by that we mean the narrative told in 'irregular' *triṣṭubhs* as excerpted by Mary Carroll Smith, or any other imagina-able nucleus, is certainly a heroic story. The *Rāmāyaṇa*, on the other hand, is rather different (see p. 51 above): the older part of the story (banishment and return) is only heroic in so far as quiescence is a form of heroism, whilst the later part (the war against the Rākṣasas) is firmly mythological, requiring only the simplest form of heroism, the ability to fight; as already remarked (p. 64 above), it is in this part that the characterization of the heroes becomes blurred. It is rather as though the *Rāmāyaṇa* had started the process of becoming what it is today at a point halfway through, omitting the conversion of 'oral songs about noteworthy human beings' into fully-fledged heroic tales. That is to say, it is rather as though the *Rāmāyaṇa* had been composed *in the manner of* an epic, rather than having evolved *as* an epic.

Like the proposal that both texts consist of an (early) nucleus surrounded by much (later) disparate material, the idea that the *Rāmāyaṇa* might actually be a secondary composition requires testing by objective criteria, as far as it is possible to devise appropriate tests. In this case, however, we find ourselves stymied. If it was indeed the case that Vālmīki composed his Rāma-story *in the manner of* an epic — presumably the *Mahābhārata* itself, for no other epic has survived, and our sources do not so much as hint at one — then we should naturally expect to find close formal correspondences between the two; and so we do. As the *Mahābhārata* contains a mixture of metres, so does the *Rāmāyaṇa*; and in addition many lines and parts of lines are held in common by both works (see Hopkins, 1901, pp. 403–45). One further area for enquiry remains in the so-called 'oral theory' of Professor A. B. Lord, itself a development from the earlier work of Milman Parry. Here, too, we seem to draw a blank; but I wish to suggest that this is because insufficient research has as yet been carried out. Formula-analysis of the two Sanskrit epics is an urgent desideratum (I am tempted to call it a desiderandum), and it may well be that statistical comparison of the *density* of formulaic construction in the *Mahābhārata* and *Rāmāyaṇa* would produce significant results.

The relevant points of Lord's thesis[32] may be summarized by quotation (Lord, 1960, pp. 4, 129): 'oral epic song . . . consists of the building of lines and half lines by means of formulas and formulaic expressions . . . By formula I mean "a group of words which is regularly employed under the same metrical conditions to express a given essential idea." This definition is Parry's . . . The written technique . . . is not compatible with the oral technique, and the two could not possibly combine to form another, a third, a "transitional" technique.'

According to this view, the frequent recurrence of 'stock phrases' or 'clichés' in a poem stamps that poem as having been originally an oral composition; their absence indicates a literary work; and there is no possible common ground between the two categories. 'Stock phrases' do certainly occur with great frequency in both the Sanskrit epics, a fact which has not gone without notice; but as yet no detailed study of them has been made. Perhaps this is no bad thing, bearing in mind Mary Carroll Smith's simple, true, but rather disquieting comment (1972, p. 3): 'Before any prolonged consideration of the Mahābhārata is possible, it is first necessary to come to terms with the irregular metrical conditions that Hopkins and several of the critical text editors noted. Once the metres are separated and "the same metrical conditions" prevail, then it will be possible to study narrative content and formulaic structure in the Mahābhārata.'

Dr Smith's own contribution to what little debate there has been proves, unfortunately, to be chimerical. Chapter Three of her thesis is entitled 'The use of oral formulaic themes in Book Three', which looks suspiciously like an attempt to use all Lord's technical terms simultaneously, and turns out to have little to say on the question of formulaic composition. I know of no other attempt to apply the principles enunciated in Lord's *The Singer of Tales* to the *Mahābhārata*, but some idea of the formulae commonly used there (and in the *Rāmāyaṇa*) may be gained from Hopkins (1901, pp. 66–72); and Ram Karan Sharma (1964, pp. 167–75) devotes the final section of his work to 'Technique[s] of Oral Poetry', acting, as it would seem, on a hint from Emeneau:[33] these pages too contain lists of some of the commonest 'stock phrases' found in the *Mahābhārata*. The *Rāmāyaṇa* has been made the subject of one attempt at formula-analysis (Sen, 1966), which, alas, not only restricts itself to a sample so small as to give no statistically reliable idea of the density of formulaic composition, but also draws that sample *in toto* from a portion of the text (Book 1) generally agreed to be not the work of Vālmīki. 'Such is Human Perversity.'

It will be evident from the above that no reasoned statement is yet possible on the question of formulaic construction in the two Sanskrit epics, either individually or in comparison. We do not have to be wholly mute, however: it is at least unarguably true that both the *Mahābhārata* and the *Rāmāyaṇa* are formulaic compositions. According to Lord's dictum of 1960, they must therefore both have been oral in origin. Yet in 1975 (p. 23), Lord has somewhat relaxed the stringency of his earlier argument, allowing the possibility that a non-oral poetry might imitate (and add to) the stock of formulae used in earlier oral verse; and he goes so far as to suggest the term 'transitional' for such a poetry. If this terminology is accepted (and there is no particular reason why it should be), the *Rāmāyaṇa* probably qualifies as a 'transitional text'. It is well known that, as compared with the *Mahābhārata*, Vālmīki's poem is stylistically quite sophisticated, making much greater use of 'expressive' vocabulary, alliteration, complex sentence-structure, etc. This probably means that its reliance on formulae is smaller: a measurable criterion. The native tradition supports the distinction, for it uses different terms to refer to the two poems (without any complete consistency, it should be said), and there does not even exist a Sanskrit equivalent for the cover-term 'epic': the *Mahābhārata* is most commonly referred to as *itihāsa* '[legendary] history', the *Rāmāyaṇa* as *kāvya* 'poetry'. More specifically, indeed, Vālmīki is seen as the founder of Sanskrit poetry: he is referred to as *ādikavi* 'the first poet', and his work is *ādikāvya* 'the first poem'. It seems very likely that these titles are justified, and that Vālmīki, whilst imitating the style of oral epic current in his day, sought consciously to improve upon it. He would thus have been a literary artist, striving individualistically for excellence, and not one of the anonymous oral poets who initiated the composition and transmission of the *Mahābhārata*.

Yet such tentative conclusions cannot but be speculative while so much basic work remains undone. Mary Carroll Smith opens her thesis with the suitably statistical comment that 'The Sanskrit epic Mahābhārata is almost eight times the size of the Iliad and Odyssey together, yet it has received less than .08% of the critical attention that Homer has had.' The task facing students of the two Sanskrit epics is thus the appropriately heroic one of redressing the balance by working 1,249 times harder.

NOTES

1. Also Bharata and Janamejaya. A 'Kṛṣṇa son of Devakī' is also mentioned (*Chāndogya-upaniṣad*, 3.17.6), but it is not possible to be certain that he is identical with the Kṛṣṇa Vāsudeva of the epic.
2. For a discussion of epic performance, see Hopkins 1901, pp. 363–67. (Details of references will be found in the Select Bibliography.)
3. I am indebted to Mrs Jean Jenkins for her information on the instruments.
4. Traditionally, the authorship of the *Mahābhārata* is ascribed to Kṛṣṇa Dvaipāyana, a (Brāhmaṇical) ṛṣi who plays a major role in the story itself; he is well known as *Vyāsa* or even *Vedavyāsa* 'the Arranger of the Vedas'.
5. The names in question (Ikṣvāku, Daśaratha, Rāma, Aśvapati, Janaka, Sītā) are discussed at length by Bulcke (1962, pp. 1–26).
6. To say that the *story* contained in the *Daśaratha-jātaka* is older than that contained in the *Rāmāyaṇa* is not to say anything about the relative age of the two *texts*. It is exceedingly unlikely that the Buddhist story was known to Vālmīki, the reputed author of the *Rāmāyaṇa*; much has been made of the existence in both of variant forms of a single stanza, but this could just as well have belonged to a third, non-extant version from which both texts drew, or to a general 'reservoir' of oral verses open for use by any poet.

F

7. The older part of the story (equivalent to the story of the *Daśaratha-jātaka*) could conceivably be founded upon a basis of history; not so the later part.

8. Dr Smith acknowledges her debt to Franklin Edgerton, especially his article, 'The Epic Triṣṭubh and its Hypermetric Varieties' (*Journal of the American Oriental Society*, 59 (1939), 159–74), and to the unpublished Ph.D. thesis of Barend A. A. J. van Nooten, '*Mahābhārata* Text Analysis with the Aid of the Digital Computer' (University of California, Berkeley, 1963).

9. This term is crucial to an understanding of the workings of Indian epic, but has the disadvantage of being utterly untranslatable: conventional translations like van Buitenen's 'Law' (see his comments, 1973, p. xli) are unfortunately likely to mislead repeatedly. *Dharma* is not something imposed upon one from outside: it is intimately one's own, and varies from individual to individual. Thus even 'duty' conveys too rigid a sense: a man's *dharma* is the right course for him to follow on Earth. A dacoit's *dharma* includes the robbing and killing of, for instance, liquor-vendors and money-lenders; but it excludes the robbing of women.

10. The deification of dacoits is not uncommon. Cf. Paul Christian Winther, 'Chambel River Dacoity: a Study of Banditry in North Central India' (unpublished Ph.D. thesis, Cornell University, 1972), p. 129: 'the dacoit who must closely duplicate the tactics of revered dacoit figures of the past is capable of being perceived as a reincarnation of one of the famous warrior heroes mentioned in the sacred texts.'

11. See further John D. Smith, 1977, but also the forthcoming work by Ebeltje Hartkamp-Jonxis, Joseph C. Miller Jr, John D. Smith and Ernst van de Wetering: *Pābūjī's Paṛ: Essays on an Indian Cloth-painting and its Function in an Oral Tradition*.

12. See Mira Reym Binford, 'Mixing in the Color of Rām of Rānujā', in *Hinduism, New Essays in the History of Religions*, ed. Bardwell L. Smith (Leiden, 1976), especially pp. 123, 128.

13. A typical bookstall pamphlet of this kind is Lakṣmīdatt Bārhaṭh, *Śrī Rāmdev Līlāmṛt Kathā* (Jodhpur, undated).

14. I must make the usual remarks on the translations given here: they (of course) try to combine readability with accuracy, and are not literal. Thus I have sometimes replaced a pronoun by its referent, etc.

15. The story at this point is being narrated by Saṃjaya to Dhṛtarāṣṭra, the father of Duryodhana, Duḥśāsana and the ninety-eight other Kauravas. The whole text of the *Mahābhārata* is put into the mouths of a number of such narrators.

16. Reading *tac ca* in support of the editor's unsupported emendation *tan na*. Another translation might be, 'and saw it though they closed their eyes'; the editor has been too literal-minded, preferring, 'and closed their eyes and did not see it'.

17. The image has a certain subtlety: mountains do not shake *much* during earthquakes.

18. Heaven, earth and the lower regions.

19. A divine bird, Viṣṇu's mount.

20. Headings of this sort are used throughout the *Mahābhārata*, but do not occur at all in the *Rāmāyaṇa*. They may introduce the words of a narrator of the story, or (when the sense 'he said' is not conveyed in the verse) of a character in the story, as is the case here. Much of what Droṇa says to Yudhiṣṭhira is repeated by the other three enemies whom the latter visits.

21. Lakṣmaṇa has something of Hanumat's impetuosity, offering for example to destroy all Rāma's enemies and so prevent the banishment, but he is relatively easily dissuaded.

22. The role of warrior prince in the epic of Pābūjī is played by the hero's companion Cādo, who acts as Pābūjī's faithful envoy and counsellor; but Cādo is comparatively lightly characterized.

23. The extent to which the two sides were viewed as equal and opposite — one forming an alternative to the other, as it were — is revealed by the well-known contrasts Sanskrit *deva-* 'god': Avestan *daēva-* 'demon', Avestan *ahura-* and early Sanskrit *asura-* 'lord, god': later Sanskrit *asura-* 'demon'. There are also cases of 'good' demons in Indian mythology: Vibhīṣaṇa in the *Rāmāyaṇa* is one such, but see further O'Flaherty, 1976, pp. 94–138.

24. The question is dealt with in detail in O'Flaherty, 1976, which appeared after the text of this article had been completed.

25. For some valuable remarks on this subject (in the epic context) see R. C. Zaehner, *Hinduism* (Oxford, 1962), pp. 106–8.

26. Obtained from Parbū Bhopo of Mārwāṛ Junction, a professional singer of the epic of Pābūjī. The story of Jaya and Vijaya is however known elsewhere: see Bulcke, 1962, pp. 633–36.

27. For the informant in question, however, it would probably be true to say that all goddesses are merely manifestations of the Goddess.

28. An initial fault is necessary, for without it the story cannot get under way at all. A particularly clear case occurs in the famous 'story of Nala' in the *Mahābhārata*, where Kali, the personification of ill-luck and degeneracy, determines to possess Nala: he has to wait for over eleven years before his opportunity arises (in the interestingly literal words of the text, 'in the twelfth year Kali saw an opening') — which occurs when Nala forgets to wash his feet before performing the twilight ceremony [3.56.2-3]. In the same story appears an inversion of the same motif: the serpent Karkoṭaka, freed from a curse by Nala's arrival, wishes to bite him in order that the venom shall torment Kali, still possessing him. But he cannot do so without instigation, and so orders Nala to 'walk forward, counting your steps for a way'. Nala, counting aloud, reaches ten — *daśa* — which the serpent is able to take as the imperative of the verb 'bite' (*daṃś-, daś-*) (The text does not explain the double meaning, merely saying, 'he bit him at the tenth step'. Van Buitenen, rather surprisingly, does not seem to have grasped the point of this phrase.)

29. Or, like the account of the Rāma-story on pp. 68–69 above, highly modern — perhaps the least serious of the possible offences.

30. But see O'Flaherty, 1976, pp. 258–71.

31. Are we to suppose that, by writing 1.1-18 of his Gospel, St John somehow succeeded in persuading the world at large of the divinity of Jesus Christ? The very sparseness of New Testament references to Christ as God argues against the suggestion that His divinization was a 'late' occurrence: later sectarian interpolators would surely have gone about their job more thoroughly. In the epic of Pābūjī, references to the divinity of the hero are exceedingly few, and references to his purpose on Earth are altogether lacking.

32. To some elements of which I have elsewhere registered my strong objections: see John D. Smith, 1977.

33. M. B. Emeneau, 'Oral Poets of South India — the Todas', *Journal of American Folklore*, 71 (1958), 313-14.

SELECT BIBLIOGRAPHY

Texts

Bhatt, G. H., and others, *The Vālmīki-Rāmāyaṇa, Critically Edited for the First Time* (Baroda, 1960–75)
Sukthankar, Vishnu S., and Belvalkar, S. K., general editors, *The Mahābhārata, for the First Time Critically Edited* (Poona, 1933–66)

Translations

Narasimhan, Chakravarthi V., *The Mahābhārata, an English Version Based on Selected Verses* (New York and London, 1965)
Shastri, Hari Prasad, *The Ramayana of Valmiki*, 3 vols (London, 1953–59)
van Buitenen, J. A. B., *The Mahābhārata, Translated and Edited* (Chicago and London, 1973–) (in progress)

Scholarly Works

Bulcke, Camille [Kāmil Bulke], *Rāma-kathā (Utpatti aur Vikās)* [in Hindi] (Prayāg, 1962)
Dumézil, Georges, *Mythe et Épopée*, 1 (Paris, 1968)
Henige, David P., *The Chronology of Oral Tradition* (Oxford, 1974)
Hopkins, E. Washburn, 'The Bhārata and the Great Bhārata', *American Journal of Philology*, 19 (1898), 1-24

Hopkins, E. Washburn, *The Great Epic of India* (New York, 1901)

Hopkins, E. Washburn, *Epic Mythology* (Strassburg, 1915)

Jacobi, Hermann, *Das Râmâyaṇa* (Bonn, 1893)

Lord, Albert B., *The Singer of Tales* (Cambridge, Massachusetts, 1960)

Lord, Albert B., 'Perspectives on Recent Work on Oral Literature', in *Oral Literature*, ed. Joseph J. Duggan (Edinburgh, 1975)

Macdonell, Arthur A., *A History of Sanskrit Literature* (London, 1900)

O'Flaherty, Wendy Doniger, *Hindu Myths* (London, 1975)

O'Flaherty, Wendy Doniger, *The Origins of Evil in Hindu Mythology* (Berkeley, 1976)

Sen, Nabaneeta, 'Comparative Studies in Oral Epic Poetry and *The Vālmīki Rāmāyaṇa*: A Report on the *Bālākaṇḍa* [sic]', *Journal of the American Oriental Society*, 86 (1966), 397–409

Sharma, Ram Karan, *Elements of Poetry in the Mahābhārata* (Berkeley, 1964)

Smith, John D., '*The Singer or the Song?* A Reassessment of Lord's "Oral Theory"', *Man*, 12 (1977), 141–53

Smith, Mary Carroll, 'The Core of India's Great Epic' (unpublished Ph.D. thesis, Harvard, 1972)

van Nooten, Barend A., *The Mahābhārata* (New York, 1971)

Winternitz, M., *A History of Indian Literature*, Vol. I, Part II. Translated by Mrs S. Ketkar and revised by the author (Calcutta, 1963)

OLD FRENCH

By D. J. A. ROSS

IT MAY BE HELPFUL to begin the account of the Old French Epic with a brief discussion of its terminology and nomenclature. The medieval epic of France is known as a *chanson de geste*. *Geste* is a key word in French epic terminology, with a number of important meanings. From Latin *gesta*, things done, deeds, it passes in Old French from neuter plural to feminine singular. A *chanson de geste* is therefore a song of deeds, a song of the deeds of heroes:

> Ainz ad mun seignur Willame un jungleur.
> En tote France n'ad si bon chantur,
> N'en bataille plus hardi fereur;
> Et de geste li set dire les chançuns . . .[1]

(My Lord William has a jongleur; there is no singer in all France so good as he nor any better fighter in battle. He knows how to sing epic songs to him.)

The corresponding verb is *chanter de geste*, to sing an epic song:

> Je sai trop bien canter de geste.
> Me volés vous oïr canter?[2]

(I can sing an epic song very well. Do you want to hear me sing?)

and:

Ledit Jehan puet . . . faire chanter de geste a Beauvés au lieu acoustumé qui que il lui plait le jour de Noel . . . sans che que aultres y puist chanter se n'est par la licence dudit Jehan.[3]

(The said John may . . . have epic songs performed in Beauvais on Christmas day by whomsoever he pleases in the usual place . . . without anyone else being able to sing there except by permission of the said John.)

Conter de geste, to tell an epic tale, is also found, sometimes in non-epic contexts:

> Conter vous voel d'antive estore
> Que li clerc tiennent en memore,
> Et conter d'une fiere geste . . .[4]

(I wish to tell you of an old story whose memory the learned keep alive and to tell of a fierce tale of war . . .)

By extension *geste* comes to mean by itself an epic account — historical or supposedly historical:

Il est escrit en l'ancïene geste . . .[5] (It is written in the old history . . .)

Ci falt la geste des Bretuns.[6] (Here ends the history of the Britons.)

Ce dist l'estoire, q'en la geste trovom . . .[7] (The story, which we find in the history, says . . .)

In particular *geste* is used of the three great cycles of Old French epic; the royal epic (*geste du roi*); the feudal epic (*geste de Döon de Maiance*); and the epics associated with Guillaume d'Orange and his family (*geste de Garin de Monglane* or *de Guillaume d'Orange*):

> N'ot que trois gestes en France la garnie;
> Du roi de France est la plus seignorie, . . .
> Et l'autre aprés, bien est droiz que gel die,
> Est de Döon a la barbe florie . . .
> La tierce geste qui molt fist a proisier
> Fu de Garin de Monglane le fier.[8]

(There were only three groups of epics in France the rich; the noblest is that of the king of France, . . . and the second after it (it is very right that I should say it) is that of Döon with the long white beard . . . The third geste, which was of great fame and worth, was that of the fierce Garin de Monglane.)

A related extension of meaning, resulting from the tendency of the heroes of the epic cycles to be related by blood, is the sense race, family or kinship-group.

> Oï avés canter de Bernart de Brubant . . .
> Et de la fiere geste dont cantent li auquant,
> Ki tant soffri de paine sor sarrasine gent.[9]

(You have heard the story of Bernart de Brubant . . . and of the fierce clan of whom some sing, who suffered so much distress at the hands of the Saracens.)

Deus me cunfunde, se la geste en desment![10] (God damn me if I am untrue to my people in this.)

Vos estez d'une geste ou il a maint princier.[11] (You are of a family in which there are many noble princes.)

Je voz affi qu'il est de franche geste.[12] (I assure you that he comes from noble kin . . .)

By a further extension of meaning to nation or people *la geste Francor* comes to mean the French, and *la sarrazine geste*, *la paiene geste* or *la geste Mahom* the Saracens.

> Li desconfit se plaignent de la geste francor,
> Qui felon sont et fier et noble poigneor . . .[13]

(The defeated complain of the men of France who are wicked and fierce and noble fighters . . .)

Tuit li meillor de la paiene geste . . .[14] (All the best of the pagan people . . .)

> 'Se Dex m'aïst, traï nos a Orable;
> Et Dex confonde la sarrazine geste!'[15]

('So help me God, Orable has betrayed us and may God destroy the Saracen people!')

> 'Par le saint Sauveor que nos tuit aoron,
> Mal est hui avenu a la geste Mahon . . .'[16]

('By the holy Saviour whom we all worship, misfortune has today befallen Mohammed's people: . . .')

The Saracens are offensively referred to as *la pute geste*:

Cent mile furent de la pute geste . . .[17] (There were a hundred thousand of the foul people.)

and *de pute geste* comes finally to mean of foul or evil character:

Un Sarazin felun de pute geste . . .[18] (A wicked Saracen of foul character . . .)

La garce de la pute geste . . .[19] (The bitch of evil nature . . .)

The term *matière de France* is also used of the Old French epic. Its source is a couplet in Jean Bodel's *Chanson des Saisnes*:

> N'en sont que trois materes a nul home entendant;
> De France et de Bretaigne et de Romme la grant . . .[20]

(There are only three subjects for anyone of understanding; France, Britain and great Rome . . .)

the *matières* of Britain and Rome being the Arthurian Romances and the Romances of Antiquity.

It is necessary in the first place to limit the subject. This account is concerned only with the epic proper, the *chanson de geste* in one of the recognized epic metres, and omits numerous epic elements in the Romances in octosyllabic rhyming couplets, though this omission may distort the picture. Even so it is virtually impossible in limited space to give a representative picture of a field which includes some eighty epics, whole or fragmentary, varying in length from under 1,000 to over 30,000 lines, whose composition in their extant form extends from about 1100 to the middle of the fourteenth century, and behind which must lie in many cases earlier traditions, in whatever form expressed, going back to Carolingian and even earlier times.

The *chanson de geste* is found for the most part in the area in which were spoken the various dialects of the *langue d'oïl*; that is to say modern France approximately north of a line running from the mouth of the Loire north of the Massif Central and ending at Geneva, French-speaking Switzerland and southern

Belgium. Most surviving *chansons de geste* were apparently composed in that area.

They were also popular with the French-speaking rulers of England, which has indeed preserved three of the earliest, the Oxford version of *La Chanson de Roland*; *La Chanson de Guillaume* and *Le Voyage de Charlemagne*.

The epic appears not to have been very popular in southern France and of the few surviving, two, *Girart de Roussillon*[21] and *Daurel et Beton*,[22] are in a curious artificial dialect with Limousin affinities.[23] A third, *Fierabras*,[24] is a straight linguistic adaptation from the corresponding northern French poem. The most interesting southern epics are the two recently discovered Roland poems, *Ronsasvals*,[25] a version of the *Chanson de Roland* aberrant in several respects, and the original and interesting poem *Roland à Saragosse*,[26] epic in form but in many ways a romance in spirit.

The French epic was also popular in northern Italy where several, including two manuscripts of the *Chanson de Roland*, have been preserved in a literary pseudo-dialect which is a mixture of French and Italian. Others, like the *Entrée de Spagne*,[27] the work of an anonymous Paduan, were composed in that same language in Italy itself.

The 'matter of France' was popular also among non-romance-speaking peoples. Particularly important are the Middle High German Roland poem *Ruolantes liet*,[28] made by a priest called Konrad probably for Henry the Lion of Saxony in the 1180s, and Wolfram von Eschenbach's *Willehalm*,[29] a fine version of the story of the battle of Larchamp, based on *Aliscans* and in many ways an improvement on its model. It was completed by Ulrich von Türheim's very lengthy *Rennewart*,[30] on the life and exploits of William's brother-in-law Rainouart, a comic kitchen boy turned knight.

Of great importance also is the Old Norse *Karlamagnussaga*,[31] a prose adaptation of a number of epics of the *geste du roy* made in the early thirteenth century for King Haakon IV of Norway. It is valuable for the study of Old French epic as it preserves stories and versions of *chansons de geste* which have not survived otherwise. Adaptations from French epic are found also in Middle English and Welsh.

The extant French epics are not easy to date closely. *Roland* itself has been dated over a range from 1070 to as late as 1150, though recent opinion is for the most part prepared to accept a dating of 1100 plus or minus five years or so. Other early epics, *Gormont et Isembart*, *La Chanson de Guillaume* and *Le Voyage de Charlemagne*, have been very variously dated between the end of the eleventh and the middle of the twelfth century.

The twelfth century was the most productive of the better surviving examples, which are mostly anonymous. In the thirteenth century a number of authors whose names are known, mostly successful 'menestrels' like Bertrand de Bar sur Aube,[32] Graindor de Brie[33] and especially Adenet le Roy,[34] have left us literary revisions of older poems which their new versions supplanted and drove out of favour.

The late thirteenth and fourteenth centuries are the period of decadence of the epic in which immensely long poems like *Lion de Bourges*[35] and *Theseus de Cologne*[36] were composed for a popular audience which still existed for such productions, but which was apparently demanding a new orientation, with such figures as the heroic artisan, the goldsmith who ends as king of Antioch, and even that contradiction the heroic *vilain*, in the charcoal burner who is knighted for his undoubted loyalty and his rather ungainly valour. This audience of the decadence could identify happily with such reflexions of itself when the aristocracy had, in a more sophisticated age, lost its taste for the simple and primitive epic.

But, though extant French epics are datable approximately in the period 1090 to 1370, evidence is to be found for the existence of epic traditions, notably that of the *Chanson de Roland*, at least to the beginning of the eleventh century, and it is likely that most of the earlier epics we possess are more or less revised from yet earlier versions.

At the time when this literature was produced in its surviving form, say from the late eleventh to the mid-thirteenth century, French narrative literature was very largely in verse. From about 1200 onwards prose narrative begins to compete strongly with verse and ultimately largely to replace it. Most of the favourite epic legends appear in a prose form in the late Middle Ages and survive in popular chapbooks down to about 1850.[37]

In its origin French epic was no doubt orally composed and it was still to a considerable extent orally diffused during the twelfth century. From about 1150 it encountered the competition of long narrative romances in octosyllabic rhyming couplets. These, unlike the epic, were largely non-formulaic and composed in a written form. They were intended to be read aloud in company and not, like the epic, the subject of a semi-dramatic musical performance. Their subtler handling of erotic themes and psychological problems won for them great and increasing popularity at the expense of that of the epic.

Up to about 1150, except for a few hagiographic works, surviving northern French literature is in epic form; and epic clearly held its own in public esteem to the end of the twelfth century. Its popularity declined during the thirteenth century when most of the surviving manuscripts were made, perhaps at the desire of patrons who wished to preserve a literature which was still to a large extent orally diffused and was going out of fashion.

Epic metres are occasionally used in other genres; in particular the alexandrine is used in stanzaic form in saints' lives and for monologues in the drama. The twelfth-century *Roman d'Alexandre*, based on Pseudo-Callisthenes and other sources, with its continuations and interpolations extending to the mid-fourteenth century, which gave its name to the alexandrine line, is in form and style a *chanson de geste*.[38] Epic elements, battle descriptions and the like, are found frequently in the earlier romances in octosyllabic rhyming couplets and epic formulas are not infrequently adapted to that form to express such subjects in octosyllables.

The content of the Old French epic cannot be wholly divorced from its ethos and these aspects are perhaps best considered together. The late system-atizers who planned the great cyclic manuscripts of the thirteenth and fourteenth centuries which have preserved a large part of the surviving *chansons de geste* recognized, as we have seen, three epic cycles into which they fitted, and sometimes forced, the poems they were copying.

The first of these, the royal epic or *geste du roi*, which Bertrand de Bar sur Aube describes as 'la plus seignorie', the noblest, usually has as its central character Charlemagne. He tends sometimes to play the part of a father-figure, directing and controlling the action but leaving heroic deeds to a considerable extent to subordinates. He intervenes in person usually only at moments of the highest tension, as, for example, in his single combat with Baligant, emir of Babylon and leader and champion of Islam, as Charles himself is champion of Christianity, which forms the climax of the latter part of the *Chanson de Roland*. The royal central figure is more rarely Charles's father, Pepin the Short or his grandfather Charles Martel. His son, Louis the Pious, appears mainly in the *geste de Guillaume d'Orange*.

Charles is accompanied by a following of warriors whose relation to him is feudal, that of vassal to lord. Most important is the group known as *les douze pers*, the twelve peers of France. The composition of the group is not stable and some of them are little more than names, while some of the leading heroes are not peers. They tend to be paired, in accordance with the Germanic institution of *compagnonage* or brotherhood in arms, in which two knights have a particularly strong mutual bond of fidelity and friendship, which does not, however, exclude their normal feudal relationship to the king. Roland and Oliver form the classic companion-pair; others, such as Ivorie and Ivon and Gerin and Gerier, are little more than pairs of like-sounding names, and take no major part in the action.[39]

The chief heroes, apart from Roland and Oliver, are Ogier the Dane, Girart de Roussillon, a hero also of the feudal epic of revolt, Richard of Normandy, Geoffrey of Anjou, and old Duke Naimes of Bavaria, the wise counsellor of Charlemagne who plays Nestor's part in the Old French epic, though, old as he is, he is as good a fighter as the younger generation.

Turpin, the fighting Archbishop of Reims, who in the *Chanson de Roland* represents the Church in every sense Militant, is a very important figure whose honour it is to be the last to die before Roland himself on the field of Roncevaux. The extremely popular Latin chronicle of Charles's Spanish wars against the Saracens, which was attributed to him in the first half of the twelfth century and is now known as the Pseudo-Turpin Chronicle, is largely responsible for the acceptance of the epic traditions as sober history by the great majority of medieval chroniclers of the history of France.

The medieval public seems to have been reluctant to accept the failure of the hero through his own fault or weakness. When things go irremediably wrong, even in the face of overwhelming odds, there must have been treason at work. And so, as Arthur needs Mordred for his downfall, the author of the *Chanson de Roland* has depicted the characteristic traitor in Roland's stepfather Ganelon. He is not lacking in courage or wisdom but his character is fatally flawed by an almost pathological jealousy of his stepson and suspicion of his motives. Later authors of epics, in the late twelfth, and thirteenth centuries, link all their villains to Ganelon, whose 'bad blood' comes out in a numerous progeny of descendant and collateral traitors, an example of the systematizing tendency of the later epic. This is particularly common in the feudal epic of revolt, where the machinations of one of the *geste Ganelon* are the frequent cause of royal injustice to the hero followed by the latter's revolt against his lord.

The basic content of the *geste du roi* is, then, the struggle of Christendom under the leadership of the King of France, in a pre-Crusade against Islam, usually, as in Roland, represented by the Moors of Spain; but not infrequently invasions from Africa are depicted, as in the *Chanson d'Aspremont*.[40] Even Scandinavian heathen, as in *Gormont et Isembart*, are regularly equated with the 'Sarazin et Escler'[41] who form the stock enemy. It is significant that when the events of the First Crusade came to be told in French verse in the first half of the twelfth century it was to the epic form that Richart le Pelerin turned in composing his *Chanson d'Antioche*, preserved only in Graindor de Douai's revision of half a century later.[42] The *chanson de geste* was the natural form for a poem about the heroic deeds of French knights fighting Saracens.

The *geste de Garin de Monglane* has as its central figure Count Guillaume d'Orange who is identifiable with the historical William, Count of Toulouse and conqueror of Barcelona, who in the year 804 retired from the world, first to the monastery of Aniane and then to his own foundation of Gellone or St Guilhem du Desert, where he died in the odour of sanctity a few years later in 812. The *geste* apparently grew up around him by successive accretions, and Garin de Monglane, whose epic story is presumably one of the latest in date, was invented to supply the family with an ancestor.

The twenty-four poems of this *geste* form what is both a family cycle and a national one. The heroes are William himself, his father Aymeri de Narbonne, his brothers Bernart de Brusbant, Guibert d'Andrenas, Hernaut de Gironde (Gerona), Bueves de Commarcis, Garin d'Ansëune and Aïmer le Chetif, and William's nephews, Bertrand and Vivien in particular.

William in the epics belongs mainly to the generation after Charlemagne and his lord is the weak and ineffectual Louis, whose ingratitude to his loyal protector is the theme of a number of the poems of this *geste*. Basically the content of the *geste de Guillaume* is the same as that of the *geste du roi*, the struggle of Christendom against Islam, but here it is shown as the unaided fight of the loyal hero and his people, deserted and abandoned by their feudal superior whose duty it was to protect and support them.

Typical epics of the *geste de Guillaume* are *Le couronnement de Louis*[43] and *Le Charroi de Nîmes*,[44] which both depict the relationship between the loyal vassal and his unsatisfactory lord, and the three versions of the battle of Larchamp or Aliscans, *La Chanson de Guillaume*[45] and *La Chevalerie Vivien*,[46] with its two alternative continuations, *Aliscans*[47] and *Foucon de Candie*,[48] The subject here is the struggle against overwhelming odds and final triumph of the hero abandoned by his lord.

The feudal epic, the *geste de Döon de Maience* has some affinities with the *geste de Guillaume* in that the hero often suffers from royal injustice, but, unlike the steadfastly loyal William, the feudal hero often allows himself to be goaded into revolt against his unjust lord. That monarch is as likely to be Charlemagne himself as Louis or some other member of the Carolingian house, and the feudal epic of revolt contrasts with the loyal, crusading spirit of the *geste du roi*.

The various versions of the story of the revolt of Girart de Roussillon[49] and his final reconciliation with his lord form the classic type of this kind of epic. *Renaut de Montauban*,[50] better known as *Les Quatre fils Aymon*, is a poem of the same type whose popularity, in debased prose versions, and, in Belgium and Sicily, in puppet plays, has lasted almost down to our own day.

In *Girart de Vienne*[51] Roland, loyal nephew of Charlemagne, meets in single combat Oliver the equally loyal nephew of the rebel count Girart, an episode which leads to the reconciliation of the Count and his lord and the faithful *compagnonage* of the two young men. This poem also makes contact with the *geste de Guillaume*, as Girart is brother not only of Renier de Gennes, father of Oliver and Aude, but also of Aymeri de Narbonne, father of Guillaume and his brothers.

In some feudal epics the theme of royal injustice, though not absent, is subordinated to the resultant struggle between the victim deprived of his fief and the recipient of unjustified royal generosity. Such a struggle between the houses of Cambrai and Vermandois is depicted in *Raoul de Cambrai*.[52]

Sub-cycles are discernible in the poems forming what is known as *La geste des Lorrains*, which is unusual in depicting a heroic family which is not of noble birth on both sides, the founder of the house, Hervis de Metz,[53] being the son of a 'riche vilain' and a duke's daughter, a *mésalliance* which would not normally be tolerated in the essentially aristocratic *chanson de geste*. Another sub-cycle of some interest is that relating the fortunes of the not easily identifiable house of Nanteuil (see note 150, below).

The ethos of the Old French epic is basically feudal and Christian in a specifically crusading form. Roland's simple profession of faith:

> Pur sun seignor deit hom susfrir destreiz
> E endurer e granz chalz e granz freiz
> Si·n deit hom perdre e del quir e del peil.[54]

(For his lord a man must suffer distress and bear great heat and great cold and lose both skin and hair for him.)

and

> Paien unt tort et crestïens unt dreit.[55]

(Pagans are wrong and Christians are right.)

are the expression in brief of the essential ethos of the Old French epic, particularly of those *chansons de geste* which belong to the *geste du roi* and the *geste de Guillaume*.

To this basic ethos must be added, especially in the feudal cycle, the mutual character of the feudal bond. The vassal owes loyalty and support to his lord but the lord also owes justice and protection to his vassal. Essentially the feudal epic of revolt depicts the outcome of the breach of the feudal contract by the lord. William's unswerving loyalty, even in the face of injustice and ingratitude, has something superhuman about it. We feel, and are meant to feel, sympathy for a Raoul de Cambrai, an Isembart or a Girart de Roussillon, victims of royal caprice, injustice or political opportunism.

A word here on Saracens and women in the epic. Saracens are wrong and, unless converted, as they not infrequently are, will come to a bad end, the devils being in regular attendance to carry off their erring souls to an unpleasant destination, but they are not usually grotesque, though some Saracen champions like Ferragut and Corsolt, are giants. Apart, however, from being on the wrong side in the religious struggle they are not necessarily bad or unchivalrous: 'Fust chrestïens, asez oüst barnet.'[56] (Were he a Christian he would be an excellent baron.)

They are depicted as idolaters, worshipping the images of a pagan trinity, Mahom, Apolin and Tervagant, the authors of the epics showing complete ignorance of the strictly monotheistic and aniconic character of Islam. Apart from this in dress, armour, tactics and feudal organization they do not differ from their Christian opponents.

A touch of imperfectly understood local colour appears in the use of Arabic titles of nobility, especially *amiral* from such Arabic titles as 'amīr al-[baḥr], *almaçor* (al-manṣur, the victorious), Algalife (al-khalīfa, Caliph) and others less easily explained such as *amurafle* and *amustant*.

Women play little part in the earlier *chansons de geste*, and their increasing importance, with the emergence of something of the ethos of courtly love, is generally a sign of lateness of date and of decadence.

Aude, Roland's betrothed and Oliver's sister, makes a brief appearance at the end of the *chanson de Roland*,[57] only to die on hearing news of the disaster and of the death of the hero.

An exception occurs in the case of Guiborc, William's wife. She was Orable, a Saracen princess, wife of Tedbald, Lord of Orange, who falls in love with the hero who has penetrated into the city in disguise, and helps him to capture it, after which she is duly converted, receives the new Christian name Guiborc at her baptism, marries the hero and remains his faithful companion thereafter. She is much more active and positive than most of the women who appear in the earlier *chansons de geste*, though the female characters in *Raoul de Cambrai* also play a significant part.

The two surviving versions of *La Prise d'Orange* are rather late in date, being composed at the end of the twelfth or in the thirteenth century, but evidence survives in a brief Latin version of the story, in the *Vita Sancti Wilhelmi* of about 1120, which makes it probable that it existed at least by the first decade of the twelfth century. William's winning of Guiborc sets something of a fashion in later epics of the *geste de Guillaume* and elsewhere, where the theme of the Saracen princess who falls in love with the hero, helps him to escape from her father's prison, flees with him and ends as a respectable Christian wife and mother, becomes an almost obligatory commonplace, rather wearisomely repeated.

The author of the *Chanson de Roland* was concerned with a problem of ethos which was of current importance at the time he composed his poem. This was the problem of power in the state and the relative rights of the individual as opposed to those of the state, which in feudal society meant the monarch as supreme overlord. This is what the trial of Ganelon is really about — feudal anarchy or a strong centralized monarchy.

The fighting is over, Roland has been avenged on the Saracens, Baligant defeated, Marsile's queen Bramimonde converted. Charles summons his barons to his palace at Aix intending to put Ganelon on trial and punish his treason. For the purpose of his argument the poet imagines a constitutional position which in fact never existed, in which the council of barons can judge one of their peers without reference to the king's wishes or honour, and Charles is bound to accept their verdict. The author, whose sympathies are clearly with the rule of law and a strong monarchy, in no way loads the dice against Ganelon but allows him to make his case in the strongest possible way. Charles begins by stating his accusation:[58]

'My lords and barons, now give just judgment for me in the case of Ganelon. He went with me to Spain and deprived me of twenty thousand of my Franks and my nephew whom you will never see again and Oliver the brave and courteous knight. He has betrayed the Twelve Peers for gain.' Ganelon said: 'May I be reckoned a scoundrel if I hide it. Roland did me wrong in gold and wealth for which I sought his death and his harm, but I do not grant that there was any treason in that.' The Franks reply: 'Now let us take counsel about it.' Ganelon stood up before the king. Handsome of body and of a fine complexion were he only loyal he would appear a fine gentleman. He sees the men of France and all the judges and thirty of his kinsmen there to support him. Then he spoke out in a loud voice: 'Barons, for the love of God listen to me! My lords, I was in the army with the emperor and I served him in good faith and affection. His nephew Roland came to hate me and assigned to me death and sorrow. I was messenger to King Marsile. By my cleverness I managed to escape. I challenged Roland the fighter and Oliver and all their comrades: Charles and his noble barons heard me do so: I have taken vengeance on them, but there is no treason in that.' The Franks reply: 'We will go and take counsel about it.'[59]

Ganelon's defence is then private revenge after challenge duly made. And it is in his own eyes a perfectly justified plea. He did indeed defy Roland and the peers when appointed to the embassy. 'Sir', said Ganelon, 'Roland is responsible for all this: I will not love him as long as I live, nor Oliver because he is his friend nor the Twelve Peers because they love him so much. I defy them here, sir, in your presence because of it.'[60]

The court is prepared to put the rights of feudal anarchy before those of the monarchy and accept the plea. The lords return to Charlemagne and say to the king 'Sir, we beg you to pardon Ganelon for this once, and then let him serve you in good faith and in affection. Let him live for he is a very noble gentleman. Never through his death will we see that lord (Roland) again or win him back for wealth.' The king said 'You are for me a pack of scoundrels'.[61]

But Charles can do nothing but accept the verdict. There is however a way out. Thierry of Anjou is prepared to let the issue go to trial by battle, himself acting as Charles's champion against Ganelon's kinsman, the huge Pinabel. But first he states his grounds for challenging the court's verdict:

'My noble lord and king, do not grieve in this way. You know that I have served you much and I have an ancestral right to speak thus. Whatever wrong Roland may have done Ganelon the fact that he was in your service should have protected him; it is with you that he has broken faith and it is you that he has injured. And for this reason I would condemn him to death by hanging and to have his body [torn in pieces] as a felon guilty of a crime. If he now has any kinsman who will give me the lie I am prepared at once to uphold my verdict with this sword which I have here at my side.' The Franks reply: 'You have spoken well.'[62]

In the sequel Thierry defeats Pinabel against the odds and Ganelon is executed. The author, who was probably a churchman, not unexpectedly comes out in favour of the rule of law against feudal anarchy. No problem was of greater current concern at the time of composition of the poem. William I, himself a most turbulent vassal of the French crown, showed that he would be master in his newly-won kingdom of England by exacting a direct oath of obedience from all vassals, the rights of intermediate lords notwithstanding. In France the Capetians struggled to impose the royal power throughout the twelfth century. Suger at the beginning of the century shows Louis VI hardly able to control the squirearchy of the Ile de France. By the end of the period Philip Augustus is ready to absorb the Anglo-Angevin continental possessions.[63]

Apart from a rather conventional epic exaggeration the powers of the heroes of French epics are in no way superhuman and the marvellous and magical play little part in the earlier and better examples. By the thirteenth century, however, in *Huon de Bordeaux*,[64] the magical powers of the fairy king Oberon, who takes under his protection the hero of what was originally an epic of revolt against Royal injustice, play a large part in his successful escape from fantastic dangers in the East and in his final triumph and reconciliation with his lord Charles. *Huon de Bordeaux* is, however, like the Old French *Roman d'Alexandre*, really a hybrid, a *chanson de geste* in form but in part an adventure–romance in content and ethos.

The epic exaggerations referred to take three forms: immense disparity of numbers, as in the last phase of the battle of Roncevaux where sixty Franks engage fifty thousand Saracens;[65] the excessive age attributed to such characters as Charlemagne: 'dous cenz anz ad e mielz . . .'[66] ('He is two hundred years old and more . . .') and extraordinary feats of strength in dealing death-blows to the enemy, as when Roland on more than one occasion bisects his opponent vertically so that his sword finally bites through his saddle and deep into his horse's spine.[67] In general, however, battles are depicted as a series of single combats each described with exactitude and obvious appreciation of the skill and prowess of the combatants.

An exception must be made in the case of Charlemagne himself, who, in the *Chanson de Roland* and some other poems, receives special marks of divine favour in the form of prophetic dreams and angelic encouragement. Nevertheless this manifestation of the Christianized marvellous is normally limited to admonition and encouragement.[68] When at the climax of the final battle of the *Chanson de Roland*, Charles, in single combat with Baligant the champion of Islam, is staggering under the blows of his gigantic enemy, the archangel Gabriel appears before him, but Baligant is not struck down by divine intervention. 'Great king, what are you about?' says the angel in what one feels can only be a disapproving tone; and Charles, recalled to a sense of his duty, splits Baligant's head open with a downward slash of his sword. It is by his own unaided human efforts that he has to fight his battle and that of his faith.[69]

In the Middle Ages the *chansons de geste* seem generally to have been accepted as having a basis of valid historical fact. Their authors not infrequently quote supposed historical sources in a rather vague and non-commital manner.

Ceo dit la geste a seint Denise.[70]

(The account (preserved) at St Denis says this . . .)

Il est escrit en la geste Francor . . .[71]

(It is written in the history of the Franks . . .)

Geste Francor trente escheles i numbre(n)t.[72]

(The history of the Franks reckons at thirty the number of companies there.)

. . . el mostier Saint Denise,
La ou les jestes de France sont escrites.[73]

(In the church of St Denis where the chronicles of France are written.)

These references to the history of 'the deeds of the Franks', and in particular to historical sources supposedly preserved in the royal monastery of St Denis or elsewhere, are a commonplace in the epics, and are for the most part to be discounted as serious references to sources, but they do indicate a degree of supposed historicity which the composer expects his audience to accept.

But perhaps the strongest confirmation that the epics were generally accepted as historical in the Middle Ages is to be found in the existence, and general acceptance, of the *Pseudo-Turpin Chronicle*.[74] This Latin prose work of the first half of the twelfth century, associated with Cluny, the Compostella pilgrimage and possibly with Pope Calixtus II, and attributed pseudonymously to the fighting archbishop, tells the story of Charles's campaigns in Spain following epic traditions, some of which, like the single combat of Roland and the Saracen giant Ferragut, survive in no other form. Its unhesitating acceptance by almost all writers of Latin and vernacular chronicle-histories of France in the Middle Ages and beyond parallels the similar acceptance of Geoffrey of Monmouth in England, and would appear to support the idea that the Middle Ages regarded the *chansons de geste* generally as factually true.[75]

What germ of real historical fact may be embedded in the *chansons de geste* is a highly controversial question. In the nineteenth century a historical basis for the epics was generally taken for granted. Heavily discounted by Bédier and his school[76] the importance of the historical element has found strong supporters in Ferdinand Lot, who never accepted Bédier's views,[77] René Louis, whose historical study of the legend of Girart de Roussillon is a model of its kind,[78] and most recently in Ramón Menéndez-Pidal, whose key work, *La Chanson de Roland y el neo-tradicionalismo*,[79] has given its name, neo-traditionalist, to one of the two current schools of thought on the origins of the French epic.

The question is really extremely difficult of solution because medieval historical sources, annals and chronicle-histories, give so few of the kind of

G

details of tactics and military practice which may well be preserved in the *chansons de geste*, with the result that there is little basis for comparison or confirmatory evidence.

What is certain, however, is that later composers and revisers of epics never hesitated to change the story which they were telling to bring it up to date, and to make military practice and civil life conform to those of contemporary twelfth-century feudal France.

For example, the only reliable and reasonably detailed account of the disaster of 15 August 778, that given in Einhard's *Vita Caroli*, describes the action as an ambush in which the Basques charged down from above on the Frankish rearguard at a point high in the Pyrenean pass, drove them in confusion down into the valley, and wiped them out.[80] The poet of the Oxford *Chanson de Roland*, working probably in about 1100, has transformed the action into a set-piece cavalry battle, in which the tactic employed is invariably the charge with couched lance resulting in the unhorsing of one or sometimes of both of the combatants, followed, when the lance is lost or broken, by engagement with the heavy sword.[81]

Now the charge with couched lance as a cavalry tactic seems to date from not earlier than about the mid-eleventh century and, for its effective employment, requires open and level ground. It could not possibly have been used by either side in the situation described by Einhard, who incidentally makes it clear that the enemy of the Franks were mountaineers, lightly armed and in consequence able easily to escape after the action. Such horses and pack animals as the Franks may have had with them, plunging and rearing in panic under the sudden attack, can only have rendered effective defence the more difficult. Yet, despite his completely up-to-date description of the fighting, the author of the Oxford *Roland* continues to describe a rocky and mountainous terrain, with high hills, deep defiles and gloomy forests, a decor perfectly suited to Einhard's account of the battle.

> Halt sunt li pui e tenebrus e grant,
> Li val parfunt e les ewes curant.[82]

(The hills are high and dark and huge and the valleys are deep and the torrents swift.)

It seems possible that the *Roland* poet was working on and transforming an earlier form of the story which may have been closer to Einhard's. Other details seem to corroborate this. On the way to Roncevaux the Saracens take up their position in a thicket at the top of the hills:

> Paien chevalchent par cez greignurs vallees, . . .
> En un bruill par sum les puis remestrent
> IIIIC milie atendent l'ajurnee.
> Deus! quel dulur que li Franceis nel sevent![83]

(The pagans ride along through the great defiles ... They remained halted in a thicket at the summit of the hills. Four hundred thousand of them await the dawn. Ah God! what a cause for grief that the French do not know of it.)

This seems to agree closely with the ambush described by Einhard but we hear no more of it, and when Oliver climbs a hill to observe the enemy he sees them advancing openly and covering the whole countryside with their vast numbers.[84]

It is not unlikely also that Gautier del Hum, who is sent by Roland to occupy the high ground, and, having clashed with the enemy and lost his force, flees down from the hills to take a part with Roland and Turpin in the final stand, was originally the leader of a flank-guard sent out to protect the upper flank of the rearguard as it made its way through the pass, but which failed to carry out its duty and prevent the ambush being effective.[85]

This brings us to the question of the time represented in the Old French epic. This is supposed to be usually the eighth and ninth centuries, especially the reigns of Charlemagne and Louis the Pious, though earlier and later periods are sometimes depicted, and some of the feudal epics are rather vaguely situated in time. It is however a Carolingian age depicted in terms of twelfth-century French feudalism, and, as we have seen in the case of the tactics in the *Chanson de Roland* and the problem of power as posed in the trial of Ganelon, the life depicted and the problems examined are those of the author's contemporaries.

The same is true in the field of armour and weapons. The knight wears a *hauberc* or shirt of mail falling to the knees and split in front and behind for convenience of riding, the resulting flaps (*pans*) being possibly secured by a strap or tie round the thigh. The *hauberc* has a hood of mail (*coife*) closed by a laced-up flap (*ventaille*). The *hauberc* is sometimes described as *doblier*, of double mesh, or *doblé en treis*, of triple mesh, also *treslis*, woven. This probably implied the wearing of two or three shirts of mail over one another for additional protection. The common adjective is *jaserenc* or *jaserent*, of Algiers.

Over the hood of the *hauberc* was worn a conical helm (*heaume agu*), probably of leather or *cuir bouilli* strengthened by an iron band round the head (*cercle*), often described as decorated with jewels set in gold (*a or gemmé*), and similar bands running from ear to ear and from nape to forehead crossing at the top of the skull. The iron band was extended from the forehead for four or five inches to form the *nasal* or nose-guard. Rather curiously the adjective usually applied to the helm is *vert*, green, which one must suppose implies a protective coating of green paint, though contemporary visual documents do not show this. The helm, which could otherwise have been rather easily knocked off, was secured to the *coife* of the *hauberc* by a lace (*lacié*).

The *broigne* (*brunia*, *byrnie*) was a simpler form of body protection consisting of small metal plates or metal rings sewn to a leather or heavy canvas doublet, offering considerable protection against a slashing blow but virtually none against the thrust of a couched lance. It is mentioned frequently but appears to be regarded as synonymous with the *hauberc*.

The knight also carried a shield (*escu*), which contemporary visual documents, miniatures and reliefs, depict as kite-shaped and about three feet six inches to four feet in length. It was designed to protect the left side of the body. It was made probably of wood with a covering of leather, and a metal rim, and it was sometimes strengthened with bands of metal crossing under the central metal boss. Its weight was supported by a strap round the neck (*guige*) and it was controlled by two loops (*enarmes*) through which the left forearm was passed.

There is no mention of heraldic devices on the shield in the *Chanson de Roland*, though the adjectival phrase *peint a flors* could indicate a primitive proto-heraldry, and in general heraldry is rarely referred to in the *chansons de geste*.[86] A grotesque face mask as boss gave its name to the *escu bocler* (*scutum bucculare*), and *bocler*, later *bouclier*, comes to be synonymous with *escu*, as does also *targe*, originally apparently a round shield. In retreat the knight slings his shield behind him to protect his back (*targe adossee*).

The legs in the early period were protected only by breeches or cloth leggings, sometimes cross-gartered. Mail leggings or trousers (*chauces*) are mentioned in the later epics as being laced on (*laciés*). Prick-spurs are worn, but no protection for hands or feet is mentioned.

The weapons of the knight in the earlier epics are normally two, the heavy lance (*lance, espiet*), used couched under the armpit and aimed so as to pierce and unhorse the opponent; and the heavy sword (*espee* or *brant*), used mainly to deal slashing blows. The shaft of the lance is called *la hanste* and is described as *de pomier*, of apple-wood, or *fraisnine* of ash. Its point is *la mure*, and it is decorated with a pennon, *gonfanon*. A common formula is *pleine sa hanste* (or *lance*), by the full length of his lance, and implies that the victor lifts his opponent out of the saddle and deposits him a full lance-length behind his horse, a feat which was evidently much admired as it is so frequently described (see note 81, above).

The sword is described as of steel and sometimes as inscribed (*brant d'acier lettré*), and famous fighters have named swords, as Roland has Durendal, Oliver Hauteclaire, and Charlemagne Joieuse. Surviving inscribed examples seem mostly to bear the name of the maker or a charm, sometimes Christianized. The sword has a hilt, or grip (*helz, heut*) and a pommel (*ponz, pomel*) or knob to prevent its falling from a hand slippery with blood and sweat. Both are usually described as of precious materials:

> 'U est vostre espee ki Halteclere ad num?
> D'or est li helz e de cristal li punz.'[87]

('Where is your sword whose name is Hauteclaire? Its hilt is of gold and its pummel of crystal.')

and relics may be set in them for the spiritual protection of the owner:

> 'En l'oriét punt asez i ad reliques.'[88]

('In the golden pummel there are many relics.')

Although the Bayeux tapestry shows extensive use of missile weapons, both by archers on foot and in the form of javelins hurled by knights on horseback, by the end of the eleventh century missiles are contemptible weapons, only to be used by a cowardly enemy unwilling to close with the hero. So in the *Chanson de Roland*, at the end of the battle when Turpin and Roland are fighting on alone surrounded by the enemy, the latter, alarmed by the sound of Charles's trumpets, cry:

> 'Li quens Rollant est de tant grant fiertet,
> Ja n'ert vencut pur nul hume carnel;
> Lançuns a lui, puis sil laissums ester!'[89]

('Count Roland is a man of such fierce courage. He will never be vanquished by any man of flesh and blood. Let us hurl weapons at him and then leave him alone.')

And they try to overwhelm the two survivors under a hail of missiles. Saracen champions in other epics are also sometimes shown carrying and using javelins but Christians never descend to this sort of tactic.

The knight is a horseman and his horse is his *destrier* (dextrarium), possibly so-called because led by the squire by his right hand, though other explanations have been suggested. Besides normal adjectives of colour, *bai, brun, gris, auferant* (compounded of *ferant* grey and Arab. *al faras* horse), etc., it is also described in terms of its origin: *norois* of Norway, *arabi*, Arabian, *d'Espagne*, Spanish. It is swift, *coranz*, and strong and fierce, *forz et fiers*. It has no barding or protection but no Christian knight would attack the horse rather than his rider, though a Saracen might descend to such baseness. The horses of great heroes are named, like their swords. Roland's is Veillantif, Marsile's Gaignun (Mastiff), Gerier's Passecerf, and Charlemagne's Tencedur.

We have many accounts of the knight arming himself for battle, a process which is always quite logical and begins with the putting on of the *hauberc* and ends with the hero seizing his lance. The amount of detail varies. A good example is to be found in the *Chanson de Roland*; the arming of the Saracen champion Baligant before his battle with Charlemagne.[90]

> Li amiralz ne se voelt demurer
> Vest une bronie dunt li pan sunt saffrét,[91]
> Lacet sun elme, ki ad or est gemmét,
> Puis ceint s'espee al senestre costét;
> Par sun orgoill li ad un num truvét,
> Pur la Carlun dunt il oït parler
> [A fait s'espee Precieuse apeller (MS.T. p. 176)]

Ço ert s'enseigne en bataille campel;
Ses cevalers en ad fait escrïer.
Pent a sun col un soen grant escut let,
D'or est la bucle e de cristal listét.
La guige en est d'un bon palie roét.
Tient sun espiét, si l'apelet Maltét,
La hanste [ad] grosse cume [est] uns tinels;
De sul le fer fust uns mulez trussét.

(The emir does not wish to waste time. He puts on a byrnie whose flaps are yellow with varnish (?), laces on his helm which is decorated with precious stones set in gold and then he girds on his sword on his left side. In his pride he has found a name for it. Because of Charles's sword of which he heard tell he has had his sword called Précieuse. That was his war-cry in a pitched battle and he made his knights shout it. He hangs a great broad shield of his about his neck; the boss is of gold and it is bordered with crystal. The belt of it is made of a good silken cloth embroidered with circles. He grasps his lance and he calls it Maltet. The shaft of it was as thick as a club and the iron head of it alone would be as much as a mule could carry.)

The problem of the manner of composition of the French epics is not a simple one. All the poems we possess have naturally reached us in a written form and therefore bear to a greater or less degree the marks of written composition. One school of thought regards the epics as having always been written compositions, the work of individual, more or less educated and even learned poets.

There is however plenty of evidence for an earlier period of oral-formulaic composition and for oral transmission even down to a fairly late date and one overlapping with the period of written transmission.

For example we are told by a reviser that Graindor de Brie, author of the original version of *La bataille Loquifer*, a late twelfth-century addition to the *geste de Guillaume*, composed the poem and taught it to his son who unwisely allowed King William of Sicily to have a copy made in written form, presumably at the son's dictation, with the distressing result that the family lost its copyright.

Ceste cançons est faite grant pieça.
Por voir vous di .c. et .l. ans a
Grandors de Brie, qui les vers en trova,
Por sa bonté si tres bien le garda,
5   C'ains a nul home ne l'aprist n'ensigna.
Maint grant avoir en ot et conquesta
Entor Sesile ou li bers conviersa.
Quant il fu mors a son fil le douna.
Li rois Guillaumes tant celui losenga,
10   Que la cançon de devers lui saça,
Ens en .i. livre le mist et saiela.
Quant il le sot, grant dolor en mena:
Puis ne fu sains tant come il dura.[92]

(This song was made a long while ago. In truth I tell you it was a hundred and fifty years back in the past. Graindor de Brie who composed the poem because it was so good took such great care of it that he never instructed or taught anyone how to sing it. He obtained and won with it great wealth in Sicily where he used to go about. When he died he gave it to his son. King William flattered him so much that he got the song out of him and put it and sealed it up in a book. He (the son of Graindor de Brie) when he knew it grieved deeply over it. He never recovered his health as long as he lived.)

The passage is important as indicating oral transmission. Graindor kept his work to himself and *taught* it to no one (l. 5) and did well as a result of his caution (ll. 6–7). At his death he gave it to his son. *Douna* (l. 8) could imply a written copy but the reference to King William[93] extracting the tale from Graindor's son and *setting it in a book* (l. 11) seems to imply rather that until then the transmission was still oral. The regrets of Graindor's son (ll. 12–13) would therefore be due to the loss of the family's copyright, which could only be preserved so long as the epic was neither *taught* (l. 5) to another jongleur, nor *recorded in written form* (l. 11).

The poem *Les deus bordeors ribauz*, 'The two rascally jesters', is a piece of cross-talk between two jongleurs accusing one another of professional incompetence. The formula is 'I know this or that poem', not 'I have a copy of it' (ll. 305–10 and 320–22):[94]

> Ge sai bien chanter a devise
> Du roi Pepin de S. Denise;
> Des Loherans tote l'estoire
> Sai ge par sens et par memoire;
> De Charlemaine et de Roulant
> Et d'Olivier le conbatant.[95]

(I well know how to sing to your liking of king Pepin of St Denis. I know both in general and word for word all the tale of the men of Lorraine, and that of Charlemagne and Roland and the good fighter Oliver.)

> De totes les chançons de geste
> Que tu savroies aconter
> Sai ge par cuer dire et conter.[96]

(I know *by heart* how to recount and tell all the epic songs you could mention.)

The emphasis on the jongleur's need for a good memory (ll. 308 and 322) recurs in a similar piece *La Contregengle*, 'The dispute' (ll. 182–83):[97]

> 'Mes les œvres dont tu te prises
> N'as tu pas encor bien aprises.'

('But you have not yet learned properly the works you are so proud of.')

The same idea occurs also in the prologues of the *chansons de geste* themselves. Jehan Bodel in the *Chanson des Saisnes*, his revision of the account of Charlemagne's wars with the Saxons,[98] says (ll. 4–5):

> Jamais vilains jougleres de cesti ne se vant!
> Car il n'en saroit dire ne les vers ne le chant.

(Let no base jongleur ever boast about [knowing] this [song] for he would not know either the poem or its music.)

Raimbert de Paris in *La chevalerie Ogier*, ll. 11859–60 says:[99]

> Cil jogleor, saciés, n'en sevent guere;
> De la canchon ont corrunpu la geste.

(Those jongleurs to be sure know nothing about it. They have spoilt the story of the song.)

So too the anonymous author of *Aiol*,[100] ll. 13–16:

> N'est pas a droit joglere qui ne set ices dis,
> Ne doit devant haut home ne aler ne venir;
> Teus en quide savoir qui en set molt petit,
> Mais je vos en dirai qui de lonc l'ai apris.

(He is no proper jongleur who does not know this tale and he should not go and come in the presence of a nobleman. There are some who think they know it who know very little about it, but I, who learned it long ago, will tell you about it.)

The exordium of *Les enfances Guillaume*, 'William's youthful exploits', is a particularly useful example of this type of statement (ll. 1–3 and 16–22):[101]

> Chanson de geste plaroit vos a entandre?
> Teis ne fut faite des lo tans Alixandre;
> Fist lai un moines de Saint Denise an France, . . .
> Uns gentis moines ki a Saint Denise ier,
> Quant il oït de Guillaume parleir,
> Avis li fut k'i fut antroblieis,
> Si nos an ait les vers renoveleis,
> Qui ont el role plus de cent ans esteis.
> Je li ai tant et promis et donnei
> Qu'i m'ait les vers ansaigniés et moustreis.

(Would you like to hear an epic story? There was never one like it since Alexander's time. A monk of St Denis in France composed it . . . A noble monk who was at St Denis — when he heard tell of William it seemed to him that the story (or he) was half forgotten; so he has revised for us the poem which has been written down in the roll for more than a hundred years. I have promised and given him so much that he has taught and showed me the poem.)

Despite the fact that in the thirteenth century, with the production of the prose *Grandes croniques de France*, St Denis did become the chief centre of French historiography, we can probably discount as a specious authentication the alleged authorship of the monk at that abbey, who in any case should hardly have taken payment for his work even had he existed; but the passage shows clearly the importance of oral transmission and the role of learning by heart and a good memory in the jongleur's profession.

Lines 16–19 of *La destruction de Romme* repeat the point:[102]

> Cil ke la chanchon fist l'ad longement gardee,
> Ains il n'en volut prendre a voir nulle darree
> Ne mul ne palefroi, mantel ne chier fourree;
> Ne onke en halte court ne fu par lui chantee.

(He who composed the song for long kept it to himself. He would indeed never take any wealth for it, neither mule nor horse nor mantle nor rich fur, nor was it ever sung by him in a great court.)

Lastly as late as about 1366 we find Petrarch writing to Boccaccio (*Epist. rerum sen.*, v, 3):[103]

'Sunt homines non magni ingenii, *magnae vero memoriae*, magnaeque diligentiae, sed maioris audaciae, qui regum ac potentum aulas frequentant, de proprio nudi, vestiti autem carminibus alienis, dumque qui et [? read quod aut] ab hoc, aut ab illo exquisitius materno praesertim charactere dictum sit, ingenti expressione pronuntiant, gratiam sibi nobilium et pecunias quaerunt, et vestes, et munera.'

(There are men of no great originality but of great powers of memory and great application, but even greater impudence, who frequent the courts of kings and great men having no literary garments of their own but clothed with the songs of others: and while they perform with great expressiveness whatever has been most finely said by one or another in the mother tongue, they seek the good graces of noblemen and money and clothing and other gifts.)

The jongleur was then a wandering performer who made his way from court to castle, from market place to village green and from fairground to tavern, wherever a possibly generous crowd might collect and throw him a few mansois or parisis for his performance. His social status was usually low and he had to scrape a precarious existence hawking about his literary wares, conjuring tricks and acrobatic feats for the amusement of such as would pay.

Some of their repertory appears in the fabliau *Le roi d'Angleterre et le jongleur d'Ely*, ll. 5–14:[104]

> Delez le trosne, dessoubs le deis,
> As fortz chastels, es riches paleis,
> Truffeur se trovent et pautonier,
> Qar mestier est de lur mestier;
> Devaunt nostre sire en pleniere cour

Sunt meint jogleur e meint lechour;
Molt bien sevent de tricherie,
D'enchauntementz e genglerie,
E font parroistre par lur grymoire
Voir come mençonge, mençonge come voire.

(Beside the throne beneath the dais in strong castles and in rich palaces jesters and rascals are to be found, for there is need of their craft — many jongleurs and many scoundrels are in our lord's presence in full court. They know plenty about trickery, magic and sleight of hand and through their cunning they make truth appear a lie and a lie the truth.)

Their character was no better than their position. They tell us themselves that whatever rich cloak or fine jewel a generous or drunken patron might throw them for a whim was drunk and diced away as soon as they had it in their hands.

A telling picture of the jongleurs' character and way of life occurs in the second version of *Le Moniage Guillaume*, ll. 1248–78.[105] William, who has turned monk in his old age and is on his way to rescue his country from the Saracen giant Isoré, goes singing of his own past deeds through the woods when some robbers overhear him. One of them, taking him for a jongleur, suggests that he is not worth robbing.

'Mien entïent, que chou est uns joglers,
Qui vient de borc, de vile u de cité,
La ou il a en la place canté.
A jouglëor pöés poi conquester,
De lor usage ai jou vëu assés:
Quant ont trois saus, quatre u cinc assanblés,
En la taverne les keurent alöer
S'en font grant joie tant com puënt durer,
Tant come il durent ne feront lasqueté;
Et quant il a le boin vin savouré
Et les vïandes qui li sont a son gré,
S'i est bien tant que il ne puet finer.
Quant voit li ostes qu'il a tout aloué,
Dont l'aparole con ja l'oïr porrés:
"Frere," fait il, "querrés aillors ostel,
Que marcëant doivent ci osteler;
Dounés moi gage de chou que vous devés."
Et cil li laisse le cauche ou le soller,
Ou sa vïele, quant il n'en puet faire el,
Ou il li ofre sa foi a afier
Qu'il revenra, s'il li veut respiter.
Tous dis fait tant que on le lait aler:
Quant est a l'uis, il se prent a l'errer

Et si vait querre ou se puist recovrer,
A chevalier, a prestre u a abé.
Boine coustume, certes, ont li jogler:
Ausi bien cante quant il n'a que disner,
Con s'il eüst quarante mars trovés;
Tous tans font joie tant com il ont santé;
Por amor Dieu, laissiés l'outre passer.'

('I know well that that's a jongleur coming from some village or town or city where he's been singing in the public square. You can't get much out of a jongleur; I've seen plenty of the way they live. When they've scraped together three shillings or four or five they run and spend them in the tavern. They have a great time so long as they [those shillings] may last. As long as they last they won't slack up. And when he's tasted the good wine and the food that's to his liking he'll remain there as long as he doesn't come to the end of it. Then when the host sees he's spent everything he speaks to him as you shall hear: "Brother," says he, "go and look for somewhere else to live. There are merchants coming who are to stay here. Give me a pledge for what you owe." And he leaves him his breeches or his shoes or his fiddle when he can't get out of it; or else he offers to swear he'll come back if he'll only give him time. In any case he does get him to let him go; and when he's out of the door he sets off and goes to see where he can get something from some knight or priest or abbot. Indeed the jongleur has a good habit: he sings as readily when he's no dinner coming as if he'd found forty marks. They're always cheerful, as long as they're well. For God's sake let him go on his way.')

The fabliau *De Saint Piere et du jougleur*,[106] in which St Peter wins all the souls in hell at dice from a jongleur whom the devil had unwisely made his door-keeper, gives another clear picture of their way of life:

Il ot un jougleor a Sens
Qui mout ert de povre riviere,
N'avoit pas sovent robe entiere.
Ne sai comment on l'apela,
Mais sovent as dez se pela;
Sovent estoit sans sa viele,
Et sanz chauces et sanz cotele,
Si que au vent et a la bise
Estoit sovent en sa chemise.
Ne cuidiez pas que je vos mente,
N'avoit pas sovent chaucemente; . . .
Et quant a la foiz avenoit
Que il uns sollerés avoit
Pertuisiez et deforetez,
Mout i ert grande la clartez,
Et mout ert povres ses ators.
En la taverne ert ses retors,

Et de la taverne au bordel;
A ces .ii. portoit le cembel.
Mes ne sai plus que vos en die
Taverne amoit et puterie,
Les dez et la taverne amoit,
Tout son gaaing i despendoit,
Toz jors voloit estre en la boule,
En la taverne ou en la houle.
.I. vert chapelet en sa teste,
Toz jors vousist que il fust feste;
Mout desirroit le diemenche,
Onques n'ama noise ne tence,
En fole vie se maintint.
Or orrez ja con li avint.
En fols peschiez mist son usage;
Quant ot vescu tout son eage,
Morir l'estut et trespasser.
Deables, qui ne puet cesser
Des genz engingnier et sousprendre,
S'en vint au cors por l'ame prendre;
.I. mois ot fors d'enfer esté,
Ainz n'avoit ame conquesté.
Quant vit le jougleor morir,
Si en corut l'ame sesir;
Por ce que morut en pechié,
Ne li a on pas chalengié.

(In Sens there was a jongleur whose condition was very poverty-stricken — often he hadn't even a whole garment to wear. I don't know his name but often he used to skin himself at dice. Often he was without his fiddle and without his breeches or coat so that he was often left standing in his shirt in the cold north wind. Don't think I'm lying to you — often he had no shoes to wear . . . And when sometimes he happened to have a pair of shoes full of holes and cut to pieces, you could see plenty of daylight through them — his clothing was very poor. His usual home was in the tavern and he moved between the tavern and the brothel. To these two places he brought along the row he made (lit. his uproar). But I can't tell you any more about him. He loved the pub and naughty girls, dice and the wineshop and that's what he spent all his earnings on. He wanted to be always in the bowling alley the pub or the knocking shop. With a green garland on his head he would have liked it always to be a holiday. He used to long very much for Sunday to come. He never liked rows or quarrels. He lived a wanton life. Now you shall hear what happened to him. He lived in sin and wanton folly and when he had come to the end of his days he had to die.

A devil who can't stop deceiving people and catching them out came to his body to take his soul. He'd been a whole month out of hell and hadn't caught a soul. When he saw the jongleur dying he came running up to seize his soul and because he died in sin no one challenged the devil's right to him.)

When we bear in mind the high cost of books in the Middle Ages, when a text-book could be regarded as adequate *cautio* or pledge for a loan which might maintain a student for some weeks, it is clear that most jongleurs, being social near-outcasts, would rarely be in a position to own one; and that if they ever did it would probably soon follow their other earnings 'tout aux tavernes et aux filles'.

The evidence in favour of oral transmission of a memorized text is therefore very strong, but there is none in the surviving documents to prove that jongleurs engaged in impromptu oral-formulaic composition after the manner of the Yugoslav *guslari*.

There is nevertheless every probability that they did, at any rate in the pre-literary period. The mere fact that the poems are written in a formulaic style would appear to point to a period of impromptu composition extending back into the past before the twelfth century. The great variability in the texts which have reached us also points to some degree of impromptu variation even after the poems were generally memorized for performance.

An additional piece of evidence is the existence of different versions of some of the *chansons de geste* which can reasonably be presumed to stem from differing oral traditions. We have two different *Moniage Guillaume* (William turned monk) poems, two versions of *La prise d'Orange*, and *La chanson de Guillaume*, *La chevalerie Vivien* and its two alternative continuations, *Aliscans* and *Foucon de Candie* all tell the same story of the battle of Larchamp or Aliscans.

The problem is complicated by the form in which these poems have reached us. The Oxford manuscript of the *Chanson de Roland* is a small parchment codex written in the region of 1150. It is at present bound with a copy of Chalcidius's Latin version of the *Timaeus*. It was already so bound in the Middle Ages as someone in the thirteenth century copied the word Chalcidius on to the blank part of the last folio of *Roland*.[107] The manuscript may well have belonged to a monastic library. Oseney has been suggested. The *Chanson de Roland* is after all a poem with a very important religious element. Otherwise most of these poems have survived in large cyclic manuscripts of the thirteenth and fourteenth centuries, though individual copies also occur.

It is difficult to discern the part of oral composition in these circumstances. It seems clear enough that the late twelfth and thirteenth century revisions of older poems by such professional *menestrels* as Adenet le Roy and Bertrand de Bar sur Aube were written compositions, though their authors still write in the traditional formulaic style, which indeed maintains itself largely unchanged, particularly in the accounts of battles and single combats, as late as such epic-type poems of the fourteenth century as *Theseus de Cologne* (see note 36, above) and the Peacock cycle of the *Romand' Alexandre*, *Les Voeux du Paon* and its continuations.[108]

It is also possible that in the decadence of the epic and of their art jongleurs may sometimes have performed from a written text belonging to a patron, or the poem may even have been divorced from its musical accompaniment entirely and read aloud by the family clerk or chaplain like a romance.

The form of the *chansons de geste* is quite characteristic and entirely different from that of the romance in octosyllabic rhyming couplets. The poem consists of an indefinite number of tirades called *laisses*, of length varying from five or six lines to over a hundred.

Very long *laisses* usually indicate a late date. The average in *Roland* is fourteen lines, and one of the strongest reasons for regarding the second part (Rainouart) of *La Chanson de Guillaume* as a later addition to an originally primitive poem is that in it seven long *laisses* in ε account for 743 lines out of 1574, nearly half the poem, whereas in the first part there are only three long laisses in ε totalling 187 lines out of 1980, less than one tenth of the whole.

The metre is either in true rhyme, with identity of the final tonic vowel and all phonemes following it throughout the *laisse*, or in assonance, with identity of final tonic vowel only.

Laisses have either masculine or feminine rhyme or assonance. A masculine rhyme or assonance ends on a tonic vowel or following consonant, a feminine one has an atonic ə following the tonic vowel, with or without intervening and following consonants. Masculine and feminine rhymes or assonances may not be mixed in the same *laisse*.

The term *laisse* was technical and is attested from the thirteenth century. For example in *Des deus bordeors ribauz* we have (ll. 88–89):[109]

> De Pertenoble le Galois
> Sai ge plus de .xl. laisses;

(I know more than forty laisses of Pertenoble le Galois.)

and in the *Berne Chansonnier*:[110]

> Com jugleire as cortois frans
> Per dousor requiert et prie
> Quant ait sa laixe fenie,
> Aïe a paisseir lou tens.

(As a jongleur asks and begs of courteous gentlemen for kindness sake when he has finished his *laisse* for help to keep alive.)

And Joinville in the *Vie de Saint Louis*[111] tells of the king's custom: 'Quant li menestrier aus riches homes venoient leans et il aportoient lour vielles aprés mangier, il atendoit a oïr ses graces tant que li menestriers eust fait sa lesse.'

(When the minstrels of powerful nobles came there and brought their fiddles with them after a meal he used to put off hearing grace till the minstrel had sung his *laisse*.)

Three different metres are found. The octosyllable, with a not entirely stable caesura after the fourth syllable, occurs only in the six-hundred-line fragment of the early poem *Gormont et Isembart*[112] and in the hundred and five lines surviving from the early twelfth century *Roman d'Alexandre* of Albéric.[113] Though attested in early saints' lives from the tenth century its use in epic is too rare for one to be able to say whether it is completely aberrant or actually the earliest verse form used, later expanded, as some scholars have suggested, to the decasyllable and the alexandrine.

The commonest epic metre is the decasyllable, with a regular caesura after the fourth syllable. This is the metre of the *Chanson de Roland* and of most of the earlier surviving epics. A six/four cut occurs occasionally but is uncommon.

The earliest surviving use of the alexandrine, with a six/six cut, is in *Le voyage de Charlemagne*, composed probably in the region of 1150, though some have dated it early in the twelfth century.[114] The alexandrine takes its name from its use in the Old French *Roman d'Alexandre* and its continuations, though these date from about 1160 at the earliest. The name is found in late medieval treatises on versification: 'Cy s'ensuivent les tailles de lignes alexandrines, et sont dittes lignes alexandrines pour ce que une ligne des fais du roy Alexandre fu faite de ceste taille, *Doctrine de la seconde retorique*.'[115]

(Here follows the form (?) of Alexandrine lines; and they are called Alexandrine lines because a line telling the deeds of king Alexander was made in this form.)

The alexandrine tends to be the more popular metre in the late period, when hybrid poems of great length and partially non-epic content like *Lion de Bourges* and *Theseus de Cologne* (see notes 35 and 36, above), were written in that form; but the decasyllable remains in use to the end of the epic period.

Both the decasyllable and the alexandrine, besides the additional ə of the feminine ending may also have an additional ə at the caesura, which is then known as epic caesura. An alexandrine with epic caesura and feminine ending has therefore fourteen syllables. Some epics, mostly of the *geste de Guillaume*, end the *laisse* with a short line of four or six syllables on a different rhyme or assonance, which is known as the *vers orphelin*.

The manner of composition of the Old French epic is formulaic and the formulaic unit is the hemistich of four or six syllables. What appear to be whole line formulas exist, but their hemistichs can also be found in other combinations.

There are both fixed and invariable formulas and variable ones. The existence of a large variety of different possible rhymes and assonances causes a high degree of variability in the formulas of the second hemistich, while that of the first hemistich tends more often towards fixity of form.

A good example is the formula already mentioned, *pleine sa hanste*, by a full lance length (he laid him on the ground behind his horse). Three passages taken at random from *La Chanson de Guillaume*[116] show its use in laisses in -i,-ɛ-ə and -a respectively.

> Pleine sa hanste del cheval l'abati . . .[117]

(By a full lance length he hurled him from his horse.)

> Pleine sa hanste l'abat mort a tere.[118]

(By a full lance length he lays him dead on the ground.)

> L'escu li freinst, e le halberc li estroad
> Pleine sa hanste l'abat mort del cheval.[119]

(He shattered his shield and pierced his hauberc; by a full lance length he hurls him dead from his horse.)

It is in fact likely that the composer worked less with invariable memorized units than with variable syntactic patterns, which could express essentially the same idea with the final word variable to suit the rhyme or assonance. The first and third examples above show how a change of word order can help to achieve this effect.[120] They also show how differences of time can be introduced by changes of tense. In the same way formulas can be varied to express changes of person and number while the basic meaning of the phrase remains the same.

It is important to realize that the formula is a linguistic unit as the word is a unit, and that a great poet can achieve the highest level of poetic production with formulas no less than with individual words. Recent study by Professor Duggan has shown that the formulas in seven of what are generally accepted as the finest episodes in the *Chanson de Roland* average 43 per cent of the whole in each scene and that 37 per cent of them occur also in the poem outside the scenes in question.[121]

It is extremely doubtful if the consequence he drew from this, that *Roland* was orally composed, necessary follows, as undoubted literary compositions, like Branch II of the *Roman d'Alexandre*, and even some as late as *Les Voeux du Paon*, still show the same formulaic composition. What is however, abundantly clear is that a great poet can compose a great poem with formulas no less than when he enjoys the greater freedom of using words individually.[122] Naturally, a mediocre poet can achieve a high degree of tedium by the same means.

The presence of repetitive patterns in the Old French epic leaps to the eye. Earlier scholars talked of 'clichés' and 'des phrases toutes faites' with a certain contempt. Since the publication of the work of Milman Parry and A. B. Lord on the Homeric and South Slavonic epic the real character of Old French epic style has been recognized. Jean Rychner[123] was the first to apply their methods to its study and considerable interest is now being shown in the question of formulaic composition though very much still remains to be done in this field.[124]

The presentation of the *chanson de geste* cannot be separated from its style and the two aspects must be considered together. Its name implies that it was a song to be sung and not a piece to be recited or read aloud. As we have seen, the performer was that itinerant entertainer the jongleur. In Old French he is usually called *jogler*, from *iocularem*, or *joglëor*, *ioculatorem*; the modern nasalized form has possibly been influenced by the verb *jangler*, to chatter or babble.

He accompanied his performance on a *vielle*, a viol or fiddle, a stringed instrument, an ancestor of the violin played with a bow. *Vielle* now means a hurdy-gurdy but the numerous medieval pictures of jongleurs at work regularly show them with a fiddle of some kind.[125]

Very little indeed is known of the music of the *chanson de geste*. All that survives is the rather solemn tune of a single line of a very coarse parody of an epic called *Audigier*, preserved in the light opera of Adam de la Hale, *Le jeu de Robin et Marion*.[126] It seems surprising that the excitement of battle and single combat could be rendered effectively to so solemn and lugubrious a tune:

It may not be typical but we also have the remark of Jean de Grouchy: 'idem cantus debet in omnibus versibus reiterari.'[127] This may well mean that the music remained unchanged line after line. This supposition seems to be supported by the verse passages in *Aucassin et Nicolette*, which, though composed in heptasyllables, have formal affinities with the epic in that they are arranged in assonanced monorhyme *laisses* of variable length and have a *vers orphelin* of four syllables at the end of the *laisse*. The music, which is preserved in the unique manuscript, consists of a pair of phrases set to the first two lines of the *laisse* and evidently intended to be repeated throughout, and a final short phrase for the *vers orphelin*. There are minor variations according as the lines have masculine or feminine ending.[128] There would therefore appear to have been no reluctance on the part of the audience to accept the monotony of musical repetition, any more than in the case of plainsong, with which our one line of *Audigier* shows some affinity.

At first sight a French epic appears to be told in an entirely inconsequential mixture of narrative tenses, past historic, imperfect, present perfect and present indicative, with a great preponderance of the last. Recent study by Dr M. Blanc[129] has reduced this apparent chaos to some degree of order and has at the same time established some interesting facts about the manner of presentation of the *chansons de geste*.

The method of performance was in fact semi-dramatic, the jongleur placing himself in time with his subject and treating it as if the events recounted are

H

actually taking place before his eyes and he is relating them to an audience much in the manner of a modern radio sports-commentator. This accounts for the very heavy preponderance of a present tense of vivid narration and present description, accompanied by parentheses in the present perfect. This last is a true compound perfect, not, as in Modern French, a colloquial substitute for the past historic. It is often used to catch up with events which have as it were outrun the speed of narration; just as the sports commentator will describe a series of movements in a game in the present tense and give their result in the present perfect: 'A passes to B, B to C who shoots — he has scored.'

The past historic, again contrary to modern usage but in keeping with that of the classical theatre of the seventeenth century, is the regular past tense for narrative in direct speech. The imperfect tense for the most part fulfils its modern functions but is often, apparently rather arbitrarily but possibly for metrical reasons, replaced by the past historic.

Narration is normally in the third person but the narrator not infrequently intervenes to comment on events, to anticipate future action, or to express a personal opinion. We have a typical example in *Le couronnement de Louis* (ll. 2081–84):[130]

> La li afient tel quinze chevalier
> Mielz lor venist qu'il l'ëussent laissié,
> Car puis en furent honi et vergoignié.
> Deus! qu'or nel set li cuens o le vis fier![131]

(There some fifteen knights pledge him their faith. It would have been better for them had they left the matter alone for afterwards they were shamed and disgraced because of it. Ah what a shame that the count of the fierce look does not know it now!)

The *chansons de geste* were rarely of such brevity as to be able to be performed in a single session. A passage in *Huon de Bordeaux* shows that for performance the epic was divided into instalments and that the jongleur expected to be paid for each:[132]

> Segnor preudomme, certes, bien le veés,
> Pres est de vespre, et je sui moult lassé.
> Or vous proi tous, si cier com vous m'avés
> Ni Auberon, ne Huon le membré,
> Vous revenés demain aprés disner;
> Et s'alons boire, car je l'ai desiré.
> Je ne puis, certes, mon coraige celer
> Que jou ne die çou que j'ai empensé:
> Moult sui joians quant je voi avesprer,
> Car je desire que je m'en puise aler.
> Si revenés demain aprés disner,
> Et si vous proi cascuns m'ait aporté
> U pan de sa chemise une maille noué,

Car en ces poitevines a poi de largeté;
Avers fu et escars qui les fit estorer,
Ne qui ains les donna a cortois menestrel.

(My lords you can surely see that it is nearly evening and that I am very tired. Now I beg you all, as you love me and Auberon and Huon the strong, to come back tomorrow after dinner; and so let's go and have a drink now for I've been wanting one. Indeed I can't hide my feelings and not say what I have in my mind. I am very glad when I see evening coming on for I want to be able to get away. So come back tomorrow after dinner and I ask each of you to bring along with you a halfpenny knotted in his shirt tail for these pennies of Poitou are worthless enough. He was a mean devil and a miser who first had them struck and so was he who ever gave them to a gentle minstrel.)

A typical example of the vivid, semi-dramatic epic style is the first account of fighting in the *Chanson de Roland*. It is also typical of the care and appreciation of detail with which the single combat is described in the French epic. It is the beginning of the battle and Roland, Charles's nephew, as commander of the Frankish rearguard, confronts his opposite number Aëlroth, nephew of the Saracen King Marsile in command of the Moorish vanguard:[133]

Li nies Marsilie, il ad a num Aelroth,
Tut premereins chevalchet devant l'ost.
1190 De noz Franceis vait disant si mals moz:
'Feluns Franceis, hoi justerez as noz;
Traït vos ad ki a guarder vos out;
Fols est li reis ki vos laissat as porz.
Enquoi perdrat France dulce sun los,
1195 Charles li magnes le destre braz del cors!'
Quant l'ot Rollant, Deus! si grant doel en out,
Sun cheval brochet, laiset curre a esforz,
Vait le ferir li quens quanque il pout.
L'escut li freint e l'obserc li desclot,
1200 Trenchet le piz, si li briset les os,
Tute l'eschine li desevret del dos,
Od sun espiét l'anme li getet fors;
Enpeint le ben, fait li brandir le cors,
Pleine sa hanste del cheval l'abat mort,
1205 En dous meitiez li ad brisét le col;
Ne leserat, ço dit, que n'i parolt:
'Ultre culvert, Carles n'est mie fol,
Ne traïsun unkes amer ne volt,
Il fist que proz qu'il nus laisad as porz,
1210 Oi n'en perdrat France dulce sun los.
Ferez i Francs, nostre est li premers colps!
Nos avum dreit, mais cist glutun unt tort.'   AOI.

(Marsile's nephew's name is Aëlroth. He rides out in front before the army. As he goes he says such wicked things of our Franks: 'Scoundrelly Franks, today you will [have to] fight our men. The man who should have protected you has betrayed you. The King is a fool to leave you here in the pass. This day sweet France will lose her good name and Charles the Great his [strong] right arm.'

When Roland hears it — God how angry he was — he spurs his horse and lets it gallop at full speed. The count goes and strikes him as hard as he can. He breaks through his shield and rips open his *hauberc*; cuts through his breast shattering the bones, and tears away his whole spine from his back. With his lance he thrusts out of him his [life and] soul. He drives it well home, makes his body swing back [in the saddle] and lays him dead a full lance-length behind his horse. He has broken his neck in two and, as he says, he will not fail to answer him. 'You scoundrel, Charles is no fool, nor was he ever one to love treason. He did well to leave us here in the pass. Today sweet France shall not lose her good name for it. Strike hard, Franks, the first blow is ours! Right is on our side but these rascals are in the wrong.')

By translating literally the present tense of vivid narration and keeping the short sentences, which rarely exceed the end-stopped lines of the original, a feature which is generally characteristic of French epic style, something of its flavour has been retained at some stylistic cost.

The passage is completely typical of the description of a single combat in a *chanson de geste*. We note the appreciative care with which the path of Roland's lance point is followed, and the resulting unhorsing and death of Aëlroth described. There are some forty such single combats described in the *Chanson de Roland* in completely formulaic language, yet with no exact repetition, and with freshness and originality in every case.

That is typical of the method of representing warfare in the French epic. The battle is broken up into a series of such descriptions of single combat. These are then punctuated by an occasional general glimpse of the battlefield. This usually begins with the formula: *La veïssiez*, There you might have seen. A typical example is in *Roland*:[134]

> La bataille est e merveillose e grant;
> Franceis i ferent des espiez brunisant.
> La veïssez si grant dulor de gent,
> Tant hume mort e nasfrét e sanglent!
> L'un gist sur l'altre e envers e adenz,
> Li sarrazin nel poënt susfrir tant,
> Voelent u nun, si guerpissent le camp;
> Par vive force les enca[l]cerent Franc.   AOI.

(The battle is terrible and great. There the Franks strike hard with their glittering lances. There you might have seen men in such great pain, so many dead and wounded and covered with blood. They lie heaped one on another face upwards and face down. The Saracens can stand it no longer; whether they like it or not they abandon the field. The Franks pursued them as hard as they could.)

Significant also are the instances of heroic abuse between the combatants, exemplified in Aëlroth's speech above and Roland's triumphant answer. Another theme frequently occurring is the lament for the dead hero. Roland's lament over Oliver as he collects the bodies of the Twelve Peers to receive the dying Turpin's blessing is a good example of these, usually brief and dignified expressions of manly grief:[135]

> Ço dit Rollant: 'Bels cumpainz Oliver,
> Vos fustes filz al duc Reiner,
> Ki tint la marche del Val de Runers.
> Pur hanste freindre e pur escuz peceier,
> Pur orgoillos veintre e esmaier,
> E pur prozdomes tenir e cunseiller,
> E pur glutun veintre e esmaier,
> En nule tere n'ad meillor chevaler.'

(Roland said: 'Oliver, fair friend, you were the son of Duke Renier who held the march of Val de Runers. For breaking a lance or shattering a shield, to vanquish and bring down the proud and to uphold and counsel worthy men and to vanquish and bring down scoundrels there is no better knight in any land.')

With its Virgilian echo[136] this is deeply moving in its noble simplicity. The lament of Charles over Roland is much longer, extending over five *laisses* and forty-three lines of speech, and totals, with descriptive matter, fifty-nine lines, from l. 2885 to l. 2942.

Another important element is the death scene of the hero. I propose to translate the death of Roland, the finest example of the kind, so will say no more here.

The *Roland* poet has a favourite method of emphasizing the significance of the episodes which he considers important. This is by means of *laisses similaires*, paired or repeated *laisses*, of which the second or second and third repeat the argument of the first, but on different assonances and consequently varying their formulas.

Usually the action does not stand still completely. Oliver asks Roland three times to call for help and three times Roland refuses.[137] Roland in his turn proposes twice to sound the horn and twice Oliver, using with intentional irony Roland's own words, refuses to approve his action.[138] Roland tries three times to break Durendal.[139] Sometimes it is not the action but the psychological viewpoint that changes, as in the three stages in the account of the death of Roland.[140]

Laisses similaires are not very widely used outside *Roland* and they may have been a favourite stylistic device of its author which others felt that they could not safely imitate without the risk of monotony.

A much commoner device in all epics is the *reprise*, the picking up of the subject of narration of a *laisse* in the first few lines of the next *laisse*, which then carries the account further.

It does not appear possible to define exactly the general social function of Old French epic, apart from the general function of literature to please, amuse, interest and excite.

We have two pieces of evidence for *chansons de geste* being sung in battle or composed by warriors. Guy of Amiens,[141] Henry of Huntingdon,[142] and Geffrei Gaimar,[143] mention the jongleur Taillefer who rode before William's army and struck the first blow at Hastings. It is not however until Wace wrote the *Roman de Rou*, a century after the event, that Taillefer is credited with singing the *Chanson de Roland* before asking for the honour of striking the first blow:[144]

> Taillefer, qui mult bien chantout,
> Sur un cheval qui tost alout,
> Devant le duc alout chantant
> De Karlemaigne et de Rollant,
> E d'Oliver e des vassals
> Qui morurent en Rencevals.

(Taillefer, who was an excellent singer, rode on a swift horse before the Duke singing of Charlemagne and Roland and Oliver and the knights who died at Roncevaux.)

William of Malmesbury had already mentioned the singing of the *Chanson de Roland* before the battle three or four decades earlier, but he makes no mention of Taillefer:[145] 'Tunc cantilena Rollandi inchoata, ut martium viri exemplum pugnaturos accenderet, inclamatoque Dei auxilio, proelium consertum.' (Then the Song of Roland was begun, so that the warlike example of a hero might arouse those who were about to fight, and then, after calling upon God for aid they joined battle.) Wace may well have combined what he found in William with the account of Taillefer in the other authors.

He could only have sung a brief passage of our existing poem or the battle would have had to be postponed until next day. The passages of Wace and William of Malmesbury are useless for dating the epic but do at least show that the idea of singing a part of an epic before battle to rouse the troops was felt to be acceptable in the third quarter of the twelfth century.

The idea that the tale of epic deeds will have a good effect on the audience occurs also in the thirteenth-century romance *Floriant et Florete*:[146]

> D'autre part sont cil conteour;
> La est des chevaliers la flour,
> Quar volentiers les escoutoient,
> Que les anciens faiz contoient
> Des preudomes qui jadis furent,

Qui se maintinrent si com durent,
Des grant batailles que il firent,
Et comment lor terre conquirent.
Tout ce li conteour contoient,
Et il volentiers les öoient,
Et se miroient es biaus dis,
S'en devenoient mieux apris;
Quar qui romanz velt escouter
Et es biaus diz se velt mirer,
Merveille est s'il ne s'en amende.

(And there too are the story-tellers. The flower of chivalry is present for they liked to hear them telling of ancient deeds of brave men who did their duty in the past and of the great battles they fought and how they won their lands. The story-tellers told all this and they were glad to hear them and to see themselves in their fine stories. And so they (the knights) became the better instructed as a result of it, for if anyone is ready to listen to a tale and to see himself in fine stories it is surprising if he is not the better for it.)

The second passage is the mention, as original author of the poem, of Bertolai de Laon, one of the knights taking part in *Raoul de Cambrai*:[147]

Bertolais dist que chançon en fera,
Jamais jougleres tele ne chantera.
Mout par fu preus et saiges Bertolais,
Et de Loon fu il nez et estrais,
Et de paraige del miex et del belais.
De la bataille vi tot le gregnor fais:
Chançon en fist, n'or[r]eis milor jamais,
Puis a esté oïe en maint palais,
Del sor Guerri et de dame Aalais
Et de Raoul, siens fu liges Cambrais,
Ces parins fu l'evesques de Biauvais.
Berniers l'ocist, par le cors saint Girvais,
Il et Ernaus cui fu liges Doais.

(Bertolai says that he will make a song about it. No jongleur will ever sing one like it. Bertolai was very brave and very wise, and he was born and bred in Laon and he was of the best and fairest descent. He saw all the greatest burden of the battle; he made a song about it, you will never hear one better. Since then it has been heard in many a palace. It was about Guerri the Fair and lady Aalais and about Raoul; Cambrai was his fief and his godfather was the bishop of Beauvais. Bernier killed him, by the body of St Gervais, he and Ernald whose fief was Douai.)

This passage has given rise to much controversy. Bédier denying Bertolai's existence as he would be inconvenient for his theory of composition by jongleur-poets working on material provided by the monks of sanctuaries mentioned in the poems.

Again what seems important is that, whatever degree of truth there may be in the tradition, the idea of such a warrior poet composing the first version of the *Chanson de Raoul de Cambrai* was evidently acceptable to the audience of the existing poem of the late twelfth century.

The chief social function of the *Chanson de Roland* is clearly to encourage the young knight to imitate that great pre-crusader Charlemagne his predecessor, and go out and fight the infidel. Whether crusade in Spain or in the East was intended is not certain. If the latter the idea of crusade could hardly have entered the Roland tradition before the preaching of the first crusade in 1095.

We have seen how the author of *Roland* was interested also in the suppression of feudal anarchy and the extension of the rule of law.

This last concern would hardly be of serious interest to those for whom the poems of the feudal cycle were composed. The frequency of the theme of the hero in revolt against royal injustice in this cycle makes it clear that its patrons had little interest in a strong monarchy or the rule of law.

Raoul de Cambrai,[148] *Girart de Roussillon*[149] and possibly the poems of the *geste de Nanteuil*[150] may be family epics, composed originally for descendants, or supposed descendants, of the heroes portrayed. The poems of the *geste de Guillaume* seem partly to form a family epic cycle associated with Guillaume de Toulouse, and partly to be imbued with the crusading anti-pagan spirit of the poems of the *geste du roi*. Inevitably there is a good deal that must be conjectural in any discussion of the social purpose of these poems of seven or eight centuries ago, and it is unwise to insist too strongly on any theory.

Some of the later revisions of epics were certainly written for the amusement of great patrons. Besides the ne'er-do-well wandering jongleur there existed also his wealthier and more respectable colleague of fixed residence and permanent employment, the *menestrel*.[151] This word, from *ministerialis*, is basically a servant of any kind but it comes to mean particularly the private entertainer or musician attached to the household of a monarch or great lord. In due course the word loses caste and, becoming synonymous with *jogler*, means any kind of entertainer, jester or musician, but several of the named authors of revised *chansons de geste* were *menestrels*.

Among them were *Adenet le Roi*[152] who wrote for Henri III, Duke of Brabant, for his two sons, Jean and Godefroy and later for Gui de Dampierre. He was responsible for the surviving versions of three *chansons de geste*; *Ogier le Danois*, *Berte au grant pié* and *Bovon de Comarchis*.[153] So too Girart d'Amiens wrote *Charlemagne*, a continuation of *Berte au grant pié* for Charles de Valois.[154]

There is not a great deal more to be said about the audience of the French epic than has emerged already. It might be performed in kings' courts or before the dregs of society in a low tavern. Traditionally the jongleur addresses his audience as *Seigneur*, My lords, but this is a piece of meaningless politeness and no indication of the character of the audience for whom the performance was intended. In the late period some authors adopted an extended style of address embracing all classes of society instead of the traditional 'Seigneur', but it was to all classes that they always addressed their song. An instance is to be found in the exordium of *Lion de Bourges*.[155]

> Seignour or faite paix, chevaillier et baron,
> Bourgois et clerc et prestre, gens de religion,
> Et je vous chanterai(t) une bonne chanson;
> Telle ne fut chantee pues le tempz Salmon.
> Oui avés chanter dou riche duc Lion
> Qui fut sire de Burge la noble region,
> Maix cil qui vous en chante[nt] n'an scevent .j. boton.

(Now be silent all, my lords, knights and barons, burghers, clerks and priests and you cloistered folk also and I will sing you a good song. None like it has been sung since Solomon's time. You have heard sing of the mighty Duke Lion who was lord of Bourges that noble province, but those who sing of him don't know a thing about it.)

Certainly the jongleur's great days were the festivities of the rich and powerful, when the tradition of largesse caused prodigal distributions of money, plate, rich furs, and the like to entertainers of every kind. We have pictures of such feasts. Two examples come from *Les enfances Godefroi*,[156] an epic of the Crusade Cycle:

> Aprés mengier viëlent li noble joglëor,
> Romans et aventures content li contëor,
> Sonent sauters et gigles, harpent cil harpëor;
> Moult valt a l'escoter qui en ot la dolchor.
> De si a l'avesprer demainent grant baudor,
> Et li quens fist doner chascun lonc son labor,
> Mantiaus, muls, palefrois, tant qu'il en a honor.

(After the meal the noble jongleurs play on their viols; the story-tellers tell romances and stories of adventure; psalteries and fiddles sound, the harpers play. It is very good to listen to for anyone who hears the sweetness of it. They are very joyful until evening was coming on and the Count had each rewarded according to his labour; [he gives them] mantles, mules, and palfreys until he is honoured by them.)

And again:[157]

> Grant joie ot en la sale environ de tos lés.
> Cil joglëor i ont lor estrumens sonés,
> Salterions e gigles, dont il i ot asés.
> Witasses li vassax les a moult bien loés;
> Il lor done mantiax et bliaus engolés,
> Pelichons vairs et gris et hermins gironés.
> Onques nus ne s'em plainst, quant il se fu tornés;
> De quanqu'il despendi est moult bien aquités.

(There was great joy throughout the hall on every side. The jongleurs have sounded their instruments there — psalteries and fiddles of which there were plenty. The knight Witasse praised them greatly. He gives them mantles and vests with collars and fur cloaks of miniver and gryse and ermine cut in triangles. Not one of them ever complained when he had left there; each of them was well paid for all that he spent.)

In the *Chanson de Guillaume* we have a more ordinary scene of everyday social life when Guiborc arranges for the entertainment of the knights she has summoned as reinforcements for her husband William:[158]

> Tuz lez demeines en ad Guiburc sevrez,
> Suz al paleis les assist al digner,
> Chançuns e fables lur fait dire e chanter;
> Guiburc meïmes les sert de vin aporter.

(Guiborc chose out all the chief lords and seated them at dinner up in the palace. She has songs sung and tales told to them. She herself serves them bringing them wine.)

I propose to end this account with four specimen passages chosen from some of the most interesting and the oldest surviving *chansons de geste*. To give adequate summaries of the action of such poems as *La Chanson de Roland*, *La Chanson de Guillaume* and *Le Voyage de Charlemagne* would lengthen this study beyond reasonable limits and be open to the objection that whatever is included much that is good has to be omitted. That applies also to this briefer selection but it is hoped that these passages will be generally accepted as both typical and outstanding.

My first passage comes from that primitive and rather uneven masterpiece the *Chanson de Guillaume*. It is, despite some disagreement[159] generally regarded as one of the oldest poems of the *Geste de Guillaume d'Orange*, and it is certainly one of the most primitive of the old French epics, with a spirit and ethos which are by turns noble, brutal, coarse, occasionally ridiculous, and even, as the passage I have tried to render shows, tender. It appears to have been influenced by a version of the *Chanson de Roland* resembling that of the Oxford manuscript.

I have selected it to show the character of William's wife, the converted Saracen princess Guiborc, and William himself in a downcast mood, together with something of the boisterous humour which also has its place in the *chanson de geste*. The only manuscript is a latish Anglo-Norman one and the text has suffered considerably from scribes who no longer understood the subtleties of the semi-dramatic presentation of the oral-formulaic style and have frequently changed tenses and lengthened and shortened lines arbitrarily. I have therefore used a past simple narrative tense pretty consistently instead of following all the tense vagaries of the text.

William has lost his army in the second stage of the battle of Larchamp with the African invader Deramed. Guiborc, who has been collecting reinforcements for him, sees him ride down the hillside towards his castle alone, a dead man flung over his saddle-bow. Her knights try to persuade her that the body is not that of her beloved nephew Vivien, but she pushes them aside and goes to meet her lord at the castle gate:[160]

'My noble lords, for the love of God I would beg you let me go. He is my lord: I must go and serve him.' She went down the steps and came to the gate and unbarred it for him. She opened it above[161] and let the Count in. He looked at her and began to question her.

'Lady Guiborc, since when did you keep my gate?' 'By my faith, Sir, it is but recently I have been doing so. Your force, my lord, Count William, is very small.'

'Sweet love, since when have you been my porter?' 'By my faith, Sir, but a short time, not for long. It is but few knights you are bringing home, Sir William.'

'Lady Guiborc, here is Guichart your nephew. You will never see Count Vivien again.' The noble lady stretched out her arms to him and he placed the dead knight in them. The body was heavy and her arms gave way under the weight. She was a woman and her flesh was weak. The corpse fell to the ground its tongue lolling out to one side, on that Thursday evening.[162]

Guiborc looked at him as he lay on the ground. His face was livid and his cheeks pale. His eyes were turned up in his head and his tongue lolled out to the left: his helm slipped down to his chin. Guiborc wept and William comforted her.

'By God, Guiborc, you have good cause for tears for they used to say in my lord's court that you were the wife of a powerful man, a bold count, a brave fighter. Now you are the wife of a worthless runaway, a cowardly count and a base fellow ready to turn tail, one who brings not a single man home from battle with him. From today you will be your own cook and your own baker; you will not belong to the proud nobility. Never will you see my nephew Vivien again. Whoever cares about it my joy is at an end, I shall never again have on earth a man's[163] honour.' William wept and Guiborc with him. The lady heard her lord's lament and forgot a part of her own sorrow. When she spoke she said very lovingly:

'Marquis William, for the love of God forgive me! It is a great grief that a man should have to weep and a great pity that he should have to lament. It was the custom of your great and noble family when they went conquering other lands, that they all met death on the field of battle. I would sooner have you die in Larchamp by the sea than that your line should be disgraced by you, and your heirs reproached after your death.' When William heard it be began to shake his head and wept tenderly and gently. He addressed Guiborc his dearly loved wife and spoke to her in the French tongue and explained to her: 'Sweet love, forgive me for the love of God. Whoever else may care about it I have good cause to weep. Three hundred and fifty years have passed since my mother bore me. I am old and feeble and cannot bear arms. God's gift he lent me has failed me — that youthful strength which cannot return, and so pagans have come to hold me in contempt; they will not flee nor turn tail for fear of me. Deramed has won the battle, taken the spoil and disarmed the dead. The pagans have embarked on their ships. The lands where I hold sway are far off and the men I should summon are strong. If I had come to Larchamp by the sea the Saracens would have turned in flight. Whoever else cares about it I am left all alone. I shall never again have on earth a man's honour.' William wept and Guiborc comforted him. 'Sir, my lord, forgive me for the love of God. Now let me tell lies by your leave.[164] I shall already have thirty thousand of them. Fifteen thousand are all ready to fight a pitched battle.' 'Where are they, Guiborc? You must not hide it from me. My dear love, tell me the truth about them!' 'Up in the palace sitting at their dinner.' Then the count laughed and ceased weeping. 'Now go and lie as much as you like, Guiborc, with my good will.' Then she went up the stairs; before she wept but then she began to sing; they looked at her and questioned her: 'Lady Guiborc, what did you find out there?'

'By God, my lords, much that was to my liking. William Hooknose has come back quite safe and sound through God's mercy; and he has won the pitched battle in the field and killed Deramed the pagan.

But in one way things have gone badly for him; he has lost his noble knights, the flower and beauty of sweet France. They have killed the famous Vivien, in pagan or in Christian lands no better knight could be born to exalt holy Christianity or to uphold and protect the Faith.

For God's sake I beg you go to Larchamp; the boats and all the ships are shattered, the wind is long in coming and they cannot get away. Upon a rock beside a creek of the sea ten thousand of the Saracens have disembarked. They have brought the gold and silver with them and taken the spoil and disarmed the dead. My lord was alone and could not remain there any longer.

Whoever [of you] would now go to Larchamp by the sea to capture those men of whom I have told you, my lord has very broad lands in his heritage and he will readily and willingly give you some of them.

And if there is any [of you] who does not wish to take lands without a wife, I still have here one hundred and sixty maidens who work my cloth of gold and silk with flower and wheel patterns. They are kings' daughters — there are none more lovely under heaven, and I have brought them up under William's protection. Let him come to me and choose the most beautiful. I will give him a wife and my lord will give him land if he fights[165] well there so as to be worthy of praise.'

There were some who were in haste to choose the most beautiful on that Thursday evening who afterwards lost their heads in Larchamp.

Guiborc herself served her lord with water. Then she seated him at a low table; for very sorrow he could not go to the highest.

Then she brought him a haunch of a wild boar. The knight took it and ate it upon the spit. He did so as it was very tender. She brought him a great loaf of fine bolted flour and on top of it two great baked cakes;[166] and she brought him also a great roast peacock. Then she brought him a great mazer full of wine — it was all she could do to hold it in her two arms.

William ate the loaf of fine bolted flour and after that the two baked cakes; he ate the whole of the great haunch of boar and drank a gallon of wine in two draughts, and ate up the whole of the two baked cakes and did not offer Guiborc a crumb of them, and all the while he did not raise his head.[167]

Guiborc saw him, shook her head and laughed until she wept with both her eyes. She addressed William in French and spoke to him: 'By the God of Glory who caused me to be converted and to whom I shall render the soul of this wretched sinner that I am, when the time comes at the great day of judgment, a man who eats a great loaf of fine bolted flour and for that does not leave the two baked cakes, and eats up the whole of a great haunch of a boar and on top of that a great roast peacock, and then drinks up a gallon of wine in two gulps, is surely one to fight a very hard war against his neighbour. He is not one to flee most vilely from the field nor is his kin in danger of being held base.'

My second piece comes again from the *Geste de Guillaume* and shows the hero in a much more ebullient mood than the last one. It is part of the lively and powerful introduction to the *Charroi de Nîmes*, a short poem in which William captures Nîmes from the Saracens by a Trojan horse device, introducing his men into the city hidden in barrels, while he himself, with his nephew Bertrand, acts the part of a merchant. In William's absence Louis has been distributing fiefs to his followers, and, with his habitual ingratitude, has failed to reward the Count for his many years of faithful service. William storms into the palace and gives his lord the most terrific tongue-lashing, reminding him of his past services and taxing him with the basest ingratitude. Louis is quickly reduced to making ignominious and cringing apologies, and, in the passage I am translating, goes on to make a series of base offers to William of fiefs that he has no right to give. William refuses them with contempt and finally settles for a fief in the Saracen occupied districts of Southern France, which he will have to win for himself. The situation is one that, in the case of a less gentlemanly character than William, could easily have led to an epic of revolt.[168]

The passage is marked by what I am convinced is an intentionally ironic use of inappropriate formulas, Louis being described as 'the noble', 'the brave' and 'the fierce' just at those points in the action where he least deserves those laudatory epithets:

'Sir William', said the fighter Louis,[169] 'by that apostle men seek in Nero's field,[170] I have yet sixty of your peers to whom I have neither promised nor given anything'. William replied, 'Sir King, there you lie. There are no peers of mine in all Christendom saving yourself who are a crowned king. I do not wish to boast myself above you. Now take those men you have named and bring them into that field there one by one mounted and armed and fully equipped for battle. If I have not killed so many and more for you, and yourself too if you wish to go there, I will never touch a foot of your heritage.' The King hears him and has bowed before him. On raising himself he has addressed him about it.

'Sir William', said the noble Louis, 'now I can see well you are a man full of anger.' 'Yes indeed', said William, 'and so were my kinsmen before me. That's how it goes with a man who serves worthless people. However much he does he gains nothing by it, but rather he becomes worse off all the time.'

'Sir William', said the brave Louis, 'now I see well you are a very angry man.' 'Yes indeed', said William, 'and so were my ancestors. That's how it goes with a man who serves a worthless lord; however much he raises him up he gains little by it himself.'

'Sir William', Louis answers him, 'you have protected and served me affectionately more than any man in my court. Come forward, I will give you a fine gift: take the land of the brave Count Fouques and three thousand knights will serve you.' 'That I will not' William answered him, 'two of the noble Count's sons are alive who will well be able to keep safe the land. Give me another fief, for I have no wish for this one.'

'Sir William', said King Louis, 'since you do not wish to hold this land and take it from the boys, take that of Aubrey the Burgundian and his stepmother Hermesant of Tori, the best woman who ever drank wine; three thousand mailed knights will serve you'. 'That I will not', said William in reply, 'there is a son of the noble Count still living, Robert is his name, but he is very little, as yet he is too young to put on his shoes or his clothes, but if God grants that he grow big and strong he will be well able to hold the whole fief'.

'Sir William', said Louis the fierce, 'since you are unwilling to disinherit that child, take the land of Berengier the Marquis then. The Count is dead, so do you take his wife; two thousand knights will serve you with glittering arms and swift horses; and they will not take a penny's worth from you.'

William hears him and goes nearly mad with anger: he began to shout in a loud voice. 'Listen to me you noble knights, hear how the man who willingly serves my just lord Louis is rewarded by him. Now I will tell you about Marquis Berengier: he was born in the Valley of Riviers; he killed a Count for whom he could not pay the blood money; he fled to the palace of Laon and there fell at the Emperor's feet and the Emperor received him gladly and gave him land and a courteous lady to wife. He served him willingly for a long time. Then it happened that the King fought a battle against the Saracens, Turks and Slavonians. It was a terrible full-scale pitched battle: the King was struck down from his horse and would never again have been able to mount, when Marquis Berengier chanced to come up. He saw his lord hard pressed in the thick of the fight and so rode up to him at full speed. In his hand he held his sword of polished steel. There he cut a ring round him as a boar does when surrounded by hounds, and then he dismounted from his swift horse to help and assist his lord. The King mounted it and he held the stirrup for him, and so the King fled like a cowardly hound. So Marquis Berengier was left there; and there we saw him killed and cut to pieces and we could not help or assist him. A noble heir survives him; he is called the little Berengier. So help me God that man who, like a scoundrelly renegade, would cheat the boy is a great fool. The Emperor wishes to give me his fief: I will not have it and I wish you all to hear it. And I must let you all know one thing, by that apostle that men seek in Rome, there is no knight in France so bold but, if he takes little Berengier's land, he will quickly lose his head to this sword of mine.' 'We thank you, sir', say the knights who belong to little Berengier. There are a hundred of them who bow to him and all go on bended knee before him.

We have seen in our extracts from *La Chanson de Guillaume* and *Le Charroi de Nîmes* that neither boisterous humour nor irony are alien to the spirit of the

French epic. My third passage is from a poem which contains a relatively small serious element and has often been classed as a parody. This was probably not the composer's whole intention, as the account of the Palestine pilgrimage of Charlemagne and his twelve peers, and of his collection of important relics for the royal monastery of St Denis is quite serious. Much of *Le Voyage de Charlemagne* is however frankly comic in a rather rough and tumble manner and serves well to illustrate the lighter side of the *chanson de geste*.

The poem was preserved in a single Anglo-Norman[171] manuscript of the thirteenth century formerly in the British Museum and now mislaid. It has been variously dated between 1060 and 1175. Probably some date between 1130 and 1160 would be plausible. It is especially interesting in form as it appears to be the oldest surviving epic in alexandrines, the metre which became increasingly popular, probably through the success of the Alexander cycle, during the thirteenth century and came to be used almost exclusively for the latest poems in epic form.

I begin with the first scene which launches the action of the poem. Charlemagne strutting about in his royal attire and boasting of his greatness is sharply cut down to size by his queen. Unfortunately his wounded vanity is too much for his sense of humour:

One day Charlemagne was in the church of St Denis: he had taken up his crown and made the sign of the cross upon his head, and girded on his sword whose pummel was of pure gold. There were dukes and lords, barons and knights there.

The Emperor Charles looked towards his wife; she was wearing a most beautiful and handsome crown. He took her by the hand and led her beneath an olive tree; in a loud voice he began to address her: 'Lady, did you ever see any man under heaven whose sword and the crown on his head so well became him? I will yet conquer cities with my lance.'

She was not tactful and she made him an unwise answer: 'Emperor,' said she, 'you may be setting your own worth too high. I do yet know of one who shows more elegantly when he wears his crown among his knights: and when he puts it on his head it suits him better.'

When Charlemagne hears it he is very angry at it; because the French heard it he is very much distressed and downcast about it. 'Now lady, where is that king? Now tell me who he is. So we will both wear our crowns on our heads together, and your friends and all your advisers shall be there, and I will send for the good knights of my court! If the French tell me that it is so then I will admit it; but if you have lied to me you will pay dearly for it, I will cut off your head with my sword of steel!'

'Emperor,' said she, 'do not be angry about it. He is richer in wealth and gold and minted coin but he is not so brave nor such a good knight as you when it is a matter of striking hard blows in battle or pursuing an enemy!'

When the Queen saw that Charles was so angry she was very sorry and wished to fall at his feet: 'Emperor,' said she, 'have pity on me for the love of God. I am your wife. I was only meaning it in play. I will clear myself if you order me to by swearing an oath or undergoing an ordeal: I will leap down from the highest tower of the city of Paris to prove to you that it was neither spoken nor imagined by me to your dishonour!'

'That you shall not,' said King Charles, 'but do you just name that king for me.'

'Emperor,' said she, 'I can not think of him now . . .'

'By my head,' said Charles, 'you will tell me his name at once or I will have that head of yours cut off.'

Now the Queen understands that she cannot get out of it; she would gladly have left the matter there but that she did not dare to change what she had said (?). 'Emperor,' said she, 'do not think me a fool; I have heard much talk of King Hugh the Strong. He is Emperor of Greece and of Constantinople, and holds all Persia as far as Cappadocia. There is no more handsome knight between here and Antioch, nor were there ever such knights as his except for yours.'

'By my head,' said Charles, 'I will yet know the truth about it! If you have lied you are surely a dead woman.'

'By my faith,' the King said to her, 'you have greatly angered me, by this you have entirely lost my affection and my good will. I still think you will lose your head from your shoulders for it. You ought not to have thought so of my might. I will never rest until I have seen him.'[172]

The pilgrimage to Jerusalem, where the patriarch showers relics on the pilgrims, is duly carried out and Charles and the peers make their way to Constantinople, the secular goal of their journey. They find the Emperor Hugh engaged in the far from royal occupation of ploughing, though with a plough and harness of pure gold. He welcomes them, impresses them with his great wealth and his wonderful revolving palace, and finally leaves Charles surrounded by his peers in thirteen separate and magnificent beds for the night.

He does not however wholly trust these strangers and sets a concealed observer to report on their conversation. Before they turn in for the night Charles encourages his peers to play the game of 'gabs' or extravagant and fantastic boasts.

When they had eaten in the royal palace and the chief officers had removed the tablecloths the squires jump up on every side in order and go off to their lodgings to rub down the horses.

King Hugh the Strong called to Charlemagne and led him aside and the twelve peers with him. He held the King by the hand and led them into a room painted with designs of flowers and decorated with precious stones of crystal. A carbuncle shines[173] and glows bright there, set in a pillar of King Goliath's day.

There are there twelve soft beds of copper and metal with velvet pillows and sheets of silken stuff: it would take twenty oxen and four carts to carry the smallest of them. The thirteenth in the middle is carved with great art. Its feet are of silver and its frame of enamel-work. Its coverlet was good, the work of Maseüs — a very noble fairy who gave it to the King — its workmanship is worth more than the Emir's[174] treasure. The King should indeed love him who gave it up to him and served him so well and provided for him nobly.

The French were in the room and saw the beds. Each of the twelve peers at once took his own. King Hugh the Strong had wine brought to them.

He was wise and strong and full of cunning: and so he had set a man in the vaulted room under a marble daïs which was hollowed out underneath. All night long he looks at them through a little hole and the carbuncle glows so that one can see as well as in May, in summer when the sun shines.

King Hugh the Strong came away and went back to his wife. Charles and the French go to bed in their own time. Now the counts and marquises will make their boasts and brags. The French were in the room and drank plenty of the wines.

And one said to the other, 'Just look how very beautiful it is! Just look at the noble palace and all this great wealth! If only it had pleased the glorious God of holy majesty that Charlemagne my lord had got all this or won it by force of arms on the field of battle!'

And Charlmagne said to them, 'I should indeed make the first boast. King Hugh the Strong has no young knight so strongly built in all his household; and let him have put on two *haubercs* and two well-shaped helms, and let him be mounted on a swift and well rested war horse ...'[175] And then let the king lend me his sword decorated with the gold pummel; and I will strike at the helms at their thickest point.[176] I will hack through the *haubercs* and the gem-studded helms and right through the lance-rest and saddle of the well-rested horse. I will drive the sword into the earth and if I let it go it will not be recovered by any living man until it is dug out from the ground at the depth of a full lance length!'

'By God,' said the spy, 'you are vigorous and strongly built! King Hugh was a fool when he gave you lodging. If I hear you speak any more such foolishness tonight I will have you sent away at early dawn tomorrow morning.'

And the Emperor said: 'Make your boast Roland, my dear nephew.'[177]

'Gladly, my lord,' said he, 'just as you say. Now tell King Hugh to lend me his ivory horn[178] and then I will go out there into that plain: my blast will be so strong and the wind of it so loud that in all the city, which is so broad and large, there will not be a gate or postern left standing, nor any object of copper or steel, however large or heavy it may be, which will not knock against another through that roaring wind.

'King Hugh will be very strong if he steps forward for he will lose his beard and have his whiskers burnt off. And he will have his great marten fur wrap twisted round his neck and his ermine cloak turned inside out on his back!'

'By God,' said the spy, 'this is a bad sort of brag. King Hugh acted like a fool when he put up such people for the night.'

'Make your boast, Sir Oliver,' said the courteous Roland.

'Gladly,' said the Count, 'provided Charles allows it. Let the King take his daughter whose hair is so golden and put us secretly in a bed in her room: if I have not her bear witness to my prowess a hundred times tonight I am quite ready to agree to lose my head tomorrow.'

'By God,' said the spy, 'you will give up long before! What you have said is most shameful; if only the King knew of it he would not love you again all his life long.'

'And you Sir Archbishop, will you make your boast with us?'

'Yes, by Charles's orders,' said Turpin. 'Let the king tomorrow take three of the best war horses which are in his city and make them gallop together out there in that plain. When they are going at full gallop I will come running so quickly from the right that I will sit on the third from me and not touch the other two. And I will hold

I

four very large apples in my hand, and I will go throwing them in the air and throwing them up and I will let the horses gallop at full speed — if one apple slips from me or a second falls from my hand let Charlemagne my lord put out the eyes from my head.'

'By God,' said the spy, 'this is a fine boast and a good one. There is nothing shameful in it directed against my lord the King.'[179]

The other peers make their boasts in due order and next morning the spy reports to King Hugh all that he has heard the Franks say in the night. The King is very naturally furious at the insulting nature of the 'gabs', and threatens his guests with death if they do not fulfil exactly to the letter those wine-engendered boastings.

However, through the virtues of the relics brought from Jerusalem, and the piety of Charles and his peers, the 'gabs' are duly performed with divine assistance. Even Oliver, who could hardly expect the deity's approval, manages to persuade the young lady to corroborate his story.

Deeply impressed by Frankish prowess the Emperor Hugh admits Charles the better man and becomes his vassal. The Emperor returns to Paris with his peers and his relics, and, having by this time forgotten his resentment and had the satisfaction of being proved right, graciously pardons his lady.

My last excerpt is from the *Chanson de Roland*. It is one of the emotional climaxes of the poem, Roland's attempt to destroy his sword Durendal that it may not fall into enemy hands and the final scene showing Roland making his peace with God by an act of contrition in accordance with the teaching of the Church, and his martyr's death.

Roland is perhaps the only literary product of the medieval French genius which is undoubtedly of the first rank, an epic able to bear comparison with any wherever produced.

A round dozen of different Turolduses have been suggested as its author, if that is what the last line of the poem:

Ci falt la geste que Turoldus declinet.[180]

really means (and it could refer to a scribe or a jongleur who had added the poem to his repertory), but none of the proposed identifications really convinces.

Whoever he was the author of *La Chanson de Roland* was a poet of the first order. Using already existing material, possibly in the form of a poem telling of the defeat of Roncevaux in a form close to Einhard's historical account of the disaster, and using also the oral-formulaic style of the jongleur, with all its repetitions and consequent danger of boredom, he succeeds in making a poem which is never boring. Even the forty or so single-combats, so accurately and appreciatively described, though their course and outcome is always very much the same, are never really repetitive. By frequent changes of assonance and consequent variations of formula he succeeds in the difficult task of saying virtually the same thing differently forty times over.

It is this subtle use of the traditional oral-formulaic style which is one of the chief marks of the poet's quality. One may say that *Roland* is a traditional oral-formulaic poem which has passed through the creative faculty of a poet of genius.

He was certainly a churchman and a man of some learning, as the Virgilian echoes in the *Roland* demonstrate, though I suspect a secular who had some personal experience of the warfare he so ably describes, rather than a monk, a man perhaps not unlike his own fighting archbishop, who felt that a poor fighter had no place on a battlefield and had better go and be a monk.[181]

He was evidently deeply concerned about the policies of the Church of the late eleventh century. We have already seen his interest in the problem of power in the state and the need to put an end to the curse of feudal anarchy and private war through the action of a strengthened central monarchy. This was the policy which the Church was at the same time pursuing through the movements of the Peace and Truce of God.

But in many ways the *Roland* is also a plea in favour of the idea of the expansion of Christianity, which was preached by Urban II at Clermont in 1095. The poet shows Charlemagne as the great pre-crusader, fighting on all fronts to extend the sway of Christianity and never ceasing from that task. The angelic summons to Charles to go to the rescue of King Vivien besieged by pagans, in the last lines of the poem,[182] is significant; the good crusader's work is never done. There are always more unbelievers to fight and to convert.

But the *Roland* poet had also a more uncommon vision in that he saw the state as an entity and an abstract idea in an age of warring individualists precariously held together by the feudal bond. At a time when loyalties were personal to one's lord he could think of 'dulce France' and 'France l'asolue', sweet France and holy France, and make his characters speak convincingly of these abstractions, though Roland himself is also the embodiment of loyalty to the feudal lord. These are ideas towards which the later Middle Ages, born of the Hundred Years War, were groping. Charles V, Bertrand du Guesclin and certainly Jeanne d'Arc would have understood. They are unlikely greatly to have affected the poet's contemporaries.

The passage we are to examine is interesting not only as an emotional climax of the poem but also as an example of the way in which the poet makes use of the epic device of *laisses similaires*, repeated *laisses* saying the same thing on a different assonance and so with different formulas.

In the three attempts of Roland to shatter his sword there is much more than mere repetition; there is a definite moral progression in Roland's attitude to Durendal in the course of the three *laisses*. In the first he is thinking of himself, *his* fame and *his* glory — no other man is fit to have *his* sword. In the second *laisse* he is still thinking of himself but rather as the true vassal who has won so many lands for Charles, his lord, with his sword — the attitude is no longer self-centred. And in the third *laisse* Roland no longer thinks of himself. Durendal is a holy sword full of relics which must not fall into pagan hands but must be kept safe by Christians. The progression is from self to others and from worldly to spiritual.

So too in the death scene itself a similar progression can, I think, be traced from the worldly action of placing himself beyond the rest and facing the enemy, to the humble confession of sin and the required act of contrition at the end.

Roland is in some ways a coarse and brutal product of a coarse and brutal age, but a poet who could use the consecrated formulas of the French epic with such delicacy and subtlety was neither brutal nor coarse.

Roland realizes that he has lost the sight of his eyes; he struggles to his feet and puts out all his strength — the colour is drained from his face. A dark grey rock stands before him; he strikes ten blows at it in sorrow and bitterness. The steel grates on the stone but does not break or become notched. 'Saint Mary help me!' said the Count, 'Ah Durendal! It was a bad day when you were forged! Since I am losing my life I can take no more care of you. With you I have won so many fights in the field and conquered so many broad lands which Charles now holds, Charles whose beard is white. May no man have you who would flee for fear of another. A very good knight has long owned you — there will never be his like in holy France.'

Roland struck at the rock of sardonyx: the steel grates on it but does not shatter or notch. When he saw that he could not break it he began to lament to himself. 'Ah, Durendal, how bright and shining you are! You glitter and flash so in the sun! Charles was in the valleys of Maurienne when God sent him word by his angel that he should give you to a count and captain. Then the noble King, Charles the Great, girt me with it. With it I won for him Anjou and Brittany, and with it I won for him Poitou and Maine. With it I won for him Normandy the free, and with it I won for him Provence and Aquitaine and Lombardy too and all Romagna; with it I won for him Bavaria and all Flanders and Burgundy and all Apulia, Constantinople too whose homage he received and in Saxony he does as he wishes. With it I won for him Scotland and Ireland and England which he held to supply his privy-purse; with it I won for him so many provinces and lands that Charles holds, Charles whose beard is white. For this sword I feel sorrow and grief: I would sooner die than that it remain in pagan hands. God and Father, do not let France be brought to shame through it.'

Roland struck at a dark grey rock and hacked off more of it than I can tell you. The sword grates on the stone but neither shatters nor breaks, and it sprang up again towards heaven. When the count sees that he will not break it he mourns over it very gently to himself: 'Ah, Durendal, how lovely you are and most holy. In the golden pommel are many relics, Saint Peter's tooth and some of Saint Basil's blood, and some hairs of my lord Saint Denis, and there is a piece of Saint Mary's garment in it too. It is not right that pagans should hold you in their power; you should be held in honour by Christians; may no man have you who would do a cowardly act! With you I shall have won very broad lands: Charles holds them whose beard is long and white; and with them the Emperor is both noble and powerful.'

Roland feels that death is overcoming him and working down from his head to his heart. He has made his way swiftly to beneath a pinetree and has lain down upon his face on the green grass. He places his sword and the horn beneath him and turns his head towards the pagan people. He has done this because he truly wishes that Charles may say and all his people too: that the noble Count died as a conqueror. He admits his guilt many times and often: in satisfaction for his sins he held out his glove to God.

Roland feels that his life is over; he is lying on a steep hill facing Spain; with one hand he has beaten his breast in contrition: 'God, I confess my guilt to your holy power — the guilt of my sins both great and small which I have committed from the hour when I was born to this day when I am struck down here.' He has held out his right-hand glove to God. Angels from heaven come down to him there.

Count Roland lay beneath a pine tree; he has turned his face towards Spain. He began to call many things to mind, so many lands he won as a knight, sweet France and the men of his line, and Charles the Great, his lord, who brought him up: he cannot help weeping and sighing. But he does not wish to forget his own spiritual needs; he admits his guilt for sin and prays God for mercy.

'True Father who never lied; you raised up Saint Lazarus from the dead and protected Daniel from the lions, protect my soul from all dangers because of the sins which I committed in my life!' He offered his right-hand glove to God, Saint Gabriel has taken it from his hand. He has gone to meet his end with head bowed upon his arm and hands joined in prayer. God sent his angel Cherubin, and with him Saint Michael of Peril by Sea, and Saint Gabriel also came to him with them; they carry away the Count's soul to Paradise.

Roland is dead: God has his soul in heaven.[183]

NOTES

1. *La Chanson de Guillaume*, edited by D. McMillan (Paris, 1949–50), i, ll. 1258–61. J.Wathelet-Willem, *Recherches sur la Chanson de Guillaume* (Paris, 1975), p. 857, in her critical text reads:
   Ainz, ad Guillelmes, mis sire, un jugleür:
   En tote France, n'ad si bon chanteür,
   N'en la bataille plus hardi fereür:
   E de la geste li set dire chançuns . . .

2. Adam le Bossu, *Le jeu de Robin et Marion*, edited by E. Langlois (Paris, 1924), ll. 743–44.

3. *Charte de l'Eglise de Beauvais*, 1367, D. Gren. 311 No. 106, Richel., quoted from F. Godefroy, *Dictionnaire de l'ancienne langue française* (Paris, 1885), IV, 268.

4. *Roman de Thebes*, edited by L. Constans (Paris, 1890), II, 106. MSS A and P, ll. 17–19.

5. *Chanson de Roland*, 3742. All quotations from this work are from *La Chanson de Roland*, edited by F. Whitehead (Oxford, 1942).

6. Wace, *Le Roman de Brut*, edited by I. Arnold (Paris, 1938–40), l. 14859.

7. *Les Narbonnais*, edited by H. Suchier (Paris, 1898), l. 926.

8. *Le Roman de Girart de Viane, par Bertrand de Bar sur Aube*, edited by P. Tarbé (Reims, 1850), pp. 1–2, ll. 11–12, 14–15, 44–45.

9. *Die Chanson Garin de Monglene*, edited by E. Schuppe (Greifswald, 1914), ll. 2 and 9–10.

10. *Chanson de Roland*, l. 788.

11. *Aye d'Avignon, chanson de geste anonyme*, edited by S. J. Borg (Geneva, 1967), l. 757.

12. *Jourdain de Blaye*, edited by P. F. Dembowski (Chicago and London, 1969), l. 1525.
13. *Jean Bodel: Saxenlied*, edited by F. Menzel and E. Stengel (Marburg, 1906–09), ll. 6263–64.
14. *Le covenant Vivien*, edited by M. W. J. A. Jonckbloet, in *Guillaume d'Orange* (The Hague, 1854), I, 163–213, l. 1582.
15. *La prise d'Orange*, edited by C. Régnier (Paris, 1967), ll. 1189–90.
16. *Döon de Maience*, edited by M. A. Pey (Paris, 1859), ll. 8066–67.
17. *La Chanson de Guillaume*, ed. cit. (note 1), l. 220. L. Wathelet-Willem, ed. cit. (note 1), p. 753, reads 'de cele p.g.' 'of that foul people . . .'.
18. Ibid., l. 3158.
19. *Blancandin et l'Orgueilleuse d'Amour*, edited by F. P. Sweetser (Geneva, 1964), l. 2019.
20. Above, note 13, ll. 6–7.
21. *Girart de Roussillon, chanson de geste*, edited by W. M. Hackett, 3 vols (Paris, 1953–55).
22. *Daurel et Beton, chanson de geste provençale*, edited by P. Meyer (Paris, 1880).
23. W. M. Hackett, *La langue de Girart de Roussillon* (Geneva, 1970)
24. I. Bekker, *Der Roman von Fierabras, provenzalisch*, Abhdl. preuss. Akad. hist. phil. Kl., Vol. x (Berlin, 1826), 129–278.
25. M. Roques, 'Ronsasvals', *Romania*, 58 (1932), 1–28 and 161–89; 66 (1935), 433–80.
26. *Roland à Saragosse, poème épique méridional du XIVᵉ siècle*, edited by M. Roques (Paris. 1956).
27. *L'Entrée d'Espagne, chanson de geste franco-italienne*, edited by A. Thomas (Paris, 1913).
28. *Das Rolandslied des Pfaffen Konrad*, edited by C. Wesle, 2nd edn (Tübingen, 1967). For the genesis of the poem between 1186 and 1189 at the court of Brunswick see H.-E. Keller, 'Changes in Old French Epic Poetry and Changes in the Taste of its Audience', in *The Epic in Medieval Society. Aesthetic and Moral Values*, edited by H. Scholler (Tübingen, 1977), p. 170 and the extensive note 58 (pp. 174–77).
29. *Wolfram von Eschenbach, Willehalm und Titurel . . .*, edited by W. Schröder and G. Hollandt (Darmstadt, 1971).
30. *Ulrich von Türheim, Rennewart . . .*, edited by A. Hübner, 2nd edn (Berlin, 1964).
31. *Karlamagnussaga*, edited by K. Unger (Christiania (Oslo), 1860). French versions by P. Aebischer, *Textes norrois et littérature française du Moyen Âge*, I (Geneva–Lille, 1954); II (Geneva, 1972). P. Aebischer, *Rolandiana Borealia: la Saga af Runzivals bardaga et ses dérivés scandinaves comparés à la Chanson de Roland* (Lausanne, 1954). P. Aebischer, *Etudes sur Otinel, de la chanson de geste à la Saga norroise . . .* (Berne, n.d., c. 1960).
32. Author of *Aimeri de Narbonne*, edited by L. Demaison (Paris, 1887), and *Girart de Vienne*, edited by F. G. Yeandle (New York, 1930).
33. Author of *La bataille Loquifer*, edited by M. Barnett, Medium Aevum Monographs, New Series, VI (Oxford, 1975).
34. Author of *Berte aus grans piés*, edited by U. T. Holmes (Chapel Hill, 1946), and *Buevon de Conmarchis*, edited by A. Henry, *Œuvres d'Adenet le Roi*, II (Bruges, 1953).
35. Unpublished. Bibliography in Bossuat (below, Bibliographical note), p. 383, nos. 4046–54.
36. Unpublished. Study by R. Bossuat, 'Theséus de Cologne', *Moyen Age*, 65 (1959), 97–133, 293–320, 539–77. Study and partial edition by E. Rosenthal, 'Theseus de Cologne' (dissertation, University of London, 1975, typescript).
37. On the late versions see G. Doutrepont, *Les mises en prose des épopées et des romans chevaleresques du XIVᵉ au XVIᵉ siècle* (Brussels, 1939).
38. Edited by E. C. Armstrong and others in the series Elliott Monographs, Nos. 23, 27 and 34–42 (Princeton, 1928–75).
39. The institution of the Twelve Peers was influential beyond the limits of the *chanson de geste* proper. The authors of the *Roman d'Alexandre* show Aristotle organizing the Macedonian's great captains, Ptolemy, Clitus, Perdiccas and the rest, in a similar group of 'douze pers de Grèce'. *The Medieval French Roman d'Alexandre*, II, edited by E. C. Armstrong and others, Princeton, Elliott Monographs 37, 1937, Branch I, ll. 669–95.
40. *La chanson d'Aspremont*, edited by L. M. Brandin, 2nd edn revised, 2 vols, c.f.m.â. (Paris, 1923–24).
41. Saracens and Slavonians.
42. *La Chanson d'Antioche . . .*, edited by P. Paris, 2 vols (Paris, 1848).
43. *Le Couronnement de Louis, chanson de geste du XIIᵉ siècle*, edited by E. Langlois, 3rd edn (Paris 1938).

44. *Le Charroi de Nîmes, chanson de geste du XIIe siècle*, edited by J. L. Perrier (Paris, c.f.m.â., 1931). New edition by D. McMillan, *Le Charroi de Nîmes. Chanson de geste du XIIe siècle* (Paris, 1978).

45. Above, note 1.

46. *La Chevalerie Vivien, chanson de geste*, edited by A. L. Terracher (Paris, 1909).

47. *Aliscans*, edited by E. Wienbeck, W. Hartnacker and P. Rasch (Halle, 1903).

48. *Folque de Candie nach den festländischen Handschriften zum ersten Male herausgegeben* von O. Schulz-Gora (Dresden and Halle, 1909–36).

49. Above, note 21.

50. *Renaut de Montauban*, edited by H. Michelant, Bibl. d. Lit. Vereins, 67 (Stuttgart, 1862), and *Les Quatre fils Aymon, chanson de geste*, edited by F. Castets (Montpellier, 1909).

51. Above, notes 8 and 32.

52. *Raoul de Cambrai, chanson de geste du XIIe siècle*, edited by P. Meyer and A. Longnon (Paris, 1882).

53. *Hervis de Mes. Vorgedicht der Lothringergeste, nach allen HSS zum erstenmal vollständig herausgegeben*, edited by E. Stengel (Dresden, 1903).

54. *Chanson de Roland*, ll. 1010–12.

55. Ibid., l. 1015.

56. Ibid., l. 899.

57. Ibid., ll. 3705–33.

58. The account of the trial of Ganelon here translated and abbreviated runs in Whitehead's edition from l. 3734 to 3974.

59. ll. 3750–79.

60. ll. 322–26.

61. ll. 3807–14.

62. ll. 3824–37.

63. See E. Köhler, *'Conseil des barons' und 'Jugement des barons'* (Heidelberg, 1968).

64. *Huon de Bordeaux*, edited by P. Ruelle (Paris and Brussels, 1960).

65. *Chanson de Roland*, ll. 1671–1701.

66. Ibid., l. 539.

67. Ibid., ll. 1321–34.

68. An exception is *Roland*, ll. 2443–75, where God repeats the miracle of Joshua; x. 12–14, staying the course of the sun that Charles's vengeance on the Saracens of Marsile may be complete.

69. Ibid., ll. 3564–620.

70. *Gormont et Isembart*, edited by A. Bayot (Paris, 1921), l. 146.

71. *Chanson de Roland*, l. 1443.

72. Ibid., l. 3262.

73. *Girart de Viane*, ed. cit. (note 8, above), pp. 45–46.

74. *Historia Caroli Magni et Rotholandi*, edited by C. M. Jones (Paris, 1936). H. M. Smyser, *The Pseudo-Turpin edited from Bibl. Nat. Fonds Latin ms. 17656 . . .* (Cambridge (Mass.), 1937). See also R. N. Walpole, *The Old French Johannes Translation of the Pseudo-Turpin*, 2 vols (Univ. California Press, 1976).

75. See I. Short, 'A study in Carolingian Legend and its Persistence in Latin Historiography (XII–XVI Centuries)', *Mittellateinisches Jahrbuch*, 7 (1970), 127–52.

76. J. Bédier, *Les Légendes Epiques*, 4 vols (Paris, 1908–13).

77. F. Lot, *Etudes sur les légendes épiques françaises* (reprint) (Paris, 1958).

78. R. Louis, *De l'histoire à la légende. Girart, Comte de Vienne*, 3 vols (Auxerre, 1946–47).

79. French version (revised), R. Menéndez-Pidal, *La Chanson de Roland et la tradition épique des Francs* (Paris, 1960). See also J. J. Duggan, *The Song of Roland, formulaic style and poetic craft* (Berkeley, 1973).

80. L. Halphen, *Eginhard, Vie de Charlemagne* (Paris, 1923), pp. 12–13.

81. D. J. A. Ross, 'Pleine sa hanste', *Medium Aevum*, 20 (1951), 1–10.

82. *Chanson de Roland*, ll. 1830–31.

83. Ibid., ll. 710, 714–16.

84. Ibid., ll. 1017–38. See D. J. A. Ross, 'L'originalité de "Turoldus": le maniement de la lance', *Cahiers de Civilisation Médiévale*, 6 (1963), 127–38.

85. Ibid., ll. 803–13 and 2035–55. D. J. A. Ross, 'Gautier del Hum, an historical element in the *Chanson de Roland*?', *Modern Language Review*, 61 (1966), 409–15. See also D. J. A. Ross, 'Before Roland: what happened 1200 years ago next August 15?', *Olifant*, March 1978, 171–90.

86. G. J. Brault, *Early Blazon* (Oxford, 1972).

87. *Chanson de Roland*, ll. 1363–64.

88. Ibid., l. 2345.

89. Ibid., ll. 2152–54.

90. Ibid., ll. 3140–54.

91. The exact meaning of the epithet sasfret or saffré is disputed. Yellow varnished seems the most likely suggestion. Some kind of dressing for the mail of the hauberc was obviously needed to preserve it from rust.

92. Quoted from E. Faral, *Les Jongleurs en France au moyen âge* (Paris, 1910), p. 179.

93. Probably either William II of Sicily (1166–89) or his father William I (1154–66).

94. A. de Montaiglon and G. Raynaud, *Recueil général et complet des Fabliaux* (Paris, 1872–90), I, 11.

95. Ibid., p. 12.

96. Ibid., p. 12.

97. Ibid., II, 262.

98. Above, note 13.

99. Quoted from E. Faral, *Les Jongleurs en France*, p. 184.

100. *Aiol, chanson de geste*, edited by J. Normand and G. Raynaud (Paris, 1877).

101. *Les Enfances Guillaume*, edited by P. Henry (Paris, 1935), pp. 3–4.

102. Quoted from Faral, op. cit., p. 178 (see note 92, above).

103. Faral, op. cit., p. 76, note 1.

104. *Recueil général*, II, 242 (see note 94, above).

105. *Les deux rédactions en vers du Moniage Guillaume*, edited by W. Cloetta, 2 vols (Paris, 1906–11), I, 101–02.

106. *Recueil général*, V, 65–66 (see note 94, above).

107. A. de la Borde and M. C. Samaran, *La Chanson de Roland, reproduction phototypique du MS. Digby 23 de la Bodleian Library d'Oxford* (Paris, 1933), pp. 23–27 and f. 72.

108. D. J. A. Ross, *Alexander Historiatus*, Warburg Institute Surveys, I (London, 1963), 14–18.

109. *Recueil général*, I, 4 (see note 94, above). The *bordeur* is showing his ignorance doubly as both *Perceval le Galois* and *Partenopeus de Blois* with which he confuses it, are romances in octosyllabic rhyming couplets.

110. Quoted from Tobler-Lommatsch, *Altfranzösisches Wörterbuch*, V, col. 80.

111. Joinville, *Histoire de Saint Louis*, edited by N. de Wailly (Paris, 1890), §668, p. 282.

112. *Gormont et Isembart*, edited by A. Bayot (Paris, 1921).

113. *The Medieval French Roman d'Alexandre*, III, edited by A. Foulet (Elliott Monographs, 38 (Princeton, 1949), 37–60.

114. *Le Voyage de Charlemagne*, edited by P. Aebischer (Geneva and Paris, 1965).

115. Quoted from F. Godefroy, *Dictionnaire de l'ancienne langue française*, VIII, Complément, p. 78.

116. Edited by D. McMillan, pp. 20, 93 and 123, and by J. Wathelet-Willem (Paris, 1975), pp. 772–73, 956–57 and 1034–35 (see note 1, above).

117. l. 421.

118. l. 2302.

119. ll. 3136–37.

120. C. W. Aspland, *Epic formulas containing the -ant forms in twelfth century French verse* (St Lucia, Queensland, 1970), especially pp. 33–44.

121. This was shown by Professor J. J. Duggan in a valuable paper read to the London Medieval Society on 20 January 1972.

122. Since this passage was written Professor Duggan's book, J. J. Duggan, *The Song of Roland. Formulaic style and poetic craft* (Berkeley, 1973), has appeared to provide us with one of the most important studies of the composition of the *chanson de geste* so far available. On the question of the formulaic style in the 'great' scenes see pp. 39–60. I feel however, that there is strong evidence of the intervention of an individual reviser in *Roland* who was concerned with such questions as power in the state. A similar point could probably be made about the surviving form of most *chansons de geste*.

123. J. Rychner, *La chanson de geste, essai sur l'art épique des jongleurs* (Geneva, 1955).

124. C. Aspland, op. cit., note 81 and J. J. Duggan, 'Formulas in the *Couronnement de Louis*' Romania, 86 (1966), 315–43. Also above, note 122.

125. See L. M. C. Randall, *Images in the margins of Gothic manuscripts* (Berkeley and Los Angeles, 1966), frontispiece and figs. 105 and 572.

126. K. Varty, *Le jeu de Robin et Marion* (London, 1959), p. 37, musical transcription by E. Hill.

127. The meaning appears to be: The same tune should be repeated in all verses. (?)

128. F. W. Bourdillon, *Aucassin et Nicolette* (Manchester, 1919) pp. xxx–xxxiii.

129. M. Blanc 'Le présent épique dans la Chanson de Roland', *Actes du Xᵉ Congrès International de Linguistique et Philologie Romanes*, Strasbourg, 1962 (Paris, 1965), pp. 565–78, and 'Time and tense in Old French narrative', *Archivum Linguisticum*, 16 (1965), 96–124. Dr Blanc is preparing a general study of the question.

130. Edited by E. Langlois, p. 65. Above, note 43.

131. ll. 2081–84.

132. Ed. cit. (see note 64), pp. 237–38 (ll. 4976–91).

133. Ed. cit., ll. 1188–1212. Cf. Duggan, op. cit., pp. 118–27.

134. Ed. cit., ll. 1653–60.

135. Ed. cit., ll. 2207–14. On this *planctus* motif see Duggan, op. cit., pp. 160–84, especially pp. 163–68 on Charles's lament for Roland.

136. Virgil, *Aeneid*, vi, 853.

137. Ed. cit., ll. 1049–81.

138. Ibid., ll. 1691–721.

139. Ibid., ll. 2297–354.

140. Ibid., ll. 2355–96. Below, pp. 124–27.

141. *Gui d'Amiens, Carmen de Hastingae Proelio* in F. Michel, *Chroniques anglo-normandes*, iii, 18. Text in Faral, *Les Jongleurs en France*, p. 275 (see note 92, above).

142. *Henrici archidiaconi Huntendunensis Historia Anglorum*, edited by T. Arnold, Rolls Series (London, 1879), vi, 30. Text ibid., p. 276.

143. *L'Estoire des Engleis by Geffrei Gaimar*, edited by A. Bell (Oxford, 1960), ll. 5265–300, pp. 167–68.

144. *Le Roman de Rou de Wace*, edited by A. J. Holden, 3 vols (Paris, 1970–73), ll. 8013–18; ii, 183.

145. William of Malmesbury, *De Gestis Regum Anglorum*, edited by W. Stubbs, Rolls Series 90 (1889), Vol. ii, 302.

146. Edited by H. F. Williams, Univ. Michigan Publ. Lang. and Lit. (Ann Arbor, 1947), ll. 6231–45.

147. Ed. cit. (see note 52, above), ll. 2442–54, pp. 83–84.

148. Ed. cit., see note 147.

149. Edited by W. M. Hackett, see note 21. On the legend in general see R. Louis, op. cit. (note 78).

150. P. Meyer, 'La Chanson de Döon de Nanteuil, fragments inédits', *Romania*, 13 (1884), 1–26; *Gui de Nanteuil, chanson de geste*, edited by J. R. McCormack (Geneva, 1970); *Aye d'Avignon, chanson de geste anonyme*, ed. S. J. Borg (Geneva, 1967); *Parise la duchesse*, ed. F. Guessard and L. Larchez (Paris, 1860); *Tristan de Nanteuil*, ed. K. V. Sinclair (Assen, 1971).

151. See E. Faral, *Les jongleurs en France*, pp. 103–18.

152. *Roi* that is *des menestrels*, a semi-official title and office bearing some resemblance to those of the kings of arms among the heralds.

153. *Les œuvres d'Adenet le Roi*, edited by A. Henry, 5 vols (Bruges, Paris, Brussels, 1951–71).

154. *Histoire Littéraire de la France*, xxxi, pp. 171 ff.

155. Unpublished MS Paris, Bibliothèque Nationale, français 22555, fol. 1, col. 1, ll. 1–6.

156. *La Chanson du Chevalier au Cygne et de Godefroi de Bouillon*, edited by C. Hippeau (Paris, 1877), p. 9, ll. 30–36.

157. Ibid., p. 60, ll. 1648–55.

158. Edited by McMillan, p. 54, ll. 1236–39. Edited by J. Wathelet-Willem, pp. 854–55.

159. Its editor, D. McMillan, dates it as late as the thirteenth century, largely on linguistic and metrical grounds, making too little allowance for the very high degree of scribal corruption which the poem has suffered. See D. McMillan, ed. cit. (see note 1), ii, 115–31. J. Wathelet-Willem, ed. cit., pp. 651–54 proposes more convincingly a date in the region of 1150 for the existing text.

160. The passage is taken from McMillan's text, ll. 1275–1432. Ed. J. Wathelet-Willem, pp. 858–73.

161. *en sus* could possibly refer to a wicket in one leaf of the gate.

162. *Joesdi al vespre* is a typical *vers orphelin* of the poem, used apparently to mark the passage of time.

163.   *Mortel* normally means mortal in all its senses, none of which make sense here. I suggest a (mortal) man's honour; the commentators are silent on this line. The formulas recur with a variant of assonance in l. 1349. J. Wathelet-Willem in her glossary, p. 1163, suggests *qui doit mourir*, which does not help much.

164.   i.e. concealing the news of William's full losses from the reinforcements she has collected.

165.   Literally, strikes.

166.   *rostiz*, roasted, but cakes are baked.

167.   Literally, his face or countenance.

168.   The text is taken from *Le Charroi de Nîmes*, edited by J. L. Perrier (Paris, 1931, reprinted 1966), ll. 278–379, pp. 9–13.

169.   *ber*, literally baron; nobleman, knight, warrior are the essential meanings of this important word. In the mouth of a woman it means husband, *Mon baron*, My lord.

170.   St Peter, the Pratum Neronis, Nero's Field on the Mons Vaticanus being the supposed site of his martyrdom.

171.   It is noteworthy that there is a tendency for the most primitive forms of the epics to be preserved on the periphery of the area of French speech. The Oxford text of *La Chanson de Roland*, *La Chanson de Guillaume* and *Le Voyage de Charlemagne* have all survived in Anglo-Norman manuscripts and the only other text of the assonanced *Chanson de Roland* is a Franco-Italian one, MS V[4] in the Biblioteca Marciana in Venice. All the purely French texts of *Roland* are of the later version in true rhyme. These peripheral areas were evidently not up to date in following literary fashions, a very fortunate circumstance.

172.   Text, ed. cit. (see note 114, above), ll. 1–52. I use Aebischer's critical text on pp. 31 and 33.

173.   The supposed luminosity of the carbuncle is a commonplace in medieval French literature.

174.   The Amiral is not particularized but was probably intended for the Sultan of Egypt.

175.   There is an anacoluthon in this long sentence.

176.   Literally dearest, most valuable.

177.   *bel*, really fair, is very frequent in such forms of address but cannot usually be translated literally.

178.   This is the horn, made from an elephant's tusk, which plays a key part in the quarrel of Roland and Oliver in the *Chanson de Roland*. It is naturally associated with Roland here also.

179.   Text, ibid., ll. 415–506, pp. 57, 59, 61 and 63.

180.   The meaning of *decliner* is itself in dispute. Usually it means, to fail, decline, come to an end, and is used of death, illness, the sun's setting, etc. There is very little evidence that it can mean tell, or relate, which is what one would like it to mean here; Here ends the tale that Turold tells. There is actually a better, though not much better, case for taking *que* as having the force of *car* and translating: Here ends the tale for Turold is in failing health.

181.   See *Roland*, ll. 1876–82. I do not believe, despite the view often expressed, that any contempt for monks is here intended by the archbishop. The *orator* has his place and function in medieval society no less than the *bellator*, and both alike contribute to the defence of that society against its enemies spiritual and temporal.

182.   ll. 3992–4001.

183.   Text from ed. cit. (see note 5, above), ll. 2297–397.

BIBLIOGRAPHICAL NOTES

To provide even a skeleton bibliography of the *chanson de geste* would lengthen this account by at least a half. I propose therefore to list the principal bibliographies in which the material can be found, having already given in the notes the best editions of the works mentioned in the text.

Basic to all study of Medieval French literature is: R. Bossuat, *Manuel Bibliographique de la Littérature française du moyen âge* (Melun, 1951). The epic is dealt with in Part 1, Chapter 2, pp. 11–88, Nos. 66–909; later versions (fourteenth and fifteenth centuries) in Part II, Chapters 2 and 3, pp. 379–87, Nos. 4015–84. Two supplementary volumes have appeared (1955; 1961).

Premier Supplément (1949–53) (Paris, 1955), pp. 21–34, Nos. 6034–191 and pp. 85–86, Nos. 6765–78.

Second Supplément (1954–60) (Paris, 1961), pp. 17–30, Nos. 7130–264 and p. 88, Nos. 7857–61.

Nineteenth-century studies in the field of French Epic are critically listed in: L. Gaultier, *Bibliographie des chansons de geste* (Paris, 1897).

Recent work is listed annually and evaluated in: *The Year's Work in Modern Language Studies*, Cambridge, Modern Humanities Research Association, 1 (1931) and yearly thereafter.

Finally on 15 August 1955 was founded *La Société Rencesvals* to co-ordinate studies in the field of epic in the romance languages. It holds colloquia, usually at two-yearly intervals, and publishes a critical bibliography: *Bulletin Bibliographique de la Société Rencesvals*, which reports on the colloquia and contains a full critical bibliography of work appearing in the field. Ten fascicules have appeared between 1958 and 1977.

MEDIEVAL SPANISH

By L. P. HARVEY

The Geographical and Historical background

IT IS HARDLY NECESSARY to describe the geographical limits of the Iberian Peninsula: the natural frontier of the Pyrenees is as clear a line as any in the world. Although the Peninsula is shared between two nations, the Spanish and the Portuguese, and four languages (Castilian and Portuguese, the two national tongues, and two other regional languages, Catalan and Basque) yet in surveying epic material we need only concern ourselves here with the epic traditions of Castilian. This is because Castilian is the only language in which we have positive evidence that true traditional epic poetry ever flourished. A hundred-line fragment of ancient date in Aragonese dialect (found at Pamplona) appears to be a version of the French theme of Roland at Roncevaux.[1] As a counterblast to this intrusive theme from north of the Pyrenees there may have been in existence in early times, as early as the twelfth century, a Leonese epic of which one Bernardo del Carpio (a fictional creation) was the hero, but the evidence (early prose accounts in Latin and Castilian, late short ballads) is less than entirely conclusive. One can understand that in the climate of ideas of the Romantic and post-Romantic periods, patriots should feel that every language worth its salt ought to have its own epic, and where no epic could be found, then epics had to be posited, to be reconstructed.

With speculation concerning such hypothetical epics in Portuguese, Basque or Catalan we need not concern ourselves. Portuguese in Renaissance times was endowed by Camões with one of the great poems in the Greco-Roman neo-Classical tradition of literary epics, *Os Lusíadas*, but that wonderful work lies outside the purview of this volume. The Basques, tough mountain warriors, as those who have had to fight their way across the Pyrenees have discovered to their cost, had their heroic songs, but there is nothing in the short history of Basque literature to indicate that they ever possessed narrative epic songs. This in spite of the fact that the faithful companion of the great hero Rodrigo 'el Cid' was clearly in contact with Basques from his epithet Alvarfáñez *Minaya* (i.e. Castilian *mi* 'my' + Basque *anai* 'brother'). There were Basque heroes, but not Basque heroic epic poems. True, we know virtually nothing of composition in Basque before the language (under the impulse of the Reformation) was first committed to writing in the sixteenth century, but the Basques are a people who preserve their ancient ways and their ancient speech most jealously, and, it is difficult to imagine that they would have forgotten an epic tradition if they had ever possessed one. The case for the existence of early Catalan epic poetry has been argued frequently. It was stated by Martín de Riquer with great persuasiveness and erudition in a paper entitled 'L'epopea medievale in Catalogna'.[2] Although he is indeed able to point to a number of considerations which render probable the existence of epic poetry created and disseminated by Catalans for Catalans, as for example the frequent occurrence of 'epic' names such as Roland and Oliver in records, he may appear to some to be too ready to identify as being distinctively Catalan what could have been simply common Provençal. It is well known that in the twelfth century it was the *langue d'oc* and not Catalan which served as the medium of artistic expression, even though what was conventionally termed 'Limousine' was often heavily Catalanized. Perhaps more importantly, Riquer claims to recognize in the *Libre dels fets* of Jaime I and the chronicles of Desclot and Montaner passages of scarcely disguised assonantal verse showing through the prosified text. Such reconstructions are persuasive, but they fall far short of constituting a rigorous proof. In the first place the nature of assonantal verse is such that one would expect the random occurrence of a few assonantal periods in any text, and secondly, even if one is prepared to accept that behind the prose lies verse, that verse was not necessarily in Catalan, but, given the ease of adaptation from one Romance vernacular to another, could well have been couched in Provençal or perhaps Aragonese. It does not seem too much to ask to see one genuine fragment of Catalan epic or at least one unambiguous reference to such a composition before proceeding to further reconstruction. The weight of evidence still points towards the possibility that within the Iberian Peninsula, Castile is the only area which has ever possessed an epic of its own.

Even in Castile, as we shall see, the amount of epic material to survive, and, as far as we can infer, the amount of epic material which ever existed, is much less than what is found in many other areas — much less than what existed in medieval France, or in Yugoslavia in relatively modern times for example. Yet this area is worth the careful attention of the comparativist, for not only are some of these epic compositions of outstanding aesthetic quality, but also the detailed scholarship which has been lavished on the Castilian material has produced findings of general interest. There is perhaps no other venerable epic tradition in the world where we can document so fully and so early the relationship between historical events and epic tradition. Although many other outstanding scholars have contributed a great deal to our knowledge of this field, all would agree that it is to the extraordinarily devoted scholarship of Ramón Menéndez Pidal that we owe the advanced state of studies on the epic in Spain.

'Wide is Castile', as the Spanish saying has it, and the areas which have come to bear the names of Old Castile and New Castile occupy almost the whole of the *Meseta Central*, from the Sierra Morena, northern frontier of Andalusia, up to the Atlantic coast round Santander. But the area of the epic tradition is narrow and circumscribed: the Southern part of Old Castile. New Castile, the area incorporated into the Christian north in some of the most daring border warfare of the eleventh century, is not a land of epic. Toledo, the ancient capital, and Madrid, the new, have neither of them evoked great epic verse. Epic is limited in the Iberian Peninsula to Castilian, and within Castilian lands it is limited to the north, to that little wedge-shaped territory of Old Castile which came to stand rather as a keystone at the head of the arch of the Spanish state. This area within its primitive boundaries stretched only as far South as the Montes de Oca in the present province of Burgos, and the consciousness of the tight feeling of group solidarity is preserved for us in the fairly late *Poema de Fernán González*:[3]

> Estonces era Castiella un pequeño rencón
> era de castellanos Montedoca mojón
> et de la otra parte Fitero fondón
> moros tenien Carraço en aquella sazón.

However, the town just to the South of the Montes de Oca, Burgos, came to be the centre of the greatest of all Spanish epics, that of Rodrigo de *Bivar* (a hamlet near Burgos), *el Cid Campeador*. Also in the modern province of Burgos, Salas de los Infantes was another centre of an epic of great renown, although not one which has survived in its primitive form. Even the clerical epic, in accordance with traditions of Spanish literary historians usually classified as a phenomenon apart, in fact flourished strictly within these limits, with Burgos as the centre: San Pedro de Arlanza, San Pedro de Cardeña, San Salvador de Oña are within the radius of sixty kilometres, and even San Millán de la Cogolla (in the province of Logroño) and Palencia (in the province of that name) are in areas immediately bordering on Burgos.

The epic tradition of Castile flourished in the full light of history. The *Poema de Mio Cid*[4] tells of events in the last two decades of the eleventh century, and Mendéndez Pidal's date for the formation of the *Poema de Mio Cid* as we have it in the unique Bivar manuscript is 1140. Voices have been raised in recent years questioning such an early dating, although the weight of scholarly opinion in Spain itself appears to be at the moment still on the side of Menéndez Pidal. Yet even if we were to take the later dates of the end of the twelfth century or beginning of the thirteenth century as suggested by Ubieto, Russell, Pattison, Smith and others,[5] we still have the phenomenon of a poem which was formed only a century after the events narrated, and this, if compared with what we find in other literatures, is a remarkably short span.

The society of the eleventh century in which the *Poema de Mio Cid* flourished was Romance-speaking, and it was Christian. The small Christian states of the northern mountainous Cantabrian chain, from Galicia in the West and from

León, through Castile itself, to Navarre, Aragon, and also the Catalan county of Barcelona, were all struggling to push back the frontier to the south at this period (besides jostling for position amongst themselves). The enemy was the Arabic-speaking Muslim. The opportunity for conquest (or for Reconquest according to one's historical perspective) was created by the collapse in the eleventh century of the central authority of the Caliphate of Cordova, and the setting up of small states, a kaleidoscopic confusion of them in the period of Petty Kingdoms (*Mulūk aṭ-ṭawā'if*).[6]

But the states pursuing the policy of Reconquest were lands the civilization of which was in many ways very deeply impregnated with the Germanic culture which had been brought to Spain by the Visigoths,[7] rulers in the Peninsula from the fifth century until the advent of the Arabs in 711. The Visigoths had brought with them their own legal code, providing for such characteristically Germanic tribal practices as trial by ordeal and battle, at first the privilege of those who could claim the special status of Goths, as opposed to the generality who, as citizens of the so-firmly rooted Roman settlements, were, of course, subject to Roman law. When the Arab invasions pushed the Christian remnants up to the infertile hills of the north, the Visigothic customary law rather than Roman legislation became the code of the resisters. A Visigothic code was also preserved by the Mozarabs of Toledo and elsewhere; it had a Latin name *Forum judicum* (or *Fuero juzgo* in Romance), and it was in Latin, but it embodied Germanic social concepts, having been granted by Receswinth and confirmed by the Council of Toledo in Visigothic times in 654.

The Visigoths had brought with them their social structures; the nucleus of loyal vassals banded to their feudal lord by ties both of obligation to serve and also of commensality (*gahlaiba*, *compaña*, 'company'), proved to be the most effective military grouping. In the eleventh century it was that part of the peninsula which preserved best the Visigothic military social order which passed most effectively to the attack when the Caliphate collapsed.

How much of their original Germanic speech they had brought with them it is difficult to tell. The way in which Germanic settlers in early days held apart from the former Roman subjects would seem to indicate a language barrier, but may be explained simply by the doctrinal differences between Arians and Catholics, and by a sentiment of contempt for the strangers they dominated. It may be inferred that part of the cultural baggage which they brought into the Iberian Peninsula was their own Germanic epic tradition. However, of this branch of Germanic poetry we know tantalizingly little. Jordanes, writing in his *Getica*,[8] *c.* A.D. 550, speaks of the narrative of an early stage of their history included 'in priscis eorum carminibus pene historico ritu'. Of this early poetry we have no direct knowledge. Since this is poetry concerned with tales of national origins, it is reasonable to assume that it was something which we would have classed as epic lays (and also, perhaps, since it would appear to have been known to Jordanes in the variant forms so characteristic of the genre). That the Goths should have had their heroic songs like those of other Teutonic tribes might be taken for granted, even if we did not have such a positive statement as this. But what of the Visigoths who actually reached Spain? They had, after all, fought their way into this western land after a protracted tour of the Roman world. Clearly they had lost much of their cultural distinctiveness on the way. Had they lost their songs and lays? May we infer, when Saint Isidore, writing for the Visigothic court of Sisebut (612–21) a manual for young men of noble rank, the *Institutionum Disciplinae*,[9] speaks of the desirability of them preferring, over soft love lyrics, the 'carmina maiorum quibus auditores provocati ad gloriam excitentur', that these 'songs of our ancestors by which those who listen may be stirred and encouraged to deeds of glory' are songs of Visigothic ancestors sung in Spain? The alternative is to imagine that he has in mind some Latin poems which might have been spoken of at the beginning of the sixth century in this way.

Between this reference of the early seventh century and the earliest Romance epic poem in the Peninsula of which we know, there is a gap of *at least* half a millennium, and to make inferences of cultural continuity over such a gap is perhaps over-bold. However, there are indications that in the Christian kingdoms of the North of Spain there took place a process of cultural identification with the Visigothic past (as representing a Golden Age when Christian Spain was free of the Muslim yoke), rather than with the more distant glories of Senecan Roman Spain. To this day most of the characteristic Spanish personal names are Germanic: Alberto, Alfonso, Alonso, Enrique, Francisco, Guillermo, Ricardo. Throughout the Middle Ages the boast of descent from Gothic blood (*sangre de godos*) was the most direct and effective claim that could be made to nobility. *Limpieza de sangre* (purity of blood) as a preoccupation of the Golden Age of Spanish culture in the sixteenth and seventeenth centuries is usually discussed by modern historians from the negative point of view that it constituted a claim that Jewish and Arab blood was absent: at the time the claim was usually couched in the positive form that Visigothic blood was present. Above all, as has been stated above, the structure of the medieval Spanish states, León, Castile, Navarre, Aragon, etc., was based on Germanic-style social relationships. The state was cemented by the bond of service owed by the lord to his king, by the vassal to his lord. Feudalism in Spain, a frontier land, was always complex. It never received the pure formulation, systemization and universality achieved elsewhere in Western Europe, but this did not mean that feudal relationships did not provide the hard bony skeleton on which the fighting strength of the Christian North relied: the secular epic, as it has survived, constitutes lively and intelligent propaganda in favour of that feudal society.

What has been said of the possible Visigothic influence on the formation of the Castilian epic may, to the sceptical mind, seem tenuous indeed. It is exasperating that the evidence about the nature of the Visigoths' own songs and poems is entirely absent. To argue entirely on the basis of ethos and political structure may seem less than convincing to the purely literary scholar. Yet some evidence internal to the extant poems might seem very persuasive. In particular the theme of the purchase of the liberty of Castile for the price of a horse, as contained in the *Poema de Fernán González*,[10] bears a striking resemblance to a story in the work already mentioned, by Jordanes, the *Getica*, to the effect that the Goths, at an earlier stage in their wanderings had been reduced to servitude on an island and had been freed for the price of a horse. There were evidently varying accounts of this servitude and of the place where this took place: 'in Brittania vel unaqualibet insularum' says Jordanes. *Brittania* is, of course, quite impossible, and one wonders whether it is the product of late garbling. The freeing of the Goths from this yoke was achieved, according to this legend, by a person unnamed, 'unius caballi praetio'.[11]

What may be the earliest reference to the Spanish story bearing a resemblance to this Gothic legend is to be found in the *Chronicle of Nájara (Crónica Najarense)*[12] dated *c.* 1150, where Count Fernán González is referred to as the man who led the Castilians out from under the yoke of Leonese rule. There is certainly no mention of the *price of a horse* here, and all that can be asserted with certainty is that when the chronicle was compiled the story of the activities of Fernán González was already the subject of narratives known to the chronicler probably from oral sources (*dicitur*).

It is the positive and explicit evidence of the *Poema de Fernán González*, dated 1250, which makes it extremely likely that this Nájara reference was in fact to the price of a horse legend. The work will be dealt with below; for our present purposes let it suffice to say that the historical Fernán González, Count of Castile (*c.* A.D. 950) was felt by Castilians to have been the ruler who established the independence of the area which we now know as Old Castile from the far more ancient neighbouring kingdom of León. In so far as this *was* achieved (and the situation was always quite fluid), it was by an astute policy of playing off one power, León, against others interested in the area, such as Navarre and the Muslim South. Geographical fact and historical and dynastic circumstance meant that Castile and León were bound to have their fates intertwined. In a long perspective one can see that whereas in the early Middle Ages León was a seat of power with Castile a border region, by the twelfth century Castile emerged as the strongest land-based power in the Iberian Peninsula, with León cut off from most of the prizes to be won in the expansion to the south which we know as the Reconquest. (At the end of the Middle Ages Columbus, based on Andalusia, the southern colonized extension of the crown of Castile, was to open up a New World which learned to speak a variety of Castilian, not,

K

of course, of Leonese.) The lions of León remain emblazoned in the Spanish national arms, but León is to this day a backwater.

Such a reversal of roles begs for an explanation, and the myth which was put to use was the myth of the *price of a horse*. In the *Poem of Fernán González* we are told that the count possessed a particularly fine horse (and, it must be added, a hawk, an element entirely absent from Jordanes's brief story) on which the king of León, Sancho Ordóñez, cast envious eyes, on an occasion when Fernán González was obliged to attend at the Leonese court. The king asked the count to sell the hawk and the horse, which Fernán González only agreed to do if the king promised that, should there be any failure to pay over to him the price, the king would incur the penalty of the price doubling for every day's delay:

> Si el aver non fuesse aquel día pagado
> siempre fues' cada día al gallarín doblado.[13]

The effect of the geometrical progression after a delay of three years is to create a debt so immense that the king is quite incapable of fulfilling his bond. The wily Fernán González then agrees to forego his price in exchange for the liberty of Castile.

It will be seen that this legend tells how Castilians were released from Leonese servitude (as had the Goths been of old) *for the price of a horse*. The *First General Chronicle*[14] which, for reasons discussed below, often echoes in its wording that of the verse epics, in fact uses the words 'servidumbre de leon e de los leoneses', seemingly echoing the 'servitude' mentioned by Jordanes. A similar situation had elicited a similar response. It is hard to imagine how the myth common to both the Goths and the Castilians can have been transmitted over the intervening centuries except through oral epics. We certainly know of no continuity of written material. A story such as this can endure for some time in the folk-memory without the aid of writing or organized oral transmission, but more than half a millennium is indeed a long time, and we must surely posit some mnemonic mechanism of transmission to bridge such a gap. We cannot exclude the possibility that the vehicle of transmission is a Latin historical text,[15] but the existence of such an ancient myth is a persuasive argument for the existence of an epic tradition.

There is no other element with alleged Visigothic connexion in any of the other Spanish epics to be compared with the 'price of a horse' motif. In the *Poema de Mio Cid* there is a tantalizing aside during the journey of the Infantes of Carrión back from Valencia to their home territory. After passing the Sierra de Miedes (a known locality) and Montes Claros (of more dubious identification), we read the puzzling lines:

> A siniestro dexan a Griza que Alamos pobló
> Allí son caños do a Elpha ençerró
>
> (ll. 2691–92)[16]

(To the left they leave Griza [one of the relatively few unidentified place-names in the *Poema*] which Alamos [presumably a masculine singular, cf. such personal names as Arnaldos] settled, there are the caves in which he shut Elpha.)

If Elpha is a creature to be shut in a cave, she may well be an *elf*-maiden, and if we are in such a Germanic world, one is led to speculate whether Alamos is not at some remove a corruption of Alanos (i.e. Alans). We are on very uncertain ground.

The Visigoths at the height of their power had never succeeded in imprinting their identity on the whole Peninsula; they came as Arian heretics to a Catholic land, and to the ways of that land they assimilated themselves. We have seen that they adopted the language of the existing inhabitants, as they had adopted their religion. And yet there remained until the end *two* communities side by side, the Visigoths and the old Roman inhabitants (including in that grouping not only the colonists of diverse origins from all over the Empire, but also the aboriginal tribesmen who, with exceptions such as the Basques, had adopted Roman ways).

The culture of the Roman community, Latin and Christian, also lived on after the Arab conquest of 711: the so-called *Mozárabes* (*musta'rib* = Arabiser) were the chief transmitters of the Roman heritage, although also inheritors of part of the Visigothic tradition: even in the Church it was the Visigothic capital of Toledo which succeeded best in preserving the ancient tradition of pre-conquest Christianity.

There is little sign that the Roman-descended community ever possessed their own epics. Some of their lyrics have survived, the most ancient texts in any Romance vernacular, as refrains appended to certain Arabic (and Hebrew) poems, the *muwashshaḥāt*. There are Latin literary compositions of scant intrinsic merit: the Latin poem on the conquest of Almería, a text associated with the Chronicle of Alfonso VII (written before A.D. 1157) and the *Carmen Campidoctoris*,[17] a Latin poem on the exploits of Rodrigo 'el Cid' written shortly after the hero's death (i.e. first half of the twelfth century). These are poor evidence from which to deduce the existence of any Mozarabic epic tradition. The Christians of Arab Spain were not lacking in courage and the martial virtues. Their soldierly qualities were so appreciated by the Muslims that when many of them were deported to North Africa a corps d'élite of palace soldiery was recruited from them. As for their courage, it had been amply demonstrated by the foolhardy exploits of the martyrs of Córdoba, who, in the ninth century had pushed the tactics of non-violent confrontation to extreme limits.[18] The Mozárabes were no tame and subjugated helot community, but, so far as we know, they had no heroic songs, and they contributed nothing to the formation of the Castilian epic.

As for the Arabs themselves, the enormous cultural importance of their presence in Spain makes it seem contradictory to say that it is difficult to demonstrate any Arabic influence on Spanish epic poetry. The Arabic poetry of *ḥamāsa*, of heroism, was written inside a poetic tradition so complex and rich in language as to make it at times inaccessible not merely to those who did not speak Arabic but also to those who lacked an elaborate literary education.

That we know almost nothing of *popular* Arabic poetry in Spain is hardly surprising: we know little of popular poetry in the Arab world at large. The Islamic orientation of native Arab scholarship has blocked the study of secular vernacular compositions of all sorts. European Arabists, faced with the problem of assimilating the subtle and extensive Arabic tradition of literary scholarship, have rarely had the courage to strike out on their own and examine phenomena despised by Arab men of letters.[19] Lane in his *Manners and Customs of the Modern Egyptians*[20] has a few fascinating paragraphs on the musical performance of narrative poetry by the *shā'irs*, singers of tales seemingly very similar in many ways to the Muslim epic singers described by Lord[21] in Yugoslavia. Galmés de Fuentes[22] has, in the study referred to below, pointed out that there are references to the singing of the songs of Antar in Spain. The Archpriest of Hita in his *Book of Good Love*[23] discussed with critical discrimination the suitability of Muslim-style musical instruments for various purposes, but with no hint of any epic function for these instruments.

In the *First General Chronicle* (begun under Alfonso X in the second half of the thirteenth century) Chapter 909[24] contains what purports to be a contemporary Arabic lament on the loss of Valencia (it was captured by Rodrigo 'el Cid' in 1094). The Arabic language of this text contains so many curious features that it has been seriously argued that it is not an original text at all, but a clumsy word-for-word *re*translation from the Castilian, the original Arabic poetic text being completely lost. The Chronicle text at this point is beyond all doubt badly garbled. This is only what one would expect where transmission has taken place at the hands of copyists who had no understanding whatsoever of the language of what they were reproducing. It really is hard to imagine why the chroniclers should have taken the most unusual step of giving the Arabic *in extenso* unless they thought that it had special authenticity. And we have to remember that the court of Alfonso contained a number of scholars of all three religions who were perfectly familiar with Arabic, both of the written and of the vernacular varieties. The best manuscripts of the *Chronicle* are splendid codices carefully written for court use. Are we to believe that these competent Arabists would have permitted pidgin jargon to be set down in a work planned to enhance national prestige? It is more likely that what we have is a version, however garbled, of a genuine vernacular lament. The *Chronicle* explicity refers to the lament as in *viessos* (verses), but from the text as given, it is not possible to recognize any known pattern of metre, or any other known form of literary artifice, even *saj'* (rhymed prose: indeed rhyme and also assonance are totally absent). There is space only to quote a single line: it is as formless from the metrical point of view as all the others. There is the widest variation in number of syllables. (To give the spelling of any of the MSS would not be very helpful; I attempt a reconstruction into a 'colloquial' form of Arabic.) 'Al-wed al-maleh mat'ak al-kebir, wed al-abyar, ma'a al-mi al-ukhar alledi kunt anta minha jit makhdūma, qad kharaj min wadih wa-yamshi ayn lish kin li-yamshi.' (The beautiful great river which was yours, the Guadalabiar, together with the other waters whereby you were served, has left its bed, and flows where it used not to flow.)

This lament in Arabic may well have been known to the Cid, the great epic hero. He, after all, was the leader of the forces which captured the city, and the lament is supposed to have been pronounced in public. We are even given the name of the wise old Moor who composed the lines: Alhuacaxi, i.e. al-Waqashī. What is quite certain is that these lines bear no connexion whatsoever with the form of the Castilian epic of the Cid.

Some effort has been made recently in Spain to resuscitate elements of Ribera's[25] thesis that the Castilian epic tradition had Arabic roots. Ribera's thesis, dating from 1915, is based on the misapprehension that references to native Spanish metres adapted into Arabic refer to epic phenomena, whereas Samuel Stern[26] has since demonstrated beyond any peradventure that these references (in Ibn Bassām) are to the lyric genre of the *muwashshah*, already mentioned above. Ribera posited the existence of what he called *fotohat* (conquest poems), but he is able to adduce no texts of specimens of this type. The attempt to revive the thesis points to the existence of poetry in the extremely simple *arjūza* metre. Lutfi 'Abd al-Badī', in his 'La poesía épica en la España musulmana'[27] attempts to claim the Castilian epic tradition itself as belonging to the Islamic orbit: 'La erudición ha reconocido la fuerza expansiva que tuvo el cuento árabe español en el cuento medieval; ha reconocido la influencia de la lírica andaluza en la lírica provenzal; ¿No es lógico que el género épico tan arraigado en la España musulmana haya influído en la poesía castellana, estando el género épico íntimamente vinculada con la vida exterior?'.

Such a line of argument would not bear much weight were it not supported by texts, and 'Abd al-Badī' backs up his hypotheses by references to an *arjūza* of just under 450 lines on the subject of the conquests of the greatest of all the sovereigns of Al-Andalus, 'Abd ar-Rahmān III, which is quoted by Ibn 'Abd Rabbihi in his '*Iqd al-Farīd*.[28] With minor modifications this thesis is repeated by a Spaniard, Francisco Marcos Marín, in *Poesía narrativa árabe y épica hispánica*.[29] The conclusion that it is 'a narrative literary work but with a strictly historical basis, simple in form, classical in language, devoid of concessions to the dialect of Al-Andalus' is one with which one could hardly disagree, but the impression created by the dull and dry mnemonic verse of this annalistic composition is in my judgement far from that of any epic poem, whether oral or literary.

Álvaro Galmés de Fuentes in his recent study entitled 'Epica árabe y épica castellana (problema crítico de sus posibles relaciones)'[30] takes the work of Marcos and 'Abd al-Badī' further. On the basis of explicit mention of popular heroic Arabic poetry performed in Spain, and also by attempting to recognize Arabic thematic elements in Castilian poems such as the *Poema de Mio Cid* and *The Seven Young Lords of Salas* (*Siete infantes de Salas*) he presents a case which is persuasive, but which falls short of being entirely compulsive. This recent work, however, has served to draw our attention to a gap in our knowledge of Arabic poetry in the Peninsula. The verse narratives of the type described by Lane in Cairo in the nineteenth century must have had their counterparts in Spain, and renewed efforts must be made to study both the living tradition of bards in Arabic lands and also to subject early references to Arabic narrative verse to a careful scrutiny.

Finally, in considering the various cultural traditions which may have contributed to the formation of the native epic tradition in Spain, we must turn to France. There is no doubt that the immensely fruitful epic cycles from North of the Pyrenees had profound influence in Spain. The opportunities for French vernacular works to become known in the Christian kingdoms of the Peninsula were present in abundance in the eleventh century. The most important single factor was the abbey of Cluny. Cluny provided the trained priests who carried through the reform of the liturgy decreed at the Council of Burgos in 1080. It might seem that this has little bearing on the evolution of an epic which is, so the accepted teachings of Spanish scholars have it, in its origins secular. The passing of the old Mozarabic liturgy was the external sign for the restaffing of most of the key posts by Frenchmen, almost all of whom were Cluny-trained. Although the difference between the new French script introduced by the French teachers and the old Mozarabic hand was not as great by any manner of means as the difference between, for example, the old Arabic-based Turkish script and the new Roman script imposed by Ataturk, the effect seems to have been almost as dramatic. In the space of a single generation, Christian Spain took up a new cultural orientation, and became more closely integrated into the intellectual currents of Western Europe. The French ecclesiastics were everywhere: in the *Poema de Mio Cid* the hero appoints a bishop for the newly-captured city: he has the obviously French name of Jerome, and although Cluny is not mentioned in the poem, Jerome seems to have a Cluniac interest in crusading:

> El obispo don Jerome so nombre es llamado,
> bien entendido es de letras e mucho acordado,
> de pie e de caballo mucho era arreziado.
> Las provezas de mio Cid andavalas demandando
> sospirando ques viesse con moros en el campo;

que sis fartas lidiando e firiendo con sus manos
a los dias del sieglo non le llorasen cristianos.[31]

(His name is Bishop Don Jerôme, he is well versed in letters, and a doughty fighter on foot and on horseback. He journeyed asking after the heroic deeds of Mio Cid, longing to meet the Moors on the battlefield. If only he could have his fill, in battle, fighting hand-to-hand, let no Christians (thereafter) bewail his fate, for the rest of time.)

Jerome in the *Poema* is a representation of a historical Jérôme de Périgord. But he is also a literary reflection of the fighting bishop Turpin of the *Chanson de Roland*. Early Spanish acquaintance with the French epic is confirmed by the chance survival of the Aragonese fragment mentioned above of what was clearly a version of the theme of Charlemagne, Roland and Oliver. This fragment was only preserved because the vellum on which it was written was reused to make a document wallet for Pamplona cathedral library. It is long enough, some hundred lines, to permit us to form some judgement of the scale and style of the whole poem now lost. (Menéndez Pidal gave it the title *Roncesvalles*, following his sensible and useful practice of giving clear titles to so many of the vaguely-denominated works which have come down to us.)

Further confirmation of the fact that French epics circulated in Spain is provided by the linguistically unusual form of some Castilian proper names ending in -os such as Arnaldos, Carlos, Gaiferos, etc., which are frequent in the narrative ballads (*romances*). The standard treatment of Latin second-declension nouns is of course for the nominative form to be lost altogether, and for an -o ending to result from the decay of accusative -um. From Carolus we would expect Carlo, as in Italian. The final -s is to be explained as due to the prestige in epic texts of the Old French nominative forms such as the *Carles li reis* as in the *Chanson de Roland*. One might suspect that the Latin nominative itself had contributed to the dissemination of these forms (cf. *Dios* in contrast to Judeo-Spanish *Dio*), but the association of these forms with heroic legend is confirmed by the ballad literature, whereas there is no evidence that forms like Gaiferos, etc., ever had any great currency in Latin.

French scholars in particular have paid careful attention to the relationship between epics and pilgrimage routes. The greatest route of them all in the West was, of course, that to Santiago in Galicia, inevitably cutting through Castilian lands The dearth of material in Castilian, apart from the special case of the *mester de clerecía* discussed below, makes the analysis of Spanish epic for connexions with pilgrim routes and cult centres difficult if not impossible, but it is entirely reasonable to suppose that the pilgrims of St James would have brought with them their epic entertainments, such as, no doubt the *Chanson de Roland*, and that these epics would sometimes have been transposed into Castilian, as happened with *Roncesvalles*. A. L. Lloyd, when questioned at the London Seminar on Epic about bilingual epic singers in modern times in the Balkans, stated that it was unusual, but not unknown, for singers in mixed border areas, such as the fringes of the Hungarian and Rumanian speech communities, to be able to perform in both tongues. It is not logically necessary to posit bilingual performers in Francien and Castilian (they would merely have been the most elegant of a number of possible channels of transmission), but given this 'Francien nominative' form of proper names, and the existence of certain common verbal formulae, the hypothesis is an attractive one. It is noteworthy that in the *Poema de Mio Cid* the formula *pleurer des yeux* is sometimes *llorar de los ojos*, the transposition we would expect, but also *plorar de los ojos*, where the unusual initial *pl-* could be due to French influence (but could also, it must be added, be due either to archaism or to the influence of other dialects in the Peninsula).

The place of the Epic within the Spanish literary tradition

In common with the other Romance languages, Spanish only gradually came to be accepted as the medium for the expression of all types of subject-matter. (One might even say that the process was not completed until the twentieth century, when the vernacular finally came to be used for liturgical purposes.) During the Middle Ages there was a linguistic division of functions, and in every sphere the vernacular was less highly esteemed than the language of culture, Latin. Setting aside the Romance refrains to Arabic *muwashshaḥāt*, since they are in the distinct Mozarabic dialect and are insubstantial, the *Poema de Mio Cid* may well be the oldest surviving Castilian text of a literary nature. (There are legal instruments in a dog Latin, more than half Romance, of earlier date, but again they can be disregarded for our present purposes.) In spite of its priority in date (twelfth century?), the *Poema* does not seem to have initiated a written literature. It belongs to an oral genre in the view of the present writer (although that view is not universally shared),[32] and appears to be an exceptional case of an oral epic for some reason set down in writing. Castilian literature proper begins in the mid-thirteenth century, and is the product of the intellectual ferment associated with the court of Alfonso X (the Wise, 1221–1252–1284). The King's own work is illustrative of the way in which at the time conventions existed whereby one language was felt suitable for one type of use, and another language for another. The *Cantigas*, devotional Marian poems in lyric form, are in Galician–Portuguese, the Peninsular idiom which had taken over and acclimatized the Provençal lyric tradition. But if the King followed tradition in not using Castilian for elegant lyric composition, his policy with regard to prose composition was quite revolutionary, and deliberately so. He wanted the principal fields of intellectual activity to be open to his Castilian subjects in their own tongue. His patronage brought into being a literature in Castilian in the spheres of law, theology and history.

Besides those works directly produced by the scholars of his court circle (and often subjected to a final stylistic retouch by the King himself), a considerable range of prose literature came into being, with a great deal of translation from Arabic as well as from Latin.

Although Castilian continued throughout the Middle Ages to have a weaker literary tradition than that of Italy and France (it was not until the so-called Golden Age of the sixteenth and seventeenth centuries that writers in Castilian overcame their inferiority complex when comparing themselves with writers in these tongues), there was no doubt from the time of Alfonso the Wise onwards that Castilian was firmly established as a vehicle of expression available for all types of use. Other dialects, once equal rivals, survive now merely in peasant speech, and only Portuguese, which once seemed gravely menaced, but is now so firmly entrenched on both sides of the Atlantic, and Catalan, without the institutional support of a nation state, but still in remarkably robust health, are in regular use for literary purposes.

The strength of the *literary* tradition in Castilian, and its antiquity, have tended to obscure the Castilian oral tradition. One of the contributions of Menéndez Pidal was to demonstrate the underground continued existence of much ballad material, which literary scholars had too readily assumed was defunct. Two key concepts in the thought of this scholar are those of *latency* and of *neo-traditionalism*. Just as he is ready to envisage sound changes (the characteristic initial f > h of Castilian for instance) as being initiated, at first rejected, only to lapse into a 'latent' state, and re-emerge predominant in a much later period (in the case of f > h, after 500 years), so too in his studies of the ballad he has succeeded in demonstrating, on the basis of his own field work and the collation of material flowing in from researches inspired by his successes, that many ballads thought extinct were still alive, perhaps amongst the gauchos of Argentina, the villages of isolated parts of Spain, or even, after an enormous lapse of time, amongst the Jewish communities descended from those Jews expelled from Spain in 1492. There is, of course, an important difference between latency as used by Menéndez Pidal in his linguistic studies, and latency as used in literary history. A recessive variant realization of a phoneme sometimes does re-emerge as dominant, but there are no documented cases of a once moribund genre re-emerging to enjoy predominance. We are dealing with curious latent *survivals*, nothing more. The allied concept of 'traditionalism' has been more fruitful. Alongside the literary tradition, a popular tradition transmits a theme in a form subject to variants and yet identifiably distinct, 'living in its variants' as Menéndez Pidal himself said of traditional ballads. The Spanish literary tradition has at all periods been in part open to the creations of popular currents, and writers of the greatest refinement have turned popular elements to their purposes. Much of the traditional heroic material of epic was transposed by dramatists of the

Golden Age into dramatic form. The polymetric versification of Golden Age plays even permitted the quotation direct of lines and passages in the heroic ballad metre within the play. In this way the stage preserved much of the ethos of heroic poetry. The puzzle posed by the *theme of honour* so beloved of Spanish dramatists is largely resolved if one bears in mind that it is anachronistically transposed from the more ancient genre.

Before the Golden Age, there is virtually no evidence that drama existed, and certainly nothing to indicate that it would fulfil the function of vehicle of national legend and myth in the way it was to do at the hands of Lope de Vega. There is, in fact, only one single fragment (the *auto de los Reyes Magos*)[33] of a dramatic nature before the fifteenth century. It is surprising that a country which was to produce so much drama, both religious and secular, should have nothing dramatic to show during the Middle Ages, and yet this is the case in so far as Castile is concerned. (In Catalonia the cultural links with the lands north of the Pyrenees led to a very different state of affairs.)

The genre which in part competed in Castile with epic poetry was not the drama but prose narrative of a historical nature. When Alfonso X's historians compiled their vernacular chronicle, they drew not only on existing historiography in the learned languages — Latin and Arabic, but also on vernacular sources of an oral nature: *romances et cantares*. It would seem that the creation of a genre, the prose chronicle, which dealt explicitly and formally with the national past, led to the decline of the large-scale epic itself.

The study of the prose chronicles has been of the greatest importance, since it has permitted the reconstruction of the plot-outline of many epics otherwise lost, and R. Menéndez Pidal has even in some cases attempted to bring back to life whole poems (as for example in his *Reliquias de la poesía épica española* in which, *inter alia,* he reconstructs the lost epic of the Seven Young Lords of Salas — *Siete infantes de Salas*). We can have faith in this method of reconstruction because a control to the process is available: the Cid epic, in a version closely related to that which has survived in the Bivar MS, was used as source-material for the *Primera Crónica General*. We are thus able in places to test in an objective way the possibility of recognizing the assonantal lines of the *mester de juglaría* behind the Alfonsine prose. Even the most sceptical scholar is forced to admit that it is possible in many places to discern the passages which were once in verse. This gives scholars more confidence when they proceed to work on other sections of the *Primera Crónica General*, or indeed on other chronicles, where other themes occur. A considerable number of epic subjects can be recognized: Bernardo del Carpio, the loves of Mainete (Charlemagne) with Galiana in Toledo, the Seven Young Lords of Salas, etc. On the other hand, some Spanish literary historians speak of long lists of epic poems, arranging them into cycles and discussing their interrelationships in a way which accords ill with the inevitably tenuous evidence for their detailed shape and structure, even if one is willing to accept that they must indeed have existed. Without the chronicle material, our knowledge of Spanish epic poetry of the ancient period would be sparse indeed.

After the thirteenth century, one finds only the lamentably decadent *Youthful exploits of the Cid (Mocedades de Rodrigo)*[34] *c.* 1350–60, apart from the small-scale ballads or romances. These latter are often aesthetically admirable, and in many ways are examples of historical narrative poetry at its best, but a *romance* is not the narrative of a whole long campaign or the adventure of a great hero, it is brief, allusive, and can narrate only a short series of incidents.

It has been assumed that the decline of the epic in Spain after the advent of vernacular history is due to the redirection of patronage, formerly available for the minstrels (*juglares*) towards the writers of prose. It may well be that the epic of the old traditional form was in decline quite independently of the advent of prose history. We lack the documentation to study the ways in which patronage was exercised. Before the period of Alfonso the Wise we do not find *juglares* playing any specially honoured role in society, certainly no quasi-priestly function such as they exercised in some other cultures. The very name, *juglar, joculator*, indicates that they were primarily entertainers. As we shall see, the creators of a clerical epic were anxious to reject the associations of minstrelsy; 'I bring you a fine craft, it is not one of minstrelsy' 'Mester traigo fermoso, non es de joglaria'.[35] If a clerical poet declares himself a *juglar*, it is as part of the topic of modesty.

Heroic poems of the ballad type continued to be composed in celebration of exploits such as those of the border warfare between Castile and Muslim Granada, right down to the end of the Middle Ages. The ballad continued to exercise its function as a channel for the dissemination of news even later than that. This minor genre of a socially (and almost always aesthetically) inferior kind continued until modern times.

As might be expected, the literary epic has been much cultivated in Spain from the Renaissance onwards, although, in spite of the amount written, little has been produced of the highest quality. There is nothing in Spanish of the calibre of *Os Lusíadas* or of *Paradise Lost*. Sometimes use was made of the learned epic to narrate contemporary historical events. Juan Rufo in his *Austriada* glorifies the royal bastard Juan de Austria, narrating his campaigns against the Moriscos and the battle of Lepanto. Ercilla's *Araucana* (1569–89) is the narrative of the Spanish conquest of the Araucanian Indians of Chile by a man who actually took part in the campaigning. The *Araucana* is by no means devoid of literary merit. Its models are Virgil and Lucan, and outside Latin literature, Ariosto. This poem is in no sense a continuation of the ancient national epic traditions; it will accordingly not be examined here.

The case of *Araucana* poses the question, relevant to the situation of the epic within Spanish literature, of the extent to which the works of the Middle Ages were known to later periods, and thus able to serve as models. Spaniards of the Renaissance had little interest in the works of the Spanish Middle Ages. An edition of the *Poema de Mio Cid* was indeed made (by Ulibarri) in 1596, but characteristically was not printed. What the sixteenth, seventeenth, and eighteenth centuries knew about the exploits of the Cid was derived either from prose chronicles or from ballads. The first printing of the *Poema* was a fruit of late eighteenth-century antiquarianism: T. A. Sánchez's *Colección de poesías castellanas anteriores al siglo XV* (Madrid, 1779). The great importance accorded to the *Poema* in recent times is the result of the scholarly and critical activity of the nineteenth century and after.

Spaniards from the end of the Middle Ages until the present have gained their knowledge of the national epic material above all else from the ballads (*romances*), and from the ballads transposed into drama.

Categories of epic poetry in Spain

It is the firmly established tradition of native Spanish scholarship to classify the medieval epic into three categories:

(1)   the secular *mester de juglaría* (craft of minstrelsy, earliest in date, flourishing in the twelfth century, decadent by the mid-fourteenth),

(2)   the *mester de clerecía* ('craft of clerisy', predominant in the thirteenth century extending into the fourteenth, written by clerics and largely on themes of interest to the clergy),

(3)   the *romances* (ballads, of which the earliest extant examples go back to the fourteenth century, a genre which flourished in its heroic form in the fifteenth century, and continued extremely popular through the sixteenth and into the seventeenth century. The form retained some life until the present day, both by the transmission of traditional texts and thanks to the work of modern literary artists).

It must be borne in mind that none of these three 'schools' or styles is exclusively epic. In the case of the second, there is a great deal of material extant which is in no way heroic (e.g. *Libro de Apolonio*). Nevertheless, in each case the epic works are the most important specimens of the style.

Each of these types of poetry has a distinctive metrical form, although there is a close family resemblance between (1) and (3), probably arising because (3) is the product of the disintegration of the long poems of (1) into short sequences of 20–100 lines.

The metre of the *mester de juglaría* has given rise to a considerable amount of discussion. We cannot be sure that we understand it fully, but in the few specimens which have survived it differs from *all* other known verse-forms in Castilian because it is not based on any exact count of syllables. According to some it is simply anisosyllabic, others see behind the unevenness a rhythmic line of a Germanic or English type. The term 'sprung-rhythm' has been used by critics with an English-speaking background.[36] The most careful studies of the metre are those of Menéndez Pidal in his edition of the *Cantar de Mio Cid*, where a statistical breakdown of metrically unambiguous lines in the unique Bivar MS shows a distribution out of a total sample of 987 as follows.[37]

Lines with number of syllables in the first hemistich and the second as follows:	Number of lines in Menéndez Pidal's sample:
7 + 7	150
6 + 7	120
7 + 8	112
6 + 8	92
8 + 7	81
5 + 7	60
8 + 8	56
5 + 8	40

Frequencies fall away in a fairly regular but steep curve from this point from 7 + 9 (27 such lines) to 5, 6, and 7 + 13 (one line each).

A strong case is thus established for the thesis that the basic form of the half line is heptasyllabic. Given the frequency of apocopation of the final *-e* and even *-o* in Old Castilian (*dio le* alternating with *diol*), seven syllables at this early period often contains the same weight of words as eight syllables of the regular octosyllabic romance, and so such a line is by no means surprising. It is noticeable that in the principal text, the *Poema de Mio Cid*, the second hemistichs approach with greater regularity to the norm than do the first hemistichs. I have suggested[38] that since this irregularity is similar to the irregularity found in those texts taken down from Serbo-Croat bards by Parry in his modern investigations when dictation was attempted, it could be that the breaking of the rhythm consequent upon the unfamiliar process led to more 'incomplete' lines before the caesura than after it, where the final assonance (see below) acted as a mnemonic device. If this were so, it might follow that the text as performed under natural conditions might have been much more regular. Nevertheless, the metrical 'irregularities' which occur even in the *mester de clerecía* make it on the whole unlikely that a text as performed would have approached a fixed 7 + 7 form.

The metre of the *mester de clerecía*: the *Libro de Alexandre*[39] gives us a clear recipe: 'Mester traigo fermoso non es de joglaria / mester es sen pecado, ca es de clerezia / fablar curso rimado por la quaderna via / a sílavas cuntadas, ca es de grant maestria.' (I bring you a fine craft, it is not one of minstrelsy. / It is a spotless craft, for it is of clerisy, / speaking in a rhymed cursus, in the four-fold path, / in syllables that are counted, for it is a matter of great skill.) The reference to counted syllables is borne out by the new line structure, not a statistical distribution curve around a mean of seven, but seven syllables exactly. The line is called the *alejandrino* in Spanish, the French alexandrine acclimatized because it was propagated by the *Libro de Alexandre* and other poems of similar learned inspiration. Given the fact that Spanish words, even at this period of frequent apocopation, are longer on average than French ones, the heptasyllabic hemistich is of equivalent effect to the French hexasyllable. The alexandrine still is used in modern Spanish poetry, some of the finest poems of the *modernista* movement employed the line, but has grown apart from the old epic line. The alexandrine still counts fourteen syllables in a complete line, whereas the *romance* epic line counts sixteen.

It will have been noted that the new line also has full rhyme and not merely assonance, and the rhymes are grouped in stanzas of four lines, whereas the old epic line maintained the same assonance sequence of varying length (*tirada* is the term for these sequences, though the term for the equivalent phenomenon in Old French, *laisse*, is also used). From the passage quoted, this stanza is called the *cuaderna vía*, which has become a regular technical term, though there seems little doubt that in the text just quoted it is not a technical term but a joke: everything clerical is automatically superior — this is a craft which is *sen pecado*, spotless, without sin, of course, being clerical, without defect, being so well constructed, and being a clerical production, it is on the four-fold path, here a four-line stanza, but a clear reference to the *quadrivium*. In view of this flippant tone, it is perhaps pressing the text too hard to deduce from it that its author saw a rigid distinction between two *mesteres*, *clerecía* and *juglaría*, but such is the interpretation frequently given to these lines.

The short stanza is undoubtedly a difficult form to handle: it falls easily into a jingle, and it is difficult to achieve sustained pathos or heroic elevation. It does not seem ideally suited for the purpose to which it was principally put, the narration of edifying hagiographic material to a popular audience, but our modern ear may be partly at fault, certainly it seems to have been taken up with great enthusiasm in the thirteenth century by poets who were much concerned to communicate with a mass audience in an agreeable form.

The *mester de clerecía* is frequently classified as 'learned', 'clerical', and therefore is regarded as being something apart from the secular tradition. Such a clear dichotomy does not seem helpful or useful. The *mester de clerecía* certainly frequently employs written source material, and makes quite sure that the audience knows that the source material is not oral by saying so: 'Cuemo diz la leyenda' (*Alexandre*, 335), 'Pero diz el escrito que bien es de creer' (*Alexandre*, 2115), and examples could easily be multiplied a hundredfold, perhaps the most striking is Berceo's line in *Santo Domingo* 'el escripto lo cuenta, nin joglar nin cedrero' 'the document says this, and no minstrel or strumming musician'.[40] Sometimes the versifier is doing little but translate into Castilian verse from a Latin life of some saint. The different ethos of the genre is marked by the fact that we now know quite a great deal about the biography of one of the principal practitioners, Berceo, a writer associated with the monastic centres of San Millán de la Cogolla and Silos, whereas we know nothing of individual secular *juglares*.

Yet there are many points of contact between the two varieties of verse. In language the heroic epithets applied to secular heroes in the secular poems are given a theological gloss in the clerical epic, so that King David is 'David tan noble rey, una fardida lança' 'a bold [wielder of the] lance', using a heroic epithet occurring frequently in the *Poema de Mio Cid*. There is nothing intrinsically strange in this, after all David *was* a hero, but when both San Millán and Santo Domingo are referred to repeatedly as 'en buen ora nado' 'born at a fortunate hour' (an epithet which had constantly been applied to Rodrigo), or when Santo Domingo is described as 'Su escapula cinta, el adalil caboso', the saint's scapulary as Brian Dutton[41] pointed out, is clearly being envisaged as his spiritual sword, and 'adalil caboso' is an epithet, 'heroic leader', very specifically belonging to the secular military epic. At times the use of expressions in new theological senses is delightfully witty. Thus bread in the well-established formula 'los que comen el tu pan' (these who eat your bread), with its secular military associations of heroic companionship (see above), has obvious sacramental associations when Santo Domingo prays to 'Padre de muchos que comen el tu pan'. At other times one must admit that these secular elements in *clerecía* poems can seem inept, and remind one of nothing so much as of the insecure modern churchman who insists at all costs on working the latest piece of trendy jargon into his theology.

A new understanding of the *mester de clerecía* has been possible only in recent years and in the light of the fundamental researches of Dutton. At last criticism can escape from the sterile round of commonplaces about learned sources, clerical inspiration, and, the ingenuousness of Berceo. Dutton has established a tight nexus of economic motivation for this poet's religious versification. It is worthwhile considering in outline the case made out concerning Berceo, if only for its possible light on the sort of motives which may have come into play in the case of secular poetry, for, to summarize baldly, Berceo wrote his poems to back up his monastery's claims to various dues and privileges and to encourage pilgrimages to it as a cult centre, producing them as vernacular analogues to the forged Latin instruments which also appeared at about that time. In this instance we can put names and dates to a process of rewriting history for the benefit of a certain sectional interest which seems to be one of the functions of the epic in general.

The location of the monastery of San Millán (Emilianus) de la Cogolla falls within the ambit of epic locations in Spain: it is in Rioja, north-east of Burgos. Emilianus the hermit, supposed to have been the founder, died in A.D. 574, but we only have documents showing a monastery functioning on the site for the tenth century, although there is no reason to doubt that there was some religious house there earlier. It grew and prospered until, at the end of the twelfth century, donations, etc. fell away, probably because of the existence of a number of rival centres at that time. Between the years 1210 and 1250 (as Dutton[42] has shown), a number of Latin documents were falsified, some of them providing favourable evidence for use in lawsuits conducted by the monastery with regard to property, titles, etc. (as for example when in 1228 the Bishop of Calahorra attempted unsuccessfully to exact episcopal dues from churches dependent on the monastery), but probably the most important forgery from the point of view of the profit of the monastery, and without any doubt the most important forgery for its repercussions in the field of epic poetry, was that which purported to give evidence that the great Castilian hero already mentioned, count Fernán González in 934 established the right of the monastery to collect an annual due from all towns in Castile and Navarre, the so-called *Votos de Fernán González*. Laying claim to *votos* of ancient date was an activity not unknown at this date and indeed much later. The epic *Poema de Fernán González* represents a rival claim on behalf of the monastery of Arlanza to these same *votos*. (To the best of my knowledge the last forgeries aimed at backing up claims to *votos* were the fabrication not of medieval deeds but of pseudo-scriptures, an account of the Second Council of Jerusalem, etc., to reinforce the claims of the distant primacy of Santiago de Compostela over the cathedral church of Granada in the 1590s.) As will be seen in the analysis of the *Vida de San Millán*, the statement of the claim to *votos* is an important element from the outset.

Our ability to establish in this way the existence of a clear economic strand in the creation of Berceo's poem (and I do not wish to suggest it was the only strand, that devotion was absent, or that it is impossible that Berceo could have believed that he was restating the essential truth) helps us to understand the sort of formative factors which may lie behind the *Poema de Mio Cid* and primitive Spanish epic, for the Cid epic contains copious mention of the gifts bestowed by the hero on the monastery of San Pedro de Cardeña. P. E. Russell[43] has described how relics of the Cid were installed in the church there, and how they were objects of pilgrimage. The nexus of material and economic interest may not have been as elaborate as in the case of the *clerecía* poems, but it is impossible to deny that it was present. A. D. Deyermond in his fundamental study of the late epic the *Mocedades de Rodrigo*[44] shows that that poem represents propaganda for the diocese of Palencia.

In suggesting that the epic poems of the *mester de juglaría* and of the *mester de clerecía* have as much to bind them together in style and in motivation as to distinguish them in metrical form, nothing has been said of the *romance*. This is to be related to the *juglaría* poems in form and largely in content. In form it consists of lines of sixteen syllables the last two of which bear assonance. There is a medial caesura so strong that in fact it is the normal typographical practice to print each hemistich as a separate 'line'. Such an octosyllabic unit is very close to that of the poems of the *mester de juglaría*, but there is this important distinction: the syllable count is strict and regular. As for the length, it is not fixed, and normally ranges from a dozen lines or so to several score (the assonance usually remaining constant throughout any given poem). Whether as a consequence of the limitations of length or as a cause is not clear, but there is a difference of perspective between the long epics and these ballads. There is no presentation of events in detail, instead there is a tendency to concentrate on the most telling episodes, with at times abrupt leaps from one stage to another of an adventure. The listener's historical knowledge or imagination must bridge the gaps.

In content there is a wide range of material. Most of the epic 'cycles' are represented: there are poems on Carolingian themes, on Bernardo de Carpio, the Cid, the Seven Young Lords of Salas etc. There are also poems which appear to arise out of contemporary events. The bloody civil strife of the fourteenth and fifteenth centuries and the constant theme of border warfare with the Moorish kingdom of Granada provided heroic subject-matter in plenty. Ancient poems of a hagiographical nature do not occur. What is not clear is the social function which underlay the creation of the early *romances* in the fourteenth century. By the fifteenth century some patronage for the performers and creators of romances was available at court. *Romances* were composed by court musicians for performance there soon after the historical events to which they allude. This can be established because, of course, court transactions are more likely to be recorded and survive: payments to musicians appear in surviving account books, whereas gifts in kind to itinerant performers were forgotten the week they were made. We can only say that the body of *romances* does not give the impression of being in the main the creation of court circles in the fifteenth century. Some ancient poems are undoubtedly the result of a process of disintegration of the longer ancient epics. Whether such fragmentary ballads, or the historical *romances* (of which some can be traced back to the first half of the fourteenth century) are older in date, it is difficult to determine.

Specimen Works

The Poema de Mio Cid

This poem survived virtually complete, only the outer leaf (or leaves) of the unique manuscript is missing. The surviving text begins *in medias res*, in a way

L

which could hardly be improved, describing the hero, Rodrigo de Bivar, weeping bitterly (no unheroic action in this tradition) as he left his Castilian home for exile incurred because of the wrath (*ira*) of his King, Alfonso VI.

In his edition of the *Poema* Menéndez Pidal judged that introductory material should be provided from the prose chronicles to tell how the Cid had just completed a mission in which, in order to collect on the King's behalf tribute payments from the semi-independent Moorish King of Seville, he was obliged to deal harshly with certain Christian freebooters who were harrying the lands of this King. The leader of the freebooters was one Garci Ordóñez, a most powerful man in the court of Alfonso VI, head of a clan known as the Bani Gómez. This information is certainly necessary to understand one aspect of the plot, the family feud between Rodrigo and the Bani Gómez, but one might equally say that it is also necessary, in order to appreciate the subtleties of the relationship between Rodrigo and his King, to know that Rodrigo had at an earlier stage in his life been official champion of the realm of Castile when, under Alfonso VI's brother, Sancho II, it had been independent of Alfonso, then King of León. When, during the siege of Zamora, Sancho died at the hands of Vellido Dolfos there were rumours that Alfonso had in some way been implicated in plotting to secure the death of his own brother (so that he could inherit his kingdom). After standing out for a long time, Rodrigo did eventually give his oath of allegiance to Alfonso, but only on a condition: that Alfonso should swear an oath at a well-known centre for oath-taking (the church of Santa Gadea) in which he stated explicitly that he had no part in the death of his brother.

Obviously such an action was not likely to endear Rodrigo to Alfonso. Alfonso had had a great indignity inflicted on him, and was hence predisposed to listen to the tales that slanderers (*mestureros*) might bear. Such slanderous accusations of failure to give proper military service to the King led to the explusion with which our manuscript opens. The tension between the King and the hero is felt throughout the poem. There is an ambiguity about the characterization of Rodrigo which was no doubt particularly attractive within the society of the twelfth century: he is depicted as a paragon of loyalty to the social hierarchy and he is at the same time rising independently thanks entirely to his personal qualities. Operating completely outside the established system, he is so successful that the hierarchy eventually has to acknowledge him.

There is an immensely important myth at work here: that of the outlaw fundamentally more deeply loyal to the underlying principles of society which expels him than are the powers-that-be in that society (compare the myth of Robin Hood). It is a myth which permits social regeneration.

The text of the *Poema*, as it has survived, opens when, driven into exile, the Cid is loyally supported by his vassals (who in fact no longer had *legal* obligations to him). The poem tells of his successful stratagems in border warfare amongst the Muslim villages of what we would now call New Castile and across into the basin of the Ebro. He successfully levies tribute and 'earns the bread' of his troops. He is astute and, where necessary, fiercely brave in combat, but, once victory was won, merciful and always ready to spare the lives of Moorish captives. In one fortified village for example, Castejón, which he decided not to hold, he intentionally refrained from destroying the fortification and, before he left, allowed a garrison of a hundred Moors to take over. We are very far indeed from an atmosphere of brutalized crusading such as we find in the *Chanson de Roland*. The description of the warfare is realistic. Numbers engaged are in all cases within the bounds of possibility. Divine intervention is absent.

Humorous interludes are provided: at the outset, finance is raised for the expedition by a variation on the gold-bar trick; chests filled with sand instead of treasure are pledged as security on a cash loan provided by two Jewish money-lenders. At the end of the first *cantar* of the three into which the poem is divided, fun is made of the Count of Barcelona who was captured when taking the field to protect his Moorish tributaries. The Count, depicted as a fop with over-nice table manners, is humiliated by being forced to accept the invaders' hospitality before he is released. These comic interludes pander to Castilian group prejudices against Jews and against Catalans, prejudices which persisted long after the date of the poem.

The continued military success of the Cid brought him down from the frontier villages on the headwaters of the Ebro and into the rich lands of the Mediterranean coastal plain. It seems contradictory at first sight that whereas in the first *cantar* the advance is narrated in minute detail, village by village — Medinaceli, Ariza, Cetina, Alhama, Bubierca, Ateca, Terrer, Calatayud — in the second the advance is sketched in broad strokes, and the major victory of the Cid's career, the long siege and eventual capture of the immensely rich city of Valencia (certainly richer many times over than any town in the Christian part of the peninsula) is accorded only a few (undeniably effective) lines. The poem is undergoing a change of focus. Narrative tension is never relaxed. We never come to take the Cid's victories for granted as we do in those tiresome epic poems in which the hero enjoys infallible divine assistance, but our attention is directed principally towards the relationship between Rodrigo and Alfonso, to whom Rodrigo continues to profess unswerving loyalty. In a rising crescendo of gifts of booty from the battlefields, the quarrel is patched up, and the peace is sealed by a plan approved by the King, and loyally if reluctantly accepted by Rodrigo, to marry off the Cid's two daughters, Elvira and Sol, to two young scions of the powerful clan led by that Garci Ordóñez whom Rodrigo had humiliated at Cabra (the King, presumably, hoping to settle a feud which divided the most powerful groups of vassals of his realm).

The third *cantar* opens with the third and last comic passage of the poem, in which these young lords, the Infantes de Carrión, disgrace themselves by their comic terror when a menagerie lion gets loose in the court (in contrast the Cid's own men stood firm, and the Cid — when he woke up — simply led the beast back to its cage in a splendid demonstration of his force of will), but its focus shifts yet again, once again ensuring that our attention does not flag.

On the military plane the Cid has had to face an enemy quite different from any he has encountered on the frontier: the hosts of North Africa, with fifty-thousand tents in the army's camp. The drum-music, obviously quite unfamiliar to the Spaniards, terrifies the Cid's womenfolk. These fearsome invaders are the Almorávides, Moorish Puritanical fanatics called in by the hard-pressed Spanish Arabs when they found themselves unable to withstand the Christian advance. The circumstances of the battles described in the poem are not, in all probability, in exact accord with what is known of the historical battles, but there must be a close relationship between the events described and the sort of encounter which took place between the Cid and the powerful armies from across the seas. Numbers are large, but not beyond the bounds of verisimilitude. Even at this stage in the poem there is no suspicion of the degree of exaggeration which sometimes characterizes near-contemporary narrative in France.

The outcome of the fighting is even more booty for the Cid, and a resounding victory.

What the Cid does not realize is that in the battle his sons-in-law once again make themselves the laughing-stock of the whole army because of their cowardice.

From this point onwards we are no longer concerned with the Cid and his battles against the Moors. The poem now turns on the relationship between the Cid and his King, and on the Cid's vindication of his family honour after it suffers a brutal attack by his sons-in-law. These young men are presumably unable to continue at court after making such a public display of their cowardice, although we are not told as much. They decide to go back home to Carrión from Valencia, taking their wives and their newly-won booty with them. On the road, in the isolated oak grove of Corpes, they first make love to the Cid's daughters, then strip and thrash them, leaving them for dead to the mercy of the wild beasts of the forest.

The shock of the brutal assault under these conditions is conveyed with great power: the double contrast between the idyllic pastoral setting, the unnatural sadism (no other word is adequate) of the young husbands, and the natural threat of the wild creatures of the forest prowling round.

The *infantes* continue on their way home to Carrión, where the Cid can only reach them to secure redress through the royal courts. The ancient institution of trial by battle means that the legal proceedings are full of physical thrills too, but we are forced to admire the astute as well as dignified way in which the hero conducts his case. Of course, the outcome of a man-to-man combat between him and any individual opponent would be so predictable that all suspense and tension would have been lost, but it is not the Cid who fights — he cannot relax his personal vigilant watch over Valencia, and sends proxies to represent him. The Cid is completely successful in these legal battles. His family's honour is entirely vindicated. The young lords of Carrión are disgraced. The Cid, who had begun the poem as a man sent out into dishonourable exile, ends it, having won his way back into the King's good grace, and having demonstrated in a court of law his superiority over the group which had originally slandered him. Finally he sees his daughters sought in marriage by the royal houses of Navarre and Aragon. There is a pleasing symmetry in the conclusion:

> Oy los reyes d'España sus parientes son.[45]

(Nowadays the Kings of Spain are related to him.)

Poema de Fernán González

Behind this *clerical* epic almost certainly there lies a juglaresque poem, but it is lost (although material from it may survive in chronicle). The clerical poem contains a chronological introduction which smacks of bookish world-histories. There are obvious clerical features, but the core of the narration is ancient Castilian legend. Fernán González, Count of Castile, fights hard to protect his tiny country. He kills Sancho, King of Navarre, in battle. At an assembly (*cortes*) convoked in León by King Sancho Ordóñez (Fernán's suzerain) Fernán sells his hawk and his horse, as described above, with the price increasing 'al gallarín doblado' (i.e. at an interest rate of 100 per cent) if it should not be paid promptly.

The intrigue on which the central argument of the poem is based is in essence that on which Corneille's dramatic version of the Cid legend relies: the hero's love for the daughter of a man he has killed. In this case the girl is Sancha, daughter of Sancho of Navarre. Sancha's love transcending blood ties, she helps Fernán in a number of adversities (treacherously lured into a trap, Fernán is imprisoned by the new King of Navarre, for example, but Sancha helps him to escape, and flees with him).

By the end of the poem, after Fernán's success in war, notably against his Christian neighbours, but also against the Moors of Cordova, he lays claim to the proceeds of his sale made to the King of León, and León, lacking the resources to pay, has to concede to Castile its liberty.

La vida de San Millán

This is a work of hagiography by a known poet, Gonzalo de Berceo, and we are in no doubt that Berceo was basing his vernacular composition on a life of Saint Emilianus in Latin by Braulio, on other works by the same writer, and on Latin archive material available to Berceo. The poem is thus ecclesiastical and 'learned'. Berceo speaks of 'reading' the poem in his very first verse (though, of course, reading could imply recitation without the actual presence of a written text). Aspects of the life of the saint are couched in military terminology more suitable to heroic epic. For instance, 'sin [(or the Devil)] waged war in him [the saint] in many guises, but by whatsoever path he advanced, he held the frontier against it'. (53) St Emilianus is described as 'sancto cavallero' (56) and the following text, which refers to his wanderings, fleeing from human company, and his emerging at last from the wilderness, is in words all of which are used in the *Poema de Mio Cid* of the military movements of the epic hero:

> Decir non vos podriemos   todas sues trasnochadas
> sin todos los logares   en qi tovo posadas
> destajarvos qeremos   de las fuertes andadas
> sacarlo de los yermos   a las tierras pobladas.[46]

> I could not narrate all the night marches
> nor all the places where he pitched camp.
> I will bring the journeying to an end
> and bring him out from the wastes into inhabited lands.

The epic tradition is clearly very much alive in such works.

This poem is wrongly named in that only the first of its three divisions is concerned with the events of the saint's *life*. The second part deals with the miracles worked by the saint. The miracles are *fazannas* (daring deeds), using the same word as is used of the deeds of the chivalric hero. The epic flavour of the third part is even more strongly marked, for it contains an account of how Castile under Fernán González came to attribute in perpetuity certain dues (*votos*) to the religious foundations of the saint, just as León attributed dues to the shrine of Saint James at Santiago de Compostela. This gives the religious poet the chance to narrate the story of how the Moorish King Abderraman exacted an annual tribute from the Christians of three score maidens, and how King Ramiro of León and Count Fernán González of Castile made their respective vows, and, in battle, with the divine intervention of Santiago, conquered and so put an end to their shameful servitude.

The *mester de clerecía* style had only a limited life in the thirteenth and early fourteenth centuries. One of the last examples of it must have been the Muslim *Poema de Yuçuf*,[47] telling the Quranic story of Joseph. This has been dated as the fourteenth and even thirteenth century, but it comes down to us in *aljamiado* manuscripts of the sixteenth. The Moriscos were more faithful to the style than were the Christians.

Amongst the Christians the epic style lived on only in the form of the relatively short *romance*.

When scholars of the Romantic period first focused their attention on the Spanish *romances*, it seemed to them that they had before them specimens of those *cantilenae*, those 'lays', which, so nineteenth-century literary theory told them, predated the formation of long epics. The findings of Spanish scholarship are quite different. It is true that some *romances* sprang, like the theoretical *cantilenae*, direct from the celebrating of a heroic deed. We have documented cases of this happening in the course of the warfare on the border of Granada. But many ancient *romances* are the product of the decay and dismemberment of long epics. When these long epics ceased to be performed, whether from lack of noble patronage or whatever reason, the most striking incidents may have continued to be recited, and were preserved in the memory of the people. They were not the product of free improvisation, as they had been when still embedded in the long primitive epics, nor were they fixed, as were the poems in *cuaderna vía*, but were 'alive in their variants', as Menéndez Pidal has said.

The story of the recovery of the remains of the Spanish *romance* (ballad) tradition by Menéndez Pidal, when it was thought by the urban intelligentsia of Spain that it was long since dead, is a remarkable and exciting chapter of Spanish scholarship. As we have seen, the diffusion of these last relics of the epic tradition in all parts of the Hispanic world, including the Americas and even the Jewish communities of North Africa and elsewhere, has been very carefully studied.[48] There is a coming and going between the ancient popular tradition (transmitting lays of Charlemagne, of the Young Lords of Salas and many others), the work of cultivated poets and the journalistic songs sung by blind minstrels at fairs. The form is sufficiently alive for the greatest poets of recent years, Antonio Machado and Federico García Lorca, each in very different ways to have made it serve his purposes.

An almost inevitable consequence of its brevity is its allusiveness and fragmentary nature. Far from being a defect, this is often a positive virtue. The *romance* preserves in serene octosyllabic hemistichs the most memorable, the unforgettable quintessential moment of an adventure. Of the many ballads which gain aesthetically from their haunting incompleteness, one could perhaps single out above all the well-known Ballad of Count Arnaldos (*romance del conde Arnaldos*):[49]

> Would that I might have such an adventure on the waters of the sea
> As there befel to Count Arnaldos, upon Saint John's morning!
> With his hawk on his wrist he set out to hunt,
> and saw a galley coming, making for the land.
> Its sails were of silk, its rigging of fine yarn,
> The sailor at the helm was singing a song
> Which becalmed the sea and lulled the winds,
> It brought the fishes in the deep swimming up to the surface;
> The birds flying in the air settled down on the mast.

Then up spoke Count Arnaldos — you will hear his very words —
I only teach my song to him who comes with me.

The cultivation of the *romance* by itinerant (often blind) professional singers (and sellers of broadsheets) certainly continued into modern times. If the practice is not now dead it must be very close to extinction. The Spanish epic tradition[50] has survived for eight hundred years.

NOTES

1. Jules Horrent, *Roncesvalles, étude sur le fragment de cantar de gesta conservé à l'Archivo de Navarra* (Pampelune) (Paris, 1951).

2. Accademia Nazionale dei Lincei, CCCLXVII, 1970, quaderno 139, *Atti del convegno internazionale sul tema: la poesia epica e la sua formazione (Roma, 1969)*, Rome, 1970. For Riquer's paper see pp. 181–91.

3. Stanza 171 of *Poema de Fernán González*, edited by R. Menéndez Pidal in *Reliquias de la poesía épica española*, pp. 34–153. See also the edition of A. Zamora Vicente, Madrid, 1954. Translation: Castile was then a tiny corner, / Montedoca was the boundary for Castilians, / and the other extreme was Fitera, / Moors at that time held Carraça.

4. *Cantar de Mio Cid*. edited by R. Menéndez Pidal, 3rd edn, 3 vols (Madrid, 1954), has long been the standard edition. It includes an excellent palaeographical edition as well as a critical edition which in the opinion of some (myself included) is too ready to reconstruct and to regularize. A cheaper one-volume edition has the title *Poema de Mio Cid*. The epic is now best studied in *Poema de Mio Cid*, edited by Ian Michael (Madrid, 1976) (see pp. 66–67 of Michael for a survey of editions).

5. Both Michael (in his edition, see note 4) and Colin Smith (in his edition, Oxford, 1972) present fully the arguments in favour of a later dating in the early thirteenth century. See these works for the by now copious bibliography on this topic.

6. For the history of this period see R. Menéndez Pidal, *La España del Cid*, 5th edition (Madrid, 1956).

7. For the Visigoths in Spain, see E. A. Thompson, *The Goths in Spain* (Oxford, 1969).

8. Jordanes, *De origine actibusque Getarum* in *Monumenta Germaniae Historica*, auctores antiqui, Vol. 5, 1 (1882), 53–138.

9. Edited by A. E. Anspach, in *Rheinisches Museum für Philologie*, 67 (1912); here see p. 557.

10. Ed. cit. in note 3 above, lines 569–74.

11. The passage is ambiguous, and may refer to peoples other than the Goths; see N. Wagner, *Getica, Untersuchungen zum Leben des Jordanes und zur frühen Geschichte der Goten* (Berlin, 1967), especially pp. 60–102 and L. P. Harvey, 'Fernán González's horse' in *Medieval Hispanic Studies presented to Rita Hamilton* (London, 1976), pp. 77–86.

12. *Crónica najarense*, ed. A. Ubieto Arteta (Valencia, 1966), 90.

13. Ed. cit., stanza 582.

14. *Primera crónica general*, edited by R. Menéndez Pidal (Madrid, 1955), see vol. II, p. 422.

15. Even the *Getica* itself, or some text derived from it, in which case the two occurrences of the legend would cease to be significant.

16. For a discussion of this passage, see R. Menéndez Pidal, *En torno al Poema de Mio Cid* (Barcelona, 1964), pp. 179–86.

17. The *Carmen Campidoctoris* was edited by Menéndez Pidal in *La España del Cid* (see note 6 above), pp. 880–84.

18. See especially, E. P. Colbert, *The martyrs of Córdoba, a study of the sources* (Washington D.C., 1962).

19. They have not been lacking altogether. See B. Heller, *Die Bedeutung des Antarromans für vergleichende Literaturgeschichte* (Leipzig, 1931) and A. Abel, 'Formation et constitution du roman d'Antar' in *La poesia epica e la sua formazione* (see note 2, above), pp. 717–33.

20. London, 1836, but I refer to the Everyman edition, p. 398.

21. Albert Lord, *The Singer of Tales*, Harvard Studies in Comparative Literature, 24 (Cambridge, Massachusetts, 1960). See also Milman Parry and Albert Lord, *Serbocroatian Heroic Songs* (Cambridge, Massachusetts and Belgrade, 1954).

22. A. Galmés de Fuentes, 'Épica árabe y épica castellana' in *La poesia epica e la sua formazione* (see note 2, above), pp. 197–259.

23. Juan Ruiz, *Libro de Buen Amor*, edited by G. Chiarini (Milan and Naples, 1964), Verses 1228–34 and 1513–17.

24. Ed. cit., supra note 14.

25. 'Épica andaluza romanceada' in *Dissertaciones y opúsculos* (Madrid, 1928), I, pp. 93–150.

26. S. M. Stern, in his Oxford doctoral thesis (1951) entitled 'The Old Andalusian *Muwashshaḥ*', edited by me in an abridged form in a volume of Stern's writings, *Hispano-Arabic Strophic Poetry* (Oxford, 1974), pp. 64–65.

27. In an unpublished Madrid doctoral dissertation. I owe the reference to F. Marcos Marín (see note 29 below, p. 39 of the Montreal, 1970 edition).

28. Ed. Cairo, 1944, Vol. IV, pp. 501–72.

29. Ed. Madrid, 1971; a shorter form of the work had appeared in Montreal, 1970, with the title *Elementos árabes en los orígenes de la épica hispánica*. See especially p. 156 of the Madrid edition.

30. See note 22, above.

31. *Poema de Mio Cid*, lines 1289–95.

32. E. De Chasca, *El arte juglaresco en el Cantar de Mio Cid* (Madrid, 1967), develops an oral-formulaic appreciation of the work, and for an up-to-date survey from this point of view see K. T. Adams, 'The Yugoslav model and the Text of the *Poema de Mio Cid*' in *Medieval Studies presented to Rita Hamilton* (London, 1976), pp. 1–10. Other recent publications, especially by British Hispanists, show a shift of opinion towards a more individualist interpretation. This is particularly clear in Colin Smith's edition of the text, Oxford, 1972, and in Smith's numerous articles. He seeks to identify an individual creator (a lawyer, able to refer to written sources, even with echoes of learned historical models such as Sallust). Smith recognizes that formulaic elements are present in the work, but regards them as inherited stylistic features of the genre; in this Smith does not differ in essentials from A. D. Deyermond, *A Literary History of Spain: the Middle Ages* (London, 1971), see especially pp. 47–49 for a succinct discussion of the state of studies on this problem. In his 1976 edition, Ian Michael appears to follow Smith in his attempts to secure a clear personal profile of an author (ed. cit., pp. 51–52). My own position is therefore a minority one.

33. The fragment may well antedate the *Poema de Mio Cid*. It has frequently been edited: see D. Gifford and F. Hodcroft, *Textos lingüísticos del medioevo español* (Oxford, 1959), pp. 37–42.

34. Palaeographic edition in A. D. Deyermond, *Epic poetry and the clergy. Studies in the Mocedades de Rodrigo* (London, 1968), pp. 221–77.

35. *El libro de Alexandre*, edited by R. S. Willis, Jr, Elliott Monographs, 32 (Paris/Princeton, 1934), pp. 2–3.

36. See R. A. Hall, 'Old Spanish stress-timed verse and Germanic superstratum', *Romance Philology*, 19 (1965–66), 227–34. The problem is discussed by A. Deyermond in his *Epic Poetry and the Clergy* (London, 1969), pp. 56–58. See also K. T. Adams, 'The metrical irregularity of the *Cantar de Mio Cid*, a restatement...', *Bulletin of Hispanic Studies*, 69 (1972), 109–19.

37. *Cantar de Mio Cid*, ed. cit., pp. 90–91.

38. 'The metrical irregularity of the *Cantar de Mio Cid*', *Bulletin of Hispanic Studies*, 60 (1963), 137–43.

39. See note 35 above.

40. *Vida de Santo Domingo de Silos*, edited by A. Andrés (Madrid, 1958), stanza 701 ab.

41. This with many other examples of *a lo divino* use of epithets is discussed by B. Dutton in his *La 'Vida de San Millán de la Cogolla' de Gonzalo de Berceo* (London, 1976), especially p. 178.

42. Op. cit., especially pp. 185–93 and 237.

43. P. E. Russell, 'San Pedro de Cardeña and the Heroic History of the Cid', *Medium Aevum*, 27 (1958), 57–79.

44. See note 34, above.

45. *Cantar de Mio Cid*, ed. cit., line 3724.

46. *Vida de San Millán* (see note 41 above), stanza 68.

47. Edited by R. Menéndez Pidal, second edition (Granada, 1952).

48. As in so many other fields, much of the spade work was done by R. Menéndez Pidal, who published a Catálogo del romancero judío-español in 1906, reproduced in *Los romances de América y otros estudios*, sixth edition (Madrid, 1958). S. G. Armistead and J. H. Silverman, in their article 'Para un gran romancero sefardí', published in *Actas del Primer Simposio de Estudios Sefardíes*, edited by I. M. Hassán (Madrid, 1970), pp. 281–94, refer to much of the recent bibliography. See also in the same volume the bibliography cited on p. 295 by Moshe Attías.

49. *Cancionero de romances* (Antwerp, n.d.), f. 193 r.

50. Professor A. D. Deyermond of Westfield College, and Dr David Hook of my own College, have been kind enough to read drafts of this chapter, and to make useful suggestions. They are in no way responsible for any of my shortcomings.

A panel of the Sutton Hoo Helmet
(restored)

MEDIEVAL GERMAN

By A. T. HATTO

THE CORPUS OF HEROIC POETRY in medieval German embraces very disparate material: the *Hildebrandslied* — a late Germanic heroic lay from the Lango-bardic of Northern Italy on an international theme (composed *c.* A.D. 650, incomplete text *c.*800); the *Nibelungenlied* — a full-scale heroic epic from within the courtly culture of *c.*1200 in an originally lyric metre; *Kudrun* — an heroic epic conceived as some sort of response to the spirit of the *Nibelungenlied* and ending not in catastrophe but in conciliation in accordance with the needs of its own generation, of less poetic worth than the *Nibelungenlied* yet of good quality (*c.*1240); and a few poems with heroes and plots inherited directly or cyclically from the Heroic Age and informed in some measure by the heroic outlook, for example the fragmentary *Wolfdietrich A* (*præ* 1250) and the *Raben-schlacht* (end of the thirteenth century).

The question of genre is thus a baffling one. It has been firmly handled only in our own day, when it has come to be realized that ancient names do not of themselves make ancient heroes, that shattering victories and rivers of blood are not in themselves expressive of heroic ethos, and that scholars' piety towards a national heritage has no power to raise its aesthetic or moral value or to recover vanished masterpieces.[1]

The *Hildebrandslied* sits fair and square within the genre of the Germanic heroic lay, however late its style. As to the Middle High German poems, the only criterion apt to our purpose is that of ethos. For in *Biterolf* (1250–1300) such illustrious names as 'Etzel' (Attila), 'Hagen', and 'Walther' are the sole elements, not excluding style, diction, metre, content and ethos, that are not sub-chivalric; but there are gradations from this to the few undoubted heroic poems. Contemporary critics are not followed here in detail in their honest struggle to establish genres, chiefly because most of the specimens, as products of the literary sub-culture post 1250, are not worth bothering one's head about, although one may agree that heroes with ancient names tend to have comrades representing the old comitatus (whatever nonsense they may be engaged in) and to this extent differ from sub-chivalric heroes. There is also a tendency for actions associated with ancient names to be told in strophic form, first in the Nibelung-strophe (since *c.*1160), then in lengthened versions (e.g. *Kudrun*; *Walther*) or in an apparently amplified structure (*Jüngeres Hildebrandslied*), but also in other strophic structures (e.g. *Rabenschlacht*, short sextets). But as was seen, the correlation is not absolute, nor are such strophes a bulwark against inundation from the sub-culture. Ethos, then, must be the decisive criterion here.

The ethos of the truly 'heroic' epic poems of medieval Germany was an inheritance from the Heroic Age (Age of Migrations) through both poetry and the feudal ethos, which had absorbed and transformed the earlier ethos.

Medieval German heroic epic cannot be discussed in the round without reference to the genre of the ancient Germanic heroic lay. Accordingly, a brief characterization of this genre is given here.

The Germanic heroic lay can be said to have been a terse, self-contained, objective, memorized poem of epic-dramatic style imbued with an heroic ethos conveyed with art in a single-stranded plot. The action marched from crisis to crisis, taking lighter matters in its stride. Peaks of action commonly erupted in bursts of tense dialogue in which words had the status of deeds. Heroic lays expressed the outlook of chieftains and the picked warriors of their comitatus. Their function was to recall the mutual obligations of lords and retainers and to flesh them for battle, whenever it might come. Bards were members of the élite for and before whom they performed, so that the whole phenomenon was a manifestation of aristocratic spirit. The mood of heroic lays is said to have been optimistic only in as far as it asserted the possibility of heroism. Typical plots show how men destined to lose go down fighting against odds, often in narrow places and sometimes, quintessentially, in a burning hall.

The metre of the heroic lay was basically a four-bar line in 4/4 time, divided at the middle by a caesura, yet tightly gripped by alliteration at the strong points heading the first three bars, with alliteration in the third bar obligatory. If the 'original' style was stichic, later historical specimens developed a variety of styles, with for example enjambement reaching as far as the caesura of the next or even later verses, or with looser or tighter bundling of verses. Historical specimens clearly show that poets sought *le mot juste* from among a 'treasure' of formulae whose underlying patterns could generate new variants beside the old. Poets sought *les mots justes* in order to perpetuate them in the memorized art-poems that were heroic lays. But the underlying formulaic elements strongly suggest that this highly artistic tradition grew from an established tradition of improvisation. As to performance, 'singing' to the harp is assured among the Goths for heroic eulogy by a passage in the historian Jordanes (v, 43) though not for the heroic lay. The evidence of *Beowulf* for Old English goes no farther than to certify that scops both played the harp and sang heroic lays (such as that of Finn): but it is inadmissible to state by simple addition that scops 'sang heroic lays to their own accompaniment on the harp', though they may well have done so despite the prime association of the harp (*hearpe*) with merry-making (cf. its kennings *gomenwudu* = *gléobéam* = lit. 'merry-making-wood').* In the North, recitation of heroic lays seems assured.

---

* Alcuin's '*ibi decet lectorem audiri, non citharistam; sermones patrum, non carmina gentilium. quid Hinieldus cum Christo?*' is equally elusive.

The time of the earliest inferred lays falls into a period when the Germani still had only Runic script confined to epigraphic and magical use. These earliest lays are attributable to the last quarter of the fourth century A.D. and are assigned to regions as far apart as Angel in Schleswig-Holstein, the ancestral seat of the Angles, and the then Gothic territories north of the Black Sea. Postulation of an Anglian Lay of Offa is more open to question than acceptance of a Gothic Lay of Ermanrik: but if it holds, the spatial interval argues for an already well-established genre. Of available specimens there are the almost complete Langobardic Lay of Hildebrand in a Bavarianized and then lightly Old Saxonized version (composed c.650, recorded c.800); the Old English Finnesburh Fragment of uncertain date (printed by George Hickes in 1705 from a parchment that was lost by the end of the seventeenth century but which is attributed to the eleventh century); a dozen or so lays in Old Icelandic in the mid-thirteenth-century Codex Regius of the Edda, together with a few other 'Eddica', the earliest attributed to the ninth century. Analysis of these last, namely *Hamdismál*, *Atlakviða*, and the fragmentary Battle of the Goths and the Huns embedded in the *Hervararsaga*, has shown that they form a bridge in style, diction and content between the Continental and later Norse traditions and indeed derive from the former. The Lays of Hildebrand and of Finnesburh are assuredly terse and dramatic: but even the most archaic Norse lays show strong tendencies towards an even more elliptic, balladesque style, in which lyrical elements, too, were to come much to the fore.

It remains to be said of the Germanic heroic lay that although for the most part historical events are discernible as having launched them, they soon take off into their own sphere of pure poetry and so could never be confused with historical poetry. Ethnic groups become individualized through their leaders and heroes; these ally themselves or clash with one another in a heroic time-continuum that often defies historical chronology; and they do so for private, mostly family, reasons.

The only surviving specimen of the heroic lay in German is the *Hildebrandslied*, the inter-tribal dissemination of which from Northern Italy to Iceland is highly representative of the genre. The plot (A 'good' father slays his 'good' son in a duel) is international, with other, more archaic, examples occurring in Old Irish, Medieval Persian and Modern Russian;[2] the cyclic legendary matter — 'Theodoric's Exile' — in which it is embedded is Ostrogothic; the actual lay was composed in Langobardic; the (incomplete) text, probably written in Fulda, was copied from a Bavarian version and has an unconvincing coating of Old (i.e. Continental) Saxon; continuing its northerly transmission, a version is discernible in Old Icelandic. On German soil, the outlines of a thirteenth-century chivalric version can be reconstructed on the basis of post-chivalric manuscripts and prints, which introduce a bathetic happy end.

It would be tempting to illustrate this unique specimen with a translation, but there is as yet insufficient agreement among scholars to warrant one in the present work. Yet the main outlines are clear.

After claiming a hearing, the bard tells us in his second verse that champions have met, one to one. Already in the next verse he names them as Hiltibrant and Hadubrant, names which, although they may never have been paired in poetry before, were so structured as inevitably to have sent a shudder through the first audience, since they imply blood-kinship. Again, in the very next verse, the poet tells us that these champions are father and son — the tightest unit in Germanic life and law — and that they stand between two armies. There is the possibility of tragedy here: and heroic lays normally end tragically. Will mutual recognition avert disaster? When the two have made their battle-gear ready, Hiltibrant as the senior man asks Hadubrant to identify himself within his kindred. Hadubrant readily complies and takes the shortest path by naming his famous father Hiltibrant, who, long ago, had gone away eastwards with Theodoric to escape the malevolence of Otacher (Odoacer). He had left a young wife in the nuptial bower and a babe without an inheritance. Hadubrant fancies his father can no longer be alive. As his source for this information Hadubrant cites 'our people, old and experienced, that are no more'. Hiltibrant foresees how things will end if he cannot establish his identity after an absence of thirty years, and it must be remembered that he must do so without loss of honour 'between two armies'. The severely controlled style of the Germanic heroic lay is magnificently apparent in the manner in which Hiltibrant grasps this nettle. Calling on God in Heaven to witness, he asserts that the man opposite him never had dealings with so nearly related a man, and offers him a torque of gold as a pledge to establish good will, if indeed not full paternal-filial love in the legal sense.[3] Following the visual indications, however, Hadubrant has understandably placed Hiltibrant as a Hunnish warrior and is accordingly on his guard against ruses. After warning Hiltibrant to keep his distance,[4] Hadubrant goes on to insult his antagonist as only having grown to be so old by constantly practising guile. The succession of verses at this point cannot be that of the original and there is probably a lacuna: but Hadubrant makes a clash inevitable by this time categorically asserting that war in the east (Pannonia) carried off his father and that by the evidence of his fine armour his interlocutor was never a warrior in exile from 'this [Ostrogothic] kingdom'. With a mighty groan, Hiltibrant accepts the calamity that is upon them, that either he must slay his son or be slain by him. He rebuts the slurs cast on his long and honourable fighting career and utters his challenge. The warriors proceed from long to short range fighting — the poet's telescoping of time is masterly, his concentration on dialogue at the expense of action has been typical of the genre — when the manuscript breaks off, with no advantage to either. Three independent lines of reasoning — the dynamics of the international plot, later allusions in German and Icelandic literature, but most of all the powerful trend of the torso itself — assure us that the outcome must have been tragic. How the poet broke the deadlock to achieve it is unknowable.

The *Hildebrandslied* unfolds a drama within the souls of two men caught in a tragic web of circumstance interacting with their formed characters, with the audience as a mute chorus apprised from the outset of the truth which the father soon learns but can share with his son only when it is too late. The style, not surprisingly in so late a lay composed on Roman soil, is highly selective of the resources of Germanic poetic diction. The use of *heiti* and kennings, for example, is restrained, as is also that of variation. A striking feature is the use of blank second half-verses as rhetorical pauses.[5]

Between the time of the *Hildebrandslied* and that of the *Nibelungenlied* great changes occurred which tend to be obscured if one dwells on the latter poem, which preserves its ancient ethos and thematic material to a remarkable degree. The Germanic heroic lay as an art form was disrupted from within and without: from within by the dissolution of the comitatus, the bearer of the heroic ethos, in the newly created Christian kingdoms and empires; from without by the victory over the old alliterative measure of assonating couplets in the manner of the Ambrosian hymns, a process completed in Upper Germany by A.D. 900. The success of assonance outside monastery walls will have shattered ancient lays lingering in memory. The lofty, austere tone, conveyed in a weighty metre capable of any rhetorical inflexion, could not survive in the new-fangled, monkish sing-song, the utmost limits of which are reached in the spirited description of the Franks joining battle in the *Ludwigslied*.[6] The old epic vocabulary, with its epithets, formulae, *heiti* and kennings, could not be accommodated in those rhythms of German which chanced to suit the Christian use of Latin.

The great extension of opportunity between the periods of the *Hildebrandslied* and the *Nibelungenlied* was the advent of narrative at book length, at first with sacred subjects, notably the life of Christ, as purveyed by clerics. At the beginning of the last quarter of the twelfth century, following hard on their colleagues in France, German clerical authors were competing for the ear of lay audiences with entertainers who could manage books, the clerics having offered first biblical, then classical narrative such as the *Alexander* lightly moralized, the entertainers on the other hand furnishing secular matter of diverse origins that brought colour, animation, humour (however coarse) and a greater variety of human moods to German poetry. By the time of the *Nibelungenlied*, narrative at book length was well-established also in the sphere of heroic poetry. In general, the most gifted and inspired exponent of book narrative proved to be the dark horse in the race, the *ministerialis*, that is, the clerically educated subservient knight who alone was able to express the outlook of the rising chivalric culture with knowledge, sympathy and enthusiasm.

The *Nibelungenlied* was not the work of a fashionable knight expressing this chivalric culture. Rather was it a magnificent attempt to assimilate an archaic theme to the prevailing culture as far as it would go without destroying it.

The bare plot of the *Nibelungenlied* has a yellowish Merovingian hue.

Having won the amazonian Queen Brunhild for King Gunther in exchange for Gunther's sister Kriemhild, the mighty King Siegfried is murdered by Gunther's vassal Hagen after a quarrel between the Queens; for which Kriemhild, at long last, avenges him.

The poem thus deals in provocation and revenge, and it must be said at once that it was not well-judged by the poet to give the provocation almost as much time as the revenge. The fault is underlined by the use of narrative material of lighter weight to gain length — material much to the liking of younger contemporaries, no doubt, but tending towards incongruity with older matter, or so it seems today.

The *Nibelungenlied* was composed at some time between 1195 and 1205. The poet's name and status are unknown. That he was one of the better sort of settled entertainers with some clerical training, a type that is well documented, is suggested by the general style of presentation and by passages favouring superior minstrels. The patron is to be sought in the old Duchy of Austria, then extending its influence west of the Enns towards the bishop's city of Passau, the authorities of which, perhaps in imitation of ecclesiastical houses in France, seem to have 'taken over' our poet's text. This they appear to have achieved in a new recension, which aligns the *Nibelungenlied* to *Die Klage*, a fabrication in a lighter metre that always follows the epic in complete manuscripts and makes the absurd claim that but for Bishop Pilgrim of Passau (971–91), who has the events recorded in Latin from the survivors of the catastrophe, there would be no poem of the Nibelungs. What we *can* believe is that Passau commanded the scriptoria which could have effected such a take-over.

In terms of his own age the poet of the *Nibelungenlied* aimed at an accommodation of traditional heroic subject-matter with newly-received chivalric notions and with the new fashion of 'biographical' romances, that is, narratives of a leading character's life. The heroic matter that was shaped into the *Nibelungenlied* tended to resist such treatment, and in the event the new courtly and chivalric elements are shattered by the ever more violent eruption of ancient ingredients. It is more generous to the poet to think that he calculated this effect from the outset rather than that his work is a naïve amalgam of two sorts of subject-matter which he was unable to reconcile. Yet, as will be seen, he was capable of naïveté when it came to harmonizing his two main sources, thus no absolute judgement can be based on such criteria. As to the 'biographical' aspect, truly, Kriemhild's awakening to love, and her death on avenging its loss, embrace all other events: but if she is named in one breath, her invincible adversary Hagen must be named in the next. It is on the clash of wills of this pair that the whole action pivots. The fairest thing one can say of a great heroic poet composing while Hartmann von Aue, doyen of Arthurian romance in Germany, was writing his classic *Iwein* is that the no less classic *Nibelungenlied* came at the last possible moment in time, and that if there was a price to pay, the poet paid it.

The *Nibelungenlied* falls into thirty-nine sections later named '*âventiuren*' — '(chivalric) adventures' — but here called 'chapters'. The action is knotted in the Fourteenth Chapter when Kriemhild publicly names Brunhild as Siegfried's concubine (we are left to think in her mistaken belief that this was so); in the Sixteenth, Hagen murders Siegfried with Gunther's assent to avenge the slur on Gunther's and his consort's honour; the 'First Part' (corresponding to a group of sources, former lays) ends with the Eighteenth, when Kriemhild declines to return to Siegfried's land and rear their son; in the Nineteenth, a sort of bridge to the 'Second Part' (which was reared on a now lost epic *Diu Nôt* in the same metre), Kriemhild gains possession of Siegfried's treasure and with it the chance of revenge, but Hagen sinks it in the Rhine; in the Twenty-second, Kriemhild weds the mighty Etzel (Attila); in the Twenty-fourth she invites Gunther and his men to Etzel's land; they arrive in the Twenty-eighth and are attacked at Kriemhild's instigation in the Thirtieth; attack follows attack, and by the end of the Thirty-eighth all of the Burgundians have fallen except Gunther and Hagen; in the Thirty-ninth Gunther and Hagen are delivered bound to Kriemhild; Hagen tricks her into having Gunther killed lest Gunther divulge where Siegfried's treasure lies, after which Kriemhild kills Hagen with her own hands on his refusal to disclose it.

How did the fatal knot come to be tied so firmly so soon?

Siegfried, prince of the Netherlands, having thrown off his gentle nurture somewhere down-Rhine, had appeared at the Burgundian court in Worms with his comitatus like the rudest of barbarians and offered to fight Gunther, win or lose, for their two kingdoms. Burgundian diplomacy, however, had won the day, and Siegfried had soon fallen in love with Kriemhild without ever having seen her and so far as the Burgundians were concerned from that time on was tamed. On report coming from Iceland of a lovely princess who would marry no man but him who could defeat her at her sports, Gunther and Siegfried had struck a bargain — Kriemhild in exchange for Brunhild — following Hagen's assessment that only Siegfried could effect this union. Siegfried, endowed with superhuman strength of the same order as Brunhild's, had defeated her under his cloak of invisibility while Gunther had gone through the motions, and he had repeated this deception on Gunther's nuptial couch in Worms; for, nettled that Siegfried no longer subserved Gunther as he had done in Iceland, Brunhild had resisted Gunther's advances and hung

M

him on the wall. Leaving Brunhild untouched (if we may so call ramming her on to the bed so that all her joints creaked), Siegfried had nevertheless taken her ring and girdle, the outwards symbols of her virginity, and on his return had handed these trophies to Kriemhild with no word of explanation. It was these tokens which Kriemhild flaunted in the Fourteenth Chapter as a means of worsting Brunhild in a dispute over their husbands' standing. As supreme arbiter in Burgundy, Gunther now called on Siegfried to justify himself, but he cut short the proceedings on Siegfried's being ready to swear that he had not boasted of sleeping with Brunhild. Hagen was absent from the scene. Had he been present, things might have run another course. Moved by his lady's tears as much as by her account and judging that the ring and girdle spoke louder at court than a royal oath, Hagen resolved to avenge his lord and lady.

These dire events grow from the interplay of figures possessing marks of individuality. A different Brunhild would not have made athletic prowess the sole test of a suitor for her hand; a different Gunther would not have accepted a wife beyond his wooing; a different Siegfried would not have duped and mastered Brunhild as the price of his own marriage; a different Hagen would have avoided murder to right his lord's seeming wrong; a different Kriemhild would have abided by the loss of her husband — and there would have been no Fall of the Nibelungs. Merely to phrase such banalities raises the equal and opposite issue as to what freedom the action gave to a gifted poet to delineate credible actors.

The issue has been much discussed. It has inspired the aphorism 'die Rolle prägt den Kopf' or 'the role determines the soul'. Clearly, had Homer gone beyond the wrath of Achilles and narrated the pillage, atrocity, sacrilege and rape at the fall of Troy he could not have afforded to ennoble some of the Achaean warriors to the extent we know he did. It has further been wittily said of the central and therefore oldest figures of the Nibelung tradition, that they must not be weighed down by too much soul, precisely because their 'characters' are so firmly aligned to stark and crucial events. This would be true if the poet had been renewing a single source for his own generation. Yet for the First Part he was attempting to harmonize two main sources (lays of Brunhild) and some minor sources (lays on young Siegfried) with, for the Second Part, a lost epic (the 'Fall of the Nibelungs'), in such a way as would please a sharply divided audience of tough veterans from the frontier waiting for time-hallowed punch-lines, and a fashionable younger set grouped about ladies with delicate feelings. The question of the poet's sources will be touched on later; but the effect of their harmonization on the portrayal of character must be mentioned here.

The Brunhild lays presented a Gunther who owed his wife to another man and who connived at murder to save his fragile honour; but the old 'Fall' presented Gunther at his last stand as a hero second to none. A modern writer who wished to bounce his anonymous public into accepting such contradictions as the expression of one and the same psyche need only rake through his text-books to find a suitable pattern of 'complexes': but the method adopted by the Nibelung poet with a live audience to appease was to say as little as possible. Such was in any case his privilege as an epic-dramatic poet. Nevertheless, the two Gunthers, the king with the yellow streak and the hero in action, do not cohere.

With Kriemhild, the poet's concern for fashion made his task hard in another way. His sources for the First Part must have lacked the whole aura of Kriem-hild's romantic involvement with Siegfried without her ever having met him, as we find it in the *Nibelungenlied*: but he decided to go with the younger generation, adepts of the Minnesang and courtly romance, even though at the end he would cause Kriemhild to take a sword and strike off Hagen's head. With Kriemhild, however, he succeeded. He offers us no glimpse that could suggest unity of the two Gunthers, even at the level of schizophrenia; but Kriemhild he presents very plausibly as one person: the blushing maiden; the fulfilled young wife; the wife so dotingly proud of her husband that she is blind to the dangers she exposes him to; the stricken widow weeping tears of blood over his grave; the widow whose excessive love is now turned to boundless hate. His unified view is conveyed in a great flash of insight at the end, when standing before Hagen who is bound at last, she espies Siegfried's sword Balmung at his side:

> Si sprach: 'sô habt ir übele   geltes mich gewert.
> sô wil ich doch behalten   daz Sîfrides swert.
> daz truoc mîn holder vriedel,   dô ich in jungest sach,
> an dem mir herzeleide   von iuwern schulden geschach'.

('You have repaid me in base coin', she said, 'but Siegfried's sword I shall have and hold! My fair lover was wearing it when last I saw him, through whom I suffered mortal sorrow at your hands!')

This displays the obverse of the coin. On one side is the ageing woman, wife to Etzel yet in truth still a widow, consumed over the years by the one desire for revenge, so that men call her a she-devil: on the other a young wife at heart, so much in love with her first husband that he is her 'fair lover' still. Halfway through the poem, Kriemhild nevertheless rather disturbingly declined to rear the pledge of Siegfried's love, and we are faced by a choice between believing her already perverse or accusing the poet of minor incompetence. Could he not have done better for a son whose main raison d'être is to give substance to Siegfried's dying reproach? — 'May God have mercy on me for ever having got a son who in years to come will suffer the reproach that his kinsmen were murderers!' The poet at this point is on the horns of a dilemma. If Kriemhild stays in Worms with her son, Hagen will surely destroy him. If she goes to the Netherlands to rear him she will walk out of the picture.

Hagen is drawn consistently throughout and is more easily visualized as one person. The Hagen who murders Siegfried in the First Part to avenge his lord's dishonour and end Siegfried's supremacy, is the same as the Hagen of the Second Part who summons up fate by killing Etzel's son before the father's eyes, thus provoking battle in the best tactical situation with Dancwart holding the door. Hagen's higher political intelligence is conveyed by the epic device of pairing him with a man of superior physique, and also artistic talent, the gentleman minstrel Volker. Hagen sinks Siegfried's treasure in the Rhine lest Kriemhild use it to hire warriors; he counsels against her marrying Etzel and against acceptance of Etzel's invitation to Hunland, only to be overriden. From start to finish he is the supreme force behind the throne, 'the type of responsible statesman who has to do what he sees is necessary'.[7] His negative qualities grow strangely from his good ones: from loyalty to his ruling house, loyalty to his army, loyalty to his comrade-in-arms. From the time the Burgundians, now styled 'Nibelungs',[8] set out for Etzel's land until the end we have surely the most extended aristeia in heroic poetry, and it is Hagen's. In it he emerges as a figure of sombre, even sinister magnificence, an indestructible erratic from a vanished stratum of culture.

On Gunther little needs to be added to what has been said incidentally. The one consistent trait in his image is that he leans on Hagen from beginning to end for political advice. All that Hagen requires of Gunther in order to transpose plan into action, whether it be murder or grand robbery, is Gunther's royal assent. Gunther rejects the first proposal that Siegfried should be made away with, partly for moral reasons: but when Hagen proposes what we miscall a 'perfect' murder, Gunther accepts it. It is fitting that in the Second Part when fate begins to close in on the Burgundians, the ancient royal epithet 'Hope of the Nibelungs' is attached not to King Gunther, but to his vassal Hagen.

It is symptomatic of their minor roles that up to this point the present writer has felt no need to name Gunther's brothers and co-kings Gernot and Giselher. Gernot is a middle-term, now paired with the senior king, now with the youngest. Giselher's role is to be 'young', in the Second Part even at an age when one might think him growing grey. Conversely in the Second Part Giselher claims to have been a tiny child when Siegfried was murdered, which is untrue. An expression of Giselher's epic 'youth' is to be tender and affectionate towards his sister in her griefs and troubles; but since he never helps her, whether to save her husband or to secure her treasure, the effect on a modern reader is one of hypocrisy. A correct approach is to regard Giselher and Gernot as supporting figures to Gunther in a triple choreography — adequate to any given scene, but problematic beyond it.

Although Siegfried is eliminated by the end of the First Part, his character oscillates between sometimes burlesque rumbustiousness and an equable, even idealized courtliness. This is not only because men who are rudely strong tend to have a comic side to them, which our poet exploited in Siegfried, but because he attempted the impossible in trying to please both sections of his audience. The uncouth, burly young Siegfried was traditional: on the other hand new romantic notions required him to be a fitting mate for the now blushing Kriemhild. The two Siegfrieds co-exist, unreconciled. The measure of the poet's concern for what young ladies of fashion might think is given by his suppression of an older tradition, well-authenticated by the *Þiðrekssaga*,[9] that Siegfried of course had to deflower Brunhild to rob her of her superhuman strength, and by his substituting a wrestling-match, with the ring and girdle not as love-tokens but as trophies; and by his conversion of the issue at law from the deed itself to mere boasting of the deed. Siegfried rises to great heights of noble feeling as his life's blood dyes the flowers: yet remorse for having violated Brunhild's freedom by leaving her body to another is absent. Such things were all in the day's work of the hero of ancient type who comes and goes in 'Siegfried' — compare how Parzival in the chivalric romance of that name risks his life to make good the consequences of an innocent kiss forced from the lips of Jeschute.

The last of the five central figures is Brunhild, whom her supernatural strength as a maiden links with Siegfried as does also her fate, since she and Siegfried, far the strongest of all, are broken by the end of the First Part. Defloration had reduced Brunhild's strength to the level of other women's: but in the fateful Fourteenth Chapter, unaware how vulnerable she had become, she had replied proudly to Kriemhild's tactless praise of Siegfried, though truthfully according to her lights. After the murder of Siegfried, Brunhild virtually fades out of the story. The once arrogant warrior-maiden is now a spent force, the guile and self-interest of others have destroyed her by opposing to her the only power capable of overwhelming her, namely Siegfried. Later Eddaic tradition shows Brynhild languishing for Sigurð's love. Whether this idea originated in the North or in the South, the extant *Nibelungenlied* is untouched by it. It is true that Siegfried had visited Brunhild in Iceland prior to Gunther's wooing expedition. Like Sigurð in the *Sigurðarkviða in skamma*, Siegfried 'knows the way'. Yet in what circumstances Siegfried had been there the text of *Nibelungenlied* does not say. This does not really matter, since Brunhild's motives are accounted for entirely in terms of power, not love. Siegfried seems to be well aware of this, since at the wooing he deflects Brunhild's attention from himself to Gunther by feigning to be Gunther's vassal. At the wedding-feast, Brunhild weeps to see Kriemhild at Siegfried's side. The reason she gives is that her sister-in-law has been ruined by marriage to a vassal. She broods over this for many years until, with unexpected results, she brings it to a head in the Fourteenth Chapter.

It has been argued that the tragedy which engulfed the semi-mythic Siegfried and Brunhild was due to their allowing themselves to be drawn from their pristine northern realm into mésalliance with lesser beings at the decadent court at Worms. The idea is not entirely valueless, especially when one compares the leading figures of the *Nibelungenlied* with those of the Eddaic Niflung lays, where all are of more archaic type and to that extent more compatible. Nevertheless, as our text stands, Siegfried sets out on his own initiative for the Burgundian court to woo Kriemhild and he it is who, without prompting, conceives and puts into execution the plan for the deception of Brunhild. This will and ability to deceive spring not from infection by a court reneging on its culture but from unbroken barbarian callousness towards the chattels women were. When Hagen tells the court how Siegfried had gained Nibelung's treasure by playing off Nibelung's two heirs against each other, we recognize that Siegfried had mastered the game of *tertius gaudens* long before coming to Worms.

The Margrave Rüdiger of Pöchlarn in old Austria came relatively late to the Nibelung action. His role is to woo Kriemhild for Etzel, his patron in exile, and (in one of those charmed moments of civilization and peace so beloved of epic poets) to entertain the Burgundians on their way to their doom. At this festivity wide-hearted Rüdiger publicly betroths his daughter to Giselher. He had not been able to win Kriemhild for Etzel without pledging himself her liege for all eventualities, so that when fighting breaks out in Hunland he is bound by feudal and personal oaths on the one hand and on the other by bonds of hospitality, friendship and a marriage lacking only consummation. The terms of the feudal oath leave him no option but to attack his lord's enemies. This Rüdiger does only after a bitter inward struggle. He avoids his friends but seeks out death. In one of the great gestures associated with Hagen, the latter, with his shield (a gift of the Margravine of Pöchlarn) hacked to pieces, asks for Rüdiger's, thus allowing Rüdiger to show his magnanimity for the last time. Martial honour is what Hagen understands best, and with this delicate appreciation of Rüdiger's feelings at having to attack his friends, he ranges himself momentarily beside the chivalric characters Erec, Iwein, Parzival, Willehalm and Rual li Foitenant as one who knows courtesy from the heart.

According to cyclic tradition, Rüdiger and Hagen had been among the group of exiles and hostages at Attila's court, which also included Walther,[10] Dietrich (Theodoric) and Hildebrand. There is thus some justification for meeting the last two in our poem, though they came to Nibelung tradition relatively late. The role of Dietrich is to maintain his neutrality between his lord Etzel and his Burgundian friends as long as he can: but though he had given timely warning of Kriemhild's weeping, his fealty compels him finally to bind Gunther and Hagen and deliver them up to Kriemhild with a plea for

mercy. He and old Hildebrand — the 'invented' hero[11] had come to stay —
had of course to be saved up for their Return to Lombardy in the Dietrich
cycle.[12] Dietrich's aloofness from the strife enabled the poet to present him in an
entirely positive light, as a gleam of hope beyond the holocaust; but his Hildebrand shows a great descent from the austere figure of the *Hildebrandslied* in that
he sets him in a somewhat comical light. The veteran warrior tries in vain to
restrain his nephew Wolfhart with a high tackle: with the result that this
charming young berserker and Dietrich's other comrades attack the Burgundians and are slain to a man, leaving the now pathetic Hildebrand to face
Dietrich with the news

In a straightforward account of the *Nibelungenlied* the question of the poet's
sources would have to be relegated to parentheses, footnotes and appendices.
They could not be passed over entirely since in their effects they obtrude
themselves on the reader so powerfully that they must be referred to if only to
save the poet's good name. In a work devoted to the comparative study of
heroic epic poetry, however, there can be no question of playing the sources
down, however brief the treatment.

For generations, hypothetical reconstructions of the prior stages of Nibelung tradition seemed more important to their makers than an appreciation
of the beauties of our poem. It was therefore not surprising that an aesthetic
reaction should come, and that it would overreach itself. The reaction coincided
with the iconoclastic desire to topple the sober 'prehistory' presented in
classic form by the gifted Swiss Germanist Andreas Heusler. But it seems to the
present writer that studies of Nibelung tradition which assume Heusler's
theories to be passé, condemn themselves to swift oblivion. Of the two — over-
simplification or over-multiplication of genetic theory on the basis of the few
surviving sources — the former is preferable as conserving rather than dis-
sipating mental energy. It has recently been shown that elements of genuine
Nibelung story were able to enter the manuscript tradition even of the classic
Nibelungenlied, the success of which ultimately put an end to the copying of all
other written versions. This should serve as a reminder. For just as in a terrain
a myriad roads and paths dwindle in number as they approach fords, bridges
and passes to negotiate rivers and mountains so the numerous strands of heroic
tradition must diminish and change direction as they come to terms with those
major features of the literary landscape known as masterpieces. This much in
defence of the bare scheme offered here.

Any reconstruction of source history must be founded upon correct assessment both of extant sources and their interrelationships. In this case — passing
from the more to the less archaic, irrespective of manuscript dating or even of
dates of composition — we have to deal in the main with the lays of Sigurð
and the Niflungs in the *Edda* (*c*.1270); the *Þiðrekssaga* (mid-thirteenth century);
and our *Nibelungenlied* (*c*.1200). The Eddaic lays have their own evolution

through time, but for the matter in hand it is not over-difficult to separate the less from the more archaic features. All that needs to be said here[13] is the following: the archaic *Brot* (*præ* 1000?) narrates the murder of Sigurð (= Siegfried) by Gunnar's (= Gunther's) brother Gothorm (= Godomaris/ Gernot) at the instigation of Brynhild through Gunnar. The beginning of the lay is missing in the Codex Regius, but the following reconstruction of the motives for Sigurð's murder is not open to serious question. In his brother-in-law Gunnar's shape, Sigurð had ridden through a wall of flame to win Brynhild for Gunnar and after three chaste nights spent with her had delivered her to him, but given her ring to his own wife Guðrún (= Kriemhild). Later during a quarrel over the status of their husbands, Guðrún had taunted Brynhild with the latter's ring. Brynhild had then told Gunnar that either he or she, or Sigurð, must die. The even more archaic *Atlakviða* (*c.*900?) narrates Atli's (Attila's) invitation to the Niflungs (= Burgundians), their sister Guðrún's (= Kriemhild's) loyal warning that her husband Atli is lusting for their treasure; their arrival, betrayal, capture and Atli's attempt to extort the treasure, which Gunnar foils first by having brave Högni killed and then by dying in the snake-pit; whereupon Guðrún wreaks vengeance on Atli. The *Þiðrekssaga* was compiled round the central figure of Þiðrek (Theodoric = Dietrich) from Low German material furnished by North German merchants. As far as the Nibelung material is concerned, the *Þiðrekssaga* presents a more archaic or less modernized version than the *Nibelungenlied*. When comparing parallel passages of two variants one must be wary of according genetic priority *automatically* to the data of one of the variants; for a fundamentally cruder variant can perhaps bring this or that refined datum of its source down to its own general level. Nevertheless, no convincing example of such coarsening or blinding of a finer element from the (reconstructed) source of the *Nibelungenlied* and the *Þiðrekssaga* has been cited for the latter; whereas refinements of cruder motifs of the source are not hard to establish for the former. The Austrian poet's unsuccessful attempt to blind the motif of Brunhild's defloration in order to please both ancients and moderns in his audience, has been referred to.[14] One further example must suffice. Our poet narrates that as Etzel and his Burgundian guests were feasting in the hall, Kriemhild had her and Etzel's son brought to table '*since there was no beginning the fighting in any other way* . . . How could a woman ever do a more dreadful thing in pursuance of her revenge?' This is all that Kriemhild does in the matter, and it cannot be called 'dreadful'. Hagen pains the father and his own lords by observing that the boy has an ill-fated look. At this point Hagen's brother Dancwart bursts into the hall to announce that the Burgundian squires have been massacred at Kriemhild's instigation. Hagen forthwith provokes battle by killing Etzel's son. Recourse to the *Þiðrekssaga* shows convincingly how our poet came to write this strange passage; for there Grimhild dares her son to buffet Högni, who then despatches him and so starts the fighting. Concern for the new proprieties *c.*1200 caused our poet to repress Kriemhild's ruthless incitement of her son. To replace it he invented the massacre of the squires. On the other hand, concern for tradition caused him to hint to the old guard that he knew what he was omitting.

In fine, the *Atlakviða* preserves a stage of motivation earlier than that of the common source of the corresponding parts of the *Þiðrekssaga* and the *Nibelungenlied*; the sister avenges her brothers on Attila, who had murdered them for their treasure; (the reconstructed) *Brot* preserves the element of Sigurð's loyalty towards Gunnar, with the implication that the defloration of Brunhild in the common source of the *Þiðrekssaga* (which keeps it) and of the *Nibelungenlied* (which manifestly blinds it) was a later coarsening on the basis of 'no smoke without a fire' and reflects a descent in ethos from aristocratic bard to plebeian minstrel. It further needs to be underlined that the quarrel between the queens as given in (the reconstructed) *Brot* was — as we have seen earlier — not over love but status.

On this basis the following bare scheme can be constructed.

A lay, probably of Burgundo–Frankish origin (fifth–sixth century) presented in a new, non-historical light: (i) the destruction of the Burgundian dynasty east of the Rhine by a raiding force of Huns (not led by Attila) of 437, and (ii) the death of Attila of 453. The historical Attila according to a citation of Priscus was found dead of a broken blood vessel beside his bride Ildico. A circumstantial combination typical of heroic legend is recorded by Marcellinus Comes seventy years later to the effect that a woman had murdered Attila with a knife. All that is now required to give the bare bones of the plot of the Burgundo–Frankish lay reflected in the *Atlakviða* is the further combination that the bride with the Germanic name murdered Attila in revenge for her brothers — 'in fact' the Burgundian dynasty shattered by the Huns — who would 'naturally' have been led by Attila. A separate Frankish lay far less strong in historical plot, stronger in elements from folk-tale, presented a hero (possibly with a dragon-slaying past) who wooed and won a battle-maiden for a king, in return for the latter's sister. This hero was later murdered because of a quarrel between the two women. Either when this lay was created or subsequently, the king's family was identified with Gunther's family in the Burgundo-Frankish lay, after which the two lays tended to attract each other. Was it rather strained even for Germanic notions of clan solidarity that the sister, who in the one lay had lost her splendid husband at her brothers' hands, should in another lay loyally avenge those brothers' deaths on their slayer? Judging by the slight signs of mutual attraction between the earliest corresponding lays in the *Edda*, the strain was not great in the archaic North: but in Upper Germany, so much more exposed to new influences, this constellation did not hold. Here the subject-matter of the two lays was powerfully interlocked by an innovation: the sister now avenges herself on her brothers — on her own blood-kin — for the loss of her first spouse. The earliest firm date that can be given to this innovation is *c.*1130, from a chance record of a Saxon singer at a Danish court who told of 'Grimhild's famous betrayal of her brothers'; yet the change must surely have been made much earlier. It has been argued plausibly that this innovation was induced by a weakening of the clan ethos which nourished the blood-feud and by a corresponding deepening of the marriage bond, in both cases under Christian influence. The substitution of the wife's revenge for Attila's vain attempt to extort treasure from the Burgundians, however, did not lead to the elimination of the fine scene in which the Burgundians prefer death to surrendering the treasure, the Burgundian treasure now being identified with the treasure left by Siegfried to Kriemhild. Powerful attraction between the two plots, those of Siegfried–Brunhild and the Fall of the Nibelungs, must, then, be assumed for Upper Germany. Nevertheless, the earliest evidence of fusion of these plots into a connected narrative in German is our *Nibelungenlied* of *c.*1200.

The First Part of the *Nibelungenlied* corresponding to the original Siegfried–Brunhild lay has inconsistencies of motivation which are best explained as due to the poet's using two irreconcilable twelfth-century variants. These will have been longer heroic lays of minstrel type rather than full-scale epics like the lost *Nôt* of *c.*1160, subsumed in the Second Part of our *Nibelungenlied* and made obsolete by it.

Themes from lost twelfth-century minstrel Lays of Young Siegfried, in which Siegfried gains Nibelung's treasure, slays a dragon and hardens his skin in its blood but for one spot between his shoulder-blades, were brilliantly framed by our poet within a vignette in the shape of Hagen's report on the newly-arrived hero, as the Burgundians look down on him through a window. The poet further activated motifs from Young Siegfried Lays in the Eighth Chapter, an episode of his own invention in which Siegfried fetches his Nibelung subjects to check Brunhild's forces in Iceland. The Young Siegfried Lays no doubt go back in part to much-debated but shadowy Frankish lays, since clear echoes of these are found in the *Edda*.

The name 'Nibelung' requires a word of explanation, since the poet uses it inconsistently. Historically, 'Nibelung' may have been the dynastic name of the Burgundians. In our poem it applies properly to them, though only in the Second Part. In the First Part is applies to a northern people, dwarfs and giants, whose eponymous founder, Nibelung, was lord of treasure of which Siegfried gained possession. From the poet's point of view, the Burgundians' acquisition of this treasure will have justified their acquisition of the name of Nibelung, although as a matter of literary history it is far more likely that the name of 'Nibelung' was extended from the Burgundians to Siegfried's subjects.

The degree of success attained by the poet in his attempt to unify his three groups of sources to the satisfaction of young and old has emerged piecemeal on the way. It is a comment on the nature of heroic epic poetry that the poet fell well short of perfection and yet produced a great poem. Like the heroes whom it portrays, the genre is robust and has the power to rise mightily above glaring defects.

The poet was very fortunate to have before him for the Second Part the lost *Nôt* of *c.*1160, a stark epic packed with terse sayings and pregnant gestures and couched in a more stichic use of the Nibelung measure, much of it visibly keyed into the fabric of the extant *Nibelungenlied* in truly medieval fashion. Without the *Nôt* (or something very like it) as a bridge to the past which he recaptured, our poet would have drowned in the chivalric sentiment of his day. With the *Nôt* as the basis for his Second Part, and by extending its spirit to the whole narrative, he made the most notable contribution to tragic poetry of his age, an age noted rather for its violent fluctuations between pessimism and optimism. This the poet achieved not least through his remarkable reticence, even his grim taciturnity, in the psychological and moral spheres. Apart from his condemnation of Hagen's treachery, which he owed to his patron, he refrains from all direct comment on the actions he depicts. At most he leaves threads dangling for thoughtful Christians to tug at if they please, notably in his fleeting allusions to the pride, arrogance or self-assurance of all who are laid low in his poem.

A scene as likely to survive translation as any is the one in which Kriemhild faces her enemy for the last time and gains the victory on the physical plane while he by remaining true to his purpose in the face of death gains it on the moral.

And now lord Gunther was bound by Dietrich. For although kings ought never to suffer such bonds, Dietrich thought that, had he let the king and his vassal go free, they would have slain all who crossed their path. Dietrich took Gunther and led him bound to Kriemhild. Thanks to Gunther's misfortune many of her own cares left her. 'Welcome, Gunther of Burgundy,' she said.

'I would salute and thank you, dearest sister,' he answered, 'if your greeting were more gracious. But I know you to be so angry that you will give Hagen and me scant welcome.'

'Queen of a most noble king,' said Dietrich, 'no knights as worthy as I have given you now were ever taken prisoner. Allow these wretched lords to profit from my entreaties.'

She declared she would gladly do so, and lord Dietrich left the heroes with tears in his eyes. But Etzel's queen was soon to exact fierce vengeance, for she robbed those matchless warriors of their lives, the one and the other. She kept them apart to add to their sufferings, and neither set eyes on the other again till she went in to Hagen with her brother's head. Kriemhild took ample vengeance on them both.

The Queen then went to visit Hagen and addressed that warrior with fierce hostility. 'If you will give me back what you have robbed me of, you may still return to Burgundy alive!'

'Your words are wasted, most noble Queen,' answered Hagen grimly. 'I have sworn never to reveal the treasure so long as one of my lords remains alive, nor shall I yield it to anyone!'

'I shall make an end!' cried the noble lady, and she commanded them to take her brother's life. They struck off his head, and she carried it to Hagen by the hair. Great was the grief it gave him.

When the unhappy man saw his lord's head, he said to Kriemhild: 'You have made an end as you desired, and things have run their course as I imagined. The noble King of Burgundy is dead, young Giselher and lord Gernot, too. Now none knows of the treasure but God and I! You she-devil, it shall stay hidden from you for ever!'

'You have repaid me in base coin,' she said, 'but Siegfried's sword I shall have and hold! My fair lover was wearing it when last I saw him, through whom I suffered mortal sorrow at your hands.' She drew it from its sheath — he was powerless to prevent it — and bent her thoughts to robbing him of life. She raised it in both hands — and struck off his head! King Etzel saw this, and great was the grief it gave him.[15]

Matters are different in the *Kudrun*, sometimes styled 'an anti-*Nibelungenlied*'.[16]

The reticence of the Nibelung poet can scarcely have meant that he affirmed the ethos of revenge at all costs; and he may have had private reservations on the assertion with which he all but concludes his poem, that 'the King's high festival had ended in sorrow, as joy must ever turn to sorrow in the end' (str. 2378). However that may be, the poet of *Kudrun* was not minded to leave any doubt as to his views on the blood-feud, and, with as little recourse to preaching as his predecessor, unfolded his own epic. After taking his audience through two generations of rapine and revenge such as Upper Germany had been experiencing since 1198, the poet of *c.*1240, employs the normal means of epic narrative to teach the superiority of conciliation over implacableness, of hope over despair — one of the world's great themes in periods of transition, and reflected in such dissimilar works as the *Oresteia*, *Njálssaga*, and the fine but little known *Broken Arrow* of the American Frontier. Though not supremely well gifted, the poet of the *Kudrun* achieved his aim through his leading character Kudrun, a princess of the third generation, whose outlook he contrasts implicitly with that of Kriemhild in the *Nibelungenlied*, with that of Kudrun's mother Hilde (whom she has to win over), and with that of old Wate (an amiable berserker of ancient stamp).

The plot of *Kudrun* is this. Hetel, King of the Hegelings, sends his vassals Fruote, Horant, Wate and others overseas to woo Hilde, daughter of the possessive Hagen, King of Ireland, whose boyhood escape from a griffin has been narrated in a first part. The party succeed in luring the princess on board, gaining her consent, and putting to sea, thanks to the shrewdness of Fruote and the wondrous singing of Horant; but they are overtaken by Hagen on the shores of Wales, where Hetel has arrived to welcome Hilde. In the ensuing battle, Hagen wounds Hetel and is wounded by Wate. Hilde pleads for her father's life, peace is made, and Wate heals the wounds by magic.

Hetel and Hilde have a son, Ortwin, and a daughter, Kudrun. The girl grows to be so lovely that many wooers appear in Hegelingen, some peaceably, others sword in hand. Of these, Herwig of Zealand finds favour. Before his and Kudrun's contracted marriage is celebrated, however, a disappointed suitor, Hartmuot, lands in Hegelingen with his father, King Ludwig of Normandy, during Hetel's and Herwig's absence and abducts Kudrun and her ladies. Alerted by Hilde, Hetel and Herwig give chase and overtake the raiders on the Wülpensand. In the bloody encounter on this island, Ludwig slays Hetel and sails home by night with his army. Disdaining to marry Kudrun without her consent, Hartmuot leaves her to his mother Gerlint's persuasions in ignorance of the latter's cruel nature. In her vain attempts to break the captive's will, Gerlint gives Kudrun ever more menial tasks, which Kudrun accepts with humble dignity, until at last she and her royal companion Hildeburg are made to wash clothes on the shore. Thirteen years raise a new generation of fighting-men to Hegelingen and Zealand, and at a word from Hilde they arm and sail for Normandy. On a fast-day at noon an angel comes to Kudrun and Hildeburg on the strand in the shape of a water-bird and hints with human voice that deliverance is near. After a reconnaissance during which Ortwin and Herwig are recognized by the fair washerwomen shivering in the March wind, the invaders launch their attack. Herwig slays Ludwig, Hartmuot is captured, Wate takes the castle by storm, kills the babes in their cradles and cuts off Gerlint's head; but Kudrun shields Hartmuot's kindly sister Ortrun from Wate's rage. In the sequel, thanks to Kudrun, her wedding to Herwig takes place together with Hartmuot's and two others, thus putting an end to old feuds, notably that with Normandy.

The three parts — Hagen's boyhood and marriage, the wooing of his daughter Hilde, and the trials and triumph of Kudrun — are of mounting length and significance. The reconciliation between Hagen and Hetel in the second part is the practical expression of Hilde's divided affections and the self-interest of two families. In the third part, reconciliation is due chiefly to a new approach to the blood-feud which was already taking shape in the young Hagen and is now perfected in his grand-daughter Kudrun. The ethical distance which the poet intends us to traverse is marked precisely by that between Wate and Kudrun. Between the Hagen of the *Nibelungenlied,* jealous of his lord's honour and power, and the grievously wronged Kriemhild there had been nothing to choose in ruthless pursuit of vengeance: between Wate and Kudrun, however, there is all the world. Wate represents an old-fashioned, ultimately Germanic way of life in a perilous world, a way of life seen by the poet as valid but not final. The poet accepted the implications of his narrative that Kudrun could not have been born nor her family's new outlook brought to fruition without Wate and what he stood for: yet he saw farther, namely that if the Hegeling story was not to end in tragedy like the *Nibelungenlied* or indeed like an earlier (lost) version of the epic of Hild,[17] then Wate's ethos must be transcended. The poet wisely does not moralize, but instead presents the grizzled Wate as a sympathetic though rugged character. Even Wate's slaughter of the babes does not mar the portrait, since, as Wate himself reminds us, a rule of the old law that had bred him and which still had a wide currency was 'extirpate or be extirpated'. The portrait is not marred because Wate is all of one piece, and it is strangely symbolic that at the physical level, once the fighting has stopped, Wate heals the wounds of both friend and foe! It does the poet much credit that the more modern figure of Kudrun, whom he places beside Wate serenely and without condemning him, is also of one piece. Mature reflection on the possibilities of Christianity amid such men and customs as prevailed enabled the poet to present Kudrun not as an insipid she-saint, but as a young woman in the round — tough and shrewd enough to stand up to Gerlint and every inch a princess, who, once she has been kissed by the two kings come to deliver her, proudly throws her washing away and makes ready to enter into her own. Despite its more hopeful message, *Kudrun* is bare of false sentiment. That this message so skilfully conveyed is not the Beatitudes at the double but something more sober and practicable is shown by the poet's careful choice of Gerlint and the defector Hergart for Wate's avenging sword. This verdict has Kudrun's final approval and is balanced by her actively saving Ortrun and the mostly chivalrous Hartmuot, whom the poet has made handsome and brave in order quietly to underline how loyal Kudrun was to Herwig during her long captivity.

The general contrast between *Kudrun* and the *Nibelungenlied* is picked out in details such as these. Kriemhild scandalizes warriors by over-stepping the line dividing feminine from masculine behaviour to the point where she usurps the sword: but Kudrun shows awareness of the limits with her repeated phrase, 'If I were a man . . .'. Kriemhild seizes the initiative to provoke destruction: but Kudrun acts to achieve a stable peace. Kriemhild broods over the murder of Siegfried for thirteen years before Etzel's proposal gives her her chance: Kudrun's captivity lasts as long before her so different opportunity arrives. In the *Nibelungenlied* Hagen seeks to extort a prophecy on his army's dark fate from swan-maidens surprised beside the Danube: but in Kudrun an angel comes freely from heaven in similar guise to hint at a happy outcome.

The manifest influence of practical Christianity on the ethos of *Kudrun* raises the question of genre. Is *Kudrun* an heroic epic? Since the poem offers not a rejection of the heroic outlook but a revision of it in a sober Christian sense, the answer must be 'yes', with the qualification that it is a unique specimen. For we are not to imagine that if an external power were to attack the pacific alliance of Hegelingen, Zealand, Normandy and Moorland, the heroes who had given so good an account of themselves would not resist manfully with Kudrun's active support after conciliation had failed. On the other hand it is equally inconceivable that in the event of victory the alliance would revert to the old outlook. This brings us to the *Willehalm* of the knight Wolfram von Eschenbach, another epic poem of unique stamp, which we must assume the *Kudrun* poet had digested as fully as he had digested the *Nibelungenlied*.

It would be tempting to include *Willehalm* in an account of medieval German heroic poetry, possibly for the first time. *Willehalm* is an heroic poem and much besides. The narrative data are from the Old French cycle of Guillaume, chiefly from the *Bataille d'Aliscans*, all undoubtedly heroic poetry:[18] what Wolfram adds is beauty and logic of structure, deep and delicate motivation of character, a profound and sensitive reading of Christianity, and a noble blend of courage under attack and compassion in victory. The style is Wolfram's own more robust version of the courtly manner, the metre is courtly couplets. *Willehalm*, lacking the last book of ten planned, is an original epic masterpiece informed by an ethos in which the heroic and the chivalric are fused. But this is not the place in which to justify a claim some might wish to disagree with.

Between the periods of the *Hildebrandslied* and the *Nibelungenlied* one can imagine first an alliterative lay and then a lay in assonating couplets on Walter of Aquitaine. Walter escapes from Attila's court with his betrothed Hildegund and some treasure not long after his fellow hostage Hagen's return to Worms on Gunther's accession; is waylaid by Gunther and his men in the Vosges; fights them to a standstill in a defile, where his back is covered, while his old comrade Hagen looks on; and either is slain (for which there is no evidence) or as in the later *Waltharius* and *Þiðrekssaga* rides triumphantly home with his woman, more like a hero of the Wild West than the hero of a Germanic lay. The alliterating lay will have been related to the Old English *Waldere* fragments; the assonating lay, an early specimen of its kind, will have furnished the plot to the Latin *Waltharius* (*c*.930), an epic poem of disputed authorship in Leonine hexameters which belongs to medieval Latin literary history. The fragments of an Austrian epic of Walther (*c*.1230–50) are too scanty to determine the position and outlook of the poem, though its style was influenced by that of the *Nibelungenlied*.

The earliest heroic romance of adventure was probably the double narrative of *Ortnit* and *Wolfdietrich* (*præ* 1250), which united separate plots by means of a dragon-slaying motif. Significantly it originated beyond the Austrian homeland of the *Nibelungenlied*, probably in Bavaria or Franconia. Wolfdietrich (thought to be derived from Theuderich, son of Clovis) slays the dragon which had killed Ortnit of Garda (misinterpreted from Garðaríki = Rurikid Russia) and marries his widow. Of concern here are the surviving five-hundred strophes of the original (*Wolfdietrich* A). King Hugdietrich of Constantinople is made by the treacherous Saben to think that his infant third son Dietrich is the issue of an incubus, and he commands his vassal Berhtung to put the boy to death. Berhtung's inward struggle between his fealty and the tender feelings inspired by his charge are described with both strength and charm. The boy miraculously survives all the old man's tests, even that of exposure to wolves, justifying the name 'Wolf'-Dietrich. Berhtung then throws in his lot with the boy and eventually regains Hugdietrich's favour. He rears Wolfdietrich with his sixteen sons. After the King's death, Saben sets Wolfdietrich's brothers against the young hero, but Wolfdietrich's and Berhtung's loyalty to each other survives every test, even the loss of Berhtung's vassals and six sons. In the rugged, yet tender-hearted Berhtung, archaic ethos and new sentiment are fused. Despite the new facet, Berhtung deserves his place beside Hagen and Wate as a vassal of the older school.

The theme of the exiled Theodoric was already sufficiently well established *c.* 650 to sustain the cyclic extension of the *Hildebrandslied*, with only the barest reference to Theodoric's wrong at Odoacer's hands and his long stay with Attila, conveyed obliquely through the circumstances of his follower Hildebrand.[19] As his epoch receded, the importance of Theodoric as a hero grew in legend, poetry and iconography, and spread in at least two waves to the Old Norse world as marked by the tenth-century runic stone of Rök in East Gotland and by the *Þiðrekssaga*, while leaving traces in Old English poetry.[20] The themes of Dietrich's Flight and Return provide a basis for cyclic extensions such as *Alpharts Tod*[21] as late as the mid-thirteenth century. Theodoric-Dietrich had in fact become the paramount hero of German heroic legend and poetry. It is, then, all the more remarkable that there is no poem of Dietrich extant which is of any aesthetic value or which even suggests how there might have been one. Despite all the reams that have been filled by the fabulations of scholars usurping the bard's role, very little has been reconstructed that could be called pregnant action of the sort which alone had power to mint a Germanic lay and live.

Whatever the features of the indefinite number of early lays on Theodoric, by the tenth century his antagonist Odoacer has been replaced by Ermanrich, destroyer of his own kin, the Harlungs,[22] so that it is fitting that Ermanrich should accede to the advice of his evil counsellor Sibech and seek the death of his 'nephew' Dietrich. Ermanrich is no longer the Visigoth of history but Holy Roman Emperor, and Dietrich is no longer the Ostrogoth. Dietrich is known instead by his dynastic name of Amelung and he is lord of Bern (Verona). The plot of the centrepiece of *Dietrichs Flucht* is modelled on that of the *Rabenschlacht*. A group of Dietrich's vassals under Hildebrand are ambushed by Ermanrich. In order to save them, Dietrich renounces his kingdom and finds shelter with Etzel. The text of the *Rabenschlacht* is more unified. In it, Dietrich on his Return with an army equipped by Etzel, leaves Elsan in Verona with two of Etzel's sons and Dietrich's young brother Dieter, all three of whom keenly desire to take part in the battle before Ravenna, where Dietrich gains the victory. The three youths elude Elsan and in their summer clothes are slain by the traitor Witege, whom Dietrich espies and chases into the sea, where a merwoman takes him below the waves. Etzel's wife Helche curses Dietrich, but when she and Etzel realize that he, too, is bereaved, they forgive him. Meanwhile Dietrich has again forfeited his kingdom.

There is no proper means of telling what of all this is ancient; yet of one thing we may be sure: not the sentiment. These two narratives, the former in couplets, the latter in sextets, were gathered together and enframed by an Austrian minstrel styling himself Heinrich der Vogler towards the end of the thirteenth century. His main purpose was political. In an interpolation he makes vigorous propaganda against the princes for the rights of the nobility, much endangered towards the end of the century. The version of the *Flucht* which he used, shorn of its irrelevant accretions, may go back to a precourtly version of the twelfth century. But the chief point of interest here is that a literate professional entertainer put sub-heroic matter, showing Dietrich's self-sacrifice for his vassals, to a contemporary purpose.

Alpharts Tod (*c*.1250; fifteenth-century MS) also had a purpose. It was aimed at the decline of chivalric custom in battle. It is a late addition to the cycle of Dietrich situated at the eve of his exile. Alphart, a young kinsman of Hilde-brand not known to earlier tradition, insists on proving his manhood by reconnoitring alone. In the field he slays seventy-two knights who come at him fairly in turn. He is then downed by Witege and Heime, famous names in Germanic heroic lore. Knowing Alphart to be superior, man to man, they attack him together, one from the front, the other from behind, in violation of oath. By fighting in this fashion these defectors from Dietrich 'break God's law', that is, the rules of Christian chivalry. The final battle, with which a better poet could have done more — compare Vivianz's last stand against odds in *Willehalm* — is comical, since there is too much talk and shilly-shallying by Witege and Heime, who ring all possible changes in their triangular situation, not excluding the fraudulent suggestion that the two should return to Erman-rich and say they had not seen Alphart. Such high-sounding old epithets as *Wielandes barn* ('Son of Wayland') sit uneasily on the heads of characters who vacillate unpredictably between the roles of veterans and old wives. The ethos is a fusion of the sub-heroic and the sub-chivalric, the style somewhat balladesque.

In *Biterolf* (*post* 1250), the assimilation of sub-heroic material to sub-chivalric romance is complete in style, metre and content. In courtly couplets as smooth, in a style as easy and as professionally competent and devoid of poetic texture as that of Rudolf von Ems, the *Biterolf* poet merges two once very different worlds. Biterolf, lord of Toledo (near which the black art was invented), owns a rare sword forged by Mime — *of Azzaria*, twenty miles from Toledo! A traveller who has hobnobbed with Etzel praises the latter's court and prowess — Etzel, it seems, is a second Arthur. Knowledge of the *Nibelungenlied* is assumed, posing the question whether the audiences to which *Biterolf* was directed could have understood even as much of that great poem as did the concocter of the *Klage*.

From this time on the little that remains of ancient heroic lore is purveyed as pure entertainment by the resurgent professionals to ravening and omnivorous audiences of rough country nobles, townsmen and then peasants, with appropriate concessions in taste. Nevertheless, we must not forget the romantic Emperor Maximilian I (1459–1519), to whose collecting zeal we owe not only unique monuments of chivalric poetry but also the *Kudrun* and manuscripts of heroic and sub-heroic poems from the *Nibelungenlied* downwards. To the detached scholar the chief value of the later narratives can serve only as material for a study of decline.

The first period of decline, which concerned the Germanic heroic lay, was briefly mentioned.[23] The second period is but a part of a general swift decline in poetry written for courtiers and urban patricians. A few courts, tiny islands of civilization in an ocean of semi-barbarism, and inspired by a great ideal, nurtured an abundance of poetic masterpieces, both short and long, of which the *Nibelungenlied* was only one. After true greatness such as this there must always be a falling-off: but here it was deeply accentuated by the effects, over sixty years, of the many-sided political struggle dating from the double election of emperors in 1198. The literary efflorescence and the high personal culture which sustained it at favoured courts was over within two generations. The *Kudrun*, written some forty years after the *Nibelungenlied*, although offering a recipe for its own harassed generation, did not and could not, succeed in its own time, the literary taste of which is indicated by its author's concession in Part i, where Hagen has 'adventures' with a griffin. The *Nibelungenlied* had led the way into a realm of puerile fantasy in the Eighth Book, in which Siegfried plays pranks on his dwarfs and giants of Nibelungland. The demonic side of Dietrich, which had drawn the condemnation of the Church, also suited the new fashion. Dietrich's battle with a giant in the *Eckenlied* is balanced by one with a dwarf in *Laurin*. Sub-heroic fabulation with its reckless pursuit of *âventiure* and contempt for form as against matter, however, repetitive, was competing with sub-chivalric narrative, which it thus came much to resemble.

Regrettably, there is as yet no technical study of the decay of German heroic poetry as a phenomenon.[24] In order to illustrate some of the factors at work it is proposed to inspect two poems, one with an ancient past and wearing as well as could be expected, the *Jüngeres Hildebrandslied*; the other slung together from existing material to suit new tastes, *Der Rosengarten*. It will serve better to take the latter first.

In the fifteenth/sixteenth-century Austrian *Rosengarten* (A), one of several free extensions of a lost thirteenth-century poem, Kriemhild challenges Dietrich with eleven of his comrades to visit her rose-garden at Worms and do battle with Siegfried and eleven others for a kiss and a garland. Dietrich accepts with the express purpose of lowering Kriemhild's pride. Appropriately, his men from Verona all win. Dietrich himself faces horny Siegfried very gingerly until his comrade Hildebrand questions his courage and so brings Dietrich's renowned Flammenwerfer action into play, which soon melts Siegfried into surrender. Hildebrand's brother Ilsan, enjoying a warrior's *moniage à la française*, hears of the challenge, leaves his cloister, joins in, slays fifty-two opponents, crams a garland over his tonsure, kisses Kriemhild's face bloody with his bristles, and returns to brethren who love him not. A rough sub-heroic ethos, themes from chivalric romance, motifs of minstrel comedy, all graced by ancient names, are here jumbled together to make an anti-romance. But just how satirical the lost original poem was meant to be we cannot know. Yet we do know that this formula succeeded hugely with later generations of all stations in life as narrative for its own sake. What must have gripped their interest was the match between the picked team from Bavaro–Austria and the Rhinelanders — with of course a twelve–nil victory for the home side. It has long been known that the obsession of cricketing fans with such things as Compton's knee (rather than, say, the Wounds of Christ) is but a scrap of shattered religiosity. In the same way, obsession with teams of picked sportsmen in *Der Rosengarten* and in modern news media alike, testifies to the relapse of the ancient cult of heroes into its crudest constituent elements. With cyclization taken to its absurdest lengths, with the old high ethos reduced to inanities, the later recensions of *Der Rosengarten* are crazy pavements assembled from defaced *disjecta membra* of a once magnificent frieze.

The *Jüngeres Hildebrandslied* is of ancient and honourable descent. How did the old Lay of Hildebrand finally emerge from the influences which nurtured a *Rosengarten* and its adaptations? First, it did not go utterly to pieces. But, second, its tragic outcome gave way to a happy end, a process which can be followed in several stages. The extant manuscript and printed sources of the fifteenth–seventeenth centuries derive from a popular balladesque version of *c.*1400, which in turn derives from a lost chivalric version of the thirteenth century. In the latter version, reflected in the *Þiðrekssaga*, the son Alebrand aims a foul ('woman's') blow at Hildebrand; but as the *Þiðrekssaga* narrates it there is already recognition and reconciliation none the less. This is an embarrassment, the beginning of a process of disintegration. Since the notion of a foul blow is chivalric, not earlier, it is reasonable to think that the original chivalric version of the thirteenth century ended with Alebrand's death. Indeed in the mid-thirteenth century, the literate entertainer Der Marnære had an item in his repertoire 'On the death of young Alebrand'. The version in the *Þiðrekssaga*, then, already shows a softening of the ending that was to win the day in the later balladesque version. In the latter, logically enough, the embarrassing foul blow was suppressed by the process of 'blinding'. '*I do not know*', says the poet, 'how the young man gave the old man a blow' — the same device of diplomatic ignorance of which the Nibelung poet had availed himself when blinding the motif of Brunhild's defloration in his source.[25] The reference to the once foul, now mighty, blow is needed in order to lead into the punchline, 'A woman taught you that blow!'.

In the later lay, the original setting between two armies, silent witnesses of dire events, has gone. The general texture is far less dense, and with the conciliatory ending a note almost of gaiety comes in. Purely linear descent from the original of the extant old *Hildebrandslied* must not be assumed. The original poem will have multiplied in variants with cross-influences. Other versions of the father-slays-son plot were current in Ireland (and probably Scotland), in Persia and in the Caucasus, if not in the intervening country, in the thirteenth century; and specific motifs of oral poetry tend to attract compatible motifs. For example, in the Old Norse, Old Irish and some Russian versions, the son is out fowling when he meets his father, symbolizing his carefree, peaceful mood.

Motifs from the old *Hildebrandslied* which seem to survive in the balladesque version, though distorted in form and context, are these. Alebrand says 'Tell me, you aged man,[26] what you are seeking in my father's (or: your) country? You wear armour bright and dazzling as though you were a king's son.[27] You want to pull the wool over my eyes, young warrior that I am'.[28] Told to stay at home and warm himself at the fire, Hildebrand retorts: 'I have had to go campaigning, campaigning and fighting all my days[29] — that is why my beard is grey'. 'You must yield to me your armour and your green shield', says Alebrand.[30] The descent in tone from the measured exchanges of the old lay is marked by Alebrand's replique on the grey beard: 'I will tear out your beard . . . so that your rose-red blood flows down your cheeks!'

The inability of thirteenth-century Christian courtly society to tolerate the father's slaying of a son in heroic poetry is in harmony with the change introduced into the tradition of *Hild* by the *Kudrun* poet or a predecessor. In the original version Hagen overtook his daughter's abductor and husband Hetel on the Wülpensand and in one variant slew and was slain by him. But in *Kudrun*, Hetel and Hagen are reconciled — on the coast of Wales — and only later is Hetel, now a father in pursuit of his daughter Kudrun's abductor, slain — on the Wülpensand.

The dramatic aspects of the *Nibelungenlied* and to a lesser degree of the *Kudrun* prompt the question as to how the dramatic mode was expressed in other ways in medieval German. Pure drama was of course absent at first, though cultivation of the dramatic aspects of the liturgy and also of folk rituals led to truly theatrical representations in the later Middle Ages. It is hard to believe that certain dialogue and dance songs of the Minnesang, that is, the courtly love-lyric, were not enacted in costume in an elevated vaudeville style before the same sort of courtly audiences as those of the *Nibelungenlied*. Otherwise, no doubt, all narrative verse, including the heroic, was rendered according to needs and possibilities with the help of the histrionic-mimetic art. It is scarcely conceivable that (as some have suggested) the *Nibelungenlied* with all its tense scenes and changing décor — 'At the cathedral door' — 'On the stair of the burning hall' — was performed in a dead-pan manner. And it would be very odd (as others have suggested) if the poet of the lost *Nôt*, on which the Nibelung poet of *c.*1200 based his second part, had chosen his epoch-making 'Nibelungstrophe' from the Danubian lyrical tradition merely in order to recite and not chant or sing it. There are neumes above the opening strophe of the heroic *Eckenlied* in the *Carmina Burana*, and the minstrel Der Marnære confirms that this poem was sung.

In the absence of clear evidence for the extemporization of medieval German heroic poetry one assumes a divorce between the composition and performance of anything that has reached us. The formulaic material is post-oral and at times eked out to an extreme of triteness. It is marvellous that the Nibelung poet can say so much so well with so wretched an epic diction. This diction is minstrel-like but also courtly in a broader sense, with the former element often tending to reassert itself as heroic poetry descends from the high level of the *Nibelungenlied* and *Kudrun*. In it there is the freedom to use pre-chivalric, in effect inherited Germanic, terms for 'warrior' (e.g. *helt*, *wîgant*, *degen*) and for matters concerned with warfare, such as chivalric authors either avoid or use with irony (though the chivalric Wolfram von Eschenbach does as he pleases).

The inner style of the medieval German heroic poems is third-personal-objective. The Nibelung poet, for example, never apostrophizes a character. He embraces his audience in his opening phrase 'We have been told in ancient tales . . .'; addresses them directly in the concluding line of this strophe 'Of such things you can now hear wonders unending . . .'; and in the final strophe of his epic takes his leave of them in person 'I cannot tell you what happened after this . . .'. The rare first person is fictional at least in as much as there are good grounds for believing the first strophe to be the work of the poet of the 'C' Recension, the last strophe the work of the man in whom we see the author of the classic version of the epic.

Regarding the status of the poets of the medieval German epics, very little is known. As part of the objective style of the epics and their nature as believed or supposed 'history', authors in this genre do not name themselves. For the mid-twelfth century it must be assumed that professional literate poets had begun their rivalry with oral poets in this field. The influence of the style of popular entertainers — '*spilliute*' or 'minstrels' — which poets of different station might also use if it suited their purpose, is strong in our genre and has left its marks even on the superior *Nibelungenlied*. It is thus difficult if not impossible to disentangle the social class or non-class to which the author of a given epic belonged. Towards the end of the thirteenth century in Austria a hack breaks anonymity in his *Buch von Bern* (*Dietrichs Flucht*) in order to harangue the nobility on a political matter, posing as author of a work of which he wrote but little.[31]

The ethos and inferred function of lays such as the *Hildebrandslied* have been discussed above.[32] Ethos and function in relation to the medieval German epic are also largely a matter of inference. It can, however, be no accident that the region in which the heroic spirit survived most robustly was the frontier province of Austria, a margraviate within living memory of the Nibelung poet of *c.*1200, who situates his Huns beyond the frontier in Hungary. The old Austrian *Nôt* must assuredly have had the function of steeling the morale of the Austrian knights of its day (*c.*1160). Of the enigmatic *Nibelungenlied* we cannot be so sure. *Kudrun* aimed at conciliation to end blood feuds — at armed pacification with honour, of course not pacificism. *Dietrichs Flucht*, with its contemporary polemic, stresses loyalty in princes towards their vassals. *Alpharts Tod* stands for fair play on the battlefield. Nothing could better illustrate the diversification of function when an archaic heroic society has ceased to exist and has left powerful heroic themes as a legacy in poetry.

The variety of heroic types, from the frank and carefree to the dour and sinister, is such that it is left to the reader to attempt his own generalizations. Some heroes were no doubt felt to be wholly admirable and exemplary: yet not all. In *Kudrun*, Wate was intended to be admirable and obsolete — that is, not to be imitated now. At leading courts of the classical and post-classical period, pure literary interest and pleasure in life's variety had overtaken and eventually submerged the functional exemplariness that had once nerved the comitatus to its duty. In some contemporary eyes — not least the Nibelung poet's — the once exemplary Kriemhild had come to be the pattern of what no woman should be. Kudrun, again, is exemplary in a more 'modern' sense.

The tendency of the Germanic heroic lay to play down magic and the supernatural as a point of style continues in serious medieval German epic. Siegfried's cloak of invisibility is used in the *Nibelungenlied* only when primary plot demands it; and his and Brunhild's superhuman strength is shown in a comic light. The poet retains the baleful prophecy of the Danubian swan-maidens that no Nibelung shall return and has Hagen test it with scientific detachment by throwing the chaplain overboard, thus provoking intervention from on high: for the non-swimmer floats miraculously. Cases of intervention in a more obviously Christian sense are the apparition of the angel in bird shape with a happy prophecy for Kudrun; the baptism of the babe by the light of candles held by unseen hands in *Wolfdietrich* A, and the swaddling-clothes of silk that will grow to his size and protect him as a man — all bordering on motifs from another genre, that of pious legend. But in *Kudrun* there is ancient magic, too. Wate, inflictor of great wounds, can heal them with a magic herb; Horant can charm the birds from the bough with his wondrous singing. In these better compositions such elements are used sparingly and effectively: but in lesser works into which the marvellous is imported wholesale from sub-chivalric romance it serves together with other criteria as a sure index of decline.

As has been seen above, medieval German heroic tradition provides a clear example of the evolution of 'lay' to 'epic'. As far as the Nibelung material was concerned, this at no stage involved mere amalgamation of existing lays. On the contrary, the first main lay of the Fall of the Nibelungs (Burgundians) was expanded into the lost epic *Nôt*, retaining its sharp outlines but with much new incident and with new characters, all duly subordinated to the main theme. The poet of *c.*1200 applied the same process to later versions of the other main source, variant lays of Siegfried and Brunhild; he skilfully inserted the briefest necessary information from further lays on Siegfried's youth in the form of a report by Hagen; and he fused the two parts into a continuous epic. *Kudrun* presents an epicized version of the old Baltic lay of *Hild* fused with a repetition of the plot of which Hild's daughter Kudrun, a new character with a new out-look, is the heroine. The process of epic growth in Germany, then, on the evidence of the only two examples that permit of convincing analysis, resembles that of crystallization. It shows organic growth about a shapely nucleus that is retained.

The textual background of German heroic poetry is probably typical of any medieval tradition. The *Hildebrand* torso is lodged on the recto of the first and the verso of the last leaves of a manuscript of theological content. Although it was an oral poem, the errors in our text reveal that it was copied from a written source. If, as is widely believed, the manuscript originated in Fulda, this would point to the antiquarian interests of Anglo-Saxon missionaries in Germany. The manuscript history of the *Nibelungenlied* is bound up with its presumed 'take-over' by the see of Passau,[33] and with innovations of group C as against group B, favouring Kriemhild against Hagen. Unlike the excellent but un-successful *Kudrun*, known to us from the unique copy in the Ambras MS compiled for an imperial connoisseur, the *Nibelungenlied* descended in many manuscripts as a classic text with only minor attrition. The first five hundred strophes of *Wolfdietrich* A, of good quality, are uniquely preserved in the Ambras MS. The Middle High German *Walther* survives only in a few frag-ments. As to the Dietrich epics and later sub-heroic narratives of adventure, earlier Middle High German versions were put out of the running by successive recensions and extensions, and thus lost. The varying quality of the manuscripts here suggests any function ranging from prompt-book to luxury edition. At the end of the tradition some texts saw the novelty of print: the *Jüngeres Hildebrandslied* was reprinted until the seventeenth century; *Das Lied vom Hürnen Seyfried* is known only from printed versions. Of all the material discussed, then, only the *Nibelungenlied* offers the possibility of a reliable text, and even this will be not the poet's but a recension which soon followed it.

NOTES

1. See H. Rupp, ' "Heldendichtung" als Gattung der deutschen Literatur des 13. Jahrhunderts', *Volk, Sprache, Dichtung*, Festgabe für Kurt Wagner (1960), pp. 9–25; W. Hoffmann, *Kudrun*. Ein Beitrag zur Deutung der nachnibelungischen Heldendichtung (Stuttgart, 1967), pp. 1–11; W. Hoffmann, *Mittelhochdeutsche Heldendichtung*, Grundlagen der Germanistik, 14 (Berlin, 1974), 1. Teil: Die Heldendichtung als Gattung der mittelhochdeutschen Literatur. The last-named work is authoritative. It relieves the present author of the need for detailed documentation. The present author is even more radical than Professor Hoffmann and can, as heir to a different literary heritage, afford to be so. The purpose of the present contribution is to inform fellow contributors to this volume, and others with the same comparativist interests, about the nature of *truly* heroic epic poetry in Medieval German. There has recently appeared *Deutsche Heldenepik in Tirol*. König Laurin und Dietrich von Bern in der Dichtung des Mittelalters. Beiträge der Neustifter Tagung des Südtiroler Kulturinstitutes. In Zusammenarbeit mit Karl H. Vigl herausgegeben von Egon Kühebacher, (Bozen, 1979). An important work, ranging far beyond what the title and sub-title indicate, by numerous leading scholars.

2. See G. Baesecke, 'Die indogermanische Verwandtschaft des Hildebrandliedes', *Nachrichten von der Gesellschaft der Wissenschaften zu Göttingen*, Phil.-Hist. Klasse, Fachgr. IV. Neuere Philologie u. Literaturgeschichte, Neue Folge, Bd. III, Nr. 5, pp. 139–53; A. T. Hatto, 'On the excellence of the "Hildebrandslied": a comparative study in dynamics', *Modern Language Review*, 68 (1973), 820–38.

3. On possible legal procedures at this point see Ute Schwab, '*arbeo laosa*. Philologische Studien zum Hildebrandlied', Basler Studien zur deutschen Sprache und Literatur, 45 (Berne, 1972), 46–57.

4. Despite Professor Schwab's arguments, loc. cit., it seems preferable to retain the MS's attribution of lines 37 ff. *mit geru scal man geba infahan,|ort widar orte* to Hadubrant, even though some of the inquits are the result of 'editing' *c.* A.D. 800 and one of them is unquestionably wrong (line 45).

5. See I. Reiffenstein, 'Zu Stil und Aufbau des Hildebrandsliedes', in *Sprachkunst als Weltgestaltung*. *Festschrift für Herbert Seidler*, Hrsg. von A. Haslinger (Salzburg–München, 1966), pp. 229–54.

6. Lines 48–54, in, for example, W. Braune, *Althochdeutsches Lesebuch*[13], bearbeitet von K. Helm (Tübingen, 1958), p. 129.

7. J. Knight Bostock, 'The message of the *Nibelungenlied*', *Modern Language Review*, 55 (1960), p. 206.

8. See p. 180, below.

9. Edited by H. Bertelsen, in 2 vols (Copenhagen, 1908–11). The *Þiðrekssaga*, compiled *c.*1250 in West Norse, retells in prose North German versions of heroic poems grouped into a 'life' of Theodoric the Great. See J. De Vries, *Altnordische Literaturgeschichte* in: Grundriss der germanischen Philologie, 15 and 16, II (Berlin, 1967), pp. 514 ff.; German translation: F. Erichsen, *Die Geschichte Thidreks von Bern*, Thule XXII (Jena, 1924).

10. See: *Ekkehards Waltharius*. Hrsg. K. Strecker (Berlin, 1907); K. Langosch, *Waltharius. Ruodlieb. Märchenepen*. Lateinische Epik des Mittelalters, mit deutschen Versen (Basel/Stuttgart, 1956); F. Norman, *Waldere* (London, 1933).

11. See p. 168, above.

12. See p. 186, below.

13. I have given the orthodox position on this much debated subject in: *The Nibelungenlied: A new translation*, Penguin Classics, L 137 (London, 1964, etc.), Appendix 4, 'The Genesis of the Poem', pp. 370–95. This appendix gives the narrative data of the Eddaic Lays and the *Þiðrekssaga* on the Nibelungen theme.

14. See p. 175, above.

15. The *Nibelungenlied*, pp. 289–90. For another rendering see D. G. Mowatt, 'The *Nibelungenlied*', Everyman's Library, 312 (London, 1962), pp. 217–18.

16. For detailed discussion see: W. Hoffmann, *Kudrun*, Ein Beitrag zur Deutung der nachnibelungischen Heldendichtung, Germanistische Abhandlungen 17 (Stuttgart, 1967); I. R. Campbell, *Kudrun*, a critical appreciation, *Anglica Germanica*, Series 2 (Cambridge, 1978).

17. For reconstructions of this lost version of *Hild* see: H. Schneider, *Germanische Heldensage* (Grundriss der germanischen Philologie, 10), 1 (Berlin, 1928), pp. 361–71, 381–84; and B. Boesch, *Kudrun*, Altdeutsche Textbibliothek, 5 (Tübingen, 1954), pp. xxxvi–xxxix (Introduction to an edition of the text).

18. For *chansons de geste* of the Guillaume Cycle, see Professor David Ross's discussion in the Old French section of the present work, pp. 80 ff., above.

19. See p. 168, above.

20. *Deor*, 18 *Ðéodric áhte prítig wintra Mǽringa burg*; *Waldere*, II, 4–10.

21. See p. 187, below.

22. On the Harlungs see G. T. Gillespie, *A catalogue of persons named in German heroic literature (700–1600), including named animals and objects and ethnic names* (Oxford, 1973), pp. 62–63. See further the entry 'Ermenrich' (pp. 37–39) and indeed the entries for the other heroes named in the present contribution.

23. See p. 169, above.

24. Such a study is implicit in Professor Hoffmann's *Mittelhochdeutsche Heldendichtung* (see footnote 1, above), but this work has no chapter specifically devoted to the theme.

25. 'I do not know whether it was his pride which made him do it' (str. 680,2). On this oral device of blinding motifs as a result of reshaping of plot, see A. T. Hatto, '*Ine weiz* . . . . Diplomatic ignorance on the part of Medieval German poets', in *German Studies, presented to Leonard Ashley Willoughby* (Oxford, 1952), pp. 98–102.

26. Compare the older *Hildebrandslied*, line 39 ('You are very wily, old Hun.').

27. Ibid., lines 46–48 ('I can well see from your armour that at home you have a good lord and were never an exile from this kingdom!').

28. Ibid., line 40 ('You lure me with fair words . . .').

29. Ibid., lines 50–51 ('I wandered summer and winter for thirty years in foreign lands and was always ranged among the shock-troops!').

30. Ibid., lines 60–61 ('Let him that can, make trial which of us two today is to yield up his arms or be master of both suits of mail!'), spoken by Hildebrand.

31. See the following paragraph

32. p. 166, above.

33. See Appendix 2, 'The manuscript tradition' to my translation of the *Nibelungenlied*, cited in note 13, above.

SERBO-CROAT

By ROBERT AUTY

AMONG THE GREAT MASS of anonymous traditional poetry in the Serbo-Croatian language the epic bulks largest and represents one of the most characteristic and aesthetically valuable contributions by the Slavs to the stock of world literature. The extent of the material, the long period of time over which the techniques and subjects have developed, and certain regional differences of theme and treatment make it difficult to provide a definition of the genre as precise and generally applicable as can be given, for example, for the Germanic lay.[1] Nevertheless, the most characteristic type of poem may be tentatively defined thus: it is a poem of about 100–300 lines, dealing with heroic persons or events, generally, though by no means necessarily, with a tragic outcome. The lines are unrhymed, of regular length, and exhibit certain characteristic rhythmic patterns. The style is conventional, relying to a great extent on formulae and repetition. The narrative is single-stranded and highly concentrated. The poems were (and to a limited extent still are) chanted (much more rarely recited) by professional singers. When chanted they are almost invariably accompanied on a stringed instrument, the single-stringed or two-stringed *gusle*, an instrument of the violin type, or (usually in Muslim areas) the two-stringed *tamburica* (*tambura*), a kind of mandolin. The singers produce the texts partly from memory, partly by improvisation. Until the nineteenth century they were handed down solely by oral tradition.

It has been estimated that about half a million lines of this kind of poetry are available in print; and that a similar quantity exists in known manuscript collections. The earliest preserved collection of any size was made in about 1720;[2] but it is only in the last 150 years or so that these songs have been systematically collected and recorded. The most valuable specimens — at any rate from the aesthetic point of view — are contained in the collection of Serbian folk poetry made by Vuk Karadžić in the first half of the nineteenth century (nine volumes, of which Volumes II–IV and VI–X contain epic poems). For a full study of the material Vuk's collection must be supplemented by that of the Matica Hrvatska (ten volumes, of which Volumes I–IV and VIII–IX contain epic poems) and, for the very characteristic Muslim songs, by those of Kosta Hörmann and of Parry and Lord. There is a very extensive scholarly literature dealing with the Serbo-Croatian epic; and, as the composition and recital of such poems has lived on to our own time, much of the scholarly treatment concerns the singers themselves, their techniques of composition and delivery, and the social background against which the whole phenomenon must be considered. Murko, 1951 (see Bibliography, p. 210, below) is a veritable encyclopædia of the Serbo-Croatian popular epic as it existed in the first third of this century; and his information is greatly amplified by Parry and Lord, 1953–54 and Lord, 1960. A good deal of work has been devoted to the origin of the historical songs and their relation to the events they describe. Pre-eminent among investigations of this kind is Maximilian Braun's study of the historical background of the Kosovo songs (Braun, 1937). As against these important questions of literary history and literary sociology less attention has been paid to the purely aesthetic analysis of the songs. It is true that a number of important studies have been devoted to their metrical analysis (Maretić, 1907, Saran, 1937, Jakobson, 1952), but it is only relatively recently that narrative technique and structure have begun to be studied in detail (Braun, 1961, Schmaus, 1953, Koljević, 1974); and on language and style much yet remains to be done.

Although various references in medieval chronicles and other texts enable us to assume the existence of heroic songs among the Serbs before the Turkish conquest we have, as Braun rightly points out, no right to assume that these were similar in form or manner to those which have been preserved from later times. The first recorded examples of such poems are found in the piscatorial idyll of Petar Hektorović (*Ribanje i ribarsko prigovaranje*) composed in 1556 and published in 1568. The two poems given there are put in the mouths of Dalmatian fishermen; they are composed in the 15–16 syllable line known as *bugarštica*, and one of them treats the hero of one of the principal Serbo-Croatian epic cycles, Kraljević Marko. Other isolated examples were recorded in the seventeenth century; and from about 1720 we have the earliest preserved collection, the Erlangen MS, which contains over 200 anonymous poems, very many of them epics, and seems to have been compiled in the Croatian Military Frontier. This is an early example of the interest in ancient and popular poetry which became widespread in central as well as western Europe in the eighteenth century. This interest is also reflected in the work of the Dalmatian Franciscan Andrija Kačić Miošić, who not only published a collection of historical poems written by himself in a manner derived from the style of the traditional heroic songs but also included among them some genuine examples besides.[3] To Vuk Stefanović Karadžić (1787–1864) we owe not only the invaluable collection of poems already referred to, but also the first identifications and descriptions of individual singers. From then onwards we have a whole mass of information about the way in which this poetry is produced and handed down. Singers of epic poems, both professional and amateur, were numerous throughout the nineteenth century, especially in Montenegro and Bosnia-Herzegovina. Indeed, in Bosnia, Herzegovina and the Sanjak of Novi Pazar we find court poets still employed by the Muslim begs and agas as late as the eve of the First

World War. Bosnia-Herzegovina remained under Turkish suzerainty until 1908 and the Sanjak until 1912. As late as the 1950s there were to be found a good number of singers who performed the traditional songs and even composed new ones.

The long-line metre (*bugarštica*) is the vehicle of a fair number of the poems recorded before 1800. Since then, however, we have exclusively poems composed in unrhymed decasyllables — the *deseterac*, which had thus even by Vuk's time become the characteristic epic metre. Although the typical song is less than 500 lines long,[4] there are a great many that exceed this norm; the Muslim songs in particular, which exhibit a number of special features, may be several thousand lines in length.

A convenient classification groups the poems according to their subject-matter. The vast majority deal, at least nominally, with events and characters from the history of the Serbs and Croats, beginning with the Turkish conquest of the Balkans in the fourteenth and fifteenth centuries and extending to the Second World War. Outside this main corpus lies a group of poems dealing with religious or mythological themes; closely associated with this group is a small number of poems dealing ostensibly with themes from Serbian history before the Turkish invasions. These have little connexion with actual history and belong mainly to the realm of legend and fairy-tale. With the Kosovo cycle the historical element becomes clear and tangible. While facts and personages are no doubt modified or invented to create a poetic reinterpretation of the events described, the historical basis is unmistakable. Although the defeat of a Serbian army on the plain of Kosovo (near Priština) in 1389 did not mark the final incorporation of Serbia in the Ottoman Empire, it came to symbolize in poetry the final eclipse of medieval Serbia. In fact a further cycle of poems deals with the rearguard actions that extended over the following century, during which the Turks inexorably pushed forward to Croatia and Hungary. These are the songs of the 'despots, voivodes and bans': their heroes include not only Serbs and Croats but Hungarians (though with Serbianized names, such as Sibinjanin Janko for John Hunyadi and Svilojević for Hunyadi's brother-in-law Szilágyi). Another extensive group of poems takes its themes from the activities of the rebels and outlaws who resisted Turkish rule in the period from the sixteenth to the eighteenth centuries: these are the songs of the hajduks and uskoks. A separate cycle commemorates the struggles of the Montenegrins against the Turks. The Serbian rebellions which led in the early nineteenth century to the re-establishment of an autonomous principality of Serbia form the subject of a further important series of songs. Such were the cycles of heroic songs current when Vuk Karadžić made his collection. To these must be added the more recent songs dealing with events of the twentieth century, notably the Balkan wars of 1912–13 and the First and Second World Wars; and also the very interesting cycle of Muslim songs from the Krajina region of north-western Bosnia which view the Christian-Turkish border struggles from the Turkish point of view.

The poems under consideration are referred to traditionally as 'songs of old time', 'ancient songs' (*starinske, stare pjesme*) or as 'heroic songs' (*junačke pjesme*). These two terms bring out the basic character and function of the poems in the eyes of those who composed and listened to them. On the one hand they represent history, or at any rate history as it had been transformed in the minds of the Serbs and Croats, expressed in the most general terms. The details of historical events are subordinated to the general picture or are changed to fit it. The broad historical picture thus presented forms a background for the portrayal of the conduct and bearing of heroes. *Junak* 'hero' is a term which constantly recurs as an appellation of the chief characters. The characteristics implied by this term have been well summarized by Braun (1961).[5] The hero is a fighter (either a professional warrior or at least a person highly skilled in armed combat); he is an individualist, relying on his own powers and with few or no ties other than those of family loyalty (interpreted in a very wide sense); honour and reputation form the mainspring of his actions: thus, chivalrous and magnanimous conduct and bearing can be as important as victory in battle. There can be no doubt that in addition to their functions of entertainment and of historical information these poems had, at least implicitly, a didactic function: the conduct and attitudes of the heroes were recommended models for the listeners to emulate according to their lights.

Although the heroes are portrayed in a great variety of situations, their specific qualities are best exemplified when they are confronted by a tragic destiny or involved in a tragic conflict. It is the first of these situations that characterizes the poems of the Kosovo cycle. The 'Emperor' (in historical fact Prince) Lazar knows that he is bound to be defeated by the superior Turkish forces. Moreover, in one poem at least, he suspects that he will be betrayed by one of his own vassals, as in fact proves to be the case. But he regards it as his duty to go into the battle, foredoomed as he is to defeat. The attitude of other Serbian heroes is similar; and when the inevitable destiny has been fulfilled by the destruction of the Serbian army we are told that

> sve je sveto, sve čestito bilo
> i milome Bogu pristupačno.[6]
> (All was holy, all was honourable and fitting in the eyes of God.)

The inevitability of death as the ultimate destiny of the hero is sometimes implied more indirectly, as in the poem *Smrt Senjanina Iva* (The Death of Ivo of Senj).[7] The mother of Ivo, who is one of the uskoks of the Adriatic port of Senj, outlaws who fought against Venice and the Turks, has a prophetic dream which, with its interpretation, takes up the first third of the poem: her son is to perish, along with many other men of Senj, at the hands of the Turks. The remainder of the poem relates the arrival of Ivo, mortally wounded, his brief narrative of the fatal expedition that was annihilated by the Turks, and his death. Though the theme of the hero's destiny is not so explicitly stated as in the Kosovo songs the hearers can have been in no doubt that it was inevitable and indeed fitting for the outlaw's life to end thus.

In many poems the hero finds himself in a tragic situation not as a result of an inevitable or expected consummation of destiny but as a result of blind chance. Such are the poems that describe fights between two heroes who, unknown to one another, are related (father and son or, more commonly, brothers). The quality of the hero generally shows itself here by his committing suicide when he realizes that he has killed a kinsman.

The songs which show their heroes' qualities in situations of dramatic tension are no doubt aesthetically the most satisfying of the Serbo-Croatian epic poems; but such masterpieces cannot be produced to order, and it is not surprising that the great mass of epic material is not of such high quality and deserves the epithet 'heroic' for no other reason than that it continually presents to us the varied adventures of persons who are universally recognized as heroes. Such poems are not necessarily tragic in their outcome. They may, but need not, portray battles. What they have in common is that they show the strength, courage, independence and magnanimity of their protagonists. The plots range from the simplest of anecdotes to complex adventure stories. Many of the themes are international ones, and supernatural elements sometimes play a part, particularly the characteristic and by no means always friendly Slavonic wood- and water-nymphs known as *vile*. It is in poems of this kind that we follow the exploits of Kraljević Marko, one of the best-known figures of South Slavonic epic and legend. Poems about him are found in the languages of all the Balkan Slavs. The historical Marko was the son of the Serbian King Vukašin and ruled as a Turkish vassal in Prilep (north-western Macedonia) from the Battle of the Maritsa (1371), in which his father perished, until his own death in 1394. History records no more about him. It is remarkable that this Turkish vassal should have become a popular hero with Serbs, Croats, Macedonians and Bulgarians. The poems about him often have an anecdotal character; humorous incidents, entirely lacking in the tragic Kosovo cycle, are frequent, as are supernatural elements: Marko is of superhuman strength, his magic horse was presented to him by a *vila*. Quarrelsome and a great drinker, he respects the Sultan, his overlord, but protects his fellow-Serbs against Turkish tyranny. Never troubled by tragic conflicts or by the burdens of destiny like the heroes of Kosovo, this extrovert figure is nevertheless also a hero, albeit *sui generis*. The ethical outlook of the songs about Marko is essentially the same as that of the Kosovo songs.[8]

The narrative structure of the poem is, as was stated at the outset, single-stranded. This does not always apply to the Muslim songs; but the uninterrupted unitary plot is an important common feature of the songs of the Christian tradition. Frequently the poem begins with a brief introduction of the principal character, sitting in his palace at a meal or, even more commonly, drinking wine. Three of the Kosovo songs provide variants of this opening: *Slavu slavi srpski knez Lazare | u Kruševcu, mjestu skrovitome* (The Serbian prince Lazar is celebrating his saint's day in Kruševac, the hidden city); *Car Lazare sjede na večeru, | pokraj njega carica Milica* (Emperor Lazar sat down to dinner; beside him was the Empress Milica); *Vino pije Musiću Stevane | u Majdanu čisto srebrnome, | u svom krasnom dvoru gospodskome* (Musić Stevan is drinking wine in Majdan [the town] of pure silver, in his fair lordly palace).[9] There often follows a dialogue, from which the nature of some tragic conflict emerges, or the fore-boding of impending disaster. The 'action' in the strict sense is often restricted to a few lines towards the end; or it may be related indirectly, in the words of messengers. Other songs plunge *in medias res*, though even here the situation may be more or less stereotyped: *Pojezdiše do dva pobratima | preko krasne Miroča planine. Ta jedno je Kraljeviću Marko, | a drugo je vojvoda Milošu* (Two sworn brothers rode across the fair mountain of Miroča. One was the king's son Marko and the other was voivode Miloš); *Konje jašu do dva pobratima, | Beg Kostadin i Kraljević Marko* (Two sworn brothers are riding on horseback, Beg Kostadin and the king's son Marko)[10] — then immediately follows a dialogue. To this type belongs also the opening with its variants: *Uranila Kosovka devojka, | uranila rano u nedelju* (The girl of Kosovo got up early, early on a Sunday morning); *Poranio Kraljeviću Marko, | poranio niz Kosovo ravno*[11] (The king's son Marko got up early and was going down the plain of Kosovo). Yet another frequent opening is an invocation of God: *Mili Bože, na svemu ti vala* ('Dear God, thanks be to Thee for everything'); *Mili Bože, čuda velikoga* ('Dear God, what a great marvel!').[12]

Just as the action can on occasion be described in retrospect, by messengers or (as in *The Death of Ivo of Senj*) by the hero himself, it is possible for it to be anticipated. This is at any rate the case in the very subtle and effective song *Prince Lazar's slava*, of which the opening has already been quoted. On the eve of the battle of Kosovo Lazar drinks a toast to one of his warriors Miloš Obilić, but accuses him of preparing to desert to the Turks and betray his lord. Obilić replies, passionately affirming his loyalty, accusing the real traitor Vuk Branko-vić, and swearing that he will kill the Turkish Sultan and, after the battle, take revenge on Vuk Branković. For the full effect of this poem the singer must rely on his hearers' knowledge of the happenings at Kosovo. All know that Vuk will indeed betray Lazar, that Miloš will keep his promise to kill the Sultan, but that the whole Serbian army will be destroyed, including Lazar himself. Although no action whatsoever takes place in this poem it is one of the most dramatic of the songs of Kosovo. Other songs are more explicit, sometimes stringing a series of incidents together. But these incidents are always seen from a single point of view; the unity of action and a certain concentrated tension are always maintained. The conclusion of a song is less frequently expressed in stereotyped terms than the beginning. Sometimes indeed the tension is relaxed by a concluding line such as *Onda bilo, sad se spominjalo* (Once it was, now we have remembered it);[13] or: *Bog sam znade je li tako bilo | a mi, braćo, da se veselimo* (God alone knows whether it was so, / but let us make merry, brothers!).[14] But it is much more common for the poem to cease abruptly with the close of the action.

The Serbo-Croatian epics, as we saw earlier, were normally chanted to the accompaniment of the single-stringed *gusle* or, in certain regions, of the *tambura* (*tamburica*), an instrument with two metal strings which are plucked. The musical accompaniment has been characterized in detail by Braun (1961, 59–62) and Murko (1951, pp. 381 ff.). All observers agree that the initial impression on the non-native observer is one of monotony and by no means immediately appealing — 'reichlich befremdend' (Braun, 1961, p. 60). Nevertheless, it is clear that within the narrow limits of a melody that is repeated line after line many and subtle variations are introduced; and even the foreign listener, once his ear is attuned, falls under the spell of the *guslar*. When a song is produced in the manner described some modification or even deformation of the normal speech-sounds results. In Serbo-Croat stress, quantity and intonation are all phonemically relevant; and it might be supposed that these factors would be suppressed by the superimposition of melody. Again, those competent to judge are agreed that this is not the case: the natural rhythms of speech, while to some extent overlaid or obscured, are still perceptible.

'Im allgemeinen gleicht sich das Versmass nach Möglichkeit dem Rhythmus der gesprochenen Rede an; der Zehnsilber wird nicht skandiert' (Braun, 1961, p. 51). The 'tension between the normal accent and the metre' (Lord, 1960, p. 37) heightens the aesthetic effect. Some performers, moreover, recite the poems without accompaniment. Although this is no doubt a later development, it is too frequent, especially in particular areas, to be disregarded. It is thus fully justified to analyse the texts from a metrical, as well as a musical, point of view; and the fact that such analysis reveals regular patterns and tendencies in the ten-syllable line is in itself significant.

The clearest and most authoritative metrical analysis of the Serbo-Croatian epic *deseterac* is that of Roman Jakobson (1966, p. 418). He characterizes the line as exhibiting certain metrical constants admitting of 'no, or only occasional, deviation', and certain tendencies. In what follows we note the most important of these characteristic features.

The basic structure is one of syllables, not of stress-groups: that is to say, the number of ten syllables is constant, and variation is introduced by the very considerable variety of stress, intonation, and quantity patterns. This is, of course, the exact opposite of the Germanic metre described above (p. 166), where the stress pattern is regular and the number of syllables variable. The line forms a syntactic unit: there is normally no enjambment. A caesura, marked by a word-boundary, occurs after the fourth syllable. The third and fourth syllables always form part of the same word-unit; this is also the case with the ninth and tenth syllables. This means that in štokavic Serbo-Croat, where no word may have final stress, the last syllable of each part of the line must be unstressed. The final cadence (i.e. the pattern of the four last syllables of the line) is clearly characterized. The ninth syllable is hardly ever an accented short; and accented longs are avoided in the seventh and eighth syllables. Within the limits imposed by these constants it is clear that a variety of rhythmical patterns are possible, some essentially trochaic, some dactylic. Without entering the controversy as to which of these rhythms is fundamental to this type of verse the foreign observer can, at any rate, observe that the intertwining of the two gives it its specific character and attraction. The metrical tendencies further characterized by Jakobson need not be recapitulated here in detail. They indicate tendencies towards trochaic rhythm and a division of the second colon into two stress-groups which are, however, so closely connected and of such varied length that they do not create a second caesura. The metrical structure that has been sketched here may be illustrated by the opening lines of *Kosovka devojka* (The Girl of Kosovo):

1	Ùranila | Kòsōvka dèvōjka, ||
	Ùranila | ràno u nèdelju,
	U nèdelju | prije jârka sûnca, ||
	Zasúkala | bȉjele rukáve, ||
5	Zasúkala | do bêlī lakátā, ||
	Na plèćima | nòsī lȅba béla, ||
	U rùkama | dvâ kondíra zlátna, ||
	U jèdnōme | làdjanē vòdicē, ||
	U drùgōme | rùmenōga vína, ||
10	Òna idē | na Kòsovo râvnō, ||
	Pa se šêćē | po rázboju mláda, ||
	Po rázboju | čèstitōga knêza, ||
	Te prèvrćē | po kȑvi junáke; ||
	Kog junáka | u žìvòtu nâdjē, ||
15	Ùmīvā ga | làdjanōm vòdicōm, ||
	Pričèšćujē | vínom cȑvenijem ||
	I zàlāžē | lȅbom bȉjelijem. ||
	Námera | je nàmerila bíla ||
	Na junáka | Òrlovića Pâvla, ||
20	Na knéževa | mláda barjaktára || ...

(The girl of Kosovo rose in the morning, rose on Sunday before the sun was hot, she rolled up her white sleeves as far as her white elbows, on her shoulders she bore white bread, in her hands were two golden pitchers, in one of them was cold water, in the other red wine, she goes to the plain of Kosovo, and she walks, the young girl, over the battlefield, over the battlefield of the honourable prince, and she turns over the heroes [lying] in blood; when she finds a hero who is still alive she washes him in the cold water, administers the red wine and gives him white bread to eat. Chance had brought her to the hero Òrlović Pavle, the prince's young standard-bearer . . .[15]

The Serbo-Croatian language exhibits a fairly considerable dialectal variety, and it is of interest to note the linguistic character of the epic songs. One of the basic differences between the dialects is in the representation of the Common Slavonic phoneme ě. By this criterion we distinguish *ekavic*, *ijekavic* and *ikavic* dialects (i.e. ě > *e, ije* and *i* respectively). The most fruitful source of the epic songs seems to be the *ijekavic*-speaking area (Herzegovina, Montenegro, parts of Bosnia). This was also the dialect-type spoken by Vuk Karadžić, and it seems at least possible that he may have adapted some of the texts which he heard to his own dialect, which was at the same time the one most frequently represented in the songs. Other collectors (particularly of the Muslim songs of Bosnia) have recorded many songs in the *ikavic* dialect. It is striking that *ijekavic* forms can be found in songs from all the areas. This is partly due, no doubt, to the spread of popular songs to new areas, in which they were not, or only partly, adapted to a new dialect. It seems, however, that the *ijekavic* dialect came to be regarded as appropriate for this kind of poem and that it was employed, sometimes imperfectly, by speakers of other dialects. Thus many poems show a dialect-mixture. This was no doubt encouraged by the fact that many words in the *ijekavic* dialect have a syllable more than they have in either of the others, and that this alternation could be exploited according to the exigencies of the metre. For example, in the lines from *Kosovka devojka* quoted above the word for 'white' occurs as *bijele* (*ijekavic*) in line 4, but as *beli* (*ekavic*) in line 5. This alternation comes to be regarded, like particular stylistic features, as part of a special epic language. To this same poetic language belongs the use, never found in ordinary speech, of the vocative in place of the nominative: for example 'Vino pije *Musiću Stevane*', 'Slavu slavi srpski knez *Lazare*'. This device also provides a convenient extra syllable when the metre requires it.

The style of these poems is highly formalized. Reference has already been made to certain stock openings and to the rarer stock conclusions. Stock epithets are also a typical feature: *bijeli dvor* (white palace), *hladna voda* (cold water — for a river), *bijeli dan* (white day), *rujno vino* (red wine), *Kosovo ravno, Kosovo polje ravno* (the plain of Kosovo) — these are but a few of the most common phrases containing stock epithets. There are many other formulaic expressions besides these. Parry has defined the epic formula as 'a group of words which is regularly employed under the same metrical conditions to express a given essential idea';[16] and Lord has shown in detail the importance of the formula in the composition and transmission of the epic songs.[17]

Very frequent, in addition to formulaic phrases, is the repetition of a line
or of a whole sequence of lines, sometimes with a slight modification to fit the
movement of the narrative. Braun[18] has shown how the song *Marko pije uz
Ramazan vino* is largely constructed round the frequent repetition, with slight
variations, of a sequence of four lines:

> Car Suleman jasak učinio:
> da s' ne pije uz Ramazan vino,
> da s' ne nose zelene dolame,
> da s' ne pašu sablje okovane,
> da s' ne igra kolom uz kadune;
> Marko igra kolom uz kadune,
> Marko paše sablju okovanu,
> Marko nosi zelenu dolamu,
> Marko pije uz Ramazan vino . . .

(The Emperor Suleyman issued an order: it was forbidden to drink wine in Ramadan,
to wear green dolmans, to gird on sheathed swords, to dance the *kolo* with the ladies;
Marko dances the *kolo* with the ladies, Marko girds on a sheathed sword, Marko
wears a green dolman, Marko drinks wine in Ramadan . . .)[19]

At each important turn of the story these lines are again repeated with the
appropriate modifications. Although this *tour de force* seems especially suited for
the boisterous songs about Kraljević Marko, the device of repetition, of a single
line or of a series, is frequently employed to heighten the dramatic effect.
A more sophisticated device is metaphor and, in particular, what may be called
the negative metaphor, which appears in passages such as the following:

> Što se bijeli u gori zelenoj?
> Al' je snijeg, al' su labudovi?
> Da je snijeg, već bi okopnio,
> labudovi već bi poletjeli.
> Nit je snijeg, nit su labudovi,
> nego šator age Hasan-age . . .

(What is shining white in the green wood? Is it snow or swans? If it were snow it
would by now have melted; swans would have flown away. It is not snow, nor yet
swans; it is Hasan Aga's tent.)[20]

On the whole the best songs are sparing in their descriptions of nature or of
outward appearance and dress. The elaborate descriptions which are found,
for instance, in some of the Muslim songs are a later feature which does not
add to the dramatic effectiveness of the poems.

To illustrate the structure of these epic songs it will be best briefly to analyse
one example. *Musić Stevan* (Vuk, II, 46), already referred to, is one of the finest
poems of the Kosovo cycle. The narrative runs as follows:

lines

1–28	Musić Stevan is drinking wine in his palace, waited on by his servant Vaistina. He says he is going to sleep, but that Vaistina must wake him at dawn on the following day so that they can keep their tryst with Prince
29–51	Lazar at Kosovo and do battle with the Turks. Musić Stevan goes to bed, Vaistina dines and drinks wine. He goes outside and sees that it is dawn
52–69	and time to go. On his way he meets Musić Stevan's wife who begs him not to wake his master; for she has had a dream prophesying the destruction of
70–89	the Serbian armies. Vaistina repeats the command of the prince and
90–103	insists on waking his master. Musić Stevan gets up, prepares himself for battle, and drinks a toast to the glory of God, to the success of his expedition
104–57	and to the Holy Cross. He departs for the battle. Arriving on the field of Kosovo, he meets a girl who tells him that she has been early to the river Sitnica and has found it full of corpses of men and horses, and of turbans and Serbian white silk caps. She gives him one of the caps; Musić Stevan realizes that he has come too late and has deserved to be cursed by his Prince. He gives the girl three golden ducats to remember him by and rides off to the
158–69	battle. He crosses the river Sitnica, joins the battle, slays three pashas, and is himself killed, together with his servant Vaistina and all his army of 12,000 men. The poem ends with the words: 'And there also our Prince perished; there the Serbs lost the kingdom of their honourable earthly monarch.'

The 'action', the battle itself, occupies eleven lines out of 169. The remainder of the poem is largely composed of dialogue. There are two turning-points: first, when the servant refuses to be deterred by the forebodings of his master's wife and, second, when Musić Stevan realizes that the battle is lost but nevertheless goes to his death in order to satisfy the demands of honour and his pledge to his Prince. The heroic attitude of the servant is repeated at a higher level by the decision of his master. Each of these turning-points finds expression in a dialogue between a man and a woman. Throughout, the poem lays stress on formal actions and on the emotions and relationships that they symbolize. The careful preparations for departure, the drinking of the final toast, the silken Serbian cap as the evidence of disaster, the gift to the girl of Kosovo as a pledge of remembrance — it is these that the poet chooses to stress, rather than the events of the battle itself: the listeners are thus assured, though not explicitly as in the poem quoted above (p. 199), that 'all was done in honour, all was holy'.

It is natural that scholars have long been preoccupied by the question: when and how did these songs first come into existence? It is perhaps not surprising that no certain answer can be given. However, some probabilities may be established. The poems that deal with events of Serbian history before the first battle of Kosovo (1389) are fanciful or legendary in character and have little connexion with real historical events. This is not true of the Kosovo cycle or of the majority of the songs dealing with the period of Turkish rule. Many of these deal with real personages and often, as in the Kosovo cycle itself, reflect historical truth at least in a general way. Braun (1937) has provided a most valuable and detailed study of the relationship of epic and history in the Kosovo poems. It thus seems at any rate probable that historical epic poems of the type which we possess first began to be composed after, but not very long after, the Turkish invasion of the Balkans in the fourteenth century. This does not exclude the possibility of earlier Serbo-Croatian epics based on historical events; but if any such existed they have not been preserved.

It has recently been persuasively argued by Sv. Matić (1964, 1972) that the songs of the Kosovo cycle are of much later origin than had hitherto been thought. They originated, he suggests, in Syrmia (Srem) in the eighteenth century, as an outgrowth of the historical interest and patriotic sentiment which characterized the monasteries of Fruška Gora at that time. If this were so, then it would be necessary to suppose that the historical memory of Kosovo had been handed down largely in the form of written chronicles which then constituted the basis and stimulus of the Kosovo epic cycle. The issue cannot be further discussed here. Even if, however, Matić's well-argued thesis were accepted, it would not change our view of the origins and development of epic composition among the Serbs. Even without the Kosovo cycle there are plenty of heroic songs which must derive from earlier times.

The comparative studies of Roman Jakobson make it seem probable that the Serbo-Croatian epic decasyllable goes back to Common Slavonic sources; but we cannot say what kind of poetry may have been written in this metre or in its prototype in prehistoric periods. More problematic is the origin of the *bugarštica*, in which the earliest preserved heroic poems are composed (see above, p. 198) and examples of which are attested from the sixteenth to the eighteenth centuries.

In the fourteenth-century Serbian principalities there existed a feudal society in which knightly vassals owed loyalty to their prince and waged war for him. Though conditions were even more primitive and less stable than, say, in Western Europe in about 1200, the circumstances were comparable. We can easily envisage a tradition of epic poetry growing up under these conditions as it had done in the west. Such a tradition may well have continued to exist in the Serbian and Bosnian principalities that survived for about a century after the first battle of Kosovo. The Serbian feudal class was, however, destroyed by the first half of the sixteenth century, and the social framework of the epic songs was transformed. They were preserved, modified, and transmitted by oral tradition in conditions which we cannot reconstruct in detail. By the nineteenth century, when the picture again becomes clearer, epic singers were numerous in the Serbian peasant society which formed the new Serbian principality after the rebellions against the Turks during the Napoleonic era. They were yet more numerous in the still Turkish province of Bosnia and in the tribal society of Montenegro. In Bosnia we know that 'court singers' of a sort existed until the eve of the First World War. The techniques of composition and performance were by no means decadent even at that period, although it must be admitted that the poems of the Balkan Wars lack the unique quality of the earlier poems. One example of these late specimens of our genre may be of interest — the poem describing the London peace conference after the First Balkan War in May 1913. We are told how the Balkan delegations were welcomed by

> Ministar engleski
> Što sa kraljem od Engleske ruča,
> Prva glava u Engleskoj slavnoj,
> Prva glava Ser Edvarde Greje . . .
> Na dvoru se otvoriše vrata,
> Na vratima kralj engleski Đorđe,
> Sav u zlatu i dragom kamenju
> Iz daleke Inđije donetom . . .
> Nasmeši se kralj engleski Đorđe,
> Pa propušta gospodu balkansku,
> Propušta je u srebrne dvore,
> Za zlatnu je trpezu dovodi
> Da je gosti do sutrašnjeg dana . . .

(The English Minister who lunches with the King of England, the first man in famous England, the first man, Sir Edward Grey . . . In the palace the door opened, in the doorway was King George of England, all in gold and precious stones brought from distant India . . . King George of England smiles, then he allows the Balkan gentlemen to pass through, to pass through into silver halls, he leads them to a golden table, that he may entertain them until the next morning . . .)

The metre and style, at least, are fully traditional.

On Murko's last expedition to Yugoslavia in 1930–32 he met 403 singers and collected information about many more. Although one of them claimed to be 120 years old, the largest age-group was of persons in their forties. Even in the 1950s, when Lord made his most recent recording expeditions, he found several singers still performing. It may, however, be doubted whether the genre can long survive in the rapidly changing society of modern Yugoslavia.

The heroic songs of the Serbs and Croats did not develop into long heroic epics, either by the process of *Aufschwellung* or by the combination of various 'lays' into a single work. It is sometimes argued that the cycle of Kosovo poems forms some kind of unity. This is so, but this unity of theme does not signify a step on the path from lay to epic. Each song is fully self-contained: and even if a knowledge of the tragedy of Kosovo is sometimes presupposed in the hearers, nevertheless no detailed plot of any of the poems leads directly on to another. The cycle remains a series of individual works. A more serious tendency towards a more complex epic structure has been noted in the Muslim songs of the Bosnian Krajina region which were studied in detail by Alois Schmaus. It is at any rate certain that in them the 'single-stranded' unitary narrative of the typical Serbo-Croatian songs has been abandoned in favour of double plots or of a single plot observed from different vantage-points. Lord points out, incidentally, that the greater length of the Muslim poems may be explained by the fact that they were frequently sung during the nights of Ramadan, when the singer had to entertain his audience until dawn. On the basis of the material available it would seem that even here we cannot speak of a fully-fledged 'epic' but only of more elaborate 'lays'.*

*In his Introduction to 'The Wedding of Smailagić Meho' by Avdo Mededović (*Serbo-Croatian Heroic Songs*, collected by Milman Parry, Vol. III, translated with introduction, notes and commentary by A. B. Lord, etc., Cambridge, Mass., 1974) under the title 'Avdo's Originality', Professor Lord claims this song of over 12,000 lines as an authentic romantic epic. At the 'Rundgespräch' of the Zentral-asiatisches Seminar of the University of Bonn, 29 September – 1 October 1980 at St Augustin bei Bonn, Professor Miroslav Kravar presented a paper entitled 'Die Hochzeit Smailagić Mehos' making the same claim. Whether Robert Auty would have accepted this song as a unique exception to his concluding remarks is something we cannot know, and the reader is left to his own conclusions. Gen. Ed.

NOTES

1. See above p. 166.
2. The Erlangen MS: see Gesemann, 1925.
3. Andrija Kačić Miošić, *Razgovor ugodni naroda slovinskoga* in *Stari pisci hrvatski*, 27, ed. T. Matić (Zagreb, 1962).
4. Braun, 1961, p. 74.
5. pp. 10–13.
6. Vuk, II, 45, 92–93.
7. Vuk, III, 31.
8. They are contained in Vuk, III, especially nos. 53–73.
9. Vuk, II, 49, iii; II, 44; II, 46.
10. Vuk, II, 60; II, 59.
11. Vuk, II, 50; II, 68.
12. Vuk, II, 74; II, 47.
13. *Razgovor ugodni* . . . (see note 3, above), 332.
14. Vuk, III, 492.
15. Vuk, II, 50. The accents on the vowels indicate quantity and intonation thus: `` — short falling; ' — short rising; ⌢ — long falling; ´ — long rising; ⁻ — length.
16. Quoted in Lord, 1960, p. 30.
17. Lord, 1960, ch. 3, 'The Formula'.
18. Braun, 1961, pp. 65–67.
19. Vuk, II, 70.
20. Vuk, III, 81. For the 'negative metaphor' in general see Felix Oinas, 'Negative parallelism in Karelian–Finnish folklore' in *Folk Narrative Congress in Helsinki 1974*, and the literature there cited.

BIBLIOGRAPHY

Texts

Gesemann, Gerhard, 1925. *Erlangenski rukopis starih srpskohrvatskih narodnih pesama*, Zbornik za istoriju, jezik i književnost, I/12 (Sremski Karlovci)

[Hektorović, Petar], 1568. *Ribanye i ribarscho prigovaranye i razliche stvari ine sloxene po Petretu Hectorovichiu Hvaraninu* (Venice). Heroic songs on pp. 12a–16a. Facsimile edition, Zagreb, 1953

Hektorović, Petar, 1968. 'Ribanje i ribarsko prigovaranje' in *Hanibal Lucić. Petar Hektorović*, ed. Marin Franičević, Pet stoljeća hrvatske književnosti, 7 (Zagreb). Heroic songs on pp. 187–92

Hörmann, Kosta, 1888–89. *Narodne pjesme Muhamedovaca u Bosni i Hercegovini*, 2 volumes (Sarajevo)

Hrvatske narodne pjesme, 1896–1942. 10 volumes (Zagreb)

Karadžić, Vuk Stefanović, 1887–1902. *Srpske narodne pjesme*, 9 volumes (Belgrade). New edition of Volumes I–IV, Belgrade, 1953–54

Parry, Milman and Albert Bates Lord, 1953–54. *Serbocroatian Heroic Songs*, 2 volumes (Cambridge, Mass., and Belgrade)

Studies

Braun, Maximilian, 1937. *'Kosovo'. Die Schlacht auf dem Amselfelde in geschichtlicher und epischer Überlieferung*, Slavisch-baltische Quellen und Forschungen herausgegeben von Reinhold Trautmann, 8 (Leipzig)

Braun, Maximilian, 1961. *Das serbokroatische Heldenlied* (Göttingen)

Jakobson, Roman, 1952. 'Studies in Comparative Slavic Metrics' in *Oxford Slavonic Papers*, 3 (Oxford), pp. 21–66

Koljević, Svetozar, 1974. *Naš junački ep* (Belgrade)

[Add. by A. P.: Koljević, Svetozar, 1980. *The epic in the making* (Oxford)]

Lord, Albert Bates, 1960. *The Singer of Tales* (Cambridge, Mass., and London)

Maretić, Tomislav, 1907. *Naša narodna epika* (Zagreb)

Matić, Svetozar, 1964. *Naš narodni ep i naš stih* (Novi Sad)

Matić, Svetozar, 1972. *Novi ogledi o našem narodnom epu* (Novi Sad)

Murko, Mathias, 1929. *La poésie populaire épique en Yougoslavie au début du XXᵉ siècle*, Travaux publiés par l'Institut d'études slaves, 10 (Paris)

Murko, Matija, 1951. *Tragom srpsko-hrvatske narodne epike. Putovanja u godinama 1930–1932*, 2 volumes, Djela Jugoslavenske akademije znanosti i umjetnosti, 41 and 42 (Zagreb)

Saran, Franz, 1934. *Zur Metrik des epischen Verses bei den Serben*, Veröffentlichungen des Slavischen Instituts an der Friedrich-Wilhelms-Universität Berlin herausgegeben von Max Vasmer, 10 (Leipzig)

Schmaus, Alois, 1953a. *Episierungsprozesse im Bereich der slavischen Volksdichtung*, Veröffentlichungen des Osteuropa-Instituts München, 4 (Munich)

Schmaus, Alois, 1953b. 'Studije o krajinskoj epici', in Rad Jugoslavenske akademije i umjetnosti, 297 (Zagreb), pp. 89–247

Subotić, Dragutin, 1932. *Yugoslav Popular Ballads* (Cambridge)

Translations

Low, D. H., 1922. *The Ballads of Marko Kraljević* (Cambridge)

Morison, W. A., 1942. *The Revolt of the Serbs against the Turks (1804–1813)* (Cambridge)

Rootham, Helen, 1920. *Kossovo. Heroic Songs of the Serbs* (Oxford)

OB UGRIAN

(Vogul and Ostyak)

By G. F. CUSHING

THE VOGUL (Mansi) and Ostyak (Hanti) peoples live in North-West Siberia. Their homeland is the Hanti–Mansi national region, immediately to the east of the Urals, where they live in small and widely-scattered settlements along the River Ob and its tributaries, hence their collective name of Ob-Ugrians. This region consists of some 550,000 square kilometres of taiga country, with immense forests and vast marshes. The climate is bleak, with long hard winters and brief summers. In this huge area, whose total population is only 125,000, the Voguls number some 6,000 and the Ostyaks 19,000.

The Ob-Ugrian languages, together with Hungarian, form the Ugrian subgroup of the Finno-Ugrian branch of the Uralic family of languages, whose homeland was probably the Kama valley region west of the Urals. The Finno-Ugrian branch divided into Finnic-Permian and Ugrian about 2000 B.C.; from this latter sub-group the Hungarian speakers broke away during the first half of the first millennium B.C., and the remaining Ugrians were mingled with various nomadic Siberian peoples. Their traces are lost until the eleventh century A.D., when Russian chronicles refer to *Jugor* and *Jugra*; at this period they seem still to have been living on the west side of the Urals, but in the following centuries they gradually moved north and east to their present habitat, as the eastward spread of the territorial name Jugria indicates. The majority of the Ugrians have lived in this region since at least the early sixteenth century, though some scattered communities survived on the European side of the Urals until a century ago. The present pattern of settlement suggests that the Voguls occupied the area west of the Ob, while the Ostyaks moved further east along its tributaries. The name 'Vogul' first appears in 1396, but 'Ostyak' is not recorded until the sixteenth century. Today, three dialects survive in each language, and differences between some of them are so great that communication between their speakers is virtually impossible, and Russian is used.

Although the linguistic relationship of the Ugrians is clearly established, their ethnic affinity causes problems. They bear little resemblance to modern Finno-Ugrian speakers elsewhere, but have certain characteristics in common with the Samoyeds. It is possible that they are the remnants of a Siberian type of race who mingled with the Ugrians — for the Urals are only seen to be a barrier to wheeled transport — and adopted their language, eventually taking it back with them to the Ob valley.

The Russians gradually penetrated Siberia, setting up trading-posts and garrisons and bringing Orthodox Christianity as part of their design to achieve domination of the region. There were numerous risings against them, for they deprived the illiterate Ugrians of their best hunting and fishing areas and exacted taxes from them. In the eyes of the Russians, and in particular of the missionaries who attempted to establish Christianity among them, they were a singularly barbarous people who indulged in strange and unseemly pagan rites and were fiercely resistant to the superior Orthodox culture. Despite increasing interest in them — for they were among the first non-Russian peoples encountered by travellers to the east of the Urals — scholarly research did not begin to bring to light their cultural inheritance until the nineteenth century. By this time the days of the Ostyaks and Voguls seemed to be numbered, and scholars regarded their task as a rescue operation to preserve the astonishing riches that were in danger of disappearing entirely. The recording of folk songs and tales was undertaken with diligence and great care; it is regrettable that much of the work of these highly competent and dedicated scholars has yet to be published. Nevertheless, the material so far made available reveals a startling contrast between the primitive bleakness of everyday life in the Ob valley and the colourful, intensely dramatic cultural inheritance of its inhabitants.

Since the heroic poetry of the Ugrians, and indeed their whole culture, is closely connected with their religious life and beliefs, some account of these must form a background to any study of their literature. The religion of the Ugrians is animistic and complex; it is capable, as the Russian missionaries discovered, of absorbing Christian elements into its sys em without undue trouble. The greatest of all spirits, Numi-Torem, the Sky-Father, is omnipotent and omniscient, while the Earth-Mother and the god of the underworld are much less clearly depicted. None of these three supreme spirits has a particular shrine or image: their presence is universal. It is with the seven children of Numi-Torem that most Ugrian worship is concerned. These children are variously described, but most of the evidence suggests that they are deified heroes, whose names are geographical locations, in other words the places where their shrines are situated. There is no definitive list of these children, though certain names appear more frequently than others. It was an Ostyak custom to make a wooden image of a dead man, dress it in his clothes and bury it after a period of one to three years; therefore it is probable that worship of the dead in the form of an image became elevated to the particular worship of heroes, who themselves gradually assumed the status of deities. This custom spread downward to lesser heroes, but never upward to the highest spirits. The family of the dead hero was naturally interested in maintaining respect for his memory and tending his shrine, and presumably quite often provided the priest or shaman whose duty it became to preserve the rites and sacrifices connected with the hero. Russian observers noted that the shaman himself might go through a process of canonization, for his successors made certain that he was accorded due respect from generation to generation, and that he too might demand sacrifices. There were numerous types of image. Some were natural stones which appeared to have human shapes, others were simply poles, and others were of wood and metal. The shrines were often in groves or inaccessible places, more especially after the arrival of the Russians and the missionaries who were intent on destroying them. Some had their own wooden huts which were kept constantly guarded. Nevertheless it is important to note that the images themselves were not the objects of worship: it was the god they represented who was all-important. Moreover these gods, who in life had been heroes, were beneficent and not evil. The shaman was usually commanded to make or to replace images. These deities had widely-differing powers; sometimes they might be impotent or even refuse to act in their essential duty as intermediaries between mere humans and Numi-Torem and they required constant worship and adoration from humans if they were to fulfil their duty. In extreme cases, when a particular deity failed to perform its proper duty, its image was destroyed, thus drawing the attention of Numi-Torem to its lapse. It is clear that the shaman had immense power: not only was he responsible for the maintenance of worship with the appropriate ceremonies and sacrifices, but he was also the only person who might perform the tasks connected with the shrine. The Russian missionary Grigori Novitsky, who visited the Ugrians early in the eighteenth century, remarks that not even the head of the tribe might enter the shrine of his local deity, but only the shaman himself.

The seven children of Numi-Torem were headed by the God of Pelim, whom the western Voguls regarded as the eldest son, and whose heroic exploits were highly esteemed by them. Yet several tales tell of his struggle for power with the youngest son, the Golden Prince, whose worship spread far more widely and who was invested with the usual powers of the first-born. This doubtless reflects a historical struggle between tribes inhabiting the Pelim and Tavda areas, resulting in the victory of the latter. After the God of Pelim, there follow the holy Prince of the River Lozva, who was concerned mainly with problems of life and health, the Old Man of the Holy Urals, the guardian of reindeer (numerous lesser heroes acted as his herdsmen), the warlike God of the Middle Sosva, who engaged in many fratricidal struggles, and Ajäs, the God of the Little Ob, whose deeds were warlike, but who is often represented as peaceful and beneficent. Next comes a female deity, Kaltes, whose relationship to Numi-Torem is confused and obscure; she was the goddess of birth and life, riches and poverty. The seventh and most frequently worshipped deity was the Golden Prince, whose shrine stood at the confluence of the two greatest rivers, the Irtysh and the Ob, where the capital of the region is now situated. His function was to look after the earth, but he shares his epithet 'golden' with Numi-Torem and at times appears in the role of sun-god.

The Vogul version of Christianity, which seems to have been acquired from priests far more ignorant than Vogul shamans, found it easy to equate Numi-Torem with God, Kaltes with Mary, and the Golden Prince with Christ. It is not surprising then to discover that some of the tales connected with these three Vogul deities have acquired Christian overtones.

Although numerous exploits are credited to the seven children of Numi-Torem, there are very many records of heroic deeds performed by lesser deities, again usually named after geographical sites and worshipped locally. Some of these adventures are as graphically recounted and as heroic as those of the major deities. The spirit-world of the Ugrians was not confined to human beings, heroes and gods. Animals and natural phenomena played an important part. The animal kingdom was as real and alive as the human one, and had a similar structure. Animals, for example, had their own shamans, who might appeal to Numi-Torem like their human counterparts. The bear, the strongest and most feared animal, was also the holiest of them and had several taboo-names; the elk, horse, reindeer and wolf, together with various birds, were also regarded as holy. Mythical animals, griffins and dragons, also appear in some tales, and even the mammoth is mentioned. Certain trees were also regarded with particular reverence.

In this world of beliefs the shaman was vitally important. He was not only the all-powerful priest and intermediary, but prophet, doctor, general advisor and, because it was he who conjured up the gods and interpreted their wishes to the people, poet and singer too. The shaman might be male or female, though the former were more in evidence, and there appears to have been no particular 'order' of shamans. J. B. Müller, writing in 1716, noted that the office was performed by the head of the family, while other observers have commented on their venerable age. It is clear, however, that those who felt themselves fitted for the task had to undergo a lengthy period of preparation before they were accepted, even though they appeared to have the right physical requirements from birth (an extra finger was such a sign, as can be seen from the usual shaman's glove). Theoretically the shaman received no payment for his services, but he was rewarded with the best meat from the sacrifice; on the other hand he undertook long journeys to beg offerings for his particular deity and advertised his powers at the same time, and there is no doubt that he lived well.

The Ugrians had no detailed calendar — the days of the week were imported from the Russians — so that there were no fixed dates for local ceremonies. The changes in the seasons, which heralded the beginning or end of the hunting and fishing seasons also, were times for major sacrifices. Local occasions, such as birth, illness and death, provided others, and the successful conclusion of a bear-hunt was the opportunity for a great festival. During the present century such festivals appear to have been institutionalized; Russian observers mention seven-yearly celebrations which include dancing, singing and play-acting without the necessity of a bear-hunt. When the gods, through the shaman, demanded sacrifices of blood, these were often of horses, which had to be bought at high prices from Russian or other traders, since they are not bred in the present-day habitat of the Ugrians. One of the more peculiar aspects of the ceremonial vocabulary of the Ugrians is its rich (and for all practical purposes useless) hippic terminology, which suggests a much earlier age and more southerly homeland. Foreign commentators imply that human sacrifices were not unknown, but for ordinary occasions the offerings generally consisted of food, smoke and various small objects.

Such is the setting of the Vogul and Ostyak heroic poems. Until the present century the majority of the Ob-Ugrians were illiterate, while today the Russian language has tended to overwhelm what remains of their languages. Thus in the Ugrian tradition the term 'literature' implies oral literature. Moreover the expected distinction between prose and verse has little meaning; instead there is a division into 'song' and 'tale', the former having musical accompaniment and the latter none. Both songs and tales may be found in the same recitation, yet even this distinction is not sharply drawn, for there exist passages of the following type:

> What little song is this, recounted by a maiden?
> What little tale is this, recounted by a maiden?[1]

The musical accompaniment was provided by two types of instrument unknown elsewhere in Western Siberia; one was a five-stringed lyre with a body shaped like a fish, and the other a swan-necked harp with nine or thirteen strings. Both are believed to have originated in Asia Minor and to have been transmitted to the Ugrians by the Iranians at a very early period.

All the oral literature so far collected falls into this category of accompanied or unaccompanied recitation. Most of it is narrative, but it includes highly dramatic scenes. As has been noted, some scholars also mention 'dramas' as such, but these are confined to pieces for bear-festivals and generally involve musical performances by masked dancers as they reconstruct the events of a great hunt. The parallel between this type of ceremonial performance and the ancient Greek Dionysiac festivals is striking.

Music of a rude kind, and even poetry, are known to this wild race, whose improvised songs are described as very striking, owing to the pantomimic skill with which they portray every incident of the narrative. Each singer pitches upon some well-known occurrence and treats it according to the promptings of his own individual taste. Frequently the same subject is handled for years in succession, more particularly if the incident is of a highly dramatic character. A bear having dug up and devoured a dead Ostiak child, the people for a long time afterwards found in this shocking occurrence a theme for their improvised minstrel, imitating with the utmost fidelity the motions of the animal, and reproducing its angry growls as the unhappy parents endeavoured to frighten it from the body.[2]

From this evidence, and from that of the texts themselves, it is obvious that drama was not highly-developed; but the songs and tales of heroes and gods display a much richer and more deeply-rooted tradition.

Heroic poetry, then, plays an important part in the Ugrian literary tradition. It is, after all, an integral part of religious observance, when the family or tribe meets together to be reminded of the power of the deity as well as to hear his commands or to ask for favours. The glory of the past heroic struggles is evoked as a standard for the present. The shaman too must maintain his own claim to respect as well as that of the deified hero he serves. It is of no consequence that the heroic songs, or parts of them, may also be used as communal entertainment. The heroic tradition predominates, and in the absence of other distinctive genres until the present century (which has seen importations from Russian) shares its form and content with songs and tales which are not specifically heroic, such as hymns of praise to the deities, invitations to the gods to attend ceremonies, and prayers to them. Some pieces of ritual texts have survived separately in the form of sung oaths or curses, work-songs or drinking-songs; their resistance to change is demonstrated admirably by the Hungarian scholar Bela Kálmán, who was noting down Vogul melodies from a young man and discovered that the text of one song was virtually identical with one collected by Munkácsi almost a century ago.[3]

The Hungarian scholar Reguly (1818–58) who made Ostyak poetry his particular field of research, was captivated by the content of the heroic songs. 'We see here a people of the far north', he wrote, 'whose mode of life suggests, in our view, that their cultural activity should have taken a totally different direction, recounting with fervent enthusiasm the warlike deeds of their ancestors and singing the sometimes catastrophic, sometimes happy fate of their heroes who, partly as gods, fought with external enemies like the Zyryans and Samoyeds and, partly as princes, waged war with their brothers and neighbours.' He adds, significantly, that Ostyak poetry does not concern itself with the inner life of the individual but 'only sings the fate of societies, towns and countries. It starts at all times from the viewpoint of an outward-looking, hard-working life and depicts its warlike movements, storms and vicissitudes. Here one does not strive through mysterious impulses, magic powers and craft to attain spiritual superiority over the world and nature, as in Finnish poetry; rather one is roused by the enchanting scenes of the imagination which conjures up brilliant deeds and successful adventures, and urged to achieve worldly dominion over peoples and lands by means of bold determination and the force of arms.'[4] This observation serves as a salutary reminder that whatever the external trappings of Ob-Ugrian heroic songs may be, their content is very much concerned with the realities of everyday life. It relates to the importance of the deified hero, his powers and the expectation of his aid. The ceremonial setting and the far from everyday language may heighten the dramatic effect, but the deeds and action do not require great effort to follow. Battle-scenes are frequent; four main causes for battle can be distinguished: revenge, particularly for the death of a near relative, wooing (the Ostyaks and Voguls are exogamous, hence it is the hero's duty to acquire a 'foreign' wife), an enemy attack, or simply the desire to make war. Boredom appears to have been a frequent, if paradoxical, spur to heroic action:

> The young warriors go into the courtyard,
> They shoot at a target. The twang of the bow-string
> Is heard by their father, Numi-Torem.
> If only somewhere
> We had a father's cause for revenge from our father
> We should pound the enemy with our fists
> Like the shell of a birch-bark barrel run dry of nourishment.[5]

But warlike action is not all, since some of the hero-gods are specifically peaceful, and their songs reflect this. In the song of the God of Pelim, the hero goes to obtain a wife and returns in peace, ending the song thus:

> Old God of Pelim,
> Since my mother bore me I have never made war,
> Since my father begat me I have never made war.
> I have no cause for vengeance on my father's side,
> I seek no cause for revenge on my mother's side.[6]

Again, the hero may visit his people, heal the sick, raise the dead, and watch over the general welfare of his people — in this instance the confusion between the Golden Prince and Christ becomes obvious. One element is notably absent from the Ugrian tradition: acquisition of land is no cause for heroic exploits, for the thinly-populated region which has been their homeland for many centuries has more than enough space for the needs of a community which depends chiefly on hunting and fishing.

The dominating figure in the song is naturally the deified hero, whose image stands in the shrine where he is worshipped. He tends to become a statuesque figure, and the shaman encourages this tendency. The effect is heightened by the dramatic method of recitation, for in most of the songs it is the deity himself who addresses the audience through the medium of the shaman, in the first person. The singer himself is not named, and references to his sources are vague in the extreme. 'Those who knew the tales, who knew the songs' handed them down. Thus the formal introduction to the song gives specific details of the name of the hero, his divine mission, the holiness of his shrine, and his exceptional powers. This is well shown in the Vogul song of the God of Lopmus:

> Holy prince of the heavenly ones,
> Holy prince of the celestial ones,
> I am called the old one, the son of Torem.
> To this my holy region of Lopmus
> My father the Great Golden One
> Has called me, and here I am.
> The myriad folk of the village,
> The myriad folk of the town
> Stand before me bareheaded.
> A king wielding a sharp-pointed sword
> Am I, the old man of Lopmus.
> A king wielding a sharp-edged sword
> Am I, the old man of Lopmus.
> All my village children who have now grown up,
> All my town children who have now grown up —
> These I defend from the hem of the robe of disease,
> These I defend from the hem of the robe of sickness:
> Behold, I am the old one of Lopmus.[7]

Other introductions may be less detailed, but the name and place are all-important. Occasionally minor characters may also be included here, but in the Vogul tradition a similar formula may be used in the middle of a poem when a new character is introduced. After such an imposing introduction, it is somewhat surprising to discover that the exploits of the hero, and indeed the hero himself, tend to be typical rather than individual and memorable. They are no more than the expected actions of a leader, and what is more, the leader of quite a small community engaged in very ordinary pursuits connected with life and work.

Nevertheless the heroes are deities, and whatever their earthly exploits may have been, and however easy it may be to relate them to historical events, they possess supernatural powers. This does not imply that they are omnipotent or even equally powerful. Clearly the children of Numi-Torem were elevated by successive generations of shamans and worshippers to an exceptional status, and this was doubtless enhanced by the penetration and acceptance of various Christian elements. But the many minor deities often behave heroically in human terms, as for example the Old Man of the source of the Sosva, who appears in the Heroic Song of the God of Jugra. He sets out on a warlike expedition along the River Sosva and arrives at the Ob, where he asks permission to visit the sacred shrine of the god Ajäs. Permission is granted, but he is warned that disaster may follow and his army may be defeated. He thereupon asks Ajäs to grant him strength, but even as he speaks his war-vessel is being smashed to pieces and his men slain. He draws his 'iron-tipped, sacred little sword', whereupon Ajäs tells him that this is useless, for he is outnumbered. He appeals once more for aid and is now successful, for Ajäs produces a giant who slays the enemy on all sides. The giant, however, is drunk with success and, full of warlike spirit, turns on the hero himself and even threatens Ajäs. At this point he receives a wound and the hero continues his fight alone, finally achieving success. Here one might expect the story to end, but instead we are brought back to the reality of the situation: although the hero is victorious, he has lost his men and his boat, and is compelled to make his way home alone. He is also warned by Ajäs never to attempt such an expedition again, for if he does, he will be punished by Numi-Torem himself. The tale is thus seen as a heroic exploit in a raid that ended in disaster, but it does not diminish the stature of the hero himself.

The war-god of Munkes (a village) is the hero of many martial adventures. There are numerous tales of his prowess, including an account of a fight with a Zyryan prince across the Urals. There are several versions of the expedition which led up to this encounter, including one which ends with his death. Asleep in a village by the Sigva, he is surprised by the enemy 'dressed uncleanly' (i.e. as a woman in menstruation, for this is the height of uncleanliness) who deprives him of his gigantic strength. Next morning he sees that the river has frozen over, and puts on his gigantic snow-shoes to cross it, all unaware that his strength has gone. As he is struggling along, the ice breaks and he is drowned. This story is unique in the Ob-Ugrian tradition, for the gods do not die. The probable explanation is that the man who died was the father of the hero and not the war-god himself, two expeditions having become confused in the course of time.

The hero, like the shaman who sings his deeds, is often distinguished from other mortals. Some are begotten by the greater deities. 'I am a man begotten by Torem and born on the third day' says the young hero-prince of the Lower Konda to his attacker.[8] He grows up rapidly: 'the garments he has worn today become superfluous (i.e. too small); tomorrow he dons new raiment. The man of the song, the man of the tale grows in this wise.'[9] As a child he becomes adept at sports and games; he may play with a miniature bow and arrow of sharp wood in the village square until he reaches the stage of killing wild beasts in the forest and can thus live by his own skill. When the young men shoot at targets, the young hero outstrips them all, and may even perform superhuman feats: in the Irtysh-Ostyak tradition the targets are seven pillars of stone, which the hero shoots out of the ground.

The hero may be orphaned in childhood, as in some tales of Pelim and Ajäs. They are brought up by foster-parents who conceal from them their real parentage and hide their fathers' armour and weapons lest they be filled too early with

P

the desire to avenge their fathers' death. There is also the uncontrollable hero, like the son of Numi-Torem who 'watches over the world'; he is the darling of his parents, but cannot be disciplined and is sent away from home, first to his elder brother, then to a 'long-haired Russian' who offers to pay for him but gets him for nothing. The Russian keeps him in a corner by the door and throws the slops over him before handing him over, again without payment, to a 'marten-like' Samoyed who harnesses him like an animal to his sleigh. The children and the old folk all mock him. Finally he is beaten and thrown on to a rubbish heap, by which time he has an adequate motive for revenge. In this story, as in others, the hero grows up suddenly. At one moment he is lamenting his fate on the rubbish heap, while at the next

> He feels his feet slipping somehow.
> As he looks at his feet
> Two snowshoes covered with reindeer-hide have somehow been fastened
>   upon them.
> As he looks at himself,
> A closely-linked armour of chain-mail has somehow been put upon him.
> He hears something rattling between his shoulders
> And as he looks
> A winged quiver furnished with seven arrows
> Is slung over his shoulders.
> As his glance falls on his left hand,
> It is somehow grasping an iron-ribbed ribbed bow.
> As his glance falls upon his right hand,
> It is somehow grasping a golden-tasselled tasselled sword.[10]

The fully-grown hero is a superhuman being, often much taller than mere mortals, and unusually handsome. One has a head 'rich in curls, beauteous with curls' and others have especially attractive plaits (such as are normally worn by the northernmost Voguls and Ostyaks to this day). They have eyes 'like ripe berries' and ears 'like reindeers' ears'. The hero's mouth is generally 'ten-toothed', and it can spit far and accurately. When he cracks his fingers, it is like the 'noise of the frozen pine as it cracks'.[11] Every hero is exceptionally strong (Ostyak *jōr* is both 'strength' and 'heroic'), and he usually gains strength in sleep and dreams from which it is difficult to rouse him. The hero of Pelim is woken by his young servant hitting him with a sword, while another says 'If you cannot wake me, pierce my thigh with a knife'.[12] The waking process may be dangerous, since the hero may kill whoever rouses him; thus in Ostyak songs the servant approaches him carefully through a hole in the roof, as though the hero were the bear in a bear-hunt. Exceptional strength and beauty are allied with a nimble mind:

Like a three-sided baler of birch-bark
So he turned his mind three ways;
Like a four-sided baler of birch-bark,
So he turned his mind four ways.[13]

Other characters in the songs and tales play very minor parts. Servants and warriors have conventional roles, spending their days in practising with bows and arrows, carrying messages, doing guard-duty and taking their turn at waking the hero. They are usually depicted as restless and ill-tempered when not fighting, and often disgruntled in battle. Their other main function is to mourn the hero when he is presumed to have died.

In battle, the hero is fully-equipped with bow and arrows, sword, axe, knife, armour and snow-shoes. The sword is the true hero's weapon and his greatest treasure. Often it is described as 'holy', because of the great deeds performed by it. It may glow miraculously or rattle loudly; indeed it is the only weapon which may be regarded as having some magic property. The other weapons may be better fashioned than average, but they are made of normal pine and birch and iron, and only the hero's skill in using them makes them particularly effective. The references to armour are interesting, for it is chain-mail (literally 'needle-costume') which the hero has probably inherited from his father and kept hidden for his own exclusive use. There is nothing strange about this except its survival, and travellers have recorded seeing chain-mail kept near the images of the gods.

The actions of the hero in war are for the most part conventional. The army has to be chosen and assembled — and here the Ostyak poems give details of the preparations, while the Vogul tradition omits them completely. There will usually be a journey to the battlefield or fortress to be attacked, in summer by boat and in winter by sledge. If the expedition is in search of a wife, there will be a sleigh loaded with money and valuables. Any battle is entirely an infantry engagement, the use of horses and cavalry being unknown. Nor is there any mention of guns, though these have been used in the Ugrian region for centuries. The battles themselves are not usually described in any detail, and the issue is most frequently decided by some act of personal heroism, a sword-duel or a wrestling-contest. Or the hero may be seized by blood-lust, in which case he may slash at friend and foe alike until he is forcibly restrained by a close relation or friend.

Magical elements may occur, but they are incidental to the action and do not normally control its progress. In the middle of one battle, the hero is caught in a pit seven fathoms deep; a maiden comes to chop firewood nearby and a splinter of wood falls into it, whereupon he picks it up, strings it with his own hair and plays a tune upon it. At this a flock of geese approaches, and one of them (a blind goose) takes a message to his horse, which dashes to his rescue.

The horse puts its head over the edge of the pit, whereupon the hero grasps the dangling reins, the horse flings up its head and lands him on its back and takes him back into the battle.

If the hero has to fight with creatures and humans possessed of magic powers — and here the Samoyeds are often depicted as enemies addicted to magic — he too will use magic, but only after his human powers have failed. The young hero-prince of the Lower Konda, faced with a long journey home, travels wearily for a long time, then stops and considers his lot. 'If I continue my journey in this wise, where shall I get to?' He changes himself into a bear, and hurries on, but this is not swift enough for him, so he becomes a snake, then flies in the shape of a hawk and runs in the form of a weasel before reaching his destination.

Heavenly intervention is also found, but not always on the side of the hero. Ajäs asks the Sky-Father for some snowshoes, bow and arrows, and is granted them, but in one Ostyak epic describing a bitter fight with a Samoyed, both fighters implore the aid of Numi-Torem and both receive it. First the Ostyak, who cannot keep up with his opponent, asks for a hill to be put in his path; this request is granted, but the Samoyed continues on his way after being struck by the hero. Twice more the obstacle is provided by Numi-Torem, and twice more the Ostyak wounds the Samoyed but cannot kill him. Just as the final blow is about to fall on the Samoyed's head, the latter prays for a river of blood into which he jumps at the last moment, demanding blood-sacrifices from the Samoyeds for his lucky escape and taunting the Ostyak for failing to win his scalp. The Ostyak then returns home, his victory having been snatched from him.

It is tempting to look outside the Ugrian tradition for an explanation of these magic and mythical elements, but there is no need to do so. The singer is the shaman, and shamans have magical powers; they too travel in mysterious ways, in order to communicate with the higher gods and bring back messages to earth. They too can change themselves into animals and birds and can perform apparently miraculous feats of healing. Moreover it is in the shaman's interest to display his hero as a superhuman character, and this he does by extending his own powers to those of the hero, helping him on difficult journeys and aiding him in battle, yet not detracting from the human virtues he must possess. Here perhaps the occasional failure of magic may be related to the shaman's own failures, and to the recognition that others may possess greater powers than his.

After the heroic deeds have been performed, the hero must demonstrate his prowess to his people. After battle, he kills his victim, turns his face to heaven, offers his soul to the Sky-Father and scalps him. He then hangs the scalp from his belt and returns home, hoists the scalp like a banner from a tree and shows it thus to all his people. Occasionally more unpleasant practices are permitted: the enemy may be sacrificed or his heart and liver taken home and eaten, a custom apparently not unknown among the early Hungarians, if Regino's chronicle is to be believed. The enemy's armour, weapons and often his wife too, are taken as spoils of war, and his gods destroyed. Here again the shaman's interest can be observed. If his hero destroys a rival shrine — and this is often accompanied by the destruction of the sacred grove in which the shrine stands — he can justifiably expect his own shrine to become more popular.

Unless they are the reason for a heroic exploit, women are given a minor role in the hero's life. Captives are roughly treated, and treacherous women even more savagely handled. One Vogul tale tells how the hero's wife forced him to undertake a fishing-trip so that she might visit her Russian lover. The two men are equally-matched, and the hero recognizes that neither of them will win, so he turns on his wife, throws her by her hair on to the ground and kicks her so hard that she disappears from sight, then falls to earth and dies. Marriage-expeditions sometimes end in a declaration of peace between two heroes of like strength, celebrated with a great feast and exchange of presents. The heroes swear solemnly that they will never fight each other again, possibly sealing the bond with blood-sacrifices and intermarriage between their families. The exogamous nature of the Ugrian tradition is clearly revealed in such accounts. Often, however, the heroic nature of a marriage-expedition lies mainly in the journey to the beloved. The bride-to-be may be carefully guarded or even married already. The young hero-prince of the Lower Konda has to overcome numerous obstacles on the way to his beloved who is shut up inside a town. He digs his way into it, then calls upon the Sky-Father for his aid. Numi-Torem responds by creating great heat for seven weeks, whereupon the lady goes down to the River Ob to bathe, leaving her clothes on the bank. The young prince crawls beneath the clothes and when she returns for them changes into a bear and carries her off in his mouth. Such accounts of seizure or elopement are common; occasionally they lead to warfare, but not always. In any event such episodes are not usually the main ones in the hero's life.

The hero, then, is an exceptional man, but his deeds do not strain the imagination of the audience or take them into realms outside their everyday life. Hunting, fishing, river-journeys, wooing and fighting local battles are the background to his exploits. The audience, if the accounts of foreign observers are to be trusted, clearly believed the songs and tales in the main. After all, they often hoped to gain something from the deified hero concerned, and realized that their requests might not be fulfilled if they did not show proper reverence. Moreover they were not unduly abashed if the deity concerned failed to respond; in this case they taught him a lesson by smashing his image. The Ob-Ugrian approach appears to have been extremely practical and down-to-earth. Life was hard, a constant struggle against largely unfavourable elements and foreign enemies, and help was sought for everyday affairs, without attempts to escape from them into fantasy. Here even the sacred animals, like the bear, do not move far outside their normal role. The bear was a taboo animal, and its name was not mentioned, but at the same time it was a dangerous enemy and had to be killed to preserve human life. The Ugrians solved this problem at their bear-festivals by mourning the death of the sacred animal but at the same time pointing out to it that it was a Russian weapon that had killed it.[14] Romantic fiction does not play a part in this tradition — and it is interesting to note that modern prose and poetry, such as there is, tends to be severely realistic.

The time element in these tales presents some peculiarities. The heroes, a number of whom are specifically designated as 'old', perform tasks that must have altered very little in the course of centuries. How much did life in North-West Siberia change until the very recent past, with the improvement of communications and the discovery of oil there? Certainly there is no lamenting of vanished glory; at most there are references to enemies, such as the Russians and Samoyeds, who try to take away the living of the people concerned by trickery. Tribal conflicts may be seen as the source of some tales, the continual struggle against foreign invaders of others, and the noble deeds of the heroes may inspire the hearers to emulate them. But some references are clearly ancient and must have seemed so to the audience. The hero's weapons and armour bear no resemblance to those used for centuries in the Ob valley, where even bears are shot with guns. Above all, as we saw earlier, the appearance of the horse and a vocabulary which suggests an intimate acquaintance with horse-breeding are totally out of place and anachronistic in an area where the horse is useless. Here there is evidence of an earlier culture in a more southerly region, where horse-breeding was part of everyday life. The Hungarian language shares with Vogul and Ostyak several ancient terms which could only have been needed in such an area. The existence of musical instruments which also came from the south and were used to accompany these songs is further evidence to support this theory. Whether the audience was unduly troubled by these elements is a matter of doubt; the vocabulary of the songs in any case is far removed from everyday language, and in this case the unusual weapons and animals might well have been regarded as of ritual significance.

The problem of language is closely connected with the composition of the heroic songs. They are all oral, and the original composers are unknown. 'Those who know the word, who know the sayings' pass them on, and the existence of a professional group of 'custodians of the mysteries' suggests that they were handed down and probably embellished by successive shamans. The antiquated language and vocabulary suggest that improvization might not have been a regular occurrence — and here the religious significance of the occasion must needs play a part. Tampering with religious texts is unacceptable. Where additions have been made, these appear to have been mainly new episodes or exploits in the hero's life; the suddenness with which these are introduced or come to an end and the lack of continuity in some tales point to this. As has been stated, the Ob-Ugrians were illiterate, and the only means of transmission was oral: that such transmission is not unknown even in societies which have long been literate was demonstrated by the Hungarian composer Kodály, who on one of his folksong-collecting expeditions noted down a song concerning an incident three centuries earlier during the Turkish occupation of Hungary; it had been preserved in one family and never committed to print.

The shaman who performed the ritual at the shrine recited as in the presence of a deity. Foreign observers note that certain parts of the whole ceremony, though not necessarily the actual heroic song or tale, were performed in an unnatural voice, generally likened to bird-sounds. Here it is unfortunate that the earlier scholars who collected songs from the Voguls and Ostyaks were concerned only with the texts and not with the musical accompaniment, for there are considerable differences between their versions and the later musical recordings. The early texts, for example, often appear to have no definable rhythm. The accompaniment, however, did provide a regular rhythm, usually of four main stresses per line, and the performer filled out the line with extra syllables of no particular meaning in order to maintain it. The melodies as recorded are felt to be monotonous, and the instruments were not used to heighten or diminish the dramatic effect. But rhythm is inherent also in the characteristic repetition of lines with the alteration of one or two words which fit the same metrical scheme. The highly-complex epithet, typical of Ostyak and Vogul verse, plays a notable part here. Such phrases as 'my twenty-crane-high-foot-limbed elder brother' are capable of considerable variation, while still keeping to the metre. Repetition of single words is also common: 'Our ageing hands have aged, our ageing feet have aged', say the warriors in one Vogul song. Such repetition is generally simple; there are none of the complications that are expected in, say, Finnish or Hebrew verse.

When the heroic song is connected with worship at a particular shrine, it follows a regular pattern. There is an introduction, sometimes lengthy, which prepares the audience to hear the deeds of the deity, and this is followed by the relation of his exploits, sometimes divided by a brief repetitive formula such as 'How can I do this? How do I know this?' or 'How they do this, only they themselves know.' This is not obligatory, and there are examples which show sudden changes without any warning. A different form of break in the narrative is afforded by the introduction of an unaccompanied section. There is also a ritual conclusion, which depends upon the nature of the ceremony. If it is to lead to sacrifice to the deity, in the hope that he will perform some service for the audience, very precise instructions will be given. In the Song of Ajäs, the hero demands three-hundred reindeer, all tied together, as a sacrifice, and also a piebald horse; the hides are to be hung up on trees, and prayers offered to Numi-Torem. Or the audience may simply receive a general blessing on their own lives and a promise of good fishing and hunting.

A notable feature of Vogul and Ostyak heroic songs is that the majority of them are recited in the first person by the shaman, in other words, he personifies the hero. As he is the intermediary between mortals and the gods, possession of the singer by the hero's spirit is not expected. Examination of several texts suggests that the narratives concerning minor heroes are more often delivered in the third person, and that these are altogether less impressive and their exploits more perfunctorily narrated. This style would also suggest that the original ritual significance of the heroic song was giving way to entertainment, and that the shaman was becoming a mere bard. After all, not all meetings of the community were for worship, and there is considerable evidence to show that the Ob-Ugrians enjoyed numerous festivals of a secular kind.

The close connexion of the heroic song with worship poses certain other problems. The repetitious nature of so many songs makes the action slow and dignified — indeed the deity summoned by the shaman in some cases instructs him not to make him move fast. Another expected feature of the ceremony is that numerous phrases and similes appear several times, not only in the same song, but transferred to quite different ones, thus helping to preserve the festal atmosphere. There is also the problem of the shaman himself. Does he perform his duties in a trance, or is he conscious of his actions throughout the ceremony? It would be too simple a solution to suggest that all the songs performed in the first person are sung in a shamanic trance, when the singer is possessed by the spirit of the hero himself. Moreover scholars who have recorded the songs did not take part in the actual ceremonies, and have taken them down in totally different circumstances. No satisfactory answer can be given to this problem.

It is clear that the Ob-Ugrian heroic songs and tales were not primarily for entertainment, but connected with worship, with vital questions of life, illness and death not far away. Nevertheless that some of them were used as entertainment is most likely, particularly since the distinction between religious ceremonial and secular festivals is not always sharply-defined. The bear-festivals, for example, were concerned with the capture and killing of a taboo animal, and the religious atmosphere was not excluded. The skin of the dead bear was laid in front of the images of the gods, and the bear-drama performed around it. Now foreign observers (who as a rule do not know the language) note that the Ob-Ugrians enjoyed telling stories and singing songs on every possible occasion. The first scholars to visit them found willing performers — and this might not have been the case had the shamans felt themselves to be sole custodians of the heritage of their own heroes. Internal evidence suggests that portions at least of well-known heroic songs were sung on hunting and fishing expeditions. And there is no doubt that religious ceremonies, as well as other festivals, lasted for a considerable time. Bear-festivals, for example, might last seven days for a male bear and five for a female, though in the present century it is recorded that some came to an end for lack of material to sing and dance. This seems to be the place where improvization of texts came into its own, particularly when it was aided by alcohol and other intoxicants. Munkácsi relates how the night was passed in singing and telling of tales, but he does not link these to the heroic songs.

The audience itself varied according to the importance of the hero and his shrine. In some cases, it would come from a long distance — and it must be remembered that distances between the tiny communities on the Ob and its tributaries are very considerable. Some were virtually family audiences, gathered to offer worship to their own ancestor. Although all males were eligible to attend, the position of women was subject to numerous rules. Menstruation represented the highest degree of uncleanliness, and women in this state were forbidden to live with their husbands or touch anything belonging to them, nor could they approach the shrines of the gods. In any case no women's clothes might be put into the shrine, and according to some observers women did not take part in Vogul sacrifices. Munkácsi notes that even if the shaman happened to be a woman, other women did not take part in the main ceremonies. (Here it is perhaps worthy of note that there is one Vogul song which has a female hero; it describes how a bear attacked a group of women picking berries, and one of them turned on it and killed it. This, however, is unusual and is not cast in the form of the normal heroic song.) But the audience for worship and for secular occasions was virtually the same one, bound by ties of kinship and language in a bleak and inhospitable world.

None of the published material of these songs is of great length. Some are a mere 300 lines long, others may have up to 3,000 lines. Moreover, since the style is so repetitive, the actual narrative is often very brief indeed. There is no lengthy introduction of the hero or dramatic building-up of actions. The episodes are brief and explicit. The material is known to the audience, as in the case of a good ballad, and doubtless any mistakes would also be noted. Moreover the relationship of the singer to the audience is not that of the entertainer or medieval *joculator*. He has a priestly function and is a power in the community, for the deity speaks and acts through him for good or evil. In one sense, as we noted earlier, he has more power than the secular head of the community, for he alone has access to the spirit-world and to the gods.

Since nothing is known of the existence of any other kind of literature in the Ob-Ugrian tradition, little can be said about the development of the heroic song. It has probably existed as long as heroes have been deified — and the absence of geographical locations outside the Ob region suggests that the songs now collected have all originated since the settlement of North-West Siberia by the Voguls and Ostyaks, though some of the elements had been brought there from an earlier homeland. The need for the tribe or community to be reminded of its corporate life and spirit must also have played a part, especially since it has been under constant threat of foreign invasion. The link between the hero and the religious life of the Ob-Ugrians has ensured the continuance of such a tradition. Paradoxically the strenuous efforts of Russian missionaries to convert the stubborn pagans gave them all the more reason to cling to their beliefs and with them their songs. The Voguls and Ostyaks were quite willing to embrace Christianity, indeed to absorb it into their own system of beliefs, if one condition could be met — that their images too might be baptized with them. Thus although scholars who first visited them in the last century and collected their songs were sure that their traditions would rapidly die out, they found a healthier state of oral literature than might have been the case if conversion to Christianity had not been attempted. The isolation of the region doubtless also played a part here; it was off the beaten track and not obviously on the way to anywhere else, and its climate was too forbidding for most foreigners to wish to settle there. Against this the fragmentation of two small languages into widely-differing dialects and the division of their speakers into tiny, scattered communities militated against the continuation of such a tradition. The speed of developments in the present century, particularly since the Russian revolution, has hastened its decline. Not only have material improvements, collectivization, new methods of animal breeding and fish-farming been introduced, but education has ensured the pre-eminence of Russian and tended to relegate the Ostyak and Vogul languages to the status of 'preserved folklore'. The heroic song belongs to the past.

The Song of the God of the Middle Sosva provides a useful example of the Vogul epic tradition. It is brief, consisting of some 329 lines, and was taken down from a shaman in Beryozov on 7 March 1889. The hero is one of the sons of Numi-Torem (either the sixth or the fourth, according to the two different references to him), and his shrine is situated on the river whose name he bears. It is in the middle of a thick forest and is protected by traps and other devices through which only the custodian of the shrine can find his way, indeed so well is it protected that some sources refer to it as a 'fortress'. The image itself is of wood, richly decorated with garments and trinkets, while around the main shrine are small sheds in which the guardian displays the gifts brought there by his followers. There is also a sacred tree, surrounded by iron-tipped arrows, for it is the duty of every male to offer at least one arrow and a little money to the god.

He is an important deity, as the formal introduction to the song declares: he is a 'famous prince, a noted prince' who dwells high above Russians and Ugrians in their boats on the river. But his warrior-servants are discontented, for they have no opportunities to display their prowess:

> Like trout in dire straits are we too in dire straits.
> Like herring in dire straits so are we in dire straits.

They pray to Numi-Torem to send them a cause of war, then the hero himself
finds that he cannot sleep:

> If I lay out a low pillow it becomes high,
> If I lay out a high pillow it becomes low.

While the hero tosses and turns within, the warriors outside spend their time
playing games, until an enemy boat is seen approaching; at this the hero is
enjoined to rise and put on his armour. This he does, then searches beneath his
pillows for his holy sword, which glitters when he places it in the middle of his
house. He goes forth to meet the enemy, but by this time half his army has
already been slain. He goes up to the enemy leader, cuts off his head and scalps
him, returning to hang up the scalp for all to see his victory. The tree on which
he hangs it — and doubtless the audience would be reminded of this — is
none other than the sacred tree outside the shrine. Throughout this part of the
song, the singer, telling his tale in the first person, reminds his audience of the
fact that the hero is a 'famous' prince, a 'noted' prince, and these epithets are
also applied to his sword.

   This, however, is the prelude to a further adventure. The hero catches sight
of two other leaders running away, and gives chase, this time taking a three-
pronged arrow. As he runs after them, he sees that all but one of his army have
been slain, and the survivor is made to stay behind while the hero continues the
chase and finally transfixes both enemies with one arrow. There is a touch of
humour in the description of their plight. The first of them says

> 'Hi, brother, why have you pulled me back?'
> The man at the back replies,
> 'Like autumn fish on a fine spit,
> Like spring fish on a fine spit,
> Behold we stand together
> On a three-pronged arrow of horn.'

Up to this point details have been scanty, but now follows a description of the
scalping of the two leaders which recalls the previous scalping, but contains
more information, and the contrast between the hero's own curly head and the
scalps of his victims is emphasized. It is as if the first account prepares the
audience for the details of the second; many of the phrases are repeated, but
with new elements inserted. The return of the hero with the new proofs of his
prowess is described in exactly the same phrases as were used in connexion
with his first heroic exploit, and again the emphasis is on his fame and name.

   There follows another chase, this time after the ordinary warriors in the
enemy army. Again the three-pronged arrow is used to effect, and three men are
transfixed. Their reactions are exactly the same as those of the two leaders, and

the description of the scalping is a virtual repetition of the previous adventure. The only new feature is the reference to the length of the chase, 'a knee-wearing, shin-wearing road'. This time, however, the hero continues his chase and transfixes four further enemies with his arrow; they are simply described by the singer as 'autumn fish on a fine spit', and the seven scalps are hung from the hero's belt. The return home is very briefly recounted, the only reference to the length of the journey back being found in the use of a verb which suggests a slow and weary gait. But the hero has clearly been away a considerable time, for he discovers his sole remaining warrior weeping for him on the assumption that he has been taken captive. The hero hangs up his new trophies, and tells the man to wash his 'famous, noted sword' and bring it back to its resting-place beneath his pillow. Here the emphasis is on the sacred nature of the hero's house (i.e. his shrine), his sword and the river in which it is to be washed. After this adventure the song appears to be moving to a ritual ending, but another exploit occurs after the hero has succeeded in sleeping a real sleep. Until this point the narrative has been comparatively homogeneous: the hero and his warriors have fought a battle and the enemy has been defeated with considerable losses on both sides. The language has been repetitive, and the hero's valour has been stressed to the audience, who might now be expected to react by making suitable offerings to him. This does not happen; instead a new adventure is told, and one well-attested from other Vogul accounts. Another enemy is reported to be building a stone dam across the sacred river, and the hero is roused by a watchman to action. On this occasion the circumstances are quite different; there is no army on either side, and no account of a fight. The hero arms himself as before (and his sword glows as it did when he set out on his first exploit), but simply goes down to where the 'old man' is building the dam and transfixes him with his three-pronged arrow. The enemy's body flies asunder, and appropriate geographical names are given to the places where the various parts of it fall. The song then ends with a formal passage declaring the sacredness of the stream and the shrine, and an injunction to the audience to maintain sacrifices there.[15]

This would appear to be an unsatisfactory ending to an otherwise well-constructed song, but perhaps the explanation is that the incident of the dam was well known to the audience and its inclusion somewhere in the narrative would be expected. Other sources tell the tale in greater detail — the enemy has come from a great distance and is feared by all around; the hero prays to the Sky-Father for assistance when he hears that his intent is to destroy him and his shrine, but receives little encouragement; finally he resorts to a simple trick, and calls to the enemy to look behind to see who is following; as he turns, the hero shoots at him. The geographical names ('Heart island, Head island, Belly hill', etc.) vary, and in one account a stream rises where the enemy collapses. That these names have been given to rocks in the Sosva river, which

in that particular part of its course is exceedingly treacherous and difficult to
navigate is borne out by one of Munkácsi's Vogul informants. Perhaps this may
be seen as an added reason for a shrine to the God of the Middle Sosva in this
place, for it was a well-used route and its dangers widely-known. This too would
explain why the hero enjoins the audience at the end of the song not to take
water from this sacred stream, but to leave it untouched so that journeys both
up and down stream may be made as easy as possible. There was a double
purpose in the song: the maintenance of the cult of the hero and the preserva-
tion of navigation on his river. Viewed in this light, the ending of the song is
highly relevant to the practical as well as the spiritual needs of the
worshippers.

By contrast, the Ostyak 'Song of the Golden Prince' has one purpose only:
to show the greatness of the hero himself. It is of considerable length — some
1340 lines — and curious in construction. It begins with a geographical
introduction which shows the hero in his wooden town on a high cape over-
looking the River Ob. It is a rich and prosperous place, with plenty of mead and
food. The hero introduces his family; he has an elder brother, whose name
suggests that he is powerful and hot-tempered, and a younger brother whose
martial prowess is mentioned. The rest of his family, who are numerous, have no
special characteristics: they are merely ordinary princes. All three brothers live
together in the town which the hero has constructed, and whose people serve
him absolutely, their feet growing weary from running to do his will. The hero,
like his Vogul counterpart, is called 'famous and noted', and he too possesses a
'golden-gleaming holy sword'. He also has a wife who in accordance with
Ob-Ugrian practice is a foreigner, a 'Sabir'.[16] This introduction sets the scene,
and suggests that all is peaceful, prosperous, and happy.

The hero now hears strange noises from across the river, and learns that his
elder brother has deserted him to build his own town; gradually the hero's
people leave him, and his herds of reindeer are driven away. Instead of taking
action, he laments his fate: 'I am become the prince of a deserted headland;
what am I to do?' Like the Vogul hero, he tries to sleep a true sleep, but cannot
find the solution to his problem. The final blow comes when his younger brother
leaves him, ostensibly because he dislikes his wife, with whom he has refused to
eat at table. 'Now', laments the hero, 'I am become a shabby dog, a cast-out cur
and nothing more.' He goes, somewhat shamefacedly, to his wife, who foresees
trouble, and confesses that the town is running out of food and drink; he asks her
almost imploringly to go to her father for more food and for armed assistance to
punish his elder brother for offending him, his younger brother for offending her.
This unheroic behaviour receives a scathing reply, 'Tell that story to a child,
and not to me!' She points out quite properly that if her father and his army
were to carry out this plan of revenge, the hero would in duty bound have to
revenge himself on them as foreigners, and this would leave her orphaned and

probably widowed too. This for the first time in the tale rouses his anger, and he hits her hard, whereupon she falls on the floor.

The hero once again considers the problem, and once again approaches his wife, this time offering her an escort. She makes the same reply, with the same result, but evidently thinks better of it, and dresses for the journey. The preparations are described in some detail, but the journey itself and the results of it are taken for granted. She returns with provisions, but is carried off by the younger brother to see the new town. She manages to evade him, and the provisions reach their destination, whereupon the hero is happy once more, with food and drink in plenty. Meanwhile the Sabir army arrives, and a terrible battle ensues in which the elder brother is killed, while the younger one fights until his strength is exhausted and secretly slips back to the hero's house. Here, like the prodigal son, he asks for refuge and pleads to be taken on as a servant. The wife, however, refuses to have anything to do with him, and he goes out again to fight the enemy and to seek a hero's death in battle. Instead he is captured, stuffed into a sack and tied to a horse's tail in utter disgrace.

Having finished the battle, the Sabirs wonder whether they should attack the hero's own town, but he is considered to be such a feeble and useless character that they go home. This is the point where the hero comes into his own at last; up to now his behaviour has been anything but heroic — he has allowed his brothers to build a rival town, he has had to ask his wife to bring foreign aid, and has always appeared as vacillating and weak. After a brief exchange with his wife, who says that she has truly prophesied events, he dresses himself carefully — and the Ostyak account describes this in detail — and goes off on his snowshoes, which give him the power to travel faster than the horses of the Sabirs. He thus arrives in their town before they arrive home, and meets his father-in-law as he returns from the expedition 'covered in Ostyak blood'. He kills him with his sword and recovers the sack in which his younger brother has been carried thither. Having undone it, he tries to revive him with fire and with water, but in vain. He then prays to Numi-Torem for aid, but only after he has prepared a sacrifice of reindeer does the Sky-Father answer his prayer by sending a lightning-flash down to the corpse to revive it. The younger brother awakes from what he believes to have been a long sleep (and this implies that he has recovered his strength), puts on armour and helps the hero to attack and defeat the Sabir leaders who have been so scornful about their sister's husband. There is a splendid confrontation between the hero and the eldest of her brothers, and a brief skirmish resulting in the complete destruction of the Sabirs. Their bodies are quartered, their town utterly destroyed by fire and the hero's revenge fulfilled. The tale ends with the return of the two brothers, now friends for life, and a description of the peace and plenty which now reign once again in the town, where once again the hero reigns supreme.

Most of the 'heroic' action takes place in the last third of the narrative, whose vocabulary contrasts sharply with the relatively simple and repetitive phrases of the Vogul tale. There are the expected references to the hero's handsome appearance and his 'curly locks', his armour and his prowess in battle, but the complex epithets bestowed on practically every character and every piece of equipment give an impression of poetic richness which is far less common in Vogul. The hero tries in vain to sleep:

> I lie on my bed, but I have no rest,
> Like a worn-out axe-handle, I twist and turn,
> Like a birchwood knife-handle, I toss and turn.
> My heart is as if pierced by a long larch-spit,
> My liver is as if gored by a sharp fir-spit.
> Hungry and thirsty I languish,
> Tongue-tied, speechless I suffer.

The construction, which appears strange in view of the long-delayed heroic action, suggests a much more dramatic approach than in the Vogul example. The main characters, the hero, the younger brother and the wife, are well portrayed, and the encounter between the bedraggled and exhausted younger brother and the unforgiving Sabir woman is graphically told. The hero's long search for a true cause for heroic deeds, his deep thoughts and inability to sleep are all forgotten in the frenzy of action when the Sabir town is burnt to the ground and the people scatter like scared fish, their mouths wide open, and he declares triumphantly that at last he has taken true revenge. The end of the song is notable in that the wife is not mentioned, though it was she who advised the hero to seek out his brother's body and try to revive it; the two brothers are left to rejoice together and to live together.[17]

The Song of the Golden Prince is not alone in having both a local and a 'national' significance. The incidents described can be related to the problems of life in the Ob valley, where raids and local skirmishes through the centuries have been numerous, and where leaders of various communities have had to struggle hard to maintain themselves in power. But the reference to 'Ostyak blood', which is repeated several times, suggests something wider. On the evidence of such songs as have been published, the Ostyaks of the Ob valley seem to have had much more sense of their corporate existence than had the Voguls, whose settlements were not so widely spaced.

How far these two examples are typical of the Vogul and Ostyak tradition is difficult to determine with any degree of certainty, since as yet not all the material collected over a century ago has seen the light of day. Moreover it is only very recently that the material available has been considered as literature; the devoted scholars who collected it were more interested in the linguistic aspects of the languages concerned, which was only natural, for it must be remembered that the relationship between Hungarian, Vogul and Ostyak, like the whole question of the existence of the Uralic language-group, was the subject of considerable and acrimonious controversy in the last century. Munkácsi's immense work on the Voguls was not published in its entirety until 1952, sixty years after its inception. Many of the discoveries of the pioneers Reguly and Pápay are still to be published. In the meantime, while linguistic research has continued apace, appreciation of the literary worth of the texts is still in its infancy, and in addition such appreciation comes exclusively from foreign scholars. In these circumstances many questions must remain unanswered and many problems await solution. Nevertheless the published material affords a tantalizing glimpse of an unexpected culture.

NOTES

1. B. Munkácsi, *Vogul népköltési gyüjtemény*, IV (Budapest, 1897).
2. Charles H. Eden, *Frozen Asia* (London, 1879), p. 153.
3. J. Boros and L. Rapcsányi, *Vendégségben őseinknél* (Budapest, 1975), p. 87.
4. *Reguly-album* (Pest, 1850), pp. 103–104.
5. B. Munkácsi, *Vogul népköltési gyüjtemény*, II (Budapest, 1892), p. 205.
6. B. Munkácsi, ibid., p. 255.
7. B. Munkácsi, ibid., p. 276.
8. B. Munkácsi, ibid., p. 233.
9. B. Munkácsi, ibid., p. 101.
10. B. Munkácsi, ibid., pp. 112–13.
11. B. Munkácsi, ibid., p. 67.
12. B. Munkácsi, *Vogul népköltési gyüjtemény*, IV (Budapest, 1897), p. 155.
13. B. Munkácsi, *Vogul népköltési gyüjtemény*, II (Budapest, 1892), p. 104.
14. Paper read by the writer to the Folklore Society on 8 December 1976, now published as 'The Bear in Ob-Ugrian Folklore', *Folklore*, 88 (1977), 146–59.
15. B. Munkácsi, *Vogul népköltési gyüjtemény*, II (Budapest, 1892), p. 160.
16. This is not the place to discuss the interpretation of the word 'Sabir'. References to the problem are to be found in Constantine Porphyrogenitus, *De Administrando Imperio*, edited by R. J. H. Jenkins, II (London, 1962), p. 147. I have accepted the solution proposed by Géza Képes in his study 'A magyar ősköltészet nyomairól' in *Az idő körvonalai* (Budapest, 1976), p. 44.
17. See A. Reguly, J. Pápay, M. Zsirai et al., *Osztják (Chanti) hősénekek*, III, 1 (Budapest, 1963).

SELECT BIBLIOGRAPHY

Texts

VOGUL

Kannisto, A., *Wogulische Volksdichtung*, edited by M. Liimola, I–V (Helsinki, 1951–59)
Munkácsi, B., *Vogul népköltési gyüjtemény*, I–IV (Budapest, 1892–1963)

OSTYAK

Pápay, J., *Osztják népköltési gyüjtemény* (Budapest and Leipzig, 1905)
Pápay, J., *Ostjakische Heldenlieder aus József Pápays Nachlass*, edited by I. Erdélyi (Budapest, 1972)

Patkanov, S., *Die Irtysch-Ostjaken und ihre Volkspoesie*, i–iii (St Petersburg, 1897–1900)
Reguly, A., Pápay, J., Zsirai, M., *et al.*, *Osztják hősénekek*, i–iii (Budapest, 1944–65)

Scholarly works

Diószegi, V., editor, *Popular beliefs and folklore tradition in Siberia* (Bloomington and
    The Hague, 1968)
Krohn, K. and A. Bán, *A finnugor népek pogány istentisztelete* (Budapest, 1908)
Väisänen, A. O., editor, *Wogulische und Ostjakische Melodien* (Helsinki, 1937)

Q

OSSETIC

(Nartä)

By H. W. BAILEY

NARTÄ TALES OF THE CAUCASUS relate feats of heroes and hence may be called
'epic'. Here the following synthesis is based almost entirely on the Nartä texts
recorded from oral recitation in the North Iranian Saka dialects of Ossetia.
The Ossetes live on both sides of the main Caucasian mountain chain with two
capital cities Dzäuägi γau (now Ordjonikidze) and K'rc'xinvali (Tskhinval).

The word Saka is here used in the widest Achaemenian sense, as it is used in
the Old Persian inscriptions. There they call Saka all the nomad tribes to their
north extending from the Ister river (the Danube) to the Iaxartes (the Syr-
daryā). In this sense, the names in Greek and Latin, the dialects of ancient
Tumshuq, Khotan and Kanchak with the loan-words in Old Indian inscriptions, the modern Iranian dialects of the Pamirs, especially the Wakhī of Wa-
khān, and the two dialects Digoron and Iron of the Ossetic amalgam of Sarm,
Alan and Arsi peoples of Iriston form part of the otherwise lost northern
Iranian Saka language.

A striking example of early Saka is the Khotan Saka *nāma-tsuta-* 'come to a
name' in the sense of 'famous' to which Ossetic Digoron *nom-dzud, non-dzud,* and
Iron *nom-dzyd* 'famous' exactly correspond both in origin and meaning, and
which has not yet been found elsewhere.

Since the Nartä tales retain features of archaic language which cannot be
explained from modern Ossetic, which is attested, apart from the brief quotation of Ioannes Tzetzes (*c.*1110–*c.*1180) and the twelfth-century inscription of
Zelenčuk, only at the end of the eighteenth century, it is important to know the
older Saka words before attempting explanation by what may be superficial
similarities in indigenous Caucasian languages which are in contact with the
Ossetes, or more remotely in Arabic or Turkish or Mongol. In reverse it is
desirable to remember that North Iranian words occur in Georgian and
Mingrelian, and especially in Chechen and Ingush, and in Armenian.

Tales of the Nartä are recorded also in the north-western Caucasian languages Qabard, Adyge, Ubykh, Abkhaz, Abaza, and less precisely in the
central-northern Chechen and Ingush, and still less precisely in the north-
eastern Avar of Daghestan; there are also tales in the Turkish of the
Caucasus.

I

The Nartä name itself, an archaic word (here called 'dialectal epic') with -rt- retained, is an excellent illustration of the importance of this wider Saka knowledge. The Digoron forms *Nartä*, *Nart*, oblique *Nartämä* and *Nartmä*, superessive *Nartbäl* exclude the plural suffix -*tä*. The word is then from **nṛtāh* 'hero'. The same word is in the older Khotan Saka *naḍaun-* from **nṛtāvan-* 'possessor of force, hero', with nominative singular *naḍe* from **nṛtā(vā)h*, nominative plural *naḍaunä* from **nṛtāvānah*, and genitive singular *naḍaunä* from **nṛtāunah*, derived from the *nṛta-* of the verbal base *nar-* 'to be skilful, active, virile'.

Before one can date the origins of these modern Ossetic Nartä oral tales there are a few facts to cite.

1. The name Soslan of one of the chief heroes is found as the name of David Soslan, consort of Queen Tamar of Georgia who died in A.D. 1212, before the Mongol devastation. Politically the Alans, one of the ancestral peoples of the Ossetes, were powerful to the north of the Caucasus till the eleventh century. They had intermarried with the Arab Muslim state of Al-Sarīr 'the Master of the Throne', the region of the Avar Qoi-su. This name Soslan is a dialectal epic form with -*ān*, distinct from Digoron and Iron. In the same way Digoron *uezdon*, *jezdon*, Iron *uäzdan* 'noble' has also this dialectal -*ān* in Iron.

2. The name of the Alan princess (*tikin Sat'inik* in the History of the Armenian historian Movsēs Xorenac'i) is in some way related to that of the chief female Nartä, lady *Satana*.

3. *doγ*, Iron *duγ* 'horse-racing, especially at funerals (*xisti doγ*)', is from North Iranian **dauga-* 'running', from either **dau-ga-* or **daug-a-*, whence it passed to Turkish, attested in A.D. 598 in Menandros Protektor (fragment 42), as δόχια among the Tourkoi (the true Turks). It is represented in later Turkish by *yoγ*.

4. The Chechen *elta* 'patron of hunting' preserves part of the Ossetic name *Eltayan* used of a giant in the Nartä tales. In the same way a part of the Ossetic name of the ruler of the Underworld *Barastur* is preserved in the Inguš and Chechen *Ešter*, *Eštur*, *Eštr*, and *Eter*, the name of the 'lord of the dead'. The name *eltayan* is dialectal epic with initial e- (not je-) and final -*an*, from older **vṛθragna-* 'the slayer of the strong man' in a dialectal form distinct from both Digoron and Iron. Armenian *Vahagn* is also from North Iranian. It has been an error to look for Turkish here.

5. The Nartä name *Ŭärxtänäg*, later *Ŭäxtänäg*, and with substitute suffix -*aka-* for the second part also *Ŭärxäg* and *Ŭälxäg*, is the older form of the Iranian name attested as early as the fifth century as *Vaxt'ank*, *Vaxt'ank* in the History

of Łazar Pʻarpecʻi, and in Georgian legends of the early sixth-century hero *Vaxtʼang Gorgasal.*

6. The title πακαθαρ *pakatʻar* occurs in the twelfth-century inscription of the Zelenčuk valley in the Kuban region. It corresponds to the Alan title in Al-Masʻūdī (ob. A.D. 956) *byʼyr* for **bayātar*, and in the Georgian Chronicle *baqatʻar* in the name *Os-baqatʻar* ʻthe Ossetic heroʼ. It is to be interpreted from **baka-* ʻtrue, sureʼ (cognate with Ossetic *bägu, bägudär* ʻsure, heroicʼ, Turfan Persian *bg* ʻsureʼ, Parthian *ʼbg* ʻinsecureʼ) and **aθra-* ʻviolent, heroʼ from *aθ-* ʻto be violentʼ, attested in the loan-word Kuchi *etre* and Agni *atra-* ʻheroʼ. The word came into Turkish as Orkhon Turkish *byatur* (with *-ur* from Iranian *-r*, older *-ra-*, as in Turkish *Babur* from Iranian *baβra-*, later *Babr* ʻtigerʼ). It was brought back from Turkish to Persian as *bahādur*, and even late Sanskrit as *bahādura-*. From this secondary Turkish, Ossetic then has taken Digoron *bäyatär*, Iron *bäyatyr*, and metathetic *qäbatyr*. The title was widely known in Byzantine Greek βαγατουρ, βογοτουρ, Old Slavonic *bogatyrĭ*, Hungarian *bátor*, and Mongol *bayatar*, later *bātar*.

The Ossetic Nartä tales are centred upon five main families, the Nartä giving their name to the whole tradition. Their genealogical table can be set out in seven generations as follows:

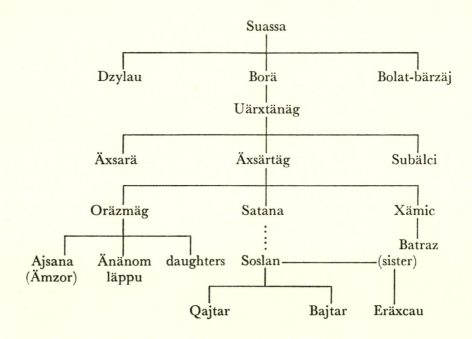

The mother of Oräzmäg and Xämic is called both Dzerassä and Sasana. Two daughters of Oräzmäg are named, one Agunda and the other Mästy-älɣyst ('angry curse'). Three wives of Soslan are cited Beduxa, Agunda, and Acyruxs.

The basis of the Nartä system is the *Ustur Xädzarä* 'the Great House', and the names of the Nartä are all epithets of their functions in the House. A selection of the names in the Nartä tales is set out first with their likely meanings. The names are not common nouns in the Ossetic dialects, and fairly certainly belong to an earlier tradition.

1. *Oräzmäg* is modified to *Uoräzmäg, Uoruzmäg, Uruzmäg* and Iron *Ŭryzmäg*. This *Oräzmäg* is plain older *ava-razmaka- 'director', which is assured by Oräzmäg's position as director and chief of the Nartä family of his generation. He is the 'chief', a 'handsome man' in build and appearance unequalled, surpassing others in ability and intelligence. From him his dependants are called *Uoräzmägetä*, Iron *Ŭryzmägtä* 'men of Oräzmäg'. He is old with a white beard. With his half-sister and wife *Satana* he is Master of the Great House. He is 'our chief *Uruzmäg*'. He has a folklore quarrel with Satana for her 'senseless words'. Together they own storehouses from which they on occasion feed the hungry Nartä men.

2. *Satana*, half-sister and wife of Oräzmäg, is the 'lady' with the archaic title *äxsijnä, äfsijnä* (rather two dialect forms of one older word than two words with different preverbs). She is the 'Lady of the House' in this precise phrase *xädzary 'fsin Satana*. Her title is rendered into Qabard by *g°aš′e* 'mistress of house, princess'. The word *Nartä* is placed before her title. She is 'our darling lady'. The name is the feminine of the masculine title, older *sātar-*, 'ruler', of which her title *äxsijnä* is a translation. A similar derivative gave the name *Sat′inik* to the Alan princess (*tikin*) in the History of Movsēs Xorenac′i (-*ik* is a common Armenian borrowed suffix to names).

Here too fits the name *Sasana*, mother of Oräzmäg and Xämic, hence an earlier Lady of the House. The base *sās-* has given the Persian name *Sāsān*, the Pontic Saka name Σασας, the name *Sasa-* on the Indo-Parthian coin, Nisa Parthian *ssn, ssnk, ssn-bwxt* and the name *Sāsān* among Šahrō's children in the *Vēs u Rāmēn* poem. The Abkhaz word *š′aš′a* 'lady' is thence a Caucasian loan-word. The high position of the Lady of the House is shown also by the Avestan *nmānō.paθnī-*, West Iranian *bān-bišn*, Armenian loan-word *bam-bišn* 'queen', Zoroastrian Pahlavī *katak-bānūk*, Pašto *mērmana*.

3. *Ajsana, Ajsäna, Asäna*, a dialectal epic word with its three long *ā*-sounds, as in *Satana*, is the name of Oräzmäg's son, who is called also *Ämzor*, the Iron equivalent of Digoron *Aznaur-*. This *aznaur-* is Georgian *aznaur* 'well-born' from Zor. Pahl. *āznāvar* 'noble'. Ajsana is the *jenceg* 'fosterling' of the smith Kurd-alägon. Assuming two dialect changes, plausible here in a proper name,

Ajsana may be older *arzānaka- 'growing child, boy', the Khotan Saka *alysānaa*- 'boy' and 'king's son', from *arz*-, *raz*- 'to grow'. Variation of -*z*- and -*s*- is known. As son of Oräzmäg he is 'son of the House', both as *arzānaka- and as *āznāvar* 'born into the high family of the Great House'. There is also a man's name *Azn*.

4. *Xämic*, Iron *Xämyc*, Inguš gen. sing. *Xamči*, is the 'lover of women' (*us üarzag*), possessing a magic tooth, the sight of which no woman can resist. He marries a woman of the *Becentä* 'dwarfs', for which he suffers much badinage. His epithet would fittingly be 'the seducer', which would lead straight to *ham-iči- with Digoron *xicä* 'amorous seduction', Iron in *äm-xīc*. Such a word is known in the Old Indian Rigvedic *vícya* 'having seduced' (10.10.6) in the story of Yama and his sister Yamī, from *ví* and *ic-ya*.

5. *Üärxtänäg*, *Üäxtänäg*, *Üärxäg*, *Üälxäg*, is the name of Subälci's father and elsewhere the ancestor of the Nartä, the grandfather of Batraz. The head of the Great House is the 'commander' or 'solemn speaker'. The base is *vark*- or *varg*- familiar in the Avestan *varaxəðra*- 'solemn ritual utterance' of the priests hostile to the Zoroastrians.

6. *Soslan*, called also Digoron *Sozuruqo*, *Sozruqo*, Iron *Sozyryko*, Chechen *Soska Solsa*, is the name of one of the two chief heroes of the generation next to Oräzmäg. His character is very fully sketched in the tales. A prominent feature of his is expressed in the epithet *närämon* 'violently virile-minded' from *nara-māna-, like *narya-manah-, Avestan *naire.manah*- modern *Nareman* 'manly-minded'. His father is called *Sosäg äldar* 'chief Sosäg' from the same base *sos*- (or *soz*-) for which a meaning 'high-spirited' may be claimed. Soslan has a folklore birth story, but as a hero of the Great House his name should be heroic.

7. *Batraz*, *Batäraz*, Iron *Batyraž*, and variants *Batradz*, *Batyradz*, Inguš *Patriž*, and *Totraz*, *Totyraž* and variant *Totradz*, *Totyradz*, Qabard *Totreš*, *Totyreš*, are the two names of the young fighting heroes of the Nartä. Batraz is son of Xämic and Totraz is son of Albeg of the Albegatä family. Both names show a second component -*rāz*, comparable to the Khotan Saka -*rāysa*- (=*rāza*-) 'directing, showing'. The first components are then *bāta*- 'feats of valour' and *tota*- 'feats of strength'.

8. *Sirdon*, Iron *Syrdon*, Inguš *Širtta* and Turkish *Širdan* (retaining the earlier -*āna*-) is given as father both Bätäg and Gätäg, and a second name Natar-Uatar and Uätär-Nätär, the variation of these names probably indicating dialectal epic words. The name *Bätäg/Gätäg* may show the two treatments of initial *ŭ*- as *b*- or *g*-, hence the name is from *vata-, an older Iranian word signifying both 'small' as in Khotan-Saka *bata*- 'small' and Zor. Pahl. *vaččak* 'child' from *vatačaka-, and 'bad' as in Zor. Pahl. *vata*- 'bad', Persian *bad*. Sirdon is the bane, but also the butt of the Nartä heroes, a trickster of the

Great House. His name is likely therefore to express this activity. In *sird-* one may see a denominative base *ser-*: *sir-* from *sai-* 'to cheat', a common development, connected with *sāi-*, Digoron *sajun* 'to cheat', possibly influenced also by the Saka verb *jēr-* found in Khotan Saka *jsīr-*: *jsīḍa-* 'to cheat', whence the loanword *tser-* in Tokhar of Kuci. The Ossetic *dzer-* is cited below in the sense of 'to seize' and might be this same word without pejorative meaning.

9.   *Borä* is the name of an unimportant actor in a few tales, and it occurs in a list, but is mainly the name of the family *Borätä, Boriatä, Boirätä, Burtä*, with an adjective *buron* 'rich', and the feminine name *Boräyäntä*, daughter of *Buräfärnyg*. The *-bor-* is also in the name *Narty Aborquayijy Buräfärnyg*. The *Borätä* are the rich Nartä family, the *qäzdyg närton mygkak*. *Boräfärnug* is the rich man par excellence. In a Russian text occurs the dyadic name *Buron-bogač* 'Buron the rich' where *buron* is glossed by Russian *bogač*. This *bōr* 'riches' has various cognates from *bau-* 'to abound, be rich'. It is not to be confused with *bōr* 'yellow' (older **balva-*) or *bōr* 'food' (older **barva-*).

10.   *Xuareldar, Xualerdar, Xuarildar,* Iron *Xorӓldar, Xory 'ldar*, is the patron of corn and fruitfulness, named from Digoron *xuar*, Iron *xor* 'corn' from the base *hvar-* of 'eating', with the second component *äldar* 'lord, owner'. His son is called *Bor-xuar ali*, Iron *Bur-xor ali* (inflected *aliji, alijy*). Digoron *xvar*, Iron *jäu* is 'millet'. The same *bōr* 'food' occurs in Zor. Pahl. *bōr, bōrak* as in the phrase *pit ut bōr* corresponding to Avestan *baourva-* and *pitu-* (Yašt 17.1). The base *barva-* is in Old Indian *bharvati* 'to chew'. In the son's name, *ali* is rather a word for 'prince' than the Muslim name ʿ*Ali*, hence a cognate of the *äl-* of *äldar* and the *āla-* of the family name *Alägatä*. The son *Bor-xuar ali* was slain by Batraz who boasted of the deed before the Ŭacamongä Bowl, whereupon in folklore fashion Xuareldar blighted the crops.

11.   *Acä* of the *Acätä* family is the father of *Acämäz* who plays the magical flute. The father's name has many variants. We find *Aci furt, Ŭazi furt, Ŭaži furt, Ŭaziji furt, Ŭazimi furt, Ŭaci furt,* Iron *Acäjy saq* ('brave') *fyrt*, in Russian script *Acamaz syn slavnogo Uaza*, Qabard *Aša*, Karačai Turkish *Ačimez* son of *Ači*, and *Ecemej* son of *Ecej*. The name of the son is *Acäti Acämäz*, Qabard *Ašamez, Ašemez*, Adyge *ašʿmez*, Abadzekh *ašmez*. A longer phrase occurs in Abkhaz Bzyb dialect *ačʿan r-ah* 'the prince of the *Ačʿan* family', translated into Russian by *vladitel' Acanov*.

In the Qabard tales the father has the dyadic epithet Russian *Aša najbolee mogučij* 'Aša the exceedingly strong'. This same Russian *mogučij* helps to render also Ossetic Digoron *ŭac-axässän congebäl* 'on his powerful-carrying arms'. The family are then named the 'strong ones'.

This same *ŭac, ac* 'strong' is also the first component of the name of *Acämäz* with the familiar *maz-* 'great', hence a compound with sequent adjective meaning 'great in strength', formed like such a name as 'Αριαμάζης in Strabo, and like a later name *Mihr-mas* with the other word *mas-* 'great'. Note how *ŭac* and *ac* alternate in the name of the Bowl *Ŭacamongä* and *Acamongä*, and in the feminine name *Ŭaciroxs* and Iron *Acyruxs*. A similar *maz-* can be detected also in the name in Čerkes *Batmǝzǝ* 'great in feats of heroism'. The heroine *Ŭadz-äftauä* consented to wed the son of Acämäz.

12. *K'armägon* is the name of a witch to whom in gratitude Oräzmäg distributed some of the booty. (The ejective *k'-* and the aspirated *k'-* are both used to replace the older Iranian *k-*, but at times the ejective *k'-* may replace the older *sk-*, as in *k'abaz*, *k'abozä*, Iron *k'abaz* 'branch', cognate with Greek σκᾶπος, Latin *scopa* 'small branch'.) The witch is the 'performer of magic' expressed by *kar-* 'to do magic' as in Ossetic *kälän*, and Old Indian *kṛtyā-*, Lithuanian *kēras*, Old Russian *čary* 'magic'. The name is thus **karmaka-* with the feminine suffix of names *-on* from *-ānā-*.

13. *Beduxa*, *Beduya*, Qabard *Bidox*, *Badax*, *Bǝdex*, is the name of one of the beautiful heroines (*räsuyd*), wife of Soslan. On Soslan's visit to the *Däl-zänxä* 'Underworld' it was Beduxa who explained to him the surprising sights he had met. She gave him also the healing leaves of the *Aza-*tree which he had gone there to seek.

Derived from the base in Digoron *bedun*, *bedujun*, participle *bett*, *bitt* 'appear, have influence' the name *bedux-* would mean 'illustrious, wonderful', or possibly 'influential', the former more suiting a lady, Soslan's wife. The final *-a* occurs in other women's names as in *Agunda*, *Akula*, *Elda*, *Satana*, *Sasana*, *Xorčeska*, as well as in the men's names *Ajsana* and *Bayodza*. This may be preferred to the derivation from **baga-duxtā* 'daughter of the distributory deity', which gave Persian *bē-duxt* and *bē-luft* for the planet Venus. From a similar verb *sah-* 'to appear' the Zor. Pahlaví has *sahīk* 'wonderful' and Persian has *sahī* used of majestic women and of lofty trees.

14. *Becentä* is the name of the family of dwarfs. There are variant forms of the name: Iron *Bycentä*, *Byšentä*, *Byšenontä*, *Bdzentä*, in Russian *Bcen*, *Bicenatä*, and most modified *Psältä*. From this *becen-* came the feminine with suffix *-on* *Becenon*, *Bycenon*, *Byšenon* and *Bycenton*. A dwarf gives his sister to Xämic as wife. The dwarf is called Digoron *Ulink'ä* 'cubit-high', and he has also the Čerkes name (in Russian script) *Aceko*, that is, in Čerkes *a* 'the' with *c'ǝk'u* 'small'. The syllable *bec-*, *byc-* is then clearly a dialectal epic word meaning 'small', and connected with Digoron *bitzeu*, *biddzeu*, *bicceu* 'child' (not found in Iron), and further from the *vata-* 'small' in Khotan Saka *bata-* 'small'. The *ulin-* of the name *Ulink'ä* is the dialectal epic word beside Digoron *ärinä*, Iron *ärin* 'elbow'.

15. *Čelaxsardton, Čelexsärtan, Čeläxsärtan, Čeläxsärton, Čiläxsärtton, Čeläxsar, Čeläsxan, Čeläxsärtäg, Jeläxsärdton, Geläxsärton,* Qabard *Džilaxstan, Džəlaqsten, Gylaxstan,* Karačai Turkish *Giljaxsyrtan,* has the usual marks of the dialectal epic name. He is one of the warlike heroes. The second component *äxsärt* is normal replacement of older *xšaθra-* 'dominion, warriorship', which is known also in the family name *Äxsärtägkatä.* The first component with its dialectal *č-, j-* is the older word *čarya-* 'warlike' in Avestan *čirya-* glossed by Zor. Pahl. *kārēčārīk,* and maintained in the Turkish loan-word *čärik, čäri* 'troop of warriors'.

16. *Maryuz,* Iron *Märyŭdz* is the name of the rich man with vast herds of horses and cattle on the plains and in the meadows. With the suffix *-uz, -ŭdz* the word is from older *marga-* 'meadow, wood', as in Avestan *marəya-,* Sogd.Manichaean *mry* 'meadow, wood' and Sogd. Buddhist *mry'* 'plain', *mryyh* 'forest', Persian *mary.* The name *Bayodza* is formed by similar suffix from *bāga-* 'plot of land, garden' suiting his possession of an enclosure called *keyog* (*kēy-* < **kāyya-*) with a folklore apple-tree.

17. *Sqäl-becän, Sqäl-beson* is a hero possessing a magic cuirass, but his wife in folklore fashion was seduced into cutting off some of the knobs, whereby it ceased to make the wearer invulnerable. The name therefore clearly contains a dialectal epic word *sqäl,* like the Digoron *äsqär,* Iron *zyär* 'armour', both also abnormal forms, and a second component *bec-, bes-* with adjectival suffixes *-än* and *-on.* This is the word found in Khotan Saka *besa-* 'shield', from older **belsa-* (**vr̥tsa-*) of the base *var-* used widely of defensive armour. The hero's name is then a description from his special dress.

18. *Qäncärgäs, Qändzärgäs* is the name of a winged seven-headed giant. He captured the Nartä Aläg and made him into a herdsman. The same story is told of Uon. The second component is well known: *cärgäs* 'eagle', Sogd. *črks,* Avestan with unpalatalized initial *kahrkāsa-,* Zor. Pahl. *karkās,* Persian *kargas,* named from the base *kark-* 'to strike' with the suffix of animals *-āsa-* (as in Digoron *robas* 'fox'). The first component can then be recognized as from *gan-* 'to seize' used of the raptor bird called in Khotan Saka *uysgana-* 'vulture', Persian *zayan.*

19. *Xorčeska* is called in Digoron *xori kizgä Xorčeska* 'Xorčeska daughter of the (lady) Sun'. The second component *-česka-* is dialectal epic and to be compared with Khotan Saka *jiśkā-* 'girl'.

20. *Subälci,* Iron *Sybälcy, Cybälc,* Qabard *Sybyl'ši,* Turkish *Sibil'či,* is a young rider, the son in old age of Uärxtänäg. The second component contains *bälci* by suffix *-i* from **balci-* 'riding', Digoron, Iron *balc,* with an adjectival first component in which may be concealed **sui-* beside *sūra-* 'strong', Khotan Saka *sūra-,* as also in Avestan *sūra-.*

21. *Selän, Šela,* Iron *Siläm, Silam* is the name of the ancestral dog, called in Digoron *xujti sär Šela* 'Šela chief of dogs'. This name **sēlama-* from older **sāramya-* belongs with Old Indian Rigvedic *sarámā-* ancestress of dogs, where the Indian tradition has *s-* in place of older *-ś-*, as found also in the Atharva-veda word *síkatā-* 'sand', Digoron *sigit,* Khotan Saka *siyatā-,* Old Persian *θikā-.* The Old Indian adjective *sārameya-* was used for 'dog'.

22. *Käntä* belongs in a somewhat confused tradition of a ruler called in Digoron *Känti sär Xuändonä, Känti Xujändag,* Iron *Kancy sär Xŭändon* beside the fuller *Känty sär Xujändon äldar,* which is found also with the titles *maligk* and *maligk paddzax* 'king emperor' in place of *äldar.*

The word *Käntä* is ambiguous, being either singular as in the Iron gen. sing. *Kancy,* or plural in *-tä.* As indicated by the Russian translation gen. plur. *Kantov,* the word *käntä* may also be collective singular for plural. In the name, the word *sär* 'chief' may be absent.

There is an Ossetic word *känt* 'building', cognate with the various words Khotan Saka *kanthā-,* Sogd. *knδh* 'city', and a loan-word from the north-west of India in Pāṇini's *kanthā.* In the name here, *Käntä* may be the same word, so that in *Känti sär* 'the chief of the *Käntä*' would resemble the old Greek title πολίαρχος.

A quite different word is introduced in the Iron phrase *Käfty sär Xŭjändon.* This same *Kaftisar* occurs in the Russian book *NEON,* where the name is placed on the *Aq dengiz* with the city *Taman,* hence on the Azov Sea. In one story *Käfty sär Xŭjändon* comes from the Underworld to visit the dying Soslan.

With the change from *Känti, Kancy* to *Käfty* a new interpretation has been introduced. The name has been taken as the genitive plural of *käf* 'fish'. In the story there is then reference to the smell of fish (*käfty smag*). The lord has *käf-dzautä* 'fishermen'. The Glossary of *NK* 1946, 581 explains *käfty, käsägty barduag* 'the ruling genius of fishes', hence the proposal to translate *käfty sär* (which is not attested in Digoron) by 'ruler of fishes'. But this is the modernized replacement of a difficult older phrase.

In *Xuändonä* I see the personal name of the ruler of the *Käntä.* The forms vary with *Xuändonä* and *Xujändag.* Here the two different suffixes *-on, -onä* and *-ag* are the usual adjectival suffixes as in Digoron *xuänxon,* and *xuänxag* 'mountainous'. The form in *-ag* excludes the word *don* 'water'. In *xuänd-, xujänd-* one would expect to see a participle in *-ant-* to a base *hau-: hu-.* For a ruler's name this points at once to the words Avestan *hvōišta-* 'most excellent', Khotan Saka *hvāṣṭa-* 'chief', Tumšuq Saka *hveṣta-,* Sogd. *xwyštr* 'superior', *γwyštk* 'revered', Munjānī *xušci, xuškye,* Ossetic Digoron *xestär* 'superior', *xestag* 'the portion of a superior', Iron *xistär.* To this will belong the Kušān Saka name *Huviṣka-.*

23. *Zeväg, Ziväg* is the seventh son of a Nartä who in folklore fashion either sits at all times in the ashes or is a boy without legs. He gains all his wishes by

direct prayer to the Autocrat of Autocrats. He marries a daughter of Borä-färnug the rich man. The name is identical with the Iron *ziväg* 'indolent', to which Digoron responds with *zinadä*, cognate with Khotan Saka *ysīta-* 'indolent'.

24. *Säuuaj, Säuaj*, Iron *Säua*, in Russian *Suaj*, Qabard *Šauej* is the heroic boy. His father's name is in the phrase *K'antdzi furt Säuuaj, K'anci furt Säuaj*, Qabard *Šauej* son of *Kanž*, but also (from Ossetic) *Dčenz*, beside Bžedux *Džandeko Sevaj*. He is for his persistence permitted to join a Nartä expedition. He is called Digoron *mink'ij*, Iron *čysyl, gycyl* 'small one', but also Iron *qäbatyr* 'hero', Qabard translated in Russian as *doblestnyj* 'splendid'. No Nartä is more 'virile' than he. His impetuosity is demonstrated. He fails to win Ŭadz-äftauä as his bride since she prefers the son of Acä, Acäti Acämäz, but he weds the daughter Agunda of Oräzmäg and so ends the vendetta between them. The horse of Säuuaj is called in Turkish *Gemuda* and in Qabard *Džamidež*, glossed by 'trusty bay', which I have not seen in Ossetic. The variation in dialectal epic names (as above under Čeläxsärdton) indicates that the horse is named the 'swift runner' from the base *čam-* 'to move fast', from which Khotan Saka has its word *tcamū* for 'locust', the swift leaping insect.

For *Säuuaj* a connexion with Khotan Saka *ṣau-* : *ṣu-* 'to cause to move (fast)' hence 'to throw, place' of any violent motion from older 'to move fast' would suit his character within the Great House. Then the two explanations by 'violent young man' and 'ugly one' from Qabard are secondary.

25. *Sopia, Sofia* is the name of a tomb. The fuller phrase is *sopiajy zäbpadz, sofiajy zäbpadz*, and *sofija-zäbpadz* 'the tomb of Sopia' to which the dying Batraz is invited. *Metri causa* there occurs also *sofijy*. A place near the village of Kazbek on the Georgian Military Road has been proposed as its site.

Sofja is a variant to the name *Safa* the 'genius of the hearth' who has a house (*xädzar*) in the sky. Since both the hearth in the floor and the tomb can be thought of as an enclosed space or box, the word *sopia, sofia, sofja, safa* recalls at once the base of the widespread Iranian *sapatā-* 'box' in Persian *sabad*, the Armenian loan-word *sapata-*, Syriac *spt-'*, Khotan Saka *savā-*, loc. sing. *savaya* 'box', Yidgha *savdö*, Kalaša loan-word *savēd-*, East Turkish *savdyč*, Russian loan-word *sapëtka* 'basket'.

At a later stage of the Nartä tradition it was thought that the Byzantine church of *Hagia Sophia* was alluded to, through a superficial similarity of sound. The *sopia* was even placed in Arabia in the phrase *Mediny sofia* 'the tomb in Medinah'.

26. *Dzerassä*, daughter of Donbettyr, one of the great lovers, was wooed by *Gätäg dony xicau* 'possessor of the water' at the river, and gave birth to Satana. But Dzerassä is the lover of Äxsärtäg, at whose death she utters a lament called

γarängä, Iron *qaräg*, a technical term. In the folklore form of a dove she seizes and carries off the apple of the Nartä.

Her name recalls the word *dzera* 'raptor' bird of prey. Both as impetuous lover and as folklore plunderer she may be the *dzerassä* 'raptrix' with a name assimilated to the bird names formed by the suffix *-āsa-*. Another name in *-assa* is that of the first ancestor of the Nartä *Suassa* which I have found only in a Russian text. It could be interpreted similarly as **s(a)uāsa-* from the *sau-: su-* in Khotan Saka *sūra-* 'strong'.

27.   The names *Agunda* and *Akula* vary for the same person, so that one would like to find a single origin for both. There are several heroines so named and they have regularly the epithet *räsuyd* 'beautiful'. If this is, as likely, a dyadic phrase the two names will derive from *ā-kau-* 'to be beautiful' with the participial suffix *-ant-* and the suffix *-la-* with the *-a* common in feminine names. This *(s)kau-* has given West Iranian *škōh* 'beauty', and more remotely Gothic *skauni-* 'beautiful'. As bringing these names within the tradition of the Great House this seems more satisfactory than isolating *Agunda* from *Akula* by calling in Greek ὑάκινθος, Zor. Pahl. *yākand*.

The name *Agunda* itself has several variants, Digoron *Agundä*, Iron *Agŭndä*, Čerkes *Akuenda*, Qabard *Aximuda*, and an uncertain Abadzex *Aguard*, Ubyx *G°enda pš'əza* 'the beautiful'.

These names have been treated at some length to show that the Iranian ecarchic system offers a consistent interpretation in all these cases.

The heroes of the Nartä tales are characterized by many epithets. Within their social system of the Great House, the *Ustur Xädzarä*, they are the Iron *uäzdan*, Digoron *uezdon*, *jezdon* 'nobles', against the *sau läg* 'black men', their inferiors, and the *xumätäg* 'common man'. They have a pride of birth, they are *närton igurd* 'of Nartä birth'. They recognize each other as friends and kinsmen.

The following epithets distinguish the Nartä heroes. They are accordingly distinguished, select, intelligent heroes, most sure (*bägudärtä*), marked out, beloved chiefs, good chiefs, the one honoured chief, excellent, handsome, strong, most able, beautiful, sound, powerful, protective, goodly, optimates, old (as meaning valiant), and the best heroes.

The family names in the Nartä tradition also fit into the Great House. Five are worthy of special notice. The first family is that of the *Äxsärtägkatä*, of which the meaning has never been obscured. It is reported that the *Äxsärtägkatä* family was few in men, but mighty in *äxsarä* 'prowess'. The two words *äxsärtäg* and *äxsarä* belong by different development to the one older word *xšaθra-*. The brother of *Äxsärtäg* was called *Äxsarä*, Iron *Äxsar*, *Äxsal*, *Äxsältär*, and *Υxsart*. In various forms this family name occurs in other Caucasian sources as Chechen and Inguš *ärxstua*, *erstxo* and Turkish *šurtuk*, a case important as showing the secondary origin in Chechen and Inguš.

The second family has an ancestor *Borä* and the family name *Boriatä, Borätä*, beside also Iron *Burtä* in a double phrase *Burtä ämä Borätä*. It is the rich family possessing *bor* 'wealth'.

The third family name is *Alägatä* with the personal name *Aläg*. From this the Georgian folk tales took *Alg-* in the geographical name *Algetʿ-i* 'the land of the *Alg* people', as they had made *Alanetʿ-i* 'land of the Alans'. *Aläg* is not important in the Nartä epic. He is carried off by the giant *Qän-cärgäs* to be a herdsman, and rescued by Batraz, who in this story is his grandson, though elsewhere Batraz is son of Xämic son of Äxsärtäg. The *Alägatä* family is said to be rich and prosperous, possessing a Great House. The basic *āla-* is likely to be a later form of **arya-* 'wealth', Zor. Pahl. *ēr*.

Just as in heroic times, according to Hesiod (Merkelbach-West (1967), fragment 203), three ancient Greek families were by simpliste technique said to be distinctively marked, the Aiakids by ἀλκή 'force', the Amuthaonids by νοῦς 'intelligence' and the Atreids by πλοῦτος 'wealth', so a tradition of uncertain date claimed heroic ability for the Äxsärtägkatä, intelligence for the Alägatä and riches for the Boriatä.

The fourth family *Acätä* is that of *Acä* father of *Acämäz*, the cultured hero, player of the magic flute.

The fifth family is the *Astä* in one tale in Digoron. Here one may wish to see the *As-* derived from older *Arsi-*, and retained elsewhere in Digoron *Asi*, Iron *Asy*, with adjective *asiag*, whence the Georgians made *Os*, and *Ovs* (the source of the name *Ossetia*).

The sense of power or force was recognized in the Greek phrase ἀλκήεντες Ἀλανοί 'powerful Alans' (Dionysios Periegetes 305), which could serve as gloss both to *Acä-tä* and *As-tä*.

There are in the basic sources some doublets, though they are eliminated from the edited sequences. Thus both Ŭarxtänäg and Ŭärxäg are the father of Subälci, being two forms of the same name, but they are also called twin brothers. Soslan is the son of Sosäg, Chechen Soska Solsa, Inguš Sioska Solsa. This hero is also called Sozuruqo (probably through Čerkes with *qo* 'son'). The names were then made into two brothers. Xämic is father of Batraz, but Batraz is also called the grandson of Aläg and Uon. The story of the death of Totraz is told also of Totraz's son Alimbeg. Of heroines of the two names Akula and Agunda similar tales are told.

II

The Nartä tales have been handed down in a form of composition called in Digoron *kadängä*, Iron *kadäg* glossed by 'a song with musical accompaniment' by Vsevolod Miller in his dictionary and in the Ossetic-Russian dictionary. The word *kadängä* is known also in the Georgian loan-word *kʻadag-i* 'herald' and *kʻadageba* 'announcement'.

For my Digoron informant the title of the performer was *kadängä-zaräg* 'singer of the work' rather than the colourless *kadängä-gänäg* 'maker of the work'.

The *kadängä* are usually in prose in their published form, but some are in verse as in the *Narti Acämäzi zar* 'the song of the Nartä Acämäz'. One text has a page of prose introduction to six following pages of verse (*IAS*, 5, 87–93). A song to Satana is placed within the story of Acämäz's wedding.

The *kadängä* is accompanied by the two-stringed fiddle *fändur*, Iron *fändyr*, played with a bow. The strings are of the hairs of a horse's tail. There existed also the *duuadäs-tänon fändyr* 'the twelve-stringed harp'. The name *fändur* is first found in Greek πάνδουρος, φάνδουρος (with other variants), and occurs in other Caucasian languages. Pictures can be seen in B. A. Galaev, *Osetinskie narodnye pesni* (Moscow, 1964), and in V. Abaev, *Iz osetinskogo ēposa*, 1939.

Two professional *kadängä*-singers are described, one Kertibi in the *Pamyatniki osetinskogo tvorchestva*, 2 (1927), preface ix–xiii, and the other Ilik'o in V. Abaev, *Iz osetinskogo ēposa*, 5.

The first is as follows. The singer Kertibi, son of Kelemet of the Kertibitä family, 1834–1914, was born in Uäqäc in Digoria and lived there till his death. He is described as taking an active part in the life of Digoria, familiar with agriculture and horse-breeding, and greatly sought after as an adviser. Then of the singer Kertibi, Dzagurti Gubädi wrote: Popular tales he knew in very great quantity; he had got them partly from his mother, partly from the old men. Most he got to know in childhood and youth. In his own narratives Kertibi gave much of the earlier history of the Ossetes, but especially of the rule of the Qabards in the North Caucasus. He usually recited his tales in winter, accompanied by his playing on the *fändur*. His tales, since he was a master of the Ossetic Digoron language, were always rich in content, the style was exceptionally light. When Kertibi recited, the whole village of Uäqäc gathered into the village meeting-place, not only the older men, but also women and children. These were particularly numerous when he played the *fändur*. So fascinatingly did Kertibi recite that the people never tired for whole days, but regretted when weariness induced him to shorten the recital. Kertibi especially loved to celebrate the Nartä heroes Soslan, Xämic, Batraz, Oräzmäg, Marguz and Sirdon. When Dzagurti Gubädi wished in 1910 to complete the collection of Kertibi's repertoire he found him too old; he had, he said, forgotten them.

Of Märγity Eprejy fyrt Ilik'o, Professor Abaev reported the following. Iliko Margiev, forty-eight years old (in 1939), enjoys the reputation of being one of the best narrators of Southern Ossetia. His repertoire is extensive and varied. His speech flows smoothly, freely and unforced. Picturesqueness and vivacity appear characteristic traits of his narrative. One feels that at the time of narration he himself experiences, together with his heroes, all the misadventures, their grief and joy. Within the story he changes suddenly from past time to the historic present and always very successfully and to the point, so that the exposition of events is animated and his hearers' attention excited. Nartä tales he cannot only narrate but also sing, accompanied by playing on the *fändyr*. The tales and the stories he heard from his father Epre and his grandfather Qandua.

Ossetic singers of *kadängä* still live on in Ossetia.

III

The world of the Nartä epic embraces the whole life of the heroic families. But there is a twofold background. There is on the one hand the concept of wide horizons and vast-extending journeys, beside on the other hand the limited mentality of the village. There is the raiding of large herds of cattle, horses and bovine cattle, in hostile lands and the search for pasture land among enemies, while the aged ancestor Aläg has only one cow. The dwellings are those of a Caucasian village even to the existence of the seven-storeyed tower. The Lady of the House discovers the making of beer from observation of plant and bird in true village folklore fashion. But Oräzmäg and Satana own storehouses which can alleviate a famine among the Nartä.

To understand the tales a knowledge of Nartä social structure is necessary, ranging from the distribution of booty from raids to the small village plots of land. There is too a religious cult in Nartä life. The heroic and the anti-heroic, the tragic and the grimly humorous alternate. The main heroes stand out with marked individuality, but the lower characters, servants, fishermen and youths, often have no names, like the protagonists in folk tales.

The Nartä have the concept of the Great Village and of the Great House. This is the type of rule that the Greeks saw as peculiarly Persian and called *oikarkhia*. The Great House has the Director and the House-Mistress with the sons or dependants as functionaries. These sons have in Ossetic the dialectal epic name of *guppur*, Iron *gŭppyr*, the *vīsō.puθra-* of the *Avesta*. Only Ajsana however is a genetic son of Oräzmäg the Director of the House. The later generation is called the 'after generation'.

Kinship terms are extensive and include *nostä* 'daughter-in-law', *fajnostä* 'brother's wife' and *ämigir* 'fellow-wife'. Xämic has two wives, but brings home a third wife the *Auari räsuyd* 'the beauty of Avaria' whom his former wives slay. Fosterage is frequent, but is expressed by Turkish terms (*jenceq*, Iron *ämcek*, and *qan*). The Georgian Geographer Vakhusht, writing in 1745, reported that the nobles (*gvarian-*) of Ossetia were *qmian-* 'possessed of *qma*-servants'. There was friction between the old (*zärond*) and the younger generation (*fäsē-väd*).

Social classes seem to be rigid. The Nartä of the three families *Boriatä*, *Äxsärtägkatä* and *Alägatä* with the families of the *Acätä* and *Astä* reveal the Nartä as *ŭezdon, jezdon*, Iron *ŭäzdan* originally a pastoralist term 'fattener of cattle', but through 'promoter, protector' has become simply 'lord or noble'. They are contrasted with the *sau läg* 'black man' in the sense of inferior. Sirdon whose father was no Nartä is a *sau läg*. Soslan's intimate friend *Saulägi furt Märäzduxt*, that is, Märäzduxt son of Sauläg, has a name meaning 'wage-paid' connected with Sogdian *mr'z*, Turkish loan-word *maraz* 'wages'. The 'noseless Sauläg' is a type of deep misfortune. The *kävdäs-ard* son 'born in a manger' implies low birth. The ordinary man is the *xumätäg*.

To be born into the Great House meant high rank. For this high birth the word *ā-zan-* was used in various Iranian languages. The Zor. Pahl. *āznāvar* 'noble' used of warriors passed to Georgian as *aznaur-i* beside the negative *u-azn-o*, whence, in Ossetic, Digoron has *aznaurtä* and Iron *Ämzoratä* of the family and *Ämzor* as a personal name, a name of Oräzmäg's son Ajsana. The name *Azn* of the Nartä is the word *āzna-* preserved in Avestan *āsna-* and Turfan Iranian plural *āznān*, glossed by Sogdian *āzāt*, and Armenian loan-word *azniu* 'noble'. The family is called *mugkag* 'the seeded' from *mugä* 'seed', as elsewhere in Iranian **marta-tauxma-* 'mortal seed' means 'mankind', in Turfan Parthian *mrdwhm *mardōhm*, Persian *mardum*, older in Sogdian *mrtxm'k*.

The *guppur* 'sons of the House' from older **visas-puθra-*, Turfan Parthian *vis-puhr*, Ṣiṇā loan-word *guš-pūr*, is used in the word with suffix *-gin guppurgintä*, *gubburgintä*, and in the compound *guppursartä*, Iron *gŭppyrsartä* to express the group.

Another term for the group of younger men is Digoron *iuonäx-sartä* 'the youths' equivalent to Iron *qal fäsiväd* 'bold descendants'. The *iuonäx-* is a derivative of the older *yuvan-* 'young'. The 'lord' or 'master' is called *äldar*, and the heroines tend to be daughters of *äldar*. It is part of the name of the Nartä *Sajnäg äldar*. The term 'village lord' (*yäu-äldar*) occurs, containing the older territorial name *gava-* of the *Avesta*.

The other end of the social scale is the slave. For this status the word used is *ŭacar*, a loan-word connected with West Iranian *vāčār* 'market'. A folklore tale of Batraz tells of him selling himself during a famine to an *äldar* 'lord', but his indignant departure when the *äldar* calls him *älxyd* 'purchased'. The tales report the carrying off of boys and girls from the Chechen and Nogai tribes. Satana has in her house a *ŭacar gumiry* 'giant slave' whom she sends to repel an unwelcome guest.

Birth in a Nartä family is all-important, but to have a name is a religious necessity since otherwise the unnamed one can have no funeral cult (*xist*). Oräzmäg's unnamed son (*änänom läppu*), killed by accident on Oräzmäg's dagger among his kin the Donbettärtä, returned from the Underworld by permission of Barastär lord of the dead to seek his father Oräzmäg and beseech him for a portion of the funeral cult.

Of the lower classes there are only a few names. The two heralds (*fedeuäg*) are Sibeka of the Lower Ward (*sinx*) and Tärazon (or Cärazon) of the Upper Ward. Two doorkeepers Tula and Tulabeg appear. There are Mäcyqo and Tepsyqo, two servants of Safa. But in the background are unnamed servants, fishermen, herdsmen, messengers, general servants. At a feast Sirdon acts as cupbearer. The wretched plight of Batraz's grandfather Bolat as herdsman of the giant's horses and of Aläg as shepherd of Qän-cärgäs is strongly expressed. Equally bad is the fate of Üärxäg labouring in the mine for the people of the Underworld. Twelve hired men serve the giant Mukara; at his mother's funeral rite Sirdon has hired servants, bakers of bread and brewers of beer.

The public life of the Nartä is conceived on the village model. They assemble for public business as a group of old men (*zärond*, cognate of Greek γέροντες, hence a gerousia), at the *nixäs*, Iron *nyxas*, the ground set apart for discussion, where they sit in a circle on stone seats. The Kʿartʿvel language of Račʿa has made *sanaxšo* from the Ossetic word, for the same concept, and other words in various Caucasian languages attest the practice.

After a raiding expedition, called a *balc*, at times lasting several years during which time the raiders were not in touch with their homes, the cattle called *fonsikond* were driven to the place called Iron *üarän fäz* 'the plain of distribution', an act of great significance in heroic times.

Public too was the sport and dancing. The 'play' (*γazun*) on horseback was the act of the rider called *jigit* in Turkish. For dancing Ossetic had the three words *semun*, *serun*, and *kafun*. The dance on their fellows' shoulders is mentioned, a feat still performed in Ossetia. Feastings are evidently a cause of much rejoicing. The feast (*mijnasä*) may last a week, as at the wedding of Acämäz. The *fezonäg* (meat on the spit) and *bägäni* (beer) are favoured food, but the Nartä had also the drink called *rong*, a name surviving in Swanetian *rang* for a honey drink. They knew also *äluton* 'boiled ale' and *sänä* 'wine'.

The Nartä are settled in three separate wards (*sinx*, Iron *syx*, possibly the old word *šayana-*, Armenian loan-word *šēn*) called Upper, Middle and Lower. A place near their settlement is called *Fäs-nart Xuzä-dzägat*, Iron *Fäs-nart Xus-dzägat*, similar to the name *Xuzmä-dzägat* in a story of the Terk-Tork. Within their region they have the usual houses, towers with courtyard and cultivated fields. The *kesenä* towers occur in other Caucasian languages, and *buru*, *bru*, Iron *byru* 'enclosure' gave the Inguš *buru* and the Avar *burav* as the name of Dzäuägi γäu (Vladikavkaz, Ordjonikidze); it recalls the Khotan Saka *prūva-* 'fortress', Kroraina *pirova*.

Five public halls of the Nartä are listed: Ancient Hall, Great Hall of the Alägatä, Oath-taking Hall of the Borätä, the Communal Hall and the Assembly Hall.

Two displays of riches appear. The *Dzyly mälikk* 'the king of Dzyl' at sacrifices and funeral feasts is seated on a chair of honour with the skin of a white bear beneath his feet, one young Nartä behind him and two at his side keeping off the flies. The rich Marɣuz has vast fields and lavish establishments.

IV

The World of the Nartä

The Nartä are greatly occupied with the world around them, which they reduced to an intelligible whole. The tales assume this background.

1.   Magic plays a large part in the tales. The general term was *kälän*, derivative of the base *kar-*. Äfsati, patron of the wild animals, gave a magic flute to his friend Acä of the Acätä family who in turn gave it to his son Acämäz. Cerek has a magic breastplate, Bidas a magic helmet. Xämic has a magic tooth irresistible to women. The Borätä have a magic ass which springs upon a woman whom a hero has cursed.

The most dangerous magic is in the wheel called Digoron *iuojnoni, uojnoni, ojnoni calx* and *Marsug*, Iron *Marsäg, Malsäg, Barsäg, Balcäg*. The full phrase is *Barsädžy calx* meaning either 'wheel of Barsäg' or the 'wheel which is Barsäg'. Two glosses are offered: 'animate wheel' and a 'powerful man'. He is called the chief Barsäg. The insulted daughter of the (lady) Sun persuades the wheel to attack Soslan.

The other Caucasian languages render this name by Qabard *žan-šerx*, Čerkes *džan-čarɔx*, Šapsug *ccijān-kušārx* (*ku* 'cart') where the first component means 'sharp'. This is like a gloss to Digoron *iuojnon* indicating the older form *vi-vāyana-* with adjectival *-on* from *vai-* 'to cut'. The name *barsäg* is then likely to have been *baršaka-* 'cutting, sharp'. The replacement of this epithet by Digoron *uäl-arvon Marsug* 'the celestial Marsug' and by a Byzantine-induced *fid iuane*, Iron *fyd juane* 'father John' is the same treatment of an unknown early word which was noticed with *sopia* above. One will think of the Turkish *Su-day* 'water mountain' for the old city name *Sogdaia*.

The most important magical possession of the Nartä however is the Bowl which reveals the hero. This cup or bowl was called *iron amongä nuazän* 'the Aryāna- cup of demonstration' in a tale of how Säua took the cup from the Terk and Turk, and gave it to the Nartä. Thereafter it was called *Narty amongä nuazän*. The glossator called the cup *qalac* 'large cup' and *dessag kʾos* 'marvellous vessel', where the *kʾos* is in Khotan Saka *kūsa-*.

The bowl is called in Digoron *ŭacamongä, ŭaci amongä* and *ŭaciamongä*, Iron *ŭacamongä* and *acamongä*. Its peculiar property was that a man spoke truth about his many feats and the liquor rose untouched to the speaker's mouth, but otherwise remained unmoved or rose partially. Batraz's feats convinced the Bowl. The Bowl was called also *nart-amongä* and *narti ŭaciamongä*.

The contents were beer (*bägäni*). The Čerkes tales however used their word *sane* of the liquor in the Bowl, which is glossed by both 'mead' and 'wine'.

The meaning of the epithet *nart-amongä* is clearly 'revealing the hero', and in *ŭacamongä* the same meaning of the verb *amonun* 'to show' indicates the meaning 'revealing the force' of the hero, with *ŭac*, like *ŭacä* 'strong, strength'.

Other ancestral treasures (called by the name *xäznatä* from Arabic *khaznah*) are three pieces of cloth intended as prizes for the young men, the *fäsiväd*. They were all claimed successfully by Xämic for his son Batraz who proved himself the boldest, the most modest at table and the most moral in family life.

With magic the witches also appear, both friendly and hostile. They are called 'sitters in the inner chamber'. A second witch can reverse the magic of the first. The witches possess a magic whip, a stroke of which can transform into animal shape. Other shape-shifting occurs when Sirdon changes into an old man and then into an old woman; Soslan becomes a whirlwind; Xuareldar becomes a bubble in a vessel of beer; Satana becomes a mist.

The magic which occurs in ancient epic of talking animals is found here also in the Nartä tales. Batraz, Soslan, Oräzmäg, Ämzor, Acämäz and Säua all talk to their horses. Soslan dying calls upon birds and beasts, and knows the language of them all.

Lots are used by the Nartä which they trust, but Sirdon is able to falsify them when the Nartä in bad times seek a leader to take them and their famished herds to an enemy's grounds.

2. The Nartä view of the world influences their tales greatly. They had a threefold division into 'the sky above', the 'earth's face' and the 'part below the earth'. The beings of the sky above are called *Ŭälimontä* and those below the earth *Dälimontä* (*mon* 'dwelling'). These three regions are contiguous. Batraz can move into the sky and dwell with the celestial smith Kurd-alägon. The genii called *izäd*, *idauäg*, and *xucau* can descend to earth, as when they visit the birthplace of Soslan and come to the assistance of Acämäz. Mountain tops are the favoured dwellings of the genii. Äfsati for example dwells on Mount Adaj.

These genii are departmental. *Fälvära* is protector of domestic cattle, *Äfsati* patron of the wild beasts, *Safa* patron of the hearth-chain. Byzantine names, Georgios as *Uas-kergi*, Theodoros as *Totur*, and Elias as *Elia* have been associated with the more archaic *izäd*. The genii in the tales mingle among the Nartä, they share their tables and their food and drink.

3. The religious beliefs of the Nartä are prominent. Just as the monster bird Iranian *paškuč* has through Georgian become the Ossetic *p'ak'undzä*, so the Iranian original of the Digoron *dziuarä*, Iron *dzŭar*, has been influenced by the Georgian *jvar-i*, Čerkes *dzuör*, Chechen *ẓara*. The Georgian *jvar-* resembles Georgian *gvar-* 'family' with *gvarian-* 'noble', from Iranian *gōhr*, so that behind Georgian *jvar-* we may see Iranian **javaθra-* with the meaning of Ossetic Digoron *dziuarä* 'thick, firm, broad' in the compounds *dziuar-väsqä* 'broad-

shoulder' and *dziuar-sar lädzäg* 'broad-headed staff' (base *gau-* 'to increase in size'). The word is used for the Greek σταυρός 'thick thing, trunk' used for the Christian cross. The Persians in their Christian texts used simply *dār* 'wood'. The concept has been dechristianized in Ossetic.

In the Nartä tales the *dzuar* is a shrine and the supernatural being who inhabits it. It is then little more than a sacred object. When Batraz's wife is denounced by the *dzuar* in a shrine, Batraz undertakes to punish the *dzuar* who flees from his shrine to the supernatural beings called *Ūacillatä*, thence to the *Safatä*, until the *Tutyrtä* effect a reconciliation. There are references to the *xucauy dzuar* 'the Autocrat's holy being', the *Narty styr dzuar* 'the Nartä's great holy being', and it occurs in the plural *dzuärttä*.

The heroic world cannot exist without its smith. In Ossetic the name of the smith (*kurd*) is handed down in a variety of forms. The basic form will be *Kurd-alägon*, but there are also *Kurd-aläg*, *Kurd-aläurgon*, *Kurd-alauärgon*, Turkish *Alaugan*. The smith is the worker with fire, hence in the Great House system the epithet is likely to suit. Evidently a word *āla-* or *āra-* from older *āθra-* 'fire' suits as part of his name. Then *aläg* is here from **āθraka-*, and *alägon* is from **āθrakāna-*. The *-urgon* may contain a word for working. The personal name of *Aläg* of the *Alägatä* family and Old Indian *ulkā* 'torch' hardly belong here.

The genii receive the epithet *ŭac*, with variants *ŭas*, *ŭaš*, Čerkes loan-word *aussi*; Inguš has a forgotten god *vac*. The non-religious meaning 'strong' is primary. The Digoron *uacä* occurs in reference to a powerful light. As a personal name *Uacä* alternates with *acä* in the name *Acätä* 'the strong family'. Infected by the Byzantine word *hagios*, the word *ŭacä* may have been modified in sense. Note the doubling of the epithet in *Ūacä Ūas-kergi* 'the strong genius Georgios'.

A group of genii who live in the waters is called Digoron *Donbettär*, *Donbettir*, Iron *Donbettyr*. The first component is plain *don* 'water'. The second component originally will have been Iranian, later forgotten. If it is from older **badra-* as in Avestan *hubaδra-* 'lucky' the *bettär* are the lucky ones, that is the rich ones or the lords of the waters. They are kinsmen of Satana and hence belong to the older stratum. The Byzantine connexion with Georgian P'et're, Greek Πέτρος cannot be original.

The highest being in the Nartä religion is called Digoron *xucau*, Iron *xŭcau* from an older Saka **hvaθyāva-* modified from **hvatāvya-* by shifted umlaut, which in turn gave Sogd. *xwt'w* **xvatāv*, Zor. Pahl. *xvatāv*, equivalent to Greek αὐτοκράτωρ. It gave the Persian *xudā* used in Muslim times to render *Allāh*.

The Nartä lord is called *xucauti xucau* 'autocrat of autocrats', a kind of superlative. He is the 'autocrat of the blue sky'. The Nartä call upon him and the *xucau* fulfils all their prayers. At Batraz's burial the *xucau* comes and sheds three tears, which become three famous shrines.

The technical word for offering is Digoron *kovun*, *kuvd*, *kuftitä*, Iron *kuvyn*, *kŭvd*, with the victim called *kosart*, Iron *kusart* (*kauš-* 'to slaughter'). For sacrifice there are also the two words Digoron *fäqqau* and *nivond*. Supplication is made on the *kuvän k'upp* 'the hill of offering'.

The oath is an important sanction, called in Digoron *ard*, *ŭasxä* and *somi*.

The word *farnä*, *farn*, Iron *farn*, adjective *färnug*, Iron *färnyg*, expresses all welfare and prosperity. A hero prays to *Farnä* for a good Nartä wife. Ŭärxäg hopes to secure *farn* for his sons by performing a *kŭvd* offering; they are *farny gŭrdtä* 'born out of the *farn*'. Digoron has also two other words for 'fortune' *fes* and *amond*.

Blessing and cursing have their place in the Nartä tales. The horse is devoted to his dead owner by a ceremony *bäx-fäldist* for which ritual texts are preserved. The same *fäldesun* is used of devoting a person to an evil fate. Thus Sirdon is devoted to be in the Underworld the servant of Soslan by the youths of the Borätä family. Similarly Soslan's sister's son devoted Barsäg to be the body-servant of Soslan in the Underworld, a reflection of a custom attested in Ossetia as when Mitdziev was sentenced in this life to attendance upon Kelemet of the Tugan family.

4.   Death, suicide and burial form part of the tales. Death is called a law (*fätk*). There is a macabre scene at the death of Soslan slain by the Barsäg wheel. Batraz refused to enter the tomb till the *xucau* attended the burial. The world of the dead is a *zindonä* 'guard-house, prison' (**zaina-dāna-*, as in Persian *zēn-dān*, with *zēn* 'watching', not *zēn* 'weapon' or *zīn* 'life') ruled by Barastur with a porter Aminon. The name Digoron *Barastur*, *Barastär*, *Barasdur*, *Baruastur*, *Baruastär*, Iron *Barastyr* will express his function as lord of the world of the dead. This was *var-* in the Avestan in a phrase *aṃrāi var*, in Turfan Parthian *'hrywr* **ahrē-var*, and Zor. Pahl. *anrāk var*. Ossetic *bara-* may stand for this *var-* and the second component *stur* will be 'the strong one, master' (comparable to the second component *stura-* in proper names in the *Avesta*). The second component *-stur*, *-stär* has been taken into Chechen and Inguš as *ešter*, *eštur*, *eštr* and *eter* 'lord of the dead'. The fuller phrase is Inguš *dela-eštr* 'the god Eštr'.

Suicide is several times reported. Sozyryko was saved by Čiläxsärdton, Äxsärtäg destroys himself. Batyradz in one story falls on his own sword. Beduγa, the first wife of Soslan, slays herself with her scissors, but is resuscitated by Soslan. Elda the younger wife of Oräzmäg dies through drinking an overdose of a sour drink.

Burial was in an *ingän*, an archaic word which is *hankana-* in the *Avesta*. The *zäbpadz* 'earth dwelling' is surmounted by a monument (*cirt*, Iron *cyrt*, Inguš *čurt*). In the story of Uas-tyrdži burying the two brothers Äxsar and Äxsärtäg, the *cyrt* was built of lime and stone with a handsome tower (*galuan*) all around. Sirdon prophesied that they would bury him in the Assembly place (*nyxas*). In the Underworld tales the hero is conceived as alive in his tomb. Thus Soslan destroyed Sirdon from his tomb. Soslan's avenger Eräxcau calls to

Soslan in his tomb that he has slain the Balsäg wheel. Barastur's consent is necessary to leave the Underworld, and return before midnight is compulsory, a common folklore feature.

5.   Customs of social intercourse include the courteous greetings according to an *äydau* 'practice' which is not to be infringed. The vendetta is a powerful sanction. It is called simply blood (*tog*) and the avenger is 'the man of blood' (*toggin*). The son of Totraz feels compelled to avenge his father on Soslan. The vendetta of Oräzmäg and K'andz is adjusted by the marriage of Oräzmäg's daughter to Säuuaj son of K'andz.

Punishments include the threat of enslavement. The guilty wives of Xämic who caused the death of his third wife are bound to the tails of wild horses and broken up, then are burned.

On the other hand the infringements of ethics in Soslan's Underworld visions are trivial village faults.

Raiding and hunting form a large part of the life of the Nartä heroes, the normal life of epic heroes. The expedition could last several years. These expeditions start at the Assembly ground of the Nartä. The younger men serve the elder as their attendants. The unnamed son of Oräzmäg challenges Oräzmäg to an expedition which leads to a great cattle raid.

6.   The world had had earlier inhabitants than the Nartä, who form the fifth generation. They conceived a series of 'earth-beings' listed as creations of the *xucau*. A dwarf of the Kämbädatä family instructed Xämic in the knowledge of earlier generations. He knew five stages, the *gumiritä*, the *ŭadmiritä*, the *eliatä* (replaced in a Glossary by *ŭäjyg*), the *kämbädatä* and the fifth the *Nartä* men. All these four names are likely to have Saka origins but with later contamination. The first name is Digoron *gumeri*, *gumeritä*, *gumiritä*, *gämeri*, *gumerä*, *gumerag läg*, Iron *gŭmir*, *gŭmiry*, *gumirytä*, to which Georgian *gmir-i* 'hero' is related. The word *gumiry* is glossed by *tyx-gänäg* 'acting with force'. Elsewhere it will be proposed that the Saka base is **vi-mīra-* 'huge' rather than a Biblical connexion with Armenian *gamir-kʿ* 'Cappadocians' and related names.

The second name Digoron *ŭadmeritä*, Iron *ŭadmiritä* is likely to have a first component *vāta-* 'strong'. The third name *eliatä* will originally have meant 'lord' with the Chechen loan-word *ela*, *eli* Batsbi *ala*, *al*, Inguš *äla* 'prince'. This is the *ali* in the name *Bor-xuar-ali*, not here affected by the Byzantine *Elias*, Digoron *Uacella*, Iron *Uacilla*.

The fourth name *Kämbädatä* and *Kambadatä* is the dwarf family evidently expressing the small size by the word *kamba-* 'little'.

The Digoron word *ŭäjug*, *uajgutä*, Iron *ŭäjig*, *ŭäjyg*, *ŭäjgŭtä* refers to the giants, deadly enemies of the Nartä. Horror stories depict them eating Nartä captives. They are so huge that the Nartä take refuge in a giant's skull. Oräzmäg escapes from a giant's cave in a sheep's skin Polyphemos-style. The son of a giant, Aläf, joins in a Nartä dance and is mutilated by Batraz. The giants live in the land beyond the mountains, the *fäs-xonx*. To reach them it is necessary to pass the clashing mountains, a folklore touch. The giants have captive Nartä as herdsmen and captive women who assist the hero. The hugeness, violence and savagery of the *ŭäjug* is the chief characteristic. One giant is called *Tuxi furt* 'son of force'. The name is therefore clearly another derivative of the base which gave Avestan *vīra-* in *hvīra-*, Old Indian *vayas-*, Latin *uīrēs* 'force'. The phrase Iron *ŭäjgŭtä ämä ŭängŭtä* combines the 'violent and the young' (*ŭängŭtä* from older *yuvan-*) like the men in Virgil, *Aeneid* 6.771 *qui iuuenes quantas ostentant aspice uires*. The Tokhara A used *wir*, plural *wire*, for 'youthful'. Comparisons with Armenian *Hayk, Hayastan*, older Iranian *vayu-* 'wind', and Sogd. *w'ywk* 'hunter' (for which the giants are not known) are out of place.

7. The career of the Nartä Soslan has been selected here to illustrate the Nartä hero. Space does not allow a life of more than one. Soslan is one of the most active and most abundantly described.

Soslan's birth is of folklore, though he is called also Sosäg's son, in Chechen Soska Solsa. His name is shown by the second syllable *-än* to be dialectal epic. In Digoron this name is often replaced by *Sozuruqo, Sozruqo*, Iron *Sozyryko* (with probably Čerkes *-qo* 'son'). Satana causes excitement to a shepherd or a horse-herd, whereby Soslan is born out of a stone. He becomes Satana's 'son whom I have not born', nor is he a son of Oräzmäg, but in one variant tale Oräzmäg is the father. Here Oräzmäg visits a cave and is bewitched by a malevolent woman dwelling in the cave. Here too Soslan is born out of a rock.

The genii come to the birth of Soslan to bestow gifts. Soon grown up he seeks adventures to test his powers. He meets the *k'obor läg* 'strong man' of Gŭm, they fight, and at the end enter into a compact of sworn brotherhood. Soslan has also another intimate friend Saulägi furt Märäzduxt.

Soslan shows his violence and force by compelling his enemies to yield up their beards to make him a fur coat, sewn for him by the women of his foes. He defeats the giant Mukara by cunning and strength. By causing the death of Sirdon's son he incurs Sirdon's undying enmity. Beduxa, his first wife, after death interprets the Underworld visions to Soslan when he descends to seek the plant *Aza*. By trickery, advised by Satana, whereby he covered his armour with bells and terrified Totraz's horse, he shot Totraz from behind. For a time Totraz was suspected of cowardice, but was cleared and honourably buried. Satana, when Soslan is absent, is attacked by foes and thrown into the Lake of the Underworld Prison. Drawn back by a message, Soslan follows her and delivers her from the Prison. In one tale Satana is to remain for ever in the Prison as punishment for her aid to Soslan in all his evil deeds. For his second wife he wedded Agunda the Beautiful. His death was brought about by the rejected daughter of the (lady) Sun through the Barsäg wheel. But Soslan's death is avenged by his sister's son Eräxcau who captured the wheel. Meantime Totradzi furt Alibeg awaits Soslan in the Underworld to slay him to avenge his father.

Soslan the great Nartä is therefore an ambivalent hero. He has many epithets. He is virile-minded (*närämon*), famous, rover, the Nartä's maintenance and support, most distinguished, heroic, light and bold man, mountain ruffian (in the opinion of Akula the Beautiful), intelligent, well-born (*xuärz-igurd*). His wonderful feats are mentioned. He is skilled in playing the *fändyr* fiddle. The rainbow, a mythic or folklore touch, is called Soslan's bow. He is a friend (*limän*) and sworn brother to the Strong man of Gŭm. In appearance he is broad-shouldered with a black mark between his shoulders, large-necked, fiery-eyed. But he has also defects, he has crooked knees, bent legs, eyes like a sieve, two pupils to the eye and a beard like the quill of a porcupine (these last features are the witness of Totraz's hostile mother). His enemies styled him forsworn and untrustworthy.

8. The whole life of a village community can be deduced from the tales. Here only a few details can find place. In village fashion the hero and heroine are seen at humble tasks. Üärxäg waters his horse, is assaulted by the sons of Soppar, his son Subälci is slain, but revivified. Satana washes clothes, is seen by the herdsman and Soslan is born from the stone. Axsä-budä's lady wife sits carding wool and spinning. The despondent Oräzmäg falls upon his chair and smashes it. Aläg has one cow. Oräzmäg and Satana have storehouses sufficient to save the starving Nartä. The old men at the Assembly place make their decisions which are called *tärxon* given at the *tärxondonä* 'place of the decision', interesting as the derivative of *tark-*, whence came also the title adopted by the Turks as *tarxan*, and known also as a royal title and name in Sogdian *tarxōn*. The Turkish title was written *ttarkana* in Khotan.

9. The feelings of the Nartä heroes are abundantly shown in the tales. It will suffice to notice their fear of ridicule which is a powerful check upon the hero. Amorous seduction is also frequently introduced. Grief at the death of a relative is made vivid in the laments. Dzerassä at the loss of her husband Äxsärtäg pulls out her hair, tears her cheeks and utters a *qaräg* 'lament' which the mountains echo. The mental qualities are constantly brought forward.

10. The dress and its materials, wool, silk, felt, and leather, are noted. The elegance of the sons of Boräfärnyg is shown by their Khorasan hats of lamb-skin, shirts of wool, leggings and boots of goat-skin. But as in all epic sources the hero's armour, both offensive and defensive, takes a large place. The various metals are worked, gold, silver, iron, steel, copper, lead, *äryau* (possibly tin) and, with these, crystal and ivory.

11. Geography has evident interest for the narrators. Many actual places are named, but there is also a list of archaic geographical names of which the precise meaning has been lost. These old names are important as indicating a possible date for the formation of the Nartä epic and so claim elucidation here.

Iron *Agŭr* has variants in Digoron *Argan-Aurgen, Agez-biaurgen, Auolɣan äma Beuolɣan, Ajgez äma Aguzni* (gen. sing.). This name may be the *Ogur*, the tribal group whence part of the Hungarians came. The Armenian historian Movsēs Dasxuranc'i mentioned the *Houn Honagour*, which is elsewhere *Honogur*. If the Digoron *Aguzni* (gen. sing. of *Aguznä* or *Aguzn*) is old it would be the *Oɣuz* Turks.

Four names are associated with artefacts. The first is *xaxiag xax idonä*, Iron *xax xärx idon*, with a variant *xäx* for *xax*. That is the 'bridle of the *Xax* (*Xärx, Xäx*) land'. In the Geography ascribed to Movsēs Xorenac'i two names are handed down in *Garš-k' K'out'-k'*, interpreted as **karš-* and **gout'-*. The first is likely to stand for the name found in Byzantine Κασαχία, replacing older Κερκέται, in Persian *Kašak*, Old Russian *Kasogi*, Ossetic *Käsäg*, adjective *käsgon*, Swanetian *mə-kšag*, 'the *Čerkes*' or 'Circassians'. The second name is then one of the many forms of the name of the Goths, in the Parthian text of the inscription of Shāhpur I, line 3 *gwt*, in the Greek text Γουθθων. The Goths were in the Crimea till many centuries later when the last of the Gothic nobles entered the Russian nobility.

The second name is in the phrase *babiag avd äftaugi* 'the seven saddle-cloths of Bāb'. Here may be the adjective to the Arabic seventh-century *al-Bāb*, *Bāb al-abwāb, al-Bāb wa 'l-abwāb*, that is Darband (not *Bābilī* 'Babylon').

The third name is in the phrase *angusag ävdust sarɣ* 'the ornamented saddle of Angus-'. This may be taken as a form of *Angust'-i*, modern *Onguštie*, later *Inguš*, who are called by the Georgians *ɣliɣwi*, by the Ossetes *qulɣa*, by the Avars *ɣalɣaj* living to the east of Dzäuägi ɣäu.

The fourth name is in the phrase *andiag nimät* 'the felt cloth of Andi', in which can be seen the present *Andi*, Avar *'andi-* of the Andi Qoi-su, but if old could refer to the Ἄνται.

A name *xati*, adjective *xatiag*, adverb *xatiagau* 'in Xatiag language' is a folklore term used of a language which the young Nartä do not know and which is known to only a few of the older Nartä. It occurs as a magical language, as when *xatiag ävzagäj* is glossed by *kalmy ävzagäj* 'in serpent's language'. The noun occurs in the phrase *xati niči zyhta* 'no one (of the young men) knew Xati', when they heard a talk between Oräzmäg and Sozyrqo *xatiagau* 'in Xatiag language'.

In the sixth century the *fortissima gens* (according to Jordanes) in the steppe land of Skuthia on the Pontic Sea was called by the Byzantine historian Ἀκάτιροι. These *Akatiroi* were later confused with the *Khazar* (*xazar, xazir*) of the north-eastern shore of the Pontic Sea as far as the Kuban region.

If the Zoroastrian *htwl* of the *Bahman Yašt* is read *Hatur* or *Xatur*, it has suffered the same confusion, since it is glossed by Pazand *Azar* and by Parsi
Persian *Xāsār*. The Ravenna geographer has also identified *Agaziri* with the
Khazar. A second case of *htwl* in the phrase *W htwl kwstk'n* *ut Xatur kōstakān
is uncertain in meaning. An Iranian *hatura-* or *xatura-* would mean 'nomad' if
connected with Ossetic Saka *xätun* 'to roam, range'; the Nartä are called *xätäg
läg* 'nomad men'. To compare *Akatiroi* would show the familiar prefix *a-* in
ethnic names (as *Mardi*, *Amardi* and the rest). In Ossetic *xati*, *xatiag* the final *-r*
would then have been dropped at an earlier stage, as a final *-š* is dropped in
Ossetic *uari* 'falcon'. Neither the *Ḥatti* of Anatolia in the second millennium
before our era nor the *Xatāy* of the Liao dynasty (from A.D. 907), the *Kitan*, are
here in question.

The name *sxuali* occurs in a phrase *sxualijy mäligk* 'king of *Sxuali*'. The Nartä
propose to drive their cattle in time of drought to the lands of this *malik*,
although they fear his hostility. A comparison of Digoron, Iron *uari* 'falcon',
Digoron *uare-cavd*, Iron *uari-cavd* 'struck by the falcon' with the Zor. Pahl.
variš, Komi (Ziryen) *variš* establishes that Ossetic has dropped a final *-š*. This
has occurred also in *sxuali*, in which one will see the equivalent of *xvalis-* in the
Russian name of the Caspian Sea *xvalisĭskoe more* (*xvalijskoe*, *xvalmskoe*). The
Byzantine name was Χοαλῖται, Χολιᾶται, Χωλιᾶται. The Armenian loan-word
xołozmik is nearer to the Old Persian *huvārazmiya*, Persian *xvārazm*, older Greek
Χοράσμιοι. If *sxuali* is thus 'Chorasmian', the Nartä were ranging north of the
Caspian Sea.

Two names wrongly assumed to be geographical are *zaliag*, *zariag* and
Digoron *zauti*, Iron *zalty*. In these the *zar-*, *zal-* should be traced to **jaθra-*
'poisonous' and *zar-* 'age-old' used respectively of the snake and the snows.

The whole of nature surrounding the Nartä, the animals, birds, beasts and
fish, and the plants, is in the background of the tales. Of the animals the horse
plays a great part. It is not originally an animal of the mountains; just as the
'cart' *uärdun*, Iron *uärdon*, as loan-word in Abkhaz *a-wardən*, and Chechen *warda*,
Inguš *wordä*, with Sogdian *wrtn*, Persian *gardūn*, belongs to the plains.

In colour the horses are grey, white, and black, and the Turkish *qulon* in
Digoron, Iron *qulon* 'of varied colour' occurs as gloss to the Iranian *ärfän*
(Armenian loan-word *erpʿn*). Breeds of horses are cited, one fine breed is called
Digoron *äfsorq*, *äfsory*, Iron *äfsury*, *ävsury* (with abnormal dialect forms), and a
second breed is *saulox*. The untamed horse is *emilläg*, Iron *jemylyk* derived like
the Armenian loan-word *amehi* 'wild' from Iranian **a-miθryaka-*.

The favourite horses of the Nartä have names. Oräzmäg's horse is called
Ärfän and *Mätran*. But the name *Ärfän* is also the name of the horses of Sozuruqo,
Soslan, and Xämic. Xämic has also a horse called *Durdura*. In the Turkish tale
Alaugan's horse is called *Gemuda* given to Šauej, in Qabard Šauej's horse is
called *Džamidež*. Another horse of Oräzmäg is called *Čerčena*. The genius

Ŭas-tyrdži rides the horse *Dzindzalasa*. There is a Qabard horse called *tx°o-ž'ije* (*tx°o* 'bay colour').

The common word for horse in Ossetic is *bäx* in which is preserved a derivative of the base *vak-* 'to move swiftly' in the form **vaxa-* 'swift', as *täx* 'stream' from *tak-* 'to flow'. It may be connected with Khotan Saka *baji* meaning probably 'horse' from **vači-* 'swift'. If the Chechen *beq'a*, plural *boq'ij* 'foal' is connected, it will derive from Iranian. The racehorse is *doγon*, Iron *duγon* 'ridden in the *doγ*', Iron *duγ* '(funeral) races'.

The birds enter at times into the tales in folklore fashion. Satana and Soslan speak to the birds.

The one plant of importance in the tales is the *Aza* for which Soslan visits the Underworld on a mission from the Seven Giants. It has the power of resuscitation. It is expected to grow in the Giants' fortress. The name *aza-bälasä* 'the Aza tree' has probably a Saka name, possibly the adjectival *-a* suffix to the verb *azun* 'to care for, treat'. Persian has an *āzā* 'mastic', perhaps in some uncertain way to be connected here.

V

The aesthetic quality of the Nartä texts can only be rightly judged by the speakers of Ossetic. I have however had two emphatic expressions of critical value. My Digoron informant Bajtuγanti Barasbi and also Professor Vaso Abaev both approved highly of the narratives in *Pamyatniki osetinskogo tvorchestva*, II (Digoron). Professor Abaev wrote highly also of the Iron reciter Ilik'o. B. Barasbi found the texts in *Iron adämon sfäldystad*, v (1941), in poor style.

The modernized *Narty Kaddžytä* (1946) in prose, and *Narty Kaddžytä* (1949) in verse, are edited texts based upon earlier records from the narrators themselves. They give a cyclic story through the generations, contradictions are absent, and variants passed over.

The direct records from narrators are in both prose and verse. In length they differ greatly, some occupy several printed pages, others fill only a page or a little more. The song of Sozyryqo of the Borätä family has one page of introduction, then continues in six pages of verse.

The long tale *Acämäz ämä Agŭndä-räsuγd* 'Acämäz and Agundä the Beautiful' contains two songs. This is the song to the House:

O Good House, the House with eight angles and four nooks; such it is, securely based, the beams fetched from the Rich Valley, the rafters from the Valley of Fortune, its hearth-chain sent from heaven. The chief is Oräzmäg of the Nartä and the House Lady is Satana. The attendant is truly Soslan, the younger sons are the Nartä's later generation. Ah, my wish would be they should live long, may they have (strong) paws like the bears, may they have (strong) horns like the stag of the Black Wood, may they have young like the birds; and merrily may they live, these our beloved younger sons!

The following prose tale of Soslan from *Pamyatniki osetinskogo tvorchestva*, II, 16–18, will suffice to indicate the style:

Soslan and Alibeg son of Totradz.

Soslan was getting booty in cattle from the Upper Road and lucky herds on the Lower Road. Once Soslan went hunting, he ranged and nowhere found anything. One day where he was, he ascended the Five Peaks mountain and thence looked out to the plain of Qum. He was looking and there appeared a black spot, behind it goes, as it were, a furrow of a plough making the black mark. Soslan looked at it long, saying 'What can it be?' Then he started towards it and came up with it, and the man was still travelling asleep upon his horse's back, and his lance drags in the ground, digging in it to the extent of a plough's furrow.

Soslan set upon him, saying 'The *xucau* (autocrat) has brought me booty in cattle'. He drew his *cerq*-sword, he struck him with all his force, and then fell backwards. Once more Soslan set upon him and he raised his bow to his forehead, loosed the arrow upon him, and he made one small wound on his forehead. The sleeping man, half-awake, rubbed himself, saying 'These midges will not let me sleep', and opened his eyes.

Soslan, on his part, was no longer bold, he was afraid. The man pulled up his horse and attacked Soslan's horse against its breast. Soslan fell backwards from his horse and drew back the length of a measure, making a line with his shoulder. After a long time he set himself to rights.

The horseman from his travelling strap loosed his lance, and he struck between Soslan's saddle and his saddle-cloth, and forced him behind the saddle, saying 'See, what kind of a mountain sparrow has the *xucau* given me?' Soslan drew out his snake's tongue, began to beseech him, and he sent him to the ground. They began to question each other, and began to know each other. To him Alibeg son of Totradz said 'So you are he whom I have long sought before? If you are Soslan, then you killed my six brothers and now there is no way but to kill you'.

Soslan began to beg 'Let me go home, there are still some affairs of mine, and those I will settle. I will intrust the women to someone. I will give the Nartä oath that this day next week I will come to you at the mound of Xäran below Ŭarpp'.

People of old were wont to be true to their word, and Alibeg son of Totradz trusted him, and he let him go and thereupon each went his way to his home. Soslan with shoulders high and head bent went in to the Lady of the House and told her that he had given the oath to Alibeg.

The Lady said to him, 'If it please the *xucau*, then he will do nothing to you. Go and get me enough wolf-skins to make a coat. Then what pleases the *xucau*, that will happen'. Soslan went out to the thorny brakes on the Terek river and there he killed many wolves; he brought them to the Lady. She made from them a coat by the day of the following week.

When the day of their meeting arrived, the Lady fastened upon his horse's neck a hundred large and a hundred small bells, put the wolf-skin on his shoulder and instructed him 'Go, be first at the Xäran mound and leave your horse, but listen for the coming of Alibeg. I will change myself into a cloudy mass and will hide you. When Alibeg comes, he will shout to you "Soslan, where are you?" Three times say nothing to him. When he turns towards home, then get upon your horse, show your courage, and yourself, and do not spare'. Soslan hid as the Lady instructed him.

At that time Alibeg son of Totradz arrived and shouted 'Soslan, where are you? Fail not your promise'. When he answered nothing to him, he struck his horse. 'So you have broken your oath', he said. He turned his face towards home.

Soslan threw himself on his horse and said to him 'See, here I am. Break not your oath. Wait for me'. The smell of the wolf-skin reached the nose of Alibeg's horse, and he took hold of the reins (he fled). Moreover the hundreds of bells of every sound poured out their noise. The horse turned from side to side, it would come no nearer, and would not be stopped. Alibeg son of Totradz first pulled the bridle to the ears, and he tore off the mane, then when he did not stop, he broke his neck and the horse died under him.

Then Soslan shot him full of arrows in his back, and he died. He heaped the booty on his horse and so he came to the Great Road. There a man with twelve mules was bringing fuel to the son of Totradz. When Soslan knew that he was servant of Alibeg, he said to him 'Go to the Urunduq Lady and say to her "Your reward for good news is for me: your son has slain Soslan. Make ready to wear mourning at the funeral ceremony". These beasts leave with me'.

The man left the mules with Soslan, he began to run, he came to the Urunduq Lady and repeated his message. The Urunduq Lady asked him, 'Where are your beasts?'. (He replied) 'The horse of the man who was coming to you to get the reward for good news was worn out, and he drives them quietly here'. 'Like what was the man?' the Urunduq Lady asked him again. He said to her 'Shoulders high, head bent, bulging forehead, with penetrating eye, on one shoulder a written sign, on the other a cross; between the shoulders a dark star, a broad-eyed man, he sat upon a yellow *alasa*-horse'. 'So my fire has become cold. It is surely Soslan himself and again my only young son he has surely slain', she said, and uttered a lamentation. The man was no longer bold, and he turned back, on his own track he returned. He ran to the road, and where is the horseman and where are the mules? Soslan had driven them to his home.

The men wished to pursue him. The Urunduq Lady said to them 'Of my sons not one was wounded in the back, but it was not for this one to die from wounding in front. Look if he is wounded behind. Then he is a coward, and bury him. He is not worthy to be buried in the (Nartä) Cemetery. Otherwise, if he is wounded in front, then he died in the *qazauat* (heroic fight); bring him to his brothers, and bury him among them'. They went in pursuit and saw the body of the horse, then they knew that it was ill luck caused by the horse and they bore him to the (Nartä) Cemetery. They buried him with honour.

The vocabulary of the Nartä tales is archaic, requiring elaborate glossaries. The proper names also are from an older stratum than the modern Digoron and Iron. Etymologizings of the popular type naturally occur.

The themes recurring in the Nartä tales are copiously varied. They cover both village life and the lives of the heroes. Thus the tales allude briefly to fighting, whether in duels or in groups, with giants or in Batraz's case with the genii, sieges, horse and cattle raiding, slaves, expeditions called *balc* of from one to seven years, hunting, horse-racing, captivity and escape, armies, field-camping, death in the waterless desert, underworld visit, underworld captivity and escape, visit to the sky, the visible appearance of the *xucau*, the domestic occasions of the hero's wife-seeking by himself or by proxies, marriage procession, feasting, gifts, friendship, death, suicide, funeral feast, demand of tax or tribute, servants, dependants, the Great House, visit to rich houses, castaway child in a box, Oräzmäg's sea journey in a box, barbarous customs, Xämic's wives tied to the tails of horses, Čeregiqo and Buräfärnyg's daughter, Batraz and Boräfärnug's woman, the indolence of Zeväg, the clashing mountains, a fur-coat of beards, Batraz's fall to earth, games with knuckle-bones, praise of old Nartä customs, metallic limbs and unfinished tempering.

The Nartä tales receive a slight poetic tinge in the many similes. These are usually short, no more than a comparison of two things. Here is a list of selected similes. The shout of a hero, the crack of a whip and the noise of a shot are like thunder. The birth of an exceptional child, the son of Oräzmäg, reaches Safa in the sky like thunder. A sword flashes like the sky's girdle, the rainbow. The blood of an enraged hero is like boiling milk. Poor racehorses are like draught oxen. The sea is like a seething cauldron. Batraz descends from the sky like an eagle of the mountains. The eagle seizes the small bird as Batraz seizes the giant's son. The giant's son shakes like a dry stalk. Arrows speed like flies. Arrows are like falling snow. The points of arrows are like porcupine's quills. The riders cross a river like an arrow. The giant rocks the cave like a cradle. The dwarf hunter turns over the carcase of the stag like a butterfly or a leaf. A horse is turned like a top. Two mountains on the way to the giants' land clash together like two rams. Agunda's stag-drawn silver coach moves like the wind. A roast on the spit cooks with a roar of a river. The falling of rocks is like a dish cooked with flour. Oräzmäg's unnamed son is bright like the *kärkusäg* flower (unknown). A face is all white like a piece of white cloth. A face is bright like the sun and shimmers like the morning mist. Hair is like winter snow, the glance warmed the heart like the autumn sun, and the eyes were like jewels. A beard is like the porcupine's quill. Dust clouds are like the black mist of rain. The steam of hot food is like the grey morning mist. In matters of violence the giant is caught on the sword's point like a top. The giant's head is taken off him like the head of a small bird. An arrow-shot youth rolls like a sheaf. The giant's son perishes like a cup of water. A raging man is like a man pursuing an enemy. The giant's son flees like a wounded deer. The feats of Batraz are like the sun's brilliance. Čeregiqo revenges himself on Boräfärnug's daughter like one winnowing corn. The troops of Agŭr are broken like gravel. In battle a body is pierced like a sieve. The sparks from a horse's hooves are like the shining sky and the clods thrown up are like ravens. A drop of blood is like red silk. A man without a horse is like a wingless bird. In distress the spirit (*uod*) is narrower than a hair. A sword cuts an anvil like curds. The giant's lips are like a scoop. A round saddle is like the carcase of a duck. A horse is clean like an egg-shell. The young men move like geese one behind the other. The woman entered the water like a duck. All these similes are largely close to the earth.

One longer simile occurs. The youthful hero asks how fine he looks on his horse. They reply 'As the early morning sun is beautiful upon the morning dew-drop on the green grass of spring, so are you fine on your horse's neck'; 'as moonlight strikes down upon the mountains, so are you fine upon your horse'; or 'as in the spring's warmth the dew-drop is beautiful upon the grass, so are you fine on your horse's back'. A somewhat shorter simile is 'As the sun's ray is beautiful upon the mountain, so is your armour; as the spring dew-drop is fair on the new grass, so is your sword'.

The negated metaphor has been found four times, as follows. 'It was not a dark mist, it was the dust of horses racing'. It was not the morning star, it was Acämäz the son of Acä'. 'It was not a ball of black mist, it was the grey horse of Alimbeg of the Alägätä family'. 'It was not the black raven, it was clods thrown up by the horse's hooves'.

Formulae and clichés are frequent. The phrase for despondency takes a variety of forms: 'With shoulder high and head bent', in four variants. The file of walkers is footstep upon footstep. A lord is amazed to find trespassers where no bird dare fly nor ant creep. To leave the Underworld the horseshoes are reversed to deceive the other inmates. A child is rejected as a servant by a ruler because the *qumiz*, fermented milk, is still moist upon his lips. Of a journey, its distance is known only to the *xucau*. There are fixed formulae for prayers.

Humour, especially in relation to Sirdon, is savage. Soslan in the Underworld, as being too virile, is thrown into the Underworld lake. At his mother's long deferred funeral feast Sirdon arranges for his tables to be overturned, and so excuses himself to his guests. Batraz falling through seven storeys of a tower into a tub of water is more humorous than mythic.

Folklore elements have been cited variously earlier. They are such cases as Oräzmäg's quarrels with Satana, the dog *selan*, the invention of beer, talking animals, nameless servants, magic, Underworld visions of village-like life, Soslan's birth from a stone, the rainbow as Soslan's bow, the child's swift growth in the cradle, resuscitations, rejuvenations, the invention of the *fändur*, the bird messengers, metallic limbs, Soslan's coat of beards, magic talk in the *xatiag* language, the stag-drawn coach, the name *Ulink'ä* 'cubit-size' for the dwarf and *Tuxi furt* 'son of strength' for a giant.

All these features contrast sharply with the heroic fighting, war, expeditions, funeral games and love-making.

Myth has left a few traces, as in the daughter of the Lady Sun, *Xorčeska*; in Batraz guest of the smith Kurd-alägon in the sky; and his descent; the Chechen

Elta and *Eltayan*. The *xucau* is a celestified autocrat like the Master of the Great House, with the genii as his attendants like an earthly court.

Though rather obscure the geographical archaic names *Agur, Aguznä, Babiag, Xati, Sxuali, Astä* would suit a period between 500 and 700 of our era. Since nomadic customs have remained from the first record almost unchanged they do not suffice to give a date. The Skuthai (Scythians) of Herodotos are similar in their nomadic life, but do not seem to have precise identity with Nartä traditions. The Nartä treasures of three pieces of cloth, and the Ŭacamongä Bowl are peculiarly of the Nartä. The autocrator of the Greeks seems to be rendered in the word *xucau*.

Highly archaic are on the other hand the *ard* 'oath', which is a normal development from a form *ṛtá-* (prominent in early Iranian texts), and the *izäd* 'spirit, genius, angel', which has developed from older *yazata-* 'recipient of worship', equally familiar in the oldest Indian texts. The word *kovun* 'to make offerings' may belong with the rare Old Indian *kubh-*.

The epic quality of the Nartä tales can be best seen in the careers of the heroes and the heroines. It is notable that the heroines stand out with distinctive names, Satana, Dzerassä, Agunda, Akula and Elda, each with a distinct character.

They thus contrast with the many nameless Nartä who move about at the assembly-place the *Nixäs*, and attend the *mijnasä* feasts, before a still dimmer background of servants.

There are two types of Hero. One is the fighting, vehement man, protector of the Nartä people. The other is found in Acämäz who shows incipient artistic traits, as a musician and lover.

The story of the Nartä ends in their destruction. In one tale they are overwhelmed by the *xucau* beneath a mountain.

SHORT BIBLIOGRAPHY OF TEXTS AND STUDIES

Schiefner, A., *Ossetische Sagen und Märchen* (St Petersburg, 1868)

Miller, Vsevolod, *Osetinskie etyudy*, I–III (Moscow, 1881–85)

Miller, Vsevolod and R. von Stackelberg, *Fünf ossetische Erzählungen im digorischen Dialekt* (St Petersburg, 1891)

Miller, Vsevolod, *Digorskie skazaniya* (Moscow, 1891)

Pamyatniki osetinskogo tvorchestva, I (1925); II (1927); III (1928) (Vladikavkaz)

Narty kaddžytä (Cxinval, 1929); (Dzaudžykau, 1946, 1949); 2nd ed. (Ordžonikidze, 1975) (=*NK*)

Abaev, V., *Iz osetinskogo ëposa* (Moscow–Leningrad, 1939)

Xussar Irystony fol'klor (Stalinir, 1940)

Iron adämon sfäldystad, v (Ordžonikidze, 1941) (= *IAS*, 5)

Abaev, V., *Osetinskiy yazyk i fol'klor*, I (Moscow–Leningrad, 1949)

Narty, ëpos osetinskogo naroda (Moscow, 1957) (= *NEON*)

Iron adämy sfäldystad, I–II (Ordžonikidze, 1961) (with large bibliography) (= *IAS*, 1)

Bgazhba, Kh. S., *Abkhazskie skazki* (Sukhumi, 1965)

Salakaya, Sh. Kh., *Abkhazskiy narodnyy geroicheskiy ëpos* (Tbilisi, 1960)

Hübschmann, H., 'Sage und Glaube der Osseten', *Zeitschrift der Deutschen Morgen-ländischen Gesellschaft*, 41 (1887), 539–67 (translation from Miller, *Osetinskie etyudy*)

Alborov, V. A., *Termin 'nart'* (Vladikavkaz, 1930)

Abaev, V., *O sobstvennykh imenakh nartovskogo ëposa* (Moscow, 1934)

Dumézil, G., *Légendes sur les Nartes* (Paris, 1930) (with bibliography)

Bleichsteiner, R., 'Rossweihe und Pferdeopfer im Totenkult der kaukasischen Völker', *Wiener Beiträge zur Kulturgeschichte und Linguistik*, 4 (Salzburg–Leipzig, 1936)

Bailey, H. W., *Journal of the Royal Asiatic Society*, 1953, 109 ff. (a note, now superseded, on the name Nart)

Dumézil, G., *Le livre des héros* (Paris, 1965) (with preface of 1959), translation of *Narty Kaddžytä*, 1946

Dumézil, G., *Mythe et épopée* (Paris, 1968), 441–575

Galaev, B. A., *Osetinskie narodnye pesni* (Moscow, 1964)

Petrosian, A. A. (editor), *Skazaniya o nartakh, ëpos narodov Kavkaza* (Moscow, 1969)

Gadagatl', A. M., *Narty, Adygskiy ëpos* (1969, 1970, Maikop)

Meremkulov, V. and Salakaya, Sh. Kh., *Narty, Abazinskiy narodnyy ëpos* (Cerkessk, 1975)

Salakaya, Sh. Kh., *Abkhazskiy Nartskiy ëpos* (Tbilisi, 1976)

Petrosian, A. A. (editor), *Narty, Adygskiy geroicheskiy ëpos* (Moscow, 1974)

S

MONGOL

The Contemporary Tradition

By C. R. BAWDEN

THE HOMELAND OF THE MONGOL EPIC is co-terminous with the geographical distribution of the main Mongol-speaking peoples. Though the Mongols are, relatively speaking, not a numerous people, they have, in the course of the last several centuries, settled over wide and not necessarily contiguous areas of Eurasia, and are to be found nowadays in three main groups. The one independent Mongolian state today is the Mongolian People's Republic (MPR), more or less identical with what used to be called Outer Mongolia. The MPR lies between the USSR and China, between the longitudes of 85 and 120 degrees east, and is inhabited for the most part by Khalkha Mongols.[1] Oirat, or west Mongol peoples, close linguistically to the Kalmucks, live in the western parts of the MPR and in Sinkiang. The half million or so square miles of the MPR are the home of less than one and a half million people. Contiguous to the MPR on its south-eastern border is the Inner Mongolian Autonomous Region of China, inhabited nowadays mainly by Chinese, but containing a substantial minority of Mongols who differ only to a minor degree in dialects, traditions, and customs from the Khalkha Mongols of the MPR. In the second area, to the north of the MPR, and within the USSR, live the Buriats. Thirdly, but separated from other Mongol groups, the Kalmucks also live in the USSR, and are found mainly in their own ASSR on the lower reaches of the Volga.

The epic, or rather, epics, may be found in each of these three areas. There are certain unifying characteristics. Thus the 'Jangar' epic, long considered to be the property of the Kalmucks, is now known to belong to the repertory of bards in several parts of the MPR, as well as among the Buriats. Rintchen, for example, published in 1965 the text of a 'Jangar' episode found in written form among the Buriats of the Kerülen river. The epic of *Han Harangui* is, so Rintchen reports, especially favoured in Mongolia, and is considered the source of the Mongol epic, and its hero, Khan Kharangui, is known as the Epic Khan. This epic has a considerable written tradition, as well as its oral tradition: manuscripts are to be found mainly among the west Mongol peoples of the MPR, but written versions were also used by the Soyot or Urianghai people of Tuva and the neighbouring Buriats, while a manuscript version was found as far eastwards as Töv aimag (Central province) of the MPR. It will, however, be the purpose of the present chapter to do no more than consider in outline the epic as it survives today in the MPR.

It was the epic as it was discovered to exist among the Kalmucks of the Volga and much later among the west Mongol peoples of the present-day MPR which first attracted the attention of travellers and scholars. Benjamin Bergmann's account of the 'Jangar' songs (*Gesänge*, as he terms them) and the Kalmuck bards (*Dschangartschi*, in his orthography) who performed them, is still of interest today. By contrast, the epic as it exists in the MPR and Inner Mongolia was relatively speaking neglected until the twenties of the present century, when N. N. Poppe collected a number of what he termed *Gesänge und Heldensagen*. These were finally published in 1955. In the introduction to his edition Poppe remarked that the heroic epic as found amongst the Khalkha Mongols was already then in a state of advanced decay. It was impossible, he said, to find among the Khalkhas such long and beautiful tales as amongst the Buriats and Oirats. The Mongolian scholar G. Rinchinsambuu, writing in 1960 and again in 1964, seems to confirm Poppe's viewpoint. He says that the Mongol heroic epic is now fated to be forgotten, and he adduces contemporary cultural and technical change, in particular the spread of school education and of literacy, to account for this. Bards have declined in number, and have forgotten their epics, and the epics themselves are becoming fragmented. In Khalkha, Inner Mongolia and Buriatia, he continues, various epics are still recited in poetic form, but generally speaking they are 'mere narratives' and have lost their 'real nature'. Rinchinsambuu does not consider this a new process. Decline set in in the mid-nineteenth century, but its slow progress has greatly accelerated in recent years.

Indeed, the gloomy forecasts of Poppe and Rinchinsambuu were already anticipated by the Buriat scholar Žamcarano in an essay on the Mongol heroic epic which appeared in 1914. Some of what he said may be quoted, as the best available account of what an epic meant to its singer and its audience:

What is our Buriat *ülger*? The *ülger* narrates in an elegant manner the famous doings of heroes — heroic men, heroic women, and heroic steeds . . . The *ülger* is properly a story about the hero's battles. But its purpose is not just recreation but also the instruction of its listeners. The *ülger* may be recited to gain some benefit, for example to cure the sick, to restore the sight of a blind person, or to promote the success of some enterprise, such as hunting or fishing. It may be lucky to recite the *ülger* on a journey. The *ülger* must be respected. Why? Because the heroes who appear in the *ülger* are not of ordinary flesh and blood but of divine origin. The Buriats say that, according to shamanist ideas, the heroes of an *ülger* are still alive, and that if the *ülger* is recited wrongly or defectively, the bard will offend the heroes. The *ülger* is not to be performed slackly. In olden times the performance of an *ülger* was accompanied by various rites of a pious nature. For example, a dish of milk would be placed on the roof, lamps and incense would be offered, a bowl overturned, or ashes scattered to see if a certain thing should be undertaken or not. Apart from that, *ülger* were not performed by day, but at night . . . That is how it was of old. Nowadays the impetus of the *ülger* is failing, and the old customs will be destroyed.

On the other hand, the contemporary Soviet critic Mikhailov puts forward quite another opinion. He writes: 'But one thing is obvious. The heroic epic lives among the Khalkhas in our day too. New narrators are constantly appearing, new examples of the heroic epic are being written down in the most widely separated corners of Mongolia.' Mikhailov seems in this context to be referring to the use of the traditional themes in modern dress, rather than to the persistence of epic in a more or less archaic form, and to this extent his opinion may well be correct.

Undoubtedly, however, research undertaken in the field in Mongolia in the last two decades has shown that, among the older generation of performers at least, the tradition of epic performance survives, though the type of audience, and the occasion for a performance, and the mood in which the listeners attend to a performance, have all undergone change. The Academy of Sciences of the MPR has sponsored a lengthy series of annual programmes of ethnographic collection, and amongst the items of popular literature recorded on tape, and to some extent already published, are epics in sufficient number to demonstrate that the epic tradition flourished in all parts of Mongolia. The best summary of the work which has been done in Mongolia, together with the most detailed survey of the epic, is due to W. Heissig. Comparatively little has yet appeared in English.

The existence of the Mongol epic as a literary genre is generally recognized today, though it would seem that some of the scholarly terminology is relatively modern and has been borrowed from Russian literary criticism. The usual word used for the epic is *tuul'*, and there is also the expression *baatarlag tuul'*, for 'heroic epic' which is apparently a translation of the Russian *geroicheskii epos*. An alternative word for the epic is *ülger*. Rinchinsambuu defines the terminology as follows:

Tuul' is the word used for the most part in west Mongolia and some other parts of Mongolia for tales, *ülger*, about manly heroes, who fight heroically with ogres or despotic khans, and the artistic exponents of these are called *tuul'ch*. In Khalkha the word *tuul'* is not used so much, and they are called *ülger* (tales), or *urt ülger* (long tales) or *huuch ülger* (tales of olden times), and the men who tell them are called *ülgerch* or *urt ülgerch* and sometimes also *huurch* (fiddlers).

Some verse tales published by Rintchen which are classified both by himself and by Heissig as 'epics' are given, in their written sources, the name of *teüke/tüüh*, a word usually nowadays meaning 'history'. Finally, the word *ülger*, as well as describing a verse epic, may, as will be mentioned below, be the name of a prose tale, and, in the form *bensny ülger*, the first element of which derives from the Chinese *pen-tzu* 本子, is the name of a particular type of long narrative in mixed prose and verse, whose subject matter will have been drawn from a literary source, usually one of the great Chinese romances. The book epic differs from the epic itself in various particulars. As each book epic has its own literary source, it will differ in plot from other book epics, whereas epics tend to have similar plots. The narrative presented in the book epic is usually a complicated one. One modern book epic, based on a stage play, retells the whole interwoven subject matter of that play, albeit in a very altered form. On the other hand, the narrative in an epic is a simple and uncomplicated one. In form the two genres contrast, for whereas an epic may mingle poetry and prose, in the book epic it seems normal to alternate prose with verse, often telling the same episode twice over in different ways. Finally, as Rintchen tells us, the mode of performance is different. The Khalkha epic bard usually recites his poem without instrumental accompaniment, 'with closed eyes, as if observing in the depths of his soul the images called forth by the magic of the verses'. The performers of the book epic, on the other hand, usually accompanied themselves on the four-stringed, bowed *huuchir*. In what follows, the book epic will not be further considered.

Though contemporary scholarship seems to prefer the term *tuul'* or *baatarlag tuul'*, the persistence of a less technical nomenclature may lead to uncertainty in defining what is, and what is not, an epic. On the one hand, one can find verse tales reprinted among tales in prose in modern printed collections of oral folk literature such as that of Nadmid. Some, if not all, of these verse narratives exhibit all the characteristics, formal and thematic, which are normally associated with what is called an epic, but are not necessarily specifically described as epics. In such circumstances, it can be difficult to define the limits of the epic without merely begging the question. On the other hand, there are prose tales which tell what is to all intents and purposes the same story as a verse epic, using the same stylistic devices — standard runs of lines, stock epithets, formulas, eulogy, and hyperbole, and narrating identical incidents. Only the verse-form may be lacking, or it may be present only in a desultory way. It is difficult to give a concrete example without going into a complex process of analysis, but one might mention a tale such as *Heviin sain Buidar* ('Buidar always good') which recounts the familiar wooing expedition to be found in many epics. Again, Nadmid has a long tale entitled *Eriin sain Egeedei mergen* ('Egeedei mergen, the best of men') which gives the immediate impression of being an 'epic' printed as prose, though retaining for the most part its metrical features. Among the episodes related is the traditional sports contest between the hero and a challenger for the hand of the princess. We may note here one remarkable parallel to the verse epic *Eriin sain Han Harangui* ('Khan Kharangui, the best of men') in that in each case the rival suitor is of divine origin. In *Egeedei mergen* he is called Tengeriin Tehshar böh, 'The Teh-yellow wrestler of Heaven', and in *Han Harangui*, Tengeriin hüü Erhem Har, 'Honoured Black, Son of Heaven'. The name Tengeriin Tehshar Böh also occurs in the verse-epic *Öödii mergen haan*. It is hardly possible in a general survey such as the present to point out the many close parallels, thematic and stylistic, between the prose tale and the verse epic, of which this a minor sample.

Egeedei mergen gives the impression of being a verse epic which was developing towards a prose form when recorded. This seems to be a normal process: as will be described later on, it is well known that bards, through age, failing memory, and so on, can find themselves unable to reproduce the whole of a verse epic, and capable of doing no more than retell some of it in a prose form. But there are other possibilities of development. In the epic *Öödii mergen haan*, for example, which because of its particular interest will be analysed more fully later on, we find retold a tale of magic, of which prose versions also exist, which is not the common stuff of the heroic epic, and which has its international versions as well. We must accept the possibility that prose märchen may become versified and so take on the epic form. An example of this process having taken place in recent years is afforded by the modern epic *Altan hundagat hüü* ('The boy with the golden goblet') which was published in 1956 with a note to the effect that it had been put into verse from a folk tale. Another, similar, case is that of the 'epic' *Bayandai haany hüü Bayandondog baatar* ('Bayandondog Baatar, son of Khan Bayandai'). This poem, described as a 'versified tale' (*shüleglesen ülger*) was composed on the basis of folklore themes by the poet M. Chimed (b. 1919) and printed in 1947. It is thus a moot point whether it should be considered an epic at all, since it is clearly a piece of art poetry. But to exclude it on those grounds alone would perhaps be a subjective and arbitrary procedure.

It cannot be stated with any precision when the genre of the Mongol epic first originated, especially as the epic does not treat of easily recognizable historical incidents. The 'Jangar' epic of the Kalmucks was well developed by the time Bergmann, who undertook his travels in 1802–1803, came into contact with it. He records a magic tale according to which, around the year 1771, a Kalmuck commoner died an untimely death, and was compensated for his unmerited shock by receiving from Erlig Khan, the king of the underworld, the gift of song. This cannot be taken literally, but it does serve to show that Bergmann's Kalmuck informants at least thought that the epic was in existence in about 1771. However, there are indications that the epic is of earlier origin. Without necessarily adopting the extreme position of the Kalmuck scholar Erdniev, who would move the date suggested by Kozin, that is, the fourteenth century, back to the second half of the first millennium B.C., one finds less difficulty in accepting Erdniev's other suggestion that what he calls the 'final' form of the 'Jangar' epic may be dated not later than the end of the sixteenth century, that is, to a time when the west Mongols still formed a united people, and the separation of the Kalmucks of the Volga and the Oirats of Kokonor had not yet taken place. However, in view of the very nature of the epic, a form passed on from bard to bard, but recreated by each individual bard, it is hard to imagine any 'final' form at all. Of the Khalkha epic we can say that it looks back to a 'feudal' time, when rival khans, possessed of great wealth in their flocks and herds, were raiding each other's lands and ravishing their peoples. According to the epics themselves, the action is situated in the remotest past, definable only by the most extreme and imaginative figures of speech — when the earth was only just formed, when the world mountain Sumeru was only a hillock, when the Milk Sea was a puddle, when the Dalai Lama was a novice. These images represent, perhaps, a primitive pictorial type of imagination, and they are not exclusive to the epic alone of literary genres, but the fact of their Buddhist terminology argues for placing the origin of at least this component part of a typical Mongol epic at not earlier than the second conversion to Buddhism, which took place in and after the last quarter of the sixteenth century. For one thing, the institution of Dalai Lama was not known until then. Reference to the Manchu emperor, in other versions of the formulaic passage which situates the epic in its time, brings the time of composition of a relevant passage of an epic somewhat further forward, to at least the middle of the seventeenth century.

Other points of detail give rough hints as to the date of origin of particular passages in an epic. The hero may, as does Khan Kharangui, use a telescope:

> When he looked through his slim black telescope,
> Made of eighty eight marrow bones,
> He saw dust the size of a little wasp
> Come up in the direction of the rising sun,
> And then vanish.

It is not certain when the telescope first reached Mongolia. In English the first use of the word is recorded in 1648, while according to the Lives of the Jebtsundamba Khutuktus, the K'ang-hsi emperor used a telescope to watch the Khutuktu leave Peking after his visit there. This seems to have been at the time when the emperor and his guest paid a visit to Wu-t'ai-shan, and such a visit is dated by *Erdeni-yin erike* to the year 1698. Thus reference to a telescope in an epic can hardly have occurred before the mid-seventeenth century.

At a moment of crisis the epic hero may sit down and have a smoke. Tobacco seems to have reached China at the beginning of the seventeenth century, and can hardly have reached the Mongols earlier. Without prejudice to Erdniev's views on the early origin of the epic, it seems that these scattered and uncertain points of historical reference point to redactions datable not earlier than the years of disorder in the sixteenth century preceding the Manchu conquest in the seventeenth, and promote the plausibility of the view that the society portrayed in the epics reflects the internal dissension and disorder of that time.

The landscape of the epic is a recognizable, though idealized, Mongolia, even though only a few real Mongol place names, notably those of the Altai and Khangai mountains, occur. The ogre, the traditional foe of the hero, may live in a fortress of cast iron, surrounded by thorny trees, and with no way in, but the hero himself, as also the princess he goes to woo, lives in what is essentially the felt tent of the Mongol nomad, constructed in the traditional way, though, in accordance with the hyperbolic style of the epic, it is of a magnificence difficult to comprehend and is described, as is the remote past itself, in a series of visual images:

> Now as for the palace
> Of young Baatar Belegt,
> It had a door of yellow gold,
> A living-serpent girth-rope,
> A skirting of black silk,
> Curtains of fine silk,
> And a fine firm base.

The hero's wealth lies in his enormous herds of sheep, horses, camels, and oxen, the usual domestic beasts of the Mongols, numbering sometimes hundreds of millions. He drinks the traditional milk drinks of the Mongols, and smokes tobacco. He recites an occasional Buddhist prayer, makes the burned offering known as the 'Thirteen burned offerings', a Buddhistic ritual, and knows how to ride, shoot with bow and arrow, and wrestle. When he comes to the princess's tent-palace, he finds it guarded, like any Mongol tent, by fierce dogs, which have to be held down by somebody belonging to the household.

Epics of the 'Jangar' type look back, too, to a golden age, when the hero and his princess could be ever young:

> There was the holy prince Jangar,
> Grandson of Tavtai tamba jilen haan,
> Great-grandson of Tavtai tah' budan haan,
> Son of Üizen aldar haan,
> Who was always twenty-five years old,
> And his queen Avai gerel,
> Who was always sixteen years old.[2]

The social order presented, rudimentary as it is, in the Mongol epic, is a monarchic one. The hero is a khan or a khan's son, owning as we have seen, enormous flocks and herds, and master of many subjects and with mighty heroes subordinated to him.[3]

Magic and religion play a part in the Mongol epic. The hero's horse, in particular, is a force to be reckoned with. It is a superequine steed, but also a superhuman adviser. It knows more than the hero, it can speak, and it can foretell the future. Typically it has:

> A swivel in every hair,
> A word in every joint.[4]

The action of the epic takes place, normally, in this world, though in an enhanced version of it, and the hero's realm is often named as a whole continent.
Influences from other worlds are apparent. Thus a rival suitor, who disputes
the princess's hand, may be presented as a denizen of the world above. In *Han
Harangui* he is *Tengeriin Hüü Erhem Har*, 'Honoured Black, Son of Heaven'.
In some epics shamans and shamanesses play a part, assisting on the side of
evil, that is, the side opposed to the hero:

> As he was returning,
> Up came a shamaness,
> Grasping a one-faced drum,
> Over the Pass of Dry Maan't.
> 'You have torn me from
> My five sons', she said,
> 'I shall struggle with you
> Till the Eight Altai Continents are destroyed,
> I shall struggle with you
> Till the Three Sunny Continents are destroyed',
> She said.
> As Hairt Har
> Came up,
> The shamaness
> Became a ground squirrel
> And ran in under him;
> He became a polecat three fathoms long,
> And ran up to her;
> She became a sparrow
> And twittered above him;
> He became a hawk and went to her from behind;
> And he seized her quickly,
> The shamaness mother,
> And put her in a sixty-fathom pit,
> And stopped it with a round stone,
> And sealed it with a flat stone . . .[5]

The appearance of shamans might suggest that the epics in which they play a
part look back to the period of the great missionary campaigns of the lamas
against the shamans, which took place around the turn of the sixteenth century,
or even earlier. But this is not to say that the epics promote Buddhism. There is
just enough use made of Buddhist words and clichés to make it apparent that
the Yellow Faith was familiar to the individual bard, but that is all. The hero is
not assisted by Buddhist deities against the shamans, nor does he fight on behalf
of the Yellow Faith, so that one cannot claim to see in the epic a model of the
victory of one religion over another.

As mentioned above, the Mongol epic is not historical in its content. The Mongols certainly have a heroic past. Their great hero is Genghis Khan, the founder of their nation and until recently an ancestral god with his own shrines, temple guardians, and liturgy. Legends about Genghis are recorded in chronicles and in oral prose literature. Other dramatic moments in the history of the Mongols are remembered in the same way, and in elegiac poetry. But none of this has become the recognizable subject matter of epic. The Mongols seem to have ignored the possibilities of historical events and to have composed their epics around imagined heroes, ogres, princesses, talking horses, external souls, and so on, all existing in a wonderful, idealized, make-believe world, situated in a remote and splendid past. The violent action of the epic is, too, always the prelude to a life of lasting pleasure, characterized by ceaseless eating and drinking.

The epic is not historical, nor is it tragic, and one wonders if it is even heroic, except in a very special sense of the word. Heroism implies effort, but it is axiomatic in the Mongol epic that, whatever happens, the hero possesses enough superhuman strength and skill and other advantages, to make his final victory a foregone conclusion. He never fails: even if he is defeated and killed in an early skirmish, he will certainly be revived, perhaps by the intervention of his wise horse, perhaps by the help of a superhuman girl. Should he succumb to premature defeat, as for example in *Öödii mergen haan*, it may be because he has disregarded the advice given him by his horse, and has fallen into a trap. From this he is rescued by a heavenly girl who is brought down to earth for the purpose by his horse. However, apart from some isolated events such as this one, which admittedly occurs in a märchen-like context rather than a truly heroic context, there never seems to be direct divine intervention in the course of the epic, such as occurs in the Homeric epic. The hero owes his ultimate invincibility to his outrageously comprehensive abilities, and to that extent one has to question the aptness of the term 'heroic', since the forces opposed to the hero are by definition bound to fail.

Speaking in general terms, one may say that the typical Mongol epic is concerned with a contest which takes place between the forces of good, represented by the hero, who is traditionally a khan or a khan's son, and the forces of evil, usually represented by an opposing khan, or an ogre, *mangas*, a creature of repulsive appearance and colour and disgusting habits, and possessing many heads. The ogre also frequently has a number of souls, which reside outside his body, and which have to be identified, located, and killed before the ogre himself can be killed. An epic involves a journey. In an epic of the 'Jangar' cycle this may be a simple adventurous journey to fetch a bride, followed by a great feast. Thus, in *Üizen aldar haany hüü, üeiin jaahan Junraa noyon* ('Ever-young prince Junraa, son of Üizen aldar khan'), the epic begins with a presentation of the hero and his heroes and his four seas. He causes a fine temple to be built. He then sets out to fetch a certain princess, overcomes a number of difficulties on the way with the help of his horse's advice, and returns, to hold a great feast. In *Zöng Belegt Baatar*, the hero is presented in the same way, followed by descriptions of his palace, his queen, his four seas, his four birds, his four precious trees, his flocks, and herds. Next the evil ogre is described, together with his vicious propensities. The ogre decides to make an assault on the hero, motivated by a dream he has had. The ogre is defeated and runs away, and is followed by the hero, who destroys him in a second battle.

In other epics, as for example *Han Harangui*, or *Gants modon honogtoi galzuu ulaan baatar*, 'The mad red hero at home in a single tree', which will be analysed below, the wooing expedition plays a more important part. The hero may set out on his journey because he has dreamed of a bride, and it may be that the princess he has dreamed of is in fact the girl to whom his parents have betrothed him before either was born. He may simply be looking for adventure: in *Han Harangui* his adventures begin when he asks his parents:

> 'Where is there
> A fair princess to take,
> A tough enemy to fight to the death with?

He may even, as in *Gants modon honogtoi*, set out with the intention of ravishing a queen rather than winning a princess.

The success of the wooing expedition, which is in itself a foregone conclusion, is decided by the holding of a sports meeting. The hero changes himself, on the occasion of his challenge, into a drivelling boy, and his magnificent steed into a mangy colt. Or he may even reduce his horse to such a size that he can hide it in his wallet and proceed on foot. He defeats the other suitor at the traditional three Mongolian national games of horse-racing, archery, and wrestling. On his return from the wooing he may leave his bride to follow on, while he goes on ahead to greet his parents. This involves him in a further expedition, for he will find his home devastated, and will discover a letter telling him what has happened and advising him not to pursue the ogre. But he sets out again to defeat the ogre and release the prisoners. On this, as on previous journeys, he may be helped by the persons he meets, often a white-haired old herdsman who, if named, may bear a Turkish-type of name such as Aksakaldai. Or the hero may engage in a duel with another warrior whom he defeats and kills, or who swears blood brotherhood with him. The hero is always victorious in the end. The ogre is killed, perhaps after his souls have been discovered and killed in succession. His body is burned and the ashes are scattered and a great feast concludes the epic.

We may summarize the action of a typical Mongol epic which follows the above pattern. *Gants modon honogtoi galzuu ulaan baatar* was recorded in 1957 by members of a students' group who were collecting folklore in the area of the

Orkhon-Selenge basin. The text was first published in 1958 and has since been reprinted for school reading use:

In ancient times there lived a hero called 'The mad red hero at home in a single tree'. His father was Khan Tungalag ('Clear') and his mother was Queen Tungalag. One day he announces to his mother that he intends to take for himself the wife of Hereestei mergen haan ('Wise Khan with a cross'), who owns velvet boots and a brown speckled horse. His mother tries to discourage him from thinking thoughts which should not be thought, but he replies: 'If a man cannot realize his aims, he will have the signs of a woman. If a horse cannot realize his leap he will have the signs of a mare. I have to go, and now I shall make ready.' His father and mother agree to let him go. The hero saddles his horse with his stiff yellow saddle which seventy men cannot lift and, embraced by his parents and seen off by his people, sets out on his journey. First he climbs to the summit of the juniper-bearing Golden Sumeru mountain, makes an offering of incense and recites all the scriptures he knows. Making his bowl-sized eyes the size of a ladle, he utters his wish that he may remain alive whatever befalls him, and turns his horse towards the blue-looking mountains.

At the frontiers of the realm of Hereestei mergen haan he changes himself into a grey hawk and swoops over the smoke-hole of the khan's tent. The khan sends out his queen to see what has cast a shadow over the cooking pot. She reports that she has seen a hawk flying away, and the khan says:

> 'Is it the soul of a hero
> From another land and banner?
> Is it an enemy
> Threatening my life?
> It must be something,
> And it may be the soul of a hero,
> Who has come to take you away.'

Next morning the hero arises and approaches the khan's tent. He changes his steed into a mangy colt and himself into a drivelling urchin. He ties up his horse to the hitching line, and it can hardly bear the weight of the rein. Taken aback at this, he 'reins back his horse like a cliff, hobbles it like a box', and taking off his bow and arrows lays them on the tent roof, which sags under the great weight. Taken aback again, for how could a khan's palace not bear the weight of a poor little boy's simple bow, he sticks the arrow into the ground and hangs the bow from it. Then he enters the tent. The khan greets him:

> 'Drivelling urchin boy,
> Where is your homeland?
> With whom is your business?
> What is your aim?'

The boy replies:

> 'My business is with you.
> My aim is your wife.
> I shall play the Three Games

> With your noble self,
> And take the queen your wife
> To my manly self.'

The khan proposes that they meet next day, as the red sun rises, and the boy agrees. Then he asks for food:

> 'A hungry man needs food,
> A thirsty man needs tea.
> Give me something to eat and drink.'

The khan replies scornfully:

> 'There is a fierce four-year-old mare
> Feeding in my herds.
> Her mane touches the skies,
> Her chest leans on the ground.
> Catch and eat her if you can,
> If not, go hungry.'

The boy catches the mare and kills and eats her. Next day the khan awaits him at the meeting place. The boy resumes his proper shape and says nonchalantly: 'When shall we start?' 'Now', says the khan, and as they prepare for the first contest, archery, all the assembled people admire them. The khan says:

> 'Will you shoot first,
> Having come from afar?
> Shall I shoot first,
> Being on my home ground?'

and the boy says 'You shoot first'.

The boy undoes his seventy-two buttons and bares his chest. Ninety bow-shots away, the khan notches his arrow and begins to draw. His arrow strikes the boy's chest and nearly fells him, but the boy

> Put his hand into his breast
> And brought out fox-white medicine
> Which works before noontide,
> Brought out sheep-white medicine
> Which works in less than a day,
> Tied these with a black scarf,
> Bound them with a yellow scarf
> Where he had been shot and wounded,
> And said: 'Is it my turn now?'

His arrow, shot from the same distance, pierces the khan's chest and sets the plains on fire. The myriad folk run up with felt to beat out the fire, and water to extinguish it, but the hero simply blows on it and puts it out. The khan gets up, healed, and says:

'The first game was yours,
The second (i.e. the horse race, which for
    some reason is omitted from this epic)
    is mine.
Let us dispute the third.'

They wrestle indecisively for a day, and then the hero's horse advises him how to throw the khan. The khan has never been thrown before and finding himself at death's door, tells the boy to take his wife and cherish her as he has done:

'Now take off my boot,
Bring out the nine-span knife,
And cut off the bowl-sized birth-mark
Which is on my back.
If you do so, I shall die,
And then you shall go.'

But the hero says:

'Seeing I have a knife of my own,
Why should I use someone else's?'

and cuts off the birthmark, so that the khan dies.[6]

Then the hero puts on the khan's boots and mounts his horse, and turns into the khan, and goes to tell the queen to get ready to leave, together with all her belongings. The queen will not leave till he has resumed his own form. Then the hero sets out with all the khan's wealth for his own land, saying to the queen:

'I have a father, Khan Tungalag.
I have a mother, Queen Tungalag.
I wonder if they are well?
I shall go on in front to see.
Stop for the night where a circle is drawn.
Stop at noon where a square is drawn,
And then come on.'

Leaving behind his own bow and arrow, and taking the ones he has captured, he goes on in advance, and finds his lands ravished. His parents' palace has vanished, and nettles are growing on the site. As he wonders what has happened, a white-mouthed rat comes out of the nettles and vomits in front of him. He rummages in the vomit and finds a square of white paper, with writing of gold, which turns out to be a letter from his father. It tells him to look for the meat of a big white wether to the right of the fireplace. If it is cooked, he should eat it; if it is not cooked, he should not. He should look for a robe of white lambskin with hair a span long on the left side. If it is still new, he should put it on; if it has got shabby, he should not. The black ogre Atgaaljin with fifteen heads has kidnapped his parents, but it would be useless to come after them.

The hero rummages in the fireplace, finds and eats the meat and puts on the robe. Then he returns to his wife, takes back his own weapons and says:

'The fifteen-headed
Black ogre Atgaaljin
Has stolen away
My father Khan Tungalag
And my mother Queen Tungalag.
I shall go after them
And if my father and mother are alive
I shall come back with them straightway.
If they have perished
I shall take my revenge.
If my bow and arrow gain in colour
Know that I am all right.
If my bow and arrow lose colour
Know that I fare badly.'

He travels for many days and nights, suffering hunger and thirst. He meets an old shepherd who greets him in proper epic fashion:

'Where are you going,
My fine boy,
With fire in your face,
With embers in your eyes,
With fat on the nape of your neck,
With marrow-bones in your shins?'

And the boy tells him his business. He has similar encounters with a horse-herd and an ox-herd and collects at their instructions the foetus-membranes of three beasts which have just produced their young. From the ox-herd he learns about the habits of the ogre when he comes back from hunting, and where the ogre's souls are. One of his three souls is an upturned black cooking-pot by the door. The second is a single anemone on the mountain which is his winter quarters. The third is the black chest in his tent. The ogre has two dogs, called (as is usual) Asar and Basar, and fierce maidservants who beat up any guests. The hero's father and mother have been put in a pit three fathoms deep inside a triple fortress.

The hero uses his membranes to throw to the dogs and delay them, and enters the ogre's palace where he turns into a drivelling boy. The maidservants illtreat him and try to throw him out before the ogre returns, but he resists them, kills the souls, and makes the maids take him to where his parents are. Sand poured into the pit enables them to climb out, and all three escape. The angry ogre pursues them and overtakes them and a wrestling match ensues. With the help of his mother and father, who strew flour beneath his feet and frozen droppings under the ogre's feet, and with the advice of his horse, the hero wins and kills the ogre, and the epic ends with a glorious feast:

So they drank spirits without putting down their goblets,
Ate meat without putting down their knives,
Made a wedding feast for a hundred days,

> And enjoyed themselves
> With a banquet for sixty days,
> And lived happily ever after
> On the golden earth.

As well as those epics whose subject matter is the wooing expedition and battles with an ogre, there are others which deal with themes of different types. The swan-maiden theme[7] is treated in some epics which have been recorded in the MPR. We find it in *Manai hushuuny Mani Badar zangi* ('The *zangi* Mani Badar from our banner'), recorded by Poppe and in *Dan tsagaan mor'toi Dansaran guiranch övgön* ('The old beggar Dansaran who had a single white horse'), recorded by Rintchen. It was also made use of by Chimed in composing his poem *Bayandondog baatar*. The epic *Jayar büridü-yin qayan* from Inner Mongolia deals with the theme of the calumniated wife, a theme known also to Mongol prose tales as well as to world-wide oral literature. *Öödii mergen haan*, recorded in Bayanhongor aimag in the MPR, uses the theme of the mare whose foals are stolen away at birth. This theme, also known internationally, is found in Mongol oral prose literature in, for example, the story *Ih baga Alim* ('Big Apple and Little Apple') in Nadmid's collection. It is worth offering a brief summary of this epic which also makes use of a variant of the calumniated wife theme.

There was once a khan called Öödii mergen who could unfailingly shoot a piece of grass off at the joint. He had a wife called Naran duut ('Sun-voiced') and a black horse which understood speech. He had tens of thousands of matching horses in his herds. One morning he arises and goes to the top of the Steel-Sumeru mountain to offer up the thirteen incense offerings and to recite the scriptures. He smokes his goose-necked pipe and has with him his huge bow and arrow which seventy men cannot lift. He sees thin red dust arising from the west and thin white dust arising from the north. As he is wondering what war can be afoot, his horse comes to say that three ogres have caught him, asked him where Öödii mergen's soul was, and finally hamstrung him. With a mighty whinny he has smashed their iron building and escaped, and has come to announce that there is a war in the west. Will the khan not go to it?

The khan sets off, shaking heaven and earth, and draws his mighty bow:

> At the red sun of morning
> He drew
> His huge striped bow
> Which seventy men could not lift,
> And when blood the size of an ox
> Had gathered on his thumb-nail,
> At the red sun of evening,
> He let it go.

He subdues the unnamed enemy. The battle is passed over in a couple of lines and seems only a device to enable the hero to return home and find his realm devastated.

As he sits weeping, his horse tells him to lift up a certain stone, and out comes a letter, yellow in colour and a fathom long. In it his wife tells him that she has put tea ready for him in his teapot, and meat on his dish, and put a piece of her golden comb in the skirt of his robe. The same three ogres have come and kidnapped herself, their son, and all their people. It is useless to come after them, as he will only lose his life. Rather he should marry the Hero Fairy Princess, daughter of the khan who rules the western continent.

Advised by his horse to eat the food and go and fetch the Hero Fairy Princess the hero changes into a ragged urchin, turns his great bow and arrow into weapons of reed grass, and his eloquent horse into a mangy colt. The khan engages him successively as a lamb-herd, a calf-herd and a scullion for the princess. One day a bitch pups, and the boy puts the pups under the princess's skirts and threatens to tell her parents that she has given birth to them. She begs him not to do so, but to get rid of the pups for her, and promises to marry him.

At this juncture there arrives another suitor, Tengeriin Teh Shar Böh ('The Yellow Teh-wrestler of Heaven'), and the boy proposes the usual sports contest to decide which of them shall marry the princess. They agree on archery, wrestling and a horse-race. The boy falls asleep at the beginning of the race, but still manages to win on his mangy colt. He asks the khan and the queen:

> 'Is the first game
> Mine?'
> And with tears in one eye,
> No tears in the other eye,
> Looking thither and weeping,
> Looking hither and laughing,
> Willy nilly,
> 'All right', they said.

Next comes the archery contest:

> They were to shoot
> Through the eye
> Of a silver pack needle,
> Through the hole
> Of a dried pelvic bone,
> Leaving nothing left
> Of sheep-sized white boulders,
> Leaving no chips
> Of ox-sized black boulders,
> And knock over
> The Grey Knoll of Encounters.

In this contest too the boy is victorious, and the khan and the queen accept it, weeping and laughing as before. Finally, in the wrestling match he throws his opponent so hard that he is buried ninety cubits deep and the khan's diviner has to sound out where he is so that he can be dug out.

T

At this point in the narrative, where one might expect the return to the devastated homeland to ensue, different material is exploited. The boy asks to join the thousand slaves and ten thousand subjects who are guarding a special mare. This mare brings forth foals:

> With teeth of the steel-jewel,
> With a head of the skull-jewel,
> With golden chest,
> With silver buttocks,
> With a tail of pearl.

She has already foaled six times and the Garuda bird has stolen the foals.

Towards dawn the guards fall asleep, the mare foals, and something swoops down and steals the foal. But the boy manages to shoot off the foal's pearly tail and a feather from the Garuda bird. The guards report that the mare has not foaled, but the boy can produce the tail and the feathers, and a general hunt for the Garuda ensues. The guards decide to take back some owl feathers and pretend to have killed the Garuda, but Öödii mergen actually finds the bird, with its head resting on one mountain, its body on another and its wings on a third, kills it and takes some feathers. He finds the seven foals and a stallion too, and drives them back to the khan's palace. But he disregards the advice given to him by his horse as to how he should behave, and so falls into a pit prepared in the tent. His horse is tightly bound and hobbled. The guards pretend that they have killed the Garuda bird, though they have failed to keep the horses. However, the princess can give them the lie.

The horse succeeds in escaping, and learns that a certain Yellow Girl belonging to the Khan of Heaven, can revive dead people. He flies up to Heaven and gets himself fattened up and hence noticed by the Yellow Girl. He persuades her to come down to earth, and she agrees to do so as long as the horse can get her back home in time for the 'mid-day mandala'. Letting down her hair into the pit she recovers Öödii mergen's bones, put them together again, reconstitutes his flesh and finally restores his life. The horse takes her back home just in time. He himself gets imprisoned by the khan of Heaven, but manages to escape.

Then Öödii mergen sets out to rescue his first wife. He goes hunting on the ogre's mountain, where he finds his game being stolen by a boy with a yellow colt. This is of course his son. The recognition is made easier by the presence of the fragment of the comb, which the boy takes to his mother. She says she will find out about the ogre's souls for them, and by pricking the ogre's child with a pack needle she discovers that one soul is a lion and tiger on the western mountain; one soul is a roebuck and roedeer on the eastern mountain; one soul is the dogs Asar and Basar at his door; one soul is his riding horse; one soul is a bronze fire which burns from his waist when he sleeps; one soul is a brown-striped snake which comes out of his nostrils and winds round his neck. She also finds out about his medium-sized and small souls.

Armed with this knowledge, father and son kill the outer souls, which makes the ogre feel ill. He calls for his wise yellow divining apparatus. This is not to be brought in by the wrong door, it must not be moved under a bitch, nor must a woman be allowed to bestride it. Of course, all these things are done to it, and the ogre disregards the omens it shows. A bronze fire comes out of his waist and father and son shoot it. Then they shoot the striped snake and finally kill the ogre. They begin a great feast, but then Öödii mergen remembers he has not killed the ogre's son. He cuts off the son's head, they kill a great spider which emerges, and all live happily ever after.

The metrical structure and the poetic style of the Mongol epic have been several times discussed in specialized literature, but must be surveyed here also. Ideally, the epic consists of a continuous piece of verse. There is no stanza-structure. The most immediately obvious characteristic of Mongol verse is that it is alliterative: lines succeed one another in groups of varying number, the first word of each line of the group beginning with the same syllable. There are also odd lines which do not alliterate with their neighbours. The linguistic phenomenon known as vowel-harmony is made use of. In Mongol the vowels are divided into two groups, one, the back-vowel series, comprising the vowels *a*, *o* or *u*, while the other, the front-vowel series, comprises the vowels *e*, *ö* or *ü*. The vowel *i* (sometimes spelled *y*) is common to both series. In general, a word may contain only vowels belonging to the group to which the first of its vowels belongs. This phenomenon seems to provide a ready linguistic base for the stylistic device of parallelism, characteristic of much Mongol verse, not only epic verse. Parallelism means here the practice of matching a line, a pair of lines or four lines with another group of the same size, in such a way that the number of words, their grammatical category, their position in the line, and their individual meaning are the same or similar, while the overall meaning conveyed by one group matches the overall meaning conveyed by the other. The effect produced by this device can be reinforced by the use of vowel harmony. The second group may at least begin with a word belonging to the opposite vowel series to that of the first group, though the contrast in vowel harmony is not normally carried right through the line. The following brief passage from *Han Harangui* may serve to illustrate what has just been described:

Alag uulyg naigatal	Trotting till the gay mountains swayed,
Altan delhiig dorgitol	Till the golden earth shook,
Höh uulyg naigatal	Till the blue mountains swayed,
Hövchin delhiig dorgitol	Till the whole world shook,
Sümber uulyg naigatal	Till Mount Sumeru swayed,
Sün dalaig dorgitol hatiruulj.	Till the Milk Sea shook.

The grammatical shape of each line is here the same. An adjective or a proper name stands in the first place, followed by a noun with an objective case-suffix, followed by a verb form ending with the suffix -*tal*/-*tol*. The initial words of lines 1 and 2 alliterate with a back-series vowel, and those of 3 and 4, and 5 and 6 respectively with vowels of the front series. This use of vowel harmony is not, however, an obligatory element in parallelism.

Parallelism is a structural device with a secondary, stylistic effect. The almost antiphonic structure of the verse produces a somewhat more emphatic tone than mere enumeration of epithets would give, though enumeration of epithets is also a device used. Thus, to stress the great numbers of beasts a hero owns, a bard may recite:

> He had blue-brown yaks
> Filling the forested ridges.
> He had dappled brown yaks
> Filling the Altai.
> He had black brown horses
> Filling the Khangai.
> He had a small brown horse
> To ride within his camp.
> He had a big black horse
> To ride at game and birds,
> And as for his Jewelled Cornelian Brown horse,
> Which he rode to war,
> It had a fine hare's spine, etc., etc.

A second device, more purely stylistic than the structural device of parallelism, is the free use of exaggeration. Indeed, so extravagant is the nature of exaggeration in the Mongol epic, and so continually is it employed, that an epic gives the impression of being an extended hyperbole. Every action and every piece of description is so heightened as to transcend the normal, everyday world to the extent that credibility is not merely suspended, but simply becomes irrelevant. If hyperbole were limited to the description of the hero and his possessions it might be considered panegyric,[8] but in fact it colours any and every scene in an epic, and seems to be a device intended to stress the unreality of the epic world and its events, rather than to bring out the special features of this or that protagonist. Hyperbolic descriptions are not individually matched to their subject. Thus the hero's body may well be described in the same or similar terms whoever he is. In *Han Harangui* we read:

> His body was made of bronze,
> His neck was made of steel,
> There was no gap between his ribs,
> There was no joint in his lower back.

In *Eriin sain Egel mergen haan* ('Egel mergen haan, the best of men'), we read of the hero that

> His body
> was made of bronze.
> His neck
> Was made of steel.

And of Zöng Belegt Baatar:

> His native body was made of steel.
> His born body was made of iron.

The horses of different heroes, too, are described in much the same way, the enumeration of characteristics in such a description recalling the similar enumeration in another poetic genre, the 'title' of a fine horse.

The effect of hyperbole, then, is not to stress individuality, but to remove all limits of credibility as to the qualities ascribed to any person, or the nature of any enterprise. The ogre, for example, must be infinitely ugly and evil:

> The nails of his feet
> Grew out towards the steppes
> And had become hooks of blue iron.
> The nails of his hands
> Grew towards the outside
> And had become hooks of steel.
> He had blue striped eyes
> And a brown striped tongue.
> He sucked people's blood
> And ate children's flesh.

The princess, on the other hand, is dazzlingly beautiful:

> She had cheeks of bright red
> With rays like the light.
> She had clear red lips
> Whose rays pierced the tent wall.
> She was called Girl Lapis Lazuli,
> And had a lovely form.
> From the ground where she stepped
> Grew up gay flowers.
> From the ground where she walked
> Spurted beams of light.
> She could look at the hairs of the beasts and count them.
> She could hold the hairs of a hat and count them.

There is little to distinguish her from Avai Gerel, the consort of Jangar:

> In her light behind her one could herd horses.
> In her light before her one could do needlework.
> She had tent-piercing brilliance,
> Bright red cheeks,
> She had tent-wall piercing rays
> And shining red cheeks.
> She had full lips,

> She had spy-glass black eyes.
> She had shell-white teeth.
> On her right cheek
> Shone the text of the Badmanyambuu.
> On her left cheek
> Shone the text of various scriptures.
> She smelled of incense
> And was eternally sixteen years old.[9]

Not only is everything highly exaggerated, but there are no medium shades, no compromises. Each character, whether hero, princess, steed, ogre, fierce maidservant and so on, is a stereotype, and is the epitome of the qualities associated with the type in all epics. The steed is wise and faithful, the ogre ugly and evil and in the end cowardly, and so on. The Mongol epic is an unsophisticated genre, in the sense that its emotional appeal is direct and primitive. The sympathies of the bard are apparent and categorical, and certainly correspond with the feelings of the audience.

Even from the few quotations given so far in translation, it will be evident that the structure and the imagery of the Mongol epic are not arbitrary, but formulaic and bound by an apparently strict tradition. Poetic ability resides in the skill with which the individual bard can combine and manipulate traditional themes and motifs, clothing them in a familiar dress of imagery and metaphor. Examination of a single epic reveals the use of runs of lines which are repeated as occasion demands. For example, in *Han Harangui* the hero is described, in part, as follows:

> With his pastures at Aihan river-bend,
> With the Gay Mountain as his back-rest,
> With his pastures at the Milk Sea,
> With Mount Sumeru as his back-rest,
> With the whole steppe as his pasture,
> With the Blue Mountain as his back-rest,
> With Khan Saikhan as his father
> With Queen Tungal as his mother.

These lines occur twice more, when the princess dreams of Khan Kharangui, and when she repeats her dream to her herdsman. In the same epic, the imposing movement of the hero and his companion is described more than once as:

> Galloping swiftly
> Below the cloudy heaven,
> Above the pointed trees,
> Not blinking their watching eyes,
> Not stemming their roaring voices.

As appeared in the brief discussion above of the use of hyperbole, epics resemble each other in that each contains descriptions of some or all of the same complex of persons and objects, and similar incidents are narrated. Though a different selection may be made from the common stock of traditional material, and this will be treated at more or less length by different bards, each action and each description will be cast in terms at least recognizable, usually broadly similar, and sometimes to all intents and purposes identical, as between one epic and another. Thus the initial formula, setting the action in its time, may be short, as in *Han Harangui*:

> At the beginning of a good era,
> At the end of a bad era.

Or it may be longer, as in *Egel mergen haan*:

> At the beginning of a good era,
> At the end of a bad era,
> In the world of the six continents,
> When the sun was just risen,
> When the leaves first spread,
> When the continents were just created,
> When the state was just formed,
> At that time.

Some formulae, such as that used when the hero, on his journey, meets someone who asks him about his purpose, have become rather stereotyped, varying the selection of actual words used, but chosen from a fairly small vocabulary, and employing only a small number of standard alliterations, arranged one way or another.

Thus, in *Han Harangui*, we have:

Shilendee shiltei	'You two poor boys,
Shilbendee chömögtei	With sinews[11] in the nape of your neck
Nüdendee tsogtoi	With marrow bones in your shins,
Nüürendee galtai[10]	With embers in your eyes,
Hoyor höörhön hüü	With fire in your face
Het nutag haana ve?	Where is your distant pasture land?
Hereg zorig hend ve?	With whom is your purpose?
Yamar hergeer yavna?	What is your business?
Yavdal uchraa helne üü.	Tell me your affairs.'

In *Gants modon honogtoi*:

Nüürendee galtai	'My fine boy,
Nüdendee tsogtoi	With fire in your face
Shilendee ööhtei	With embers in your eyes,

Shilbendee chömögtei	With fat on the nape of your neck,
Sain hüü chi	With marrow bones in your shin,
Haa hürch yavna?	Where are you going?'

and:

Nüdendee tsogtoi	'Boy, looking like a hero,
Nüürendee galtai	With embers in your eyes,
Shilendee ööhtei	With fire in your face,
Shilbendee chömogtei	With fat on the nape of your neck,
Sain eriin baidaltai hüü	With marrow bones in your shin.
Sain yavj baina uu?	Are you well?
Hereg zorig hend ve?	With whom is your purpose?
Hetiin sanaa haana ve?	Where is your far thought?'

In *Egel mergen haan*:

Nüürendee galtai	'Alert young fellow,
Nüdendee tsogtoi	Smart of stature,
Shilendee gereltei	With fire in your face
Shilbendeen chömögtei	With embers in your eyes,
Gav hiisen nuruutai	With light in the nape of your neck,
Shav hiisen band'	With marrow bones in your shin,
Al' haany albat ve?	What khan's subject are you?
Alsyn hereg hend ve?	With whom is your distant purpose?
Hen haany albat ve?	Which khan's subject are you?
Hetiin zorig hend ve?	With whom is your far business?'

A formula may have the same overall shape, but be different in vocabulary and alliteration. Thus in *Han Harangui*, describing the speed of a journey, we read:

Yeren yösön jiliin gazryg	Covering ninety-nine years' journey
Yeren jösön saraar tovchilj	In ninety-nine months,
Yeren yösön saryn gazryg	Covering ninety-nine months' journey
Yeren yösön ödröör tovchilj	In ninety-nine days,
Yeren yösön ödriin gazryg	Covering ninety-nine days' journey
Yeren yösön tsagaar tovchilj.	In ninety-nine hours.

And, in *Erdene Havhan Soyoo*:

Gurvan jiliig	He covered three years
Gurvan saraar	In three months,
Gurvan saryg	Three months
Gurvan honogoor	In three days,
Gurvan honogiig	Three days
Gurvan tsagaar tovchlood yavjee.	In three hours.

Finally, a favourite type of formula can be found applied to more than one object. For example, in *Öödii mergen haan*, the hero's bow is:

Dalan hün daadaggüi	The huge striped
Danhar ereen	Bow and arrow
Num sumaa	Which seventy men could not lift.

In *Gants modon honogtoi* the same type of attribute is applied to the saddle:

Dalan hün daadaggüi	His stiff yellow saddle
Dargar shar emeelee	which seventy men could not lift.

In a 'Jangar' episode, it is applied to a dish and a porcelain pot:

Dalan hün daadaggüi	In his huge black dish
Danhar har tevsheereen	Which seventy men could not lift,
Dalan hün daadaggüi	In his sea-porcelain pot
Dalai gangar shaazangaaraa	Which seventy men could not lift.

In *Egel mergen haan*, it is applied to the tent door:

Dalan hün	His broad yellow door
Damjilj daadaggüi	Which seventy men
Daldgai shar üüdee	Could not lift up together.

And in *Han Harangui*, as in the 'Jangar' episode, it is applied to a porcelain pot, and also to the tent door:

Dalan hün damjilj daadaggüi	Taking the sea white porcelain pot
Dalai tsagaan shaazang avaad.	which seventy men could not lift up together.

and

Dalan hün damjlaad daadaggüi	Lifting up the sea-quilted door
Dalai shirmel üüdii n' örgöj.	Which seventy men could not lift up together.

As well as descriptions, episodes which were no doubt familiar to and expected by, an epic audience, would be narrated according to a formulaic pattern using runs of lines which, while in detail different one from the other, show considerable overall resemblance. Thus, in the archery contest which forms part of the wooing expedition, the antagonists either shoot at each other, or, more commonly, shoot at a series of targets which they agree upon in advance. All the targets must be hit consecutively by one arrow. In any individual epic where this incident occurs, the targets may be listed as many as three or even four times, once when the arrangements are made, and twice or

three times more, depending on the number of archers, as each of the antagonists fires his arrow. In *Egel mergen haan* the arrangements are made as
follows:

> They said: 'How shall we shoot?'
> And said to each other: 'Let us shoot
> Through the eye of a golden packneedle,
> Through the hole in a silver coin,
> Through the hole in a dried pelvic bone,
> Through the joint of a white grass
> Leaving nothing left
> Of sheep-sized white boulders,
> Turning ox-sized white boulders
> To ash.'

In *Han Harangui* the arrangements are as follows:

> 'Nearest of all
> We shall shoot sheep-sized white boulders
> Leaving nothing left.
> We shall shoot ox-sized black boulders
> To bits
> Beyond that.
> Beyond that
> We shall heap up sixty carts of firewood
> And shoot it till there is nothing to use as a toothpick.
> Beyond that
> We shall stick up packneedles of gold and silver
> And shoot through their eyes.
> Beyond that we shall stick up a pelvic bone
> And shoot through its hole.
> Beyond that we shall make a gap
> That an ox-cart can go through
> In the north-facing Örvön black cliff.
> Beyond that we shall ignite
> A little fire,
> And then catch the arrow and stop it.'

The antagonists fulfil most, or in the case of the hero, all of these conditions,
and the hero's arrow may prove itself even mightier than required. In *Egel
mergen haan* it finally slithers for ninety-nine years before being stopped. In
Han Harangui the hero's companion chases after the arrow and just manages
to catch it and stop it with his 'cunning black lasso'.

The epic is essentially a verse-form meant to be presented orally. However,
as early as 1927, when Poppe collected eight items, not one of these was
entirely in verse, each containing a certain proportion of prose passages. Today,

through age and failing memory, bards may be found to be no longer capable of repeating the whole of an epic which they once knew, and when they have not been able to pass on their skill to a pupil the epic is in danger of disappearing. The woman-bard Mangal recorded the epic *Ar zamba tivüg ezlenhen törsön Aguina Ulaan haan* ('The red khan Aguina, born ruling the continent of North Jambudvipa'), in the 1960s, but she could only recite the first part properly, resuming the remainder in prose narrative. She was aged seventy-five at the time. Mangal said:

'I learned this epic when I was young. It was a very long epic. I have forgotten some of it. It was a beautiful epic, in alliterated verse, recited to a melody. Now I haven't the voice to do it any more.'

Generally speaking, though, it is said that a bard finds difficulty in reciting an epic in any other way than the accustomed one. Both Vladimirtsov and Rintchen have remarked upon this fact, and I myself noticed that an epic retold in an ordinary voice after a recitation to the proper melody was by no means the same text, but at times more of a paraphrase.

Epics may be performed in a number of ways. Rintchen has written briefly on this subject and scattered information may be found elsewhere. The present author, in the years 1967–68, heard four types of performance. These were:

(1)   Straightforward recitation without any chant or melody.
(2)   Intonation without instrumental accompaniment.
(3)   Singing to the self-accompaniment of a plucked instrument.
(4)   Singing to the self-accompaniment of a bowed instrument.

It is also possible for an epic to be recited to the rhythmical tapping of some object, perhaps the bard's tobacco pipe, though I did not have the good fortune to hear this. A bard Jal, from whom the epic *Bürged Baatar*, 'Eagle Hero', was taken down, and published in 1967, performed in this manner, and said that his elder brother, a bard who knew an episode from *Han Harangui*, had done the same.

1.   The epic which the author heard recited without chant or melody was called *Zöng Belegt Baatar*, and it was delivered by a member of a writers' circle in the town of Darhan in January 1968. The text I heard was almost identical with a printed version at my disposal, and though I failed to establish the fact conclusively, it seemed likely that the performer had learned it from the book. This is indeed a respectable way for a bard to acquire an epic: the existence of manuscripts, especially manuscripts of *Han Harangui*, has been referred to above. We may note here the evidence given by a bard named Dum of Gov' Altai aimag. Dum made a recording of a 'Jangar' episode in 1966 and stated that he had learned it at the age of 22 from a mendicant lama. The lama had

recited it from a 'sutra' he carried with him, and had also taught Dum seven stories as well.

The performer at Darhan used an ordinary speaking voice, and there was nothing, except for the effect of verse, to distinguish this performance from the oral narration of prose tales which I heard from the lips of semi-professional story tellers, in Hovd and in Ulan Bator. I have indeed some reservations as to whether this is really a traditional way of reciting an epic at all. It is interesting to note that Dr Caroline Humphrey also recorded an epic in 1974 from a herdsman in Arhangai aimag which was also apparently a non-musical performance, but of which she says: 'The epic was chanted at a fast rate, rather than pronounced in an ordinary speaking voice, but it was not accompanied by any music.' The epic recorded at Darhan was not chanted.

2.   The second type of delivery was heard from a bard named Gongor, a member of the Bayasgalant am'dral herding co-operative at Manhan sum in Hovd aimag and was recorded by the author in September 1967. Mr Gongor told me that he had learned the epic, called *Ezen tenger haan* ('Khan Lord Heaven'), from his parents, but that he had supplied the melody, or chant, himself. It is difficult to characterize a metrical performance in writing, but Gongor used an insistent if rather monotonous chant, characterized by (a) a strong rhythm, in which stress-groups similar to those of the iambic and the trochaic feet of English verse could be recognized. The transition from one type of stress to the other occasioned a somewhat jerky effect; (b) shifts of stress within a word, apparently at the demands of the metrical stress pattern. It was very noticeable that a word which in normal speech would be stressed on the first syllable (and in Mr Gongor's non-musical repetition of his epic was so stressed) could be heavily stressed on the second if occasion demanded; (c) extension of a single vowel to become two vowels, or of a closed syllable to become two syllables, as for example the extension of the word *sümber* to sound *süm-m be-er*; (d) the emphatic pronunciation of certain consonants, particularly *n* and *m*, but also *r*, to the extent that they became syllable-carriers. A similar type of performance was that of Dügersüren, a woman-bard from Dorno Gov' aimag, reciting a part of the epic *Höhöö deglen* ('Grey Heron'). The recording I was able to hear was less than ideally clear, but indicated that Dügersüren made use of the same vocal devices as did Gongor.

Unaccompanied chants were also used by Namilan, a Dörvöd singer from Uvs aimag in reciting a part of 'Jangar', and by Zodov of the same aimag in reciting a part of *Bum Erdene*, but in these west Mongolian performances I missed the characteristic distortions made use of by Gongor. The rhythms seemed even more insistent than Gongor's, but proceeded without demanding, for example, stress shifts. A feature of Namilan's performance, absent from Gongor's, but to be found also in the singing of Bataa, to be mentioned below, was the use of a short ululating refrain at the end of each section of his epic, followed by a short pause, which in turn was followed by an exclamation at the beginning of the next section. Namilan's performance, as I heard it on tape in Ulan Bator, is reproduced on pp. 125 ff. of the collection 'Jangaryn tuul's'. The two versions do not completely coincide, nor is there any indication in the printed text of the refrain and the exclamation.

3.   The third type of delivery was heard from Bataa, a bard from the Bayat people, a west Mongolian minority living in Uvs aimag. Bataa is said to be able to perform a version of *Han Harangui* for a month on end, but when the author heard him in the autumn of 1967 he was recording an excerpt from *Bum Erdene*, having been invited to the Institute of Language and Literature in Ulan Bator to have his repertory taped. Bataa sang, using an insistent rhythm and a repetitive melody, to his own accompaniment on the *tovshuur*, a two-stringed, plucked instrument. His performing style does not seem to have been reduced to notation, but would appear to differ very little from that of another west Mongolian bard, S. Choisüren, which has been. Choisüren's performance is scored for voice and *tovshuur*, and is set in two flats and 4/4 time, varying occasionally to 5/4 and 2/4. The accompaniment is indicated throughout as a pair of quavers. The second of each pair is the B flat below middle C, and the first is the B an octave higher, or the neighbouring C. The basic unit in the bar is the quaver, a 4/4 bar consisting of 6 quavers and a crochet, or else 8 quavers. There is usually one syllable of the text to each musical note, so that the overall effect is one of compelling regularity. This is a very simple metrical structure when compared, for example, to the so-called 'long song' (*urtyn duu*), a favourite folk-song form in Mongolia, which is characterized by long florid passages which interrupt the delivery of the text. Bataa also made use of a refrain to end a section of his epic, but this was less obvious in his performance than in Namilan's.

4.   An epic may also be sung to the self-accompaniment of a bowed instrument. Rintchen describes the use of the four-stringed *huuchir*, the instrument of Luvsan huurch, whose repertory he recorded and published, together with the 170 different melodies used by the bard in performing his epic *Bodi mergen haan*.[12] Another bard whom Rintchen knew, and who also played the *huuchir*, was Norov, who, he says, was one of some tens of bards who used to perform in public in Ulan Bator down to the thirties of this century. A bard may also accompany himself on the two-stringed *morin huur*, or horse-headed fiddle. In 1967 the author heard a performance by a young singer named Tseveenaravdan, a west Mongol bard and member of the Zahchin people, who lived in a brigade of Manhan sum and was aged 18 at the time. Tseveenaravdan had learned his epic from another bard, while his fiddle had been made by his own father. His performance can best be described by referring to the similar style

displayed in the performance, on track I A 1 of Hungaroton records LPX
18013–14, of a legend about the origin of the *morin huur*. The instrumental line
functions mainly as a rhythmical support, but it is more varied, both in melody
and in tone, than Bataa's. There are instrumental interludes, which serve to
break the epic up into shorter units.

The normal way to become a singer of epics seems to have been imitation and
study of an established bard, and the motivation to do so was fascination with
the epic genre. Thus Parchen, the informant of Vladimirtsov, heard the epic
Ergel Türgel performed at the local court when he was nine years old, by a bard
called Sügsüü. The young boy was very interested and began to memorize the
epic and to imitate the singer. He learned *Bum Erdene* simply by listening to
performances of the bard Buural Sesren, and surprised and gratified the older
bard by singing it to him. Sesren is said to have exclaimed: 'Now my favourite
epic will not die with me' and to have given the lad a ceremonial scarf as a
reward, with tears in his eyes. A fantastic account of Parchen's initiation as a
bard is given by the late Ralph Fox, who tells how at the age of twelve Parchen
was pasturing his father's flocks when a giant rode up upon a dragon and
asked him if he would like to become a singer of epic tales. He told him to
sacrifice the largest and best white goat to the King of the Dragons. Then he
struck the boy on the shoulder and left him, and when Parchen awoke (for it
might all have been a dream) a wolf was eating the goat. This account, which
recalls Bergmann's story of the origin of the 'Jangar' epic, has no basis in truth,
but is not entirely valueless. It seems to be a literary borrowing from the account
given by Vladimirtsov of how the bard Eeten Gonchig was said to have received
his gift.

However, even though there were manuscript copies of certain epics, it was
by listening to, and learning from, another bard, that a bard normally extended
his repertory. Very often the gift ran in families. W. Heissig has collected
together most of the currently available information on this point, and concludes that 'the singers of heroic songs were persons especially predestined by
inclination, imagination, disposition and partly also by family tradition'.[13]
We may refer here once again to Gongor and Tseveenaravdan. Mr Gongor told
me that he had learned his epic from his father and mother, and that he used to
rock his child to sleep by reciting the epic, as his own parents had done with him.
Tseveenaravdan had learned his epic, *Galuu Baatar* ('Goose Hero'), from a local
bard named Erentsen, who had died in 1966 at the age of seventy-five. He had
learned another tale, which he recited in prose, from another narrator named
Tsend, a herdsman of the same brigade, who was aged fifty-three.

Both Vladimirtsov and Rintchen speak of there having been 'professional'
bards among the Mongols, though it is clear that many bards had other sources
of income and occupations. Parchen, for example, would take rewards for his
art from the local nobility, but he had beasts of his own, and also did some

farming and went hunting now and again. Luvsan huurch was trained at home as a bone-setter and fortune-teller as well as a singer, and later on gained something of a medical training in a Buriat lamasery, so that he could treat his audience as well as entertain them. Today the bard, like the story-teller, is even more of a part-timer. Gongor and Tseveenaravdan were members of a herding co-operative. Bataa, by 1967 already an oldish man, had been a herder as a boy. He had done odd jobs around a lamasery and after the revolution of 1921, as well as acquiring some animals of his own, he had been employed by the state in various minor capacities. The contemporary bard seems no longer to have a large or regular audience for his epics. Gongor performed for a few acquaintances in the hotel of his co-operative, and afterwards sang with no audience but a tape-recorder belonging to the Institute of Language and Literature. Bataa performed in the academic surroundings of the Institute itself. Of the few bards whom I heard in 1967–68, only Tseveenaravdan, who took part in a small public concert in the brigade of which he was a member, had anything like a public audience.

The richness of the material recorded in the last decades in Mongolia may, alas, be the last flowering of a dying art. Thus of the thirty-two 'Jangar' singers listed in 'Jangaryn tuul's', only a few seem to have been living in 1968, the year of publication, and most of these were elderly. The youngest of those for whom the year of birth is given was born in 1939. The next youngest was born in 1920, while several others were born between 1880 and 1912. The bards from whom Khalkha epics were recorded and published in the collection *Halh ardyn tuul'* also seem generally to have been elderly. Thus Dum was born in 1901, the 'old' bard Has was fifty-two when he sang in 1966, Dashdavaa was seventy-three, and so on. But whatever may happen, it is at least reassuring to know that the tape-recorder, in the hands of our Mongolian colleagues, has been able to preserve an oral tradition reaching back at least into the previous century, when the masters of the elderly bards of today will have been performing.

NOTES

1. For a detailed survey of the distribution of the Mongols of the MPR see Hamayon, 1970.
2. Zagdsüren, 1968, p. 29, in the epic *Bogd noyon Jangar*.
3. Nor do the khan's subjects play any significant part in the action of an epic. Nevertheless the epic may be considered a popular genre, since it appealed to all levels of society and drew its bards, almost without exception, from the ordinary people.
4. Horloo, p. 79, in the epic *Egel mergen haan*.
5. Horloo, p. 149.
6. The motif of the man who can be killed only by a particular weapon or one he supplies himself may be found elsewhere in Mongol literature, for example in a popular tale relating to the first Jebtsundamba Khutuktu, told by O. Lattimore in his book *Mongol Journeys*, and in Mongol chronicles, so for example *Erdeni-yin tobči* and *Altan tobči*, in the passage concerned with the duel between Genghis Khan and the ruler of the Tangut people. It occurs also in a popular ritual known as the 'Offering of the Fox'.

7. See A. T. Hatto, 'The Swan Maiden: a Folk-tale of North Eurasian Origin?', *Bulletin of the School of Oriental and African Studies*, 24 (1961), 326–52.
8. The description of the hero at the beginning of an epic concentrates upon his parentage, his name, his physical make-up and appearance, his homeland, his subordinate heroes or ministers, and his possessions, including his flocks and herds, his palace and his horse, and sometimes also his queen. It is during the course of the epic that his powers become apparent as he employs them.
9. Zagdsüren, 1968, pp. 35–36, in the epic *Bogd Jangar haan*.
10. These two lines, alliterating in *nü-* have a *locus classicus* in the *Secret History of the Mongols*, paragraph 82.
11. Or, perhaps, 'glass', the Mongol word *shil* being ambiguous.
12. Rintchen, 1960, Introduction, and 1965, p. vii.
13. Heissig, 1972, p. 356.

SELECT BIBLIOGRAPHY

Altan hundagat hüü, in *Ardyn aman zohiolyn emhtgel* (Ulan Bator, 1956)

Bawden, C. R., *The Jebtsundamba Khutuktus of Urga*. Asiatische Forschungen, 9 (Wiesbaden, 1961)

Bawden, C. R., 'The Theme of the Calumniated Wife in Mongolian Popular Literature', *Folklore*, 74 (Autumn 1963), 488–97

Bergmann, B., *Nomadische Streifereien unter den Kalmüken in den Jahren 1802 und 1803* (Riga, 1804–1805, reprinted 1969)

Chimed, M., *Bayandondog Baatar (Shüleglesen ülger)* (Ulan Bator, 1947)

Dashdorj, D. and I. Gür-rentsen, *Ardyn aman zohioloos* (Ulan Bator, 1958) (Contains: *Heviin sain Buidar, Gants modon honogtoi galzuu Ulaan baatar*)

Velikii pevets 'Jangara' (Elista, 1969) (Contains U. E. Erdniev, 'K voprosu o vremeni vozniknoveniya eposa Jangar')

Fox, R., 'Conversation with a Lama', *New Writing*, 2 (1936), 179–88

Hamayon, R. and M. Helffer, 'A propos de "Musique populaire mongole", enregistrements de Lajos Vargyas (coffret de deux disques Hungaroton Unesco co-opération, LPX 18013–14)', *Études mongoles*, 4 (1973), 145–80

Hamayon, R., 'Mongols: hommes et langues', *Études mongoles*, 1 (1970), 9–51

Heissig, W., 'Die Aufzeichnung von Volksliteratur in der mongolischen Volksrepublik', *Zeitschrift der Deutschen Morgenländischen Gesellschaft*, Supplementa 1, XVII. *Deutscher Orientalistentag 1968, Vorträge, Teil 2*, 754–71

Heissig, W., *Geschichte der mongolischen Literatur* (Wiesbaden, 1972)

Heissig, W., 'Innermongolische Arbeiten zur mongolischen Literaturgeschichte und Folkloreforschung', *Zeitschrift der Deutschen Morgenländischen Gesellschaft*, 115 (1965), 153–99

Heissig, W., 'Zur Frage der individuellen Idiomatik der Rhapsoden', *Zentralasiatische Studien*, 6 (1972), 145–228

Horloo, P., *Halh ardyn tuul'* (Ulan Bator, 1967) (Contains: *Eriin sain Han Harangui, Eriin sain Egel mergen haan, Eriin sain Erinchin mergen hüü, Hairt Har, Bogd noyon Jangar, Erdene Havhan soyoo, Öödii mergen haan, Bürged baatar*)

Humphrey, C. and B. Damdin, 'Gurvan nastai gunan ulaan baatar', *Journal of the Anglo-Mongolian Society*, 2, 1 (June 1975), 32–59

Jayar büridü-yin qayan in *Γurban nasutai yunayan ulayan bayatur* (Huhhot, 1956)

Kara, G., *Chants d'un barde mongol* (Budapest, 1970)

Mikhailov, G. I., 'K voprosu ob evolutsii mongol'skogo geroicheskogo eposa' in *Tyurko-mongol'skoe yazykoznanie i folkloristika* (Moscow, 1960)

Nadmid, J., *Mongol ardyn ülger* (Ulan Bator, 1957)

Poppe, N., 'Das mongolische Heldenepos', *Zentralasiatische Studien*, 2 (1968), 183–200

Poppe, N., 'Die mongolische Heldensage Khilen Galdzü', *Zentralasiatische Studien*, 6 (1972), 229–72

Poppe, N., *Khalkha-mongol'skii geroicheskii epos* (Moscow–Leningrad, 1937, reprinted Gregg, 1971)

Poppe, N., *Mongolische Epen* I–II. *Übersetzung der Sammlung B. Rintchen. Folklore mongol, livre deuxième; livre troisième*, Asiatische Forschungen, 42 and 43 (Wiesbaden, 1975)

Poppe, N., *Mongolische Epen* III. *Übersetzung der Sammlung G. Rinčinsambuu, Mongol ardyn baatarlag tuul's*, Asiatische Forschungen, 47 (Wiesbaden, 1975)

Poppe, N., *Mongolische Epen* IV. *Übersetzung der Sammlung P. Xorloo, Xalx Ardyn Tuul'*, Asiatische Forschungen, 48 (Wiesbaden, 1975)

Poppe, N., *Mongolische Volksdichtung* (Wiesbaden, 1955)

Rinchinsambuu, G., 'Mongol ardyn baatarlag tuul's', *Studia Folklorica*, I, 7 (Ulan Bator, 1960)

Rinchinsambuu, G., 'Mongol tuuliig üeleh asuudal' in *Studia Mongolica*, IV, 10–21 (Ulan Bator, 1964)

Rintchen, [B.], *Folklore mongol, livres* I–IV, Asiatische Forschungen, 7. 11. 12. 15 (Wiesbaden, 1960–65)

Schmidt, I. J., *Die Taten Bogda Gesser Chan's* (St Petersburg, Leipzig, 1839; reprinted Berlin, 1925)

Tsoloo, J. and U. Zagdsüren, 'Baruun Mongolyn baatarlag tuul's', *Studia Folklorica*, IV, 2 (Ulan Bator, 1966)

Veit, V., 'Siregetü-yin mergen qaγan, Ein Epos aus der Inneren Mongolei', *Zentralasiatische Studien*, 6 (1972), 63–144

Vladimirtsov, B. Ia., *Mongolo-oiratskii geroicheskii epos* (St Petersburg, Moscow, 1923, reprinted Gregg, 1971)

Zagdsüren, U., 'Jangaryn tuul's', *Studia Folklorica*, IV, 15 (Ulan Bator, 1968) (Contains fifteen 'Jangar' episodes)

Zagdsüren, U. and S. Luvsanvandan, *Mongol ardyn baatarlag tuul'syn uchir* (Ulan Bator, 1966) (Contains: Rintchen: *Manai ardyn tuul's*; Zagdsüren: *Tuul'ch M. Parchiny am'dral uran büteeliin tuhai*; Vladimirtsov: *Oirad mongolyn baatarlag tuul's* (Mongol translation of the introduction to Vladimirtsov's monograph); A. V. Burdukov: *Oirad Halimagiin tuul'chid*; T. A. Burdukova: *Oiradyn nert tuul'ch Parchin*; Žamcarano: *Mongolyn baatarlag tuul'syn tuhai temdeglel*)

KIRGHIZ

Mid-nineteenth century

By A. T. HATTO

THE MOST NUMEROUS PEOPLE of the present-day Socialist Soviet Republic of Kirgizia bears a name of great antiquity. The ethnonym 'Kirghiz' is said to be discernible in ancient Chinese records for a people north of the Eastern Huns. Kirghiz — more properly *Kırkız* — are named in the famous Turkic runic inscriptions of the early eighth century and they are placed north of the Eastern Türk, at which time it seems the Kırkız had their own runic script.

In A.D. 840 the Kırkız erupted from Siberia and shattered the empire of the more civilized Uigur in Mongolia but failed to exploit their victory, since *c.*920 the Khitan forced them to retire. Kirghiz are referred to in Arabic chronicles of the ninth to eleventh centuries. In the *Secret History of the Mongols*, '*Kirgisut*' are located among the forest peoples of the north at the time of their subjugation by Jochi, son of Chinggis-khan, in 1207 (§239). Since the late sixteenth century at least, the Russians reported the Kirghiz name in the Upper Yenisei region and on into the eighteenth century, though some confusion between 'Kirghiz' subsections of other tribes and the Kirghiz there has not yet been altogether disentangled. There can, however, be little doubt that the name of the present-day Kirghiz was inherited from the Old Kirghiz of the Yenisei, but the question which remains as yet unanswered is *how*? — Transmitted by what ethnic units? — Of what strength? The Russians at first referred to those now known as 'Kazakh' and 'Kirghiz' as 'Kirghiz' jointly, without differentiation. Then, since the early eighteenth century, as the identity of their nearer neighbours the Kazakh became clearer, the Russians used the term *Kirgiz-kaysaki* for these, whereas *Kara Kırgız* came to be employed for the tribes of the T'ien Shan Mountains, whom, or some of whom, the Manchu[1] and the Kalmak had named *Burut* since at least *c.*A.D. 1700 and the Chinese possibly since the fourth century as *Po-lu* or *Pu-lu*. It has yet to be disproved that a 'Burut' element makes up the vast bulk of those known as 'Kirghiz' today. The Russians also referred to the Kara Kırgız as *Dikokamennie Kirgizy*, that is 'Kirghiz of the wild rocks'. It is quite possible that the element *kara*, literally 'black', in the name *Kara-kırgız* was expressive of the Kazakh neighbours' scorn of a people that had no khans of the 'white' Chinggisid 'bone' or stock, had been only recently and superficially converted to Islam, and altogether led a more wretched existence than the Kazakhs.

The Russified Kazakh princeling Chokan Chingisovich Valikhanov (1835–65) sought eagerly for traditions of Kirghiz migrations from the north yet found none — except for an implication in a passage from heroic epic, which, as I shall show, was the result of retouching in an antiquarian spirit.[2]

In 1959, the number of Kirghiz living in the Soviet Union was estimated as approaching a million. Of these, more than 800,000 lived in Kirgizia, over 90,000 in Uzbekistan, and 26,000 in Tadzhikistan. Outside the Soviet Union, some 70,000 are thought to be living in Sinkiang — an invaluable parallel source for Kirghiz heroic poetry, should it occur to someone to record it. There were until 1978 about three-thousand Kirghiz in the Afghan Pamir, and, of course, no few in Kazakhstan. At the time when he was recording his epic texts in the mid-nineteenth century, V. V. Radlov (W. Radloff, 1837–1918) estimated the number of Kirghiz as far in excess of 300,000. They were grouped notionally into a Left and Right Wing comprising many tribes, both great and small. These divisions persist even now in the memories of old men. With their often contradictory help, ambitious attempts have been made to follow tribal structure down to minor clans and families. In Radlov's time the largest political entities were loose confederacies of tribes led by rich *manap* or *biy*. There is no evidence that the neo-Kirghiz ever had Khans.

The mid-nineteenth-century Kirghiz were chiefly nomadic herdsmen, who through the year grazed a succession of high pastures in the very mountainous region within which they were penned by mightier peoples, most memorably and painfully by the Kalmak overlords until the Jungarian state was destroyed by the Chinese in 1758. The beasts the Kirghiz herded were the *beš tülük* ('of the five coats'): horses, large horned cattle, camels, goats and sheep. As mountaineers and nomads they despised the 'Sart' or sedentary plainsmen and town-dwellers, regarding them as fit only to be plundered. Thus their civilized neighbours tended to regard the Kirghiz as little more than brigands, though for such adventurous travellers as the English architect T. W. Atkinson they were brigands of charm. From the illustrations to Atkinson's books and from the sketches of Valikhanov a vivid impression can be gained of the Kirghiz habitat, of their yurts, equipment and dress, and of the persons of some of their chieftains.

If we are to be guided by the content and tone of the epics, the crucial group-experience of the Kirghiz was no dramatic migration such as some have dreamt of, but perennial competition for pastures with the Kalmak, who largely shared their mode of subsistence. This struggle, bitter enough while the Kalmak were masters, was accentuated in Kirghiz eyes by the Kalmaks' speaking an alien Mongol tongue, practising the Lamaist Buddhist religion and, like the Chinese who finally subdued them, delighting in pork. Kirghiz heroic poetry breathes hatred and loathing of the jabbering, idol-worshipping Kalmak who ride to battle with legs of pork at their saddle-bows. Only superficially Muslims themselves, the Kirghiz were proud of the difference.

The plots of the epics to which Section I now offers a general introduction, are analysed in Section II below (pp. 318–24). Some readers might wish to peruse this latter section first.

I

In the mid-nineteenth century, Kirghiz poetry was entirely oral, for only the odd mullah was literate. Within this oral tradition, heroic epic dominated. Indeed it was claimed by Valikhanov, exaggeratedly, that the cyclic development of *Manas* had become so vast that it was drawing Kirghiz poetry and folklore to itself in an oral encyclopedia. In the words of Radlov, more soberly, all other lore was grouping itself round *Manas* 'just as in a saturated salt solution the new crystals, separated out on evaporation, group themselves round a large crystal nucleus in the liquid, or iron-filings arrange themselves about a magnetic pole'.

Heroic epic was always couched in verse rich in epithets, formulae and more or less memorized 'runs'. The mixed prose-and-verse form current among the Kazakhs and Özbegs was absent. Drama as a distinct form was wholly lacking. The dramatic mode was expressed as an undifferentiated ingredient of heroic narrative performed with histrionic effects. The epic of *Joloy*, taken from the Soltu tribe, surprisingly, is in part mock-epic (5,000 lines). It also contains a satirical Catalogue of Heroes and Heroines.[3] The narrative of *Töštük*, couched in the same diction and metre as those of the more strictly heroic epics, with its Underworld subject-matter is already in the mid-nineteenth-century version moving towards the fantastic twentieth-century version of Sayakbay, who loads on to the old shamanistic hero-tale more than it can bear.[4] As far as I am aware, the only genre of poetry other than heroic epic recorded by a scholar of the mid-nineteenth century is the Lament for a Dead Warrior. Two examples were recorded by Radlov: but even if these had not been extant, the genre could have been inferred from the Lament for the Dead Manas improvised by his widow Kanıkey in Radlov's sixth episode from *Manas*. The metre of the two recorded laments and of Kanıkey's lament for Manas is that of the epic, and their diction overlaps strongly with epic diction.

Apart from heroic epic and lament, Radlov names the following genres as current in the mid-nineteenth century: 'proverbs and old sayings in the most marvellously intricate rhymes, love-songs, historical songs, songs sung in rivalry,[5] wedding-songs . . . even comic songs', for the most part capable of improvisation.

A remarkable development of the middle decades of the present century is the recasting of Central Asian epic matter in operatic form, including the epics of the Kirghiz *Manas*-cycle.

Kirghiz heroic poetry, though alive today, is probably moribund. Like all heroic traditions of the Soviet Union it is under close political scrutiny. Sedentarization spells the end of herder-nomadism in the wild regions that fostered the tradition. Modern forms of communication are also having their effect. It is symptomatic of the present state of the tradition that the greatest bard of the recent past, Sayakbay Karalaev (b. 1894) became a celebrated radio personality.

By a sad irony, the licensed collecting zeal of Kirghiz patriots and intellectuals in the twenties and thirties of this century proved self-frustrating and must long remain so, since it led to an accumulation of material so uncritical and so vast — four million lines are said to have been recorded — that even if teams of first-class scholars were there to edit and analyse it, the task could not be accomplished in our time. Thus, of this twentieth-century material only a few longer episodes from live bardic performances, probably recorded under laboratory conditions, have been published and they were published in cheap popular editions, virtual chap-books, with bridging passages sometimes in prose. There is also an ambitious harmonized version of the *Manas*-cycle in four volumes; but this is almost useless for scholarly purposes since one cannot tell where the version of one bard ends and that of another begins or where an educated poet-harmonizer has furnished links and embellishments. While it is of great interest in itself and also for the purposes of this investigation to see from these twentieth-century recordings how traditional heroic material has been accommodated first by Sagymbay Orozbakov (1867–1930) to Pan-Islamic and then by Sayakbay to contemporary ideology, for the reasons given no attempt will be made here to present the twentieth-century material as such, though it will be drawn upon where appropriate. Despite the failure of the men of the twenties and thirties to restrain their bards from unmanageable inflation of themes, they made invaluable observations on live performances and on the antecedents, apprenticeship and careers of living or recent bards.

Thanks to the interest of the two great travellers Radlov and Chokan Valikhanov, some 23,000 lines of mid-nineteenth-century Kirghiz heroic poetry distributed over a variety of themes are on record. The greater share of almost 20,000 lines falls to Radlov, of which 12,454 are from the cycle of the national hero Manas (9,449 for Manas himself, 3,005 for his son Semetey); 5,322 for Joloy; and 2,146 for Er Töstük. These recordings were published by Radlov in 1885.

A further 3,251 lines (according to the numeration in my edition)[6] had been collected by Valikhanov in 1856, but the precious manuscript was lost sight of until Professor A. Margulan discovered it in 1964.[7] Until then only the first third of it had been available since 1902 in Valikhanov's stylish but at times somewhat inaccurate prose rendering 'Kukotay'. Valikhanov's recording of 1856 most fortunately runs parallel to Radlov's episode 1, 4) 'Bok-murun'.[8] Both variants have as their theme 'The Memorial Feast for Kökötöy-khan' (*Kökötöydün ašı*), celebrated also in twentieth-century epic. Valikhanov's variant is referred to here as *Kökötöy* for short (though Kökötöy-khan has died by line 164).

It is this mid-nineteenth-century material that will be surveyed below.

Radlov recorded his texts in 1862 while with the Bugu and in 1869 when among the Sary Bagysh and Soltu tribes. Like the German verse-translation in a separate volume which came out in the same year of 1885, Radlov's Kirghiz texts are hasty, but they yield to the normal processes of editing. In his introduction Radlov shows himself astonishingly well-aware of the implications of Kirghiz oral heroic tradition for the Homeric problem and he anticipated Milman Parry in important matters of principle. Yet, as was said, Radlov's texts and translations leave something to be desired. For all his unique merits as the great pioneer of Turkology, Radlov was not a first-rate textual scholar and probably least so in Kirghiz. One's gratitude and admiration for his irreplaceable thesaurus of Kirghiz texts is thus tempered with sorrow at his indifferent management of some of them, for which the absence of a reliable dictionary, the haste required by his vast enterprises, and the imaginary need to translate into verse, may be held in part responsible. As to Valikhanov, whereas he was understandably more shaky on Homer, as a grandson of the last Khan of the Kazakh Middle Horde he showed a finer grasp of Kirghiz heroic diction and indeed translated it into flexible poetic prose that often echoed the structure of the original. Yet Valikhanov was no textual scholar, and was not above tampering with the text.

It is only in the above sense that the word 'text' applies to what were in fact ephemeral oral improvisations. It is paradoxical that one should have to edit Radlov's recordings critically. Furthermore, Radlov himself was well aware of the distorting effect on his bard of dictation to long-hand, *tête-à-tête*. His remarks on this point reveal a desire for some instantaneous form of sound-recording — which was in fact being developed by Edison at that time.

The method of composition and performance was that of improvisation on traditional themes in terms of well-worn formulae.

Bards inflected their voices to suit the subject-matter of the moment, and accompanied their performances with traditional histrionic gestures acquired by study. Normally, *akın* (bards in the widest sense) performed to a musical accompaniment on the *komuz*, a three-stringed instrument which seems to have been plucked, not bowed like the Kazakh *kobız*. But specialists in *Manas*, known as *manasčı*, usually dispensed with such musical accompaniment and sang with changes of musical mode in sympathy with the content. For the mid-nineteenth century, Radlov notes that the singer availed himself of two melodies, the one in a quicker tempo serving for the narration of facts, the other a solemn recitative in a slower tempo for dialogue. Concerning twentieth-century bards, K. Rakhmatullin states that they frequently varied the melody according to what was being narrated. Although competitive performances (*aytıš*) of *akın* are known in other contexts, epic was delivered by a single bard. The overriding technique of composition and performance was improvisation on a formulaic basis; nevertheless longer memorized 'runs' or purple patches were often incorporated. Of such by far the most remarkable are the set Invocations of the Forty Companions by Manas in moments of need or peril occurring in each major episode of the cycle. Once or twice in the texts there is a verbal overlap between Manas's 'Forty Companions' and the Forty *Čilten* or 'Helping spirits' commanded by *bakšı* in a great part of Central Asia. Moreover *manasčı* used to recite epic as a therapeutic means, notably for barrenness and childbirth, in which they again resemble the *bakšı*. When one adds to this the fact that it was normal for *manasčı* to begin their bardic careers only on being summoned in a vision by Manas and his men and that novices would even sleep at Manas's supposed tomb in the Talas Valley, the shamanistic background of their vocation and style of performance becomes clear. The legend of the bard Keldibek Barıboz, said to have lived from 1757 to the 1880s, completes the picture, since it implies possession of the bard by the hero he sings, as the Tibetan bard was possessed by the spirit of Geser or the Ostyak by that of his hero. — 'Before Keldibek began a performance of *Manas* he told the herdsmen that they might come to the camp without fear because their cattle would go home by themselves, and no one — neither man nor wild beast — could steal even the last sheep whilst he was singing *Manas*. But when he began to sing, the yurt trembled, a mighty hurricane arose amid whose murk and din supernatural horsemen, Companions of Manas, flew down so that the earth shuddered beneath their horses' hooves.' Nevertheless, to those versed in such matters it will come as no surprise that bards who received their call from Manas were also trained in their art by senior *manasčı* for years. To bards and audiences alike this was no contradiction.

The Keldibek legend captures the spell-binding swiftness and ecstasy with which the Kirghiz bards delivered their epics, yet despite the frenzied style of improvisation, Kirghiz heroic epic was narrated mostly in an objective third-personal convention in apparent contrast to the above-mentioned facts and their reflection in legend pointing to a more shamanistic style in the past. It is as though with increasing objectivity third-personal narration had ousted the first-personal except in the ecstatic 'Invocations of the Forty Companions', in which the hero naturally speaks in the first person. Such an explanation, however, would be facile. As can be seen from Ostyak and Ainu epic (not to mention Books Nine to Twelve of the *Odyssey*) a very high degree of objectivity can be attained in heroic narrative in the first person. It is unlikely that third-personal narrative in Kirghiz epic emerged entirely from first-personal narrative. In view of the long history of the Turkic-speaking peoples and of the fact that even their most archaic off-shoot, the Yakut, had a highly developed third-personal epic style in the *oloŋxo*, often with marked shamanistic content, it is more likely that a first-personal shamanistic tradition centred on the cult of Manas fused with an already well established tradition of narrative in the third person.

Other interesting features in the use of persons are occasional apostrophe of a hero to express the bard's and the audience's sympathy, as in Homer, or the attachment of the possessive particle of the second person familiar (despite the plurality of listeners) to the name or epithet of a favourite character, as for example:

> Er Manastay baatırıŋ
> Özübekni tüzötkön!

('*Your beloved* warrior Manas taught a lesson to the Özbegs!',
Kökötöy, 3242 f.)

The implication in the latter instance is that the hero thus designated is dear to each single member of the audience. Another device more rarely used by the bard to convey sympathy was to add the possessive particle of the first person to a character's name, as in Čakanım '*my* Čakan' (referring to Manas's old mother).

Radlov regarded the diction of the Kirghiz epics as absolutely contemporary. Compared with the diction of Homer, who was much in Radlov's thoughts at the time, his assessment may be relatively true. But Radlov was not firm enough in his Kirghiz to judge this question reliably. The magnificent Kirghiz–Russian dictionary of K. K. Yudakhin designates no few words and expressions as 'epic'. The implication would seem to be that even if the Kirghiz knew the vocabulary of *Manas* by heart they distinguished certain of its epithets and formulae as not in ordinary use. The bard of *Kökötöy* in particular used words of Mongol and Persian origin not listed in Yudakhin's dictionary. My impression is that the mid-nineteenth-century bard's striving for a highly ornate diction embraced the archaic as well as the exotic.

Consideration of the style of Kirghiz epic performance naturally led to mention of various types of bard. What was said above must be supplemented now.

The traditional name for an improvisator–performer of epic was *jomokču*, from *jomok* 'heroic song'. Only in the twentieth century did *manasčı* ('specialists in *Manas*') and *semeteyči* ('specialists in *Semetey* and *Seytek*') arise. *ırčı* (from *ır* 'song') normally did not improvise epic and only knew some passages by heart. The *ırčı* partly overlapped with the *akın* — poet–improvisators, even educated men, who did not concern themselves with epic. The creative *jomokču* or *manasčı*, who was expected to be able to sing the 'whole' of *Manas*, has been likened to the Greek ἀοιδός and the uncreative *irči* to the ῥαψῳδός.

Epic singers were always of the male sex and usually came from the lower strata. Instances are known of the sons or nephews of celebrated bards also becoming bards.

The extant *Manas*-material of the mid-nineteenth century falls into four groups: A, *The Birth of Manas* (1, 1); B, *Almambet, Er Kökčö and Ak-erkeč* (1, 2), — *Bok-murun* (1, 4), *Köz-Kaman* (1, 5), *The Birth of Semetey* (1, 6), *Semetey* (1, 7); C, *Battle between Manas and Kökčö* etc. (1, 3); D, *Kökötöy*. Groups A, C, and D each have a distinct bard and date. Whether Group B was recorded from one bard or from one and the same school of bards remains to be resolved.[9]

The number of variables in Manas's flimsy pedigree suggests at least five different traditions in eastern Kirgizia alone for this one topic. On the basis of twentieth-century material, Soviet scholars tend to distinguish two major schools of *manasči*: but this may be due to an illusion created by the overpowering figures of Sagymbay and Sayakbay. Such a grouping would in any case leave out of account the possibility of discrepant traditions among the many tribal groups not represented in the recorded texts, not least the Kirghiz of Sinkiang, of whose heroic poetry nothing seems to have been recorded.

The occasions on which epic poetry was performed ranged from the casual and informal to the festive and ritual. The Kirghiz nomadized in large groups, and there were ample opportunities for entertainment at their encampments should a bard be of their number. On the other hand, well-known bards, who according to Radlov formed a professional caste, were summoned to such formal gatherings as weddings and above all funeral repasts, which were held by wealthy clans on fixed days. To one familiar with the passages in Homer and *Beowulf* in which bards are shown performing at court, it seems a loss that no *jomokču* is featured in the White Pavilion in either of the two extant versions of the *Memorial Feast for Kökötöy-khan*. Nor is Manas's Warrior-Companion Irči-uul (whose name contains the element 'singer') ever shown performing in the older poems.

The professional bards were eminently fostered by the patronage of the sultans and other men of means. Bards were adept in alluding in their preludes to notables who were present or in connecting the latters' lineages with those of the epic heroes, but they could change their tune when faced with a plebeian audience. The relationship of the bard to his audience both high and low was indeed a vital one, for he sought to discover a theme that would suit their mood, while they in turn incited him to feats of virtuosity with their applause. At such peaks of fervour, when the bard and his listeners were as one, the patron would rise, peel off a costly robe and throw it to the triumphant performer. In Radlov's day, clearly, the intimate equilibrium between bard, patron and audience, so typical of well-established oral traditions of poetry, was still in being. Allusions in the two variants of *Kökötöy* to the anti-Chinese uprising of Jaŋır-kojo in 1822–28 show that the exiled Muslim merchants of Kashgar and their friends in Kokand had found a way of turning Kirghiz heroic poetry to their own account. It would be of interest to know whether this was achieved through connexions with the tribal leaders or directly with the bards.

The nineteenth-century Kirghiz epic poems are for the most part informed by an unmistakably 'heroic' ethos. It is an ethos that binds a warlike lord — *törö* — to his companions or retainers — *čoro* — and it is an ethos that is as frank as it is free. The lord expects obedience and courage from his followers, and they expect leadership and courage from their lord and will rebuke him to his face if he falls short. The bond has variations both subtle and strong. In the episode of *Köz-kaman*, Serek, one of Manas's Forty, resents the favoured position of the Oirot prince Almambet, the outsider who has become Manas's milk-brother and right-hand man. Serek picks a quarrel with Almambet and receives Almambet's horse-lash across his cheek, but in dread of his lord refrains from paying back the blow and addresses himself to Manas with a demand for justice. Manas's reply is that of a leader of men:

> 'The nobly born Almambet
> In his rage will strike you, Serek,
> In his rage will strike me, Manas.'
> Then cried Serek, passionately weeping —
> 'Oh, what are you saying, my lord?
> Always, always
> Do you side with Almambet!'
> Wiping the blood from Serek's cheek
> Manas rode out with his comrade
> To feast with his new-found kinsmen . . . (I, 5), 1410 ff.)

With its greater length and looser, more rapid style of composition and delivery, Kirghiz epic offers fewer pithy formulations of the heroic ethos, for example, than the Germanic lay.[10] Yet formulations occur in Kirghiz which leave little to choose between the two traditions for compactness and absoluteness. One such example is found in the episode of *Bok-murun*[11] in which Manas formulates the mutual debt between himself and his Companions:

> 'I heaped up corslets for your sakes, Comrades,
> Die amid lance-thrusts for my sake, Comrades;
> I heaped up swords for your sakes, Comrades,
> Perish together for my sake, Comrades!' (I, 4), 2143 ff.)

The freedom of the lame master-armourer within his allegiance to his lord emerges from a passage in the same poem. At the height of a battle, Manas sends to the smith to demand a shattered sword that was to have been reforged: if it is not ready the smith shall die! The old man brings the sword to Manas in person, riding the many miles between:

'Have you made my sword, Master?
Have you forged my corslet, Master?'
The lame artificer gave answer:
'I have made your sword, Hothead,
I have forged your corslet, Hothead.
I will tell you the nature of the sword, Hothead.
Not enduring the forging, Hothead,
My spirit was much tormented, Hothead.
Not enduring the filing, Hothead,
Fifty files were shattered, Hothead.
Not enduring the blows, Hothead,
My sledge-hammers were shattered, Hothead,
Not enduring the pressure
My 'Children'[12] could not abide it, Hothead.
So that the blade should be yellow, I thought,
I tempered its edge with venom, Hothead —
Do not swing it at yourself, Hothead!
Thrust it where strife is hard, Hothead!' (I, 4), 1680 ff.)

There never was a risk that the smith would lose his life over the sword, since the bond that unites the two is a sure one.

Relations between warriors and their womenfolk are of a piece with their relations with one another, for women had a respected place in Kirghiz heroic society. Warrior-maidens, sometimes conceived of as swan-battle-maidens as in the epic of Manas's only son Semetey, are widely known in Central Asian heroic epic and story. As in other heroic traditions, heroes' wives in Kirghiz epic often have clairvoyant powers, and their dreams and forebodings are disregarded in the same way by menfolk who have to show blind courage. In *Köz-kaman*, Manas's favourite wife Kanıkey urges that the time is inauspicious for war-like deeds and tries to hold her husband back from his raid against the Kalmak. Manas's reply is to seize his twelve-stranded lash and bring it down on Kanıkey so that her silk tunic splits at the seams and its pearls and coral are strewn on the path. With peals of laughter she chides Manas and sends him with a blessing on his way. Another of Manas's wives, Akılay, seeks to detain him with the same portents, but in response to his angry blow curses him and his enterprise. Manas of course rides into the trouble foreseen by Kanıkey, but with prayers to his protecting spirit she averts the effects of Akılay's curse. It is Kanıkey again who at her lord's death will lament him in verse, give birth to his only son Semetey, heroically save Semetey from his presumably half-Kalmak cousins, and, finally, rear the boy to vengeance.

The tough ethos conveyed through the characters of heroes and heroines of epic poetry is convincingly referred by Radlov to the need of the Kirghiz of his day to be ready to fight at any time for their survival. In order to ward off sudden attack they nomadized not in auls like the Kazakh but in whole tribes, taking all their herds. Their life on a permanent war footing explains both the ethos of their heroic poetry and that poetry's 'epic time', according to which heroes of the mythic, the historic and most recent personal pasts are merged in one continuum.

As befits a people who lacked the institution of the khanate, genealogies in Kirghiz epic (but only here) are of the haziest. The only certain forbear of Manas in the songs is his father Jakıp (i.e. Yakub or Jacob). The names of his mother and grand-father fluctuate. The only hero with an established three-tier pedigree is Kökčö, son of Aydar-khan son of Kambar-khan. Although Kirghiz tribes are rarely named in the heroic songs, Radlov was able to record that the bards complimented illustrious patrons by linking their ancestors with heroes of epic. Since there are no extant examples it would be hazardous to guess how this was done; but it may well have been worked into the beginning of a performance when a bard was warming up.[13]

It has already been noted that novice *manasčı* repaired to the so-called 'Tomb of Manas' as part of their initiation. Whether this is a reflection of a more widespread cult of heroes that was later monopolized by Manas does not emerge.

The mere 'knocking out' and resuscitation of heroes[14] must blur the feeling for tragedy. Grief for the dead is channelled into set laments based, as was said, on a separate genre, a genre which is ancient in Turkic poetry.[15] In one episode the grief of Manas's steed, hound and falcon for their dead master is movingly conveyed:

> White-Bay, steed of Er Manas,
> Before the Palace of the Day,
> Before the Palace of the Night
> Drank no water with a 'Gulp!'
> Champed no millet with a 'Crunch!'.
> Flies had drained his ribs of blood:
> On guard before the shrine he neighed.
> At the foot of Manas' Tomb
> The gaunt image of White-bay —
> Before the Palace of the Day,
> Before the Palace of the Night
> Gazing up at heaven he whinnied:
> Skin and bone, White-bay was gaunt.

Fastened to his golden leash,
Fenced in by his silver cangue
The White-gerfalcon of Manas
Struck the geese and set them cackling,
Struck the swans and set them whooping,
Piled them in three lowly hills —
Did not tear and eat the game.
Above the Palace of the Day
Gazing up to heaven she screamed.
Her ears like spikes, her nipples forty,
The hero's White-borzoi was there:
From the sands she seized the kulan,
From the slopes the mountain ram,
Twisting double seized the maral,
Piled them in three lowly hills —
Did not tear and eat the game.
Gazing up to heaven she howled:
Barren she, her teats run dry.[16]

Faced with the death of their lord, the Companions are less lyrical, since one of their number takes it upon himself stoically to counsel the others to carry on, leaving us with the sense that the survival of the tribe, not that of its greatest leader, is the most important thing. In the twentieth-century variants the supremely tragic figure is Almambet, the alien bosom-friend of Manas and object of unending jealousy among the retinue.

When Radlov considered the role of supernatural and unnatural elements in Kirghiz epic, what struck him most was their subordination as ornament and background to the natural and realistic, especially where human characterization is concerned. Indeed, in nineteenth-century Kirghiz epic the powers of the warriors are for the most part heroically human. Yet in certain crises their powers may be shamanistically superhuman. In the episode in which he battles with Er Kökčö, Manas and his steed Ak-kula have powers of flight equal to those of Er Kökčö and his mount, though in the neutralization of firearms Er Kökčö is superior (1, 3), 231 ff.). Allusion has already been made to the shamanistic nature of Manas's Invocation of the Forty and to his capacity to revive from seeming death, even after giving the death-rattle (1, 5), 2420). In the latter case, however, older shamanistic notions merge with more recent Islamic lore of Central Asia, for Manas owes his come-back against Kökčö-köz to a protecting spirit or holyman, Kan Kojo of Mecca. In another episode in which Manas revives after being laid to rest in his tomb he is watched over by angels from Heaven. The epithets of Almambet — 'Kite of the Hills' and 'Grey-mane He-wolf' — are, as a pair, clearly shamanistic, yet although shamanistic traits are prominent in Almambet in the twentieth-century recordings, chiefly traits of a dreaded weather-shaman, they are relatively few and restrained in nineteenth-century Kirghiz epic, which serves to underline the exceptional courage of a man who fights doggedly on, though his body be full of arrows and his lord has fled the field. As to the women, their gift of second sight is matched by the magic of their drugs, in need of which their men so obstinately place themselves.

The mid-nineteenth-century epics in the Kirghiz tongue are seemingly not concerned with the Kirghiz. They are instead concerned with the 'Nogoy'. In Kirghiz epic of this time the Nogoy stood to the Kirghiz rather as Homer's Achaeans stood to the Greeks. Yet the Nogoy were heroes of a Heroic Age which, unlike the Greek Heroic Age, reached almost into the present, in this case the mid-nineteenth century. The Kirghiz bards seem to have inherited the Nogoy from the Kazakhs, whose legends took them from the historic Nogoy. The Nogoy or Nogay of history were a group of Tatar tribes who assumed the name of the great emir Nogay after his defeat and death in 1299. They were a southern constituent of the Golden Horde. Nogay's brilliant achievements grew in legend until in the fifteenth century it was fabled that the Khans of the White Horde were his descendants.

In Kirghiz epic of the mid-nineteenth century, however, this was all forgotten. There the Nogoy were idealized Kirghiz projected into a continuum spanning the past and near-present. That Kirghiz are so prominent by name in twentieth-century versions of *Manas* is entirely due to patriotic, even nationalistic tampering with the tradition.

Furthermore, from what has been said above concerning the summons of the bard from on high, of attendance by the novice at Manas's tomb and of the presentation of heroes both ancient and modern as contemporaries, it is clear that the Kirghiz of the mid-nineteenth century did not question the historicity of *Manas*, however it may have been with such fantastic 'epics' as *Töštük*. The immediacy of the traces left by Manas and his Companions in Kirghiz place-names was enhanced by that of the hero's possession of the bard. There was an expectation that Manas and his men could, even would return.

Although Kirghiz epic is precise in its time-sequences within a given action, it shows further weakness in periodization when it turns the originally historical Agıš (a Nogay mirza, son of Yamgurchi, fl. 1521) into a tribal ancestor who lives in a cave, and then makes him the contemporary of Manas and his men.[17]

Thus the times presented in the episodes of *Manas* were no golden age that was over and done with. The far-flung conquests attributed to Manas and his Nogoy express a belief in what the Kirghiz were imagined once to have been and might yet be again. The epic dream of the Kirghiz held, and perhaps still holds out to them consolation for an indefinite present of weakness, and also hope of a more splendid future. Implicit in the mid-nineteenth-century material (which is harshly existential), this outlook had become explicit by the twenties of this century, and even the version of Sayakbay, recorded in the thirties, is strongly imbued with Kirghiz nationalism, which expressed itself chiefly as hostility towards the still 'feudal' Chinese and Kalmak, on the lines laid down by tradition. Light is perhaps thrown on these attitudes by a question put to Dr Rémy Dor by one of the Kirghiz of the Afghan Pamir during his recent field-work among them: 'Are there descendants of Manas still living in the Soviet Union?'[18]

If the heroes and heroines of mid-nineteenth-century Kirghiz epic were grouped in a tableau they would form a steep pyramid with Manas for apex and the others ranged below him in degrees till at its base there would be most of his Forty, who though named in his Invocations with single unchanging epithets to characterize their functions, scarcely ever play an individual part in action. Yet this picture needs correcting in one particular. The pathos of Almambet, the Mongol exile and intruder into Nogoy–Kirghiz society, is such that he tends often to steal the limelight from his lord, a tendency greatly enhanced in the twentieth century.

Features shared by the Nogoy and shared with heroes of some other heroic traditions are these. 'Heroes' to Kirghiz audiences, the Nogoy are 'men' to one another — the word er covers both shades of meaning and may also be used as an honorific, as in 'Er Manas'. The more formidable heroes, however, often have metaphorical epithets that derive their force from birds or beasts of prey: from the dread but indeterminate feline kabılan (normally rendered as 'Tiger'), less frequently from the Lion; the Wolf; the Stallion; the Bull; the Golden Eagle; the Falcon; the Hawk; the Kite. Paired, the (Grey-mane He-) Wolf and the Kite (of-the-Hills) form an archaic shamanistic epithet for Almambet as we have seen (p. 311 above). Whether the animal names of the poisoners Kaman-köz ('Pig-eye') and Kökčöö-köz ('Jackal-eye') of the earliest discernible version of Köz-kaman would have sounded more heroic in pre-Islamic times, as perhaps 'Boar-eye', is unclear.[19] On the other hand 'Grey-mane' for 'Wolf', the animal symbol par excellence of steppe-warriors, is ancient and well-attested.

Heroes utter dire threats of total destruction and extirpation in the form: 'If I do not do this and that (e.g., take your winged steed, your White Pavilion, seize your daughters by their white wrists . . .), may my name wither!' The notion that a warrior's name should perish in the event of his threat not being fulfilled is sometimes taken for granted so that the formula then runs merely 'If I do not do this and that . . .'. Negatively, then, fame is identified with a hero's very existence. But positively action is undertaken in the first place not in order to gain kudos but to gain booty, either from rapacity or in revenge. In the giving of Khan Kökötöy's Funeral Repast, however, the pursuit of fame and the discharge of a moral duty towards the dead are merged. At such feasts, as at feasts among Celtic warriors, great care had to be shown by the host lest any hero receive a cut from the joint inappropriate to his standing, an ancient custom of the steppe not confined to those of Turkic speech. A motive for unprovoked raiding can be the fine fettle of steeds grown sleek whilst heroes frowst.

Dwellers of the T'ien Shan, the 'Nogoy', like other heroic mountaineers, despise the plainsman.[20]

What is the gain of all this fighting? A comment by Radlov is revealing. He likens the forays and battles of the nomads of Kirghiz epic to the violent flooding of a river that 'covers broad stretches of country, demolishes places of cultivation and culture, but having reached the peak of its strenuous expansion always flows back into its old bed. We witness battle upon battle yet no tangible outcome of the vast exertion of force. We see heroes pass from the scene and recognize in their offspring a new race who in fresh battles achieve only what their parents achieved and thus squander their strength vainly once again'.[21] Yet the free will of the heroes in action is unhampered by any presentiment of futility. The ancient figure of Kudai, who writes the fates of warriors in his Book as in the more primitive Siberian hero-tales, merges with an Allah who hears the prayers of the good.

After these general remarks some heroes and heroines can be considered individually.

It has emerged that Manas is the paramount hero and indeed a national hero who enshrined the virtues and best hopes of the Kirghiz. But the interesting thing about him and the tradition which he incorporates is that his superlative traits are tempered with human frailty, with the result that such hyperbolic absurdities as we meet with in Firdusi's Rustum or the Georgian Amiran are largely absent. An intriguing example, baffling as life itself, is found in *Köz-kaman*, where Manas's steed Ak-kula carries him from the field at the height of the battle against the Kalmak whilst he apparently accepts the situation, until his friend Almambet, more seriously wounded than he, rides back to rebuke and rally him. The commander's seeming lapse gains emphasis from the fact that his standard-bearer's mount has been hobbled to prevent sudden flight. Manas chides his friend in turn for his lack of faith and leads his men to victory. The aura that surrounds him has suffered no detriment, his humanity has gained mysteriously. As with Almambet, the bards invest Manas with pathos — the pathos of an only son.[22] The precariousness of Manas's existence was emphasized at his conception, since prior to it (following the bard of Radlov's first episode)[23] his mother had long been barren. Manas's epithet 'Tiger-born'[24] (conferred by bards of later episodes) may rest on his mother's having drunk tiger-soup during her pregnancy with magical intent, as Sagymbay will relate in extenso; but in any case it portends his fierceness as a warrior.

Another epithet 'Blood-born' (also known from bards of later episodes) refers
to his having descended from the womb grasping a blood-clot, a portent of
conquest. In his boyhood and youth Manas has the epithet 'Hothead' or
'Madcap', he is rebellious towards his father Jakıp and is capable of laying
hands on him. Towards his Companions, Manas is magnanimous and indulgent,
towards his wives kind-hearted so long as they do not cite their omens to turn
him from his path. As to his appearance, 'his face is like that of the bear in the
forest, his head like that of the tiger on the mountain-spur'. His steed 'Ak-kula
beneath him is like the lofty green shoulder of Mount Bölčör, our lord seated
upon him is like a god touching the sky above its pass . . .'.

By now Almambet is known to the reader in outline. It is above all in virtue of
Almambet that one can claim for Kirghiz epic a maturity often lacking in
other traditions. For if intolerance of the Kalmak is perpetuated in Kirghiz epic,
this is transcended in the person of Manas's most loyal and self-sacrificing
friend, a former 'Kalmak'[25] for whom Čakan's withered breasts flow again that
he may become the milk-brother of her only son. The upshot of the contrast
with Manas's kalmakized cousin Kökčö-köz is that a Kalmak upbringing may
ruin a man of Nogoy stock, whereas assimilation of good Kalmak material to
the Nogoy way of life can make a man. Almambet's outstanding courage and
his shamanistic aspects have been touched upon, also his imperious correction
of the fractious Serek, as befits a Chinggisid of the 'White Bone'. Another
aspect of his unusually rich character is illuminated by his dealings with
Kökčö, with whose prudent wife he maintained a pure relationship founded
upon mutual respect, a relationship inspired on both sides solely by the best
interests of Kökčö.

Er Kökčö, the epitome of mean khans, marks the opposite pole to Manas,
who by his munificence gains the outstanding vassal whom Kökčö loses.
Kökčö, moreover, publicly upbraids the wife whose shrewd counsels for the
good of his tribe he fails to appreciate, and he adds insult to injury by suffering
others to slander her.

The young Bok-murun, natural son of the hero Töštük and adoptive son of
Kökötöy-khan, fulfils the latter's dying Behest with exemplary competence.[26]
He accompanies his invitations to the heroes with threats — none of which he
needs to carry out since they all accept. Any other exploits that Bok-murun
had to his name seem to have been obliterated by progressive assimilation of
Kökötöy to the *Manas*-cycle.[27]

The figure of Khan Kökötöy himself is expressive both of the Kirghiz
idealization of the Khans whom history denied them and of their veneration
for the old and wise. Kökötöy is introduced in Valikhanov's variant as 'the
Father of the teeming Nogoy', and his Behest for his people is far-sighted.

Another venerable figure is that of the Kazakh hero Er Košoy, to whom
(before Manas) victorious raids to the East were attributed, so that he came to

be associated in epic with the historical Muslim leader Janır-kojo.[28] Despite his great age, Košoy is a formidable wrestler, the only man on Manas's side who can take on the infidel Joloy; but this he declines to do until Manas's wife Kanıkey has given him a stout new pair of breeches. An intriguing aspect of Košoys' character is that when he is invited to face Joloy he excuses himself with a catalogue of his 'defeats', which proves to be a sly form of boasting.

Er Töštük rides his famous winged steed Čal-kuyruk ('Grey-tail')[29] through the Underworld to recover his soul, which his father, the mean Khan Eleman, has jeopardized too frivolously. If *Töštük* is obviously shamanistic in origin, the playing down of Töštük's intelligence and command of supernatural powers in favour of his physical prowess must be regarded as 'heroization'. In any case, *Töštük* is not an epic but a hero-tale inflated by every device of epic diction.

Beside the mean khans Kökčö and Eleman, there is the feckless khan Jakıp, Manas's father. Although Jakıp undertakes the arduous wooing of a wife for Manas, he breaks faith with her after Manas's death and joins Abeke and Köböš, his sons by a presumably Kalmak wife,[30] in their attempt to kill the new-born Semetey and possess Kanıkey. Only in the *Birth of Manas*, recorded from a bard of the Sary Bagysh, does Jakıp seem fit to sire a hero.

Kirghiz respect for age may have led to the dissociation of Köz-kaman from Kökčö-köz, with whom the most archaic allusion links him as a poisoner, and to his transformation into a father who does what he can to thwart his son's treacherous intentions as far as he is aware of them. In this, he shows himself to be a Nogoy who 'remembers'[31] and has become the antithesis of his son, who may have the excuse of a Kalmak mother.[32]

The Sino-Kalmak antagonists Joloy, Konur-bay and Nes Kara merge in their formidable nastiness, except that Joloy has gigantic, even gargantuan qualities. Among the Soltu tribe Radlov took down an epic in which Joloy, astonishingly, is featured as a Nogoy khan. In this roystering epic-cum-mock-epic, as it had better be called, Joloy's phenomenal strength is neutralized by his gluttony and drunkenness, while the narration of his loves provokes the use of Radlov's Latin. But for his heroic wives Ak Saykal and Ak Kanıš, Joloy and all his race would have perished.

Ak Saykal, Ak Kanıš, Ak Erkeč, Čakan and Kanıkey form a gallery of heroic wives who reflect the high status of Turkic noblewomen which they had always enjoyed in the nomadic regions of Central Asia. Ak Erkeč could persist in meeting Almambet even after her honour had been impugned, in order to persuade him not to leave her pusillanimous lord. Kanıkey knows that she will receive the lash for her pains, yet she insists on warning Manas of the danger that threatens him, and when the lash falls smiles with an indulgence free from all servility:[33] we accept her as the same woman who on the nuptial couch had stabbed Manas in the arm for taking liberties. Like Ak Erkeč, Kanıkey seeks to strengthen the bonds that link her lord with his friends by feasting them and bestowing fine gifts, such as Košoy's wrestling-breeches. Her qualities are enhanced by contrast with those of her co-wives the shrewish Akılay and the dull Kara-börük, both of whom Manas picked up on the way, whereas he acquired Kanıkey by regular marriage.

With recordings ranging from 1856 to 1869, development of the mid-nineteenth-century Kirghiz epic tradition can only be inferred, not observed.

The clearly marked plots of *Almambet, Er Kökčö and Ak Erkeč* and of *Köz-kaman*, taken down as episodes of the *Manas*-cycle, are such as with few changes could have been performed as independent lays.[34] Despite their clearly marked beginnings and ends, *The Birth of Semetey* and *Semetey* could be regarded as a sub-divided unity based on a widespread Siberian plot of a son's vengeance for the slaying of his father and his disinheritance.[35] Thus it is possible that these episodes, as they now are, have been integrated into *Manas* by the process of cyclization. Valikhanov writes of the paramouncy of Manas and refers to his epic as 'encyclopedic'. The vast recordings of the twentieth century confirm this tendency, though even today *Manas* has failed to engulf every heroic or near-heroic theme.[36] Despite their phenomenal eloquence, the great bards Sagymbay and Sayakbay have contributed not a little to the decadence of Kirghiz epic by the pursuit of quantity at the expense of quality, quite apart from their tendentiousness. The episodes recorded in the mid-nineteenth century lack the 'literary' polish of Sagymbay's and Sayakbay's variants, but as heroic poetry possess vigorous qualities no longer typical of those variants. These qualities may be summed up as boldness in the bard's shift of attention from theme to theme, detail to detail, and the instant conviction with which he applies traditional formulae to this matter. By contrast, narrative movement in the twentieth-century versions is planned as in a book-epic or novel: threads are dropped and resumed later in a highly self-conscious manner; the use of formulae tends to be lame and even wearisome — especially do the epithets, vital elements of any vigorous heroic tradition, seem mechanically or pretentiously applied in contexts of rationalized narrative. A modern Kirghiz listener, however, might reject this evaluation and prefer to find his pleasure in the astounding feats of virtuosity performed by modern bards exploiting to their limits the rich alliterations, rhymes, chimes, and other ornaments bequeathed to them by tradition.[37]

Development from the mid-nineteenth century to the earlier decades of the twentieth, then, implied a deepening of immanent cyclic tendencies and greater rationalization in terms of book epic (with a marked increase of explicit characterization), for which possibly the Homeric poems and certainly the Persian *dāstān* via Özbeg and Kazakh, and ultimately the European novel will have served as models. The adaptation of themes from *Manas* in opera has already received mention.

II

The themes of Kirghiz heroic poetry are compounded of what the Kirghiz and their ancestors had lived through and of wishful compensation for their confinement in their mountain fastness by stronger powers. On the one hand there are raids and migrations; struggles for supremacy within ruling clans, with treachery, long knives and poison; there are feasting and funeral games; the joys and sorrows of an exiled warrior; and, at the margin, the experiences of a more archaic type of shaman-warrior in the Underworld. On the other hand, there are conquests of much of the known world such as no confederacy that bore the name of 'Kirghiz' could ever have accomplished, not even in the long-forgotten ninth century.

I shall attend here only to those nineteenth-century episodes of *Manas* which I have studied closely.[38] This procedure is well-advised, since attention to the details of epic texts has led to some surprising reversals of judgement. For example, my readers may agree that it is of some importance to know whether a heroine is shown as a faithful or unfaithful wife, or whether an uncle, the central figure of a whole episode, is guilty or innocent of poisoning the main hero. Yet such issues have been falsified in the past by failure to approach the original.

Radlov's *Birth of Manas* (1, 1) recorded in Tokmak in 1869, has, as he rightly surmised, little firm tradition behind it. It names the hero's father and mother, Jakıp-khan and Čıyrıčı; and it states that as a child Manas was reared in concealment, though it offers no reason. On comparison with other texts even 'Čıyrıčı' (which elsewhere has the variant 'Čıyırdı') turns out to be one of three names acquired by the originally nameless 'old woman', that is 'senior wife' of Jakıp-khan, the other two being 'Čakan' and 'Bagdı-döölöt'. The rest of the brief song, which was improvised in answer to Radlov's enquiry about the *Birth*, consists mainly of *topoi* and vague raiding itineraries.

After fourteen years of married life, Čıyırčı conceives only when Jakıp, a more resolute character here than elsewhere, has the *saadak* ('bow-and-arrow-case') bound to her thighs, after which she conceives a heroic man-child. In this version, the traditional epithet is absent according to which Manas, like Chinggis-khan in the thirteenth century and the son of king Mahāsena in Buddhist legend of *c*. A.D. 300, descends from the womb grasping a blood-clot.[39] A second epithet, not entirely confined to Manas — 'Tiger-born'[40] — is also absent from Radlov's *Birth*.

The remainder of the *Birth of Manas* deals with the hero's rapid growth to early manhood and the conquering expeditions against non-Muslims to east and west which he plans to mount. Unlike itineraries in some other texts, those outlined here tend to be wild: local place-names of Kirgizia and Kazakhstan are jumbled together with irrelevant and remote ones like 'Medina's Desert'.

In view of the wishful 'Great Expedition' to Pekin of twentieth-century versions, it is interesting that there is twice mention here of setting out for Pekin; but all that is claimed to have been achieved is the driving of the Chinese of Kashgar towards (Uch-)Turfan, and those of (Uch-)Turfan towards Aksu, that is, locally in an east–north–east direction along the southern foothills of the Kokshaal Tau Range, a reminiscence in epic of the events of Jaŋır-kojo's Rising.[41] Another interesting feature of the *Birth* is that Manas will overcome all, not only Chinese and Kalmak, but also 'Kazakh' and 'Kirghiz', these last because, as elsewhere, Manas is conceived of as a Khan of the epic 'Nogoy'. The Russian Protector is passed over in silence.

Radlov's second episode (1, 2), recorded in 1862 among the Bugu tribe, is that of *Almambet, Er Kökčö and Ak Erkeč*, the simple action of which I have compared elsewhere with a far more intricate sequence in the medieval German *Nibelungenlied*.[42] Here, the Oirot prince Almambet, impelled by longing for Islam, comes to the shores of Lake Issyk, meets the Khan Er Kökčö and is converted. Failing to convert his father the Oirot Khan and his people, Almambet slays them in their myriads and becomes an exile in the service of Kökčö. Thanks to Almambet's auspicious nature, Kökčö's people prosper as never before, but his Forty Comrades are overshadowed. They therefore conspire and accuse Almambet before Kökčö of sleeping with Kökčo's senior wife Ak Erkeč, who is as politic as she is lovely. The junior wife, Buuday-bek, who is as silly as she is lovely, corroborates the trumped-up charge. Almambet's magnificent response is to shout for arak as though he were lord there — for arak which ought to have been offered him on entering the Khan's yurt. Kökčö furiously dismisses him, but with dire threats Almambet demands as reward for his services Kökčö's personal accoutrements and 'Tekeči's Steed' — a steed known in nineteenth-century Kirghiz epic only as a fabulous prize, either in threats or in boasts. While no man stirs under Almambet's dread aspect, Kökčö withholds the gifts. Almambet leaves in his own good time. Ak Erkeč, whose feelings for the youthful Almambet are (if anything) maternal goes out to him to persuade him to wait, and then returns to her feeble spouse with the wise advice to meet Almambet's just demands and so ensure their prosperity. But the mean Khan delays too long, so that when he at last sallies out with the gifts, Almambet is gone. Almambet is to become the friend of a more generous lord, the friend of a Khan who on sight will offer just such gifts as Kökčö has withheld, the friend of no other than the great Er Manas.

Kökötöy and *Bok-murun* are variants of one and the same notional poem — in the realm of oral improvised re-creation there can of course be no such thing as 'the same poem'. The two variants are structurally very close yet vary greatly in the ways in which the two bards realize the potentialities of the largely shared structure. Elsewhere I have attempted to convey the shared situation in terms of an image which has analogies in the bardic terminology of other traditions: 'It is as though the bards held switches in their hands whose buds they could charm into leaves, side-shoots, blossoms or whole sprays, or let sleep, at will.'[43] *Kökötöy* and *Bok-murun* have some eleven major narrative constituents in common and they employ them virtually in the same order.

The major theme of the Memorial Feast for Kökötöy-khan (*Kökötöy*) is the ancient Inner Asian theme of the Funeral — here Memorial — Feast for a Hero, with Horse-race, Games and Heroic Brawling, such as are reflected in the Twenty-third Book of the *Iliad*. The eleven constituents are briefly these: the death of the aged Kökötöy (richly developed in *Kökötöy*, badly skimped in *Bok-murun*); assumption of leadership by Kökötöy's adoptive son Bok-murun, true son of Er Töštük and a fairy, the announcement of his Itinerary to the venue of the Feast, and his invitation to the Muslim and Infidel heroes; arrival of the guests, dominated by Manas; the attempt by the Infidel to extort the famous steed Maniker from Bok-murun; the Horse-race (Start); the Games; the Horse-race (Finish); the disputed Result and Melee; Manas's preparation for war, including the Forging of his Sword; invasion of the Infidel Joloy's lands ending in his death; the return of Manas and his men with booty.[44]

The youthful Bok-murun bears in common with the youthful Tibetan Joru, later to become the great Geser, a name that means 'Snot-nose', chosen to confuse the evil spirits until discarded for a 'man's name' on performance of a first heroic exploit. In *Kökötöy* and *Bok-murun*, the young man acquits himself splendidly by accomplishment of the Itinerary, but then allows his Feast to be taken over by Manas without demur. Destined as son of the great Töštük to perform feats of arms, Bok-murun performs none, and meekly submits to Manas. Thus the two variants show an advanced stage of the assimilation to the *Manas*-cycle of a once independent theme.

The Itinerary in *Bok-murun* is a realistic nomadizing route running fundamentally W.–E. from old Sairam via the Talas and Chu valleys, Karkara and the Ili to a venue between Old and New Kulja. That of Kökötöy, on the other hand, runs N.E. from, probably, Uch Turfan over the Turgen-Aksu Pass past Tarbagatay to the upper reaches of the Black Irtysh on the western slopes of the Altai, whence it plunges into myth and mystery. Bok-murun and his Nogoy are to 'go in to the *tüpkü kan*' — 'the Khan deep down at the roots, i.e. "ancestral"' — for the Repast. This is the only mention of such a personage in Kirghiz epic; and the tradition of the twentieth-century bards places the famous Feast not in the Altai but in the Karkara region. But just such a Turkic khan living in an ancestral cave in the 'Dugin Mountains' (localized in the Altai) do we find in early Chinese sources quoted in a book published in 1851 by Father Hyacinth (N. Ya. Bichurin); and this book and this passage were known to and quoted by Chokan Valikhanov in an essay on the Western Chinese Frontier. In his eager search for ancient traditions of the Kazakh and Kirghiz, the young reconnaissance officer may unwittingly have given his bard an indication of what he hoped to find; or, far less likely, the bard had it from another visiting antiquarian. In his writings Valikhanov frankly avowed that he was seeking oral traditions on the supposed migration of Kirghiz southward from their ancient homeland in the Minussinsk Depression to their present habitat in the T'ien Shan region, and confessed that he had found no such traditions — save this one memorial journey in *Kökötöy*.[45]

There are other indications of innocent antiquarian interference by Valikhanov with the text for which we owe him so much.[46]

An unusual feature of this theme, well attested by both *Kökötöy* and *Bok-murun*, is the association of the aged hero Er Košoy with the Rising of Janır-kojo against the Chinese in 1822–28. Here Košoy and other heroes of epic with old historical names, but now ahistorical figments of the imagination, are found in recordings of 1856 and 1862 at a holy war cheek by jowl with the recently historical Janır although there were Kirghiz greybeards still alive who had fought in the Rising. We recall the belief that Manas would come again. Was there some epico-religious machinery that could project the old heroes into present strife when needed?

The theme of Radlov's fifth episode from the *Manas*-cycle, *Köz-kaman* (1, 5), recorded in 1862 among the Bugu, is the struggle for the Khanate within a ruling clan. It bears a typological resemblance, born of life on the steppe, to the struggle for supremacy of Temujin, the future Chinggis, with his Tayiči'ut cousins in the *Secret History*, a resemblance which is deepened by the fact that the would-be usurpers in both cases show signs of foreign influence, that is, from the nomadic viewpoint, have grown degenerate. In the case of the Tayiči'ut this may go no farther than their tendency to adopt Manchu and above all Chinese (with some Turkic) styles: but in *Köz-kaman* Manas's cousins, headed by the treacherous Kökčö-köz, have succumbed altogether to Sino-Kalmak culture and ethos.

From the extant text of *Köz-kaman*, as with the texts of *Kökčö* and *Kökötöy*, it is possible to see how an earlier version might have been independent of the *Manas*-cycle.

The plot of *Köz-kaman* is as follows. Manas has three wives, Kara-börük, Akılay, and Kanıkey, of whom only the favourite, Kanıkey, was acquired by the approved marriage with bride-money. Manas plans to raid the Kalmak khans Ay-khan of the Altai and Kün-khan of the 'Kün-kay'. Akılay utters a curse on him, but both Kanıkey and Manas's steed Ak-kula warn him against setting out. A strange messenger arrives from the Kalmak lands to announce the approach of Manas's unsuspected uncle Köz-kaman and the latter's sons. In answer to Manas's enquiry, his father Jakıp confirms that he once had such a brother but that this brother was captured by the Kalmak at a tender age. Thereupon Manas, sadly aware of having to all appearances been 'alone from his nest' — the only son of an only son and last hope of his clan — warmly welcomes his new-found kinsmen, feasts them and converts them to Islam. Köz-kaman then invites Manas and his Forty to a return feast. The clairvoyant Kanıkey and his far-sighted friend Almambet try in vain to frustrate the invitation. At the feast, Kökčö-köz strikes Manas with his steel, but without effect — we must assume that Kanıkey's prayers, countering Akılay's curse, were heard by Manas's guardian spirit. Köz-kaman, who was no party to this attack, pacifies the revellers. Manas now summons his Forty with intent to raid the Kalmak, and Kökčö-köz conspires with Ay-khan against Manas. On reconnaissance among the Kalmak, whose Mongol tongue as an Oirot prince he naturally speaks, Almambet enters the yurt of Altın-ay, daughter of Ay-khan, and swears to abduct her. Battle is then joined with the Kalmak with all its intrigues and vicissitudes till Manas and his men win the victory. After hunting together, Manas, Köz-kaman and their retainers feast. Kökčö-köz hands Manas poisoned arak. Manas rides out, is shot in the hand by Kökčö-köz and falls with a death-rattle. But Kökčö-köz's hope of taking Manas's place both as Khan and as husband to the lovely Kanikey is not to be fulfilled. Kanıkey revives Manas with her medicaments. He goes to Mecca and revives his slain Companions with prayer. Kanıkey has a dream which in Altın-ay's interpretation portends the birth of a heroic son, the future Semetey, hero of his own epic of that name. Manas kills the sons of Köz-kaman and in his anti-Kalmak rage would also have made an end of Altın-ay, Almambet's destined bride, had Kanıkey not prevented him.

The content of *Köz-kaman* is a precipitate of the centuries old struggle for existence between Kirghiz and Kalmak, and it is significant that its entire action is situated on a single axis of great length ranging from the Altai Mountains, haunt of the 'idolatrous' Kalmak in the north-east, to holy Mecca in the south-west, with the major part of the activity naturally falling inside Kirghiz lands. At the beginning, the aggressive élan of Manas impels him north-eastwards towards the hated Kalmak and he is not checked by the warnings of wife or steed. But Köz-kaman's messenger riding south-eastwards penetrates into Manas's region. There are comings and goings along the axis until the messenger is followed towards the south-west by Köz-kaman and his clan. After a pause devoted to their assimilation, Manas resumes his thrust to the north-east using their knowledge of the way and, through a series of real places that give way on the approach to the Altai to a series of mythical places — the Valley of the Kazılık Bird, the banks of the River-where-Snow-never-falls — he penetrates in turn into the Kalmak domain. 'Knocked-out' by Kökčö-köz's poison on the way back, he is wafted south-westwards to Mecca, the rear-base of his faith and magical power. Revived, he proceeds north-eastwards once again and settles accounts with Köz-kaman's sons.

The bard is to be commended on the unusual clarity of the structure of this episode. The structure of the two *Semetey*-episodes which follow is no less clear.

The existential features of the old *Manas*-cycle are pronounced. They reflected the precarious situation of the Kirghiz tribes. In the episodes examined hitherto, Manas was the only son of a man who had 'lost' his only brother, and Manas's milk-brother Almambet was also an only son. Manas's son Semetey and Semetey's son Seytek are also only sons. In Semetey and Seytek the crisis of the clan's survival is intensified by attempts to kill them at birth.

Just as Jakıp's long-lost brother Köz-kaman turned up with his Kalmakized sons in the episode in order to demonstrate Manas's vulnerability as an 'Only One' — Manas welcomed his treacherous cousins with open arms — so now in the *Birth of Semetey* two characters not met with before, Manas's half-brothers Abeke and Köböš, are produced in order to illustrate Semetey's vulnerability. If twentieth-century tradition vouches for that of the nineteenth century at this point, Abeke and Köböš are sons of the feckless Jakıp and a Kalmak wife, and so count as true kinsmen no more than did the poisoner Kökčö-köz and his brothers. The twentieth-century bard Sagymbay is much too conscious of how things are done in books suddenly to produce Abeke and Köböš for the *Semetey*-action, for he narrates not only their birth but also the foretelling of their conception at the same time as those of Manas. The introduction of the twins Abeke and Köböš in the mid-nineteenth-century *Birth of Semetey* is thus an element of archaic epic style using a limelighting technique. 'Figures standing in darkness can be illuminated at half or full strength and returned to half-light or total darkness, as required.'[47]

The bare bones of the two *Semetey* episodes are in keeping with this rough yet powerful technique. Each is an elaboration of a plot found sporadically between the Samoyeds in the west and the Oroch in the east in which an attempt to 'put out a man's fire' — the camp-fire stands for the *stirps* — is frustrated by his womenfolk and sometimes a loyal retainer.

In the *Birth of Semetey*, the babe is spirited away into exile by his mother Kanıkey and his grandmother Bagdidöölöt, who, incensed at her husband Jakıp's alliance with the twins, reverts to the name of Čakan. Jakıp and the twins, however, burn Manas's yurt *with smoke-vent*. When Semetey returns to the site as a young man to claim his heritage, a nail from this smoke-vent pierces his steed's hoof to remind Semetey to exact vengeance. The *arbak* (ancestor spirits) who have now been joined by the spirit of Manas are as yet behind the young warrior.

Semetey duly reclaims his heritage, and the women slake their thirst for traitors' blood. But in the next episode, *Semetey*, the hero shows a turbulent nature that will prove his undoing. Sensing this danger Manas's Forty Companions decline to go raiding with him, at which he impiously slays them. He then elopes with Ay-čürök, who is regularly betrothed to Kökčö's son Ümütöy,[48] by *kalym*. A sacrifice to Manas fails: outraged by his conduct the ancestor-spirits have abandoned him. A gigantic hero Er Kiyas defeats and slays

Semetey despite the devoted aid of his Companion Kül-čoro. On the advice of the contrasted figure of Semetey's other Companion, Kan-čoro, Er Kıyas burns Semetey's corpse so that he must die for ever. Ay-čürök, a swan-battle-maiden possessed of all the qualities of the Old Irish Scáthach, Emer and the Germanic Hild in one, could have revived Semetey, had he beeen left unburned. But now, as the wife of Kıyas, all she can do for Semetey's line is to save the child in her womb. This she achieves at his birth in a brief scene to be set beside other great moments in epic. When Kıyas comes with his sword to take off Seytek's 'apple-head', the magnificent Ay-čürök threatens to don her swan-mask and fly to her father Akın-khan and fetch his armies. Seytek is saved. Together with Kül-čoro, who has survived mutilation and degradation, Seytek exacts vengeance later for the slaying of his father, vengeance in which Kanıkey and Ay-čürök cannot fail to share. The episode ends with the implied hope that Seytek will live in harmony with the *arbak* and continue Manas's line and rule.[49]

The episodic poems of the *Manas*-cycle in the mid-nineteenth century are thus clearly the product of a fine epic style and tradition, the richest and ripest of all that is on record in a Turkic tongue. Its evolution must have taken many generations. Just how many generations is a matter for speculation in the absence of reliable evidence. For it does not seem to be realized by those who adduce the *Majmūʿ at-Tavarikh* of Saif ad-Din, which V. V. Bartold stigmatized as a hotch-potch of pseudo-history and one of whose sections is enlivened with *Manas*, that the onus rests on them to prove that the *Manas*-material was not interpolated as political propaganda into the source of the late eighteenth-century and nineteenth-century manuscripts. If this bowdlerized *Manas*-material were proved to be an authentic product of the sixteenth century, the question would then arise: How did a Kipchak (Özbeg) warrior (Manas), written about in Tajik (Persian), become the paramount hero of the Burut or Kirghiz? To a sceptical mind it seems more probable that we have to do with an eighteenth-century forgery calculated to inspire respect in the Kirghiz tribes for the Kipchak rulers of Kokand.[50]

NOTES

1.   See Eva S. Kraft, *Zum Dsungarenkrieg im 18. Jahrhundert. Bericht des Generals Funingga.* Aus einer mandschurischen Handschrift übersetzt und an Hand der chinesischen Akten erläutert (Leipzig, 1953), p. 18 (A.D. 1718), et passim.

2.   See below, pp. 320 f.

3.   See the Bibliography, infra.

4.   *Er Töštük*, Aytuuču S[ayakbay] Karalaev, with an introduction by Dzh. Tashtemirov (Frunze, 1956). Sayakbay's version was translated into French by P. Boratav, *Er Töshtük, le géant des steppes.* Introduction et notes par P. Boratav et L. Bazin (Paris, 1965).

5.   *aytıš*: see below, p. 305.

6.   *The Memorial Feast for Kökötöy-khan. Kökötöydün ašı* (Bibliography, infra).

7. See 'The Kirgiz original of *Kukotay* found', in the Bibliography, below. Since his announcement in 1965, Professor Margulan has published a reduced facsimile edition, unfortunately on paper which obstructs the resolution of many problems of detail: *Šokan jane 'MANAS'*. 'Manas' jırını Šokan jazıp alyan nuskası tuuralı zertteu (Alma Ata, 1971). (With an introduction of 116 pages in Kazakh.) This was followed by a loose Kazakh paraphrase: *Köketaydıŋ ertegisi* (Alma Ata, 1973).

8. In his *Obraztsy/Proben*, v, see Bibliography, below.

9. *Memorial Feast*, Appendix 3 'Manas's Invocations of his Forty Companions. A. Grouping of Bards'. The individuality of the bard of Group C (Radlov I, 3) has been confirmed beyond question by an investigation, partly still in press, of the second and longer part of this recording. See Bibliography below, Hatto, A. T., 'The marriage, death . . .'.

10. See the German section of this volume, pp. 166 f.

11. See below, pp. 319 ff.

12. I can now give the solution to the problem posed in *Memorial Feast*, Commentary, note 2754: the smith's bellows and his sons who work them merge in a single identity.

13. See above, p. 307.

14. See below, p. 322.

15. Excerpts made towards the end of the eleventh century by Kāshgharī from western Turkic heroic laments have been published by C. Brockelmann, 'Alttürkestanische Volkspoesie', I, *Asia Major*, Introductory Volume (1923) = Hirth Anniversary Volume, pp. 3 ff.

16. Radlov, *Obraztsy*, v, I, 3), 2070 ff.

17. See 'Köz-kaman', II (the Bibliography, infra), pp. 278 f. and note 226, and *Memorial Feast*, p. 144 (note 618).

18. Communicated during a conversation in London in May 1976. The first volume of Dr Dor's researches into the life and oral literature of the Pamir Kirghiz appeared as *Contribution à l'étude des Kirghiz du Pamir Afghan*. Cahiers Turcica 1 (Paris, 1975). See now R. Dor and C. M. Naumann, *Die Kirghisen des afghanischen Pamir* (Graz, 1978), copiously and splendidly illustrated. Dr Naumann has brought valuable ecological expertise to this theme.

19. See 'Köz-kaman', II, pp. 246 ff.

20. See above, p. 301.

21. *Proben*, v, p. x.

22. See below, p. 323.

23. See below, p. 318.

24. See below, p. 318.

25. In 'Almambet, Kökčö', etc. (Bibliography, below) Almambet is referred to as an 'Oirot'. The (West Mongol) Oirot empire preceded the (West Mongol) Jungarian or Kalmak empire. It is quite in order, then, in our poems that Almambet should be abused as a 'Kalmak' by Manas's jealous Companions.

26. See below, pp. 321 f.

27. See below, p. 317 and p. 320.

28. See above, p. 308 and below, p. 321.

29. I confess to not having questioned Valikhanov's rendering of *Čal-kuyruk* as *plamyakhvost* ('flame-tail') in '*Kukotay* and *Bok-murun*', II, p. 561.

30. This relationship is only *inferred* for the mid nineteenth-century texts. Jakıp places himself on the level of the Kalmakized Kökčö-köz by his use of poison against Semetey.

31. See above, p. 315.

32. Köz-kaman was taken to the Kalmak country when a boy. With regard to Kalmak women, the Kirghiz were faced with a nice dilemma: on the one hand they considered them more passionate lovers than Kirghiz women; on the other Kalmak women were likely to bear them degenerate sons,

33. See above, p. 309.

34. See below, pp. 319 and 321 f.

35. See below, pp. 323 f.

36. Apart from *Töstük* there are: *Er Tabıldı*; *Kurmanbek*; *Janıš*, *Bayıš*; available in popular editions.

37. Kirghiz epic diction will be dealt with in detail in Volume II of the present work.

38. See Bibliography, below, p. 326.

39. See above, p. 315.

40. See above, p. 314.

41. See below, p. 321.
42. 'Almambet, Er Kökčö', etc., pp. 169–70.
43. *Memorial Feast*, p. 98.
44. For a more detailed analysis and comparison see *Memorial Feast*, Appendix 2.
45. *Memorial Feast*, pp. 91 ff.
46. Ibid.
47. Quoted from my paper 'Plot and Character in Old Kirghiz Epic' at the Royal Asiatic Society on 10 June 1976, now published in a modified form in *Die mongolischen Epen. Bezüge, Sinndeutung und Überlieferung* (Ein Symposium). Herausgegeben von Walther Heissig = Asiatische Forschungen, Bd. 68 (Wiesbaden, 1979), pp. 95–112. In its modified form this paper was read to fellow members of the Rundgespräch des Sonderforschungsbereichs 12 'Zentralasien' (25–27 September 1978) in the University of Bonn.
48. Ümütöy is left in darkness in 'Almambet, Kökčö etc.', thus another instance of the 'limelighting technique'.
49. See 'Semetey', I and II, in the Bibliography, below.
50. See *Memorial Feast*, pp. 90 f.

BIBLIOGRAPHY

I. TEXTS

(Recorded in 1856) *The Memorial feast for Kökötöy-khan. Kökötöydün ašı.* A Kirghiz epic poem edited for the first time from a photocopy of the unique manuscript [of Chokan Chingisovich Valikhanov], with translation and commentary, by A. T. Hatto, London Oriental Series, 33 (Oxford, 1977)

(Recorded in 1862 and 1869) V. V. Radlov, (W. Radloff), *Obraztsy narodnoy literatury severnykh tyurkskikh plemen*, v (1885) Narechie dikokamennykh kirgizov. (The translation into German verse appeared in the same year at St Petersburg under the title *Proben der Volkslitteratur der nördlichen türkischen Stämme*, v: Der Dialect der Kara-Kirgisen)

II. DISCUSSION AND INTERPRETATION

Hatto, A. T., 'The Birth of Manas', *Asia Major*, New Series, 14 (1969), 217–41

Id., '*Kukotay* and *Bok Murun*: a comparison of two related heroic poems of the Kirgiz', *Bulletin of the School of Oriental and African Studies*, 32 (1969), Part I, pp. 344–78; Part II, pp. 541–70

Id., 'Almambet, Er Kökčö and Ak Erkeč. An episode from the Kirgiz Heroic Cycle of Manas, a.d. 1862', *Central Asiatic Journal*, 13 (1969), 161–98

Id., 'Köz-kaman', *Central Asiatic Journal*, 15 (1971), Part I, pp. 81–101; Part II, pp. 241–83

Id., 'The Kirgiz original of *Kukotay* found'. Communication to the *Bulletin of the School of Oriental and African Studies*, 34 (1971), 379–86

Id., 'Semetey', *Asia Major*, New Series, 18, 2 (1973), 154–80 = Part I; 19, 2 (1974), 1–36 = Part II

Id., 'The Catalogue of heroes and heroines in the Kirgiz *Joloi-kan*', in *Tractata Altaica* (Festschrift for Denis Sinor) (Wiesbaden, 1976), pp. 237–60

Id., 'The marriage, death and return to life of Manas: a Kirghiz epic poem of the mid-nineteenth century', in two parts, *Turcica*, (Louvain, Paris, Strasbourg, 1980, 1981)

Russian studies of *Manas*, which in the Soviet period have focused almost entirely on the productions of the twentieth-century bards, can be followed in the very full bibliography of *Kirgizskiy geroicheskiy épos MANAS* (Voprosy izucheniya éposa narodov SSR.), edited by M. I. Bogdanova, V. M. Zhirmunskiy and A. A. Petrosyan (Moscow, 1961), in which the late Professor Zhirmunskiy's contribution 'Vvedenie v izuchenie éposa "Manas" ' (pp. 85–196) is authoritative. The late Nora K. Chadwick discussed aspects of Radlov's Kara-Kirgiz texts in Part 1 of Vol. III of her and her husband H. Munro Chadwick's *Growth of Literature* (Cambridge, 1940, reprinted 1968), entitled 'The Oral literature of the Tatars', which was reprinted virtually unchanged in *Oral epics of Central Asia* (Cambridge, 1969) together with a valuable Second Part by V. M. Zhirmunskiy entitled 'Epic songs and singers in Central Asia' (pp. 271–348), including a Bibliographical Survey and Bibliographical References. To this may be added: A. T. Hatto, 'Ḥamāsa' (*quasi* 'Heroic epic') iv. — Central Asia, *Encyclopaedia of Islam* (1965); A. T. Hatto, *Shamanism and epic poetry in Northern Asia*. Foundation Day Lecture, 1970. School of Oriental and African Studies, University of London, 1970, passim.

AINU

By C. J. DUNN

THE AINU lived and, in so far as they survive, still live to the north of the main island of Japan in Hokkaidō, Sakhalin, and in the southernmost Kuriles. They are also reported to have once inhabited the southern Aleutians and Kamchatka. In the further distant past they were certainly on the mainland of Japan and may have been one of the tribes dispossessed by the Japanese in historical times. Even the name of Mt Fuji has been said by some to be an Ainu word meaning 'sacred fire'. The language of the Ainu has generally been thought to be unrelated to any nearby tongue; Naert, however, and some others[1] believe that Ainu has Indo-Aryan connexions.

The present situation of the Ainu and their culture is the result of a century in which the policy has been their assimilation into the Japanese population. Their language has no official status and is fast disappearing, and the ethnic individuality of the Ainu, with their hairiness and other characteristics which distinguish them from the Japanese, is more and more difficult to observe because it is being diluted by intermarriage. Traditional Ainu ways of life, religion, and architecture have been replaced by Japanese ones, except for some officially encouraged tourist attractions in the form of imitation Ainu villages and rows of shops selling souvenirs. However, the work of authors both non-Japanese (such as Batchelor, Munro, and Piłsudski) and Japanese, of whom the most important was the late Kindaichi Kyōsuke, who has been followed by younger workers anxious to record the remnants of the tradition before they go for ever, has meant that a considerable amount of information about the Ainu way of life has been preserved.[2]

The latitude of the northernmost cape of Hokkaidō is that of Montreal. Winters are long, with deep persistent snow; summers are mild. There are no monsoon rains, and the climate and general environment are more like those of northern Europe than mainland Japan, which tends towards the sub-tropical.

The culture of the Ainu of Hokkaidō was basically of the stone-age when the Japanese became fully aware of them in the seventeenth century. Although the Ainu learned some agriculture over the next two hundred years, their traditions remained almost entirely those of the hunting, fishing and collecting age, with no metal industry. It followed that iron objects (derived almost entirely from Japan), especially swords and armour (though these did not need to be of iron), were counted as great treasures, and famous swords bore individual names. Great significance was attached to the possession of rare objects of this sort, which were typically stored in the roof rafters of the Ainus' ceiling-less abodes.

The traditional Ainu culture was based on religion, and one of the constant ingredients of this religion was the belief that *kamui* (gods or spirits) were everywhere and that all animals were a sort of god, or possessed the attributes of gods.[3] Natural phenomena, such as thunder, were also gods. Every human being had at least one of these gods or spirits attached to him, to act as a protector or guardian spirit. The quality of a person was linked with the quality of his guardian, or guardians (for some people had more than one). Women in particular might become protected by some special spirit. Kindaichi mentions an old woman who won the favour of a water-god, who gave her the ability to preside successfully at difficult births. She thus became a prosperous midwife. Another was possessed by the spirit of lasciviousness of the ocean, so that she would sing erotic songs to the rhythm of the waves. Women were the great wielders of magic power, at least in Hokkaidō, if not in more northern areas of Ainu-land, as they are in Japan, and those protected (or possessed) by powerful spirits such as those of spiders or snakes were particularly potent. One such had both a spider and a serpent to look after her, and she had recourse to one or the other according to circumstances. When she was called in to cure a chief's wife, the spider was invoked first, but was then superseded by the serpent which spoke from the woman's mouth, explained the reason for the illness, and offered to cure the sick woman in return for a silk robe which she possessed. The sick woman's husband, however, explained that she had often said that she would not part with it even at the cost of her life, and so she was allowed to die. Silk robes were, of course, derived from Japan and formed part of personal treasure.

The most spectacular aspect of Ainu religion was the bear-cult. A bear-cub would be lovingly reared by a human community, even being suckled by the women, to be later killed by arrows and having its neck crushed between treetrunks. Its head was afterwards exposed as an object of worship. Among typical cult objects were *inau*, pieces of wood with patterns of half-removed shavings, set up to represent gods and to be sacrificed to and worshipped. The skill in woodcarving demonstrated in the manufacture of *inau* was common among the Ainu, and it is often mentioned as a quiet fireside occupation for the long winter evenings.

In addition there seems to have been a supreme god, the ancestor of the Ainu, or the source of their culture, called Okikurumi, who at one time lived with his wife on earth, but had returned at some time to the sky, whence he had originally come.

The literature was completely oral, for the Ainu had no writing, and it was very rich. A considerable amount has been preserved, either by transcription into the Japanese syllabary, or, more satisfactorily, into roman letters, or, in more recent years, by recording on tape.

The greater part of the oral literature consists of songs or recitations of various sorts, with or without rhythmical accompaniment of beaten sticks or the like. Musical instruments — Jew's harps and strings — seem to have been played solo and not for accompanying chanting. There were incantations, lullabies, love songs, and, most elaborate of all, the various narrative pieces known to the Ainu of Hokkaidō as *yukar*. There were two sorts of these, *kamui yukar*, meaning *yukar* relating to the gods, and *ainu yukar*, those relating to men, which in fact constitute the heroic poetry, the Ainu epic. In Sakhalin these two genres were known respectively as *oina* and *hauki*. The texts of a certain number of prose tales have also survived, bearing witness to a great deal of informal story-telling at the fireside, for which ordinary language was used.[4]

The Ainu do not appear to have possessed any form of drama, but did have some ceremonial dances.

There is a certain amount of evidence, and there are also some grounds for conjecturing that the Ainu epic (*ainu yukar*) was derived from the *kamui yukar* or *oina*, possibly within the last two or three hundred years, and that it still maintains some features of this form. Excellent selections of *kamui yukar* available for study are those in the NHK (Japan Broadcasting Corporation) collection of *Traditional Ainu Music*, and in Kubodera's recent work.[5] Some of the material published by Batchelor and Piłsudski belongs to this category. Of the twenty examples in the NHK collection nearly all are of the characteristic sort of *kamui yukar*, namely songs sung as in the first person by animals, birds, plants, and other gods, particular examples being boar, rabbit, owl, a wicked male bear, a green dove, the thunder god, the cuckoo, sparrow, snipe, mouse, grasshopper, river sprite, snow god, frog, coxcomb (plant), boat-god and flying squirrel. A characteristic element of these *kamui yukar* is the use of a burden before each phrase of the narrative, one such being *hankiri kiri hankiri kiri*, which occurs in a first-person tale of a mouse killed by children and given a funeral feast at which the crow and the stork quarrel and kill each other.[6]

In these *kamui yukar* the god, whoever he may be, tells his own story, except that in those in which the superior god, Okikurumi, appears, he does not tell his own story but is referred to by name. I would like to linger a while on one which is narrated by Okikurumi's wife,[7] because it seems to represent the sort of *kamui yukar* from which the epic may have sprung. The refrain in it is *hore houre*, repeated not quite so monotonously as is *hankiri kiri* in the example above; perhaps this decrease in use of the constantly repeated rhythmic element is a step towards the epic, which has no refrain.

The legend narrated in this instance relates that the god Okikurumi had a stockade in Hokkaidō. Once, when the district was visited by famine, Okikurumi's wife took pity on the inhabitants and, making herself invisible, distributed food to them. So beautiful were her hands (apparently they could be seen holding the food) that a foolish fellow seized hold of them and dragged her into his house. Full of wrath, Okikurumi took his wife back to heaven. In the song, his soft-hearted wife describes her homesickness for the Sisirimuka, 'our river', and how Okikurumi drew in the fire pictures of her beloved scenes; they were reflected in the sky and she could gaze upon them to her heart's content.

Kindaichi asserts that all *kamui yukar* are told in the first person, as is this one by Okikurumi's wife. Batchelor's verse pieces[8] do not seem to comply with this pattern, but his material may be suspect in detail. Most of those included in the NHK collection are also in the first person. One of the verse pieces preserved by Piłsudski,[9] which would fit into the category of *kamui yukar*, is in the first person, as is another Sakhalin piece, part of which Kindaichi has published in Japanese translation.[10] All except the last two have the repeated refrain.

The most accessible example of the long epic has been published by Kindaichi under the title of *Kutune Shirka*. This great work (his shorter version runs to 7,035 lines)[11] is also in the first person. The hero is not the god Okikurumi but a human being, known as Poiyaumpe (Poiyaumbe), although this name only occurs in the epic when someone addresses him. His name implies something like 'young lad from the main island', and with him as hero the story is not in the world of spirits or the gods — although, of course, his protective deities still operate — but in that of fighting between more or less normal human beings. The incantatory refrain or burden as found in *kamui yukar* is absent.

All these narrative pieces, whether *kamui yukar* or *ainu yukar*, have a rhythmical pattern which consists of lines with two beats, as can be demonstrated in the first three lines of *Kutune Shirka*:

> Irésu yúpi
> irésu sápo
> iréshpa híne . . .

There is no use of rhyme, assonance or alliteration, and the syllable-count for each line, while not fixed, seems to average five.

The Ainu epic and the method of reciting it are described in various Japanese accounts since early in the eighteenth century. For instance, in 1737[12] it was recorded that story-telling was part of the entertainment offered when tribute was given to the Japanese at the headquarters at Matsumae, in the south of Hokkaidō.

In 1784 a description of Ainu-land includes the passage: 'When they are drunk they lie on their backs and with each hand they beat their chest and sing something like a song. Persons listening beat out the rhythm, and praise the singer. Their pleasure is quite without reserve.'

Y

In 1789, an author relates that he had to beach his ship on the Kurile island of Etorofu, and his Ainu shipmates chanted a piece and danced when they were safely ashore, even though they had nothing to eat.

In 1794 another Japanese 'stayed the night at a wretched inn in Poropetsu. I heard that three of the Ainu performed. I gave them some drink, which pleased them. One lay on the floor, and started to beat his breast and sing. The other two beat out the rhythm with firewood'.

In 1808 it is reported thus: 'For chanting they always lie on the floor, beat on their breasts with their hands, and chant in the throat, half grunting, half retching, with a wrinkled voice, slower, more relaxed than a Buddhist priest reciting sutras, faster than the chanting of *nō* plays. Listeners join in from time to time to help the chanter, half growling, half coughing; or they take "moustache lifters"[13] or something and take up the rhythm by beating with them. . . . Those who are good at chanting, in the winter, when fishing and hunting are impossible, invite each other and sing for days on end. When they hear of famous deeds, they cannot help exclaiming such things as "Don't be defeated!" "Fight well!" and so on. Women in the audience may weep at tragic moments.'[14]

More recent performances seem to have become more respectable, though no doubt a little lubrication was still desirable. Kindaichi's blind informant, Wakarpa, travelled to Tokyo and no doubt worked in an academic atmosphere. Women appear originally not to have been concerned with tales featuring a male hero; since, as we know from the alternative version of the long epic collected from a female informant, women have come to learn them, as well as being performers of *menoko-yukar*, stories with a woman as the main character. Recent photographs indicate that a largely spurious Ainu village for tourists puts on performances, which are modelled apparently on spectacular *geisha* shows in Tokyo and Kyoto. There does not seem to be a recording of a chanter working at high pressure, although some are available which give what is presumably a very pale image of the style of performance.[15]

A modern description of *kamui yukar* recited by a woman, says that she 'recited from memory, in Ainu, a good forty minutes of *yukar*. She used facial expressions. Some parts she sang, others she treated as vocal dialogue, clearly indicating that at least two persons were talking. Now she spoke in a loud angry voice; now she whispered. She sighed, halted, and stumbled. She closed her eyes, then looked skyward and off into the distance through the windows and out of the door.' The reciter had learned this *yukar* from her uncle, in whose house she had been brought up.[16]

Having given an account of the place held by the epic in Ainu literature, and referred to its method of performance, I must now turn to the epic itself.

I have said above that the long epic with a human hero which is most accessible at the moment was published by Kindaichi in 1931. It is called *Kutune*

Shirka from the name of a precious sword-sheath.[17] Arthur Waley published a partial translation of it.[18] This *yukar* in fact exists in three printed versions; for some time after Kindaichi had collected the one which Waley translated, he heard of an old woman who knew the same story, and he obtained the second version from this woman's daughter. The third version appears in *Kutune Shirka*, published in Monbetsu in Hokkaidō in 1965. It was written down by Nabezawa Motozō, as the version which he chanted. I was also able to hear (but not copy) a recording of him chanting this epic. It shows considerable variation from his printed text. In fact, chanters are said to have memorized not words, but a succession of scenes, which they described in epic style.

The story[19] is of the hero Poiyaumpe, who lives in a house in the care of his elder brother and sister, who are called by Waley 'foster brother' and 'foster sister'. There is another person there too, his brother Kamui Otopush — the godlike Otopush. These four characters become involved in an immense series of battles over the possession of a golden[20] sea otter. As the tale unfolds we learn more of this marvellous possession, but do not in fact hear of its origin until about line 1200, when the hero, after an extremely prolonged encounter with a personage trying to get the otter away from him, comes ashore to be addressed by a chieftain whose voice 'like the cuckoo' came down from the top of a beach-watching tower. 'A thing that was before once again has come in this world. In the past the lady of Kanesantaun had as attendants a pair of golden sea otters. The male sea otter dived and sought its food in the mouth of the Ishkar river.' The lady seeking to recapture her otter is known as the wicked lady of Ishkar. She is unsuccessful, and the hero and his brothers and sister are reunited, and hold a banquet. This is interrupted in what we may call the Waley version by two armoured men. For the rest of the story one cannot do better than quote from Waley's summary:

A long battle follows in which the foster-brother and Otopush were both knocked out. I use the term advisedly because they were not exactly killed. The gods, we are told afterwards, did not accept their souls, and later on they came to life again. The hero, aided by magic animals carved on his sword-sheath, which come to life and take part in the battle, kills for good and all the rock-clad and the quicksilver-clad opponents.

In the next episode a messenger suddenly arrives, asking for help for a lady whom I am going to call Miss Malinger, which is what her name (Nishap-tashum) literally means. She is the sister of a chieftain belonging to the Ishkar confederacy. Having second sight she knew that if her clan went with the other confederates to recover the otter, they would all be killed by the Hero; so she pretended to be ill, and her brother delayed the departure of his army till it was discovered that she was only shamming. Consequently he was late in coming to the aid of his allies, who were furious and decided to hang Miss Malinger. The messenger, who suddenly arrived at the banquet, had come to ask for the Hero's aid. The Hero at once leaves the banquet and arrives in time to cut Miss Malinger down. They fall in love and he carries her back

as his bride. Soon, however, an enemy carries her off while the Hero is out hunting.
There are more battles; Miss Malinger is recovered and the Hero leaves her at home
while he goes out to make a final clearance of his enemies.

While he lies on the ground, exhausted by many battles, a beautiful girl appears
and bending over him sings:

> If such a hero
> Fell to my hand
> What a boon to my village!

At this moment Miss Malinger, knowing by instinct that he is in danger, appears
at his side and casts a spell upon the beautiful girl. The hero steps up to the girl
from behind and undoes one by one the strings of her bodice. The passage that
follows is strange and terrible:

> Her young breasts
> That were like two snowballs
> I fondled with my hand.
> She looked back over her shoulder
> And cried out, 'Is it you?
> I thought you were dead.'
> But while she was saying these words
> I hewed her limb from limb,
> And heard the swish of her soul,
> Her evil soul as it rose.
> Then Malinger came to me and said,
> 'Woman should do battle with women
> And this my evil sister
> Should have fallen to my hand.
> But now that, before I could slay her,
> A godlike hero
> Has meted punishment
> We have no more to fear;
> Let us go back to our home.'
> But I thought to myself,
> 'Where is this village of Peshutun
> That the girl said she came from?
> If without destroying it
> I were not to go back home,
> Would it not be said I was afraid?'
> That was what I thought to myself.[21]

There seems to be no reason why the story should have ended there, but
Kindaichi thinks that his blind informant, Wakarpa, ran out of memory at this
point. He thought the epic was potentially longer, and we now know that this
belief was justified (see note 19).

Kindaichi's alternative version, which was collected in the female informant's home in Hokkaidō, has 8,223 lines as against the blind man's 7,035, and
even then it is in only four sections with three battle-stories, whereas the
blind man's has nine sections, with eight battles. The alternative version is
thus much longer and more leisurely. Yet there is clearly a close relationship
between the two, for the same phrases occur in both, and similar episodes.

Kindaichi's account of the collecting of the long version is that there was an
old woman, who had the reputation of being a great chanter. She herself was
too old to recite the story to him, but her daughter was able to dictate it to him
in a week in 1927. It is said to show the influence of the daughter's everyday
speech, with a good deal of modern language.

Throughout both versions we can observe vivid figures and descriptions.
When the ship through which the hero chased the thief ran ashore, some
sailors from it were to be seen, as if putting out dog's heads. The Ainu words are
ukosetasapa roshkikane, which is analysable, Kindaichi says, into *uko* = 'together',
seta 'dog', *sapa* 'head', *roshki* 'erect', *kane* 'while'. A robber comes down through
the smokehole to the upper beams 'like starlight slipping down'. When the hero
chases this intruder at one time they fly through the air 'like birds with hands',
men sprawl on the floor 'spread like mats', waves are 'like sideways mountains'.
These vivid images are set against a realistic topography of mountains, rivers
and gravel tracks, the details of which are lovingly described. The Ainu were
very attached to their environment, as indeed one would expect of men who
relied on hunting and gathering for their livelihood. Two strange and formidable figures who break into the feast, the rock-armour man and quicksilver
man, are joined into one in the corresponding passage in the alternative version,
where 126 lines correspond to 76 of the blind man's version, and he is accompanied by an equally poisonous female.

Someone unknown fell thump on to the watch-tower and burst into the porch.
Throwing up the hanging curtain over on to its back some being of unknown shape
hurled itself into the yard. I watched it as it came in and saw that it was the poison
man well known in rumour. I thought, as was said, that he would be a small man; he
seemed, however, like a small mountain sprouting legs and sprouting arms. His
fiercely poisoned armour went to the tips of his hands. The surface of his armour was
like rocks with streams between. In the streams poisoned water and poisoned bubbles
flowed down. In spaces between the rocks fierce poisoned thorns stood spikily up.
From the barbs of the thorns poisoned bubbles dripped. I gazed upon him and
wondered what one could do to kill him. He was covered all over with fearful
growths of fearful things. Like a forest of magic swords spiky rocks covered his armour,
and his sword was as long as a lance. Behind him came a poison woman with fiercely
poisoned armour. Poisoned bubbles stood on the tips of spiky thorns. On her back a
poisoned iron ring she bore, tied to her with poisoned rope. She followed close behind
the poison man. A terrifying smell of poison swept through the house like a great
wind. I feared that very soon I would lose consciousness. No sooner did the poison

man enter the house than he gazed around and his mouth was full of laughter. When he spoke, his voice rumbled and rumbled in the depths of his throat like the tide sweeping in to sea caverns.[22]

Kindaichi claimed to know of the existence of some eighty examples of epic tales with human heroes which had not been written down, and from 1959 onwards he and some others produced several printed texts,[23] which are listed in Bibliography D, below. The beginnings seem to follow a pattern, that of a person reaching adulthood, someone who has been brought up in some part of a great house, where he had no knowledge of the outside world. In the blind man's version of *Kutune Shirka* the hero has been carving objects. For the first time he takes cognizance of the household treasures which have come down from his ancestors, treasures in this case including the famous sword from whose sheath the epic takes its name, but which does not come into action until about halfway through the story, possibly when the otter itself is losing some of its importance to the narrative. There are also various handguards, armour, and the like. It is also characteristic that the hero is always the last reserve in a fight, and it is he who wins, only after his comrades have been defeated.

An element deriving in a way from the previous two, those of the newly-emerging hero and his position as a reserve, involves his being left behind in a house while others go out and fight.

In a work dated 1808[24] there is the first reference to the word *yukar* in Japanese, and there are summaries of more than one example of these narratives. One begins thus:

A prosperous chieftain died and his child was living in someone else's house. On the beaches nearby some whales were caught. The master of the house had relatives there, and sent this child there and had him beg for fat.

Another summary has a similar starting-point:

The chief of a certain place was highly appreciated and had great family treasures. When he died he left one daughter and two sons. The chief of Ishkar prepared some sweet wine and invited the three to drink it. At first they were reluctant to go, but after two or three messengers had come, they thought that it would be difficult to persist in their refusal. However, they were still suspicious and decided that there was no need for all three to go, so two would accede to the invitation and the third, the younger boy, would stay behind and guard the house.

Needless to say, he eventually has to get out the family treasures — sword, armour, bow, arrows, quiver box, etc. — and rescue his kin after many a long battle. Later on in the story, when they have to conceal themselves from the enemy, they leave the house in charge of a house-minder. The description of this woman is striking, even though we only have the nineteenth-century

Japanese translation, and demonstrates the ease and effectiveness with which the imagery of nature is used in such descriptions:

The enemy peered in through the window, and all there was to see was a strange-looking old woman at the fireside. As they peered closely at her, they saw that her eyes shone like the sun, her white hair was like snow collected on withered autumn leaves in the mountains. The wrinkles on her face were like the white waves rising in a winter sea. The remains of the tattooing round her mouth was like the thick vegetation in the summer on a cape rising from the rock-beating waves, the opening of her nostrils was like the coming and going of the steam from a stag shaking its antlers in the depths of a cave in the rocky mountains. Her breath as she drew it flashed sparks enough to make one think that they were the flying ashes of a burning mountain. Though her form was that of a human being, the more they looked at her, the more they thought she looked unlike a being of this world. A feeling of awe penetrated their bodies; after one glance at her they were unable to take their eyes off her, and as they gazed the hair on their bodies stood on end, and they stayed in a state of confusion.

It is also quite to be expected that the religious beliefs and practices of the Ainu should take their place in their epic. For example, to return to the golden otter story, the various protective or possessing deities show their presence in it. The hero has the powerful thunder god on his side, and when he goes out to meet the foe, the thunder rolls (but the deity does not seem to go so far as to hurl thunderbolts). The sea otter itself is such a one, and was stolen from its possessor (or possessee), who wants to get it back. When the strange rock-armour and quicksilver men pick their quarrel, and defeat his friends, the hero is helped by some more of his gods whose images he wears on his equipment, from which they come to life and fight — a wild boar from the hilt of his sword, a dragon from the sword guard, a 'summer-fox', whatever that may be, from the scabbard. Gods may be prayed to for recovery, for example, from the poisoning from the scratches dealt by the rock-armour man. When men die, they are known as gods, and they go up to the sky, with noise of swishing. There are two sorts of death, one final and one temporary; in the latter case some such word as 'likely to return' is used at the time of death, and the character returns with no particular ceremony after some hundreds of lines.

The examples of the Ainu epic that have been discussed up to now have a male hero. Early descriptions suggest that the traditional reciters of these were men. It is noteworthy, however, that women (for example Kindaichi's female informant) now seem to be active in preserving the old memories. The existence of *menoko yukar*, women's *yukar*, has already been mentioned, along with the fact that these were narrated by women. One preserved in the NHK collection[25] starts with the woman saying: 'My brother brought me up, cared for me well and loved me,' reflecting the normal role of the main character as one who at first is of minor importance. However this heroine uses women's weapons in the long fights which ensue. She has, it seems, prophetic dreams:

I fell into a deep sleep, my head pillowed on my sewing. Was it a dream or a vision, I suddenly found myself outside the house. Behind the house had risen a thick mist, and beyond it I could see a great host of men standing, bearing arms.

In her dream she hears them plan an attack on her village, and wakes to warn her brother. This starts off a huge and typical battle, lasting in this case for six summers and six winters, in which her brother seems to be replaced by her husband-to-be, Sanputounkuru, as the main contestant on the good side. A shadowy figure called Esanottomat tries to become intimate with the heroine by combing her hair against her will. This seems to lead to another period of unconsciousness, from which the heroine awakens to find herself and Sanputounkuru lying naked by a fallen tree.

I collected leaves from the trees and plants nearby and worked them with my hands to make some sort of garment to clothe me. Then I took out my secret girdle[26] and brandished it twice and brandished it thrice, and made for Sanputounkuru some clothing, a helmet and even his sword. He joyfully stretched out his hands and received them. He put them on and firmly tied the string of his helmet.

He was ready to start fighting again.

It is to be expected that Ainu-land, bordering as it does on the great shamanistic cultures of Siberia, should itself have within it shamanistic elements. Piłsudski (1909) has a remarkable article on the practices and formation of the shaman in Sakhalin. It may be that the intoxication that seems to have been necessary for good performance at the recitation of the epic produces a sort of light trance of a shamanistic sort. It is possible, however, that, as one moves southward from Sakhalin through the various islands of Japan down to the Ryūkyū chain, there is a greater tendency for the intermediary between god and man to be female. Certainly this is, or was, normal in Japan. When it comes to *menoko yukar*, the heroine appears to have been something of a shamaness. In the example that has been summarized above she has prophetic dreams and is able to project herself from her body and see her naked body lying beside a tree. Kindaichi[27] reports on another *yukar*, collected in fact in Sakhalin, the heroine of which is quite clearly a shamaness. It is linked with the epic because of the pattern of a child brought up in the recesses of a house, to emerge at the beginning of the story to maturity. She reaches the age of young womanhood, and looks for the first time into an old bag her granny had left behind. This is described at some length, and also its contents, which, instead of the sword and military equipment of the male hero, are a small drum with a string loop, a gold drum-stick, a gold hat. With the help of this clearly shamanistic equipment she 'thickens her magic' and sees a scene of desolation and the marks of the passage of a 'magic woman'. For 2,000 lines the story goes on, and is summarized by Kindaichi as culminating in a struggle between the young sorceress and this magic woman, as a result of which the old one is defeated and the hero — who he is Kindaichi does not say — saved.

In conclusion, let us return to the golden sea otter. This passage demonstrates many of the special qualities of the Ainu epic — its fantasy, its imagery, its love for the environment and its bellicosity — and one cannot but regret that a culture that could produce such things is on the verge of extinction.

As the souls of the dead, those who were really dead, rose to the skies, the sound of their ascent echoed and re-echoed. The foundations of this land below were shaken and rocked by the sound, and a feeling of grief arose within me. At this time once more through the high smoke-hole something came in as quiet as starlight, and dropped on to the upper rafter. I heard a hand being placed on the Golden Sea Otter. In astonishment I once more threw the servant's clothes I was wearing on the floor. Once more I donned my own garb. On the upper rafter the Golden Sea Otter slipped from my hand; at the high smoke-hole it slipped from my grasp; on the timbers of the roof-ridge it slipped from me again. Then up into the sky the thief flew away. I drew my sword and went after him, but the feeling of touching him with my great sword I did not feel. My left hand grappled with him like a two-hooked, a three-hooked grappling iron. My great sword passed beneath him and sent out sparks like the sparks of a fire rising. My great sword passed above him and sent out sparks like the sparks of a fire rising. He thus escaped from my grasp and from my sword, slipping and dodging away like the wind. Up into the sky like birds with hands we went. Through the god-sky we sped, and over the man-earth. Along the beloved stream behind my village, I sped like a god, I sped like a spirit, riding on the face of the wind that blows down the stream. But from this fearsome man, what island could he come from, who can he be to elude me so, I could not recapture the Golden Sea Otter. Thus I came out to the mouth of my beloved stream. What did I see? Such things passed all my thoughts! In the cove of our village, at the entrance to this cove, lay a great war vessel,[28] with chains hanging from port and starboard sides. Towards this vessel he swiftly flew. On the stern-board he turned aside my sword; at the bottom of the ship he turned aside my sword; in desperation he plunged in through a porthole. Through the porthole too I jumped. In the hull of the ship, what men were there? Through the hull of the ship I brandished my sword. Some I pursued, some I let go in the places I went through. Many men crawled grovelling on the floor, or fell as though spread like mats ... At this moment of all moments the great ship raised its sails and over the face of the sea they made it move. All at once, toward the open sea they made the vessel move. During this time, once more, he leapt out through the ship-window. On the floor of the stern, he escaped my striking sword. On the deck he eluded my sword blows, but on the prow-wings the Golden Sea Otter I recaptured. After that, I hacked them all to dismembered corpses and scattered them, villains all! In truth I had admired his way of seeking the Golden Sea Otter, and from this man of Ponmoshiri, with my sword-tip hissing through the air, I had recaptured the Golden Sea Otter![29]

NOTES

1. e.g. Lindquist, 1960. Present-day Japanese experts favour a proto-Mongol origin for the Ainu language.
2. Slava Ranko (pseud.) 'Pioneers in the study of the Ainu language and folklore', *Maratto*, no. 2 (June 1977), 17–25 has a good historical account.
3. See 'Inter-species communication and the Ainu way of life' by Slava Ranko, *Maratto*, no. 1 (March 1977), for a longer account of the Ainu and their gods, summarized from Japanese sources.
4. Two important collections of such stories are *Asai* (1972) (in Japanese) and *Kayano* (1974) (Ainu in Japanese syllabic transcription with Japanese translation).
5. Kubodera, 1977. Nos. 7 and 70 of the *kamui yukar* in this work appear in English versions in Slava Ranko, *Maratto*, no. 1, pp. 1 and 15.
6. NHK 1965, p. 469, recording no. 58; NHK 1976, side 8A, track 1.
7. NHK 1965, p. 436, recording no. 56.
8. e.g. Batchelor, 1938, pp. 118 ff.
9. Piłsudski, 1912, pp. 12 ff.
10. Kindaichi, 1961, pp. 216 ff.
11. Kindaichi, 1931; Vol. II gives the Ainu text, with Japanese translation, of two versions of this long epic. Vol. I has explanatory material, with a grammar of Ainu, and quotes, for example, early references to the Ainu and their epic.
12. This and subsequent references to early reports of *yukar* are selected from Kindaichi Vol. I (1931), chap. 7, pp. 351–76.
13. See Munro, 1962, p. 39.
14. See illustrations to no. 95 in Izumi Seiichi, *Ainu no sekai* (The world of the Ainu) (Tokyo, 1968).
15. e.g. in NHK 1967, side 8A, track 4, 8B 1 and 9A 1.
16. Hilger, 1971, pp. 36–37.
17. There is some doubt about the meaning of this name. *Sirka* (*shirka*) is a decorated scabbard, and, according to Kindaichi, *kutu* (*-ne* is a copula used here attributively) is a plant with a hollow stem, giant knotweed. Slava Ranko (see note 19), however, interprets it as 'curved sheath', that is, one that is curled in spirals towards its tip. The nomenclature may be connected with the old Japanese habit of presenting the Ainu with swords with much decoration but useless blades. See also *Shupne shirka* in Bibliography D.
18. Waley, 1951.
19. A synopsis of Kindaichi's first version is given in 'The Ainu heroic epic *Kutune Shirka*', *Maratto*, no. 3 (September 1977), pp. 26–48. The pseudonymous author Slava Ranko mentions two further, unpublished versions, one of which has 15,368 lines (compared with Kindaichi's 7,035 and 8,223, and Nabezawa's 6,775) and so can probably be thought of as the nearest to a definitive form.
20. Slava Ranko, *Maratto*, no. 2 (June 1977), p. 45 has doubts about this translation and suggests either 'metal' or 'marvellous'.
21. Waley, 1963, pp. 205–207, quoted with permission of George Allen & Unwin (Publishers) Ltd.
22. Kindaichi, 1931, Vol. II, p. 700, line 2114 to p. 704, line 2203.
23. Kindaichi, *Ainu jojishi yūkara-shū* (1959–75).
24. Kindaichi, 1931, I, pp. 356 ff.
25. NHK 1965, pp. 489 ff.
26. Munro, 1962, pp. 141 ff.
27. Kindaichi, 1961, pp. 216 ff.
28. Is this war vessel Japanese or from the Asian Continent? Is this epic a memory of some attack from overseas? Slava Ranko is inclined to accept Chiri's theory of a connexion with the so-called Okhotsk culture. See *Maratto*, no. 2, pp. 30–33.
29. Kindaichi, 1931, Vol. II, p. 296, line 929 to p. 305, line 1007.

BIBLIOGRAPHIES

A. Catalogues

Hickman, B., *A catalogue of books dealing with the Ainu in the Library of the School of Oriental and African Studies, University of London* (with a foreword by Professor C. J. Dunn) (London, SOAS [1975]), iv + 30 pp.

Matsui, Masato and Shimanaka, Katsumi, *Research resources on Hokkaidō, Sakhalin and the Kuriles at the East West Centre Library*, Occasional Papers, no. 9 (Honolulu East West Centre Library, 1967), vii + 266 pp.

Taguchi, Kirsten Yumiko, *An annotated catalogue of Ainu material in the East Asian Institute of Aarhus University*, Scandinavian Institute of Asian Studies monograph series, no. 20 (Lund, Student litteratur, 1974), 136 pp.

B. Select bibliography of western language works (those containing important excerpts of Ainu literature are asterisked)

Batchelor, John, *The Ainu and their folk-lore* (London, The Religious Tract Society, 1901)*
    An Ainu–English–Japanese dictionary (including a grammar of the Ainu language), 4th edition (Tokyo, Iwanami shoten, 1938) [4], xxvii, ii, [1], 145, [1], 581; 100 pp.*

Hilger, M. Inez, *Together with the Ainu: a vanishing people* (Norman, University of Oklahoma Press, 1971)

Kodama, Sakuzaemon, *Ainu historical and anthropological studies* (Sapporo, Hokkaidō University School of Medicine, 1970), 295 pp.

Lindquist, Ivar, *Indo-European features in the Ainu language* (Lund, 1960)

Munro, Neil Gordon, *Ainu cult and creed*. Edited with a preface and additional chapter by B. Z. Seligman. Introduction by H. Watanabe (London, 1962), xviii + 182 pp.

Naert, Pierre, *La situation linguistique de l'Aïnou; 1. Aïnou et Indoeuropéen* (Lund, 1958), 234 pp.

Piłsudski, Bronislav, 'Der Schamanismus bei den Ainu-Stämmen von Sachalin', *Globus*, 95 (1909), 72–78
    Materials for the study of the Ainu language and folklore (Cracow, Imperial Academy of Sciences, 1912), xxvi, [2]; 242 pp.*

'Slava Ranko' (pseudonym), *Maratto*, (715 Tenth Ave, San Francisco, Calif., 94118, U.S.A., 1977–   )*

Waley, Arthur, 'Kutune shirka; the Ainu epic' in *Bottegue Oscure*, Quaderno VII, pp. 214–36 (Rome, 1951), partially reprinted in Arthur Waley, *The secret history of the Mongols and other pieces* (London, 1963)*

Watanabe, Hitoshi, *The Ainu Ecosystem: environment and group structure* (Seattle and London, 1973), ix + 170 pp.

C. Select bibliography of Japanese language works

Asai, Tōru (editor), *Ainu no mukashibanashi* [Ainu tales of old] (Tokyo, NHK, 1973), 271 + 12 pp.

Chiri, Mashiho, *Bunrui Ainugo Jiten* [Ainu subject dictionary], Vol. I, *Shokubutsu-hen* [Plants], Vol. II, *Dōbutsu-hen* [Animals], Vol. III, *Ningen-hen* [Human beings]. Nihon jōmin bunka kenkyūjo, I (Tokyo, 1953), 30 + 394 pp.; II, 1962, 18 + 235 + 105 pp.; III, 1954, 7 + 711 pp. + 2 pl.

Institute for the Study of North Eurasian Cultures, Hokkaidō University, *Hoppō Bunka Kenkyū* [Studies of Northern culture] (Sapporo, Japan, 1939–   )

Kayano, Shigeru, *Wekaperu-shū taisei* [Collection of Wekaperu, Ainu tales], Vol. I (Tokyo, Arudō, 1974), 9 + 291 pp.

Kindaichi, Kyōsuke, *Ainu jojishi yūkara no kenkyū* [Study of yukar, the Ainu epic], 2 vols (Tokyo, Tōyō Bunko, 1931 (1967)), 14 + 534 pp.; xx + 1,024 pp.

Ainu bunka-shi [Cultural history of the Ainu] (Tokyo, Sanseidō, 1961), 10 + 576 pp.

Ainu jojishi yūkara-shū [Collection of *yukar*, the Ainu epic], Vols I–IX (Tokyo, Sanseidō, 1959–75), 456 + 478 + 500 + 375 + 338 + 401 + 362 + 309 + 411 pp.

Kubodera, Itsuhiko, *Ainu jojishi shin'yō, seiden no kenkyū* [Ainu narrative poetry: study of songs of gods and religious tradition] (Tokyo, Iwanami-shoten, 1977), xiv + 790 pp.

Monbetsu-chō kyōdoshi kenkyū-kai [Association for the study of local history, Monbetsu, Hokkaidō] ed. *Ainu jojishi Kutune Sirka* [Kutune Sirka, an Ainu epic] (Sapporo, Monbetsu . . . , 1965), 259 pp.

Ainu no jojishi [Ainu narrative poetry] (Sapporo, Monbetsu . . . , 1969), 614 pp.

Nihon hōsō kyōkai (NHK: Japan Broadcasting Corporation] *Ainu dentō ongaku* [Ainu traditional music] (Tokyo, NHK, 1965), 566 + 4 discs

Ainu ongaku [Ainu music] (Tokyo, NHK, 1967). Album of 10 long-playing discs plus booklet, 55 pp.

D. *List of printed versions with romanized transcriptions of epics with a human hero*

Explanation of symbols:
1. (a) Ainu Title;   (b) translation of title
2. Where text is to be found:
>   Batchelor = *An Ainu–English–Japanese Dictionary*, 1938
>   Kinkyu   = Kindaichi, *Ainu jojishi yūkara no kenkyū*
>   Kinshu   = Kindaichi, *Ainu jojishi yūkara shū*
>   Monshi   = Monbetsu chō kyōdoshi kenkyū-kai, *Ainu no jojishi*
>   Monjo   = Monbetsu chō kyōdoshi kenkyū-kai, *Ainu jojishi Kutune Sirka*
>   Piłsudski = *Materials for the study of Ainu language and folklore*, 1912

3. (a) line for line Japanese translation;   (b) free translation
4. Length in lines
5. Notes

I   1(a) *Akeusutu wanresu* (b) The tale of the wicked uncle; 2. Kinshu VII, pp. 281–356; 3(a); 4. 1,858

II   1(a) *Huri hayokpe* (b) Eagle armour; 2. Monshi, pp. 205–58; 3(a); 4. 1,375

III   1(a) *Imonka-oyan-mat* (b) The lady with the bird helmet; 2. Monshi, pp.

407–53; 3(a); 4. 1,198; 5. *menoko-yukar*, perhaps better considered as *kamui-yukar*

IV 1(a) *Ipe wen kinra* (b) Eating madness; 2. Monshi, pp. 261–328; 3(a); 4. 1,791

V 1(a) *Iyochi unmat* (b) The lady from Iyochi; 2. Kinshi, VI, pp. 27–390; 3(a); 4. 8,920; 5. Iyochi is said to be Yoichi, west of Otaru. It has a stockade-site, said to be full of snakes; the many swords left behind by the young lord of Iyochi are said to have turned into these

VI 1(a) *Iyochi-un-mat* (b) The lady from Iyochi; 2. Monshi, pp. 371–404; 3(a); 4. 878

VII 1(a) *Kamuikarsapa kamuikartumam* (b) God-made head, god-made body; 2. Kinshu, III, pp. 379–488; 3(a); 4. 2,587; 5. Title is name of famous armour

VIII 1(a) *Kemka Karip* (b) The bloody ring; 2. Kinshu, IV, pp. 37–362; 3(a); 4. 7,961; 5. Women used a ring with sharpened edge, or with blades, as a weapon

IX 1(a) *Kina chishinap mun chishinap* (b) The grass effigy; 2. Kinshu IX, pp. 23–229; 3(a); 4. 5,063

X 1(a) *Kutune Shirka* (b) The knot-weed scabbard; 2. Kinkyu, II, pp. 345–608; 3(a); 4. 7,035; 5. This is the version of the long epic partly translated by Waley, and summarized in *Maratto*, no. 3. See notes 17, 18, 19

XI 1(a) *Kutune shirka* (b) The knot-weed scabbard; 2. Kinkyu, II, pp. 609–950; 3(a); 4. 8,223; 5. This is Kindaichi's second version

XII 1(a) *Kutune sirka* (b) The knot-weed scabbard; 2. Monjo; 3(a); 4. 6,775; 5. A shorter version than those in Kinkyu

XIII 1(a) *Nishimakunmat* (b) The lady from Nishimak; 2. Kinshu, V, pp. 27–328; 3(a); 4. 7,238

XIV 1(a) *Nitay-pa kaye* (b) He who bends and breaks the tops of the trees in the woods; 2. Monshi, pp. 135–202; 3(a); 4. 1,759

XV 1(a) *Ponsamorunkur* (b) The little Japanese; 2. Kinshu, III, pp. 37–358; 3(a); 4. 7,080; 5. The hero is Poiyaumpe; his brother is known as 'the little Japanese' from his fine equipment

XVI 1(a) *Sak-somo-ayep a-koyki* (b) The defeat of the wicked dragon; 2. Monshi, pp. 331–68; 3(a); 4. 981

XVII 1(a) *Seta chiresu, wenpe chiresu* (b) Reared with the dogs, reared by evil men; 2. Monshi, pp. 563–614; 3(a); 4. 1,361

XVIII 1(a) *Shupne shirka* (b) The reed scabbard; 2. Kinshu, VIII, pp. 25–115; 3(a); 4. 2,203. 5. Wakarpa version; see *kutune shirka* for similar sword-name

XIX 1(a) *Shupne shirka* (b) The reed scabbard; 2. Kinshu, VIII, pp. 141–300; 3(a); 4. 3,868; 5. Chiri Yoshie's version

XX 1(a) *Tupesan kamimanit otumi oshma* (b) The story of the battle of the eight skewers; 2. Kinshu, IX, pp. 253–399; 3(a); 4. 3,587

XXXI 1(a) *Uchiu ninkari* (b) The story of the ear-ring; 2. Kinshu, VII, pp. 31–261; 3(a); 4. 5,712

XXII 1(a) *Wakka sak sukup, ape sak sukup* (b) Reared without water, reared without fire; 2. Monshi, pp. 457–560; 3(a); 4. 2,820

Additional items

XXIII   1(a) *Poiyaumpe*; 2. Batchelor, pp. 106–45; 3(b) (English); 5. This is in prose, but has typical *yukar* content

XXIV   1(a) *Rurupun niśpa ućas koma* (b) The rich man of Rurupa; 2. Piłsudski, pp. 12–24; 3(a) (b) (English). 5. Recited rhythmically, but probably local to Sakhalin and not a *yukar*

Note: While this chapter was in proof, the following important work on the Ainu epic appeared: Philippi, Donald L., *Songs of gods, songs of humans* (Princeton and Tokyo, 1979), xiv + 417 pp.

EAST AFRICAN

The Bahima Praise Poems

By H. F. MORRIS

The Background

THE HOMELAND OF THE BAHIMA lies in the short-grass uplands to the west of
Lake Victoria in what is now western Uganda and north-western Tanzania,
where for centuries they have grazed their herds of long-horned cattle. Writers
of the nineteenth, and first half of the present centuries, generally accepted
without question that these people were Hamitic in origin and had entered
Uganda from the north-east a number of centuries ago as conquering warriors
and had imposed their domination upon the indigenous Bantu cultivators.
Today such theories are treated with caution, and little more can be said in
this respect with any degree of certainty than that, when, probably in the
fifteenth century, the various small kingdom states emerged in this area,
traditionally coming into existence on the disintegration of the large Bacwezi
kingdom, the Bahima already occupied a dominant position in their social
organization. It is with the Bahima of one of these kingdom states — Ankole —
that we are here concerned.[1]

The kingdom of Ankole, from small beginnings in the south-east of the
present district at around the close of the fifteenth century, spread steadily
northwards and westwards during the eighteenth and nineteenth centuries,
incorporating neighbouring kingdoms, until by the end of the nineteenth
century, when British influence first made itself felt, it was the most powerful
state in the area. Ankole's pasture-lands were famed for their excellence and
here the Bahima, with their vast herds, still preserved a dominant social
position and separate cultural identity to a far greater extent than elsewhere in
Uganda. They were, however, a minority in the kingdom, the inhabitants of
which comprised two distinct groups, the pastoralist Bahima (singular,
Muhima) and the agriculturalist Bairu (singular, Mwiru). In personal appearance, the two peoples were easily distinguishable, the typical Muhima,
tall and slender with a comparatively light coloured skin, standing in contrast
to the darker coloured, more negroid Mwiru.

It was, however, in the cultures of the two peoples that the most fundamental
difference lay. The Muhima was essentially a pastoralist and his whole life
centred around his cattle herds, each member of which with its pedigree was
known to him, and with them he would periodically move his settlement to

find fresh pasture. From his herds the Muhima derived most of what he needed to maintain himself and his family, for his diet consisted almost exclusively of milk, butter, cattle blood, and occasionally the meat of slaughtered calves. The Mwiru, on the other hand, was an agriculturalist who engaged in various crafts such as metal working and pottery. To him the ownership of female cattle was forbidden and he did not share in the cattle culture of the Bahima. Both these people, or classes of society, had their part to play in the traditional organization of the kingdom and were inter-dependent upon each other. At the head of society was the Omugabe who was believed to be descended from the legendary Bacwezi and also, according to some authorities, to possess certain semi-divine powers, such as that of rain-making.[2] He chose his chiefs from among his relatives and prominent Bahima, and these were given areas of the kingdom to administer and were responsible for bringing their followers with their spears and bows to fight in the ever recurrent campaigns waged by the Omugabe against his neighbours with the plunder of cattle as the principal aim.

The Bahima were the warriors and the leaders of society and on them the Bairu relied for protection. The Bairu, for their part, provided much that the Bahima needed and did not themselves produce, such as craftwork and beer. They also performed for the Bahima certain menial work in their kraals, such as hut building. In return, the Bairu received presents and patronage from their social superiors. There was, moreover, a certain amount of social mobility between the two sections of the community. Although it has been stated that inter-marriage between Bahima and Bairu was forbidden, this, if it had been so in the distant past, was no longer true by the late nineteenth century. By that time it had become not uncommon for a promising Mwiru who had distinguished himself to be given a Muhima wife and cattle: his children would then adopt a Muhima way of life and they, or at any rate their descendants, would be looked upon, both by themselves and others, as Bahima. Whatever ethnic differences there may have been between Bahima and Bairu, the main distinction between them had become one of social class and the following of a distinctive mode of life. To be a Muhima meant to possess wealth — for cattle were the principal form of wealth known to society — social prestige and position, and, above all, a culture which centred exclusively around cattle.

An administrative station was first set up by the British in Ankole in 1898 and three years later a formal Agreement was concluded between the Omugabe and his principal chiefs on the one hand and the British Crown on the other. Ankole was thenceforth, until the ending of British rule in 1962, administered as a district of the Uganda Protectorate through a Native Government of which the Omugabe was the head.[3] Under Uganda's Independence Constitution Ankole was given the status of a federal kingdom which she retained until

1967 when the Uganda Government abolished the institution of kingship and established a unitary state.

At the outset the British administration worked through the Bahima chiefs whose sons were educated in the schools of the Church Missionary Society. But it was not long before the new régime began to undermine the existing social order. The establishment of schools, even in the remotest areas, gave the Bairu the opportunity, of which they avidly availed themselves, of obtaining an education which enabled them to compete with the Bahima for positions of authority. Soon after the Second World War a spirit of bitterness, said to have been hitherto unknown, had become evident between Bahima and Bairu, the latter resenting any surviving aspects of privilege enjoyed by the traditional ruling class.[4] If the spread of education, coupled with the general egalitarian outlook of the colonial administration in the latter decades of its existence, played a vital part in undermining Bahima dominance, there were also economic forces working relentlessly to the same effect. Throughout the present century the growth of cash crops has steadily eclipsed cattle-keeping as the main source of the district's wealth. This century has not been a happy one for Ankole's pastoralists. The ravages of rinderpest, which had devasted Ankole's herds at the close of the nineteenth century and in the early years of the present century, were followed in the succeeding decades by the remorseless inroads of the tsetse fly. The result has been the emigration from the district of many Bahima, with their herds, as large areas of what had traditionally been the best grazing lands had to be closed as unfit for pasture.

From the outset of the colonial regime, leading Bahima adapted themselves to the new cultural environment (though still retaining their love of cattle), becoming a highly educated élite, sophisticated and generally westernized in outlook, among their own people. The bulk of the Bahima, on the other hand, have remained indifferent to the attractions of education and the twentieth-century way of life, and, except in so far as cattle raiding can no longer be an occupation, they follow almost unchanged the way of life of their ancestors. Like them, they continue to live in kraals consisting of temporary beehive huts surrounded by their cattle to which they devote their lives, ever on the move, so far as the authorities permit, to find fresh pasture. Their herds are un-economically large and, by modern standards relatively unproductive both in meat and milk and are consistently over-grazing the limited pasture-lands available. But the Muhima has resisted the exhortations of the veterinary authorities to improve the quality of his herds or to sell his beasts, for the Muhima values his cattle for other than modern economic reasons, for example on account of the beauty and grace of their horns, and he has little incentive to deplete his herds by sale, since he has little need for money save to pay his taxes and to buy the coloured cloth with which he clothes himself. It is among these unsophisticated Bahima, still living the traditional way of life, that the

z

heroic tradition, and in particular the composition and recitation of the praise poems, still flourishes.[5] Before turning to the praise poems themselves, something must briefly be said about the language spoken in Ankole.

Runyankore is, like the neighbouring Bantu languages, a highly flexible language having the capacity to convey considerable subtlety in meaning. It also has a wide range of vocabulary, which is, as is to be expected, particularly rich in words relating to the traditional cattle culture. Nevertheless, there is a considerable borrowing both from Luganda[6] and from English. This process, which is particularly noticeable in the praise poems, has meant the absorption into the language of foreign words in a Runyankore form permitting their adaptation to the grammatical and tonal structure of Runyankore. Runyankore is the common language of both Bahima and Bairu, though certain comparatively minor differences in pronunciation exist between the two peoples. Nevertheless, much of the vocabulary concerning cattle has tended to be used almost exclusively by the Bahima, and, since it has been the speech of the agriculturalists, who have formed the bulk of the population, which has been taught in schools and been represented in the body of written literature which has grown up during the present century, there is a considerable vocabulary dealing with cattle which has fallen out of general use and is now only familiar to the unsophisticated Bahima. The appearance of this vocabulary in the praise poems gives the impression that the language of these poems is archaic, since much of it is unintelligible to most Bairu and indeed to many educated Bahima. In fact, however, the composer of a praise poem, though he is constantly choosing striking or unusual words for poetic effect, does not, it would seem, consciously strive after the archaic: his language is, in general, that spoken by his associates, Bahima who have had little or no education as understood in western terms.

Two important aspects of Runyankore must be mentioned on account of their importance in the structure of the praise poems. The first is that the language is tonal, certain words being distinguishable in meaning on account of the tone they bear: there are three tones, one high, one falling and one low. The second is that of the five vowels in the language each appears in two forms, one long and one short.

Runyankore, being a Bantu language, like all such languages, operates its noun and verb systems through a regular series of alliterative prefixes attached to stems. Nouns consist of a class prefix — which may, or may not, be preceded by an initial vowel — and a stem, and every noun can be allocated to a class according to its prefix. Furthermore, these class prefixes (of which there are sixteen in all) can, in most cases, be paired, one of the pair denoting singularity and the other plurality; for example *O-mu-gabe*, a king, *A-ba-gabe*, kings. There are certain underlying ideas contained in each class prefix: for example, nouns with the singular *Mu* prefix and the plural *Ba* prefix include most of those which indicate human beings, whilst the *Ka* and *Bu* prefixes may indicate smallness. For each of the series of class prefixes, there are also one or more pronominal prefixes by which other words, including demonstratives, possessives, and verbs, are brought into grammatical relationship with the noun.

Verbs, moreover, often comprise not only a pronominal prefix, but also tense signs and object infixes. Sentences may, accordingly, be made up as follows:

O-mu-riisa	a-	ka-	reeta	e-n-te
(Class 1)	(class I pronominal prefix) (far past tense sign)	(stem)		(class 9)
The herdsman	brought			the cow
A-ba-riisa	ba-	ka-	reeta	e-n-te
The herdsmen	brought			the cow
A-ba-riisa	ba-ka-gi-reeta			
The herdsmen	brought it (gi being the class 9 object infix in agreement with ente)[7]			

The Literary Tradition of the Bahima

The literary tradition of the Bahima is exclusively oral, for writing was unknown in Ankole until the impact of western civilization at the end of the last century and, as yet, no significant body of Runyankore written literature has been produced. The body of oral literature is wide in its range, including proverbs and riddles; folk tales, of which the most popular are the Hare cycle, in which the cunning hare outwits the other animals, and the Ishe-Katabazi cycle describing the comical adventures of the foolish, but endearing, hero and his son; stories of historical and legendary heroes; and praise poems.[8] Prose and poetry both play their part, but where the heroic tradition is to the fore the latter replaces the former. For example, there are stories of historical heroes which start as narratives in prose, but in which the teller switches to metric recitation when highlighting the heroic deeds of the hero. In the praise poems — the subject of this essay — where the heroic tradition is most fully — indeed extravagantly — developed, the form is invariably metric and the delivery is given in an appropriately flamboyant manner which will be described later.[9] The heroic and metric portion of the oral literature stands apart from the rest as to content, in which the heroes and their actions are larger than life, as to formal structure and as to mode of delivery: it is this part of the literature that is the most highly appreciated by the Bahima. Yet all these types of the oral literature have this in common: they are the product of the ordinary members of the Bahima community by whom they are remembered and recited, or in the case of the praise poems composed and recited, as inclination dictates or circumstance requires. There is no tradition of a bardic class — even in connexion with the Omugabe's court — and the oral literature is that of the people, the story teller or reciter performing for the enjoyment of himself and his associates or neighbours.

The Nature of the Praise Poems[10]

The praise poems fall into two categories, depending on whether they are composed by men or women. It is with the poems composed and recited by men that we are here concerned and these are of two types, those known as *ebyevugo*,[11] in which the composer boasts of his deeds of heroism in battle, and those known as *ebirahiro*,[12] in which the composer boasts of the splendour of his cattle.[13] Women's praise poems are similar in structure to those of the men, but the ethos of their composition and recitation is very different, and they do not play so important a part in the social life of the Bahima. In the first place, the poems corresponding to men's *ebyevugo* are not concerned with deeds of heroism, but rather with praise of feminine beauty and virtue, nor is self-adulation so all pervading, since praise is freely given to the composer's companions.[14] In the second place, they are not delivered in the flamboyant manner of the men's recitations, which will be referred to later: instead, they are quietly recited in a sitting position, usually to the accompaniment of the enanga harp. Since this art form thus lacks the main heroic characteristics of the praise poems of the men, I do not propose to deal with it further in this essay.[15]

Traditionally every Muhima would be expected, as occasion demanded, to compose praise poems boasting of the virtues he attributed to himself as a warrior and performer of deeds of heroism. These he would recite, firstly in battle to keep up his own and his companions' courage, secondly on certain particular occasions, as when he received a chieftainship from the Omugabe, or when appearing before his prospective father-in-law the night before he received his bride, and thirdly for the general entertainment of his friends at social gatherings. These *ebyevugo* are not, and are not intended to be understood as being, factual accounts of what the hero actually accomplished, though evidently in the past, when warfare and cattle raiding were still endemic, it was a war-like exploit of the hero which provided the pretext and inspiration for his boasts. They are, and are accepted by the audience as being, extravagant boasts, epitomizing the traditional virtues of the young Muhima male. The ethos of these poems is essentially heroic and the doings of the hero are larger than life. He overcomes the hosts of the enemy, who flee in terror before him, his companions are rescued, their cattle saved, and that of the enemy plundered. All this the hero accomplishes through his courage and his skill in the use of the bow, the spear, and the art of wrestling. There is no question of supernatural aid: the valour of the hero is such that of this he would have no need.[16] The hero normally associates his companions with him in his deeds of heroism, but the

part they play is subordinate to his. A typical line of an *ekyevugo* in the traditional style runs as follows:

> I Who Prepare For Battle pushed my way to the enemy's rear and with
> me was the Bringer Of Sorrow.

The hero is the embodiment of the ideal Muhima warrior and the attributes of such a warrior may be discerned from a study of the praise names
which the composer invents for himself, a new one usually being chosen for
each line of the *ekyevugo*. Some of the praise names which may be encountered,
with the attributes they attach to the hero, are as follows. The hero should be
handsome and young with the speed, agility and tirelessness of youth:

> I who am pleasing in appearance,
> I who do not waste my manhood,
> I who gambol as a calf,
> I who am agile,
> I who take myself over mountains,
> I whom the foe does not weary,
> I who seek no rest.

The hero is, of course, a warrior, one to whom battle is a joy in itself:

> I who am drawn to battle as cattle are drawn to pasture,
> I who am in the forefront of the battle,
> I who heap up the dead,
> I who cause much blood to flow,
> I who push aside the spears,
> I who am not reluctant in battle,
> I who speak not of flight,
> I who keep the fire of battle alight within me,
> I who stand like a snake poised to strike,
> I who am unyielding before young warriors,
> I who have the scars of battle.

He is impatient for battle and the very sight of the foe fills him with fury:

> I who do not wait for dawn to break,
> I who search out the foe,
> I who am black with anger,
> I who need hosts of the enemy to fight.

He is, of course, without fear:

> I who do not fear black iron,
> I who do not tremble
> I who need no protection
> I who am not alarmed by the footsteps of the plunderers.

He is single-minded in his pursuit of glory:

> I who cannot be diverted from my purpose,
> I who do not give way in matters of cattle,
> I who do not slacken as a rope loses its tautness
> I who cannot be dissuaded from battle,
> I who seek no avoidance of difficulties.

Towards the enemy he is remorseless and over the body of his fallen adversary he triumphs and recites his own praises:

> I who bring disaster to the enemy,
> I who inflict pain on the foe.

He is, of course, highly skilled in the use of his weapons:

> I who draw tight the bow,
> I who do not miss my mark,
> I who do not fail to throw the foe.

The Muhima warrior is an individualist, and he is one who knows no modesty. Indeed, as we have seen, the art of self-praise is a necessary accomplishment:

> I who am praised,
> I who do not despise myself,
> I who am second to none,
> I who excel among warriors,
> I who am admired.

Although the hero's companions are associated with the hero in his deeds of valour, he has no need of their help:

> I who fight alone,
> I who seek no help.

On the other hand, he has a duty of loyalty to his companions, who depend upon him:

> I who protect my companions,
> I who give my companions courage,
> I whose aid is sought,
> I who redeem my companions,
> I who have no need to redeem my companions (because I
>   do not allow them to be captured),
> I who do not permit the cattle or the chief to be taken,
> I who keep my word.

So too, he is impetuous and scorns the counsels of caution:

> I who waste no time in the attack,
> I who depend not on the advice of others,
> I who am direct in attack,
> I who cannot be dissuaded from battle.

Nevertheless, deviousness and tactical skill are also to be admired:

> I whose decisions are wise,
> I who take the foe by surprise,
> I who encircle the foe,
> I who am vigilant,
> I who am invisible,
> I who do not disclose my plans,
> I who am unpredictable,

The *ekyevugo* is essentially a personal, topical and, indeed, ephemeral composition. The composer, inspired by some outstanding event, uses it as the background for an *ekyevugo*. While the event is still fresh in the minds of his associates, his *ekyevugo* will be especially popular. Then compositions by the same man or another, dealing with more recent events, may supplant it in the public's popularity: certainly it would be unlikely to survive its composer, for it is poems in one's own praise, not in the praise of another, that a Muhima wishes to recite.[17] Yet, although the *ebyevugo* today, as in the past, are based upon incidents which are more or less contemporaneous with their composition, the spirit which inspires them, together with the underlying themes in their content, belong to a past age — that of the warrior and the cattle raid — which ended three-quarters of a century ago. Virtually no Bahima survive with personal knowledge of pre-colonial times, nor have the Bahima during this century resisted the new forces of civil order: they are, in general, a law-abiding people, no more addicted to acts of violence — whether it be homicide or cattle raiding — than their neighbours. Yet, a nostalgic memory of the past, and of the old values which it represented, survives: the ideal qualities of the Muhima youth, which the poet attributes to himself when composing his praises and which are applauded by his audience when he recites them, are those of a warrior acting in the social setting of the last century. Contemporary incidents providing an occasion for an *ekyevugo*, perhaps mere scuffles with strangers at a watering place, appear in the *ekyevugo* as battles of heroic proportions.

This can best be illustrated by turning to the *ebyevugo* composed in connexion with the coronation of the Omugabe Gasyonga II in 1945. The accession of the Omugabe was disputed by a pretender to the throne and the situation was, for the Bahima, highly evocative of the old wars of succession which, during the

eighteenth and nineteenth centuries, had almost invariably followed the death
of an Omugabe. In actual fact, there were no disorders, the Omugabe being
peaceably crowned and the dispute disposed of in a court of law. Nevertheless,
the large number of *ebyevugo* which these events inspired describe fighting and
bloodshed. Such *ebyevugo* deal with the journeys which the Bahima made from
all over the kingdom to attend the coronation ceremonies as though they were
military exercises. Places which the hero passed on the way are named and
here engagements are purported to take place with the enemy forces of the
pretender which are scattered by the prowess of the hero. The following is a
short extract from one such *ekyevugo*:

> I Who Am Not Easily Startled defeated the foe with the strength of
> youth together with Kabinda;
> At Kanyina-bairagura I escaped safe from danger;
> I Who Am Not Perplexed despised those who confronted me amid my
> cattle together with Rubengye.
> At Bweitimba they applauded my assault and with me was Rukuhiza;
> At Twemyambi I was praised by all and with me was Rutetebya.
> The cowardly ones feared they would be wounded;
> I Who Assault The Foe was chosen from among the three hundred
> fighters together with Kawikoma;
> I Who Announce Myself left them dead on the battle-field.[18]

The *ebyevugo* are metric compositions, the rhythm consisting of a series of
stressed syllables more or less evenly spaced throughout each verse, the most
favoured type of syllable to bear a stress being one containing a long vowel.
For example:

> R(u)tashoroorwa bakaandekura nkabaanza
> R(u)tariimbik(a) ebikoomi nkabyeetuuram(u).[19]

Each verse, which is known as an *enkome* and forms an entity for the purpose of
delivery, is composed of a number of lines, usually varying from two to five.
The lines of an *enkome* tend to balance one another as regards the incidence of
stress, the nature of the stress-bearing syllables and, to some extent, the structure
of the component words. The degree to which this is carried out depends upon
the individual style of the composer, for example:

> Rutúúmana nkabyeemá Magyeegye na Majuungu
> Rushiíjana nkabirohá Mareebwa na Marwiíja
> R(u)táágir(a) okabyooreká Maziinga na Mareengye
> R(u)tashoróórwa nkazaagiz(a) ámaguundu Magyeenza na Magiimbi.[20]

A line is normally a self-contained entity as far as the sense is concerned, each
line describing a separate piece of action on the part of the hero or one of his
companions. A translation of the *enkome* quoted above[21] will make this clear.

I Who Heap Up The Dead attacked them at Magyeegye and Majuungu;
I The Attacker repulsed them at Mareebwa and Marwiiga;
You Who Call For Your Spear drove them towards Maziinga and
    Mareengye;
I Who Am Not Rejected wore out the warriors at Magyeenza and
    Magiimbi.

Of the various devices which the composer uses to give a poetic content to an *ekyevugo*, as well as to heighten its heroic content, the use of praise names is the most outstanding. Bahima during the course of their lives are given praise names, sometimes several, which refer to some characteristic which they possess or to some event in which they have taken part.[22] These praise names are composed of the honorific prefix *Ru* attached usually to a verbal relative stem: for example Rutomora, He who leads the attack. Sometimes the praise name forms a compound, a noun being added to the verbal stem: e.g. Rusheeshangabo, He who disperses the warriors. In composing an *ekyevugo*, however, the poet invents praise names for himself (though those of his companions are usually their own) and frequently each line of an enkome introduces the hero with a new praise name which often reflects the action which the line describes, for example: Rujwiga nkahigisa oburakare na Runyabyoma (I, The Angry One, fought with great fury and so did He Who Is Of Iron). Great ingenuity is shown by the composer in the construction of these praise names. Unusual verbs are chosen and converted into praise names with a metaphorical meaning. Many are inspired by the daily life of the poet's beloved cattle, for example:

Ruseeturwa-mpaka, I who am drawn to battle as cattle are led to pasture (from the
    passive of the stem -*seetura* 'to lead cattle to pasture' and the noun *empaka*
    'a contest');
Rushiijana, I who attack the enemy as a bull mounts a cow (from -*shiijana* 'to
    mate' of cattle);
Rukina, I who gambol like a calf, i.e. I who am quick or agile (from -*kina* 'to
    gambol');
Rutazaagira, I who do not stay idle (from the stem -*zaagira* 'to stand still' (of cattle)
    with the negative relative particle, *ta*).

In composing these praise names, the poet makes much use of litotes, for example:

Rutaruuma, I who have not got elephantiasis, i.e. I who am agile;
Rutashaijuuka, I who am not emasculated;
Rutakundirwa, I who am not loved (by the enemy);
Rutacungura, I who do not (have to) to redeem (my companions), i.e. I do not
    allow them to be captured;
Rutiina-mpora, I who am slow to fear;
Rutasiraara-mu-rugamba, I who am not reluctant in battle.

The search for the unusual and the striking, which is so characteristic in the construction of praise names, applies, in general, to the whole of an *ekyevugo*. Everyday nouns and verbs tend to be avoided and circumlocutions are frequently employed. Thus we find, for example, rifles described as 'the strikers of elephants' (*enkuba-njojo*) and as 'those which strike from afar' (*enkubira-haraingwa*) and warriors described as 'the savours of the cattle' (*abajuna-nte*). Most marked in this respect is the wealth of expressions used for the spear, the most important of the Muhima warrior's traditional weapons. Though there is constant reference throughout the *ebyevugo* to this weapon, the ordinary word for spear, *eicumu*, comparatively rarely occurs: instead we get, among others, the following poetic alternatives:

> *Enyarwanda*, the cattle of Rwanda (whose long pointed horns suggest
>   spears to a Muhima)
> *enshoro* 'sharp points';
> *orubango* 'spear shaft';
> *amashorongo-nyondo* 'things sharpened with the hammer';
> *ebyoma-biiragura* 'black iron';
> *enyabya-bikungu* 'the breakers of anthills'.[23]

This avoidance of the commonplace often takes the form in modern *ebyevugo* of the use of Luganda and English words (in Runyankore form) in place of the familiar Runyankore ones.

A conciseness of style is one of the characteristics of the *ebyevugo* and a line is often composed of little more than a verb in the far past tense[24] together with praise, place or proper names. A typical line takes the following form:

> Rutahindukirana   nkashumuurura Nyabongi   na
> I Who Keep My Word   started the fight at Nyabongi together with
>   Ruhambisa-njungu.
>   The Ravisher With The Spear.

Nouns, apart from praise, place and proper names, are used sparingly, and it is frequently left to the subject or object prefixes attached to the verbal stem to express the meaning of nouns which are themselves omitted. This, however, produces considerable obscurity, no doubt intentionally. For example, we find the line

> Rutembana akagaasira omu buranga na Rutigira
> He Who Goes In To The Attack shouted in the face of them and so did He
>   Who Will Not Give Way.

Here the object infix *ga*, which is used with *Ma* class plural nouns, precedes the verbal stem *-asira* and all we know for certainty is that it refers to a noun in this class: it might be *amasyo* 'herds', *amamanzi* 'warriors', *amacumu* 'spears', or any of the large number of other *Ma* class nouns which would fit in the context. Only the composer can know with complete certainty which noun is intended, but one well versed in the idiom of the *ebyevugo* will be able to say with confidence that in this particular case it was in the face of the *spears* that Rutembana shouted.

The manner in which these *ebyevugo* are recited is distinctive and well suited to their heroic content. The most oustanding characteristic of the manner of performance is the speed at which the recitation takes place. The reciter, who is known as an *omwevugi*,[25] has to deliver each *enkome* without pause for breath. Since it is the line, and not the *enkome*, which is an entity from the point of view of sense, it is possible for the *omwevugi* to vary the length of the *enkome*, choosing the number of lines at which to make his breath pause according to his lung capacity. An *enkome* does not usually exceed four or five lines.[26] At the beginning of the *enkome*, the high tones in the early part of the line are accentuated, thus keeping up the pitch of the *omwevugi*'s voice until near the end. Towards the end, and very markedly during the last part of the last line, the pitch of the *omwevugi*'s voice tails away. At the end of the *enkome*, the *omwevugi* snaps his finger and thumb[27] and the audience greets this with the chorus of '*Eee*'. In delivering an *ekyevugo*, the *omwevugi* stands with a spear in his right hand held horizontal above the shoulder or with the spear planted in the ground and his right arm outstretched. As he recites, he takes small paces backwards and forwards and marks the stresses with his heel and small forward movements with his outstretched arm or spear. He recites, of course, from memory whether or not the composition is his own. The length of an *ekyevugo* varies considerably, a usual length being of about eighty to a hundred lines.[28] The *omwevugi* may, however, omit or add *enkome* or interchange the sequence of lines as he thinks fit and the more important the occasion the more likely he is to provide the fullest version.

Many of the special occasions on which *ebyevugo* were recited, particularly when in the midst of battle, can no longer occur in present-day conditions.[29] Nevertheless, the recitation of these praise poems is still a popular pastime among the Bahima herdsmen as a form of entertainment in the evenings. Here the *omwevugi* has an audience (the members of which are themselves composers of such poems) which understands and appreciates, not merely the art employed in the composition, but also the circumstances which have given rise to the particular poem and the elliptical references which it contains. They applaud the composer's ingenuity in devising enigmatic references to topical events and striking turns of phrase and praise names, but above all the *omwevugi* is judged by his skill in recitation — his speed and capacity to encompass long *enkome* within one breath, without pause between words or lines, without faltering and without permitting the pitch of his voice to fall appreciably until the latter part of the last line.

The observations made above have been in respect of the *ebyevugo*, but many of them are equally applicable to the *ebirahiro* — the poems in praise of the composer's cattle. These are, in general, virtually identical to the *ebyevugo* in so far as metric structure, division into lines and *enkome* and mode of recitation are concerned. Furthermore, both art forms make use of praise names and heightened language and employ metaphor, circumlocution and enigmatic references by way of prefixes without the nouns with which these stand in grammatical agreement. On the other hand, there are significant differences between the *ebyevugo* and the *ebirahiro*. In the first place, there arises the question as to whether the *ebirahiro*, as well as the *ebyevugo*, can be classed as heroic. Here we are dealing with the activities of cattle and not of heroes. Nevertheless, cattle are so vital and integral a part of the traditional way of life of the Muhima warrior — for it was the raiding of cattle that motivated his aggressive exploits and the protection of his herds that inspired defensive action — that the heroic ethos runs through the *ebirahiro* as well as the *ebyevugo*. The praise names (formed like those of the cattle's owners with the honorific prefix *Ru* attached normally to a verbal relative stem) glorify the members of the herd and often attribute almost warrior-like propensities to the beasts, for example:

> She who prevents other cattle approaching her;
> She who is not dissuaded from fighting.

So too the actions of the cattle are frequently likened to those of warriors, for example:

> At Rwekubo near Kinanga, the herd walked proudly having killed a
> loaned beast;
> At Maka-abiri near Rubirizi, at Mukora-iguru near Garumuri, they
> pressed me like challenging warriors.

The cattle which the composer praises are his cows, for to a Muhima a bull is of comparatively little importance and indeed most bull calves are killed at birth to conserve their mother's milk. The pedigree of each cow of the herd is well known to the owner and, when a cow is not referred to in the *ebirahiro* by its praise name, it is given the name which it bears on account of its colour or markings (for which Runyankore has a wide range of words), together with a reference to the colour name of its mother. Often the name contains reference to the colour of the cow's grandmother or of even more remote antecedents. The actual colour name, apart from that of the most remote ancestor mentioned, is not, in fact, given, but instead the genitive particle (-*a* 'of') in agreement with the noun class of the appropriate colour name. Thus we get:

Ga rwa bihogo[30] (for Mayenje ga ruhuuzimu rwa bihogo)
The spotted cow, (daughter) of the grey cow with white spots, (daughter)
    of the strawberry cow.

The praise names for the most part describe the cow's beauty and to the Muhima
this lies above all in the grace of her long horns. Hence, we get, for example,
such varied praise names as:

> She whose horns stand out above the herd,
> She whose horns are as straight as planks,
> She whose horns are as polished reeds,
> She whose horns encircle like handcuffs,
> She who lifts up her horns brown as the enkuraijo tree.

One of the differences which are to be found between the *ebyevugo* and
the *ebirahiro* is that the former are devoid of any sentimental content. The hero
is a warrior and his sole purpose is the overthrow of the enemy. There is no
place in the *ebyevugo* for romance or tenderness, nor have women any part to
play in the events of which they tell. When a Muhima composes an *ekirahiro*
the position is very different. Here he is telling of his cattle, each of which is
dear to him and, however large his herd, is known to him individually, and
here we find expressed affection and tenderness. Such sentiments appear in
lines such as:

> They stand still, graceful with their encircling horns,
> Like queens preparing their curls . . .
> They have spent the day at the Muziizi trees of Katooma;
> When they return home loneliness vanishes.

So too, we find pathos as, for example, when the owner finds his precious beasts
dying as a result of disease or drought.[31] Lyricism and romantic sentiment,
which in so many literary traditions find expression in poetry devoted to the
adulation of women, for the Bahima find an outlet in these compositions devoted
to the praise of cattle.[32]

    There is another point of difference between *ebyevugo* and *ebirahiro* composed
at the present time. As has been mentioned, modern *ebyevugo* are largely expressed in terms of a vanished way of life — that of the cattle raid: the setting
of the *ebirahiro* — that of the daily life of the Muhima and his cattle — is, on
the other hand, still of present-day relevance.

The Development of the Tradition of Praise Poetry

The tradition of the composition and recitation of praise poems is, no doubt,
one of considerable antiquity, which may well reach back to the formation in
this area, five or more centuries ago, of the small kingdom states, intermittently

engaged in warfare for the augmentation of their herds. Our knowledge of the social life in these kingdoms in previous centuries is, however, too slender to make conjecture as to the origin and development of the poetic tradition profitable. We have, however, references in the stories of historical heroes of the past to the recitation of praises in battle, and a particularly striking one occurs in the story of Muguta, a prince of Buhweju[33] at the close of the seventeenth century. Buhweju at this time was subordinate to Bunyoro and when a king of Bunyoro died, so the story tells us, the king of Buhweju would be sent for and, decked in ceremonial beads, would be led with his followers to the capital of the new king of Bunyoro and there executed. Muguta, whose praise names were 'The son of Butaho who leaps in the air when spears are breaking, the speedy one, who inflicts deadly injuries, whose shield excels all others', was determined to break the tyranny of Bunyoro and, when the king was to be sent for execution, he took his place together with his followers, the Nkondomi. When they reached the place of execution, they were bound and an axe was placed before each of them. Muguta's page then began to recite his master's praises, whereupon Muguta was lifted up into the clouds which thundered forth and the Banyoro captors were overpowered and executed with their own axes.

The praise poems are, as has already been indicated, topical in their inspiration and ephemeral in their popularity. This, coupled with the fact that the literary tradition is entirely oral, makes any assessment of the development of this art form hazardous, since data in the form of surviving examples from past generations are slight. Indeed, were we entirely dependent for examples of these poems upon those recited by the Bahima who composed them in their own praise, we would obviously have no material pre-dating the present generation. Fortunately, however, it appears to have been the common practice for Bairu dependants in the kraals of the Bahima to have learnt the praise poems of their masters and to have passed them on, though usually in a fragmentary form. As a result, one can still find men who can recite *ebyevugo* which date back to the second half of the last century. The earliest example which I have encountered is one concerning the invasion of Buhweju by the Omugabe Mutambuka in about the year 1865,[34] the first *enkome* of which states:

> I Who Am Praised thus held out in battle among foreigners along
>   with The Overthrower;
> I Who Ravish Spear In Each Hand stood out resplendent in my
>   cotton cloth;
> I Who Am Quick was drawn from afar by lust for the fight and with me
>   was The Repulser Of Warriors;
> I Who Encircle The Foe, with Bitembe, brought back the beasts from
>   Bihanga;
> With Bwakwakwa, I fought at Kaanyabareega,
> Where Bantura started a song that we might overcome them.

An extract from a later *ekyevugo*, dealing with a disturbance which took place in the south-west of the district in 1910,[35] after the establishment of the British administration, but before it had made any appreciable impact on the social life of the Bahima, at any rate in this remote part of the district, runs as follows:

> I The Destroyer surrounded the kraals of the unsuspecting and He Who
>   Fears Not The Spears was with me;
> I Who Overthrow The Foe vociferously drew my arrows from their
>   sheath . . .
> I Who Do Not Fear The Hosts Of Kakamba, together with Rusikabagomi,
> I Who Weary The Foe brought lamentation at dawn.
>
> I Who Fell The Foe drove before me the fleers at Bukuba;
> I Who Am Not Swallowed Up strode among the kraals.

The examples quoted above should be sufficient to show the general pattern of the nineteenth-century *ekyevugo*, which remains today the framework within which contemporary *ebyevugo* are, subject to varying degrees of modification, constructed. Is the art form now, however, in decline? In one sense it undoubtedly is. The whole way of life, social and economic, of the society to which the praise poems belong is, and has been during the greater part of this century, in decline. It was already anachronistic during the colonial period and an independent African state is even less likely to show tolerance towards a semi-nomadic society, resistant, on the one hand, to the forces of education and other modern aspects of social welfare and, on the other, to efficient methods of cattle husbandry. Throughout the greater part of this century, the *ebyevugo* have, as has been mentioned earlier, drawn their inspiration largely from an aspect of the traditional way of life which had already become a memory of the past — that of the cattle raid. Bahima, once they have received modern education, with very few exceptions are completely divorced from any real understanding of this traditional art of composition and recitation. When selected *abeevugi* are brought in to perform at civic functions,[36] they recite before an audience to which even the language in which the *ebyevugo* are expressed is largely incomprehensible, whilst it is quite unable to fathom the allusions and obscurities of meaning in which the recitations abound. The performances are applauded as tours de force and as quaint survivals of the people's traditional past, but as little more. The art of the praise poem cannot hope to survive the society which produced it, and its extinction is unlikely to be delayed beyond the lifetime of the present generation.

Nevertheless, among the Bahima still living what is basically the traditional way of life among their cattle, the composition of *ekyevugo* remains very much a live and flourishing art. Furthermore, the art form has shown a marked capacity to develop and reflect the present-day experiences of the Bahima. True, the underlying theme remains the cattle raid and the heroic virtues of the warrior of a past age, but this is, nevertheless, transposed into a contemporary setting. This is largely done by a device, which can be highly effective, of interposing between *enkome* of the traditional type, with praise names and deeds of heroic valour, *enkome* which are purely descriptive. The whole effect is heightened by the use of words borrowed from Luganda or English. A good example[37] is an *ekyevugo* about the coronation of the Omugabe Gasyonga II in 1945 composed by Mr Patrick Kirindi. The poem, which consists of 114 lines, opens with four *enkome* of the conventional type; then follow eleven *enkome* of a descriptive nature, then one conventional *enkome*, then eight descriptive *enkome* and lastly two conventional *enkome*.[38] The four, fifth, sixth and seventh *enkome* are given below. The fifth and sixth *enkome* describe the preparations at headquarters in Mbarara of the invitations to be sent out for the celebrations and the seventh describes the appearance of the Bahima who had come into Mbarara for the festivities. The English words typing, printing press, linotype, and cyclostyle are little changed in the Runyankore, though they are absorbed into the pattern of the language.[39]

> I Who Suffer No Pain, with The Scourge Of The Warriors, inflicted
>   injuries on the enemy;
> He Who Is Not Despised and He Who Comes To Grips With His
>   Adversary shouted on the riverland;
> He Who Fails Not To Overthrow The Foe and He Who Is Slow To
>   Show Fear made the cannons roar;
> I Who Do Not Lose My Manhood recited in the midst of the warriors.
>
> The letters were sent out by The Disperser Of Warriors;
> The typing was done by Mashunju;
> The handwriting was perfected by Kazoora;
> 'Agandi'[40] was sent out from Nyamitanga.
>
> The letters went through the printing press;
> They passed through the linotype;
> The cyclostyling was done by Manaase;
> Murumba's letter was taken by Kabwita.
>
> The clothes which they wore were white;
> The cloth was edged with fringes;
> The spears they held were silver and black;
> Their hair was cut in large tufts;
> Their ankle-rings were adorned with beads.

Adaptation of the traditional pattern has not basically affected either the metric structure of the poems or the manner of their recitation. Nor has it circumscribed the composer, but rather widened his scope, in his search for the unusual or startling word or turn of phrase, or for the elliptical or obscure

allusion. What one does find, however, in many modern *ebyevugo* is a considerable amount of borrowing of turns of phrase, or even complete lines, from other
contemporary praise poems. But this may be no new development and poets in
the past may have drawn upon the compositions of others: with our limited
knowledge of the poems of the nineteenth century, of this, as of so much else
concerning the development of this art form, we are ignorant.

An Appreciation of Some Examples

As will be clear from the examples already quoted, the actual deeds of the
hero recounted in an *ekyevugo*, heroic though they may be, are somewhat stereotyped and limited in imaginative range. It is not here that the poetic beauty
of the *ebyevugo* mainly lies, but in the choice of diction in the description of
these deeds and in the fertile imagery and subtle allusion which the poet
employs:[41] to convey this in bare unannotated translations is difficult, if not
impossible. It is, however, proposed to examine extracts from translations of
three praise poems, the first an *ekyevugo*, called the Ekirimbi, dating from the
second decade of this century, the second an *ekyevugo* about the Second World
War and the third an *ekirahiro* composed at about the same time as the *Ekirimbi*.

(i)   *The* Ekirimbi

During the early years of the British administration in Ankole, a number of
Bahima, unable to adapt themselves to the new regime, migrated with their
herds across the frontier into German East Africa. One of these emigrés was a
chief called Kijoma who died a few years later leaving two sons, Kakonya and
Rutabindwa. During the First World War, the British administration in
Uganda encouraged those Bahima who had left their native land to return,
and Kakonya, with about a hundred followers and 1,400 head of cattle, decided
to leave German territory for Ankole. Kakonya's men were known as the
Ekirimbi (an arrow sheath) and one of them, Ruhanantuka, composed this
ekyevugo, of which he is, of course, the hero, describing the journey of these
would-be warriors back to Ankole. The *ekyevugo*, which consists of eighty-four
lines,[42] is constructed purely in the traditional style of the nineteenth-century
compositions. Each line, with only two exceptions, begins with a praise or
place name and normally ends with the name of a companion who is thus
associated, though in a subordinate position, with the valour of the composer.
Line after line recounts the heroic actions of the hero and there is here no sign
of the innovations which we would expect to find some twenty years later, such
as the interposing of purely descriptive verses. Yet, though the time may not
have come for concessions in form to be made to a changing society in which
warfare has become a thing of the past, the story which the *ekyevugo* tells is

AA

already divorced from factual reality, even when every allowance has been made for the gross exaggeration or invention of heroic valour inherent in all the praise poems of whatever period. To the composer the Ekirimbi's journey was a military exercise achieved in the face of fearful opposition and conducted as, no doubt, a Muhima would consider that such an undertaking *should* be conducted. But in fact no bullets assailed the Ekirimbi, no spears flew and no cannon had to be silenced as the *ekyevugo* tells us, for, though, no doubt, the German authorities made considerable difficulties for the Ekirimbi, their passage was a peaceful one.

The Ekirimbi is a typical *ekyevugo* of its time and possesses a fair degree of inventiveness and ingenuity, both in its use of praise names and in elliptical allusion in the body of the lines. In the opening *enkome* the conventional dedication is pronounced — the dedication to battle in the cause of the leader.

> I Who Give Courage To My Companions!   (1)[43]
> I Who Am Not Reluctant In Battle made a vow!   (2)

Then follow these eight *enkome*:

> I Who Am Not Reluctant In Battle made a vow at midnight and with me
>   was The Tamer Of Recruits;   (3)
> I Who Am Not Loved By The Foe was full of fury when the enemy were
>   reported.   (4)
>
> I Who Am Vigilant called up the men at speed together with The
>   Pain Bringer;   (5)
> I found The Giver Of Courage in secret conference.   (6)
>
> I Whose Decisions Are Wise, at me they directed their attack and with
>   me was Rwamisooro;   (7)
> I Who Overthrow The Foe returned to the fight as they attacked us.   (8)
>
> I Who Am Nimble withstood the bullets together with The Lover Of
>   Battle;   (9)
> I Who Am Invisible appeared with The Infallible One.   (10)
>
> I Who Grasp My Weapons Firmly was sent in advance to Ruyanja
>   together with The Overthrower;   (11)
> I Who Seek No Avoidance Of Difficulties drew my bow.   (12)
>
> I Who Do Not Tremble drew my bow with The One Who Tightens
>   His Bow-string;   (13)
> I Who Crouch For The Attack, they brought me back for my sandals
>   together with The Tall One;[44]   (14)
> I Who Do Not Disclose My Plans fought furiously and with me was
>   The Brave One;   (15)
> I Who Do Not Miss The Mark crossed over noiselessly together with
>   The Spear Thrower.   (16)

I Who Am Not Reluctant In Battle was with The One Eager For
 Plunder;   (17)
I Who Attack On All Sides appeared with The One Who Exhausts
 The Foe.   (18)

I Who Move Forward To The Attack took the track of the Ekirimbi
 together with The Bringer Of Sorrow;   (19)
I Who Am In The Forefront Of The Battle tracked them down at Migyera
 together with The One Who Depends Not On The Advice Of
 Others.   (20)

Each line is here introduced with a praise name and many of the lines consist
of no more than the praise name of the hero, the name of a companion associated with the action and verbal form; nouns are few and much of the meaning
of the line is conveyed by the means of prefixes attached to the verbal stem. An
example of this is to be seen in line twelve which illustrates well the economy in
the use of words and the range of meaning which the composer can convey by
inference. The line, in fact, consists of two words only — *Rutashungura nkabukyengyeramu*; the first word is the praise name (I who seek no avoidance of difficulties) and the second is built up as follows: *n* (I) *ka* (far past tense infix) *bu*
('it', an object infix in agreement with some noun of the *Bu* class) *kyengyera*
(verbal stem meaning 'to sink down or disappear') *mu* (adverbial suffix,
'within'). It is clear that the omitted noun is *obuta* 'a bow', and *nkabukyengyeramu*
thus means literally, 'I disappeared within the bow', a figurative way of saying,
'I drew my bow', the idea conveyed being that, as the archer crouches to draw
his bow, he is lost to sight behind it. Incidentally, the word is repeated in the
next line, a common device for emphasis. The praise names which the composer
has invented for himself in these lines are formed from a variety of verbal
stems which give a good idea of the range of verbs which a composer may
draw on and to which he imparts an heroic significance. The majority are
negative forms with the familiar implication of litotes. Thus:

ll. 3, 17,   I who am not reluctant in battle (from the negative of the stem *-siraara*
 'to go unwillingly')
l. 4,   I who am not loved (by the foe) (from the negative of the passive prepositional form of the stem *-kunda* 'to love')
l. 5,   I who am vigilant (from the negative of the stem *-hwekyera* 'to doze')
l. 10,   I who am invincible (from the negative of the passive of the stem *-baasa*
 'to be able')
l. 11,   I who grasp my weapons firmly (a compound formed from the negative of
 the stem *-anjuka*, to be delirious and the noun *engaro*, fingers, meaning
 literally 'I who am not delirious in the fingers')
l. 12,   I who seek no avoidance of difficulties (from the negative of the stem
 -hingura 'to pass by')

l. 13,   I who do not tremble (from the negative of the stem -*tungura* 'to shiver with fever')

l. 16,   I who do not miss the mark (from the negative of the stem -*tsyama* 'to go astray')

l. 20,   I who am in the forefront of the battle (a compound formed from the negative of the passive of the prepositional form of the stem -*reeba* 'to see', with the adverb *enyima* 'behind' meaning literally 'I who am not seen behind')

The other praise names of the hero, which are formed from the affirmative form of the verbal stem, are:

l. 7,   I whose decisions are wise (from the stem -*bogoka* 'to take the right path')

l. 8,   I who overthrow (the foe) (from the causative of the stem -*kumbagara* 'to fall over')

l. 9,   I who am nimble (from the stem -*kina* 'to gambol', of a calf)

l. 14,   I who crouch for the attack (from the stem -*erota* 'to crouch')

l. 15,   I who do not disclose my plans (from the reflexive stem -*ebinda* 'to be secretive', literally 'to fold oneself over')

l. 18,   I who attack on all sides (from the stem -*hindura* 'to turn', meaning literally 'I who turn them (the enemy) round)

l. 19,   I who move forward to the attack (from the stem -*shambuʒa* 'to step forward')

Of the striking turns of phrase employed in these lines, undoubtedly the most forceful is that in line 5: the hero calls up his companions for the fight and the idea of the speed and urgency with which they responded to his call is conveyed by an adverbial phrase which means literally 'with a breaking of testicles'. Another striking example of imagery is found in line 7 which means literally 'they attacked me so that I might be as a thing which is chopped into many pieces'. Another poetic circumlocutory phrase which, in fact, does not owe its inspiration to the composer, for it is, or was until recently, in general use, is that of 'the time of the preventing of the elephants' for midnight (line 3): this was the time when it was necessary to scare away the elephants which might be damaging the crops.

There follows an *enkome*, the lines of which are introduced, not with praise names but place names.

> At Kashaka, my rattle bell[45] rang out and with me was Rwamisooro; (21)
> At Rubumba, I found their courage deserting them. (22)

This *enkome* is in the traditional style, the names of places at which the purported action takes place being interspersed during an *ekyevugo*, the lines beginning with place names normally being paired as in this case.

The *ekyevugo* continues during the next twenty-five *enkome* to recount the deeds of the hero and his companions as they make their way northwards towards Ankole:

I Whose Aid is Sought was assailed by bullets which left me unscathed
    and with me was The Fortunate One;   (23)
I Who Stand Firm in Battle defeated them utterly and so did The One
    Who Needs No Protection.   (24)

I Who Am Clear Headed faced the spears together with The Ceaseless
    Fighter;   (25)
I Who Am Agile came up alongside them and with me was Katwaza...   (26)

I Who Fight Alone strove with men swift of foot and so did Katemba;   (33)
I Who Am Eager For Battle, with The One Who Seeks No Help, captured
    a slave girl.   (34)

I heard your cries, You Who Seek No Help;   (35)
I Who Encourage My Companions, I Who Fight Unceasingly, with The
    Seeker Of The Foe, carried off all their cattle.   (36) (37)

At Karambi, I and The Scourge Of The Warriors rejected the counsels
    of the middle-aged;   (38)
At Rufunda, they sent me off and I outpaced them...   (39)

I Who Am Not Put To Flight passed on to the battle at Rufunza and
    so did Katemba;   (57)
I Who Do Not Tremble set to work with my spear.   (58)

At Kanyabihara, I turned them back with the spear together with
    The Tracker;   (59)
At Ibaare, I got before them to the cattle and He Who Draws Tight His Bow
    was with me;   (60)
I Who Do Not Ask For Help stood fast in the narrow way.   (61)

The following observations may be made on these lines. Enough has already
been said about the construction of praise names and reference will only be
made to that in line 34, 'I who am eager for battle'. This praise name means
literally 'I who have been sharpened as a point is put to the end of a stake'.
The reference in line 23 to bullets splashing off the hero like water is interesting.
It was a common belief during the early part of this century over much of East
Africa that warriors could by charms be made invulnerable to the bullets of the
enemy which would turn to water, a belief which was to be so potent a factor in
the Maji-Maji rebellion in German East Africa in 1905–1906. It does not,
however, appear that the hero is here attributing to himself any supernatural
invulnerability, but is merely employing the normal inordinate exaggeration
to describe his heroism. As is usual, the noun (*amasasi* 'bullets') is not expressed
and is left to be inferred from the subject prefix, the literal rendering being
'they (i.e. the bullets) beat upon me there and splashed off (like water)'. The
phrase for the cutting down of the enemy in line 24 is a telling one — 'I broke
them (the foe) as to the calves of the legs'. Good examples of circumlocutions are

to be found in line 34 where the word used for slave girl means 'the one with long hair', female slaves not being permitted to cut their hair; in line 38 where the counsels of the middle aged are expressed as 'counsels in the manner of those that are twisted' because those who gave them were no longer upright in body like the youthful hero; and in line 33 where the phrase for 'striving among the swift' means literally 'striving among the legs of he-goats', the implication being, of course, that the enemy were as swift as goats in their flight.

It has already been observed that, although references to spears are ever recurrent, the references are usually made either through the employment of prefixes or by means of the use of metaphor or circumlocution. Examples of the avoidance of the use of the every-day word for 'spears' which occur in these lines are as follows. In line 58 the word for 'spear' — *enkuraijo* — is, in fact, that for a certain tree from which spear shafts are made and the phrase *nkarangiza enkuraijo* ('I set to work with my spear') means literally 'I announced myself with the enkuraijo tree'. In the following line, the word *enyarwanda* is used which, as has been mentioned, means 'the long-horned cattle from Rwanda'. In lines 25 and 26, reference to 'spears' is supplied by the prefix *ga* and the lines read literally:

> I Who Am Clear Headed, they (the spears) brought their faces
>   (before me) . . .
> I Who Am Agile, I came upon them (the spears) on their sides . . .

Just as direct mention of spears is avoided, so is that of cattle, in that the word *ente* 'cows' seldom occurs. In line 60 a substitute is found in *enkoroogi* — the special herd which an owner keeps near his kraal for his daily milk. In line 37 we get a compression similar to that referred to above in line 12, the line consisting merely of a praise name and the verbal form: *tukazibanyuunyaho* 'we sucked them (the enemy) dry there of them (their cattle)'.

Finally the Ekirimbi reach Ankole and in the last *enkome* the hero dedicates himself for service in the cause of the Omugabe and presents himself to the Chief Minister, Nuwa Mbaguta, who was known from the large boots which he was in the habit of wearing by the nickname of Big Boots:

> At Kanshengo, I was among crowds and with me was The Tamer Of
>   Recruits;   (81)
> I told The Giver Of Courage the secrets of fighting and also The One
>   Who Plants His Spear Firmly.   (82)
> I, with The One Who Is Quick To Vanquish, made a vow in the royal
>   enclosure;   (83)
> I Who Drive The Foe Before Me visited Big Boots and with me was The
>   Irresistible One.   (84)

(ii) *An* ekyevugo *about the Second World War*

It is hardly surprising that the outbreak of war in 1939 should have inspired the composition of *ebyevugo* and news of the progress of the fighting, though far afield, provided ample scope for accounts of heroism in the traditional style, which now for the first time for many years had genuine warfare for their background. In fact, however, the war did not directly affect the Bahima: few were recruited for the armed forces (and it was not upon the experiences of those who were that the composers of the *ebyevugo* drew) and there was, of course, no fighting in Uganda itself, but the military ethos was once more in vogue and the *ekyevugo* here examined is a typical product. It is, furthermore, one which gives a fascinating glimpse of how Britain's struggle in the early years of defeat appeared to the Bahima.

The *ekyevugo*, composed by Rugira-ngaro[46] consists of seventy-six lines. It opens with three lines in the purely traditional manner, in which the composer, giving himself praise names, dedicates himself to the Omugabe's service. In the rest of the composition, however, one sees how far the form of the mid-century *ekyevugo* may depart from the traditional pattern illustrated by the Ekirimbi. Many of the *enkome* are purely descriptive, devoid of praise names. There are interspersed, as is usual in modern compositions, *enkome* of the more conventional type, but none of these is in self praise and, after the opening lines, the composer plays no part in the action which purports to have taken place. Yet the underlying theme remains the traditional one of exaggerated boasts of heroism. Even the European authorities, with whose actions much of the *ekyevugo* is concerned, act like Bahima warriors, and throughout the Bahima are associated with these Europeans in the struggle, as is exemplified by the reference to the royal drum which personified the kingdom (see lines 29, 56).

If there have been changes in the form of the *ekyevugo* from the traditional pattern, the poetic devices employed remain much the same. As in the earlier *ebyevugo*, there is the choice of unusual words and the searching out of striking verbal stems, often with a metaphorical meaning, for the formation of praise names, the circumlocutions (airmen are 'those born in the sky') and the allusions and obscurities. So too, we get the sense of force and drama conveyed by the minimum use of words, as, for example in the line (55) *Encwekye n'omuzaire bikaingana*, meaning literally 'those who had borne no children and those who were parents were equal to one another', since all were now childless: indeed a striking description of wholesale slaughter. Effective use is made of the virtual repetition of lines. Thus we get two *enkome* ending respectively with the lines (56 and 64) *Abazaarwa-iguru Mengo baatebya oburwani na Mushaija-omwe* 'At Mengo airmen brought news of the battle together with Mushaija-omwe, and *Abazaarwa-iguru Mengo bayegamba amaitiro na Mushaija-omwe* 'At Mengo airmen boasted of the killing together with Mushaija-omwe'.[47]

There are certain words and phrases which, having once occurred in an *ekyevugo*, acquire, usually on account of the striking way in which they describe some contemporary phenomenon, a popularity with, and familiarity to, the Bahima audiences and are made use of by other composers, cropping up again and again in *ebyevugo* of the same period. An example of such a phrase in this *ekyevugo* is *Bushakaaza-itaka* (line 50) 'The place where they thatch with earth'. This refers to the headquarters of the White Fathers' Mission at Nyami-tanga, the buildings of which stand prominently on a hill and are roofed with red tiles baked on the premises. So too, there is the reference in lines 72 and 73 to *Bururu* 'the lady with the gun'. This character makes her appearance in other *ebyevugo* of the period[48] and it is said that her origin lies in a certain Miss Brewer (Bururu is the Runyankore form of this name) of the Church Missionary Society who was in the habit of travelling about with a shot-gun: the sight of a woman so armed made such an impression upon the Bahima that she entered into their *ebyevugo*.[49]

I Who Am Dauntless made a vow!   (1)
I Who Am Slow To Fear dedicated myself to the Omugabe;   (2)
I Who Am Not Secretive asserted the truth . . .   (3)

The Missions[50] sent us to the battle;   (6)
The County Chiefs rose up arrayed;   (7)
The letters kept on going backwards and forwards . . .   (8)
As dawn broke the soldiers[51] stood erect.   (11)

They who make no blood-brotherhood with the enemy made fast their
      determination;   (12)
In their instruction, in their play, they learnt the arts of war;   (13)
In their factory at Bufundi, the hammers rang out all night;[52]   (14)
In their workshop at Mengo, they handled their rifles as they faced one
      another.   (15)

Hitler gathered together his forces;   (16)
Britain rose up ready for war;   (17)
They vowed on the first day saying: . . .   (18)

'Start in the ninth month';   (20)
'At home in England words are finished'.   (21)

'You Bahima collect your youth';   (22)
'You Baganda collect your boys'; . . .   (23)
'Guard carefully your weapons as the warriors assemble.'   (25)

He Who Is Not Dissuaded From Fighting seized bomb and cannon . . .   (26)
Mushaija-omwe[53] was blinded by tears . . .   (29)
He Who Is Not Overtaken From Behind attacked and they fell . . .   (31)

The double-barrelled rifles[54] were aimed at the navel;   (36)
The sword blades were pushed through the collar-bone;   (37)
In Britain blood flowed up to the roofs;   (38)
The corpses blocked the way as they piled up at Kakika . . .   (39)

The Provincial Commissioner carried guns which pushed through at
     Bukongo;   (46)
He Who Assaults The Foe lifted high his head as he bled;   (47)
He Who Is Not To Be Found Among The Fleers was stretched out in
     pain;   (48)
He Who Accepts No Dictation rushed out snatching two rifles;   (49)
At the place of the thatching with earth they burnt their bricks as the
     dawn broke;   (50)
He Who Does Not Lack Cattle lifted high his head as he laughed.   (51)

At Entebbe the cannons roared;   (52)
In England there was utter destruction;   (53)
Worsening of weather appeared on the horizon;   (54)
The parents and the childless were as one;   (55)
At Mengo airmen brought news of the battle together with
     Mushaija-omwe.   (56)

Barikitaasi stood firm on the battlefield and so did Runyamosho;   (57)
He Who Accepts No Dictation rushed in among the spears and so did
     He Who Reaches To The Sky;   (58)
The veterinary officials prevented the cattle being plundered together
     with Kamuregye . . .   (59)

The Governor beat down the foe with the rifle butts;   (65)
King George made the cannons roar;   (66)
Runyamosho returned to the fight . . .   (67)
The enemy pressed around the gates of the kraals;   (69)
The fighting surrounded the District Commissioner.   (70)

The Provincial Commissioner carried nine hundred rifles;   (71)
Bururu forced the enemy to flee,   (72)
As they cried: 'Lady with your gun spare us';   (73)
In the midst of the battle they strode over the corpses;   (74)
Blood splashed around their necks;   (75)
They grappled with the foe and thus they fought on to disperse them.   (76)

(iii)   *Abatangaaza, an* ekirahiro

This *ekirahiro* was composed in about the year 1918 by Kagarame, the Chief
Herdsman of the Omugabe Kahaya II,[55] and concerns one of the Omugabe's
herds, the Abatangaaza (the Marvellous Ones). Members of the herd are
introduced and their beauty described mainly by the use of praise names.

Then, while grazing in Buganda, they are attacked by rinderpest, a disease which destroyed so many of the Bahima's herds at this time. They return to Ankole only to suffer from drought. Then, in the closing *enkome*, water is found and the surviving cattle are saved.

The praise names used give a fair indication of the aesthetic standards by which a Muhima assesses his cattle, and length and elegance of a cow's horns are seen to be her most valued attributes. So too, leanness of body is to be desired (see lines 10 and 48), an approach towards cattle breeding not likely to endear itself to the veterinary authorities. Moreover, a lively and aggressive nature is to be applauded in a cow; thus, She who gives blows and bruises (line 37) and She whose horns are for no mere display (but may be used for fighting other cattle) (line 47).

The account of the suffering of the cattle is told with deep feeling and pathos. The composer, as he sees his beloved cattle die, compares their fate to that of the seventy Ankole princes who, when fighting against the usurper Mukwenda in the 1870s, were lured by a Muganda chief, an ally of Mukwenda, into a house which was then set on fire burning them to death. He is heartbroken as he hears their groans and sees the flies gather around their carcasses. This inspires him (line 22) to a piece of particularly fertile and elaborate imagery conveyed by the use of merely three words — *Gyoogi yaatamu ebikaito* 'Blue-fly put on his boots'. The word *gyoogi* is, in fact, a Runyankore form of the English word 'jersey' and is applied to a policeman on account of the navy-blue jersey which, with his boots, is a conspicuous part of his uniform. The application is thus extended to the flies, similar not only in colour to the policeman's uniform but also in their behaviour, for, like the police, they come gathering around a dead body. Blue-fly is now on duty and in earnest, and he therefore has put on his boots.

At Katunguru near Rurangizi, She Who Teases laid back her horns and so
    did She Who Approaches The Fighters;   (1)
At Kahama near Kambarango, we deceived The One Who Drives Back
    The Others with the calf of The One Whose Horns Are Well
    Spread pretending it were hers.[56]   (2)

At Rwenfukuzi near Ndeego, the lazy ones of Mugina marvelled at the
    white patch on the daughter of The One With The Blaze On Her
    Forehead as she gambolled;   (3)
At Kabura and Nyansheko, they marvelled at the horns of the strawberry
    beast of Rwakitungu, She Whose Horns Are Not Stunted.   (4)

At Kiyegayega near Migina, the varied herd made a noise as they went
    to Rusheesha;   (5)
At Rwekubo near Kinanga, the herd walked proudly having killed a
    loaned beast.   (6)

She Whose Horns Stand Out Above The Herd gave birth and so did
    She Who Has Straightened Her Horns;   (7)
She Who Prevents Others' Approaching became friendly with The One
    Whose Horns Are As Straight As Planks.   (8)

At Akabaare at Nyamukondo's, they prepared their camps;   (9)
At Igwanjura and Wabinyonyi, they had slim bodies. . .   (10)

At Shagama and Rwabigyemano, they displayed the tips of their horns;   (14)
At Bunonko in Rwanda,[57] they danced about and played in the light
    rain;   (15)
At Nsikizi in Rwanda, they prevented the bell of The Leader from
    ringing.   (16)

At Burunga at the home of The One Who Is Not Dissuaded From
    Fighting,   (17)
At Rwoma and Ihondaniro, they returned facing Kaaro;[58]   (18)
At Nyumba and Rwemiganda, they were patient in death;   (19)
At Obukomago and Nyambindo, they died as the princes died in
    Buganda;   (20)
Alas! I am heartbroken by the groaning of The One Who Returns
    Home With Pride.   (21)

At Katebe and Muzaire, Blue-fly put on his boots;   (22)
At Rwomugina and Rwobusisi, he found them grazing in the noon-tide;   (23)
That was when they amazed the Bagina of Ntuuga near Mugore;   (24)
Who asked whether She Whose Horns Reach Across The Watering
    Troughs and She Whose Horns Are Like Polished Reeds were
    produced by the daughter of The One Whose Horns Penetrate The
    Bushes . . .   (25)
At Endongo near Bwarukuba, they grazed while they were feverish;   (31)
At Rugushuru near Mirekaano, they brought me into a land recently
    scorched by the sun . . .   (32)

All at Mukande, the heedless ones, wished to struggle at the watering-
    trough,   (41)
The Breaker, the tawny cow of Kaniaga and The Leader, the brown cow
    of the Mender Of Broken Bones;[59]   (42)
The Swift One gambolled at Buyonza;   (43)
Her horns disappeared from the sight of the proud.   (44)

I said: 'She Who Lifts Up Her Horns Brown As The Enkuraijo Tree and
    the granddaughter of The Strawberry One have slept without water;
    I have gone to and fro with The One Free From Disease';   (45)
They pleased those who met them having come from Obuyonza and
    drunk water on the way to Emiriti;   (46)
She Whose Horns Are For No Mere Display ran as they returned home;
    the milkers avoided The Restless One;   (47)
The slim cows of Rwaburanga had horns pointing upwards.   (48)

NOTES

1. Ankole is a district in south-western Uganda, lying astride the equator and bordered on the south by Tanzania and Rwanda. See S. R. Karugire, *A History of the Kingdom of Nkore* (Oxford, 1971); H. F. Morris, *A History of Ankole* (Nairobi, 1962).
2. Karugire, op. cit., chapter 2, plays down such aspects of the Omugabe-ship and, in particular, rejects the assertion that the Omugabe was a rain-maker.
3. From 1955 the Omugabe was, in theory at any rate, a purely constitutional ruler.
4. Fortunately this bitterness never reached the pitch which it did in the neighbouring state of Rwanda between Bahutu and Batutsi, a people resembling in many ways the Bahima and with whom the Bahima frequently intermarried. In Rwanda civil strife at the end of Belgian rule and after independence resulted in the near-extermination of the Batutsi.
5. The material which forms the basis of this essay was collected during field work among the Bahima in the 1950s. In this work I was given invaluable assistance by Mr Patrick Kirindi, a Muhima magistrate who is exceptional among the Bahima intelligentsia in that he has a deep knowledge of, and interest in, the traditional literature of his people.
6. The language of the Baganda who, during the present century have exercised a predominant cultural and political influence in Uganda as a whole.
7. Or, for example:

E-ki-cuncu ki-ri-ija,	the lion will come
A-ka-cuncu ka-ri-ija,	the small lion will come
O-bu-cuncu bu-ri-ija,	the small lions will come.

8. The praise poem is to be found dispersed over a large part of sub-Saharan Africa. For an admirable review of African praise poetry in the light of published material available, see Ruth Finnegan, *Oral Literature in Africa* (Oxford, 1970), chapter 5.
9. Whether the term 'epic' can be justifiably applied to this poetry is controversial. Ruth Finnegan, op. cit., pp. 108–10, does not regard epic as being a typical African poetic form and considers that the 'panegyric' poetry concentrates far more on the laudatory and apostrophic side than on the narrative and cannot really qualify as 'epic' poetry in the normal sense of the word. Jan Knappert, 'The Epic in Africa', *Journal of the Folklore Institute*, 6 (1967), 171–90, would, on the other hand, apply the description of 'epic' to the praise poems of the Bahima, among others.
10. For a fuller account of the praise poems with annotated translations, see H. F. Morris, *The heroic recitations of the Bahima of Ankole* (Oxford, 1964).
11. Singular, *ekyevugo*, formed from the reflexive verbal stem *-evuga*, 'to speak of oneself' and thus 'to boast'.
12. Singular, *ekirahiro*, formed from the verbal stem *-rahira*, 'to vow'.
13. The Batutsi of Rwanda, who also practise the art of poetic compositions in self praise, have compositions called *icyiivugo* (boasts) and *amazina y iinka* (names of cattle) which bear many resemblances to the *ebyevugo* and *ebirahiro* respectively of the Bahima; see A. Coupez and Th. Kamanzi, *Littérature de Cour au Rwanda* (Oxford, 1970).
14. The content of the women's poems in praise of cattle is broadly the same as that to be found in men's *ebirahiro*.
15. For a brief account of women's praise poems, with some examples, see H. F. Morris, 'The praise poems of Bahima women', *African Language Studies*, 6 (1965), 52–66.
16. In the stories of historical heroes the latter are sometimes credited with the power to lift themselves into the air and from there to shoot down on the enemy (see p. 360 below), but I have found no reference to this in the *ebyevugo*.
17. But see p. 360 below.
18. From an *ekyevugo* composed by Katunguka. Two other *ebyevugo* dealing with the coronation are given in Morris, *The Heroic Recitations of the Bahima of Ankole*, chapter 5.
19. Stressed syllables have been italicized, elided vowels shown in brackets and all long vowels written double, even when not so represented in the official orthography. For an analysis of the metric structure, see Morris, op. cit., pp. 32–39.
20. High tones marked with an acute accent; other conventions as in the preceding footnote.
21. Taken from the Omusingano, an *ekyevugo* of 88 lines, see Morris, op. cit., pp. 64–77.
22. These acquired praise names are in complete contrast to the personal names of a deprecatory

nature often given by parents to their children to ward off evil: e.g. Tinkamanyire, I have not yet known sorrow (but I will), Tinkakabire, I have not yet wept (but I will), Katondwaki, For what purpose has this little thing been created?

23. See A. T. Hatto's foreword to my *Heroic Recitations of the Bahima of Ankole* (note 10 above), pp. ix–x, where comparison is made with German epic diction.

24. This tense is identified by the tense prefix *ka* and refers to an action which took place at least two days ago.

25. Plural, *abeevugi*.

26. In Mpororo, the western part of the present district, an *enkome* was by tradition normally of two lines only. Elsewhere, it usually varied from two to five lines.

27. A gesture known as *enkome* from which the verse gets its name.

28. I have not myself heard one recited of more than 130 lines.

29. Though the recitation of a praise poem by a son-in-law-to-be is still required by old-fashioned Bahima.

30. Spotted one of grey one with white spots of strawberry cow.

31. See, for example, p. 373 below.

32. Lyricism is also evident in the *ebyevugo* of women referred to briefly above, in which the praises of the composer's female companions are recited.

33. Buhweju was a small mountainous kingdom in the north-west of what is now Ankole and was incorporated into the latter in 1901.

34. It was composed by Rwanyindo, Chief Minister of Mutambuka's nephew, Tajungye. For this fragment of 14 lines, see Morris, op. cit., pp. 41–45.

35. The government chief, Rwenkaranga, and most of his 300 followers were killed in an encounter with Rugarama, the traditional ruler of the area whom Rwenkaranga had displaced. The *ekyevugo* was composed by one of Rugarama's followers and was recited to me in 1955 by Komire; it consists of 40 lines.

36. When performances of the traditional arts are organized, it is usual for the Bahima to be represented by *abeevugi* and the Bairu by dancers.

37. For another example, see the extracts from the *ekyevugo* about the Second World War given at pp. 370 f. below.

38. For the whole *ekyevugo*, see Morris, op. cit., pp. 90–103.

39. The fifth and sixth *enkome* in Runyankore are as follows:

> Amabarúha gakaragiirwá Rusheesha
> Táipu ekateerwa Mashunju
> Ákacúmu kakasiimirwá Kazoora
> Ágándi bakagooherezá Nyamitanga.
>
> Gakateerwa ómuri printing préss
> Gakaraba ómuri linotýpe
> Cyclostyle ekaronderwa Manaase
> Éryá Murumba rikatwarwa Kabwita.

40. A vernacular newspaper published by the White Fathers' Mission at Nyamitanga.

41. To say that the factual content of the *ebyevugo* is stereotyped is in itself not necessarily a serious criticism of their poetic content. Many of the greatest love poems of western Europe factually say little more than 'My lady is very beautiful and I love her greatly', the poet's art and our appreciation depending upon the manner in which he expresses and elaborates this well worn theme.

42. See Morris, op. cit., pp. 51–64. It was recited to me in 1954.

43. These figures indicate the line numbers of the *ekyevugo*.

44. The sense of this line is somewhat obscure. Literally, the meaning is 'they caused me to turn for the sandals', and the implication would seem to be that in the eagerness of his attack the hero had shed his sandals.

45. Worn round the ankle.

46. Transcribed in Runyankore by Mr Patrick Kirindi.

47. For other examples of the pairing of lines see lines 22, 23 and 47, 51.

48. Other *ebyevugo* containing references to this lady and to 'Bushakaaza-itaka' which I have come across are later in date and it may be that the references in this *ekyevugo* are the original ones.

49.   Furthermore, children were sometimes called 'Akabururu', Little Brewer.
50.   The Church Missionary Society and the White Fathers' Mission.
51.   Here, as in other *ebyevugo*, the ordinary word for 'soldiers', *abaisherukare*, is replaced by *ebikara* ('the big things, black as charcoal'). This word was originally applied to the Nube soldiers employed by the Imperial British East Africa Company with whom the Bahima came into contact towards the end of the last century and remember as ferocious and predatory.
52.   Literally, 'spent the night complaining'.
53.   One of the names of Bagyendanwa, the royal drum, meaning 'the unique one'.
54.   Literally, the guns with two mouths.
55.   See Morris, op. cit., pp. 104–13. The *ekirahiro* consists of 48 lines.
56.   When a cow has lost its calf and refuses to give milk, the herdsman brings the skin of the dead calf or of another and, rubbing it against the cow, persuades her to give him her milk.
57.   Rwanda Orwera in Ankole, not the former Belgian Rwanda.
58.   Kaaro-karungi (the beautiful land), the old name for the Omugabe's kingdom.
59.   The praise name of the Omugabe Kahaya II.

THE CONTRIBUTORS

AUTY, ROBERT
M.A. (Cantab and Oxon), DrPhil. (Münster), D.Litt. (Oxon); F.B.A. Chairman, Modern Humanities Research Association, 1968–73. Late Professor of Comparative Slavonic Philology, University of Oxford.

BAILEY, SIR HAROLD W.
M.A. (West Australia), M.A. and D.Phil. (Oxon); Honorary Doctor: West Australia, Australian National University, University of Oxford; F.B.A., Danish Academy, Norwegian Academy, Swedish Vitterhets Historie och Antikvitets Akademien, Membre de l'Institut de France, Académie des Inscriptions et Belles-Lettres, Australian Academy of the Humanities; Past President of the Philological Society, the Royal Asiatic Society, The Society of Afghan Studies, President of the Mithraic Society. Professor Emeritus of the University of Cambridge.

BAWDEN, C. R.
M.A. and Ph.D. (Cantab); Professor of Mongolian, University of London.

CUSHING, G. F.
M.A. (Cantab), Ph.D. (London). Professor of Hungarian Language and Literature, University of London.

DUNN, C. J.
B.A. and Ph.D. (London). Professor of Japanese, University of London.

HAINSWORTH, J. B.
M.A. (Oxon), Ph.D. (London). Fellow of New College, Oxford, and University Lecturer in Greek and Latin Literature.

HARVEY, L. P.
M.A. and D.Phil. (Oxon). Cervantes Professor of Spanish, University of London.

HATTO, A. T.
M.A.* (London); Corresponding Member, the Finno-Ugrian Society. Professor Emeritus of German in the University of London.

MORRIS, H. F.
LL.B. and M.A. (Dublin), Ph.D. (London). Reader in African Law, School of Oriental and African Studies, University of London.

ROSS, D. J. A.
B.A. (Cantab), M.A. and Ph.D. (London). Professor Emeritus of French, University of London.

SMITH, JOHN D.
M.A. and Ph.D. (Cantab). Lecturer in Sanskrit, University of London.